# THE COMPLETE
# RUGBY UNION
## COMPENDIUM

# THE COMPLETE
# RUGBY UNION
## COMPENDIUM

KEITH YOUNG

First published in Great Britain in 2015 by
ARENA SPORT
An imprint of Birlinn Limited
West Newington House
10 Newington Road
Edinburgh
EH9 1QS

www.arenasportbooks.co.uk

This updated edition published in 2015

ISBN: 978-1-909715-40-0
eBook ISBN: 978-0-85790-326-6

*British Library Cataloguing-in-Publication Data*
A catalogue record for this book is available on request from the
British Library.

Plate section images: Fotosport, InphoSport Photography and Arena Sport Archive

Designed and typeset by Polaris Publishing, Edinburgh

Printed and bound by T. J. International Ltd, Padstow

***The author and publisher are grateful to Lockton Companies LLP
for a subvention in aid of publication.***

*To my wife, Phil*

# ACKNOWLEDGEMENTS

I would like to thank my three sons, Gareth, Brendan and Damian for their support over the last couple of years, and a special thanks to my daughter Gwenda who gave me advice on the writing of the narrative section of the *Compendium*.

I am indebted to Nigel Owens who kindly agreed to write the foreword, and I also thank Jerry White and Cecil McCabe for their help.

Finally, a special note of thanks to my literary agent, Jonathan Williams who offered such meticulous attention to detail during the editing phase of the book, and to Peter Burns at Arena Sports for bringing together this project so expertly.

*Keith Young, 2015*

# CONTENTS

# FOREWORD
## BY NIGEL OWENS

I first met Keith Young in Dublin at the signing of my autobiography, *Half Time*. He showed me the manuscript of his *Rugby Compendium* and I was amazed at the level of detail and research. When he asked me to write the foreword, I was more than happy to do so.

Keith has been a rugby enthusiast for over fifty years, and a mathematician by training; he has combined these passions to produce a book that contains a wealth of information that will delight not only rugby enthusiasts, but also anyone who is interested in sports generally and sporting statistics. This book contains data on every rugby union International (Test) match played by each of the major rugby-playing nations, laid out in a simple to read format.

There is also an analysis of the head-to-head records of the top twenty-one teams, and a summary of the results of each of the World Cup tournaments since 1987. Augmenting all this is a wonderful trivia section.

This publication is a must for the rugby enthusiast. It is more than a statistical reference book: it is a valuable compendium that would be a welcome addition to any sports fan's collection.

# EXPLANATORY NOTES

## THE TEN MAJOR RUGBY NATIONS

The ten major rugby nations are those defined as TIER 1 teams by the International Rugby Board, now known as World Rugby. They are:

Argentina, Australia, England, France, Ireland, Italy, New Zealand, Scotland, South Africa and Wales.

The first section of this book contains a brief history of each of the ten teams and a match by match record of all the internationals played by each country.

In addition, it also includes a summary of each nation's head to head matches.

## FORMAT OF EACH MATCH RECORD

Each match is recorded on a single line, divided into eight columns as follows:

*Column 1* The match sequence in chronological order (1,2,3...)
*Column 2* The exact date of the match (day/month/year)
*Column 3* The opposing team (opponents)
*Column 4* The tournament / trophy code
*Column 5* The match status (home 'H', away 'A' or neutral 'N' ground)
*Column 6* The match venue (name and/or location of the stadium)
*Column 7* The match result (win 'W', loss 'L' or draw 'D')
*Column 8* The final score (points for, points against)

# THE OTHER ELEVEN RUGBY NATIONS

Seven Tier 2 and four Tier 3 teams, as presently defined by World Rugby, have been selected on the basis of having competed in the 2011 World Cup and/or qualified for the 2015 World Cup. They are:

## TIER 2
Canada, Fiji, Japan, Romania, Samoa, Tonga and United States

## TIER 3
Georgia, Namibia, Russia and Uruguay.

Section two of this book contains a brief history of each of the eleven teams and a summary of each nation's head to head matches.

## THE POINTS SYSTEM

|                  | Try | Convert | Pen Goal | Drop G | Goal from Mark |
|------------------|-----|---------|----------|--------|----------------|
| up to 1890-1891  | 1   | 2       | 2        | 3      | 3              |
| 1891-1893        | 2   | 3       | 3        | 4      | 4              |
| 1893-1905        | 3   | 2       | 3        | 4      | 4              |
| 1905-1948        | 3   | 2       | 3        | 4      | 3              |
| 1948-1971        | 3   | 2       | 3        | 3      | 3              |
| 1971-1977        | 4   | 2       | 3        | 3      | 3              |
| 1977-1992        | 4   | 2       | 3        | 3      | discontinued   |
| 1992 onwards     | 5   | 2       | 3        | 3      | discontinued   |

# THE LIONS

In many publications, various teams representing the four Home Nations on tour to the Southern Hemisphere during the early twentieth century were called Great Britain and later the British Isles. It wasn't until the 1950s that they became known as Lions.

For consistency, and to avoid confusion, the name Lions has been used in this book for all the matches played by the four Home Nations touring teams.

However, there is one exception. In 1904 a touring Anglo-Welsh team played three Tests against New Zealand; the Lions name has not been used in these matches.

# ABBREVIATIONS AND ACRONYMS

*a.e.t* – after extra time

*SANZAR* – South Africa, New Zealand, Australia Rugby

# TOURNAMENT & TROPHY ABBREVIATIONS

| MAIN TOURNAMENTS | CODE | ON TOUR |
|---|---|---|
| | | *(Away Team)* |
| 4 NATIONS | 4N | |
| 4 NATIONS & CALCUTTA CUP | 4N-CC | |
| 5 NATIONS | 5N | |
| 5 NATIONS & CALCUTTA CUP | 5N-CC | |
| 5 NATIONS & QUAICH TROPHY | 5N-CQ | |
| 5 NATIONS & MILLENNIUM TROPHY | 5N-MT | |
| 6 NATIONS | 6N | |
| 6 NATIONS & CALCUTTA CUP | 6N-CC | |
| 6 NATIONS & QUAICH TROPHY | 6N-CQ | |
| 6 NATIONS & GARIBALDI TROPHY | 6N-GG | |
| 6 NATIONS & MILLENNIUM TROPHY | 6N-MT | |
| ADMIRAL WILLIAM BROWN CUP | ABC | ABC-T |
| ANTIM CUP | AC | AC-T |
| TROPHEE DES BICENTENAIRES | BIC | BIC-T |
| BLEDISLOE CUP | Bled | Bled-T |
| CALCUTTA CUP | CC | |
| COOK CUP | CKC | CKC-T |
| CENTENARY QUAICH TROPHY | CQT | |
| CONSUR CUP | CSC | |
| DAVE GALLAHER TROPHY | DGT | DGT-T |
| DOUGLAS HORN TROPHY | DHT | DHT-T |
| SIR EDMUND HILLARY SHIELD | EHS | EHS-T |
| FREEDOM CUP | FC | FC-T |
| FIRA EUROPEAN CUP (1952-54) | FEC | |
| FIRA EUROPEAN TROPHY (1936-38) | FET | |
| FIRA CHAMPIONSHIP (from 1965) | FIRA | |
| GIUSEPPE GARIBALDI TROPH | GGT | |
| HOPETOUN CUP | HC | HC-T |
| INVESTEC CHALLENGE CUP | ICC | ICC-T |
| FRIENDLY INTERNATIONALS | Int | Int-T |
| CENTENARY INTERNATIONAL | Int-C | |
| JAMES BEVAN TROPHY | JBT | JBT-T |
| LANSDOWNE CUP | LC | LC-T |

# MAIN TOURNAMENTS

| MAIN TOURNAMENTS | CODE | ON TOUR *(Away Team)* |
|---|---|---|
| LIONS / SOUTH AFRICA SERIES (from 2009) | LSA | |
| LATIN CUP (1995-97) | LTC | |
| MANDELA CHALLENGE PLATE | MCP | MCP-T |
| MEDITERRANEAN CUP (1955-93) | MED | |
| MILLENNIUM TROPHY | MT | |
| MT-T OLYMPIC GAMES / pre-OLYMPIC GAMES | OG | pOG |
| PAN AMERICAN CHAMPIONSHIP (from 1995) | PAC | |
| PUMA TROPHY | PT | PT-T |
| PRINCE WILLIAM CUP | PWC | PWC-T |
| RUGBY CHAMPIONSHIP | RC | |
| RUGBY CHAMPIONSHIP & BLEDISLOE CUP | RC-B | |
| RUGBY CHAMPIONSHIP & FREEDOM CUP | RC-F | |
| RUG. CHAMP. & MANDELA CHALLENGE PLATE | RC-M | |
| RUGBY CHAMPIONSHIP & PUMA TROPHY | RC-P | |
| SOUTH AMERICAN CHAMPIONSHIP | SAC | |
| TRI NATIONS | TN | |
| TRI NATIONS & BLEDISLOE CUP | TN-B | |
| TRI NATIONS & FREEDOM CUP | TN-F | |
| TRI NATIONS & MANDELA CHALLENGE PLATE | TN-M | |
| TOM RICHARDS TROPHY | TRT | |
| WEBB ELLIS WORLD CUP FINAL | WCf | |
| WORLD CUP QUALIFYING ROUNDS | WCQ | |
| WORLD CUP POOL STAGES | WCp | |
| WORLD CUP PLAY-OFFS | WCpo | |
| WORLD CUP QUARTER-FINALS | WCqf | |
| WORLD CUP SEMI-FINALS | WCsf | |
| WORLD CUP THIRD / FOURTH PLACE | WC34 | |

# THE MAJOR NATIONS

# ARGENTINA

In 1899, four rugby-playing clubs in Buenos Aires got together and formed the River Plate Rugby Football Union. This led to the birth of the Argentina national team that played its first International match against a touring Great Britain XV in 1910, and lost by 28 points to 3. Seventeen years elapsed before they played their next four games, this time against a touring Great Britain XV in 1927. All four games were lost.

Five years later, in July 1932, the Junior Springboks visited Buenos Aires and they too defeated the home side in both games played. Argentina finally tasted success in their ninth match, away to Chile in Valparaiso, when they beat the home side in both matches by margins of nearly thirty points. In 1949, Argentina hosted France, and although losing both matches, they acquitted themselves well in their first encounter against a major nation. The South American Championship began in 1951 with Argentina, the hosts, winning the tournament by defeating Uruguay, Brazil and Chile. When France returned in 1954, the Argentinians were soundly beaten in both matches. The second South American Championship, held in Chile in 1958, was again won by Argentina: Peru and Uruguay were well beaten, but Chile did offer some resistance. In 1960, on their third visit, France exposed the huge gap between Five Nations rugby and South American rugby when they won all three matches. The Argentinians were again South American champions in 1961 and 1964, demolishing all opposition.

In 1965, Argentina embarked on their first tour outside South America, when they travelled to South Africa to play two Internationals. The team lost against Rhodesia (now Zimbabwe) in their first game, but in their second match in Johannesburg they avenged their four previous defeats to the Junior Springboks. The team's impressive power and stamina won them the nickname 'Los Pumas'. During the period 1968 to 1979, Argentina played a total of twenty-two matches against seven of the eight IRB founding members. Despite winning only five of these games and drawing three more, the Pumas gained tremendously from the experience, and proved that they could now compete with the best.

They continued to challenge the top teams throughout the 1980s, defeating Australia in Brisbane in 1983, and again, at home in Buenos Aires, in 1987. They also defeated France on three occasions at home: in 1985, 1986 and 1988. However, the highlight of the decade occurred on 2 November 1985, when the Pumas held the mighty All Blacks to a 21-all draw in Buenos Aires. They could now face the 1987 World Cup with some confidence of reaching the quarter-final, but an unexpected loss to Fiji at the pool stage thwarted those ambitions. Worse was to follow at the next two World Cup competitions, in 1991 and 1995, when they finished bottom of their pool.

However the Pumas did have some success in the early 1990s: ten successive wins between September 1992 and October 1993 included a first win over France on French soil, but the run was eventually ended by a 2-0 series loss to South Africa. Proving their resilience, the Pumas staged a comeback in June 1994 with a 2-0 series win over Scotland in Buenos Aires. A drawn series with England in May/June 1997, followed by another drawn series with Australia in November, enhanced Argentina's reputation as a Tier 1 nation. This formed the basis of their success in the 1999 World Cup. In that tournament, the Argentinians reached the quarter-final stage by eliminating Ireland in a play-off, their first win against a full Irish side, and two years later, in 2001, they defeated the Welsh in Cardiff. The Argentinians were not so successful at the 2003 World Cup, when they were eliminated at the pool stage of the tournament.

Argentina registered wins against all the Six Nations teams between 2004 and 2007; these included a 2-0 home series win against Wales in June 2006, followed by another series win, also at home, against Ireland in May and June 2007. The kind of form that the team was exhibiting enabled them to reach the semi-final stage of the 2007 World Cup by eliminating Ireland at the pool stage, and going on to overcome Scotland in the quarter-final. Their winning streak was cut short, however, by a defeat to South Africa (the World Cup winners of 2007) in the semi-final. Yet not all was lost: the Pumas ended on a high note as they beat France, the host nation, in the 3rd/4th place play-off match.

Such success aided Argentina's aspiration of gaining entry to the Tri Nations tournament, but poor results against Tier 1 teams in 2008 and 2009 did little to help their cause. However, on 14 September 2009, SANZAR (which stands for South Africa, New Zealand and Australia Rugby) issued a provisional invitation to Argentina to join an expanded Southern Hemisphere competition. The invitation contained certain conditions and also took into account that the existing TV rights did not expire until 2010.

Three wins in ten matches against Tier 1 sides, in 2010 and 2011, was no improvement on Argentina's performance in the previous two years, but in spite of this, at a meeting in Buenos Aires on 23 November 2011, it was decided that a new competition called The Rugby Championship should be formed. The competition would comprise the three Tri Nations teams (Australia, New Zealand and South Africa) and Argentina, with the first tournament starting in August 2012.

During 2012 the Pumas won three matches from six against the Northern Hemisphere Tier 1 teams, but in the inaugural Southern Hemisphere Rugby Championship they lost five out of the six matches, with one drawn game against South Africa, in Mendoza. Argentina's only victory against a Tier 1 country in 2013 was against Italy in November. This sole win followed a disastrous sequence of six straight defeats in the 2013 Rugby Championship.

In the less demanding South American Championship, a tournament that was established in 1951, the Pumas have been champions thirty-four times and, in fact, between 1951 and 2013 they did not lose a single game. A new tournament was instituted in 2014, the Consur Cup, which involved Argentina, who were seeded, and Uruguay and Chile, the top two teams of the previous year's South American Championship. The Pumas were easy winners of the inaugural competition.

Later in June, they lost twice to Ireland and once to Scotland but worse was to come in the 2014 Rugby Championship, when they lost the first five matches of the competition. There was some compensation, however: they won their final match against Australia, and finished the year in style by defeating both Italy and France on their autumn tour of the Northern Hemisphere.

The 2015 Rugby Championship, which was reduced from the normal six matches to

three, turned out to be Argentina's most successful campaign to date when they defeated South Africa in Durban, by 37 points to 25, to finish in third place for the first time.

Argentina's good form continued in the 2015 World Cup when they qualified for the semi-final by defeating Ireland by 43 points to 20. However, they failed to reach the final when they were beaten by a well-drilled Wallaby team. The Pumas were also defeated in the play-off match for third place when they lost to a determined South African team by 24 points to 13.

# ARGENTINA

## HEAD TO HEAD RESULTS TO 31 OCTOBER 2015

|  | P | W | D | L | % | F | A |
|---|---|---|---|---|---|---|---|
| **v TIER 1 Teams** | | | | | | | |
| v Australia | 25 | 5 | 1 | 19 | 22.0 | 387 | 673 |
| v England | 19 | 4 | 1 | 14 | 23.7 | 282 | 488 |
| v France | 48 | 13 | 1 | 34 | 28.1 | 754 | 1169 |
| v Ireland | 16 | 6 | 0 | 10 | 37.5 | 326 | 351 |
| v Italy | 20 | 14 | 1 | 5 | 72.5 | 496 | 344 |
| v New Zealand | 22 | 0 | 1 | 21 | 2.3 | 294 | 881 |
| v Scotland | 15 | 9 | 0 | 6 | 60.0 | 268 | 309 |
| v South Africa | 22 | 1 | 1 | 20 | 7.9 | 423 | 803 |
| v Wales | 15 | 5 | 0 | 10 | 33.3 | 350 | 428 |
| **Sub-Total** | **202** | **57** | **6** | **139** | **29.7** | **3580** | **5446** |
| | | | | | | | |
| **v TIER 2/3 Group** | | | | | | | |
| v Canada | 8 | 6 | 0 | 2 | 75.0 | 262 | 137 |
| v Fiji | 4 | 3 | 0 | 1 | 75.0 | 130 | 96 |
| v Japan | 5 | 4 | 0 | 1 | 80.0 | 205 | 139 |
| v Romania | 8 | 8 | 0 | 0 | 100.0 | 317 | 97 |
| v Samoa | 4 | 1 | 0 | 3 | 25.0 | 82 | 111 |
| v Tonga | 1 | 1 | 0 | 0 | 100.0 | 45 | 16 |
| v United States | 8 | 8 | 0 | 0 | 100.0 | 247 | 119 |
| v Georgia | 4 | 4 | 0 | 0 | 100.0 | 141 | 37 |
| v Namibia | 3 | 3 | 0 | 0 | 100.0 | 194 | 36 |
| v Russia | 0 | 0 | 0 | 0 | 0.0 | 0 | 0 |
| v Uruguay | 40 | 40 | 0 | 0 | 100.0 | 1702 | 405 |
| **Sub-Total** | **85** | **78** | **0** | **7** | **91.8** | **3325** | **1193** |
| **v TIER 3 Selection** | | | | | | | |
| v Brazil | 13 | 13 | 0 | 0 | 100.0 | 1054 | 47 |
| v Chile | 37 | 37 | 0 | 0 | 100.0 | 1716 | 243 |
| v Paraguay | 17 | 17 | 0 | 0 | 100.0 | 1382 | 65 |
| v Spain | 4 | 4 | 0 | 0 | 100.0 | 149 | 75 |
| **Sub-Total** | **71** | **71** | **0** | **0** | **100.0** | **4301** | **430** |
| | | | | | | | |
| **v Other Teams** | **46** | **13** | **4** | **29** | **32.6** | **546** | **774** |
| **All Internationals** | **404** | **219** | **10** | **175** | **55.4** | **11752** | **7843** |

| No | Date | Opponents | Tmt | | Match Venue | Result | |
|----|------|-----------|-----|---|-------------|--------|---|
| 1 | 12-Jun-10 | Gt Britain XV | Int | H | Polo Ground Flores, Buenos Aires | L | 3-28 |
| 2 | 31-Jul-27 | Gt Britain XV | Int | H | Estadio G.E.B.A., Buenos Aires | L | 0-37 |
| 3 | 7-Aug-27 | Gt Britain XV | Int | H | Estadio G.E.B.A., Buenos Aires | L | 0-46 |
| 4 | 14-Aug-27 | Gt Britain XV | Int | H | Estadio G.E.B.A., Buenos Aires | L | 3-34 |
| 5 | 21-Aug-27 | Gt Britain XV | Int | H | Estadio G.E.B.A., Buenos Aires | L | 0-43 |
| 6 | 16-Jul-32 | Jnr Springboks | Int | H | Ferro Carril Oeste Stadium, B Aires | L | 0-42 |
| 7 | 23-Jul-32 | Jnr Springboks | Int | H | Ferro Carril Oeste Stadium, B Aires | L | 3-34 |
| 8 | 16-Aug-36 | Gt Britain XV | Int | H | Estadio G.E.B.A., Buenos Aires | L | 0-23 |
| 9 | 20-Sep-36 | Chile | Int-T | A | Estadio Playa Ancha, Valparaiso | W | 29-0 |
| 10 | 27-Sep-36 | Chile | Int-T | A | Estadio Playa Ancha, Valparaiso | W | 31-3 |
| 11 | 21-Aug-38 | Chile | Int | H | Estadio G.E.B.A., Buenos Aires | W | 33-3 |
| 12 | 29-Aug-48 | Oxford & Cam. | Int | H | Estadio G.E.B.A., Buenos Aires | L | 0-17 |
| 13 | 5-Sep-48 | Oxford & Cam. | Int | H | Estadio G.E.B.A., Buenos Aires | L | 0-39 |
| 14 | 28-Aug-49 | France | Int | H | Estadio G.E.B.A., Buenos Aires | L | 0-5 |
| 15 | 4-Sep-49 | France | Int | H | Estadio G.E.B.A., Buenos Aires | L | 3-12 |
| 16 | 9-Sep-51 | Uruguay | SAC | H | Estadio G.E.B.A., Buenos Aires | W | 62-0 |
| 17 | 13-Sep-51 | Brazil | SAC | H | Estadio G.E.B.A., Buenos Aires | W | 72-0 |
| 18 | 16-Sep-51 | Chile | SAC | H | Estadio G.E.B.A., Buenos Aires | W | 13-3 |
| 19 | 24-Aug-52 | Ireland XV | Int | H | Estadio G.E.B.A., Buenos Aires | D | 3-3 |
| 20 | 31-Aug-52 | Ireland XV | Int | H | Estadio G.E.B.A., Buenos Aires | L | 0-6 |
| 21 | 29-Aug-54 | France | Int | H | Ferro Carril Oeste Stadium, B Aires | L | 8-22 |
| 22 | 12-Sep-54 | France | Int | H | Ferro Carril Oeste Stadium, B Aires | L | 3-30 |
| 23 | 26-Aug-56 | Oxford & Cam. | Int | H | Estadio G.E.B.A., Buenos Aires | L | 6-25 |
| 24 | 16-Sep-56 | Oxford & Cam. | Int | H | Estadio G.E.B.A., Buenos Aires | L | 3-11 |
| 25 | 11-Sep-58 | Peru | SAC | N | Stade Français, Santiago | W | 44-0 |
| 26 | 15-Sep-58 | Uruguay | SAC | N | Estadio Sausalito, Viña del Mar | W | 50-3 |
| 27 | 18-Sep-58 | Chile | SAC | A | Prince of Wales Country Club, Santiago | W | 14-0 |
| 28 | 12-Sep-59 | Jnr Springboks | Int | H | Estadio G.E.B.A., Buenos Aires | L | 6-14 |
| 29 | 3-Oct-59 | Jnr Springboks | Int | H | Estadio G.E.B.A., Buenos Aires | L | 6-20 |
| 30 | 23-Jul-60 | France | Int | H | Estadio G.E.B.A., Buenos Aires | L | 3-37 |
| 31 | 6-Aug-60 | France | Int | H | Estadio G.E.B.A., Buenos Aires | L | 3-12 |
| 32 | 17-Aug-60 | France | Int | H | Estadio G.E.B.A., Buenos Aires | L | 6-29 |
| 33 | 7-Oct-61 | Chile | SAC | N | Camino Carrasco Polo Club, Montevideo | W | 11-3 |
| 34 | 12-Oct-61 | Brazil | SAC | N | Camino Carrasco Polo Club, Montevideo | W | 60-0 |
| 35 | 14-Oct-61 | Uruguay | SAC | A | Camino Carrasco Polo Club, Montevideo | W | 36-3 |
| 36 | 15-Aug-64 | Uruguay | SAC | N | San Pablo Athletic Ground, São Paulo | W | 25-6 |
| 37 | 19-Aug-64 | Brazil | SAC | A | San Pablo Athletic Ground, São Paulo | W | 30-8 |
| 38 | 22-Aug-64 | Chile | SAC | N | San Pablo Athletic Ground, São Paulo | W | 30-8 |
| 39 | 8-May-65 | Rhodesia | Int-T | A | Police Grounds, Salisbury | L | 12-17 |
| 40 | 19-Jun-65 | Jnr Springboks | Int-T | A | Ellis Park, Johannesburg | W | 11-6 |

# ARGENTINA

| No | Date | Opponents | Tmt | | Match Venue | Result | |
|----|------|-----------|-----|---|-------------|--------|---|
| 41 | 11-Sep-65 | Oxford & Cam. | Int | H | Estadio G.E.B.A., Buenos Aires | D | 19-19 |
| 42 | 18-Sep-65 | Oxford & Cam. | Int | H | Estadio G.E.B.A., Buenos Aires | L | 3-9 |
| 43 | 26-Sep-65 | Chile | Int-T | A | Prince of Wales Country Club, Santiago | W | 23-11 |
| 44 | 24-Sep-66 | SA Gazelles | Int | H | Estadio G.E.B.A., Buenos Aires | L | 3-9 |
| 45 | 1-Oct-66 | SA Gazelles | Int | H | Estadio G.E.B.A., Buenos Aires | L | 15-20 |
| 46 | 27-Sep-67 | Uruguay | SAC | H | Club Atlético San Isidro, Buenos Aires | W | 38-6 |
| 47 | 30-Sep-67 | Chile | SAC | H | Club Atlético San Isidro, Buenos Aires | W | 18-0 |
| 48 | 14-Sep-68 | Wales XV | Int | H | Estadio G.E.B.A., Buenos Aires | W | 9-5 |
| 49 | 28-Sep-68 | Wales XV | Int | H | Estadio G.E.B.A., Buenos Aires | D | 9-9 |
| 50 | 13-Sep-69 | Scotland XV | Int | H | Estadio G.E.B.A., Buenos Aires | W | 20-3 |
| 51 | 27-Sep-69 | Scotland XV | Int | H | Estadio G.E.B.A., Buenos Aires | L | 3-6 |
| 52 | 4-Oct-69 | Uruguay | SAC | N | Prince of Wales Country Club, Santiago | W | 41-6 |
| 53 | 11-Oct-69 | Chile | SAC | A | Prince of Wales Country Club, Santiago | W | 54-0 |
| 54 | 13-Sep-70 | Ireland XV | Int | H | Ferro Carril Oeste Stadium, B Aires | W | 8-3 |
| 55 | 20-Sep-70 | Ireland XV | Int | H | Ferro Carril Oeste Stadium, B Aires | W | 6-3 |
| 56 | 17-Jul-71 | SA Gazelles | Int-T | A | Boet Erasmus Stadium, Port Elizabeth | L | 6-12 |
| 57 | 7-Aug-71 | SA Gazelles | Int-T | A | Loftus Versfeld Stadium, Pretoria | W | 12-0 |
| 58 | 28-Aug-71 | Oxford & Cam. | Int | H | Ferro Carril Oeste Stadium, B Aires | W | 11-3 |
| 59 | 4-Sep-71 | Oxford & Cam. | Int | H | Ferro Carril Oeste Stadium, B Aires | W | 6-3 |
| 60 | 10-Oct-71 | Chile | SAC | N | Camino Carrasco Polo Club, Montevideo | W | 20-3 |
| 61 | 12-Oct-71 | Brazil | SAC | N | Camino Carrasco Polo Club, Montevideo | W | 50-6 |
| 62 | 16-Oct-71 | Paraguay | SAC | N | Camino Carrasco Polo Club, Montevideo | W | 61-0 |
| 63 | 17-Oct-71 | Uruguay | SAC | A | Camino Carrasco Polo Club, Montevideo | W | 55-6 |
| 64 | 21-Oct-72 | SA Gazelles | Int | H | Ferro Carril Oeste Stadium, B Aires | L | 6-14 |
| 65 | 4-Nov-72 | SA Gazelles | Int | H | Ferro Carril Oeste Stadium, B Aires | W | 18-16 |
| 66 | 8-Sep-73 | Romania | Int | H | Ferro Carril Oeste Stadium, B Aires | W | 15-9 |
| 67 | 15-Sep-73 | Romania | Int | H | Ferro Carril Oeste Stadium, B Aires | W | 24-3 |
| 68 | 14-Oct-73 | Paraguay | SAC | N | Clube Atlético Ground, São Paulo | W | 98-3 |
| 69 | 16-Oct-73 | Uruguay | SAC | N | Clube Atlético Ground, São Paulo | W | 55-0 |
| 70 | 20-Oct-73 | Brazil | SAC | A | Clube Atlético Ground, São Paulo | W | 96-0 |
| 71 | 21-Oct-73 | Chile | SAC | N | Clube Atlético Ground-São Paulo | W | 60-3 |
| 72 | 10-Nov-73 | Ireland XV | Int-T | A | Lansdowne Road, Dublin | L | 8-21 |
| 73 | 24-Nov-73 | Scotland XV | Int-T | A | Murrayfield, Edinburgh | L | 11-12 |
| 74 | 20-Jun-74 | France | Int | H | Ferro Carril Oeste Stadium, B Aires | L | 15-20 |
| 75 | 29-Jun-74 | France | Int | H | Ferro Carril Oeste Stadium, B Aires | L | 27-31 |
| 76 | 21 Sep 75 | Uruguay | SAC | N | Estadio del Colegio San José, Asunción | W | 30-15 |
| 77 | 25-Sep-75 | Paraguay | SAC | A | Estadio del Colegio San José, Asunción | W | 93-0 |
| 78 | 27-Sep-75 | Brazil | SAC | N | Estadio del Colegio San José, Asunción | W | 64-6 |
| 79 | 28-Sep-75 | Chile | SAC | N | Estadio del Colegio San José, Asunción | W | 45-3 |
| 80 | 19-Oct-75 | France | Int-T | A | Stade de Gerland, Lyon | L | 6-29 |

| No | Date | Opponents | Tmt | Match Venue | | Result | |
|----|------|-----------|-----|-------------|---|--------|---|
| 81 | 25-Oct-75 | France | Int-T | A | Parc des Princess, Paris | L | 21-36 |
| 82 | 16-Oct-76 | Wales XV | Int-T | A | National Stadium, Cardiff | L | 19-20 |
| 83 | 30-Oct-76 | NZ XV | Int | H | Ferro Carril Oeste Stadium, B Aires | L | 9-21 |
| 84 | 6-Nov-76 | NZ XV | Int | H | Ferro Carril Oeste Stadium, B Aires | L | 6-26 |
| 85 | 25-Jun-77 | France | Int | H | Ferro Carril Oeste Stadium, B Aires | L | 3-26 |
| 86 | 2-Jul-77 | France | Int | H | Ferro Carril Oeste Stadium, B Aires | D | 18-18 |
| 87 | 24-Oct-77 | Brazil | SAC | H | Estadio Monumental José Fierro, Tucumán | W | 78-6 |
| 88 | 28-Oct-77 | Uruguay | SAC | H | Estadio Monumental José Fierro, Tucumán | W | 70-0 |
| 89 | 29-Oct-77 | Paraguay | SAC | H | Estadio Monumental José Fierro, Tucumán | W | 77-3 |
| 90 | 30-Oct-77 | Chile | SAC | H | Estadio Monumental José Fierro, Tucumán | W | 25-10 |
| 91 | 14-Oct-78 | England XV | Int-T | A | Twickenham, London | D | 13-13 |
| 92 | 24-Oct-78 | Italy | Int-T | A | Stadio Mario Battaglini, Rovigo | L | 6-19 |
| 93 | 8-Sep-79 | NZ XV | Int-T | A | Carisbrook, Dunedin | L | 9-18 |
| 94 | 15-Sep-79 | NZ XV | Int-T | A | Athletic Park, Wellington | L | 6-15 |
| 95 | 4-Oct-79 | Uruguay | SAC | N | Stade Français, Santiago | W | 19-16 |
| 96 | 6-Oct-79 | Chile | SAC | A | Stade Français, Santiago | W | 34-15 |
| 97 | 7-Oct-79 | Paraguay | SAC | N | Estadio Sausalito, Viña del Mar | W | 76-13 |
| 98 | 9-Oct-79 | Brazil | SAC | N | Stade Français, Santiago | W | 109-3 |
| 99 | 27-Oct-79 | Australia | Int | H | Ferro Carril Oeste Stadium, B Aires | W | 24-13 |
| 100 | 3-Nov-79 | Australia | Int | H | Ferro Carril Oeste Stadium, B Aires | L | 12-17 |
| 101 | 9-Aug-80 | World XV | Int | H | Ferro Carril Oeste Stadium, B Aires | W | 36-22 |
| 102 | 1-Nov-80 | Fiji | Int | H | Ferro Carril Oeste Stadium, B Aires | W | 34-22 |
| 103 | 8-Nov-80 | Fiji | Int | H | Ferro Carril Oeste Stadium, B Aires | W | 38-16 |
| 104 | 30-May-81 | England | Int | H | Ferro Carril Oeste Stadium, B Aires | D | 19-19 |
| 105 | 6-Jun-81 | England | Int | H | Ferro Carril Oeste Stadium, B Aires | L | 6-12 |
| 106 | 3-Oct-81 | Canada | Int | H | Estadio G.E.B.A., Buenos Aires | W | 35-0 |
| 107 | 14-Nov-82 | France | Int-T | A | Stade Municipal de Toulouse, Toulouse | L | 12-25 |
| 108 | 20-Nov-82 | France | Int-T | A | Parc des Princess, Paris | L | 6-13 |
| 109 | 23-Nov-82 | Spain | Int-T | A | Campo Ciudad Universitaria, Madrid | W | 28-19 |
| 110 | 25-Jun-83 | World XV | Int | H | Club Atlético Atlanta, Buenos Aires | W | 28-20 |
| 111 | 16-Jul-83 | Chile | SAC | H | Club Atlético San Isidro, Buenos Aires | W | 46-6 |
| 112 | 20-Jul-83 | Paraguay | SAC | H | Club Atlético San Isidro, Buenos Aires | W | 43-3 |
| 113 | 23-Jul-83 | Uruguay | SAC | H | Club Atlético San Isidro, Buenos Aires | W | 29-6 |
| 114 | 31-Jul-83 | Australia | Int-T | A | Ballymore Oval, Brisbane | W | 18-3 |
| 115 | 7-Aug-83 | Australia | Int-T | A | Cricket Ground, Sydney | L | 13-29 |
| 116 | 22-Jun-85 | France | Int | H | Ferro Carril Oeste Stadium, B Aires | W | 24-16 |
| 117 | 29-Jun-85 | France | Int | H | Ferro Carril Oeste Stadium, B Aires | L | 15-23 |
| 118 | 17-Sep-85 | Uruguay | SAC | N | Estadio General Pablo Rojas, Ascunción | W | 63-16 |
| 119 | 19-Sep-85 | Chile | SAC | N | Estadio General Pablo Rojas, Ascunción | W | 59-6 |
| 120 | 21-Sep-85 | Paraguay | SAC | A | Estadio General Pablo Rojas, Ascunción | W | 102-3 |

| No | Date | Opponents | Tmt | Match Venue | Result | |
|----|------|-----------|-----|-------------|--------|---|
| 121 | 26-Oct-85 | New Zealand | Int | H Ferro Carril Oeste Stadium, B Aires | L | 20-33 |
| 122 | 2-Nov-85 | New Zealand | Int | H Ferro Carril Oeste Stadium, B Aires | D | 21-21 |
| 123 | 31-May-86 | France | Int | H Vélez Sarsfield Stadium, Buenos Aires | W | 15-13 |
| 124 | 7-Jun-86 | France | Int | H Vélez Sarsfield Stadium, Buenos Aires | L | 9-22 |
| 125 | 6-Jul-86 | Australia | Int-T | A Ballymore Oval, Brisbane | L | 19-39 |
| 126 | 12-Jul-86 | Australia | Int-T | A Cricket Ground, Sydney | L | 0-26 |
| 127 | 3-May-87 | Uruguay | Int-T | A Estadio Gran Parque Central, Montevideo | W | 38-3 |
| 128 | 24-May-87 | Fiji | WCp | N Rugby Park, Hamilton | L | 9-28 |
| 129 | 28-May-87 | Italy | WCp | N Lancaster Park Oval, Christchurch | W | 25-16 |
| 130 | 1-Jun-87 | New Zealand | WCp | A Athletic Park, Wellington | L | 15-46 |
| 131 | 17 Aug 87 | Spain | Int | H Estadio José Maria Minella, Mar del Plata | W | 40-12 |
| 132 | 27-Sep-87 | Uruguay | SAC | N Stade Français, Santiago | W | 41-21 |
| 133 | 30-Sep-87 | Paraguay | SAC | N Stade Français, Santiago | W | 62-4 |
| 134 | 3-Oct-87 | Chile | SAC | A Stade Français, Santiago | W | 47-9 |
| 135 | 31-Oct-87 | Australia | Int | H Vélez Sarsfield Stadium, Buenos Aires | D | 19-19 |
| 136 | 7-Nov-87 | Australia | Int | H Vélez Sarsfield Stadium, Buenos Aires | W | 27-19 |
| 137 | 18-Jun-88 | France | Int | H Vélez Sarsfield Stadium, Buenos Aires | L | 15-18 |
| 138 | 25-Jun-88 | France | Int | H Vélez Sarsfield Stadium, Buenos Aires | W | 18-6 |
| 139 | 5-Nov-88 | France | Int-T | A Stade de la Beaujoire, Nantes | L | 9-29 |
| 140 | 11-Nov-88 | France | Int-T | A Stade Lille-Métropole, Villeneuve | L | 18-28 |
| 141 | 24-Jun-89 | Italy | Int | H Vélez Sarsfield Stadium, Buenos Aires | W | 21-16 |
| 142 | 15-Jul-89 | New Zealand | Int-T | A Carisbrook, Dunedin | L | 9-60 |
| 143 | 29-Jul-89 | New Zealand | Int-T | A Athletic Park, Wellington | L | 12-49 |
| 144 | 8-Oct-89 | Brazil | SAC | N Estadio Charrúa, Montevideo | W | 103-9 |
| 145 | 10-Oct-89 | Chile | SAC | N Estadio Charrúa, Montevideo | W | 36-9 |
| 146 | 12-Oct-89 | Paraguay | SAC | N Estadio Charrúa, Montevideo | W | 75-7 |
| 147 | 14-Oct-89 | Uruguay | SAC | A Estadio Charrúa, Montevideo | W | 34-14 |
| 148 | 8-Nov-89 | United States | WCQ | H Vélez Sarsfield Stadium, Buenos Aires | W | 23-6 |
| 149 | 30-Mar-90 | Canada | WCQ | A Swanguard Stadium, Burnaby Lake, BC | L | 6-15 |
| 150 | 7-Apr-90 | United States | WCQ | A Harder Stadium, Santa Barbara, CA | W | 13-6 |
| 151 | 16-Jun-90 | Canada | WCQ | H Vélez Sarsfield Stadium, Buenos Aires | L | 15-19 |
| 152 | 28-Jul-90 | England | Int | H Vélez Sarsfield Stadium, Buenos Aires | L | 12-25 |
| 153 | 4-Aug-90 | England | Int | H Vélez Sarsfield Stadium, Buenos Aires | W | 15-13 |
| 154 | 27-Oct-90 | Ireland | Int-T | A Lansdowne Road, Dublin | L | 18-20 |
| 155 | 3-Nov-90 | England | Int-T | A Twickenham, London | L | 0-51 |
| 156 | 10-Nov-90 | Scotland | Int-T | A Murrayfield, Edinburgh | L | 3-49 |
| 157 | 6-Jul-91 | New Zealand | Int | H Vélez Sarsfield Stadium, Buenos Aires | L | 14-28 |
| 158 | 13-Jul-91 | New Zealand | Int | H Vélez Sarsfield Stadium, Buenos Aires | L | 6-36 |
| 159 | 15-Aug-91 | Chile | SAC | A Prince of Wales Country Club, Santiago | W | 41-6 |
| 160 | 21-Sep-91 | Uruguay | SAC | H Club Atlético San Isidro, Buenos Aires | W | 32-9 |

| No | Date | Opponents | Tmt | | Match Venue | Result | |
|---|---|---|---|---|---|---|---|
| 161 | 28-Sep-91 | Paraguay | SAC | A | Estadio del Colegio San José, Asunción | W | 37-10 |
| 162 | 1-Oct-91 | Brazil | SAC | H | Belgrano Stadium, Buenos Aires | W | 84-6 |
| 163 | 4-Oct-91 | Australia | WCp | N | Stradey Park, Llanelli | L | 19-32 |
| 164 | 9-Oct-91 | Wales | WCp | A | National Stadium, Cardiff | L | 7-16 |
| 165 | 13-Oct-91 | Western Samoa | WCp | N | Sardis Road, Pontypridd | L | 12-35 |
| 166 | 4-Jul-92 | France | Int | H | Vélez Sarsfield Stadium, Buenos Aires | L | 12-27 |
| 167 | 11-Jul-92 | France | Int | H | Vélez Sarsfield Stadium, Buenos Aires | L | 9-33 |
| 168 | 26-Sep-92 | Spain | Int | H | Vélez Sarsfield Stadium, Buenos Aires | W | 38-10 |
| 169 | 24-Oct-92 | Spain | Int-T | A | Campo Ciudad Universitaria, Madrid | W | 43-34 |
| 170 | 31-Oct-92 | Romania | Int-T | A | Stadionul 23 August, Bucharest | W | 21-18 |
| 171 | 14-Nov-92 | France | Int-T | A | Stade de la Beaujoire, Nantes | W | 24-20 |
| 172 | 15-May-93 | Japan | Int | H | Estadio G.E.B.A., Buenos Aires | W | 30-27 |
| 173 | 22-May-93 | Japan | Int | H | Ferro Carril Oeste Stadium, B Aires | W | 45-20 |
| 174 | 2-Oct-93 | Brazil | SAC | A | Clube Atlético Ground, São Paulo | W | 114-3 |
| 175 | 11-Oct-93 | Chile (SAC) | WCQ | H | Estadio G.E.B.A., Buenos Aires | W | 70-7 |
| 176 | 16-Oct-93 | Paraguay (SAC) | WCQ | H | Estadio G.E.B.A., Buenos Aires | W | 51-3 |
| 177 | 23-Oct-93 | Uruguay (SAC) | WCQ | A | Estadio Gran Parque Central, Montevideo | W | 19-10 |
| 178 | 6-Nov-93 | South Africa | Int | H | Ferro Carril Oeste Stadium, B Aires | L | 26-29 |
| 179 | 13-Nov-93 | South Africa | Int | H | Ferro Carril Oeste Stadium, B Aires | L | 23-52 |
| 180 | 28-May-94 | United States | WCQ | A | George Allen Memorial Field, Long Beach | W | 28-22 |
| 181 | 4-Jun-94 | Scotland | Int | H | Ferro Carril Oeste Stadium, B Aires | W | 16-15 |
| 182 | 11-Jun-94 | Scotland | Int | H | Ferro Carril Oeste Stadium, B Aires | W | 19-17 |
| 183 | 20-Jun-94 | United States | WCQ | H | Ferro Carril Oeste Stadium, B Aires | W | 16-11 |
| 184 | 8-Oct-94 | South Africa | Int-T | A | Boet Erasmus Stadium, Port Elizabeth | L | 22-42 |
| 185 | 15-Oct-94 | South Africa | Int-T | A | Ellis Park, Johannesburg | L | 26-46 |
| 186 | 4-Mar-95 | Uruguay | PAC | H | Ferro Carril Oeste Stadium, B Aires | W | 44-3 |
| 187 | 10-Mar-95 | Canada | PAC | H | Ferro Carril Oeste Stadium, B Aires | W | 29-26 |
| 188 | 30-Apr-95 | Australia | Int-T | A | Ballymore Oval, Brisbane | L | 7-53 |
| 189 | 6-May-95 | Australia | Int-T | A | Football Stadium, Sydney | L | 13-30 |
| 190 | 27-May-95 | England | WCp | N | Kings Park Stadium, Durban | L | 18-24 |
| 191 | 30-May-95 | Western Samoa | WCp | N | Basil Kenyon Stadium, East London | L | 26-32 |
| 192 | 4-Jun-95 | Italy | WCp | N | Basil Kenyon Stadium, East London | L | 25-31 |
| 193 | 24-Sep-95 | Paraguay | SAC | A | Estadio de las Fuerzas, Asunción | W | 103-9 |
| 194 | 30-Sep-95 | Chile | SAC | A | Prince of Wales Country Club, Santiago | W | 78-3 |
| 195 | 8-Oct-95 | Uruguay | SAC | H | Tacuru Social Club Posadas, Misiones | W | 52-37 |
| 196 | 14-Oct-95 | Romania | LTC | H | Ferro Carril Oeste Stadium, B Aires | W | 51-16 |
| 197 | 17-Oct-95 | Italy | LTC | H | Estadio Monumental José Fierro, Tucumán | W | 26-6 |
| 198 | 21-Oct-95 | France | LTC | H | Ferro Carril Oeste Stadium, B Aires | L | 12-47 |
| 199 | 8-Jun-96 | Uruguay | Int-T | A | Camino Carrasco Polo Club, Montevideo | W | 37-18 |
| 200 | 22-Jun-96 | France | Int | H | Ferro Carril Oeste Stadium, B Aires | L | 27-34 |

| No | Date | Opponents | Tmt | | Match Venue | | Result |
|----|------|-----------|-----|---|-------------|---|--------|
| 201 | 29-Jun-96 | France | Int | H | Ferro Carril Oeste Stadium, B Aires | L | 15-34 |
| 202 | 14-Sep-96 | United States | PAC | N | Twin Elms Rugby Park, Nepean, Ontario | W | 29-26 |
| 203 | 18-Sep-96 | Uruguay | PAC | N | Mohawk Sports Park, Hamilton, Ontario | W | 54-20 |
| 204 | 21-Sep-96 | Canada | PAC | A | Fletcher's Field, Markham, Toronto | W | 41-21 |
| 205 | 9-Nov-96 | South Africa | Int | H | Ferro Carril Oeste Stadium, B Aires | L | 15-46 |
| 206 | 16-Nov-96 | South Africa | Int | H | Ferro Carril Oeste Stadium, B Aires | L | 21-44 |
| 207 | 14-Dec-96 | England | Int-T | A | Twickenham, London | L | 18-20 |
| 208 | 31-May-97 | England | Int | H | Ferro Carril Oeste Stadium, B Aires | L | 20-46 |
| 209 | 7-Jun-97 | England | Int | H | Ferro Carril Oeste Stadium, B Aires | W | 33-13 |
| 210 | 21-Jun-97 | New Zealand | Int-T | A | Athletic Park, Wellington | L | 8-93 |
| 211 | 28-Jun-97 | New Zealand | Int-T | A | Rugby Park, Hamilton | L | 10-62 |
| 212 | 13-Sep-97 | Paraguay | SAC | H | Aranduroga Rugby Club, Corrientes | W | 78-0 |
| 213 | 27-Sep-97 | Uruguay | SAC | A | Camino Carrasco Polo Club, Montevideo | W | 56-17 |
| 214 | 4-Oct-97 | Chile | SAC | H | Estadio La Carrodilla, Mendoza | W | 50-10 |
| 215 | 18-Oct-97 | Romania | LTC | N | Stade Jacques Fouroux, Auch | W | 45-18 |
| 216 | 22-Oct-97 | Italy | LTC | N | Stade Antoine Béguère, Lourdes | D | 18-18 |
| 217 | 26-Oct-97 | France | LTC | A | Stade Maurice Trélut, Tarbes | L | 27-32 |
| 218 | 1-Nov-97 | Australia | Int | H | Ferro Carril Oeste Stadium, B Aires | L | 15-23 |
| 219 | 8-Nov-97 | Australia | Int | H | Ferro Carril Oeste Stadium, B Aires | W | 18-16 |
| 220 | 13-Jun-98 | France | Int | H | Vélez Sarsfield Stadium, Buenos Aires | L | 18-35 |
| 221 | 20-Jun-98 | France | Int | H | Vélez Sarsfield Stadium, Buenos Aires | L | 12-37 |
| 222 | 8-Aug-98 | Romania | Int | H | Estadio Gabino Sosa, Rosario | W | 68-22 |
| 223 | 15-Aug-98 | U. States(PAC) | WCQ | H | Cricket and Rugby Club, Buenos Aires | W | 52-24 |
| 224 | 18-Aug-98 | Uruguay (PAC) | WCQ | H | Club Atlético San Isidro, Buenos Aires | W | 55-0 |
| 225 | 22-Aug-98 | Canada (PAC) | WCQ | H | Cricket and Rugby Club, Buenos Aires | W | 54-28 |
| 226 | 15-Sep-98 | Japan | Int-T | A | Prince Chichibu Memorial Ground, Tokyo | L | 29-44 |
| 227 | 3-Oct-98 | Paraguay | SAC | A | Estadio del Colegio San José, Asunción | W | 59-0 |
| 228 | 10-Oct-98 | Chile | SAC | A | Prince of Wales Country Club, Santiago | W | 25-17 |
| 229 | 17-Oct-98 | Uruguay | SAC | H | Club Atlético San Isidro, Buenos Aires | W | 30-14 |
| 230 | 7-Nov-98 | Italy | Int-T | A | Stadio Comunale Beltrametti, Piacenza | L | 19-23 |
| 231 | 14-Nov-98 | France | Int-T | A | Stade de la Beaujoire, Nantes | L | 14-34 |
| 232 | 21-Nov-98 | Wales | Int-T | A | Stradey Park, Llanelli | L | 30-43 |
| 233 | 5-Jun-99 | Wales | Int | H | Ferro Carril Oeste Stadium, B Aires | L | 26-36 |
| 234 | 12-Jun-99 | Wales | Int | H | Ferro Carril Oeste Stadium, B Aires | L | 16-23 |
| 235 | 21-Aug-99 | Scotland | Int-T | A | Murrayfield, Edinburgh | W | 31-22 |
| 236 | 28-Aug-99 | Ireland | Int-T | A | Lansdowne Road, Dublin | L | 24-32 |
| 237 | 1-Oct-99 | Wales | WCp | A | Millennium Stadium, Cardiff | L | 18-23 |
| 238 | 10-Oct-99 | Samoa | WCp | N | Stradey Park, Llanelli | W | 32-16 |
| 239 | 16-Oct-99 | Japan | WCp | N | Millennium Stadium, Cardiff | W | 33-12 |
| 240 | 20-Oct-99 | Ireland | WCpo | N | Stade Félix Bollaert, Lens | W | 28-24 |

| No | Date | Opponents | Tmt | | Match Venue | Result | |
|---|---|---|---|---|---|---|---|
| 241 | 24-Oct-99 | France | WCqf | N | Lansdowne Road, Dublin | L | 26-47 |
| 242 | 3-Jun-00 | Ireland | Int | H | Ferro Carril Oeste Stadium, B Aires | W | 34-23 |
| 243 | 17-Jun-00 | Australia | PT-T | A | Ballymore Oval, Brisbane | L | 6-53 |
| 244 | 24-Jun-00 | Australia | PT-T | A | Canberra Stadium, Canberra | L | 25-32 |
| 245 | 12-Nov-00 | South Africa | Int | H | Estadio Monumental A V Liberti, B Aires | L | 33-37 |
| 246 | 25-Nov-00 | England | Int-T | A | Twickenham, London | L | 0-19 |
| 247 | 19-May-01 | Uruguay | PAC | N | Richardson Stadium, Kingston, Ontario | W | 32-27 |
| 248 | 23-May-01 | United States | PAC | N | Mohawk Sports Park, Hamilton, Ontario | W | 44-16 |
| 249 | 26-May-01 | Canada | PAC | A | Fletcher's Field, Markham, Toronto | W | 20-6 |
| 250 | 23-Jun-01 | New Zealand | Int-T | A | Jade Stadium, Christchurch | L | 19-67 |
| 251 | 14-Jul-01 | Italy | Int | H | Ferro Carril Oeste Stadium, B Aires | W | 38-17 |
| 252 | 10-Nov-01 | Wales | Int-T | A | Millennium Stadium, Cardiff | W | 30-16 |
| 253 | 18-Nov-01 | Scotland | Int-T | A | Murrayfield, Edinburgh | W | 25-16 |
| 254 | 1-Dec-01 | New Zealand | Int | H | Estadio Monumental A V Liberti, B Aires | L | 20-24 |
| 255 | 28-Apr-02 | Uruguay | SAC | H | Estadio Bautista Gargantini, Mendoza | W | 35-21 |
| 256 | 1-May-02 | Paraguay | SAC | H | Estadio Bautista Gargantini, Mendoza | W | 152-0 |
| 257 | 4-May-02 | Chile | SAC | H | Estadio Bautista Gargantini, Mendoza | W | 57-13 |
| 258 | 15-Jun-02 | France | Int | H | Vélez Sarsfield Stadium, Buenos Aires | W | 28-27 |
| 259 | 22-Jun-02 | England | Int | H | Vélez Sarsfield Stadium, Buenos Aires | L | 18-26 |
| 260 | 29-Jun-02 | South Africa | Int-T | A | P A M Brink Stadium, Springs | L | 29-49 |
| 261 | 2-Nov-02 | Australia | PT | H | Estadio Monumental, River Plate, B Aires | L | 6-17 |
| 262 | 16-Nov-02 | Italy | Int-T | A | Stadio Flaminio, Rome | W | 36-6 |
| 263 | 23-Nov-02 | Ireland | Int-T | A | Lansdowne Road, Dublin | L | 7-16 |
| 264 | 27-Apr-03 | Paraguay | SAC | N | Estadio Luis Franzini, Montevideo | W | 144-0 |
| 265 | 30-Apr-03 | Chile | SAC | N | Estadio Luis Franzini, Montevideo | W | 49-3 |
| 266 | 3-May-03 | Uruguay | SAC | A | Estadio Luis Franzini, Montevideo | W | 32-0 |
| 267 | 14-Jun-03 | France | Int | H | Vélez Sarsfield Stadium, Buenos Aires | W | 10-6 |
| 268 | 20-Jun-03 | France | Int | H | Vélez Sarsfield Stadium, Buenos Aires | W | 33-32 |
| 269 | 28-Jun-03 | South Africa | Int-T | A | EPRFU Stadium, Port Elizabeth | L | 25-26 |
| 270 | 18-Aug-03 | Fiji | Int | H | Estadio Olimpico Château Carreras, Córdoba | W | 49-30 |
| 271 | 23-Aug-03 | United States | PAC | H | Cricket and Rugby Club, Buenos Aires | W | 42-8 |
| 272 | 27-Aug-03 | Uruguay | PAC | H | Club Atlético San Isidro, Buenos Aires | W | 57-0 |
| 273 | 30-Aug-03 | Canada | PAC | H | Cricket and Rugby Club, Buenos Aires | W | 62-22 |
| 274 | 10-Oct-03 | Australia | WCp | A | Telstra Stadium, Sydney | L | 8-24 |
| 275 | 14-Oct-03 | Namibia | WCp | N | Central Coast Stadium, Gosford, NSW | W | 67-14 |
| 276 | 22-Oct-03 | Romania | WCp | N | Aussie Stadium, Sydney | W | 50-3 |
| 277 | 26-Oct-03 | Ireland | WCp | N | Adelaide Oval, Adelaide | L | 15-16 |
| 278 | 25-Apr-04 | Chile | SAC | A | Prince of Wales Country Club, Santiago | W | 45-3 |
| 279 | 28-Apr-04 | Uruguay | SAC | N | Prince of Wales Country Club, Santiago | W | 69-10 |
| 280 | 1-May-04 | Venezuela | SAC | N | Prince of Wales Country Club, Santiago | W | 147-7 |

| No | Date | Opponents | Tmt | | Match Venue | Result | |
|----|------|-----------|-----|---|-------------|--------|---|
| 281 | 12-Jun-04 | Wales | Int | H | Estadio Monumental José Fierro, Tucumán | W | 50-44 |
| 282 | 19-Jun-04 | Wales | Int | H | Vélez Sarsfield Stadium, Buenos Aires | L | 20-35 |
| 283 | 26-Jun-04 | New Zealand | Int-T | A | Waikato Stadium, Hamilton | L | 7-41 |
| 284 | 20-Nov-04 | France | Int-T | A | Stade Vélodrome, Marseille | W | 24-14 |
| 285 | 27-Nov-04 | Ireland | Int-T | A | Lansdowne Road, Dublin | L | 19-21 |
| 286 | 4-Dec-04 | South Africa | Int | H | Vélez Sarsfield Stadium, Buenos Aires | L | 7-39 |
| 287 | 23-Apr-05 | Japan | Int | H | Cricket and Rugby Club, Buenos Aires | W | 68-36 |
| 288 | 8-May-05 | Chile | SAC | H | Club Monte Grande, Buenos Aires | W | 48-13 |
| 289 | 15-May-05 | Uruguay | SAC | H | Club Los Matreros, Buenos Aires | W | 27-21 |
| 290 | 11-Jun-05 | Italy | Int | H | Estadio Padre Ernesto Martearena, Salta | W | 35-21 |
| 291 | 17-Jun-05 | Italy | Int | H | Estadio Olimpico Château Carreras, Córdoba | L | 29-30 |
| 292 | 5-Nov-05 | South Africa | Int | H | Vélez Sarsfield Stadium, Buenos Aires | L | 23-34 |
| 293 | 12-Nov-05 | Scotland | Int-T | A | Murrayfield, Edinburgh | W | 23-19 |
| 294 | 19-Nov-05 | Italy | Int-T | A | Stadio Luigi Ferraris, Genova | W | 39-22 |
| 295 | 3-Dec-05 | Samoa | Int | H | Cricket and Rugby Club, Buenos Aires | L | 12-28 |
| 296 | 11-Jun-06 | Wales | Int | H | Estadio Raúl Conti, Puerto Madryn | W | 27-25 |
| 297 | 17-Jun-06 | Wales | Int | H | Vélez Sarsfield Stadium, Buenos Aires | W | 45-27 |
| 298 | 24-Jun-06 | New Zealand | Int | H | Vélez Sarsfield Stadium, Buenos Aires | L | 19-25 |
| 299 | 1-Jul-06 | Chile (SAC) | WCQ | A | Prince of Wales Country Club, Santiago | W | 60-13 |
| 300 | 8-Jul-06 | Uruguay (SAC) | WCQ | H | Club Atlético San Isidro, Buenos Aires | W | 26-0 |
| 301 | 11-Nov-06 | England | Int-T | A | Twickenham, London | W | 25-18 |
| 302 | 18-Nov-06 | Italy | Int-T | A | Stadio Flaminio, Rome | W | 23-16 |
| 303 | 25-Nov-06 | France | Int-T | A | Stade de France, Paris | L | 26-27 |
| 304 | 26-May-07 | Ireland | Int | H | Estadio Brig General E. López, Santa Fe | W | 22-20 |
| 305 | 2-Jun-07 | Ireland | Int | H | Vélez Sarsfield Stadium, Buenos Aires | W | 16-0 |
| 306 | 9-Jun-07 | Italy | Int | H | Estadio Malvinas Argentinas, Mendoza | W | 24-6 |
| 307 | 18-Aug-07 | Wales | Int-T | A | Millennium Stadium, Cardiff | L | 20-27 |
| 308 | 7-Sep-07 | France | WCp | A | Stade de France, Paris | W | 17-12 |
| 309 | 11-Sep-07 | Georgia | WCp | N | Stade de Gerland, Lyon | W | 33-3 |
| 310 | 22-Sep-07 | Namibia | WCp | N | Stade Vélodrome, Marseille | W | 63-3 |
| 311 | 30-Sep-07 | Ireland | WCp | N | Parc des Princess, Paris | W | 30-15 |
| 312 | 7-Oct-07 | Scotland | WCqf | N | Stade de France, Paris | W | 19-13 |
| 313 | 14-Oct-07 | South Africa | WCsf | N | Stade de France, Paris | L | 13-37 |
| 314 | 19-Oct-07 | France | WC34 | A | Parc des Princess, Paris | W | 34-10 |
| 315 | 15-Dec-07 | Chile | SAC | H | Estadio San Martin de San Juan, San Juan | W | 79-8 |
| 316 | 31-May-08 | Uruguay | SAC | A | Estadio Charrúa, Montevideo | W | 43-8 |
| 317 | 7-Jun-08 | Scotland | Int | H | Estadio Gigante de Arroyito, Rosario | W | 21-15 |
| 318 | 14-Jun-08 | Scotland | Int | H | Vélez Sarsfield Stadium, Buenos Aires | L | 14-26 |
| 319 | 28-Jun-08 | Italy | Int | H | Estadio Olimpico Château Carreras, Córdoba | L | 12-13 |
| 320 | 9-Aug-08 | South Africa | Int-T | A | Coca Cola Park, Johannesburg | L | 9-63 |

13

| No | Date | Opponents | Tmt | | Match Venue | Result | |
|----|------|-----------|-----|---|-------------|--------|---|
| 321 | 8-Nov-08 | Chile | SAC | A | Prince of Wales Country Club, Santiago | W | 71-3 |
| 322 | 8-Nov-08 | France | Int-T | A | Stade Vélodrome, Marseille | L | 6-12 |
| 323 | 15-Nov-08 | Italy | Int-T | A | Stadio Olimpico, di Torino | W | 22-14 |
| 324 | 22-Nov-08 | Ireland | Int-T | A | Croke Park, Dublin | L | 3-17 |
| 325 | 20-May-09 | Chile | SAC | N | Estadio Charrúa, Montevideo | W | 89-6 |
| 326 | 23-May-09 | Uruguay | SAC | A | Estadio Charrúa, Montevideo | W | 33-9 |
| 327 | 6-Jun-09 | England | Int-T | A | Old Trafford, Manchester | L | 15-37 |
| 328 | 13-Jun-09 | England | Int | H | Estadio Padre Ernesto Martearena, Salta | W | 24-22 |
| 329 | 14-Nov-09 | England | Int-T | A | Twickenham, London | L | 9-16 |
| 330 | 21-Nov-09 | Wales | Int-T | A | Millennium Stadium, Cardiff | L | 16-33 |
| 331 | 28-Nov-09 | Scotland | Int-T | A | Murrayfield, Edinburgh | W | 9-6 |
| 332 | 21-May-10 | Uruguay | SAC | N | Parque Mahuida CARR La Reina, Santiago | W | 38-0 |
| 333 | 23-May-10 | Chile | SAC | A | Parque Mahuida CARR La Reina, Santiago | W | 48-9 |
| 334 | 12-Jun-10 | Scotland | Int | H | Estadio Monumental José Fierro, Tucumán | L | 16-24 |
| 335 | 19-Jun-10 | Scotland | Int | H | Estad. Mundialista J M Minella, Mar d. Plata | L | 9-13 |
| 336 | 26-Jun-10 | France | Int | H | Vélez Sarsfield Stadium, Buenos Aires | W | 41-13 |
| 337 | 13-Nov-10 | Italy | Int-T | A | Stadio Marc'Antonio Bentegodi, Verona | W | 22-16 |
| 338 | 20-Nov-10 | France | Int-T | A | Stade de la Mosson, Montpellier | L | 9-15 |
| 339 | 28-Nov-10 | Ireland | Int-T | A | Aviva Stadium, Dublin | L | 9-29 |
| 340 | 22-May-11 | Chile | SAC | H | Cataratus Rugby Club, Puerto Iguazu | W | 61-6 |
| 341 | 25-May-11 | Uruguay | SAC | H | Tacuru Social Club Posadas, Misiones | W | 75-14 |
| 342 | 20-Aug-11 | Wales | Int-T | A | Millennium Stadium, Cardiff | L | 13-28 |
| 343 | 10-Sep-11 | England | WCp | N | Otago Stadium, Dunedin | L | 9-13 |
| 344 | 17-Sep-11 | Romania | WCp | N | Rugby Park Stadium, Invercargill | W | 43-8 |
| 345 | 25-Sep-11 | Scotland | WCp | N | Wellington Regional Stadium, Wellington | W | 13-12 |
| 346 | 2-Oct-11 | Georgia | WCp | N | Arena Manawatu, Palmerston North | W | 25-7 |
| 347 | 9-Oct-11 | New Zealand | WCqf | A | Eden Park, Auckland | L | 10-33 |
| 348 | 20-May-12 | Uruguay | SAC | N | Parque Mahuida CARR La Reina, Santiago | W | 40-5 |
| 349 | 23-May-12 | Brazil | SAC | N | Parque Mahuida CARR La Reina, Santiago | W | 111-0 |
| 350 | 26-May-12 | Chile | SAC | A | Parque Mahuida CARR La Reina, Santiago | W | 59-6 |
| 351 | 9-Jun-12 | Italy | Int | H | Estadio S. Juan del Bicentenario, San Juan | W | 37-22 |
| 352 | 16-Jun-12 | France | Int | H | Estadio Olimpico Château Carreras, Córdoba | W | 23-20 |
| 353 | 23-Jun-12 | France | Int | H | Estadio Monumental José Fierro, Tucumán | L | 10-49 |
| 354 | 18-Aug-12 | South Africa | RC | A | Newlands Stadium, Cape Town | L | 6-27 |
| 355 | 25-Aug-12 | South Africa | RC | H | Estadio Malvinas Argentinas, Mendoza | D | 16-16 |
| 356 | 8-Sep-12 | New Zealand | RC | A | Westpac Stadium, Wellington | L | 5-21 |
| 357 | 15-Sep-12 | Australia | RC-P | A | Skilled Park, Robina, Gold Coast, Q'land | L | 19-23 |
| 358 | 29-Sep-12 | New Zealand | RC | H | Estadio Ciudad de la Plata, La Plata | L | 15-54 |
| 359 | 6-Oct-12 | Australia | RC-P | H | Estadio Gigante de Arroyito, Rosario | L | 19-25 |
| 360 | 10-Nov-12 | Wales | Int-T | A | Millennium Stadium, Cardiff | W | 26-12 |

| No | Date | Opponents | Tmt | Match Venue | Result | |
|-----|-----------|-------------|-------|-----------------------------------------------------|---|-------|
| 361 | 17-Nov-12 | France | Int-T | A Grand Stade, Lille Métropole | L | 22-39 |
| 362 | 24-Nov-12 | Ireland | ABC-T | A Aviva Stadium, Dublin | L | 24-46 |
| 363 | 27-Apr-13 | Uruguay | SAC | A Estadio Charrúa, Montevideo | W | 29-18 |
| 364 | 1-May-13 | Chile | SAC | N Estadio Charrúa, Montevideo | W | 85-10 |
| 365 | 4-May-13 | Brazil | SAC | N Estadio Charrúa, Montevideo | W | 83-0 |
| 366 | 8-Jun-13 | England | Int | H Estadio Padre Ernesto Martearena, Salta | L | 3-32 |
| 367 | 15-Jun-13 | England | Int | H Vélez Sarsfield Stadium, Buenos Aires | L | 26-51 |
| 368 | 22-Jun-13 | Georgia | Int | H Estadio S. Juan del Bicentenario, San Juan | W | 29-18 |
| 369 | 17-Aug-13 | South Africa | RC | A FNB Stadium, Soweto, Johannesburg | L | 13-73 |
| 370 | 24-Aug-13 | South Africa | RC | H Estadio Malvinas Argentinas, Mendoza | L | 17-22 |
| 371 | 7-Sep-13 | New Zealand | RC | A Waikato Stadium, Hamilton | L | 13-28 |
| 372 | 14-Sep-13 | Australia | RC-P | A Patersons Stadium, Perth | L | 13-14 |
| 373 | 28-Sep-13 | New Zealand | RC | H Estadio Ciudad de la Plata, La Plata | L | 15-33 |
| 374 | 5-Oct-13 | Australia | RC-P | H Estadio Gigante de Arroyito, Rosario | L | 17-54 |
| 375 | 9-Nov-13 | England | ICC-T | A Twickenham, London | L | 12-31 |
| 376 | 16-Nov-13 | Wales | Int-T | A Millennium Stadium, Cardiff | L | 6-40 |
| 377 | 23-Nov-13 | Italy | Int-T | A Stadio Olimpico, Rome | W | 19-14 |
| 378 | 17-May-14 | Uruguay | CSC | A Estadio Parque Artigas, Paysandú | W | 65-9 |
| 379 | 24-May-14 | Chile | CSC | A Estadio S. Carlos de Apoquindo, Santiago | W | 73-12 |
| 380 | 7-Jun-14 | Ireland | ABC | H Estadio Centenario, Resistencia | L | 17-29 |
| 381 | 14-Jun-14 | Ireland | ABC | H Estadio Monumental José Fierro, Tucumán | L | 17-23 |
| 382 | 21-Jun-14 | Scotland | Int | H Estadio Olimpico Château Carreras, Córdoba | L | 19-21 |
| 383 | 16-Aug-14 | South Africa | RC | A Loftus Versfeld Stadium, Pretoria | L | 6-13 |
| 384 | 23-Aug-14 | South Africa | RC | H Estadio Padre Ernesto Martearena, Salta | L | 31-33 |
| 385 | 6-Sep-14 | New Zealand | RC | A McLean Park, Napier | L | 9-28 |
| 386 | 13-Sep-14 | Australia | RC-P | A Skilled Park, Robina, Gold Coast, Q'land | L | 25-32 |
| 387 | 27-Sep-14 | New Zealand | RC | H Estadio Ciudad de la Plata, La Plata | L | 13-34 |
| 388 | 4-Oct-14 | Australia | RC-P | H Estadio Malvinas Argentinas, Mendoza | W | 21-17 |
| 389 | 8-Nov-14 | Scotland | Int-T | A Murrayfield, Edinburgh | L | 31-41 |
| 390 | 14-Nov-14 | Italy | Int-T | A Stadio Luigi Ferraris, Genova | W | 20-18 |
| 391 | 22-Nov-14 | France | Int-T | A Stade de France, Paris | W | 18-13 |
| 392 | 16-May-15 | Uruguay | CSC | A Estadio Charrúa, Montevideo | W | 36-14 |
| 393 | 23-May-15 | Paraguay | CSC | A Estadio Feroes de Cu, Ascuncion | W | 71-7 |
| 394 | 17-Jul-15 | New Zealand | RC | A Rugby League Park, Christchurch | L | 18-39 |
| 395 | 25-Jul-15 | Australia | RC-P | H Estadio Malvinas Argentinas, Mendoza | L | 9-34 |
| 396 | 8-Aug-15 | South Africa | RC | A Kings Park Stadium, Durban | W | 37-25 |
| 397 | 15-Aug-15 | South Africa | RC | H Vélez Sarsfield Stadium, Buenos Aires | L | 12-26 |
| 398 | 20-Sep-15 | New Zealand | WCp | N Wembley Stadium, London | L | 16-26 |
| 399 | 25-Sep-15 | Georgia | WCp | N Kingsholm, Gloucester | W | 54-9 |
| 400 | 4-Oct-15 | Tonga | WCp | N Leicester Stadium, Leicester | W | 45-16 |

| No | Date | Opponents | Tmt | | Match Venue | Result | |
|----|------|-----------|-----|---|-------------|--------|---|
| 401 | 11-Oct-15 | Namibia | WCp | N | Leicester Stadium, Leicester | W | 64-19 |
| 402 | 18-Oct-15 | Ireland | WCqf | N | Millennium Stadium, Cardiff | W | 43-20 |
| 403 | 25-Oct-15 | Australia | WCsf | N | Twickenham, London | L | 15-29 |
| 404 | 31-Oct-15 | South Africa | WC34 | N | Olympic Stadium, London | L | 13-24 |

# AUSTRALIA

In 1884, the first New Zealand representative side visited Australia, winning all nine matches against provincial sides. Four years later, in 1888, a team drawn from the four unions, known at that time as Great Britain, set off on a first-ever rugby tour to Australia and New Zealand. They played sixteen matches in Australia, winning fourteen and drawing two. No Internationals were played on that tour, but in 1899, on a second visit to Australia, four Internationals were played. The Aussies won the first Test by 13 points to 3, but lost the series 3-1. A loss in their first International against New Zealand in 1903 was followed the next year by a 3-0 series loss to the touring Great Britain side. Nicknamed the 'Wallabies' on their first tour of Britain in 1908-09, the Australian team lost by 9 points to 6 to Wales in the first International, but was successful against England in the second. Between 1905 and 1914, Australia played New Zealand thirteen times but won only two of those games.

From the end of the First World War to 1928, Australia played twenty-four Internationals against a New Zealand XV and three Internationals against a South African XV. Neither opponent accepted these games as full Internationals, but on their 1927-28 Northern Hemisphere tour all five International matches played were recognized as full Internationals. The Wallabies defeated Ireland, Wales and France for the first time on that tour, but lost to both England and Scotland. Then, in 1929, the Aussies won a first-ever home series against All Blacks, by defeating them in all three Internationals.

In 1931, the Bledisloe Cup, a competition between Australia and New Zealand, was founded and in 1932 the All Blacks won the inaugural series, held in Australia, 2-1. On their first tour of South Africa in 1933 the Wallabies lost a series of five Internationals 3-2, and between 1936 and 1938 they lost three further series to their Southern Hemisphere rivals.

With the outbreak of the Second World War, Australia's 1939 Northern Hemisphere tour was cancelled. It was eventually re-scheduled for the 1947-48 season and it proved to be quite successful for the Wallabies as they lost only to Wales and to France in the five Internationals played. In 1948 Australia was invited to join the International Rugby Board (IRB), which led to the inaugural meeting of the Australian RFU in November 1949. In June of that year the Wallabies shared a three-match series with the New Zealand Maoris, and in September they regained the Bledisloe Cup, last won in 1934, by winning the series 2-0, this time on New Zealand soil.

The 1950s was a poor decade for Australia, with only seven wins in thirty-five matches, which included: two 2-0 series losses to the Lions in 1950 and 1959; a 3-1 series loss to the Springboks in 1953; and a 2-0 series loss again to South Africa in 1956. Their lowest point occurred on their 1958 Northern Hemisphere tour when they lost all five matches against the Northern Hemisphere Five Nations teams.

The 1960s and early 1970s weren't much better for the team in their encounters with the Lions, South Africa and New Zealand: they suffered another 2-0 series loss to the Lions in 1966, three series losses to the Springboks, in 1961, 1969 and 1971, losing all nine Internationals, and four Bledisloe series losses to the All Blacks in 1962, 1964, 1967 and 1968. However, on the credit side the Wallabies did draw the 1963 series with South Africa 2-2, and followed it with a 2-0 win over the Springboks in the 1965 series. Despite these positive results, between 1966 and 1974 the Aussies won only seven games out of thirty-eight played.

An improvement in the 1980s included their own 'grand slam' of four wins against the Home Nations in 1984. The Wallabies also reached the semi-final of the inaugural World Cup in 1987. That achievement was bettered in 1991 when they won the trophy by defeating England, the host nation, in the final at Twickenham.

Between 18 August 1990 and 4 July 1993, the Wallabies played twenty matches and won eighteen. That run was bettered in the three-year period 1998 to 2000, when a superb Australian side won thirty Internationals out of thirty-six. Their run of victories included a second World Cup triumph in Cardiff in 1999. The dawn of the new millennium saw the Wallabies continuing their success and in 2001 they achieved a 2-1 series win against the Lions, followed by a second successive Tri Nations title, and the retention of the Bledisloe Cup for the fourth time in a row. However, this phenomenal run eventually ended in disappointment: a third World Cup trophy eluded them in 2003, when they lost to England in the final in Sydney.

During the period November 2004 to November 2005, results were mixed for the team: a sequence of six wins was followed by a run of seven losses, which included a loss of all four matches in the 2005 Tri Nations campaign. Five defeats in thirteen Internationals during 2006 was something of an improvement on the previous two years, but losing to England in the quarter-final of the 2007 World Cup was another big disappointment for the team.

In the three Tri Nations championships held between 2008 and 2010, the Aussies won only six times in eighteen matches, but bounced back in 2011 by winning their third title. The Wallabies then lost to Ireland in the 2011 World Cup pool match, but defeated South Africa in the quarter-final, before losing to New Zealand in the semi-final. They soon recovered by taking bronze in defeating Wales in the play-off match for third place. The Tri Nations tournament was expanded in 2012 when Argentina was invited to join and the tournament which was subsequently renamed The Rugby Championship: Australia finished in second place on points difference in that first year. A 2-1 series defeat to the Lions in 2013 was followed by a mediocre Rugby Championship campaign, which yielded only two wins in six games.

The team's fortunes were mixed in 2014: an impressive 3-0 home series win against France was followed by just two wins in six in the Rugby Championship, and one win in four on their autumn tour of the Northern Hemisphere.

Australia's performance has been poor in the sixteen Tri Nations tournaments held annually between 1996 and 2011: only three titles have been won, in 2000, 2001 and 2011. However, the team's performance against the All Blacks in the Bledisloe Cup series has been even worse: the Wallabies have won only twelve titles to New Zealand's forty-four in the tournament's history (between 1931 and 2015). Australia secured the Rugby Championship for the first time in 2015 when they won all three games against their Southern Hemisphere opponents in a truncated tournament. However, they lost to New Zealand in a Bledisloe Cup match a week after the tournament.

The Wallabies topped a ferociously competitive pool in the 2015 World Cup by defeating Wales and host nation England. The quarter-final against Scotland was, however, extremely close with Australia finally scraping home in the last minute by 35 points to 34. After overcoming a spirited Argentinian team in the semi-final, the Wallabies finally succumbed to their old enemy, New Zealand, in the final, and lost by 34 points to 17.

# AUSTRALIA

## HEAD TO HEAD RESULTS TO 31 OCTOBER 2015

| v TIER 1 Teams | P | W | D | L | % | F | A |
|---|---|---|---|---|---|---|---|
| v Argentina | 25 | 19 | 1 | 5 | 78.0 | 673 | 387 |
| v England | 44 | 25 | 1 | 18 | 58.0 | 940 | 674 |
| v France | 46 | 26 | 2 | 18 | 58.7 | 991 | 802 |
| v Ireland | 32 | 21 | 1 | 10 | 67.2 | 657 | 453 |
| v Italy | 16 | 16 | 0 | 0 | 100.0 | 565 | 217 |
| v New Zealand | 155 | 42 | 7 | 106 | 29.4 | 2160 | 3160 |
| v Scotland | 29 | 20 | 0 | 9 | 69.0 | 706 | 364 |
| v South Africa | 81 | 35 | 1 | 45 | 43.8 | 1415 | 1572 |
| v Wales | 39 | 28 | 1 | 10 | 73.1 | 912 | 596 |
| v Lions | 23 | 6 | 0 | 17 | 26.1 | 248 | 414 |
| **Sub-Total** | **490** | **238** | **14** | **238** | **50.0** | **9267** | **8639** |
| | | | | | | | |
| **v TIER 2/3 Group** | | | | | | | |
| v Canada | 6 | 6 | 0 | 0 | 100.0 | 283 | 60 |
| v Fiji | 20 | 17 | 1 | 2 | 87.5 | 574 | 234 |
| v Japan | 4 | 4 | 0 | 0 | 100.0 | 220 | 58 |
| v Romania | 3 | 3 | 0 | 0 | 100.0 | 189 | 20 |
| v Samoa | 5 | 4 | 0 | 1 | 80.0 | 204 | 58 |
| v Tonga | 4 | 3 | 0 | 1 | 75.0 | 167 | 42 |
| v United States | 8 | 8 | 0 | 0 | 100.0 | 368 | 78 |
| v Georgia | 0 | 0 | 0 | 0 | 0.0 | 0 | 0 |
| v Namibia | 1 | 1 | 0 | 0 | 100.0 | 142 | 0 |
| v Russia | 1 | 1 | 0 | 0 | 100.0 | 68 | 22 |
| v Uruguay | 1 | 1 | 0 | 0 | 100.0 | 65 | 3 |
| **Sub-Total** | **53** | **48** | **1** | **4** | **91.5** | **2280** | **575** |
| | | | | | | | |
| **v Other Teams** | | | | | | | |
| v South Korea | 1 | 1 | 0 | 0 | 100.0 | 65 | 18 |
| v Spain | 1 | 1 | 0 | 0 | 100.0 | 92 | 10 |
| v New Zealand Maori | 16 | 8 | 2 | 6 | 56.3 | 240 | 203 |
| v New Zealand XV | 24 | 6 | 0 | 18 | 25.0 | 257 | 459 |
| v South African XV | 3 | 0 | 0 | 3 | 0.0 | 30 | 69 |
| v Pacific Islanders | 1 | 1 | 0 | 0 | 100.0 | 29 | 14 |
| **Sub-Total** | **46** | **17** | **2** | **27** | **39.1** | **713** | **773** |
| | | | | | | | |
| **All Internationals** | **589** | **303** | **17** | **269** | **52.9** | **12260** | **9987** |

| No | Date | Opponents | Tmt | Match Venue | Result | |
|----|------|-----------|-----|-------------|--------|---|
| 1 | 24-Jun-99 | Lions | Int | H Cricket Ground, Sydney | W | 13-3 |
| 2 | 22-Jul-99 | Lions | Int | H Exhibition Ground, Brisbane | L | 0-11 |
| 3 | 5-Aug-99 | Lions | Int | H Cricket Ground, Sydney | L | 10-11 |
| 4 | 12-Aug-99 | Lions | Int | H Cricket Ground, Sydney | L | 0-13 |
| 5 | 15-Aug-03 | New Zealand | Int | H Cricket Ground, Sydney | L | 3-22 |
| 6 | 2-Jul-04 | Lions | Int | H Cricket Ground, Sydney | L | 0-17 |
| 7 | 23-Jul-04 | Lions | Int | H Exhibition Ground, Brisbane | L | 3-17 |
| 8 | 30-Jul-04 | Lions | Int | H Cricket Ground, Sydney | L | 0-16 |
| 9 | 2-Sep-05 | New Zealand | Int-T | A Tahuna Park, Dunedin | L | 3-14 |
| 10 | 20-Jul-07 | New Zealand | Int | H Cricket Ground, Sydney | L | 6-26 |
| 11 | 3-Aug-07 | New Zealand | Int | H The Gabba Cricket Ground, Brisbane | L | 5-14 |
| 12 | 10-Aug-07 | New Zealand | Int | H Cricket Ground, Sydney | D | 5-5 |
| 13 | 12-Dec-08 | Wales | Int-T | A Arms Park, Cardiff | L | 6-9 |
| 14 | 9-Jan-09 | England | Int-T | A Rectory Field, Blackheath | W | 9-3 |
| 15 | 25-Jun-10 | New Zealand | Int | H Cricket Ground, Sydney | L | 0-6 |
| 16 | 27-Jun-10 | New Zealand | Int | H Cricket Ground, Sydney | W | 11-0 |
| 17 | 2-Jul-10 | New Zealand | Int | H Cricket Ground, Sydney | L | 13-28 |
| 18 | 16-Nov-12 | United States | Int-T | A St Ignatius, California Field, Berkeley | W | 12-8 |
| 19 | 6-Sep-13 | New Zealand | Int-T | A Athletic Park, Wellington | L | 5-30 |
| 20 | 13-Sep-13 | New Zealand | Int-T | A Carisbrook, Dunedin | L | 13-25 |
| 21 | 20-Sep-13 | New Zealand | Int-T | A Lancaster Park Oval, Christchurch | W | 16-5 |
| 22 | 18-Jul-14 | New Zealand | Int | H Sports Ground, Sydney | L | 0-5 |
| 23 | 1-Aug-14 | New Zealand | Int | H The Gabba Cricket Ground, Brisbane | L | 0-17 |
| 24 | 15-Aug-14 | New Zealand | Int | H Sports Ground, Sydney | L | 7-22 |
| 25 | 24-Jul-20 | N.Z. XV | Int | H Sports Ground, Sydney | L | 15-26 |
| 26 | 31-Jul-20 | N.Z. XV | Int | H Sports Ground, Sydney | L | 6-14 |
| 27 | 7-Aug-20 | N.Z. XV | Int | H Sports Ground, Sydney | L | 13-24 |
| 28 | 25-Jun-21 | S.A. XV | Int | H Royal Agricultural Showground, Sydney | L | 10-25 |
| 29 | 27-Jun-21 | S.A. XV | Int | H Royal Agricultural Showground, Sydney | L | 11-16 |
| 30 | 2-Jul-21 | S.A. XV | Int | H University Ground, Sydney | L | 9-28 |
| 31 | 3-Sep-21 | N.Z. XV | Int-T | A Lancaster Park Oval, Christchurch | W | 17-0 |
| 32 | 24-Jun-22 | N.Z Maori | Int | H Royal Agricultural Showground, Sydney | L | 22-25 |
| 33 | 26-Jun-22 | N.Z Maori | Int | H Royal Agricultural Showground, Sydney | W | 28-13 |
| 34 | 8-Jul-22 | N.Z Maori | Int | H University Ground, Sydney | L | 22-23 |
| 35 | 29-Jul-22 | N.Z. XV | Int | H Royal Agricultural Showground, Sydney | L | 19-26 |
| 36 | 5-Aug-22 | N.Z. XV | Int | H Royal Agricultural Showground, Sydney | W | 14-8 |
| 37 | 7-Aug-22 | N.Z. XV | Int | H Royal Agricultural Showground, Sydney | W | 8-6 |
| 38 | 16-Jun-23 | NZ Maori | Int | H Royal Agricultural Showground, Sydney | W | 27-23 |
| 39 | 23-Jun-23 | NZ Maori | Int | H Royal Agricultural Showground, Sydney | W | 21-16 |
| 40 | 25-Jun-23 | NZ Maori | Int | H Royal Agricultural Showground, Sydney | W | 14-12 |

| No | Date | Opponents | Tmt | | Match Venue | Result | |
|----|------|-----------|-----|---|-------------|--------|---|
| 41 | 25-Aug-23 | N.Z. XV | Int-T | A | Carisbrook, Dunedin | L | 9-19 |
| 42 | 1-Sep-23 | N.Z. XV | Int-T | A | Lancaster Park Oval, Christchurch | L | 6-34 |
| 43 | 15-Sep-23 | N.Z. XV | Int-T | A | Athletic Park, Wellington | L | 11-38 |
| 44 | 5-Jul-24 | N.Z. XV | Int | H | Royal Agricultural Showground, Sydney | W | 20-16 |
| 45 | 12-Jul-24 | N.Z. XV | Int | H | Royal Agricultural Showground, Sydney | L | 5-21 |
| 46 | 16-Jul-24 | N.Z. XV | Int | H | Royal Agricultural Showground, Sydney | L | 8-38 |
| 47 | 13-Jun-25 | N.Z. XV | Int | H | Royal Agricultural Showground, Sydney | L | 3-26 |
| 48 | 20-Jun-25 | N.Z. XV | Int | H | Royal Agricultural Showground, Sydney | L | 0-4 |
| 49 | 23-Jun-25 | N.Z. XV | Int | H | Royal Agricultural Showground, Sydney | L | 3-11 |
| 50 | 19-Sep-25 | N.Z. XV | Int-T | A | Eden Park, Auckland | L | 10-36 |
| 51 | 10-Jul-26 | N.Z. XV | Int | H | Royal Agricultural Showground, Sydney | W | 26-20 |
| 52 | 17-Jul-26 | N.Z. XV | Int | H | Royal Agricultural Showground, Sydney | L | 6-11 |
| 53 | 20-Jul-26 | N.Z. XV | Int | H | Royal Agricultural Showground, Sydney | L | 0-14 |
| 54 | 29-Jul-26 | N.Z. XV | Int | H | Royal Agricultural Showground, Sydney | L | 21-28 |
| 55 | 12-Nov-27 | Ireland | Int-T | A | Lansdowne Road, Dublin | W | 5-3 |
| 56 | 26-Nov-27 | Wales | Int-T | A | Arms Park, Cardiff | W | 18-8 |
| 57 | 17-Dec-27 | Scotland | Int-T | A | Murrayfield, Edinburgh | L | 8-10 |
| 58 | 7-Jan-28 | England | Int-T | A | Twickenham, London | L | 11-18 |
| 59 | 22-Jan-28 | France | Int-T | A | Stade Colombes, Paris | W | 11-8 |
| 60 | 5-Sep-28 | N.Z. XV | Int-T | A | Athletic Park, Wellington | L | 12-15 |
| 61 | 8-Sep-28 | N.Z. XV | Int-T | A | Carisbrook, Dunedin | L | 14-16 |
| 62 | 15-Sep-28 | N.Z. XV | Int-T | A | Lancaster Park Oval, Christchurch | W | 11-8 |
| 63 | 22-Sep-28 | N.Z Maori | Int-T | A | Athletic Park, Wellington | L | 8-9 |
| 64 | 6-Jul-29 | New Zealand | Int | H | Cricket Ground, Sydney | W | 9-8 |
| 65 | 20-Jul-29 | New Zealand | Int | H | Exhibition Ground, Brisbane | W | 17-9 |
| 66 | 27-Jul-29 | New Zealand | Int | H | Cricket Ground, Sydney | W | 15-13 |
| 67 | 30-Aug-30 | Lions | Int | H | Cricket Ground, Sydney | W | 6-5 |
| 68 | 9-Sep-31 | N.Z Maori | Int-T | A | Showgrounds Oval, Palmerston North | W | 14-3 |
| 69 | 12-Sep-31 | New Zealand | Bled-T | A | Eden Park, Auckland | L | 13-20 |
| 70 | 2-Jul-32 | New Zealand | Bled | H | Cricket Ground, Sydney | W | 22-17 |
| 71 | 16-Jul-32 | New Zealand | Bled | H | Exhibition Ground, Brisbane | L | 3-21 |
| 72 | 23-Jul-32 | New Zealand | Bled | H | Cricket Ground, Sydney | L | 13-21 |
| 73 | 8-Jul-33 | South Africa | Int-T | A | Newlands Stadium, Cape Town | L | 3-17 |
| 74 | 22-Jul-33 | South Africa | Int-T | A | Kingsmead Ground, Durban | W | 21-6 |
| 75 | 12-Aug-33 | South Africa | Int-T | A | Ellis Park, Johannesburg | L | 3-12 |
| 76 | 26-Aug-33 | South Africa | Int-T | A | Crusaders Ground, Port Elizabeth | L | 0-11 |
| 77 | 2-Sep-33 | South Africa | Int-T | A | Springbok Park, Bloemfontein | W | 15-4 |
| 78 | 11-Aug-34 | New Zealand | Bled | H | Cricket Ground, Sydney | W | 25-11 |
| 79 | 25-Aug-34 | New Zealand | Bled | H | Cricket Ground, Sydney | D | 3-3 |
| 80 | 5-Sep-36 | New Zealand | Bled-T | A | Athletic Park, Wellington | L | 6-11 |

| No | Date | Opponents | Tmt | | Match Venue | Result | |
|----|------|-----------|-----|---|-------------|--------|---|
| 81 | 12-Sep-36 | New Zealand | Bled-T | A | Carisbrook, Dunedin | L | 13-38 |
| 82 | 23-Sep-36 | N.Z Maori | Int-T | A | Showgrounds Oval, Palmerston North | W | 31-6 |
| 83 | 26-Jun-37 | South Africa | Int | H | Cricket Ground, Sydney | L | 5-9 |
| 84 | 17-Jul-37 | South Africa | Int | H | Cricket Ground, Sydney | L | 17-26 |
| 85 | 23-Jul-38 | New Zealand | Bled | H | Cricket Ground, Sydney | L | 9-24 |
| 86 | 6-Aug-38 | New Zealand | Bled | H | Exhibition Ground, Brisbane | L | 14-20 |
| 87 | 13-Aug-38 | New Zealand | Bled | H | Cricket Ground, Sydney | L | 6-14 |
| 88 | 14-Sep-46 | New Zealand | Bled-T | A | Carisbrook, Dunedin | L | 8-31 |
| 89 | 25-Sep-46 | N.Z Maori | Int-T | A | Rugby Park, Hamilton | L | 0-20 |
| 90 | 28-Sep-46 | New Zealand | Bled-T | A | Eden Park, Auckland | L | 10-14 |
| 91 | 14-Jun-47 | New Zealand | Bled | H | Exhibition Ground, Brisbane | L | 5-13 |
| 92 | 28-Jun-47 | New Zealand | Bled | H | Cricket Ground, Sydney | L | 14-27 |
| 93 | 22-Nov-47 | Scotland | Int-T | A | Murrayfield, Edinburgh | W | 16-7 |
| 94 | 6-Dec-47 | Ireland | Int-T | A | Lansdowne Road, Dublin | W | 16-3 |
| 95 | 20-Dec-47 | Wales | Int-T | A | Arms Park, Cardiff | L | 0-6 |
| 96 | 3-Jan-48 | England | Int-T | A | Twickenham, London | W | 11-0 |
| 97 | 11-Jan-48 | France | Int-T | A | Stade Colombes, Paris | L | 6-13 |
| 98 | 4-Jun-49 | N.Z Maori | Int | H | Cricket Ground, Sydney | L | 3-12 |
| 99 | 11-Jun-49 | N.Z Maori | Int | H | Exhibition Ground, Brisbane | D | 8-8 |
| 100 | 25-Jun-49 | N.Z Maori | Int | H | Cricket Ground, Sydney | W | 18-3 |
| 101 | 3-Sep-49 | New Zealand | Bled-T | A | Athletic Park, Wellington | W | 11-6 |
| 102 | 24-Sep-49 | New Zealand | Bled-T | A | Eden Park, Auckland | W | 16-9 |
| 103 | 19-Aug-50 | Lions | Int | H | The Gabba Cricket Ground, Brisbane | L | 6-19 |
| 104 | 26-Aug-50 | Lions | Int | H | Cricket Ground, Sydney | L | 3-24 |
| 105 | 23-Jun-51 | New Zealand | Bled | H | Cricket Ground, Sydney | L | 0-8 |
| 106 | 7-Jul-51 | New Zealand | Bled | H | Cricket Ground, Sydney | L | 11-17 |
| 107 | 21-Jul-51 | New Zealand | Bled | H | The Gabba Cricket Ground, Brisbane | L | 6-16 |
| 108 | 26-Jul-52 | Fiji | Int | H | Cricket Ground, Sydney | W | 15-9 |
| 109 | 9-Aug-52 | Fiji | Int | H | Cricket Ground, Sydney | L | 15-17 |
| 110 | 6-Sep-52 | New Zealand | Bled-T | A | Lancaster Park Oval, Christchurch | W | 14-9 |
| 111 | 13-Sep-52 | New Zealand | Bled-T | A | Athletic Park, Wellington | L | 8-15 |
| 112 | 22-Aug-53 | South Africa | Int-T | A | Ellis Park, Johannesburg | L | 3-25 |
| 113 | 5-Sep-53 | South Africa | Int-T | A | Newlands Stadium, Cape Town | W | 18-14 |
| 114 | 19-Sep-53 | South Africa | Int-T | A | Kingsmead Ground, Durban | L | 8-18 |
| 115 | 26-Sep-53 | South Africa | Int-T | A | Crusaders Ground, Port Elizabeth | L | 9-22 |
| 116 | 6-Jun-54 | Fiji | Int | H | Exhibition Ground, Brisbane | W | 22-19 |
| 117 | 26-Jun-54 | Fiji | Int | H | Cricket Ground, Sydney | L | 16-18 |
| 118 | 20-Aug-55 | New Zealand | Bled-T | A | Athletic Park, Wellington | L | 8-16 |
| 119 | 3-Sep-55 | New Zealand | Bled-T | A | Carisbrook, Dunedin | L | 0-8 |
| 120 | 17-Sep-55 | New Zealand | Bled-T | A | Eden Park, Auckland | W | 8-3 |

AUSTRALIA

| No | Date | Opponents | Tmt | Match Venue | Result | |
|---|---|---|---|---|---|---|
| 121 | 26-May-56 | South Africa | Int | H Cricket Ground, Sydney | L | 0-9 |
| 122 | 2-Jun-56 | South Africa | Int | H Exhibition Ground, Brisbane | L | 0-9 |
| 123 | 25-May-57 | New Zealand | Bled | H Cricket Ground, Sydney | L | 11-25 |
| 124 | 1-Jun-57 | New Zealand | Bled | H Exhibition Ground, Brisbane | L | 9-22 |
| 125 | 4-Jan-58 | Wales | Int-T | A Arms Park, Cardiff | L | 3-9 |
| 126 | 18-Jan-58 | Ireland | Int-T | A Lansdowne Road, Dublin | L | 6-9 |
| 127 | 1-Feb-58 | England | Int-T | A Twickenham, London | L | 6-9 |
| 128 | 15-Feb-58 | Scotland | Int-T | A Murrayfield, Edinburgh | L | 8-12 |
| 129 | 9-Mar-58 | France | Int-T | A Stade Colombes, Paris | L | 0-19 |
| 130 | 14-Jun-58 | N.Z Maori | Int | H Exhibition Ground, Brisbane | W | 15-14 |
| 131 | 28-Jun-58 | N.Z Maori | Int | H Cricket Ground, Sydney | D | 3-3 |
| 132 | 5-Jul-58 | N.Z Maori | Int | H Olympic Park Stadium, Melbourne | L | 6-13 |
| 133 | 23-Aug-58 | New Zealand | Bled-T | A Athletic Park, Wellington | L | 3-25 |
| 134 | 6-Sep-58 | New Zealand | Bled-T | A Lancaster Park Oval, Christchurch | W | 6-3 |
| 135 | 20-Sep-58 | New Zealand | Bled-T | A Epsom Showgrounds, Auckland | L | 8-17 |
| 136 | 6-Jun-59 | Lions | Int | H Exhibition Ground, Brisbane | L | 6-17 |
| 137 | 13-Jun-59 | Lions | Int | H Sports Ground, Sydney | L | 3-24 |
| 138 | 10-Jun-61 | Fiji | Int | H Exhibition Ground, Brisbane | W | 24-6 |
| 139 | 17-Jun-61 | Fiji | Int | H Cricket Ground, Sydney | W | 20-14 |
| 140 | 1-Jul-61 | Fiji | Int | H Olympic Park Stadium, Melbourne | D | 3-3 |
| 141 | 5-Aug-61 | South Africa | Int-T | A Ellis Park, Johannesburg | L | 3-28 |
| 142 | 12-Aug-61 | South Africa | Int-T | A Boet Erasmus Stadium, Port Elizabeth | L | 11-23 |
| 143 | 26-Aug-61 | France | Int | H Cricket Ground, Sydney | L | 8-15 |
| 144 | 26-May-62 | New Zealand | Bled | H Exhibition Ground, Brisbane | L | 6-20 |
| 145 | 4-Jun-62 | New Zealand | Bled | H Cricket Ground, Sydney | L | 5-14 |
| 146 | 25-Aug-62 | New Zealand | Bled-T | A Athletic Park, Wellington | D | 9-9 |
| 147 | 8-Sep-62 | New Zealand | Bled-T | A Carisbrook, Dunedin | L | 0-3 |
| 148 | 22-Sep-62 | New Zealand | Bled-T | A Eden Park, Auckland | L | 8-16 |
| 149 | 4-Jun-63 | England | Int | H Sports Ground, Sydney | W | 18-9 |
| 150 | 13-Jul-63 | South Africa | Int-T | A Loftus Versfeld Stadium, Pretoria | L | 3-14 |
| 151 | 10-Aug-63 | South Africa | Int-T | A Newlands Stadium, Cape Town | W | 9-5 |
| 152 | 24-Aug-63 | South Africa | Int-T | A Ellis Park, Johannesburg | W | 11-9 |
| 153 | 7-Sep-63 | South Africa | Int-T | A Boet Erasmus Stadium, Port Elizabeth | L | 6-22 |
| 154 | 15-Aug-64 | New Zealand | Bled-T | A Carisbrook, Dunedin | L | 9-14 |
| 155 | 22-Aug-64 | New Zealand | Bled-T | A Lancaster Park Oval, Christchurch | L | 3-18 |
| 156 | 29-Aug-64 | New Zealand | Bled-T | A Athletic Park, Wellington | W | 20-5 |
| 157 | 19-Jun-65 | South Africa | Int | H Cricket Ground, Sydney | W | 18-11 |
| 158 | 26-Jun-65 | South Africa | Int | H Lang Park, Brisbane | W | 12-8 |
| 159 | 28-May-66 | Lions | Int | H Cricket Ground, Sydney | L | 8-11 |
| 160 | 4-Jun-66 | Lions | Int | H Lang Park, Brisbane | L | 0-31 |

| No | Date | Opponents | Tmt | | Match Venue | Result | |
|-----|-----------|--------------|--------|---|-----------------------------------------|---|-------|
| 161 | 3-Dec-66 | Wales | Int-T | A | Arms Park, Cardiff | W | 14-11 |
| 162 | 17-Dec-66 | Scotland | Int-T | A | Murrayfield, Edinburgh | L | 5-11 |
| 163 | 7-Jan-67 | England | Int-T | A | Twickenham, London | W | 23-11 |
| 164 | 21-Jan-67 | Ireland | Int-T | A | Lansdowne Road, Dublin | L | 8-15 |
| 165 | 11-Feb-67 | France | Int-T | A | Stade Colombes, Paris | L | 14-20 |
| 166 | 13-May-67 | Ireland | Int | H | Cricket Ground, Sydney | L | 5-11 |
| 167 | 19-Aug-67 | New Zealand | Bled-T | A | Athletic Park, Wellington | L | 9-29 |
| 168 | 15-Jun-68 | New Zealand | Bled | H | Cricket Ground, Sydney | L | 11-27 |
| 169 | 22-Jun-68 | New Zealand | Bled | H | Ballymore Oval, Brisbane | L | 18-19 |
| 170 | 17-Aug-68 | France | Int | H | Cricket Ground, Sydney | W | 11-10 |
| 171 | 26-Oct-68 | Ireland | Int-T | A | Lansdowne Road, Dublin | L | 3-10 |
| 172 | 2-Nov-68 | Scotland | Int-T | A | Murrayfield, Edinburgh | L | 3-9 |
| 173 | 21-Jun-69 | Wales | Int | H | Cricket Ground, Sydney | L | 16-19 |
| 174 | 2-Aug-69 | South Africa | Int-T | A | Ellis Park, Johannesburg | L | 11-30 |
| 175 | 16-Aug-69 | South Africa | Int-T | A | Kings Park Stadium, Durban | L | 9-16 |
| 176 | 6-Sep-69 | South Africa | Int-T | A | Newlands Stadium, Cape Town | L | 3-11 |
| 177 | 20-Sep-69 | South Africa | Int-T | A | Free State Stadium, Bloemfontein | L | 8-19 |
| 178 | 6-Jun-70 | Scotland | Int | H | Cricket Ground, Sydney | W | 23-3 |
| 179 | 17-Jul-71 | South Africa | Int | H | Cricket Ground, Sydney | L | 11-19 |
| 180 | 31-Jul-71 | South Africa | Int | H | Exhibition Ground, Brisbane | L | 6-14 |
| 181 | 7-Aug-71 | South Africa | Int | H | Cricket Ground, Sydney | L | 6-18 |
| 182 | 20-Nov-71 | France | Int-T | A | Stade Municipal de Toulouse, Toulouse | W | 13-11 |
| 183 | 27-Nov-71 | France | Int-T | A | Stade Colombes, Paris | L | 9-18 |
| 184 | 17-Jun-72 | France | Int | H | Cricket Ground, Sydney | D | 14-14 |
| 185 | 25-Jun-72 | France | Int | H | Ballymore Oval, Brisbane | L | 15-16 |
| 186 | 19-Aug-72 | New Zealand | Bled-T | A | Athletic Park, Wellington | L | 6-29 |
| 187 | 2-Sep-72 | New Zealand | Bled-T | A | Lancaster Park Oval, Christchurch | L | 17-30 |
| 188 | 16-Sep-72 | New Zealand | Bled-T | A | Eden Park, Auckland | L | 3-38 |
| 189 | 19-Sep-72 | Fiji | Int-T | A | Buckhurst Park, Suva | W | 21-19 |
| 190 | 23-Jun-73 | Tonga | Int | H | Cricket Ground, Sydney | W | 30-12 |
| 191 | 30-Jun-73 | Tonga | Int | H | Ballymore Oval, Brisbane | L | 11-16 |
| 192 | 10-Nov-73 | Wales | Int-T | A | National Stadium, Cardiff | L | 0-24 |
| 193 | 17-Nov-73 | England | Int-T | A | Twickenham, London | L | 3-20 |
| 194 | 25-May-74 | New Zealand | Bled | H | Cricket Ground, Sydney | L | 6-11 |
| 195 | 1-Jun-74 | New Zealand | Bled | H | Ballymore Oval, Brisbane | D | 16-16 |
| 196 | 8-Jun-74 | New Zealand | Bled | H | Cricket Ground, Sydney | L | 6-16 |
| 197 | 24-May-75 | England | Int | H | Cricket Ground, Sydney | W | 16-9 |
| 198 | 31-May-75 | England | Int | H | Ballymore Oval, Brisbane | W | 30-21 |
| 199 | 2-Aug-75 | Japan | Int | H | Cricket Ground, Sydney | W | 37-7 |
| 200 | 17-Aug-75 | Japan | Int | H | Ballymore Oval, Brisbane | W | 50-25 |

| No | Date | Opponents | Tmt | | Match Venue | Result | |
|-----|-----------|---------------|---------|---|----------------------------------------|---|-------|
| 201 | 6-Dec-75 | Scotland | Int-T | A | Murrayfield, Edinburgh | L | 3-10 |
| 202 | 20-Dec-75 | Wales | Int-T | A | National Stadium, Cardiff | L | 3-28 |
| 203 | 3-Jan-76 | England | Int-T | A | Twickenham, London | L | 6-23 |
| 204 | 17-Jan-76 | Ireland | Int-T | A | Lansdowne Road, Dublin | W | 20-10 |
| 205 | 31-Jan-76 | United States | Int-T | A | Glover Field Anaheim, Los Angeles | W | 24-12 |
| 206 | 12-Jun-76 | Fiji | Int | H | Cricket Ground, Sydney | W | 22-6 |
| 207 | 19-Jun-76 | Fiji | Int | H | Ballymore Oval, Brisbane | W | 21-9 |
| 208 | 26-Jun-76 | Fiji | Int | H | Cricket Ground, Sydney | W | 27-17 |
| 209 | 24-Oct-76 | France | Int-T | A | Stade du Parc Lescure, Bordeaux | L | 15-18 |
| 210 | 30-Oct-76 | France | Int-T | A | Parc des Princes, Paris | L | 6-34 |
| 211 | 11-Jun-78 | Wales | Int | H | Ballymore Oval, Brisbane | W | 18-8 |
| 212 | 17-Jun-78 | Wales | Int | H | Cricket Ground, Sydney | W | 19-17 |
| 213 | 19-Aug-78 | New Zealand | Bled-T | A | Athletic Park, Wellington | L | 12-13 |
| 214 | 26-Aug-78 | New Zealand | Bled-T | A | Lancaster Park Oval, Christchurch | L | 6-22 |
| 215 | 9-Sep-78 | New Zealand | Bled-T | A | Eden Park, Auckland | W | 30-16 |
| 216 | 3-Jun-79 | Ireland | Int | H | Ballymore Oval, Brisbane | L | 12-27 |
| 217 | 16-Jun-79 | Ireland | Int | H | Cricket Ground, Sydney | L | 3-9 |
| 218 | 28-Jul-79 | New Zealand | Bled | H | Cricket Ground, Sydney | W | 12-6 |
| 219 | 27-Oct-79 | Argentina | Int-T | A | Ferro Carril Oeste Stadium, B Aires | L | 13-24 |
| 220 | 3-Nov-79 | Argentina | Int-T | A | Ferro Carril Oeste Stadium, B Aires | W | 17-12 |
| 221 | 24-May-80 | Fiji | Int-T | A | National Stadium, Suva | W | 22-9 |
| 222 | 21-Jun-80 | New Zealand | Bled | H | Cricket Ground, Sydney | W | 13-9 |
| 223 | 28-Jun-80 | New Zealand | Bled | H | Ballymore Oval, Brisbane | L | 9-12 |
| 224 | 12-Jul-80 | New Zealand | Bled | H | Cricket Ground, Sydney | W | 26-10 |
| 225 | 5-Jul-81 | France | Int | H | Ballymore Oval, Brisbane | W | 17-15 |
| 226 | 11-Jul-81 | France | Int | H | Cricket Ground, Sydney | W | 24-14 |
| 227 | 21-Nov-81 | Ireland | Int-T | A | Lansdowne Road, Dublin | W | 16-12 |
| 228 | 5-Dec-81 | Wales | Int-T | A | National Stadium, Cardiff | L | 13-18 |
| 229 | 19-Dec-81 | Scotland | Int-T | A | Murrayfield, Edinburgh | L | 15-24 |
| 230 | 2-Jan-82 | England | Int-T | A | Twickenham, London | L | 11-15 |
| 231 | 4-Jul-82 | Scotland | Int | H | Ballymore Oval, Brisbane | L | 7-12 |
| 232 | 10-Jul-82 | Scotland | Int | H | Cricket Ground, Sydney | W | 33-9 |
| 233 | 14-Aug-82 | New Zealand | Bled-T | A | Lancaster Park Oval, Christchurch | L | 16-23 |
| 234 | 28-Aug-82 | New Zealand | Bled-T | A | Athletic Park, Wellington | W | 19-16 |
| 235 | 11-Sep-82 | New Zealand | Bled-T | A | Eden Park, Auckland | L | 18-33 |
| 236 | 9-Jul-83 | United States | Int | H | Cricket Ground, Sydney | W | 49-3 |
| 237 | 31-Jul-83 | Argentina | Int | H | Ballymore Oval, Brisbane | L | 3-18 |
| 238 | 7-Aug-83 | Argentina | Int | H | Cricket Ground, Sydney | W | 29-13 |
| 239 | 20-Aug-83 | New Zealand | Bled | H | Cricket Ground, Sydney | L | 8-18 |
| 240 | 22-Oct-83 | Italy | Int-T | A | Stadio Mario Battaglini, Rovigo | W | 29-7 |

| No | Date | Opponents | Tmt | | Match Venue | Result | |
|----|------|-----------|-----|---|-------------|--------|---|
| 241 | 13-Nov-83 | France | Int-T | A | Stade Marcel Michelin, Clermont Ferrand | D | 15-15 |
| 242 | 19-Nov-83 | France | Int-T | A | Parc des Princes, Paris | L | 6-15 |
| 243 | 9-Jun-84 | Fiji | Int-T | A | National Stadium, Suva | W | 16-3 |
| 244 | 21-Jul-84 | New Zealand | Bled | H | Cricket Ground, Sydney | W | 16-9 |
| 245 | 4-Aug-84 | New Zealand | Bled | H | Ballymore Oval, Brisbane | L | 15-19 |
| 246 | 18-Aug-84 | New Zealand | Bled | H | Cricket Ground, Sydney | L | 24-25 |
| 247 | 3-Nov-84 | England | Int-T | A | Twickenham, London | W | 19-3 |
| 248 | 10-Nov-84 | Ireland | Int-T | A | Lansdowne Road, Dublin | W | 16-9 |
| 249 | 24-Nov-84 | Wales | Int-T | A | National Stadium, Cardiff | W | 28-9 |
| 250 | 8-Dec-84 | Scotland | Int-T | A | Murrayfield, Edinburgh | W | 37-12 |
| 251 | 15-Jun-85 | Canada | Int | H | Cricket Ground, Sydney | W | 59-3 |
| 252 | 23-Jun-85 | Canada | Int | H | Ballymore Oval, Brisbane | W | 43-15 |
| 253 | 29-Jun-85 | New Zealand | Bled-T | A | Eden Park, Auckland | L | 9-10 |
| 254 | 10-Aug-85 | Fiji | Int | H | Ballymore Oval, Brisbane | W | 52-28 |
| 255 | 17-Aug-85 | Fiji | Int | H | Cricket Ground, Sydney | W | 31-9 |
| 256 | 1-Jun-86 | Italy | Int | H | Ballymore Oval, Brisbane | W | 39-18 |
| 257 | 21-Jun-86 | France | Int | H | Cricket Ground, Sydney | W | 27-14 |
| 258 | 6-Jul-86 | Argentina | Int | H | Ballymore Oval, Brisbane | W | 39-19 |
| 259 | 12-Jul-86 | Argentina | Int | H | Cricket Ground, Sydney | W | 26-0 |
| 260 | 9-Aug-86 | New Zealand | Bled-T | A | Athletic Park, Wellington | W | 13-12 |
| 261 | 23-Aug-86 | New Zealand | Bled-T | A | Carisbrook, Dunedin | L | 12-13 |
| 262 | 6-Sep-86 | New Zealand | Bled-T | A | Eden Park, Auckland | W | 22-9 |
| 263 | 17-May-87 | Korea | Int | H | Ballymore Oval, Brisbane | W | 65-18 |
| 264 | 23-May-87 | England | WCp | H | Concord Oval, Sydney | W | 19-6 |
| 265 | 31-May-87 | United States | WCp | H | Ballymore Oval, Brisbane | W | 47-12 |
| 266 | 3-Jun-87 | Japan | WCp | H | Concord Oval, Sydney | W | 42-23 |
| 267 | 7-Jun-87 | Ireland | WCqf | H | Concord Oval, Sydney | W | 33-15 |
| 268 | 13-Jun-87 | France | WCsf | H | Concord Oval, Sydney | L | 24-30 |
| 269 | 18-Jun-87 | Wales | WC34 | N | Rotorua International Stadium, Rotorua | L | 21-22 |
| 270 | 25-Jul-87 | New Zealand | Bled | H | Concord Oval, Sydney | L | 16-30 |
| 271 | 31-Oct-87 | Argentina | Int-T | A | Vélez Sarsfield Stadium, Buenos Aires | D | 19-19 |
| 272 | 7-Nov-87 | Argentina | Int-T | A | Vélez Sarsfield Stadium, Buenos Aires | L | 19-27 |
| 273 | 29-May-88 | England | Int | H | Ballymore Oval, Brisbane | W | 22-16 |
| 274 | 12-Jun-88 | England | Int | H | Concord Oval, Sydney | W | 28-8 |
| 275 | 3-Jul-88 | New Zealand | Bled | H | Concord Oval, Sydney | L | 7-32 |
| 276 | 16-Jul-88 | New Zealand | Bled | H | Ballymore Oval, Brisbane | D | 19-19 |
| 277 | 30-Jul-88 | New Zealand | Bled | H | Concord Oval, Sydney | L | 9-30 |
| 278 | 5-Nov-88 | England | Int-T | A | Twickenham, London | L | 19-28 |
| 279 | 19-Nov-88 | Scotland | Int-T | A | Murrayfield, Edinburgh | W | 32-13 |
| 280 | 3-Dec-88 | Italy | Int-T | A | Stadio Flaminio, Rome | W | 55-6 |

| No | Date | Opponents | Tmt | Match Venue | Result | |
|----|------|-----------|-----|-------------|--------|---|
| 281 | 1-Jul-89 | Lions | Int | H Football Stadium, Sydney | W | 30-12 |
| 282 | 8-Jul-89 | Lions | Int | H Ballymore Oval, Brisbane | L | 12-19 |
| 283 | 15-Jul-89 | Lions | Int | H Football Stadium, Sydney | L | 18-19 |
| 284 | 5-Aug-89 | New Zealand | Bled-T | A Eden Park, Auckland | L | 12-24 |
| 285 | 4-Nov-89 | France | BIC-T | A Stade de la Meinau, Strasbourg | W | 32-15 |
| 286 | 11-Nov-89 | France | BIC-T | A Stade Nord-Lille, Métropole | L | 19-25 |
| 287 | 9-Jun-90 | France | BIC | H Football Stadium, Sydney | W | 21-9 |
| 288 | 24-Jun-90 | France | BIC | H Ballymore Oval, Brisbane | W | 48-31 |
| 289 | 30-Jun-90 | France | BIC | H Football Stadium, Sydney | L | 19-28 |
| 290 | 8-Jul-90 | United States | Int | H Ballymore Oval, Brisbane | W | 67-9 |
| 291 | 21-Jul-90 | New Zealand | Bled-T | A Lancaster Park Oval, Christchurch | L | 6-21 |
| 292 | 4-Aug-90 | New Zealand | Bled-T | A Eden Park, Auckland | L | 17-27 |
| 293 | 18-Aug-90 | New Zealand | Bled-T | A Athletic Park, Wellington | W | 21-9 |
| 294 | 22-Jul-91 | Wales | Int | H Ballymore Oval, Brisbane | W | 63-6 |
| 295 | 27-Jul-91 | England | Int | H Football Stadium, Sydney | W | 40-15 |
| 296 | 10-Aug-91 | New Zealand | Bled | H Football Stadium, Sydney | W | 21-12 |
| 297 | 24-Aug-91 | New Zealand | Bled-T | A Eden Park, Auckland | L | 3-6 |
| 298 | 4-Oct-91 | Argentina | WCp | N Stradey Park, Llanelli | W | 32-19 |
| 299 | 9-Oct-91 | Western Samoa | WCp | N Pontypool Park, Pontypool | W | 9-3 |
| 300 | 12-Oct-91 | Wales | WCp | A National Stadium, Cardiff | W | 38-3 |
| 301 | 20-Oct-91 | Ireland | WCqf | A Lansdowne Road, Dublin | W | 19-18 |
| 302 | 27-Oct-91 | New Zealand | WCsf | N Lansdowne Road, Dublin | W | 16-6 |
| 303 | 2-Nov-91 | England | WCf | A Twickenham, London | W | 12-6 |
| 304 | 13-Jun-92 | Scotland | Int | H Football Stadium, Sydney | W | 27-12 |
| 305 | 21-Jun-92 | Scotland | Int | H Ballymore Oval, Brisbane | W | 37-13 |
| 306 | 4-Jul-92 | New Zealand | Bled | H Football Stadium, Sydney | W | 16-15 |
| 307 | 19-Jul-92 | New Zealand | Bled | H Ballymore Oval, Brisbane | W | 19-17 |
| 308 | 25-Jul-92 | New Zealand | Bled | H Football Stadium, Sydney | L | 23-26 |
| 309 | 22-Aug-92 | South Africa | Int-T | A Newlands Stadium, Cape Town | W | 26-3 |
| 310 | 31-Oct-92 | Ireland | Int-T | A Lansdowne Road, Dublin | W | 42-17 |
| 311 | 21-Nov-92 | Wales | Int-T | A National Stadium, Cardiff | W | 23-6 |
| 312 | 4-Jul-93 | Tonga | Int | H Ballymore Oval, Brisbane | W | 52-14 |
| 313 | 17-Jul-93 | New Zealand | Bled-T | A Carisbrook, Dunedin | L | 10-25 |
| 314 | 31-Jul-93 | South Africa | Int | H Football Stadium, Sydney | L | 12-19 |
| 315 | 14-Aug-93 | South Africa | Int | H Ballymore Oval, Brisbane | W | 28-20 |
| 316 | 21-Aug-93 | South Africa | Int | H Football Stadium, Sydney | W | 19-12 |
| 317 | 9-Oct-93 | Canada | Int-T | A Kingsland Rugby Park, Calgary | W | 43-16 |
| 318 | 30-Oct-93 | France | BIC-T | A Stade du Parc Lescure, Bordeaux | L | 13-16 |
| 319 | 6-Nov-93 | France | BIC-T | A Parc des Princes, Paris | W | 24-3 |
| 320 | 5-Jun-94 | Ireland | Int | H Ballymore Oval, Brisbane | W | 33-13 |

| No | Date | Opponents | Tmt | | Match Venue | Result | |
|-----|----------|---------------|-------|---|----------------------------------------|---|-------|
| 321 | 11-Jun-94 | Ireland | Int | H | Football Stadium, Sydney | W | 32-18 |
| 322 | 18-Jun-94 | Italy | Int | H | Ballymore Oval, Brisbane | W | 23-20 |
| 323 | 25-Jun-94 | Italy | Int | H | Olympic Park Stadium, Melbourne | W | 20-7 |
| 324 | 6-Aug-94 | Western Samoa | Int | H | Football Stadium, Sydney | W | 73-3 |
| 325 | 17-Aug-94 | New Zealand | Bled | H | Football Stadium, Sydney | W | 20-16 |
| 326 | 30-Apr-95 | Argentina | Int | H | Ballymore Oval, Brisbane | W | 53-7 |
| 327 | 6-May-95 | Argentina | Int | H | Football Stadium, Sydney | W | 30-13 |
| 328 | 25-May-95 | South Africa | WCp | A | Newlands Stadium, Cape Town | L | 18-27 |
| 329 | 31-May-95 | Canada | WCp | N | Boet Erasmus Stadium, Port Elizabeth | W | 27-11 |
| 330 | 3-Jun-95 | Romania | WCp | N | Danie Craven Stadium, Stellenbosch | W | 42-3 |
| 331 | 11-Jun-95 | England | WCqf | N | Newlands Stadium, Cape Town | L | 22-25 |
| 332 | 22-Jul-95 | New Zealand | Bled-T | A | Eden Park, Auckland | L | 16-28 |
| 333 | 29-Jul-95 | New Zealand | Bled | H | Football Stadium, Sydney | L | 23-34 |
| 334 | 9-Jun-96 | Wales | Int | H | Ballymore Oval, Brisbane | W | 56-25 |
| 335 | 22-Jun-96 | Wales | Int | H | Football Stadium, Sydney | W | 42-3 |
| 336 | 29-Jun-96 | Canada | Int | H | Ballymore Oval, Brisbane | W | 74-9 |
| 337 | 6-Jul-96 | New Zealand | TN-B | A | Athletic Park, Wellington | L | 6-43 |
| 338 | 13-Jul-96 | South Africa | TN | H | Football Stadium, Sydney | W | 21-16 |
| 339 | 27-Jul-96 | New Zealand | TN-B | H | Suncorp Stadium, Brisbane | L | 25-32 |
| 340 | 3-Aug-96 | South Africa | TN | A | Free State Stadium, Bloemfontein | L | 19-25 |
| 341 | 23-Oct-96 | Italy | Int-T | A | Stadio Plebiscito, Padova | W | 40-18 |
| 342 | 9-Nov-96 | Scotland | Int-T | A | Murrayfield, Edinburgh | W | 29-19 |
| 343 | 23-Nov-96 | Ireland | Int-T | A | Lansdowne Road, Dublin | W | 22-12 |
| 344 | 1-Dec-96 | Wales | Int-T | A | National Stadium, Cardiff | W | 28-19 |
| 345 | 21-Jun-97 | France | BIC | H | Football Stadium, Sydney | W | 29-15 |
| 346 | 28-Jun-97 | France | BIC | H | Ballymore Oval, Brisbane | W | 26-19 |
| 347 | 5-Jul-97 | New Zealand | Bled-T | A | Lancaster Park Oval, Christchurch | L | 13-30 |
| 348 | 12-Jul-97 | England | CKC | H | Football Stadium, Sydney | W | 25-6 |
| 349 | 26-Jul-97 | New Zealand | TN-B | H | Cricket Ground, Melbourne | L | 18-33 |
| 350 | 2-Aug-97 | South Africa | TN | H | Suncorp Stadium, Brisbane | W | 32-20 |
| 351 | 16-Aug-97 | New Zealand | TN-B | A | Carisbrook, Dunedin | L | 24-36 |
| 352 | 23-Aug-97 | South Africa | TN | A | Loftus Versfeld Stadium, Pretoria | L | 22-61 |
| 353 | 1-Nov-97 | Argentina | Int-T | A | Ferro Carril Oeste Stadium, B Aires | W | 23-15 |
| 354 | 8-Nov-97 | Argentina | Int-T | A | Ferro Carril Oeste Stadium, B Aires | L | 16-18 |
| 355 | 15-Nov-97 | England | CKC-T | A | Twickenham, London | D | 15-15 |
| 356 | 22-Nov-97 | Scotland | Int-T | A | Murrayfield, Edinburgh | W | 37-8 |
| 357 | 6-Jun-98 | England | CKC | H | Suncorp Stadium, Brisbane | W | 76-0 |
| 358 | 13-Jun-98 | Scotland | HT | H | Football Stadium, Sydney | W | 45-3 |
| 359 | 20-Jun-98 | Scotland | HT | H | Ballymore Oval, Brisbane | W | 33-11 |
| 360 | 11-Jul-98 | New Zealand | TN-B | H | Cricket Ground, Melbourne | W | 24-16 |

| No | Date | Opponents | Tmt | Match Venue | Result | |
|----|------|-----------|-----|-------------|--------|---|
| 361 | 18-Jul-98 | South Africa | TN | H Subiaco Oval, Perth | L | 13-14 |
| 362 | 1-Aug-98 | New Zealand | TN-B | A Jade Stadium, Christchurch | W | 27-23 |
| 363 | 22-Aug-98 | South Africa | TN | A Ellis Park, Johannesburg | L | 15-29 |
| 364 | 29-Aug-98 | New Zealand | Bled | H Football Stadium, Sydney | W | 19-14 |
| 365 | 18-Sep-98 | Fiji | WCQ | H Parramatta Stadium, Sydney | W | 66-20 |
| 366 | 22-Sep-98 | Tonga | WCQ | H Bruce Stadium, Canberra | W | 74-0 |
| 367 | 26-Sep-98 | Samoa | WCQ | H Ballymore Oval, Brisbane | W | 25-13 |
| 368 | 21-Nov-98 | France | BIC-T | A Stade de France, Paris | W | 32-21 |
| 369 | 28-Nov-98 | England | CKC-T | A Twickenham, London | W | 12-11 |
| 370 | 12-Jun-99 | Ireland | LC | H Ballymore Oval, Brisbane | W | 46-10 |
| 371 | 19-Jun-99 | Ireland | LC | H Subiaco Oval, Perth | W | 32-26 |
| 372 | 26-Jun-99 | England | CKC | H Stadium Australia, Sydney | W | 22-15 |
| 373 | 17-Jul-99 | South Africa | TN | H Suncorp Stadium, Brisbane | W | 32-6 |
| 374 | 24-Jul-99 | New Zealand | TN-B | A Eden Park, Auckland | L | 15-34 |
| 375 | 14-Aug-99 | South Africa | TN | A Newlands Stadium, Cape Town | L | 9-10 |
| 376 | 28-Aug-99 | New Zealand | TN-B | H Stadium Australia, Sydney | W | 28-7 |
| 377 | 3-Oct-99 | Romania | WCp | N Ravenhill, Belfast | W | 57-9 |
| 378 | 10-Oct-99 | Ireland | WCp | A Lansdowne Road, Dublin | W | 23-3 |
| 379 | 14-Oct-99 | United States | WCp | N Thomond Park, Limerick | W | 55-19 |
| 380 | 23-Oct-99 | Wales | WCqf | A Millennium Stadium, Cardiff | W | 24-9 |
| 381 | 30-Oct-99 | South Africa | WCsf | N Twickenham, London | W | 27-21 |
| 382 | 6-Nov-99 | France | WCf | N Millennium Stadium, Cardiff | W | 35-12 |
| 383 | 17-Jun-00 | Argentina | PT | H Ballymore Oval, Brisbane | W | 53-6 |
| 384 | 24-Jun-00 | Argentina | PT | H Canberra Stadium, Canberra | W | 32-25 |
| 385 | 8-Jul-00 | South Africa | MCP | H Colonial Stadium, Melbourne | W | 44-23 |
| 386 | 15-Jul-00 | New Zealand | TN-B | H Stadium Australia, Sydney | L | 35-39 |
| 387 | 29-Jul-00 | South Africa | TN | H Stadium Australia, Sydney | W | 26-6 |
| 388 | 5-Aug-00 | New Zealand | TN-B | A Westpac Trust Stadium, Wellington | W | 24-23 |
| 389 | 26-Aug-00 | South Africa | TN | A ABSA Stadium, Durban | W | 19-18 |
| 390 | 4-Nov-00 | France | BIC-T | A Stade de France, Paris | W | 18-13 |
| 391 | 11-Nov-00 | Scotland | HT-T | A Murrayfield, Edinburgh | W | 30-9 |
| 392 | 18-Nov-00 | England | CKC-T | A Twickenham, London | L | 19-22 |
| 393 | 30-Jun-01 | Lions | TRT | H The Gabba Cricket Ground, Brisbane | L | 13-29 |
| 394 | 7-Jul-01 | Lions | TRT | H Colonial Stadium, Melbourne | W | 35-14 |
| 395 | 14-Jul-01 | Lions | TRT | H Stadium Australia, Sydney | W | 29-23 |
| 396 | 28-Jul-01 | South Africa | TN | A Minolta Loftus Stadium, Pretoria | L | 15-20 |
| 397 | 11-Aug-01 | New Zealand | TN-B | A Carisbrook, Dunedin | W | 23-15 |
| 398 | 18-Aug-01 | South Africa | TN | H Subiaco Oval, Perth | D | 14-14 |
| 399 | 1-Sep-01 | New Zealand | TN-B | H Stadium Australia, Sydney | W | 29-26 |
| 400 | 1-Nov-01 | Spain | Int-T | A Campo Ciudad Universitaria, Madrid | W | 92-10 |

| No | Date | Opponents | Tmt | Match Venue | Result | |
|---|---|---|---|---|---|---|
| 401 | 10-Nov-01 | England | CKC-T | A | Twickenham, London | L | 15-21 |
| 402 | 17-Nov-01 | France | BIC-T | A | Stade Vélodrome, Marseille | L | 13-14 |
| 403 | 25-Nov-01 | Wales | Int-T | A | Millennium Stadium, Cardiff | W | 21-13 |
| 404 | 22-Jun-02 | France | BIC | H | Colonial Stadium, Melbourne | W | 29-17 |
| 405 | 29-Jun-02 | France | BIC | H | Stadium Australia, Sydney | W | 31-25 |
| 406 | 13-Jul-02 | New Zealand | TN-B | A | Jade Stadium, Christchurch | L | 6-12 |
| 407 | 27-Jul-02 | South Africa | TN | H | The Gabba Cricket Ground, Brisbane | W | 38-27 |
| 408 | 3-Aug-02 | New Zealand | TN-B | H | Telstra Stadium, Sydney | W | 16-14 |
| 409 | 17-Aug-02 | South Africa | TN-M | A | Ellis Park, Johannesburg | L | 31-33 |
| 410 | 2-Nov-02 | Argentina | PT-T | A | River Plate Stadium, Buenos Aires | W | 17-6 |
| 411 | 9-Nov-02 | Ireland | LC-T | A | Lansdowne Road, Dublin | L | 9-18 |
| 412 | 16-Nov-02 | England | CKC-T | A | Twickenham, London | L | 31-32 |
| 413 | 23-Nov-02 | Italy | Int-T | A | Stadio Luigi Ferraris, Genova | W | 34-3 |
| 414 | 7-Jun-03 | Ireland | LC | H | Subiaco Oval, Perth | W | 45-16 |
| 415 | 14-Jun-03 | Wales | Int | H | Telstra Stadium, Sydney | W | 30-10 |
| 416 | 21-Jun-03 | England | CKC | H | Telstra Dome, Melbourne | L | 14-25 |
| 417 | 12-Jul-03 | South Africa | TN | A | Newlands Stadium, Cape Town | L | 22-26 |
| 418 | 26-Jul-03 | New Zealand | TN-B | H | Telstra Stadium, Sydney | L | 21-50 |
| 419 | 2-Aug-03 | South Africa | TN | H | Suncorp Stadium, Brisbane | W | 29-9 |
| 420 | 16-Aug-03 | New Zealand | TN-B | A | Eden Park, Auckland | L | 17-21 |
| 421 | 10-Oct-03 | Argentina | WCp | H | Telstra Stadium, Sydney | W | 24-8 |
| 422 | 18-Oct-03 | Romania | WCp | H | Suncorp Stadium, Brisbane | W | 90-8 |
| 423 | 25-Oct-03 | Namibia | WCp | H | Adelaide Oval, Adelaide | W | 142-0 |
| 424 | 1-Nov-03 | Ireland | WCp | H | Telstra Dome, Melbourne | W | 17-16 |
| 425 | 8-Nov-03 | Scotland | WCqf | H | Suncorp Stadium, Brisbane | W | 33-16 |
| 426 | 15-Nov-03 | New Zealand | WCsf | H | Telstra Stadium, Sydney | W | 22-10 |
| 427 | 22-Nov-03 | England | WCf | H | Telstra Stadium, Sydney (a-e-t) | L | 17-20 |
| 428 | 13-Jun-04 | Scotland | HT | H | Telstra Dome, Melbourne | W | 35-15 |
| 429 | 19-Jun-04 | Scotland | HT | H | Telstra Stadium, Sydney | W | 34-13 |
| 430 | 26-Jun-04 | England | CKC | H | Suncorp Stadium, Brisbane | W | 51-15 |
| 431 | 3-Jul-04 | Pacific Islands | Int | H | Adelaide Oval, Adelaide | W | 29-14 |
| 432 | 17-Jul-04 | New Zealand | TN-B | A | Westpac Stadium, Wellington | L | 7-16 |
| 433 | 31-Jul-04 | South Africa | TN | H | Subiaco Oval, Perth | W | 30-26 |
| 434 | 7-Aug-04 | New Zealand | TN-B | H | Telstra Stadium, Sydney | W | 23-18 |
| 435 | 21-Aug-04 | South Africa | TN | A | ABSA Stadium, Durban | L | 19-23 |
| 436 | 6-Nov-04 | Scotland | HT-T | A | Murrayfield, Edinburgh | W | 31-14 |
| 437 | 13-Nov-04 | France | BIC-T | A | Stade de France, Paris | L | 14-27 |
| 438 | 20-Nov-04 | Scotland | HT-T | A | Hampden Park, Glasgow | W | 31-17 |
| 439 | 27-Nov-04 | England | CKC-T | A | Twickenham, London | W | 21-19 |
| 440 | 11-Jun-05 | Samoa | Int | H | Telstra Stadium, Sydney | W | 74-7 |

# AUSTRALIA

| No | Date | Opponents | Tmt | | Match Venue | | Result |
|----|------|-----------|-----|---|-------------|---|--------|
| 441 | 25-Jun-05 | Italy | Int | H | Telstra Dome, Melbourne | W | 69-21 |
| 442 | 2-Jul-05 | France | BIC | H | Suncorp Stadium, Brisbane | W | 37-31 |
| 443 | 9-Jul-05 | South Africa | MCP | H | Telstra Stadium, Sydney | W | 30-12 |
| 444 | 23-Jul-05 | South Africa | MCP-T | A | Ellis Park, Johannesburg | L | 20-33 |
| 445 | 30-Jul-05 | South Africa | TN | A | Securicor Loftus Stadium, Pretoria | L | 16-22 |
| 446 | 13-Aug-05 | New Zealand | TN-B | H | Telstra Stadium, Sydney | L | 13-30 |
| 447 | 20-Aug-05 | South Africa | TN | H | Subiaco Oval, Perth | L | 19-22 |
| 448 | 3-Sep-05 | New Zealand | TN-B | A | Eden Park, Auckland | L | 24-34 |
| 449 | 5-Nov-05 | France | BIC-T | A | Stade Vélodrome, Marseille | L | 16-26 |
| 450 | 12-Nov-05 | England | CKC-T | A | Twickenham, London | L | 16-26 |
| 451 | 19-Nov-05 | Ireland | LC-T | A | Lansdowne Road, Dublin | W | 30-14 |
| 452 | 26-Nov-05 | Wales | Int-T | A | Millennium Stadium, Cardiff | L | 22-24 |
| 453 | 11-Jun-06 | England | CKC | H | Telstra Stadium, Sydney | W | 34-3 |
| 454 | 17-Jun-06 | England | CKC | H | Telstra Dome, Melbourne | W | 43-18 |
| 455 | 24-Jun-06 | Ireland | LC | H | Subiaco Oval, Perth | W | 37-15 |
| 456 | 8-Jul-06 | New Zealand | TN-B | A | Jade Stadium, Christchurch | L | 12-32 |
| 457 | 15-Jul-06 | South Africa | TN-M | H | Suncorp Stadium, Brisbane | W | 49-0 |
| 458 | 29-Jul-06 | New Zealand | TN-B | H | Suncorp Stadium, Brisbane | L | 9-13 |
| 459 | 5-Aug-06 | South Africa | TN-M | H | Telstra Stadium, Sydney | W | 20-18 |
| 460 | 19-Aug-06 | New Zealand | TN-B | A | Eden Park, Auckland | L | 27-34 |
| 461 | 9-Sep-06 | South Africa | TN-M | A | Ellis Park, Johannesburg | L | 16-24 |
| 462 | 4-Nov-06 | Wales | Int-T | A | Millennium Stadium, Cardiff | D | 29-29 |
| 463 | 11-Nov-06 | Italy | Int-T | A | Stadio Flaminio, Rome | W | 25-18 |
| 464 | 19-Nov-06 | Ireland | LC-T | A | Lansdowne Road, Dublin | L | 6-21 |
| 465 | 25-Nov-06 | Scotland | HT-T | A | Murrayfield, Edinburgh | W | 44-15 |
| 466 | 26-May-07 | Wales | JBT | H | Telstra Stadium, Sydney | W | 29-23 |
| 467 | 2-Jun-07 | Wales | JBT | H | Suncorp Stadium, Brisbane | W | 31-0 |
| 468 | 9-Jun-07 | Fiji | Int | H | Subiaco Oval, Perth | W | 49-0 |
| 469 | 16-Jun-07 | South Africa | TN-M | A | Newlands Stadium, Cape Town | L | 19-22 |
| 470 | 30-Jun-07 | New Zealand | TN-B | H | Cricket Ground, Melbourne | W | 20-15 |
| 471 | 7-Jul-07 | South Africa | TN-M | H | Telstra Stadium, Sydney | W | 25-17 |
| 472 | 21-Jul-07 | New Zealand | TN-B | A | Eden Park, Auckland | L | 12-26 |
| 473 | 8-Sep-07 | Japan | WCp | N | Stade de Gerland, Lyon | W | 91-3 |
| 474 | 15-Sep-07 | Wales | WCp | A | Millennium Stadium, Cardiff | W | 32-20 |
| 475 | 23-Sep-07 | Fiji | WCp | N | Stade de la Mosson, Montpellier | W | 55-12 |
| 476 | 29-Sep-07 | Canada | WCp | N | Stade Chaban-Delmas, Bordeaux | W | 37-6 |
| 477 | 6-Oct-07 | England | WCqf | N | Stade Vélodrome, Marseille | L | 10-12 |
| 478 | 14-Jun-08 | Ireland | LC | H | Telstra Dome, Melbourne | W | 18-12 |
| 479 | 28-Jun-08 | France | BIC | H | ANZ Stadium, Sydney | W | 34-13 |
| 480 | 5-Jul-08 | France | BIC | H | Suncorp Stadium, Brisbane | W | 40-10 |

| No | Date | Opponents | Tmt | | Match Venue | Result | |
|----|------|-----------|-----|---|-------------|--------|---|
| 481 | 19-Jul-08 | South Africa | TN-M | H | Subiaco Oval, Perth | W | 16-9 |
| 482 | 26-Jul-08 | New Zealand | TN-B | H | ANZ Stadium, Sydney | W | 34-19 |
| 483 | 2-Aug-08 | New Zealand | TN-B | A | Eden Park, Auckland | L | 10-39 |
| 484 | 23-Aug-08 | South Africa | TN-M | A | The ABSA Stadium, Durban | W | 27-15 |
| 485 | 30-Aug-08 | South Africa | TN-M | A | Coca Cola Park, Johannesburg | L | 8-53 |
| 486 | 13-Sep-08 | New Zealand | TN-B | H | Suncorp Stadium, Brisbane | L | 24-28 |
| 487 | 1-Nov-08 | New Zealand | Bled | N | So Kon Po Stadium, Hong Kong | L | 14-19 |
| 488 | 8-Nov-08 | Italy | Int-T | A | Stadio Euganeo, Padova | W | 30-20 |
| 489 | 15-Nov-08 | England | CKC-T | A | Twickenham, London | W | 28-14 |
| 490 | 22-Nov-08 | France | BIC-T | A | Stade de France, Paris | W | 18-13 |
| 491 | 29-Nov-08 | Wales | JBT-T | A | Millennium Stadium, Cardiff | L | 18-21 |
| 492 | 13-Jun-09 | Italy | Int | H | Canberra Stadium, Canberra | W | 31-8 |
| 493 | 20-Jun-09 | Italy | Int | H | Etihad Stadium, Docklands, Melbourne | W | 34-12 |
| 494 | 27-Jun-09 | France | BIC | H | ANZ Stadium, Sydney | W | 22-6 |
| 495 | 18-Jul-09 | New Zealand | TN-B | A | Eden Park, Auckland | L | 16-22 |
| 496 | 8-Aug-09 | South Africa | TN-M | A | Newlands Stadium, Cape Town | L | 17-29 |
| 497 | 22-Aug-09 | New Zealand | TN-B | H | ANZ Stadium, Sydney | L | 18-19 |
| 498 | 29-Aug-09 | South Africa | TN-M | H | Subiaco Oval, Perth | L | 25-32 |
| 499 | 5-Sep-09 | South Africa | TN-M | H | Suncorp Stadium, Brisbane | W | 21-6 |
| 500 | 19-Sep-09 | New Zealand | TN-B | A | Westpac Stadium, Wellington | L | 6-33 |
| 501 | 31-Oct-09 | New Zealand | Bled | N | National Olympic Stadium, Tokyo | L | 19-32 |
| 502 | 7-Nov-09 | England | CKC-T | A | Twickenham, London | W | 18-9 |
| 503 | 15-Nov-09 | Ireland | LC-T | A | Croke Park, Dublin | D | 20-20 |
| 504 | 21-Nov-09 | Scotland | HT-T | A | Murrayfield, Edinburgh | L | 8-9 |
| 505 | 28-Nov-09 | Wales | JBT-T | A | Millennium Stadium, Cardiff | W | 33-12 |
| 506 | 5-Jun-10 | Fiji | Int | H | Canberra Stadium, Canberra | W | 49-3 |
| 507 | 12-Jun-10 | England | CKC | H | Subiaco Oval, Perth | W | 27-17 |
| 508 | 19-Jun-10 | England | CKC | H | ANZ Stadium, Sydney | L | 20-21 |
| 509 | 26-Jun-10 | Ireland | LC | H | Suncorp Stadium, Brisbane | W | 22-15 |
| 510 | 24-Jul-10 | South Africa | TN-M | H | Suncorp Stadium, Brisbane | W | 30-13 |
| 511 | 31-Jul-10 | New Zealand | TN-B | H | Etihad Stadium, Docklands, Melbourne | L | 28-49 |
| 512 | 7-Aug-10 | New Zealand | TN-B | A | AMI Stadium, Christchurch | L | 10-20 |
| 513 | 28-Aug-10 | South Africa | TN-M | A | Loftus Versfeld Stadium, Pretoria | L | 31-44 |
| 514 | 4-Sep-10 | South Africa | TN-M | A | Vodacom Park Stadium, Bloemfontein | W | 41-39 |
| 515 | 11-Sep-10 | New Zealand | TN-B | H | ANZ Stadium, Sydney | L | 22-23 |
| 516 | 30-Oct-10 | New Zealand | Bled | N | So Kon Po Stadium, Hong Kong | W | 26-24 |
| 517 | 6-Nov-10 | Wales | JBT-T | A | Millennium Stadium, Cardiff | W | 25-16 |
| 518 | 13-Nov-10 | England | CKC-T | A | Twickenham, London | L | 18-35 |
| 519 | 20-Nov-10 | Italy | Int-T | A | Stadio Artemio Franchi, Florence | W | 32-14 |
| 520 | 27-Nov-10 | France | BIC-T | A | Stade de France, Paris | W | 59-16 |

| No | Date | Opponents | Tmt | | Match Venue | Result | |
|----|------|-----------|-----|---|-------------|--------|---|
| 521 | 17-Jul-11 | Samoa | Int | H | ANZ Stadium, Sydney | L | 23-32 |
| 522 | 23-Jul-11 | South Africa | TN-M | H | ANZ Stadium, Sydney | W | 39-20 |
| 523 | 6-Aug-11 | New Zealand | TN-B | A | Eden Park, Auckland | L | 14-30 |
| 524 | 13-Aug-11 | South Africa | TN-M | A | Kings Park Stadium, Durban | W | 14-9 |
| 525 | 27-Aug-11 | New Zealand | TN-B | H | Suncorp Stadium, Brisbane | W | 25-20 |
| 526 | 11-Sep-11 | Italy | WCp | N | North Harbour Stadium, Albany | W | 32-6 |
| 527 | 17-Sep-11 | Ireland | WCp | N | Eden Park, Auckland | L | 6-15 |
| 528 | 23-Sep-11 | United States | WCp | N | Wellington Regional Stadium, Wellington | W | 67-5 |
| 529 | 1-Oct-11 | Russia | WCp | N | Trafalgar Park, Nelson | W | 68-22 |
| 530 | 9-Oct-11 | South Africa | WCqf | N | Wellington Regional Stadium, Wellington | W | 11-9 |
| 531 | 16-Oct-11 | New Zealand | WCsf | A | Eden Park, Auckland | L | 6-20 |
| 532 | 21-Oct-11 | Wales | WC34 | N | Eden Park, Auckland | W | 21-18 |
| 533 | 3-Dec-11 | Wales | JBT-T | A | Millennium Stadium, Cardiff | W | 24-18 |
| 534 | 5-Jun-12 | Scotland | HT | H | Ausgrid Stadium, Newcastle, NSW | L | 6-9 |
| 535 | 9-Jun-12 | Wales | JBT | H | Suncorp Stadium, Brisbane | W | 27-19 |
| 536 | 16-Jun-12 | Wales | JBT | H | Etihad Stadium, Docklands, Melbourne | W | 25-23 |
| 537 | 23-Jun-12 | Wales | JBT | H | Football Stadium, Sydney | W | 20-19 |
| 538 | 18-Aug-12 | New Zealand | RC-B | H | ANZ Stadium, Sydney | L | 19-27 |
| 539 | 25-Aug-12 | New Zealand | RC-B | A | Eden Park, Auckland | L | 0-22 |
| 540 | 8-Sep-12 | South Africa | RC-M | H | Patersons Stadium, Perth | W | 26-19 |
| 541 | 15-Sep-12 | Argentina | RC-P | H | Skilled Park, Robina, Gold Coast, Q'land | W | 23-19 |
| 542 | 29-Sep-12 | South Africa | RC-M | A | Loftus Versfeld Stadium, Pretoria | L | 8-31 |
| 543 | 6-Oct-12 | Argentina | RC-P | A | Estadio Gigante de Arroyito, Rosario | W | 25-19 |
| 544 | 20-Oct-12 | New Zealand | Bled | H | Suncorp Stadium, Brisbane | D | 18-18 |
| 545 | 10-Nov-12 | France | BIC-T | A | Stade de France, Paris | L | 6-33 |
| 546 | 17-Nov-12 | England | CKC-T | A | Twickenham, London | W | 20-14 |
| 547 | 24-Nov-12 | Italy | Int-T | A | Stadio Artemio Franchi, Florence | W | 22-19 |
| 548 | 1-Dec-12 | Wales | JBT-T | A | Millennium Stadium, Cardiff | W | 14-12 |
| 549 | 22-Jun-13 | Lions | TRT | H | Suncorp Stadium, Brisbane | L | 21-23 |
| 550 | 29-Jun-13 | Lions | TRT | H | Etihad Stadium, Docklands, Melbourne | W | 16-15 |
| 551 | 6-Jul-13 | Lions | TRT | H | ANZ Stadium, Sydney | L | 16-41 |
| 552 | 17-Aug-13 | New Zealand | RC-B | H | ANZ Stadium, Sydney | L | 29-47 |
| 553 | 24-Aug-13 | New Zealand | RC-B | A | Westpac Stadium, Wellington | L | 16-27 |
| 554 | 7-Sep-13 | South Africa | RC-M | H | Suncorp Stadium, Brisbane | L | 12-38 |
| 555 | 14-Sep-13 | Argentina | RC-P | H | Patersons Stadium, Perth | W | 14-13 |
| 556 | 28-Sep-13 | South Africa | RC-M | A | Newlands Stadium, Cape Town | L | 8-28 |
| 557 | 5-Oct-13 | Argentina | RC-P | A | Estadio Gigante de Arroyito, Rosario | W | 54-17 |
| 558 | 19-Oct-13 | New Zealand | Bled-T | A | Forsyth Barr Stadium, Dunedin | L | 33-41 |
| 559 | 2-Nov-13 | England | CKC-T | A | Twickenham, London | L | 13-20 |
| 560 | 9-Nov-13 | Italy | Int-T | A | Stadio Olimpico di Torino, Torino | W | 50-20 |

| No | Date | Opponents | Tmt | Match Venue | | Result | |
|----|------|-----------|-----|-------------|---|--------|---|
| 561 | 16-Nov-13 | Ireland | LC-T | A | Aviva Stadium, Dublin | W | 32-15 |
| 562 | 23-Nov-13 | Scotland | HT-T | A | Murrayfield, Edinburgh | W | 21-15 |
| 563 | 30-Nov-13 | Wales | JBT-T | A | Millennium Stadium, Cardiff | W | 30-26 |
| 564 | 7-Jun-14 | France | BIC | H | Suncorp Stadium, Brisbane | W | 50-23 |
| 565 | 14-Jun-14 | France | BIC | H | Etihad Stadium, Docklands, Melbourne | W | 6-0 |
| 566 | 21-Jun-14 | France | BIC | H | Football Stadium, Sydney | W | 39-13 |
| 567 | 16-Aug-14 | New Zealand | RC-B | H | ANZ Stadium, Sydney | D | 12-12 |
| 568 | 23-Aug-14 | New Zealand | RC-B | A | Eden Park, Auckland | L | 20-51 |
| 569 | 6-Sep-14 | South Africa | RC-M | H | Patersons Stadium, Perth | W | 24-23 |
| 570 | 13-Sep-14 | Argentina | RC-P | H | Skilled Park, Robina, Gold Coast, Q'land | W | 32-25 |
| 571 | 27-Sep-14 | South Africa | RC-M | A | Newlands Stadium, Cape Town | L | 10-28 |
| 572 | 4-Oct-14 | Argentina | RC-P | A | Estadio Malvinas Argentinas, Mendoza | L | 17-21 |
| 573 | 11-Oct-14 | New Zealand | RC-B | H | Suncorp Stadium, Brisbane | L | 28-29 |
| 574 | 8-Nov-14 | Wales | JBT-T | A | Millennium Stadium, Cardiff | W | 33-28 |
| 575 | 15-Nov-14 | France | BIC-T | A | Stade de France, Paris | L | 26-29 |
| 576 | 22-Nov-14 | Ireland | LC-T | A | Aviva Stadium, Dublin | L | 23-26 |
| 577 | 29-Nov-14 | England | CKC-T | A | Twickenham, London | L | 17-26 |
| 578 | 18-Jul-15 | South Africa | RC-M | H | Suncorp Stadium, Brisbane | W | 24-20 |
| 579 | 25-Jul-15 | Argentina | RC-P | A | Estadio Malvinas Argentinas, Mendoza | W | 34-9 |
| 580 | 8-Aug-15 | New Zealand | RC-B | H | Stadium Australia, Sydney | W | 27-19 |
| 581 | 15-Aug-15 | New Zealand | Bled-T | A | Eden Park, Auckland | L | 13-41 |
| 582 | 5-Sep-15 | United States | Int-T | A | Soldier Field, Chicago | W | 47-10 |
| 583 | 23-Sep-15 | Fiji | WCp | N | Millennium Stadium, Cardiff | W | 28-13 |
| 584 | 27-Sep-15 | Uruguay | WCp | N | Villa Park, Birmingham | W | 65-3 |
| 585 | 3-Oct-15 | England | WCp | N | Twickenham, London | W | 33-13 |
| 586 | 10-Oct-15 | Wales | WCp | N | Twickenham, London | W | 15-6 |
| 587 | 18-Oct-15 | Scotland | WCqf | N | Twickenham, London | W | 35-34 |
| 588 | 25-Oct-15 | Argentina | WCsf | N | Twickenham, London | W | 29-15 |
| 589 | 31-Oct-15 | New Zealand | WCf | N | Twickenham, London | L | 17-34 |

# ENGLAND

The very first rugby International was played at Raeburn Place in Edinburgh on 27 March 1871, when Scotland defeated England in a challenge match. Scotland won by one goal and one try to one try; that is, four points to one if we adopt the scoring system of the time. Four years later, England played their first game against Ireland at the Oval in London, winning by seven points to nil. Another six years elapsed before they played Wales for the first time, in Blackheath in 1881. They also won that match by the huge margin of thirty points to nil. England were very successful in those early years, losing only six times in their first forty-five Internationals to the end of the 1892 season.

In 1883 a tournament contested by England, Ireland, Scotland and Wales was launched and called the Four (or Home) Nations Championship and with it the Triple Crown, a mythical trophy won by the team that defeated the other three competitors: England were Triple Crown winners in 1883 and in 1884.

In 1910 the French team was invited to participate in the Four Nations Championship, which was renamed the Five Nations Championship. If a team won all four matches in a season, it was then said to have achieved the Grand Slam. England's next period of success came on either side of the First World War, when the team won five Grand Slams in seven seasons between 1913 and 1924, losing only twice over twenty-eight matches.

In the next match, in January 1925, a sequence of nine wins was ended when England lost for the second time to New Zealand, but in 1928 the team achieved a sixth Grand Slam title.

In 1931 the French were expelled from the competition when they contravened the amateur status of the game, so in 1932, the tournament reverted to its original name: the Home Nations Championship. After a period of fifteen years, France was readmitted and the Home Nations Championship again became the Five Nations Championship in 1947. England had to wait ten years before winning their seventh Grand Slam in 1957, and a further twenty-three years before achieving an eighth success in 1980. However, wins against South Africa in 1969 and 1972, and against both New Zealand and Australia in 1973, made up for the lean times experienced on the domestic front during the 1960s, 1970s and 1980s.

Hosting the World Cup in 1991 provided the much-needed catalyst for the English team to improve, and they certainly rose to the challenge that year. In March 1991 the team was crowned Grand Slam champions, and World Cup runners-up to Australia in November.

This was followed by a second successive Grand Slam in 1992, and a home win against South Africa later that year. A rare win against New Zealand, also at Twickenham, followed in November 1993. Winning their eleventh Grand Slam in 1995 was a big incentive for England to perform well in the 1995 World Cup, held in South Africa. In that tournament they defeated Australia, the holders, in the quarter-finals, before losing to New Zealand the semi-final. The team also lost to France in the play-off for third place.

England commenced the new Millennium in 2000 by winning the inaugural Six Nations Championship title (an expanded Five Nations Championship with the entry of Italy). This was followed by an unprecedented sequence of wins, which started with an away victory against South Africa in Bloemfontein on 24 June 2000.

In forty-three matches up to 21 February 2004, England lost only three times: once to Ireland in 2001, and twice to France in 2002 and 2003. During that period they recorded one run of eleven consecutive wins and another of fourteen. The loss to Ireland in 2001 and to France in 2002 denied them the Grand Slam in both years. A sole defeat to Wales in 1999, and to Scotland in 2000, had also denied England two earlier Grand Slams.

In 2003 the English finally achieved the Grand Slam that had eluded them for four years, and topped that by winning the biggest prize of all, the World Cup, the following October. Winning the competition by defeating Australia, the host nation, on their home ground at the Telstra Stadium in Sydney, was the high point of English rugby history.

England's fortunes took a turn for the worse in 2004, when over a span of fifteen Six Nations matches between 2004 and 2006 they won on only seven occasions. The year 2006 was a particularly disappointing for the team as they suffered a sequence of seven consecutive defeats. The following year also started badly with just four wins from ten matches up to August. The English team's fortune changed in the 2007 World Cup, when they reached their third final, before losing to South Africa in an extremely close game. The period 2008 to 2010 was again a lean time for England, with only fourteen wins in thirty-two games. Things got better in 2011, when the English team won the first four matches in the Six Nations Championship, but failed to win the Grand Slam when they lost to Ireland in Dublin.

Elimination by France in the 2011 World Cup quarter-final was followed by an encouraging 2012 Six Nations campaign in which England's only loss in the Championship was to Wales, the team that went on to win the Grand Slam. After losing three times to South Africa and once to Australia later that year, the English produced a magnificent display in December 2012, when they defeated the All Blacks at Twickenham by 38 points to 21. The team was again denied a Grand Slam in 2013, when they were beaten by Wales in the final match of the tournament.

In the 2014 Six Nations Championship England lost the first match, but won the next four, only to be denied the title by finishing as runners-up, to Ireland, on points difference. Three months later, on the tour to New Zealand, the English team's run of four wins in the Six Nations campaign came to an end, when they suffered three consecutive defeats to the home side. The losing sequence was extended to five in November when they lost for the fourth successive time to the All Blacks and then to the Springboks a week later. However, a win against the Wallabies in the final match of 2014 did ease the situation.

In the 2015 Six Nations Championship, England, as in the previous year, with four wins, had to settle for the runners-up spot again, when the team lost on points difference to Ireland.

In the 2015 Rugby World Cup, England became the first host nation in the history of the competition to be eliminated at the pool stage. Drawn in the so called 'pool of death' they narrowly lost to Wales, but were well beaten by Australia.

# ENGLAND

## HEAD TO HEAD RESULTS TO 31 OCTOBER 2015

|  | P | W | D | L | % | F | A |
|---|---|---|---|---|---|---|---|
| **v TIER 1 Teams** | | | | | | | |
| v Argentina | 19 | 14 | 1 | 4 | 76.3 | 488 | 282 |
| v Australia | 44 | 18 | 1 | 25 | 42.0 | 674 | 940 |
| v France | 101 | 55 | 7 | 39 | 57.9 | 1592 | 1269 |
| v Ireland * | 130 | 75 | 8 | 47 | 60.8 | 1505 | 1069 |
| v Italy | 21 | 21 | 0 | 0 | 100.0 | 842 | 266 |
| v New Zealand | 40 | 7 | 1 | 32 | 18.7 | 560 | 969 |
| v Scotland * | 133 | 73 | 18 | 42 | 61.7 | 1547 | 1132 |
| v South Africa | 37 | 12 | 2 | 23 | 35.1 | 592 | 780 |
| v Wales * | 127 | 58 | 12 | 57 | 50.4 | 1621 | 1484 |
| **Sub-Total** | **652** | **333** | **50** | **269** | **54.9** | **9421** | **8191** |
| **v TIER 2/3 Group** | | | | | | | |
| v Canada | 6 | 6 | 0 | 0 | 100.0 | 273 | 73 |
| v Fiji | 6 | 6 | 0 | 0 | 100.0 | 245 | 94 |
| v Japan | 1 | 1 | 0 | 0 | 100.0 | 60 | 7 |
| v Romania | 5 | 5 | 0 | 0 | 100.0 | 335 | 24 |
| v Samoa | 7 | 7 | 0 | 0 | 100.0 | 244 | 100 |
| v Tonga | 2 | 2 | 0 | 0 | 100.0 | 137 | 30 |
| v United States | 5 | 5 | 0 | 0 | 100.0 | 253 | 52 |
| v Georgia | 2 | 2 | 0 | 0 | 100.0 | 125 | 16 |
| v Namibia | 0 | 0 | 0 | 0 | 0.0 | 0 | 0 |
| v Russia | 0 | 0 | 0 | 0 | 0.0 | 0 | 0 |
| v Uruguay | 2 | 2 | 0 | 0 | 100.0 | 171 | 16 |
| **Sub-Total** | **36** | **36** | **0** | **0** | **100.0** | **1843** | **412** |
| **v Other Teams** | | | | | | | |
| v Netherlands | 1 | 1 | 0 | 0 | 100.0 | 110 | 0 |
| v Pacific Islanders | 1 | 1 | 0 | 0 | 100.0 | 39 | 13 |
| v President's XV | 1 | 0 | 0 | 1 | 0.0 | 11 | 28 |
| v New Zealand Natives | 1 | 1 | 0 | 0 | 100.0 | 7 | 0 |
| **Sub-Total** | **4** | **3** | **0** | **1** | **75.0** | **167** | **41** |
| **All Internationals** | **692** | **372** | **50** | **270** | **57.4** | **11431** | **8644** |

* excludes points scored before the introduction of the modern points system

41

| No | Date | Opponents | Tmt | | Match Venue | Result | |
|----|------|-----------|-----|---|-------------|--------|---|
| 1 | 27-Mar-71 | Scotland | Int | A | Raeburn Place, Edinburgh | L | 1-4 |
| 2 | 5-Feb-72 | Scotland | Int | H | Kennington Oval, London | W | 8-3 |
| 3 | 3-Mar-73 | Scotland | Int | A | Hamilton Crescent, Glasgow | D | 0-0 |
| 4 | 23-Feb-74 | Scotland | Int | H | Kennington Oval, London | W | 3-1 |
| 5 | 15-Feb-75 | Ireland | Int | H | Kennington Oval, London | W | 7-0 |
| 6 | 8-Mar-75 | Scotland | Int | A | Raeburn Place, Edinburgh | D | 0-0 |
| 7 | 13-Dec-75 | Ireland | Int | A | Leinster CC, Rathmines, Dublin | W | 4-0 |
| 8 | 6-Mar-76 | Scotland | Int | H | Kennington Oval, London | W | 4-0 |
| 9 | 5-Feb-77 | Ireland | Int | H | Kennington Oval, London | W | 8-0 |
| 10 | 5-Mar-77 | Scotland | Int | A | Raeburn Place, Edinburgh | L | 0-3 |
| 11 | 4-Mar-78 | Scotland | Int | H | Kennington Oval, London | D | 0-0 |
| 12 | 11-Mar-78 | Ireland | Int | A | Lansdowne Road, Dublin | W | 7-0 |
| 13 | 10-Mar-79 | Scotland | CC | A | Raeburn Place, Edinburgh | D | 3-3 |
| 14 | 24-Mar-79 | Ireland | Int | H | Kennington Oval, London | W | 11-0 |
| 15 | 30-Jan-80 | Ireland | Int | A | Lansdowne Road, Dublin | W | 4-1 |
| 16 | 28-Feb-80 | Scotland | CC | H | Whalley Range, Manchester | W | 9-3 |
| 17 | 5-Feb-81 | Ireland | Int | H | Whalley Range, Manchester | W | 8-0 |
| 18 | 19-Feb-81 | Wales | Int | H | Richardson's Field, Blackheath | W | 30-0 |
| 19 | 19-Mar-81 | Scotland | CC | A | Raeburn Place, Edinburgh | D | 4-4 |
| 20 | 6-Feb-82 | Ireland | Int | A | Lansdowne Road, Dublin | D | 2-2 |
| 21 | 4-Mar-82 | Scotland | CC | H | Whalley Range, Manchester | L | 0-2 |
| 22 | 16-Dec-82 | Wales | 4N | A | St Helen's, Swansea | W | 10-0 |
| 23 | 5-Feb-83 | Ireland | 4N | H | Whalley Range, Manchester | W | 6-1 |
| 24 | 3-Mar-83 | Scotland | 4N-CC | A | Raeburn Place, Edinburgh | W | 2-1 |
| 25 | 5-Jan-84 | Wales | 4N | H | Cardigan Fields, Leeds | W | 5-3 |
| 26 | 4-Feb-84 | Ireland | 4N | A | Lansdowne Road, Dublin | W | 3-0 |
| 27 | 1-Mar-84 | Scotland | 4N-CC | H | Rectory Field, Blackheath | W | 3-1 |
| 28 | 3-Jan-85 | Wales | 4N | A | St Helen's, Swansea | W | 7-4 |
| 29 | 7-Feb-85 | Ireland | 4N | H | Whalley Range, Manchester | W | 2-1 |
| 30 | 2-Jan-86 | Wales | 4N | H | Rectory Field, Blackheath | W | 5-3 |
| 31 | 6-Feb-86 | Ireland | 4N | A | Lansdowne Road, Dublin | W | 1-0 |
| 32 | 13-Mar-86 | Scotland | 4N-CC | A | Raeburn Place, Edinburgh | D | 0-0 |
| 33 | 8-Jan-87 | Wales | 4N | A | Stradey Park, Llanelli | D | 0-0 |
| 34 | 5-Feb-87 | Ireland | 4N | A | Lansdowne Road, Dublin | L | 0-6 |
| 35 | 5-Mar-87 | Scotland | 4N-CC | H | Whalley Range, Manchester | D | 1-1 |
| 36 | 16-Feb-89 | N Z Natives | Int | H | Rectory Field, Blackheath | W | 7-0 |
| 37 | 15-Feb-90 | Wales | 4N | H | Crown Flatt, Dewsbury | L | 0-1 |
| 38 | 1-Mar-90 | Scotland | 4N-CC | A | Raeburn Place, Edinburgh | W | 6-0 |
| 39 | 15-Mar-90 | Ireland | 4N | H | Rectory Field, Blackheath | W | 3-0 |
| 40 | 3-Jan-91 | Wales | 4N | A | Rodney Parade, Newport | W | 7-3 |

| No | Date | Opponents | Tmt | | Match Venue | Result | |
|----|------|-----------|-----|---|-------------|--------|---|
| 41 | 7-Feb-91 | Ireland | 4N | A | Lansdowne Road, Dublin | W | 9-0 |
| 42 | 7-Mar-91 | Scotland | 4N-CC | H | Athletic Ground, Richmond | L | 3-9 |
| 43 | 2-Jan-92 | Wales | 4N | H | Rectory Field, Blackheath | W | 17-0 |
| 44 | 6-Feb-92 | Ireland | 4N | H | Whalley Range, Manchester | W | 7-0 |
| 45 | 5-Mar-92 | Scotland | 4N-CC | A | Raeburn Place, Edinburgh | W | 5-0 |
| 46 | 7-Jan-93 | Wales | 4N | A | Arms Park, Cardiff | L | 11-12 |
| 47 | 4-Feb-93 | Ireland | 4N | A | Lansdowne Road, Dublin | W | 4-0 |
| 48 | 4-Mar-93 | Scotland | 4N-CC | H | Headingley Stadium, Leeds | L | 0-8 |
| 49 | 6-Jan-94 | Wales | 4N | H | Upper Park, Birkenhead Park | W | 24-3 |
| 50 | 3-Feb-94 | Ireland | 4N | H | Rectory Field, Blackheath | L | 5-7 |
| 51 | 17-Mar-94 | Scotland | 4N-CC | A | Raeburn Place, Edinburgh | L | 0-6 |
| 52 | 5-Jan-95 | Wales | 4N | A | St Helen's, Swansea | W | 14-6 |
| 53 | 2-Feb-95 | Ireland | 4N | A | Lansdowne Road, Dublin | W | 6-3 |
| 54 | 9-Mar-95 | Scotland | 4N-CC | H | Athletic Ground, Richmond | L | 3-6 |
| 55 | 4-Jan-96 | Wales | 4N | H | Rectory Field, Blackheath | W | 25-0 |
| 56 | 1-Feb-96 | Ireland | 4N | H | Meanwood Road, Leeds | L | 4-10 |
| 57 | 14-Mar-96 | Scotland | 4N-CC | A | Old Hampden Park, Glasgow | L | 0-11 |
| 58 | 9-Jan-97 | Wales | 4N | A | Rodney Parade, Newport | L | 0-11 |
| 59 | 6-Feb-97 | Ireland | 4N | A | Lansdowne Road, Dublin | L | 9-13 |
| 60 | 13-Mar-97 | Scotland | 4N-CC | H | Fallowfield, Manchester | W | 12-3 |
| 61 | 5-Feb-98 | Ireland | 4N | H | Athletic Ground, Richmond | L | 6-9 |
| 62 | 12-Mar-98 | Scotland | 4N-CC | A | Powderhall, Edinburgh | D | 3-3 |
| 63 | 2-Apr-98 | Wales | 4N | H | Rectory Field, Blackheath | W | 14-7 |
| 64 | 7-Jan-99 | Wales | 4N | A | St Helen's, Swansea | L | 3-26 |
| 65 | 4-Feb-99 | Ireland | 4N | A | Lansdowne Road, Dublin | L | 0-6 |
| 66 | 11-Mar-99 | Scotland | 4N-CC | H | Rectory Field, Blackheath | L | 0-5 |
| 67 | 6-Jan-00 | Wales | 4N | H | Kingsholm, Gloucester | L | 3-13 |
| 68 | 3-Feb-00 | Ireland | 4N | H | Athletic Ground, Richmond | W | 15-4 |
| 69 | 10-Mar-00 | Scotland | 4N-CC | A | Inverleith, Edinburgh | D | 0-0 |
| 70 | 5-Jan-01 | Wales | 4N | A | Arms Park, Cardiff | L | 0-13 |
| 71 | 9-Feb-01 | Ireland | 4N | A | Lansdowne Road, Dublin | L | 6-10 |
| 72 | 9-Mar-01 | Scotland | 4N-CC | H | Rectory Field, Blackheath | L | 3-18 |
| 73 | 11-Jan-02 | Wales | 4N | H | Rectory Field, Blackheath | L | 8-9 |
| 74 | 8-Feb-02 | Ireland | 4N | H | Welford Road, Leicester | W | 6-3 |
| 75 | 15-Mar-02 | Scotland | 4N-CC | A | Inverleith, Edinburgh | W | 6-3 |
| 76 | 10-Jan-03 | Wales | 4N | A | St Helen's, Swansea | L | 5-21 |
| 77 | 14-Feb-03 | Ireland | 4N | A | Lansdowne Road, Dublin | L | 0-6 |
| 78 | 21-Mar-03 | Scotland | 4N-CC | H | Athletic Ground, Richmond | L | 6-10 |
| 79 | 9-Jan-04 | Wales | 4N | H | Welford Road, Leicester | D | 14-14 |
| 80 | 13-Feb-04 | Ireland | 4N | H | Rectory Field, Blackheath | W | 19-0 |

| No | Date | Opponents | Tmt | | Match Venue | Result | |
|----|------|-----------|-----|---|-------------|--------|---|
| 81 | 19-Mar-04 | Scotland | 4N-CC | A | Inverleith, Edinburgh | L | 3-6 |
| 82 | 14-Jan-05 | Wales | 4N | A | Arms Park, Cardiff | L | 0-25 |
| 83 | 11-Feb-05 | Ireland | 4N | A | Mardyke, Cork | L | 3-17 |
| 84 | 18-Mar-05 | Scotland | 4N-CC | H | Athletic Ground ,Richmond | L | 0-8 |
| 85 | 2-Dec-05 | New Zealand | Int | H | Crystal Palace, London | L | 0-15 |
| 86 | 13-Jan-06 | Wales | 4N | H | Athletic Ground, Richmond | L | 3-16 |
| 87 | 10-Feb-06 | Ireland | 4N | H | Welford Road, Leicester | L | 6-16 |
| 88 | 17-Mar-06 | Scotland | 4N-CC | A | Inverleith, Edinburgh | W | 9-3 |
| 89 | 22-Mar-06 | France | Int | A | Parc des Princess, Paris | W | 35-8 |
| 90 | 8-Dec-06 | South Africa | Int | H | Crystal Palace, London | D | 3-3 |
| 91 | 5-Jan-07 | France | Int | H | Athletic Ground, Richmond | W | 41-13 |
| 92 | 12-Jan-07 | Wales | 4N | A | St Helen's, Swansea | L | 0-22 |
| 93 | 9-Feb-07 | Ireland | 4N | A | Lansdowne Road, Dublin | L | 9-17 |
| 94 | 16-Mar-07 | Scotland | 4N-CC | H | Rectory Field, Blackheath | L | 3-8 |
| 95 | 1-Jan-08 | France | Int | A | Stade Colombes, Paris | W | 19-0 |
| 96 | 18-Jan-08 | Wales | 4N | H | Ashton Gate, Bristol | L | 18-28 |
| 97 | 8-Feb-08 | Ireland | 4N | H | Athletic Ground, Richmond | W | 13-3 |
| 98 | 21-Mar-08 | Scotland | 4N-CC | A | Inverleith, Edinburgh | L | 10-16 |
| 99 | 9-Jan-09 | Australia | Int | H | Rectory Field, Blackheath | L | 3-9 |
| 100 | 16-Jan-09 | Wales | 4N | A | Arms Park, Cardiff | L | 0-8 |
| 101 | 30-Jan-09 | France | Int | H | Welford Road, Leicester | W | 22-0 |
| 102 | 13-Feb-09 | Ireland | 4N | A | Lansdowne Road, Dublin | W | 11-5 |
| 103 | 20-Mar-09 | Scotland | 4N-CC | H | Athletic Ground, Richmond | L | 8-18 |
| 104 | 15-Jan-10 | Wales | 5N | H | Twickenham, London | W | 11-6 |
| 105 | 12-Feb-10 | Ireland | 5N | H | Twickenham, London | D | 0-0 |
| 106 | 3-Mar-10 | France | 5N | A | Parc des Princess, Paris | W | 11-3 |
| 107 | 19-Mar-10 | Scotland | 5N-CC | A | Inverleith, Edinburgh | W | 14-5 |
| 108 | 21-Jan-11 | Wales | 5N | A | St Helen's, Swansea | L | 11-15 |
| 109 | 28-Jan-11 | France | 5N | H | Twickenham, London | W | 37-0 |
| 110 | 11-Feb-11 | Ireland | 5N | A | Lansdowne Road, Dublin | L | 0-3 |
| 111 | 18-Mar-11 | Scotland | 5N-CC | H | Twickenham, London | W | 13-8 |
| 112 | 20-Jan-12 | Wales | 5N | H | Twickenham, London | W | 8-0 |
| 113 | 10-Feb-12 | Ireland | 5N | H | Twickenham, London | W | 15-0 |
| 114 | 16-Mar-12 | Scotland | 5N-CC | A | Inverleith, Edinburgh | L | 3-8 |
| 115 | 8-Apr-12 | France | 5N | A | Parc des Princess, Paris | W | 18-8 |
| 116 | 4-Jan-13 | South Africa | Int | H | Twickenham, London | L | 3-9 |
| 117 | 18-Jan-13 | Wales | 5N | A | Arms Park, Cardiff | W | 12-0 |
| 118 | 25-Jan-13 | France | 5N | H | Twickenham, London | W | 20-0 |
| 119 | 8-Feb-13 | Ireland | 5N | A | Lansdowne Road, Dublin | W | 15-4 |
| 120 | 15-Mar-13 | Scotland | 5N-CC | H | Twickenham, London | W | 3-0 |

| No | Date | Opponents | Tmt | | Match Venue | Result | |
|----|------|-----------|-----|---|-------------|--------|---|
| 121 | 17-Jan-14 | Wales | 5N | H | Twickenham, London | W | 10-9 |
| 122 | 14-Feb-14 | Ireland | 5N | H | Twickenham, London | W | 17-12 |
| 123 | 21-Mar-14 | Scotland | 5N-CC | A | Inverleith, Edinburgh | W | 16-15 |
| 124 | 13-Apr-14 | France | 5N | A | Stade Colombes, Paris | W | 39-13 |
| 125 | 17-Jan-20 | Wales | 5N | A | St Helen's, Swansea | L | 5-19 |
| 126 | 31-Jan-20 | France | 5N | H | Twickenham, London | W | 8-3 |
| 127 | 14-Feb-20 | Ireland | 5N | A | Lansdowne Road, Dublin | W | 14-11 |
| 128 | 20-Mar-20 | Scotland | 5N-CC | H | Twickenham, London | W | 13-4 |
| 129 | 15-Jan-21 | Wales | 5N | H | Twickenham, London | W | 18-3 |
| 130 | 12-Feb-21 | Ireland | 5N | H | Twickenham, London | W | 15-0 |
| 131 | 19-Mar-21 | Scotland | 5N-CC | A | Inverleith, Edinburgh | W | 18-0 |
| 132 | 28-Mar-21 | France | 5N | A | Stade Colombes, Paris | W | 10-6 |
| 133 | 21-Jan-22 | Wales | 5N | A | Arms Park, Cardiff | L | 6-28 |
| 134 | 11-Feb-22 | Ireland | 5N | A | Lansdowne Road, Dublin | W | 12-3 |
| 135 | 25-Feb-22 | France | 5N | H | Twickenham, London | D | 11-11 |
| 136 | 18-Mar-22 | Scotland | 5N-CC | H | Twickenham, London | W | 11-5 |
| 137 | 20-Jan-23 | Wales | 5N | H | Twickenham, London | W | 7-3 |
| 138 | 10-Feb-23 | Ireland | 5N | H | Welford Road, Leicester | W | 23-5 |
| 139 | 17-Mar-23 | Scotland | 5N-CC | A | Inverleith, Edinburgh | W | 8-6 |
| 140 | 2-Apr-23 | France | 5N | A | Stade Colombes, Paris | W | 12-3 |
| 141 | 19-Jan-24 | Wales | 5N | A | St Helen's, Swansea | W | 17-9 |
| 142 | 9-Feb-24 | Ireland | 5N | A | Ravenhill, Belfast | W | 14-3 |
| 143 | 23-Feb-24 | France | 5N | H | Twickenham, London | W | 19-7 |
| 144 | 15-Mar-24 | Scotland | 5N-CC | H | Twickenham, London | W | 19-0 |
| 145 | 3-Jan-25 | New Zealand | Int | H | Twickenham, London | L | 11-17 |
| 146 | 17-Jan-25 | Wales | 5N | H | Twickenham, London | W | 12-6 |
| 147 | 14-Feb-25 | Ireland | 5N | H | Twickenham, London | D | 6-6 |
| 148 | 21-Mar-25 | Scotland | 5N-CC | A | Murrayfield, Edinburgh | L | 11-14 |
| 149 | 13-Apr-25 | France | 5N | A | Stade Colombes, Paris | W | 13-11 |
| 150 | 16-Jan-26 | Wales | 5N | A | Arms Park, Cardiff | D | 3-3 |
| 151 | 13-Feb-26 | Ireland | 5N | A | Lansdowne Road, Dublin | L | 15-19 |
| 152 | 27-Feb-26 | France | 5N | H | Twickenham, London | W | 11-0 |
| 153 | 20-Mar-26 | Scotland | 5N-CC | H | Twickenham, London | L | 9-17 |
| 154 | 15-Jan-27 | Wales | 5N | H | Twickenham, London | W | 11-9 |
| 155 | 12-Feb-27 | Ireland | 5N | H | Twickenham, London | W | 8-6 |
| 156 | 19-Mar-27 | Scotland | 5N-CC | A | Murrayfield, Edinburgh | L | 13-21 |
| 157 | 2-Apr-27 | France | 5N | A | Stade Colombes, Paris | L | 0-3 |
| 158 | 7-Jan-28 | Australia | Int | H | Twickenham, London | W | 18-11 |
| 159 | 21-Jan-28 | Wales | 5N | A | St Helen's, Swansea | W | 10-8 |
| 160 | 11-Feb-28 | Ireland | 5N | A | Lansdowne Road, Dublin | W | 7-6 |

| No | Date | Opponents | Tmt | | Match Venue | Result | |
|----|------|-----------|-----|---|-------------|--------|---|
| 161 | 25-Feb-28 | France | 5N | H | Twickenham, London | W | 18-8 |
| 162 | 17-Mar-28 | Scotland | 5N-CC | H | Twickenham, London | W | 6-0 |
| 163 | 19-Jan-29 | Wales | 5N | H | Twickenham, London | W | 8-3 |
| 164 | 9-Feb-29 | Ireland | 5N | H | Twickenham, London | L | 5-6 |
| 165 | 16-Mar-29 | Scotland | 5N-CC | A | Murrayfield, Edinburgh | L | 6-12 |
| 166 | 1-Apr-29 | France | 5N | A | Stade Colombes, Paris | W | 16-6 |
| 167 | 18-Jan-30 | Wales | 5N | A | Arms Park, Cardiff | W | 11-3 |
| 168 | 8-Feb-30 | Ireland | 5N | A | Lansdowne Road, Dublin | L | 3-4 |
| 169 | 22-Feb-30 | France | 5N | H | Twickenham, London | W | 11-5 |
| 170 | 15-Mar-30 | Scotland | 5N-CC | H | Twickenham, London | D | 0-0 |
| 171 | 17-Jan-31 | Wales | 5N | H | Twickenham, London | D | 11-11 |
| 172 | 14-Feb-31 | Ireland | 5N | H | Twickenham, London | L | 5-6 |
| 173 | 21-Mar-31 | Scotland | 5N-CC | A | Murrayfield, Edinburgh | L | 19-28 |
| 174 | 6-Apr-31 | France | 5N | A | Stade Colombes, Paris | L | 13-14 |
| 175 | 2-Jan-32 | South Africa | Int | H | Twickenham, London | L | 0-7 |
| 176 | 16-Jan-32 | Wales | 4N | A | St Helen's, Swansea | L | 5-12 |
| 177 | 13-Feb-32 | Ireland | 4N | A | Lansdowne Road, Dublin | W | 11-8 |
| 178 | 19-Mar-32 | Scotland | 4N-CC | H | Twickenham, London | W | 16-3 |
| 179 | 21-Jan-33 | Wales | 4N | H | Twickenham, London | L | 3-7 |
| 180 | 11-Feb-33 | Ireland | 4N | H | Twickenham, London | W | 17-6 |
| 181 | 18-Mar-33 | Scotland | 4N-CC | A | Murrayfield, Edinburgh | L | 0-3 |
| 182 | 20-Jan-34 | Wales | 4N | A | Arms Park, Cardiff | W | 9-0 |
| 183 | 10-Feb-34 | Ireland | 4N | A | Lansdowne Road, Dublin | W | 13-3 |
| 184 | 17-Mar-34 | Scotland | 4N-CC | H | Twickenham, London | W | 6-3 |
| 185 | 19-Jan-35 | Wales | 4N | H | Twickenham, London | D | 3-3 |
| 186 | 9-Feb-35 | Ireland | 4N | H | Twickenham, London | W | 14-3 |
| 187 | 16-Mar-35 | Scotland | 4N-CC | A | Murrayfield, Edinburgh | L | 7-10 |
| 188 | 4-Jan-36 | New Zealand | Int | H | Twickenham, London | W | 13-0 |
| 189 | 18-Jan-36 | Wales | 4N | A | St Helen's, Swansea | D | 0-0 |
| 190 | 8-Feb-36 | Ireland | 4N | A | Lansdowne Road, Dublin | L | 3-6 |
| 191 | 21-Mar-36 | Scotland | 4N-CC | H | Twickenham, London | W | 9-8 |
| 192 | 16-Jan-37 | Wales | 4N | H | Twickenham, London | W | 4-3 |
| 193 | 13-Feb-37 | Ireland | 4N | H | Twickenham, London | W | 9-8 |
| 194 | 20-Mar-37 | Scotland | 4N-CC | A | Murrayfield, Edinburgh | W | 6-3 |
| 195 | 15-Jan-38 | Wales | 4N | A | Arms Park, Cardiff | L | 8-14 |
| 196 | 12-Feb-38 | Ireland | 4N | A | Lansdowne Road, Dublin | W | 36-14 |
| 197 | 19-Mar-38 | Scotland | 4N-CC | H | Twickenham, London | L | 16-21 |
| 198 | 21-Jan-39 | Wales | 4N | H | Twickenham, London | W | 3-0 |
| 199 | 11-Feb-39 | Ireland | 4N | H | Twickenham, London | L | 0-5 |
| 200 | 18-Mar-39 | Scotland | 4N-CC | A | Murrayfield, Edinburgh | W | 9-6 |

| No | Date | Opponents | Tmt | | Match Venue | Result | |
|----|------|-----------|-----|---|-------------|--------|---|
| 201 | 18-Jan-47 | Wales | 5N | A | Arms Park, Cardiff | W | 9-6 |
| 202 | 8-Feb-47 | Ireland | 5N | A | Lansdowne Road, Dublin | L | 0-22 |
| 203 | 15-Mar-47 | Scotland | 5N-CC | H | Twickenham, London | W | 24-5 |
| 204 | 19-Apr-47 | France | 5N | H | Twickenham, London | W | 6-3 |
| 205 | 3-Jan-48 | Australia | Int | H | Twickenham, London | L | 0-11 |
| 206 | 17-Jan-48 | Wales | 5N | H | Twickenham, London | D | 3-3 |
| 207 | 14-Feb-48 | Ireland | 5N | H | Twickenham, London | L | 10-11 |
| 208 | 20-Mar-48 | Scotland | 5N-CC | A | Murrayfield, Edinburgh | L | 3-6 |
| 209 | 29-Mar-48 | France | 5N | A | Stade Colombes, Paris | L | 0-15 |
| 210 | 15-Jan-49 | Wales | 5N | A | Arms Park, Cardiff | L | 3-9 |
| 211 | 12-Feb-49 | Ireland | 5N | A | Lansdowne Road, Dublin | L | 5-14 |
| 212 | 26-Feb-49 | France | 5N | H | Twickenham, London | W | 8-3 |
| 213 | 19-Mar-49 | Scotland | 5N-CC | H | Twickenham, London | W | 19-3 |
| 214 | 21-Jan-50 | Wales | 5N | H | Twickenham, London | L | 5-11 |
| 215 | 11-Feb-50 | Ireland | 5N | H | Twickenham, London | W | 3-0 |
| 216 | 25-Feb-50 | France | 5N | A | Stade Colombes, Paris | L | 3-6 |
| 217 | 18-Mar-50 | Scotland | 5N-CC | A | Murrayfield, Edinburgh | L | 11-13 |
| 218 | 20-Jan-51 | Wales | 5N | A | St Helen's, Swansea | L | 5-23 |
| 219 | 10-Feb-51 | Ireland | 5N | A | Lansdowne Road, Dublin | L | 0-3 |
| 220 | 24-Feb-51 | France | 5N | H | Twickenham, London | L | 3-11 |
| 221 | 17-Mar-51 | Scotland | 5N-CC | H | Twickenham, London | W | 5-3 |
| 222 | 5-Jan-52 | South Africa | Int | H | Twickenham, London | L | 3-8 |
| 223 | 19-Jan-52 | Wales | 5N | H | Twickenham, London | L | 6-8 |
| 224 | 15-Mar-52 | Scotland | 5N-CC | A | Murrayfield, Edinburgh | W | 19-3 |
| 225 | 29-Mar-52 | Ireland | 5N | H | Twickenham, London | W | 3-0 |
| 226 | 5-Apr-52 | France | 5N | A | Stade Colombes, Paris | W | 6-3 |
| 227 | 17-Jan-53 | Wales | 5N | A | Arms Park, Cardiff | W | 8-3 |
| 228 | 14-Feb-53 | Ireland | 5N | A | Lansdowne Road, Dublin | D | 9-9 |
| 229 | 28-Feb-53 | France | 5N | H | Twickenham, London | W | 11-0 |
| 230 | 21-Mar-53 | Scotland | 5N-CC | H | Twickenham, London | W | 26-8 |
| 231 | 16-Jan-54 | Wales | 5N | H | Twickenham, London | W | 9-6 |
| 232 | 30-Jan-54 | New Zealand | Int | H | Twickenham, London | L | 0-5 |
| 233 | 13-Feb-54 | Ireland | 5N | H | Twickenham, London | W | 14-3 |
| 234 | 20-Mar-54 | Scotland | 5N-CC | A | Murrayfield, Edinburgh | W | 13-3 |
| 235 | 10-Apr-54 | France | 5N | A | Stade Colombes, Paris | L | 3-11 |
| 236 | 22-Jan-55 | Wales | 5N | A | Arms Park, Cardiff | L | 0-3 |
| 237 | 12-Feb-55 | Ireland | 5N | A | Lansdowne Road, Dublin | D | 6-6 |
| 238 | 26-Feb-55 | France | 5N | H | Twickenham, London | L | 9-16 |
| 239 | 19-Mar-55 | Scotland | 5N-CC | H | Twickenham, London | W | 9-6 |
| 240 | 21-Jan-56 | Wales | 5N | H | Twickenham, London | L | 3-8 |

| No | Date | Opponents | Tmt | | Match Venue | Result | |
|----|------|-----------|-----|---|-------------|--------|---|
| 241 | 11-Feb-56 | Ireland | 5N | H | Twickenham, London | W | 20-0 |
| 242 | 17-Mar-56 | Scotland | 5N-CC | A | Murrayfield, Edinburgh | W | 11-6 |
| 243 | 14-Apr-56 | France | 5N | A | Stade Colombes, Paris | L | 9-14 |
| 244 | 19-Jan-57 | Wales | 5N | A | Arms Park, Cardiff | W | 3-0 |
| 245 | 9-Feb-57 | Ireland | 5N | A | Lansdowne Road, Dublin | W | 6-0 |
| 246 | 23-Feb-57 | France | 5N | H | Twickenham, London | W | 9-5 |
| 247 | 16-Mar-57 | Scotland | 5N-CC | H | Twickenham, London | W | 16-3 |
| 248 | 18-Jan-58 | Wales | 5N | H | Twickenham, London | D | 3-3 |
| 249 | 1-Feb-58 | Australia | Int | H | Twickenham, London | W | 9-6 |
| 250 | 8-Feb-58 | Ireland | 5N | H | Twickenham, London | W | 6-0 |
| 251 | 1-Mar-58 | France | 5N | A | Stade Colombes, Paris | W | 14-0 |
| 252 | 15-Mar-58 | Scotland | 5N-CC | A | Murrayfield, Edinburgh | D | 3-3 |
| 253 | 17-Jan-59 | Wales | 5N | A | Arms Park, Cardiff | L | 0-5 |
| 254 | 14-Feb-59 | Ireland | 5N | A | Lansdowne Road, Dublin | W | 3-0 |
| 255 | 28-Feb-59 | France | 5N | H | Twickenham, London | D | 3-3 |
| 256 | 21-Mar-59 | Scotland | 5N-CC | H | Twickenham, London | D | 3-3 |
| 257 | 16-Jan-60 | Wales | 5N | H | Twickenham, London | W | 14-6 |
| 258 | 13-Feb-60 | Ireland | 5N | H | Twickenham, London | W | 8-5 |
| 259 | 27-Feb-60 | France | 5N | A | Stade Colombes, Paris | D | 3-3 |
| 260 | 19-Mar-60 | Scotland | 5N-CC | A | Murrayfield, Edinburgh | W | 21-12 |
| 261 | 7-Jan-61 | South Africa | Int | H | Twickenham, London | L | 0-5 |
| 262 | 21-Jan-61 | Wales | 5N | A | Arms Park, Cardiff | L | 3-6 |
| 263 | 11-Feb-61 | Ireland | 5N | A | Lansdowne Road, Dublin | L | 8-11 |
| 264 | 25-Feb-61 | France | 5N | H | Twickenham, London | D | 5-5 |
| 265 | 18-Mar-61 | Scotland | 5N-CC | H | Twickenham, London | W | 6-0 |
| 266 | 20-Jan-62 | Wales | 5N | H | Twickenham, London | D | 0-0 |
| 267 | 10-Feb-62 | Ireland | 5N | H | Twickenham, London | W | 16-0 |
| 268 | 24-Feb-62 | France | 5N | A | Stade Colombes, Paris | L | 0-13 |
| 269 | 17-Mar-62 | Scotland | 5N-CC | A | Murrayfield, Edinburgh | D | 3-3 |
| 270 | 19-Jan-63 | Wales | 5N | A | Arms Park, Cardiff | W | 13-6 |
| 271 | 9-Feb-63 | Ireland | 5N | A | Lansdowne Road, Dublin | D | 0-0 |
| 272 | 23-Feb-63 | France | 5N | H | Twickenham, London | W | 6-5 |
| 273 | 16-Mar-63 | Scotland | 5N-CC | H | Twickenham, London | W | 10-8 |
| 274 | 25-May-63 | New Zealand | Int-T | A | Eden Park, Auckland | L | 11-21 |
| 275 | 1-Jun-63 | New Zealand | Int-T | A | Lancaster Park Oval, Christchurch | L | 6-9 |
| 276 | 4-Jun-63 | Australia | Int-T | A | Sports Ground, Sydney | L | 9-18 |
| 277 | 4-Jan-64 | New Zealand | Int | H | Twickenham, London | L | 0-14 |
| 278 | 18-Jan-64 | Wales | 5N | H | Twickenham, London | D | 6-6 |
| 279 | 8-Feb-64 | Ireland | 5N | H | Twickenham, London | L | 5-18 |
| 280 | 22-Feb-64 | France | 5N | A | Stade Colombes, Paris | W | 6-3 |

| No | Date | Opponents | Tmt | | Match Venue | Result | |
|----|------|-----------|-----|---|-------------|--------|---|
| 281 | 21-Mar-64 | Scotland | 5N-CC | A | Murrayfield, Edinburgh | L | 6-15 |
| 282 | 16-Jan-65 | Wales | 5N | A | Arms Park, Cardiff | L | 3-14 |
| 283 | 13-Feb-65 | Ireland | 5N | A | Lansdowne Road, Dublin | L | 0-5 |
| 284 | 27-Feb-65 | France | 5N | H | Twickenham, London | W | 9-6 |
| 285 | 20-Mar-65 | Scotland | 5N-CC | H | Twickenham, London | D | 3-3 |
| 286 | 15-Jan-66 | Wales | 5N | H | Twickenham, London | L | 6-11 |
| 287 | 12-Feb-66 | Ireland | 5N | H | Twickenham, London | D | 6-6 |
| 288 | 26-Feb-66 | France | 5N | A | Stade Colombes, Paris | L | 0-13 |
| 289 | 19-Mar-66 | Scotland | 5N-CC | A | Murrayfield, Edinburgh | L | 3-6 |
| 290 | 7-Jan-67 | Australia | Int | H | Twickenham, London | L | 11-23 |
| 291 | 11-Feb-67 | Ireland | 5N | A | Lansdowne Road, Dublin | W | 8-3 |
| 292 | 25-Feb-67 | France | 5N | H | Twickenham, London | L | 12-16 |
| 293 | 18-Mar-67 | Scotland | 5N-CC | H | Twickenham, London | W | 27-14 |
| 294 | 15-Apr-67 | Wales | 5N | A | Arms Park, Cardiff | L | 21-34 |
| 295 | 4-Nov-67 | New Zealand | Int | H | Twickenham, London | L | 11-23 |
| 296 | 20-Jan-68 | Wales | 5N | H | Twickenham, London | D | 11-11 |
| 297 | 10-Feb-68 | Ireland | 5N | H | Twickenham, London | D | 9-9 |
| 298 | 24-Feb-68 | France | 5N | A | Stade Colombes, Paris | L | 9-14 |
| 299 | 16-Mar-68 | Scotland | 5N-CC | A | Murrayfield, Edinburgh | W | 8-6 |
| 300 | 8-Feb-69 | Ireland | 5N | A | Lansdowne Road, Dublin | L | 15-17 |
| 301 | 22-Feb-69 | France | 5N | H | Twickenham, London | W | 22-8 |
| 302 | 15-Mar-69 | Scotland | 5N-CC | H | Twickenham, London | W | 8-3 |
| 303 | 12-Apr-69 | Wales | 5N | A | National Stadium, Cardiff | L | 9-30 |
| 304 | 20-Dec-69 | South Africa | Int | H | Twickenham, London | W | 11-8 |
| 305 | 14-Feb-70 | Ireland | 5N | H | Twickenham, London | W | 9-3 |
| 306 | 28-Feb-70 | Wales | 5N | H | Twickenham, London | L | 13-17 |
| 307 | 21-Mar-70 | Scotland | 5N-CC | A | Murrayfield, Edinburgh | L | 5-14 |
| 308 | 18-Apr-70 | France | 5N | A | Stade Colombes, Paris | L | 13-35 |
| 309 | 16-Jan-71 | Wales | 5N | A | National Stadium, Cardiff | L | 6-22 |
| 310 | 13-Feb-71 | Ireland | 5N | A | Lansdowne Road, Dublin | W | 9-6 |
| 311 | 27-Feb-71 | France | 5N | H | Twickenham, London | D | 14-14 |
| 312 | 20-Mar-71 | Scotland | 5N-CC | H | Twickenham, London | L | 15-16 |
| 313 | 27-Mar-71 | Scotland | Int-C | A | Murrayfield, Edinburgh | L | 6-26 |
| 314 | 17-Apr-71 | President's XV | Int-C | H | Twickenham, London | L | 11-28 |
| 315 | 15-Jan-72 | Wales | 5N | H | Twickenham, London | L | 3-12 |
| 316 | 12-Feb-72 | Ireland | 5N | H | Twickenham, London | L | 12-16 |
| 317 | 26-Feb-72 | France | 5N | A | Stade Colombes, Paris | L | 12-37 |
| 318 | 18-Mar-72 | Scotland | 5N-CC | A | Murrayfield, Edinburgh | L | 9-23 |
| 319 | 3-Jun-72 | South Africa | Int-T | A | Ellis Park, Johannesburg | W | 18-9 |
| 320 | 6-Jan-73 | New Zealand | Int | H | Twickenham, London | L | 0-9 |

| No | Date | Opponents | Tmt | | Match Venue | Result | |
|-----|-----------|-------------|--------|---|--------------------------------|--------|-------|
| 321 | 20-Jan-73 | Wales | 5N | A | National Stadium, Cardiff | L | 9-25 |
| 322 | 10-Feb-73 | Ireland | 5N | A | Lansdowne Road, Dublin | L | 9-18 |
| 323 | 24-Feb-73 | France | 5N | H | Twickenham, London | W | 14-6 |
| 324 | 17-Mar-73 | Scotland | 5N-CC | H | Twickenham, London | W | 20-13 |
| 325 | 15-Sep-73 | New Zealand | Int-T | A | Eden Park, Auckland | W | 16-10 |
| 326 | 17-Nov-73 | Australia | Int | H | Twickenham, London | W | 20-3 |
| 327 | 2-Feb-74 | Scotland | 5N-CC | A | Murrayfield, Edinburgh | L | 14-16 |
| 328 | 16-Feb-74 | Ireland | 5N | H | Twickenham, London | L | 21-26 |
| 329 | 2-Mar-74 | France | 5N | A | Parc des Princess, Paris | D | 12-12 |
| 330 | 16-Mar-74 | Wales | 5N | H | Twickenham, London | W | 16-12 |
| 331 | 18-Jan-75 | Ireland | 5N | A | Lansdowne Road, Dublin | L | 9-12 |
| 332 | 1-Feb-75 | France | 5N | H | Twickenham, London | L | 20-27 |
| 333 | 15-Feb-75 | Wales | 5N | A | National Stadium, Cardiff | L | 4-20 |
| 334 | 15-Mar-75 | Scotland | 5N-CC | H | Twickenham, London | W | 7-6 |
| 335 | 24-May-75 | Australia | Int-T | A | Cricket Ground, Sydney | L | 9-16 |
| 336 | 31-May-75 | Australia | Int-T | A | Ballymore Oval, Brisbane | L | 21-30 |
| 337 | 3-Jan-76 | Australia | Int | H | Twickenham, London | W | 23-6 |
| 338 | 17-Jan-76 | Wales | 5N | H | Twickenham, London | L | 9-21 |
| 339 | 21-Feb-76 | Scotland | 5N-CC | A | Murrayfield, Edinburgh | L | 12-22 |
| 340 | 6-Mar-76 | Ireland | 5N | H | Twickenham, London | L | 12-13 |
| 341 | 20-Mar-76 | France | 5N | A | Parc des Princess, Paris | L | 9-30 |
| 342 | 15-Jan-77 | Scotland | 5N-CC | H | Twickenham, London | W | 26-6 |
| 343 | 5-Feb-77 | Ireland | 5N | A | Lansdowne Road, Dublin | W | 4-0 |
| 344 | 19-Feb-77 | France | 5N | H | Twickenham, London | L | 3-4 |
| 345 | 5-Mar-77 | Wales | 5N | A | National Stadium, Cardiff | L | 9-14 |
| 346 | 21-Jan-78 | France | 5N | A | Parc des Princess, Paris | L | 6-15 |
| 347 | 4-Feb-78 | Wales | 5N | H | Twickenham, London | L | 6-9 |
| 348 | 4-Mar-78 | Scotland | 5N-CC | A | Murrayfield, Edinburgh | W | 15-0 |
| 349 | 18-Mar-78 | Ireland | 5N | H | Twickenham, London | W | 15-9 |
| 350 | 25-Nov-78 | New Zealand | Int | H | Twickenham, London | L | 6-16 |
| 351 | 3-Feb-79 | Scotland | 5N-CC | H | Twickenham, London | D | 7-7 |
| 352 | 17-Feb-79 | Ireland | 5N | A | Lansdowne Road, Dublin | L | 7-12 |
| 353 | 3-Mar-79 | France | 5N | H | Twickenham, London | W | 7-6 |
| 354 | 17-Mar-79 | Wales | 5N | A | National Stadium, Cardiff | L | 3-27 |
| 355 | 24-Nov-79 | New Zealand | Int | H | Twickenham, London | L | 9-10 |
| 356 | 19-Jan-80 | Ireland | 5N | H | Twickenham, London | W | 24-9 |
| 357 | 2-Feb-80 | France | 5N | A | Parc des Princess, Paris | W | 17-13 |
| 358 | 16-Feb-80 | Wales | 5N | H | Twickenham, London | W | 9-8 |
| 359 | 15-Mar-80 | Scotland | 5N-CC | A | Murrayfield, Edinburgh | W | 30-18 |
| 360 | 17-Jan-81 | Wales | 5N | A | National Stadium, Cardiff | L | 19-21 |

| No | Date | Opponents | Tmt | | Match Venue | Result | |
|----|------|-----------|-----|---|-------------|--------|---|
| 361 | 21-Feb-81 | Scotland | 5N-CC | H | Twickenham, London | W | 23-17 |
| 362 | 7-Mar-81 | Ireland | 5N | A | Lansdowne Road, Dublin | W | 10-6 |
| 363 | 21-Mar-81 | France | 5N | H | Twickenham, London | L | 12-16 |
| 364 | 30-May-81 | Argentina | Int-T | A | Ferro Carril Oeste Stadium, B Aires | D | 19-19 |
| 365 | 6-Jun-81 | Argentina | Int-T | A | Ferro Carril Oeste Stadium, B Aires | W | 12-6 |
| 366 | 2-Jan-82 | Australia | Int | H | Twickenham, London | W | 15-11 |
| 367 | 16-Jan-82 | Scotland | 5N-CC | A | Murrayfield, Edinburgh | D | 9-9 |
| 368 | 6-Feb-82 | Ireland | 5N | H | Twickenham, London | L | 15-16 |
| 369 | 20-Feb-82 | France | 5N | A | Parc des Princess, Paris | W | 27-15 |
| 370 | 6-Mar-82 | Wales | 5N | H | Twickenham, London | W | 17-7 |
| 371 | 15-Jan-83 | France | 5N | H | Twickenham, London | L | 15-19 |
| 372 | 5-Feb-83 | Wales | 5N | A | National Stadium, Cardiff | D | 13-13 |
| 373 | 5-Mar-83 | Scotland | 5N-CC | H | Twickenham, London | L | 12-22 |
| 374 | 19-Mar-83 | Ireland | 5N | A | Lansdowne Road, Dublin | L | 15-25 |
| 375 | 19-Nov-83 | New Zealand | Int | H | Twickenham, London | W | 15-9 |
| 376 | 4-Feb-84 | Scotland | 5N-CC | A | Murrayfield, Edinburgh | L | 6-18 |
| 377 | 18-Feb-84 | Ireland | 5N | H | Twickenham, London | W | 12-9 |
| 378 | 3-Mar-84 | France | 5N | A | Parc des Princess, Paris | L | 18-32 |
| 379 | 17-Mar-84 | Wales | 5N | H | Twickenham, London | L | 15-24 |
| 380 | 2-Jun-84 | South Africa | Int-T | A | Boet Erasmus Stadium, Port Elizabeth | L | 15-33 |
| 381 | 9-Jun-84 | South Africa | Int-T | A | Ellis Park, Johannesburg | L | 9-35 |
| 382 | 3-Nov-84 | Australia | Int | H | Twickenham, London | L | 3-19 |
| 383 | 5-Jan-85 | Romania | Int | H | Twickenham, London | W | 22-15 |
| 384 | 2-Feb-85 | France | 5N | H | Twickenham, London | D | 9-9 |
| 385 | 16-Mar-85 | Scotland | 5N-CC | H | Twickenham, London | W | 10-7 |
| 386 | 30-Mar-85 | Ireland | 5N | A | Lansdowne Road, Dublin | L | 10-13 |
| 387 | 20-Apr-85 | Wales | 5N | A | National Stadium, Cardiff | L | 15-24 |
| 388 | 1-Jun-85 | New Zealand | Int-T | A | Lancaster Park Oval, Christchurch | L | 13-18 |
| 389 | 8-Jun-85 | New Zealand | Int-T | A | Athletic Park, Wellington | L | 15-42 |
| 390 | 18-Jan-86 | Wales | 5N | H | Twickenham, London | W | 21-18 |
| 391 | 15-Feb-86 | Scotland | 5N-CC | A | Murrayfield, Edinburgh | L | 6-33 |
| 392 | 1-Mar-86 | Ireland | 5N | H | Twickenham, London | W | 25-20 |
| 393 | 15-Mar-86 | France | 5N | A | Parc des Princess, Paris | L | 10-29 |
| 394 | 7-Feb-87 | Ireland | 5N | A | Lansdowne Road, Dublin | L | 0-17 |
| 395 | 21-Feb-87 | France | 5N | H | Twickenham, London | L | 15-19 |
| 396 | 7-Mar-87 | Wales | 5N | A | National Stadium, Cardiff | L | 12-19 |
| 397 | 4-Apr-87 | Scotland | 5N-CC | H | Twickenham, London | W | 21-12 |
| 398 | 23-May-87 | Australia | WCp | A | Concord Oval, Sydney | L | 6-19 |
| 399 | 30-May-87 | Japan | WCp | N | Concord Oval, Sydney | W | 60-7 |
| 400 | 3-Jun-87 | United States | WCp | N | Concord Oval, Sydney | W | 34-6 |

| No | Date | Opponents | Tmt | | Match Venue | Result | |
|----|------|-----------|-----|---|-------------|--------|---|
| 401 | 8-Jun-87 | Wales | WCqf | N | Ballymore Oval, Brisbane | L | 3-16 |
| 402 | 16-Jan-88 | France | 5N | A | Parc des Princess, Paris | L | 9-10 |
| 403 | 6-Feb-88 | Wales | 5N | H | Twickenham, London | L | 3-11 |
| 404 | 5-Mar-88 | Scotland | 5N-CC | A | Murrayfield, Edinburgh | W | 9-6 |
| 405 | 19-Mar-88 | Ireland | 5N | H | Twickenham, London | W | 35-3 |
| 406 | 23-Apr-88 | Ireland | MT | A | Lansdowne Road, Dublin | W | 21-10 |
| 407 | 29-May-88 | Australia | Int-T | A | Ballymore Oval, Brisbane | L | 16-22 |
| 408 | 12-Jun-88 | Australia | Int-T | A | Concord Oval, Sydney | L | 8-28 |
| 409 | 16-Jun-88 | Fiji | Int-T | A | National Stadium, Suva | W | 25-12 |
| 410 | 5-Nov-88 | Australia | Int | H | Twickenham, London | W | 28-19 |
| 411 | 4-Feb-89 | Scotland | 5N-CC | H | Twickenham, London | D | 12-12 |
| 412 | 18-Feb-89 | Ireland | 5N-MT | A | Lansdowne Road, Dublin | W | 16-3 |
| 413 | 4-Mar-89 | France | 5N | H | Twickenham, London | W | 11-0 |
| 414 | 18-Mar-89 | Wales | 5N | A | National Stadium, Cardiff | L | 9-12 |
| 415 | 13-May-89 | Romania | Int | A | Stadionul 23 August, Bucharest | W | 58-3 |
| 416 | 4-Nov-89 | Fiji | Int | H | Twickenham, London | W | 58-23 |
| 417 | 20-Jan-90 | Ireland | 5N-MT | H | Twickenham, London | W | 23-0 |
| 418 | 3-Feb-90 | France | 5N | A | Parc des Princess, Paris | W | 26-7 |
| 419 | 17-Feb-90 | Wales | 5N | H | Twickenham, London | W | 34-6 |
| 420 | 17-Mar-90 | Scotland | 5N-CC | A | Murrayfield, Edinburgh | L | 7-13 |
| 421 | 28-Jul-90 | Argentina | Int-T | A | Vélez Sarsfield Stadium, Buenos Aires | W | 25-12 |
| 422 | 4-Aug-90 | Argentina | Int-T | A | Vélez Sarsfield Stadium, Buenos Aires | L | 13-15 |
| 423 | 3-Nov-90 | Argentina | Int | H | Twickenham, London | W | 51-0 |
| 424 | 19-Jan-91 | Wales | 5N | A | National Stadium, Cardiff | W | 25-6 |
| 425 | 16-Feb-91 | Scotland | 5N-CC | H | Twickenham, London | W | 21-12 |
| 426 | 2-Mar-91 | Ireland | 5N-MT | A | Lansdowne Road, Dublin | W | 16-7 |
| 427 | 16-Mar-91 | France | 5N | H | Twickenham, London | W | 21-19 |
| 428 | 20-Jul-91 | Fiji | Int-T | A | National Stadium, Suva | W | 28-12 |
| 429 | 27-Jul-91 | Australia | Int-T | A | Football Stadium, Sydney | L | 15-40 |
| 430 | 3-Oct-91 | New Zealand | WCp | H | Twickenham, London | L | 12-18 |
| 431 | 8-Oct-91 | Italy | WCp | H | Twickenham, London | W | 36-6 |
| 432 | 11-Oct-91 | United States | WCp | H | Twickenham, London | W | 37-9 |
| 433 | 19-Oct-91 | France | WCqf | A | Parc des Princess, Paris | W | 19-10 |
| 434 | 26-Oct-91 | Scotland | WCsf | A | Murrayfield, Edinburgh | W | 9-6 |
| 435 | 2-Nov-91 | Australia | WCf | H | Twickenham, London | L | 6-12 |
| 436 | 18-Jan-92 | Scotland | 5N-CC | A | Murrayfield, Edinburgh | W | 25-7 |
| 437 | 1-Feb-92 | Ireland | 5N-MT | H | Twickenham, London | W | 38-9 |
| 438 | 15-Feb-92 | France | 5N | A | Parc des Princess, Paris | W | 31-13 |
| 439 | 7-Mar-92 | Wales | 5N | H | Twickenham, London | W | 24-0 |
| 440 | 17-Oct-92 | Canada | Int | H | Wembley Stadium, London | W | 26-13 |

| No | Date | Opponents | Tmt | | Match Venue | Result | |
|-----|-----------|---------------|--------|---|----------------------------------|---|-------|
| 441 | 14-Nov-92 | South Africa | Int | H | Twickenham, London | W | 33-16 |
| 442 | 16-Jan-93 | France | 5N | H | Twickenham, London | W | 16-15 |
| 443 | 6-Feb-93 | Wales | 5N | A | National Stadium, Cardiff | L | 9-10 |
| 444 | 6-Mar-93 | Scotland | 5N-CC | H | Twickenham, London | W | 26-12 |
| 445 | 20-Mar-93 | Ireland | 5N-MT | A | Lansdowne Road, Dublin | L | 3-17 |
| 446 | 27-Nov-93 | New Zealand | Int | H | Twickenham, London | W | 15-9 |
| 447 | 5-Feb-94 | Scotland | 5N-CC | A | Murrayfield, Edinburgh | W | 15-14 |
| 448 | 19-Feb-94 | Ireland | 5N-MT | H | Twickenham, London | L | 12-13 |
| 449 | 5-Mar-94 | France | 5N | A | Parc des Princess, Paris | W | 18-14 |
| 450 | 19-Mar-94 | Wales | 5N | H | Twickenham, London | W | 15-8 |
| 451 | 4-Jun-94 | South Africa | Int-T | A | Loftus Versfeld Stadium, Pretoria | W | 32-15 |
| 452 | 11-Jun-94 | South Africa | Int-T | A | Newlands Stadium, Cape Town | L | 9-27 |
| 453 | 12-Nov-94 | Romania | Int | H | Twickenham, London | W | 54-3 |
| 454 | 10-Dec-94 | Canada | Int | H | Twickenham, London | W | 60-19 |
| 455 | 21-Jan-95 | Ireland | 5N-MT | A | Lansdowne Road, Dublin | W | 20-8 |
| 456 | 4-Feb-95 | France | 5N | H | Twickenham, London | W | 31-10 |
| 457 | 18-Feb-95 | Wales | 5N | A | National Stadium, Cardiff | W | 23-9 |
| 458 | 18-Mar-95 | Scotland | 5N-CC | H | Twickenham, London | W | 24-12 |
| 459 | 27-May-95 | Argentina | WCp | N | Kings Park Stadium, Durban | W | 24-18 |
| 460 | 31-May-95 | Italy | WCp | N | Kings Park Stadium, Durban | W | 27-20 |
| 461 | 4-Jun-95 | Western Samoa | WCp | N | Kings Park Stadium, Durban | W | 44-22 |
| 462 | 11-Jun-95 | Australia | WCqf | N | Newlands Stadium, Cape Town | W | 25-22 |
| 463 | 18-Jun-95 | New Zealand | WCsf | N | Newlands Stadium, Cape Town | L | 29-45 |
| 464 | 22-Jun-95 | France | WC34 | N | Loftus Versfeld Stadium, Pretoria | L | 9-19 |
| 465 | 18-Nov-95 | South Africa | Int | H | Twickenham, London | L | 14-24 |
| 466 | 16-Dec-95 | Western Samoa | Int | H | Twickenham, London | W | 27-9 |
| 467 | 20-Jan-96 | France | 5N | A | Parc des Princess, Paris | L | 12-15 |
| 468 | 3-Feb-96 | Wales | 5N | H | Twickenham, London | W | 21-15 |
| 469 | 2-Mar-96 | Scotland | 5N-CC | A | Murrayfield, Edinburgh | W | 18-9 |
| 470 | 16-Mar-96 | Ireland | 5N-MT | H | Twickenham, London | W | 28-15 |
| 471 | 23-Nov-96 | Italy | Int | H | Twickenham, London | W | 54-21 |
| 472 | 14-Dec-96 | Argentina | Int | H | Twickenham, London | W | 20-18 |
| 473 | 1-Feb-97 | Scotland | 5N-CC | H | Twickenham, London | W | 41-13 |
| 474 | 15-Feb-97 | Ireland | 5N-MT | A | Lansdowne Road, Dublin | W | 46-6 |
| 475 | 1-Mar-97 | France | 5N | H | Twickenham, London | L | 20-23 |
| 476 | 15-Mar-97 | Wales | 5N | A | National Stadium, Cardiff | W | 34-13 |
| 477 | 31-May-97 | Argentina | Int-T | A | Ferro Carril Oeste Stadium, B Aires | W | 46-20 |
| 478 | 7-Jun-97 | Argentina | Int-T | A | Ferro Carril Oeste Stadium, B Aires | L | 13-33 |
| 479 | 12-Jul-97 | Australia | CKC-T | A | Football Stadium, Sydney | L | 6-25 |
| 480 | 15-Nov-97 | Australia | CKC | H | Twickenham, London | D | 15-15 |

| No | Date | Opponents | Tmt | | Match Venue | Result | |
|----|------|-----------|-----|---|-------------|--------|---|
| 481 | 22-Nov-97 | New Zealand | Int | H | Old Trafford, Manchester | L | 8-25 |
| 482 | 29-Nov-97 | South Africa | Int | H | Twickenham, London | L | 11-29 |
| 483 | 6-Dec-97 | New Zealand | Int | H | Twickenham, London | D | 26-26 |
| 484 | 7-Feb-98 | France | 5N | A | Stade de France, Paris | L | 17-24 |
| 485 | 21-Feb-98 | Wales | 5N | H | Twickenham, London | W | 60-26 |
| 486 | 22-Mar-98 | Scotland | 5N-CC | A | Murrayfield, Edinburgh | W | 34-20 |
| 487 | 4-Apr-98 | Ireland | 5N-MT | H | Twickenham, London | W | 35-17 |
| 488 | 6-Jun-98 | Australia | CKC-T | A | Suncorp Stadium, Brisbane | L | 0-76 |
| 489 | 20-Jun-98 | New Zealand | Int-T | A | Carisbrook, Dunedin | L | 22-64 |
| 490 | 27-Jun-98 | New Zealand | Int-T | A | Eden Park, Auckland | L | 10-40 |
| 491 | 4-Jul-98 | South Africa | Int-T | A | Norwich Park, Newlands, Cape Town | L | 0-18 |
| 492 | 14-Nov-98 | Netherlands | WCQ | H | McAlpine Stadium, Huddersfield | W | 110-0 |
| 493 | 22-Nov-98 | Italy | WCQ | H | McAlpine Stadium, Huddersfield | W | 23-15 |
| 494 | 28-Nov-98 | Australia | CKC | H | Twickenham, London | L | 11-12 |
| 495 | 5-Dec-98 | South Africa | Int | H | Twickenham, London | W | 13-7 |
| 496 | 20-Feb-99 | Scotland | 5N-CC | H | Twickenham, London | W | 24-21 |
| 497 | 6-Mar-99 | Ireland | 5N-MT | A | Lansdowne Road, Dublin | W | 27-15 |
| 498 | 20-Mar-99 | France | 5N | H | Twickenham, London | W | 21-10 |
| 499 | 11-Apr-99 | Wales | 5N | N | Wembley Stadium, London | L | 31-32 |
| 500 | 26-Jun-99 | Australia | CKC-T | A | Stadium Australia, Sydney | L | 15-22 |
| 501 | 21-Aug-99 | United States | Int | H | Twickenham, London | W | 106-8 |
| 502 | 28-Aug-99 | Canada | Int | H | Twickenham, London | W | 36-11 |
| 503 | 2-Oct-99 | Italy | WCp | H | Twickenham, London | W | 67-7 |
| 504 | 9-Oct-99 | New Zealand | WCp | H | Twickenham, London | L | 16-30 |
| 505 | 15-Oct-99 | Tonga | WCp | H | Twickenham, London | W | 101-10 |
| 506 | 20-Oct-99 | Fiji | QFpo | H | Twickenham, London | W | 45-24 |
| 507 | 24-Oct-99 | South Africa | WCqf | N | Stade de France, Paris | L | 21-44 |
| 508 | 5-Feb-00 | Ireland | 6N-MT | H | Twickenham, London | W | 50-18 |
| 509 | 19-Feb-00 | France | 6N | A | Stade de France, Paris | W | 15-9 |
| 510 | 4-Mar-00 | Wales | 6N | H | Twickenham, London | W | 46-12 |
| 511 | 18-Mar-00 | Italy | 6N | A | Stadio Flaminio, Rome | W | 59-12 |
| 512 | 2-Apr-00 | Scotland | 6N-CC | A | Murrayfield, Edinburgh | L | 13-19 |
| 513 | 17-Jun-00 | South Africa | Int-T | A | Minolta Loftus Stadium, Pretoria | L | 13-18 |
| 514 | 24-Jun-00 | South Africa | Int-T | A | Free State Stadium, Bloemfontein | W | 27-22 |
| 515 | 18-Nov-00 | Australia | CKC | H | Twickenham, London | W | 22-19 |
| 516 | 25-Nov-00 | Argentina | Int | H | Twickenham, London | W | 19-0 |
| 517 | 2-Dec-00 | South Africa | Int | H | Twickenham, London | W | 25-17 |
| 518 | 3-Feb-01 | Wales | 6N | A | Millennium Stadium, Cardiff | W | 44-15 |
| 519 | 17-Feb-01 | Italy | 6N | H | Twickenham, London | W | 80-23 |
| 520 | 3-Mar-01 | Scotland | 6N-CC | H | Twickenham, London | W | 43-3 |

| No | Date | Opponents | Tmt | | Match Venue | Result | |
|----|------|-----------|-----|---|-------------|--------|---|
| 401 | 13-Jun-87 | Australia | WCsf | A | Concord Oval, Sydney | W | 30-24 |
| 402 | 20-Jun-87 | New Zealand | WCf | A | Eden Park, Auckland | L | 9-29 |
| 403 | 11-Nov-87 | Romania | FIRA | H | Stade Armandie, Agen | W | 49-3 |
| 404 | 16-Jan-88 | England | 5N | H | Parc des Princess, Paris | W | 10-9 |
| 405 | 6-Feb-88 | Scotland | 5N | A | Murrayfield, Edinburgh | L | 12-23 |
| 406 | 20-Feb-88 | Ireland | 5N | H | Parc des Princess, Paris | W | 25-6 |
| 407 | 19-Mar-88 | Wales | 5N | A | National Stadium, Cardiff | W | 10-9 |
| 408 | 18-Jun-88 | Argentina | Int-T | A | Vélez Sarsfield Stadium, Buenos Aires | W | 18-15 |
| 409 | 25-Jun-88 | Argentina | Int-T | A | Vélez Sarsfield Stadium, Buenos Aires | L | 6-18 |
| 410 | 5-Nov-88 | Argentina | Int | H | Stade de la Beaujoire, Nantes | W | 29-9 |
| 411 | 11-Nov-88 | Argentina | Int | H | Stade Nord Lille Métropole | W | 28-18 |
| 412 | 26-Nov-88 | Romania | FIRA | A | Stadionul Giuleşti-V Stănescu, Bucharest | W | 16-12 |
| 413 | 21-Jan-89 | Ireland | 5N | A | Lansdowne Road, Dublin | W | 26-21 |
| 414 | 18-Feb-89 | Wales | 5N | H | Parc des Princess, Paris | W | 31-12 |
| 415 | 4-Mar-89 | England | 5N | A | Twickenham, London | L | 0-11 |
| 416 | 18-Mar-89 | Scotland | 5N | H | Parc des Princess, Paris | W | 19-3 |
| 417 | 17-Jun-89 | New Zealand | Int-T | A | Lancaster Park Oval, Christchurch | L | 17-25 |
| 418 | 1-Jul-89 | New Zealand | Int-T | A | Eden Park, Auckland | L | 20-34 |
| 419 | 4-Oct-89 | Lions XV | Int | H | Parc des Princess, Paris | L | 27-29 |
| 420 | 4-Nov-89 | Australia | BIC | H | Stade de la Meinau, Strasbourg | L | 15-32 |
| 421 | 11-Nov-89 | Australia | BIC | H | Stade Nord Lille Métropole | W | 25-19 |
| 422 | 20-Jan-90 | Wales | 5N | A | National Stadium, Cardiff | W | 29-19 |
| 423 | 3-Feb-90 | England | 5N | H | Parc des Princess, Paris | L | 7-26 |
| 424 | 17-Feb-90 | Scotland | 5N | A | Murrayfield, Edinburgh | L | 0-21 |
| 425 | 3-Mar-90 | Ireland | 5N | H | Parc des Princess, Paris | W | 31-12 |
| 426 | 24-May-90 | Romania | FIRA | H | Stade Jacques Fouroux, Auch | L | 6-12 |
| 427 | 9-Jun-90 | Australia | BIC-T | A | Football Stadium, Sydney | L | 9-21 |
| 428 | 24-Jun-90 | Australia | BIC-T | A | Ballymore Oval, Brisbane | L | 31-48 |
| 429 | 30-Jun-90 | Australia | BIC-T | A | Football Stadium, Sydney | W | 28-19 |
| 430 | 3-Nov-90 | New Zealand | Int | H | Stade de la Beaujoire, Nantes | L | 3-24 |
| 431 | 10-Nov-90 | New Zealand | Int | H | Parc des Princess, Paris | L | 12-30 |
| 432 | 19-Jan-91 | Scotland | 5N | H | Parc des Princess, Paris | W | 15-9 |
| 433 | 2-Feb-91 | Ireland | 5N | A | Lansdowne Road, Dublin | W | 21-13 |
| 434 | 2-Mar-91 | Wales | 5N | H | Parc des Princess, Paris | W | 36-3 |
| 435 | 16-Mar-91 | England | 5N | A | Twickenham, London | L | 19-21 |
| 436 | 22-Jun-91 | Romania | FIRA | A | Stadionul 23 August, Bucharest | W | 33-21 |
| 437 | 13-Jul-91 | United States | Int-T | A | Observatory Park, Denver, Colorado | W | 41-9 |
| 438 | 20-Jul-91 | United States | Int-T | A | Colorado Springs | W | 10-3 |
| 439 | 4-Sep-91 | Wales | Int | A | National Stadium, Cardiff | W | 22-9 |
| 440 | 4-Oct-91 | Romania | WCp | H | Stade de la Méditerranée, Béziers | W | 30-3 |

| No | Date | Opponents | Tmt | | Match Venue | | Result |
|-----|----------|----------------|--------|---|------------------------------------------|---|-------|
| 601 | 20-Oct-07 | South Africa | WCf | N | Stade de France, Paris | L | 6-15 |
| 602 | 2-Feb-08 | Wales | 6N | H | Twickenham, London | L | 19-26 |
| 603 | 10-Feb-08 | Italy | 6N | A | Stadio Flaminio, Rome | W | 23-19 |
| 604 | 23-Feb-08 | France | 6N | A | Stade de France, Paris | W | 24-13 |
| 605 | 8-Mar-08 | Scotland | 6N-CC | A | Murrayfield, Edinburgh | L | 9-15 |
| 606 | 15-Mar-08 | Ireland | 6N-MT | H | Twickenham, London | W | 33-10 |
| 607 | 14-Jun-08 | New Zealand | Int-T | A | Eden Park, Auckland | L | 20-37 |
| 608 | 21-Jun-08 | New Zealand | Int-T | A | AMI Stadium, Christchurch | L | 12-44 |
| 609 | 8-Nov-08 | Pacific Islands | Int | H | Twickenham, London | W | 39-13 |
| 610 | 15-Nov-08 | Australia | CKC | H | Twickenham, London | L | 14-28 |
| 611 | 22-Nov-08 | South Africa | Int | H | Twickenham, London | L | 6-42 |
| 612 | 29-Nov-08 | New Zealand | EHS | H | Twickenham, London | L | 6-32 |
| 613 | 7-Feb-09 | Italy | 6N | H | Twickenham, London | W | 36-11 |
| 614 | 14-Feb-09 | Wales | 6N | A | Millennium Stadium, Cardiff | L | 15-23 |
| 615 | 28-Feb-09 | Ireland | 6N-MT | A | Croke Park, Dublin | L | 13-14 |
| 616 | 15-Mar-09 | France | 6N | H | Twickenham, London | W | 34-10 |
| 617 | 21-Mar-09 | Scotland | 6N-CC | H | Twickenham, London | W | 26-12 |
| 618 | 6-Jun-09 | Argentina | Int | H | Old Trafford, Manchester | W | 37-15 |
| 619 | 13-Jun-09 | Argentina | Int-T | A | Estadio Padre Ernesto Martearena, Salta | L | 22-24 |
| 620 | 7-Nov-09 | Australia | CKC | H | Twickenham, London | L | 9-18 |
| 621 | 14-Nov-09 | Argentina | Int | H | Twickenham, London | W | 16-9 |
| 622 | 21-Nov-09 | New Zealand | EHS | H | Twickenham, London | L | 6-19 |
| 623 | 6-Feb-10 | Wales | 6N | H | Twickenham, London | W | 30-17 |
| 624 | 14-Feb-10 | Italy | 6N | A | Stadio Flaminio, Rome | W | 17-12 |
| 625 | 27-Feb-10 | Ireland | 6N-MT | H | Twickenham, London | L | 16-20 |
| 626 | 13-Mar-10 | Scotland | 6N-CC | A | Murrayfield, Edinburgh | D | 15-15 |
| 627 | 20-Mar-10 | France | 6N | A | Stade de France, Paris | L | 10-12 |
| 628 | 12-Jun-10 | Australia | CKC-T | A | Subiaco Oval, Perth | L | 17-27 |
| 629 | 19-Jun-10 | Australia | CKC-T | A | ANZ Stadium, Sydney | W | 21-20 |
| 630 | 6-Nov-10 | New Zealand | EHS | H | Twickenham, London | L | 16-26 |
| 631 | 13-Nov-10 | Australia | CKC | H | Twickenham, London | W | 35-18 |
| 632 | 20-Nov-10 | Samoa | Int | H | Twickenham, London | W | 26-13 |
| 633 | 27-Nov-10 | South Africa | Int | H | Twickenham, London | L | 11-21 |
| 634 | 4-Feb-11 | Wales | 6N | A | Millennium Stadium, Cardiff | W | 26-19 |
| 635 | 12-Feb-11 | Italy | 6N | H | Twickenham, London | W | 59-13 |
| 636 | 26-Feb-11 | France | 6N | H | Twickenham, London | W | 17-9 |
| 637 | 13-Mar-11 | Scotland | 6N-CC | H | Twickenham, London | W | 22-16 |
| 638 | 19-Mar-11 | Ireland | 6N-MT | A | Aviva Stadium, Dublin | L | 8-24 |
| 639 | 6-Aug-11 | Wales | Int | H | Twickenham, London | W | 23-19 |
| 640 | 13-Aug-11 | Wales | Int | A | Millennium Stadium, Cardiff | L | 9-19 |

| No | Date | Opponents | Tmt | Match Venue | Result | |
|-----|---------|-------------|---------|-------------------------------------------------|---|-------|
| 641 | 27-Aug-11 | Ireland | Int | A Aviva Stadium, Dublin | W | 20-9 |
| 642 | 10-Sep-11 | Argentina | WCp | N Otago Stadium, Dunedin | W | 13-9 |
| 643 | 18-Sep-11 | Georgia | WCp | N Otago Stadium, Dunedin | W | 41-10 |
| 644 | 24-Sep-11 | Romania | WCp | N Otago Stadium, Dunedin | W | 67-3 |
| 645 | 1-Oct-11 | Scotland | WCp | N Eden Park, Auckland | W | 16-12 |
| 646 | 8-Oct-11 | France | WCqf | N Eden Park, Auckland | L | 12-19 |
| 647 | 4-Feb-12 | Scotland | 6N-CC | A Murrayfield, Edinburgh | W | 13-6 |
| 648 | 11-Feb-12 | Italy | 6N | A Stadio Olimpico, Rome | W | 19-15 |
| 649 | 25-Feb-12 | Wales | 6N | H Twickenham, London | L | 12-19 |
| 650 | 11-Mar-12 | France | 6N | A Stade de France, Paris | W | 24-22 |
| 651 | 17-Mar-12 | Ireland | 6N-MT | H Twickenham, London | W | 30-9 |
| 652 | 9-Jun-12 | South Africa | Int-T | A Kings Park Stadium, Durban | L | 17-22 |
| 653 | 16-Jun-12 | South Africa | Int-T | A Ellis Park, Johannesburg | L | 27-36 |
| 654 | 23-Jun-12 | South Africa | Int-T | A Nelson Mandela Bay Stadium, Pt Elizabeth | D | 14-14 |
| 655 | 10-Nov-12 | Fiji | Int | H Twickenham, London | W | 54-12 |
| 656 | 17-Nov-12 | Australia | CKC | H Twickenham, London | L | 14-20 |
| 657 | 24-Nov-12 | South Africa | Int | H Twickenham, London | L | 15-16 |
| 658 | 1-Dec-12 | New Zealand | EHS | H Twickenham, London | W | 38-21 |
| 659 | 2-Feb-13 | Scotland | 6N-CC | H Twickenham, London | W | 38-18 |
| 660 | 10-Feb-13 | Ireland | 6N-MT | A Aviva Stadium, Dublin | W | 12-6 |
| 661 | 23-Feb-13 | France | 6N | H Twickenham, London | W | 23-13 |
| 662 | 10-Mar-13 | Italy | 6N | H Twickenham, London | W | 18-11 |
| 663 | 16-Mar-13 | Wales | 6N | A Millennium Stadium, Cardiff | L | 3-30 |
| 664 | 8-Jun-13 | Argentina | Int-T | A Estadio Padre Ernesto Martearena, Salta | W | 32-3 |
| 665 | 15-Jun-13 | Argentina | Int-T | A Vélez Sarsfield Stadium, Buenos Aires | W | 51-26 |
| 666 | 2-Nov-13 | Australia | CKC | H Twickenham, London | W | 20-13 |
| 667 | 9-Nov-13 | Argentina | ICC | H Twickenham, London | W | 31-12 |
| 668 | 16-Nov-13 | New Zealand | EHS | H Twickenham, London | L | 22-30 |
| 669 | 1-Feb-14 | France | 6N | A Stade de France, Paris | L | 24-26 |
| 670 | 8-Feb-14 | Scotland | 6N-CC | A Murrayfield, Edinburgh | W | 20-0 |
| 671 | 22-Feb-14 | Ireland | 6N-MT | H Twickenham, London | W | 13-10 |
| 672 | 9-Mar-14 | Wales | 6N | H Twickenham, London | W | 29-18 |
| 673 | 15-Mar-14 | Italy | 6N | A Stadio Olimpico, Rome | W | 52-11 |
| 674 | 7-Jun-14 | New Zealand | EHS-T | A Eden Park, Auckland | L | 15-20 |
| 675 | 14-Jun-14 | New Zealand | EHS-T | A Forsyth Barr Stadium, Dunedin | L | 27-28 |
| 676 | 21-Jun-14 | New Zealand | EHS-T | A Waikato Stadium, Hamilton | L | 13-36 |
| 677 | 8-Nov-14 | New Zealand | EHS | H Twickenham, London | L | 21-24 |
| 678 | 15-Nov-14 | South Africa | Int | H Twickenham, London | L | 28-31 |
| 679 | 22-Nov-14 | Samoa | Int | H Twickenham, London | W | 28-9 |
| 680 | 29-Nov-14 | Australia | CKC | H Twickenham, London | W | 26-17 |

| No | Date | Opponents | Tmt | | Match Venue | Result | |
|-----|-----------|-----------|-------|---|------------------------------------|---|-------|
| 681 | 6-Feb-15 | Wales | 6N | A | Millennium Stadium, Cardiff | W | 21-16 |
| 682 | 14-Feb-15 | Italy | 6N | H | Twickenham, London | W | 47-17 |
| 683 | 1-Mar-15 | Ireland | 6N-MT | A | Aviva Stadium, Dublin | L | 9-19 |
| 684 | 14-Mar-15 | Scotland | 6N-CC | H | Twickenham, London | W | 25-13 |
| 685 | 21-Mar-15 | France | 6N | H | Twickenham, London | W | 55-35 |
| 686 | 15-Aug-15 | France | Int | H | Twickenham, London | W | 19-14 |
| 687 | 22-Aug-15 | France | Int | A | Stade de France, Paris | L | 20-25 |
| 688 | 5-Sep-15 | Ireland | Int | H | Twickenham, London | W | 21-13 |
| 689 | 18-Sep-15 | Fiji | WCp | H | Twickenham, London | W | 35-11 |
| 690 | 26-Sep-15 | Wales | WCp | H | Twickenham, London | L | 25-28 |
| 691 | 3-Oct-15 | Australia | WCp | H | Twickenham, London | L | 13-33 |
| 692 | 10-Oct-15 | Uruguay | WCp | H | Manchester City Stadium, Manchester | W | 60-3 |

# FRANCE

Although a French representative team competed, and won a gold medal, at the 1900 Summer Olympics in Paris, France's first official International did not take place until 1 January 1906, when they played New Zealand in Paris. They lost that match by 38 points to 8, and exactly four years later, on 1 January 1910, they faced Wales in the inaugural Five Nations Championship, which they lost by 49 points to 14.

The following year brought France their first victory, when they beat Scotland at Stade Colombes in Paris. France's triumph was short lived: they lost their next eighteen games and it wasn't until after the First World War that they finally registered a win, against Ireland in Dublin on 3 April 1920. A few months later, in October, France beat the United States and followed that victory with another win over Scotland in January 1921.

In 1924, France competed in the Olympic Games for the second time and, following a semi-final triumph over Romania, the French lost to the United States in the final.

Then, in 1927, France beat England by 3 points to nil in Paris, and a year later they finally defeated Wales, also in Paris, by 8 points to 3. In 1931, the French were expelled from the Five Nations Championship, accused of professionalism at a time when Rugby Union was strictly amateur. They were subsequently readmitted in 1947.

France played nineteen matches between 1954 and 1956 and lost only four: on three occasions to Wales and once to Scotland. During those three years they also achieved a famous victory against New Zealand, in February 1954. In 1958 the French toured South Africa and won the series by winning the second match after drawing the first. A year later, the French team won their first Five Nations Championship, a feat they repeated with back-to-back titles in 1961 and 1962. They secured another Five Nations title in 1967, and a first Grand Slam in 1968, closing out a very successful decade.

France's second Grand Slam came in 1977. In fact, from October 1975 to the end of 1978 France played twenty-five International matches and lost only four. Yet another Grand Slam was achieved in 1981, and a fourth in 1987, which augured well for France in the 1987 World Cup competition. They certainly rose to the occasion, performing strongly until the final, when they lost to New Zealand, the host nation, by 29 points to 9.

While England seemed to dominate the early part of the 1990s, the French came roaring back near the end of the decade, winning two consecutive Grand Slams in 1997 and 1998.

From 1965 to 1997 France also competed in a European tournament known as the Fédération Internationale de Rugby (FIRA). They played in all twenty-six competitions, securing the title on twenty occasions.

France's performance in the 1991 World Cup competition was, by their standard, disappointing: they were knocked out in the quarter-final by England. Their performance in the 1995 World Cup, however, was much better and, in the play-off for third place, they gained a revenge win over England after narrowly losing to the host nation, and eventual winners, South Africa, in the semi-final.

In 1999, France, commonly referred to as 'Les Bleus', reached the World Cup final for the second time, after defeating New Zealand in the semi-final, only to lose to Australia, in the final, by 35 points to 12. France reached the semi-final of the 2003 World Cup held in Australia, but were well beaten by England, the eventual winners, by 24 points to 7. They also lost to New Zealand in the third place play-off. In the 2007 World Cup, which they hosted, despite losing to Argentina in the pool game, they qualified for the quarter final and reached the semi-final by defeating New Zealand at the Millennium Stadium in Cardiff. They lost to England in that semi-final and subsequently lost to Argentina in the third place play-off at Parc des Princess in Paris.

The French did perform better in the 2011 World Cup by reaching the final for the third time, after defeating Wales in the semi-final. In the final they narrowly lost by just one point to the host nation, and tournament favourites, New Zealand.

The French team was the most consistent in the first twelve seasons of the Six Nations Championship held between 2000 and 2011, winning forty-three Internationals out of sixty: an impressive success rate of just under 72%. During that period they also won three Grand Slams: in 2002, 2004 and 2010. However, the team's success rate fell to below 47% during the next three Six Nations Championships held between 2012 and 2014, when they managed only six wins and two draws from fifteen matches.

Furthermore, during the period 2000 to 2013, France registered only thirteen wins and two draws out of a total of forty-five International matches against the Southern Hemisphere giants, Australia, New Zealand and South Africa, making for an even lower success rate of 31.1%.

Another disappointing year for the French came in 2014 when, after finishing in fourth place in the Six Nations Championship, they suffered three losses to the Wallabies on their summer tour of Australia. They did, however, gain some revenge in November when they defeated the Aussies by 29 points to 26 in the Stade de France, but this was short-lived: they lost just a week later to Argentina at the same venue. Les Bleus finished in fourth place for the second year in succession in the 2015 Six Nations Championship.

France, despite losing to Ireland, qualified for the next stage of the 2015 Rugby World Cup as pool runners-up. In the quarter-final however, they were completely outplayed by New Zealand, losing by 62 points to 13.

# FRANCE

## HEAD TO HEAD RESULTS TO 31 OCTOBER 2015

| v TIER 1 Teams | P | W | D | L | % | F | A |
|---|---|---|---|---|---|---|---|
| v Argentina | 48 | 34 | 1 | 13 | 71.9 | 1169 | 754 |
| v Australia | 46 | 18 | 2 | 26 | 41.3 | 802 | 991 |
| v England | 101 | 39 | 7 | 55 | 42.1 | 1269 | 1592 |
| v Ireland | 93 | 55 | 7 | 31 | 62.9 | 1508 | 1084 |
| v Italy | 36 | 33 | 0 | 3 | 91.7 | 1069 | 382 |
| v New Zealand | 56 | 12 | 1 | 43 | 22.3 | 726 | 1407 |
| v Scotland | 89 | 52 | 3 | 34 | 59.7 | 1262 | 1073 |
| v South Africa | 39 | 11 | 6 | 22 | 35.9 | 578 | 783 |
| v Wales | 93 | 43 | 3 | 47 | 47.8 | 1338 | 1384 |
| **Sub-Total** | **603** | **298** | **30** | **275** | **51.9** | **9762** | **9484** |
| **v TIER 2/3 Group** | | | | | | | |
| v Canada | 9 | 8 | 0 | 1 | 88.9 | 315 | 119 |
| v Fiji | 9 | 9 | 0 | 0 | 100.0 | 359 | 111 |
| v Japan | 3 | 3 | 0 | 0 | 100.0 | 128 | 68 |
| v Romania | 50 | 40 | 2 | 8 | 82.0 | 1315 | 462 |
| v Samoa | 3 | 3 | 0 | 0 | 100.0 | 104 | 41 |
| v Tonga | 5 | 3 | 0 | 2 | 60.0 | 149 | 75 |
| v United States | 7 | 6 | 0 | 1 | 85.7 | 181 | 93 |
| v Georgia | 1 | 1 | 0 | 0 | 100.0 | 64 | 7 |
| v Namibia | 2 | 2 | 0 | 0 | 100.0 | 134 | 23 |
| v Russia | 0 | 0 | 0 | 0 | 0.0 | 0 | 0 |
| v Uruguay | 0 | 0 | 0 | 0 | 0.0 | 0 | 0 |
| **Sub-Total** | **89** | **75** | **2** | **12** | **85.4** | **2749** | **999** |
| **v Tier 3 Selection** | | | | | | | |
| v Czechoslovakia * | 2 | 2 | 0 | 0 | 100.0 | 47 | 9 |
| v Germany ** | 15 | 13 | 0 | 2 | 86.7 | 298 | 89 |
| v Côte d'Ivoire | 1 | 1 | 0 | 0 | 100.0 | 54 | 18 |
| v Zimbabwe | 1 | 1 | 0 | 0 | 100.0 | 70 | 12 |
| **Sub-Total** | **19** | **17** | **0** | **2** | **89.5** | **469** | **128** |
| **v Other Teams** | **11** | **5** | **0** | **6** | **45.5** | **137** | **155** |
| **All Internationals** | **722** | **395** | **32** | **295** | **56.9** | **13117** | **10766** |

* 1956-68      ** 1927-38

| No | Date | Opponents | Tmt | Match Venue | Result | |
|----|------|-----------|-----|-------------|--------|---|
| 1 | 1-Jan-06 | New Zealand | Int | H Parc des Princess, Paris | L | 8-38 |
| 2 | 22-Mar-06 | England | Int | H Parc des Princess, Paris | L | 8-35 |
| 3 | 5-Jan-07 | England | Int | A Athletic Ground, Richmond | L | 13-41 |
| 4 | 1-Jan-08 | England | Int | H Stade Colombes, Paris | L | 0-19 |
| 5 | 2-Mar-08 | Wales | Int | A Arms Park, Cardiff | L | 4-36 |
| 6 | 30-Jan-09 | England | Int | A Welford Road, Leicester | L | 0-22 |
| 7 | 23-Feb-09 | Wales | Int | H Stade Colombes, Paris | L | 5-47 |
| 8 | 20-Mar-09 | Ireland | Int | A Lansdowne Road, Dublin | L | 8-19 |
| 9 | 1-Jan-10 | Wales | 5N | A St Helen's, Swansea | L | 14-49 |
| 10 | 22-Jan-10 | Scotland | 5N | A Inverleith, Edinburgh | L | 0-27 |
| 11 | 3-Mar-10 | England | 5N | H Parc des Princess, Paris | L | 3-11 |
| 12 | 28-Mar-10 | Ireland | 5N | H Parc des Princess, Paris | L | 3-8 |
| 13 | 2-Jan-11 | Scotland | 5N | H Stade Colombes, Paris | W | 16-15 |
| 14 | 28-Jan-11 | England | 5N | A Twickenham, London | L | 0-37 |
| 15 | 28-Feb-11 | Wales | 5N | H Parc des Princess, Paris | L | 0-15 |
| 16 | 25-Mar-11 | Ireland | 5N | A Mardyke, Cork | L | 5-25 |
| 17 | 1-Jan-12 | Ireland | 5N | H Parc des Princess, Paris | L | 6-11 |
| 18 | 20-Jan-12 | Scotland | 5N | A Inverleith, Edinburgh | L | 3-31 |
| 19 | 25-Mar-12 | Wales | 5N | A Rodney Parade, Newport | L | 8-14 |
| 20 | 8-Apr-12 | England | 5N | H Parc des Princess, Paris | L | 8-18 |
| 21 | 1-Jan-13 | Scotland | 5N | H Parc des Princess, Paris | L | 3-21 |
| 22 | 11-Jan-13 | South Africa | Int | H Route du Médoc, Le Bouscat, Bordeaux | L | 5-38 |
| 23 | 25-Jan-13 | England | 5N | A Twickenham, London | L | 0-20 |
| 24 | 27-Feb-13 | Wales | 5N | H Parc des Princess, Paris | L | 8-11 |
| 25 | 24-Mar-13 | Ireland | 5N | A Mardyke, Cork | L | 0-24 |
| 26 | 1-Jan-14 | Ireland | 5N | H Parc des Princess, Paris | L | 6-8 |
| 27 | 2-Mar-14 | Wales | 5N | A St Helen's, Swansea | L | 0-31 |
| 28 | 13-Apr-14 | England | 5N | H Stade Colombes, Paris | L | 13-39 |
| 29 | 1-Jan-20 | Scotland | 5N | H Parc des Princess, Paris | L | 0-5 |
| 30 | 31-Jan-20 | England | 5N | A Twickenham, London | L | 3-8 |
| 31 | 17-Feb-20 | Wales | 5N | H Stade Colombes, Paris | L | 5-6 |
| 32 | 3-Apr-20 | Ireland | 5N | A Lansdowne Road, Dublin | W | 15-7 |
| 33 | 10-Oct-20 | United States | Int | H Stade Colombes, Paris | W | 14-5 |
| 34 | 22-Jan-21 | Scotland | 5N | A Inverleith, Edinburgh | W | 3-0 |
| 35 | 26-Feb-21 | Wales | 5N | A Arms Park, Cardiff | L | 4-12 |
| 36 | 28-Mar-21 | England | 5N | H Stade Colombes, Paris | L | 6-10 |
| 37 | 9-Apr-21 | Ireland | 5N | H Stade Colombes, Paris | W | 20-10 |
| 38 | 2-Jan-22 | Scotland | 5N | H Stade Colombes, Paris | D | 3-3 |
| 39 | 25-Feb-22 | England | 5N | A Twickenham, London | D | 11-11 |
| 40 | 23-Mar-22 | Wales | 5N | H Stade Colombes, Paris | L | 3-11 |

| No | Date | Opponents | Tmt | Match Venue | Result | |
|----|------|-----------|-----|-------------|--------|---|
| 41 | 8-Apr-22 | Ireland | 5N | A Lansdowne Road, Dublin | L | 3-8 |
| 42 | 20-Jan-23 | Scotland | 5N | A Inverleith, Edinburgh | L | 3-16 |
| 43 | 24-Feb-23 | Wales | 5N | A St Helen's, Swansea | L | 8-16 |
| 44 | 2-Apr-23 | England | 5N | H Stade Colombes, Paris | L | 3-12 |
| 45 | 14-Apr-23 | Ireland | 5N | H Stade Colombes, Paris | W | 14-8 |
| 46 | 1-Jan-24 | Scotland | 5N | H Stade Pershing, Vincennes, Paris | W | 12-10 |
| 47 | 26-Jan-24 | Ireland | 5N | A Lansdowne Road, Dublin | L | 0-6 |
| 48 | 23-Feb-24 | England | 5N | A Twickenham, London | L | 7-19 |
| 49 | 27-Mar-24 | Wales | 5N | H Stade Colombes, Paris | L | 6-10 |
| 50 | 4-May-24 | Romania | OGsf | H Stade Colombes, Paris | W | 61-3 |
| 51 | 18-May-24 | United States | OGf | H Stade Colombes, Paris | L | 3-17 |
| 52 | 1-Jan-25 | Ireland | 5N | H Stade Colombes, Paris | L | 3-9 |
| 53 | 18-Jan-25 | New Zealand | Int | H Stade des Ponts, Jumeaux, Toulouse | L | 6-30 |
| 54 | 24-Jan-25 | Scotland | 5N | A Inverleith, Edinburgh | L | 4-25 |
| 55 | 28-Feb-25 | Wales | 5N | A Arms Park, Cardiff | L | 5-11 |
| 56 | 13-Apr-25 | England | 5N | H Stade Colombes, Paris | L | 11-13 |
| 57 | 2-Jan-26 | Scotland | 5N | H Stade Colombes, Paris | L | 6-20 |
| 58 | 23-Jan-26 | Ireland | 5N | A Ravenhill, Belfast | L | 0-11 |
| 59 | 27-Feb-26 | England | 5N | A Twickenham, London | L | 0-11 |
| 60 | 5-Apr-26 | Wales | 5N | H Stade Colombes, Paris | L | 5-7 |
| 61 | 26-Dec-26 | N Z Natives | Int | H Stade Colombes, Paris | L | 3-12 |
| 62 | 1-Jan-27 | Ireland | 5N | H Stade Colombes, Paris | L | 3-8 |
| 63 | 22-Jan-27 | Scotland | 5N | A Murrayfield, Edinburgh | L | 6-23 |
| 64 | 26-Feb-27 | Wales | 5N | A St Helen's, Swansea | L | 7-25 |
| 65 | 2-Apr-27 | England | 5N | H Stade Colombes, Paris | W | 3-0 |
| 66 | 17-Apr-27 | Germany | Int | H Stade Colombes, Paris | W | 30-5 |
| 67 | 15-May-27 | Germany | Int | A Frankfurt | L | 16-17 |
| 68 | 2-Jan-28 | Scotland | 5N | H Stade Colombes, Paris | L | 6-15 |
| 69 | 22-Jan-28 | Australia | Int | H Stade Colombes, Paris | L | 8-11 |
| 70 | 28-Jan-28 | Ireland | 5N | A Ravenhill, Belfast | L | 8-12 |
| 71 | 25-Feb-28 | England | 5N | A Twickenham, London | L | 8-18 |
| 72 | 18-Mar-28 | Germany | Int | A Hanover | W | 14-3 |
| 73 | 9-Apr-28 | Wales | 5N | H Stade Colombes, Paris | W | 8-3 |
| 74 | 31-Dec-28 | Ireland | 5N | H Stade Colombes, Paris | L | 0-6 |
| 75 | 19-Jan-29 | Scotland | 5N | A Murrayfield, Edinburgh | L | 3-6 |
| 76 | 23-Feb-29 | Wales | 5N | A Arms Park, Cardiff | L | 3-8 |
| 77 | 1-Apr-29 | England | 5N | H Stade Colombes, Paris | L | 6-16 |
| 78 | 28-Apr-29 | Germany | Int | H Stade Colombes, Paris | W | 24-0 |
| 79 | 1-Jan-30 | Scotland | 5N | H Stade Colombes, Paris | W | 7-3 |
| 80 | 25-Jan-30 | Ireland | 5N | A Ravenhill, Belfast | W | 5-0 |

| No | Date | Opponents | Tmt | | Match Venue | | Result | |
|----|------|-----------|-----|---|-------------|---|--------|---|
| 81 | 22-Feb-30 | England | 5N | A | Twickenham, London | | L | 5-11 |
| 82 | 6-Apr-30 | Germany | Int | A | Berlin | | W | 31-0 |
| 83 | 21-Apr-30 | Wales | 5N | H | Stade Colombes, Paris | | L | 0-11 |
| 84 | 1-Jan-31 | Ireland | 5N | H | Stade Colombes, Paris | | W | 3-0 |
| 85 | 24-Jan-31 | Scotland | 5N | A | Murrayfield, Edinburgh | | L | 4-6 |
| 86 | 28-Feb-31 | Wales | 5N | A | St Helen's, Swansea | | L | 3-35 |
| 87 | 6-Apr-31 | England | 5N | H | Stade Colombes, Paris | | W | 14-13 |
| 88 | 19-Apr-31 | Germany | Int | H | Stade Colombes, Paris | | W | 34-0 |
| 89 | 17-Apr-32 | Germany | Int | A | Frankfurt | | W | 20-4 |
| 90 | 26-Mar-33 | Germany | Int | H | Parc des Princess, Paris | | W | 38-17 |
| 91 | 25-Mar-34 | Germany | Int | A | Hanover | | W | 13-9 |
| 92 | 24-Mar-35 | Germany | Int | H | Parc des Princess, Paris | | W | 18-3 |
| 93 | 17-May-36 | Germany | FET | A | Berlin | | W | 19-14 |
| 94 | 1-Nov-36 | Germany | Int | A | Hanover | | W | 6-3 |
| 95 | 18-Apr-37 | Germany | Int | H | Parc des Princess, Paris | | W | 27-6 |
| 96 | 17-Oct-37 | Italy | FET | H | Parc des Princess, Paris | | W | 43-5 |
| 97 | 27-Mar-38 | Germany | Int | A | Frankfurt | | L | 0-3 |
| 98 | 15-May-38 | Romania | FET | A | Stadionul ANEF, Bucharest | | W | 11-8 |
| 99 | 22-May-38 | Germany | FET | N | Stadionul Dinamo, Bucharest | | W | 8-5 |
| 100 | 25-Feb-40 | British Army | Int | H | Parc des Princess, Paris | | L | 3-36 |
| 101 | 1-Jan-45 | British Army | Int | H | Parc des Princess, Paris | | W | 21-9 |
| 102 | 28-Apr-45 | Empire XV | Int | A | Athletic Ground, Richmond | | L | 6-27 |
| 103 | 22-Dec-45 | Wales XV | Int | A | St Helen's, Swansea | | L | 0-8 |
| 104 | 1-Jan-46 | Empire XV | Int | H | Parc des Princess, Paris | | W | 10-0 |
| 105 | 26-Jan-46 | Ireland XV | Int | A | Lansdowne Road, Dublin | | W | 4-3 |
| 106 | 10-Mar-46 | Kiwis | Int | H | Stade Colombes, Paris | | L | 9-14 |
| 107 | 22-Apr-46 | Wales XV | Int | H | Stade Colombes, Paris | | W | 12-0 |
| 108 | 1-Jan-47 | Scotland | 5N | H | Stade Colombes, Paris | | W | 8-3 |
| 109 | 25-Jan-47 | Ireland | 5N | A | Lansdowne Road, Dublin | | W | 12-8 |
| 110 | 22-Mar-47 | Wales | 5N | H | Stade Colombes, Paris | | L | 0-3 |
| 111 | 19-Apr-47 | England | 5N | A | Twickenham, London | | L | 3-6 |
| 112 | 1-Jan-48 | Ireland | 5N | H | Stade Colombes, Paris | | L | 6-13 |
| 113 | 11-Jan-48 | Australia | Int | H | Stade Colombes, Paris | | W | 13-6 |
| 114 | 24-Jan-48 | Scotland | 5N | A | Murrayfield, Edinburgh | | L | 8-9 |
| 115 | 21-Feb-48 | Wales | 5N | A | St Helen's, Swansea | | W | 11-3 |
| 116 | 29-Mar-48 | England | 5N | H | Stade Colombes, Paris | | W | 15-0 |
| 117 | 15-Jan-49 | Scotland | 5N | H | Stade Colombes, Paris | | L | 0-8 |
| 118 | 29-Jan-49 | Ireland | 5N | A | Lansdowne Road, Dublin | | W | 16-9 |
| 119 | 26-Feb-49 | England | 5N | A | Twickenham, London | | L | 3-8 |
| 120 | 26-Mar-49 | Wales | 5N | H | Stade Colombes, Paris | | W | 5-3 |

# FRANCE

| No | Date | Opponents | Tmt | Match Venue | Result | |
|---|---|---|---|---|---|---|
| 121 | 28-Aug-49 | Argentina | Int-T | A Estadio G.E.B.A, Buenos Aires | W | 5-0 |
| 122 | 4-Sep-49 | Argentina | Int-T | A Estadio G.E.B.A, Buenos Aires | W | 12-3 |
| 123 | 14-Jan-50 | Scotland | 5N | A Murrayfield, Edinburgh | L | 5-8 |
| 124 | 28-Jan-50 | Ireland | 5N | H Stade Colombes, Paris | D | 3-3 |
| 125 | 25-Feb-50 | England | 5N | H Stade Colombes, Paris | W | 6-3 |
| 126 | 25-Mar-50 | Wales | 5N | A Arms Park, Cardiff | L | 0-21 |
| 127 | 13-Jan-51 | Scotland | 5N | H Stade Colombes, Paris | W | 14-12 |
| 128 | 27-Jan-51 | Ireland | 5N | A Lansdowne Road, Dublin | L | 8-9 |
| 129 | 24-Feb-51 | England | 5N | A Twickenham, London | W | 11-3 |
| 130 | 7-Apr-51 | Wales | 5N | H Stade Colombes, Paris | W | 8-3 |
| 131 | 12-Jan-52 | Scotland | 5N | A Murrayfield, Edinburgh | W | 13-11 |
| 132 | 26-Jan-52 | Ireland | 5N | H Stade Colombes, Paris | L | 8-11 |
| 133 | 16-Feb-52 | South Africa | Int | H Stade Colombes, Paris | L | 3-25 |
| 134 | 22-Mar-52 | Wales | 5N | A St Helen's, Swansea | L | 5-9 |
| 135 | 5-Apr-52 | England | 5N | H Stade Colombes, Paris | L | 3-6 |
| 136 | 17-May-52 | Italy | FEC | A Arena Civica, Milan | W | 17-8 |
| 137 | 10-Jan-53 | Scotland | 5N | H Stade Colombes, Paris | W | 11-5 |
| 138 | 24-Jan-53 | Ireland | 5N | A Ravenhill, Belfast | L | 3-16 |
| 139 | 28-Feb-53 | England | 5N | A Twickenham, London | L | 0-11 |
| 140 | 28-Mar-53 | Wales | 5N | H Stade Colombes, Paris | L | 3-6 |
| 141 | 26-Apr-53 | Italy | Int | H Stade de Gerland, Lyon | W | 22-8 |
| 142 | 9-Jan-54 | Scotland | 5N | A Murrayfield, Edinburgh | W | 3-0 |
| 143 | 23-Jan-54 | Ireland | 5N | H Stade Colombes, Paris | W | 8-0 |
| 144 | 27-Feb-54 | New Zealand | Int | H Stade Colombes, Paris | W | 3-0 |
| 145 | 27-Mar-54 | Wales | 5N | A Arms Park, Cardiff | L | 13-19 |
| 146 | 10-Apr-54 | England | 5N | H Stade Colombes, Paris | W | 11-3 |
| 147 | 24-Apr-54 | Italy | FEC | A Stadio Olimpico, Rome | W | 39-12 |
| 148 | 29-Aug-54 | Argentina | Int-T | A Ferro Carril Oeste Stadium, B Aires | W | 22-8 |
| 149 | 12-Sep-54 | Argentina | Int-T | A Ferro Carril Oeste Stadium, B Aires | W | 30-3 |
| 150 | 8-Jan-55 | Scotland | 5N | H Stade Colombes, Paris | W | 15-0 |
| 151 | 22-Jan-55 | Ireland | 5N | A Lansdowne Road, Dublin | W | 5-3 |
| 152 | 26-Feb-55 | England | 5N | A Twickenham, London | W | 16-9 |
| 153 | 26-Mar-55 | Wales | 5N | H Stade Colombes, Paris | L | 11-16 |
| 154 | 10-Apr-55 | Italy | Int | H Stade Lesdiguières, Grenoble | W | 24-0 |
| 155 | 14-Jan-56 | Scotland | 5N | A Murrayfield, Edinburgh | L | 0-12 |
| 156 | 28-Jan-56 | Ireland | 5N | H Stade Colombes, Paris | W | 14-8 |
| 157 | 24-Mar-56 | Wales | 5N | A Arms Park, Cardiff | L | 3-5 |
| 158 | 2-Apr-56 | Italy | Int | A Stadio Silvio Appiani, Padova | W | 16-3 |
| 159 | 14-Apr-56 | England | 5N | H Stade Colombes, Paris | W | 14-9 |
| 160 | 16-Dec-56 | Czechoslovakia | Int | H Stade Municipal de Toulouse, Toulouse | W | 28-3 |

69

| No | Date | Opponents | Tmt | | Match Venue | | Result | |
|-----|-----------|--------------|--------|---|-------------------------------------|---|---|-------|
| 161 | 12-Jan-57 | Scotland | 5N | H | Stade Colombes, Paris | | L | 0-6 |
| 162 | 26-Jan-57 | Ireland | 5N | A | Lansdowne Road, Dublin | | L | 6-11 |
| 163 | 23-Feb-57 | England | 5N | A | Twickenham, London | | L | 5-9 |
| 164 | 23-Mar-57 | Wales | 5N | H | Stade Colombes, Paris | | L | 13-19 |
| 165 | 21-Apr-57 | Italy | Int | H | Stade Armandie, Agen | | W | 38-6 |
| 166 | 19-May-57 | Romania | Int | A | Stadionul 23 August, Bucharest | | W | 18-15 |
| 167 | 15-Dec-57 | Romania | Int | H | Stade du Parc Lescure, Bordeaux | | W | 39-0 |
| 168 | 11-Jan-58 | Scotland | 5N | A | Murrayfield, Edinburgh | | L | 9-11 |
| 169 | 1-Mar-58 | England | 5N | H | Stade Colombes, Paris | | L | 0-14 |
| 170 | 9-Mar-58 | Australia | Int | H | Stade Colombes, Paris | | W | 19-0 |
| 171 | 29-Mar-58 | Wales | 5N | A | Arms Park, Cardiff | | W | 16-6 |
| 172 | 7-Apr-58 | Italy | Int | A | Stadio Arturo Collana, Naples | | W | 11-3 |
| 173 | 19-Apr-58 | Ireland | 5N | H | Stade Colombes, Paris | | W | 11-6 |
| 174 | 26-Jul-58 | South Africa | Int-T | A | Newlands Stadium, Cape Town | | D | 3-3 |
| 175 | 16-Aug-58 | South Africa | Int-T | A | Ellis Park, Johannesburg | | W | 9-5 |
| 176 | 10-Jan-59 | Scotland | 5N | H | Stade Colombes, Paris | | W | 9-0 |
| 177 | 28-Feb-59 | England | 5N | A | Twickenham, London | | D | 3-3 |
| 178 | 29-Mar-59 | Italy | Int | H | Stade Marcel Saupin, Nantes | | W | 22-0 |
| 179 | 4-Apr-59 | Wales | 5N | H | Stade Colombes, Paris | | W | 11-3 |
| 180 | 18-Apr-59 | Ireland | 5N | A | Lansdowne Road, Dublin | | L | 5-9 |
| 181 | 9-Jan-60 | Scotland | 5N | A | Murrayfield, Edinburgh | | W | 13-11 |
| 182 | 27-Feb-60 | England | 5N | H | Stade Colombes, Paris | | D | 3-3 |
| 183 | 26-Mar-60 | Wales | 5N | A | Arms Park, Cardiff | | W | 16-8 |
| 184 | 9-Apr-60 | Ireland | 5N | H | Stade Colombes, Paris | | W | 23-6 |
| 185 | 17-Apr-60 | Italy | Int | A | Stadio Omobono Tenni, Treviso | | W | 26-0 |
| 186 | 5-Jun-60 | Romania | Int | A | Stadionul Dinamo, Bucharest | | L | 5-11 |
| 187 | 23-Jul-60 | Argentina | Int-T | A | Estadio G.E.B.A., Buenos Aires | | W | 37-3 |
| 188 | 6-Aug-60 | Argentina | Int-T | A | Estadio G.E.B.A., Buenos Aires | | W | 12-3 |
| 189 | 17-Aug-60 | Argentina | Int-T | A | Estadio G.E.B.A., Buenos Aires | | W | 29-6 |
| 190 | 7-Jan-61 | Scotland | 5N | H | Stade Colombes, Paris | | W | 11-0 |
| 191 | 18-Feb-61 | South Africa | Int | H | Stade Colombes, Paris | | D | 0-0 |
| 192 | 25-Feb-61 | England | 5N | A | Twickenham, London | | D | 5-5 |
| 193 | 25-Mar-61 | Wales | 5N | H | Stade Colombes, Paris | | W | 8-6 |
| 194 | 2-Apr-61 | Italy | Int | H | Stade Municipal, Chambéry | | W | 17-0 |
| 195 | 15-Apr-61 | Ireland | 5N | A | Lansdowne Road, Dublin | | W | 15-3 |
| 196 | 22-Jul-61 | New Zealand | Int-T | A | Eden Park, Auckland | | L | 6-13 |
| 197 | 5-Aug-61 | New Zealand | Int-T | A | Athletic Park, Wellington | | L | 3-5 |
| 198 | 19-Aug-61 | New Zealand | Int-T | A | Lancaster Park Oval, Christchurch | | L | 3-32 |
| 199 | 26-Aug-61 | Australia | Int-T | A | Cricket Ground, Sydney | | W | 15-8 |
| 200 | 12-Nov-61 | Romania | Int | H | Parc Municipal des Sports, Bayonne | | D | 5-5 |

| No | Date | Opponents | Tmt | Match Venue | Result | |
|-----|------|-----------|-----|-------------|--------|---|
| 201 | 13-Jan-62 | Scotland | 5N | A Murrayfield, Edinburgh | W | 11-3 |
| 202 | 24-Feb-62 | England | 5N | H Stade Colombes, Paris | W | 13-0 |
| 203 | 24-Mar-62 | Wales | 5N | A Arms Park, Cardiff | L | 0-3 |
| 204 | 14-Apr-62 | Ireland | 5N | H Stade Colombes, Paris | W | 11-0 |
| 205 | 22-Apr-62 | Italy | Int | A Stadio Mompiano, Brescia | W | 6-3 |
| 206 | 11-Nov-62 | Romania | Int | A Stadionul 23 August, Bucharest | L | 0-3 |
| 207 | 12-Jan-63 | Scotland | 5N | H Stade Colombes, Paris | L | 6-11 |
| 208 | 26-Jan-63 | Ireland | 5N | A Lansdowne Road, Dublin | W | 24-5 |
| 209 | 23-Feb-63 | England | 5N | A Twickenham, London | L | 5-6 |
| 210 | 23-Mar-63 | Wales | 5N | H Stade Colombes, Paris | W | 5-3 |
| 211 | 14-Apr-63 | Italy | Int | H Stade Lesdiguières, Grenoble | W | 14-12 |
| 212 | 15-Dec-63 | Romania | Int | H Stade Municipal de Toulouse, Toulouse | D | 6-6 |
| 213 | 4-Jan-64 | Scotland | 5N | A Murrayfield, Edinburgh | L | 0-10 |
| 214 | 8-Feb-64 | New Zealand | Int | H Stade Colombes, Paris | L | 3-12 |
| 215 | 22-Feb-64 | England | 5N | H Stade Colombes, Paris | L | 3-6 |
| 216 | 21-Mar-64 | Wales | 5N | A Arms Park, Cardiff | D | 11-11 |
| 217 | 29-Mar-64 | Italy | Int | A Stadio Comunale Ennio Tardini, Parma | W | 12-3 |
| 218 | 11-Apr-64 | Ireland | 5N | H Stade Colombes, Paris | W | 27-6 |
| 219 | 25-Jul-64 | South Africa | Int-T | A P A M Brink Stadium, Springs | W | 8-6 |
| 220 | 17-Oct-64 | Fiji | Int | H Stade Colombes, Paris | W | 21-3 |
| 221 | 29-Nov-64 | Romania | Int | A Stadionul Dinamo, Bucharest | W | 9-6 |
| 222 | 9-Jan-65 | Scotland | 5N | H Stade Colombes, Paris | W | 16-8 |
| 223 | 23-Jan-65 | Ireland | 5N | A Lansdowne Road, Dublin | D | 3-3 |
| 224 | 27-Feb-65 | England | 5N | A Twickenham, London | L | 6-9 |
| 225 | 27-Mar-65 | Wales | 5N | H Stade Colombes, Paris | W | 22-13 |
| 226 | 18-Apr-65 | Italy | Int | H Stade de la Croix du Prince, Pau | W | 21-0 |
| 227 | 28-Nov-65 | Romania | FIRA | H Stade de Gerland, Lyon | W | 8-3 |
| 228 | 15-Jan-66 | Scotland | 5N | A Murrayfield, Edinburgh | D | 3-3 |
| 229 | 29-Jan-66 | Ireland | 5N | H Stade Colombes, Paris | W | 11-6 |
| 230 | 26-Feb-66 | England | 5N | H Stade Colombes, Paris | W | 13-0 |
| 231 | 26-Mar-66 | Wales | 5N | A Arms Park, Cardiff | L | 8-9 |
| 232 | 9-Apr-66 | Italy | FIRA | A Naples | W | 21-0 |
| 233 | 27-Nov-66 | Romania | FIRA | A Stadionul Republicii, Bucharest | W | 9-3 |
| 234 | 14-Jan-67 | Scotland | 5N | H Stade Colombes, Paris | L | 8-9 |
| 235 | 11-Feb-67 | Australia | Int | H Stade Colombes, Paris | W | 20-14 |
| 236 | 25-Feb-67 | England | 5N | A Twickenham, London | W | 16-12 |
| 237 | 26-Mar-67 | Italy | FIRA | H Stade Félix Mayol, Toulon | W | 60-13 |
| 238 | 1-Apr-67 | Wales | 5N | H Stade Colombes, Paris | W | 20-14 |
| 239 | 15-Apr-67 | Ireland | 5N | A Lansdowne Road, Dublin | W | 11-6 |
| 240 | 15-Jul-67 | South Africa | Int-T | A Kings Park Stadium, Durban | L | 3-26 |

| No | Date | Opponents | Tmt | Match Venue | Result | |
|----|------|-----------|-----|-------------|--------|---|
| 241 | 22-Jul-67 | South Africa | Int-T | A Free State Stadium, Bloemfontein | L | 3-16 |
| 242 | 29-Jul-67 | South Africa | Int-T | A Ellis Park, Johannesburg | W | 19-14 |
| 243 | 12-Aug-67 | South Africa | Int-T | A Newlands Stadium, Cape Town | D | 6-6 |
| 244 | 25-Nov-67 | New Zealand | Int | H Stade Colombes, Paris | L | 15-21 |
| 245 | 10-Dec-67 | Romania | FIRA | H Stade Marcel Saupin, Nantes | W | 11-3 |
| 246 | 13-Jan-68 | Scotland | 5N | A Murrayfield, Edinburgh | W | 8-6 |
| 247 | 27-Jan-68 | Ireland | 5N | H Stade Colombes, Paris | W | 16-6 |
| 248 | 24-Feb-68 | England | 5N | H Stade Colombes, Paris | W | 14-9 |
| 249 | 23-Mar-68 | Wales | 5N | A Arms Park, Cardiff | W | 14-9 |
| 250 | 5-May-68 | Czechoslovakia | FIRA | A Stadion Krč, Prague | W | 19-6 |
| 251 | 13-Jul-68 | New Zealand | Int-T | A Lancaster Park Oval, Christchurch | L | 9-12 |
| 252 | 27-Jul-68 | New Zealand | Int-T | A Athletic Park, Wellington | L | 3-9 |
| 253 | 10-Aug-68 | New Zealand | Int-T | A Eden Park, Auckland | L | 12-19 |
| 254 | 17-Aug-68 | Australia | Int-T | A Cricket Ground, Sydney | L | 10-11 |
| 255 | 9-Nov-68 | South Africa | Int | H Stade du Parc Lescure, Bordeaux | L | 9-12 |
| 256 | 16-Nov-68 | South Africa | Int | H Stade Colombes, Paris | L | 11-16 |
| 257 | 1-Dec-68 | Romania | FIRA | A Stadionul 23 August, Bucharest | L | 14-15 |
| 258 | 11-Jan-69 | Scotland | 5N | H Stade Colombes, Paris | L | 3-6 |
| 259 | 25-Jan-69 | Ireland | 5N | A Lansdowne Road, Dublin | L | 9-17 |
| 260 | 22-Feb-69 | England | 5N | A Twickenham, London | L | 8-22 |
| 261 | 22-Mar-69 | Wales | 5N | H Stade Colombes, Paris | D | 8-8 |
| 262 | 14-Dec-69 | Romania | FIRA | H Stade Maurice Trélut, Tarbes | W | 14-9 |
| 263 | 10-Jan-70 | Scotland | 5N | A Murrayfield, Edinburgh | W | 11-9 |
| 264 | 24-Jan-70 | Ireland | 5N | H Stade Colombes, Paris | W | 8-0 |
| 265 | 4-Apr-70 | Wales | 5N | A National Stadium, Cardiff | L | 6-11 |
| 266 | 18-Apr-70 | England | 5N | H Stade Colombes, Paris | W | 35-13 |
| 267 | 29-Nov-70 | Romania | FIRA | A Stadionul Giuleşti-V Stănescu, Bucharest | W | 14-3 |
| 268 | 16-Jan-71 | Scotland | 5N | H Stade Colombes, Paris | W | 13-8 |
| 269 | 30-Jan-71 | Ireland | 5N | A Lansdowne Road, Dublin | D | 9-9 |
| 270 | 27-Feb-71 | England | 5N | A Twickenham, London | D | 14-14 |
| 271 | 27-Mar-71 | Wales | 5N | H Stade Colombes, Paris | L | 5-9 |
| 272 | 12-Jun-71 | South Africa | Int-T | A Free State Stadium, Bloemfontein | L | 9-22 |
| 273 | 19-Jun-71 | South Africa | Int-T | A Kings Park Stadium, Durban | D | 8-8 |
| 274 | 20-Nov-71 | Australia | Int | H Stade Municipal de Toulouse, Toulouse | L | 11-13 |
| 275 | 27-Nov-71 | Australia | Int | H Stade Colombes, Paris | W | 18-9 |
| 276 | 11-Dec-71 | Romania | FIRA | H Parc des Sports de Sauclières, Béziers | W | 31-12 |
| 277 | 15-Jan-72 | Scotland | 5N | A Murrayfield, Edinburgh | L | 9-20 |
| 278 | 29-Jan-72 | Ireland | 5N | H Stade Colombes, Paris | L | 9-14 |
| 279 | 26-Feb-72 | England | 5N | H Stade Colombes, Paris | W | 37-12 |
| 280 | 25-Mar-72 | Wales | 5N | A National Stadium, Cardiff | L | 6-20 |

| No | Date | Opponents | Tmt | | Match Venue | Result | |
|----|------|-----------|-----|---|-------------|--------|---|
| 281 | 29-Apr-72 | Ireland | Int | A | Lansdowne Road, Dublin | L | 14-24 |
| 282 | 17-Jun-72 | Australia | Int-T | A | Cricket Ground, Sydney | D | 14-14 |
| 283 | 25-Jun-72 | Australia | Int-T | A | Ballymore Oval, Brisbane | W | 16-15 |
| 284 | 26-Nov-72 | Romania | FIRA | A | Stadionul 1 Mai, Constanta | W | 15-6 |
| 285 | 13-Jan-73 | Scotland | 5N | H | Parc des Princess, Paris | W | 16-13 |
| 286 | 10-Feb-73 | New Zealand | Int | H | Parc des Princess, Paris | W | 13-6 |
| 287 | 24-Feb-73 | England | 5N | A | Twickenham, London | L | 6-14 |
| 288 | 24-Mar-73 | Wales | 5N | H | Parc des Princess, Paris | W | 12-3 |
| 289 | 14-Apr-73 | Ireland | 5N | A | Lansdowne Road, Dublin | L | 4-6 |
| 290 | 27-Oct-73 | Japan | Int | H | Stade du Parc Lescure, Bordeaux | W | 30-18 |
| 291 | 11-Nov-73 | Romania | FIRA | H | Stade de la Chamberliére, Valence | W | 7-6 |
| 292 | 19-Jan-74 | Ireland | 5N | H | Parc des Princess, Paris | W | 9-6 |
| 293 | 16-Feb-74 | Wales | 5N | A | National Stadium, Cardiff | D | 16-16 |
| 294 | 2-Mar-74 | England | 5N | H | Parc des Princess, Paris | D | 12-12 |
| 295 | 16-Mar-74 | Scotland | 5N | A | Murrayfield, Edinburgh | L | 6-19 |
| 296 | 20-Jun-74 | Argentina | Int-T | A | Ferro Carril Oeste Stadium, B Aires | W | 20-15 |
| 297 | 29-Jun-74 | Argentina | Int-T | A | Ferro Carril Oeste Stadium, B Aires | W | 31-27 |
| 298 | 13-Oct-74 | Romania | FIRA | A | Stadionul 23 August, Bucharest | L | 10-15 |
| 299 | 23-Nov-74 | South Africa | Int | H | Stade Municipal de Toulouse, Toulouse | L | 4-13 |
| 300 | 30-Nov-74 | South Africa | Int | H | Parc des Princess, Paris | L | 8-10 |
| 301 | 18-Jan-75 | Wales | 5N | H | Parc des Princess, Paris | L | 10-25 |
| 302 | 1-Feb-75 | England | 5N | A | Twickenham, London | W | 27-20 |
| 303 | 15-Feb-75 | Scotland | 5N | H | Parc des Princess, Paris | W | 10-9 |
| 304 | 1-Mar-75 | Ireland | 5N | A | Lansdowne Road, Dublin | L | 6-25 |
| 305 | 21-Jun-75 | South Africa | Int-T | A | Free State Stadium, Bloemfontein | L | 25-38 |
| 306 | 28-Jun-75 | South Africa | Int-T | A | Loftus Versfeld Stadium, Pretoria | L | 18-33 |
| 307 | 19-Oct-75 | Argentina | Int | H | Stade de Gerland, Lyon | W | 29-6 |
| 308 | 25-Oct-75 | Argentina | Int | H | Parc des Princess, Paris | W | 36-21 |
| 309 | 23-Nov-75 | Romania | FIRA | H | Stade du Parc Lescure, Bordeaux | W | 36-12 |
| 310 | 10-Jan-76 | Scotland | 5N | A | Murrayfield, Edinburgh | W | 13-6 |
| 311 | 7-Feb-76 | Ireland | 5N | H | Parc des Princess, Paris | W | 26-3 |
| 312 | 6-Mar-76 | Wales | 5N | A | National Stadium, Cardiff | L | 13-19 |
| 313 | 20-Mar-76 | England | 5N | H | Parc des Princess, Paris | W | 30-9 |
| 314 | 12-Jun-76 | United States | Int-T | A | Rockne Stadium, Northfield, Chicago | W | 33-14 |
| 315 | 24-Oct-76 | Australia | Int | H | Stade du Parc Lescure, Bordeaux | W | 18-15 |
| 316 | 30-Oct-76 | Australia | Int | H | Parc des Princess, Paris | W | 34-6 |
| 317 | 14-Nov-76 | Romania | FIRA | A | Stadionul Giuleşti-V Stănescu, Bucharest | L | 12-15 |
| 318 | 5-Feb-77 | Wales | 5N | H | Parc des Princess, Paris | W | 16-9 |
| 319 | 19-Feb-77 | England | 5N | A | Twickenham, London | W | 4-3 |
| 320 | 5-Mar-77 | Scotland | 5N | H | Parc des Princess, Paris | W | 23-3 |

| No | Date | Opponents | Tmt | Match Venue | Result | |
|-----|---------|-------------|-------|--------------------------------------------------|---|-------|
| 321 | 19-Mar-77 | Ireland | 5N | A Lansdowne Road, Dublin | W | 15-6 |
| 322 | 25-Jun-77 | Argentina | Int-T | A Ferro Carril Oeste Stadium, B Aires | W | 26-3 |
| 323 | 2-Jul-77 | Argentina | Int-T | A Ferro Carril Oeste Stadium, B Aires | D | 18-18 |
| 324 | 11-Nov-77 | New Zealand | Int | H Stade Municipal de Toulouse, Toulouse | W | 18-13 |
| 325 | 19-Nov-77 | New Zealand | Int | H Parc des Princess, Paris | L | 3-15 |
| 326 | 10-Dec-77 | Romania | FIRA | H Stade Marcel Michelin, Clermont Ferrand | W | 9-6 |
| 327 | 21-Jan-78 | England | 5N | H Parc des Princess, Paris | W | 15-6 |
| 328 | 4-Feb-78 | Scotland | 5N | A Murrayfield, Edinburgh | W | 19-16 |
| 329 | 18-Feb-78 | Ireland | 5N | H Parc des Princess, Paris | W | 10-9 |
| 330 | 18-Mar-78 | Wales | 5N | A National Stadium, Cardiff | L | 7-16 |
| 331 | 3-Dec-78 | Romania | FIRA | A Stadionul Dinamo, Bucharest | W | 9-6 |
| 332 | 20-Jan-79 | Ireland | 5N | A Lansdowne Road, Dublin | D | 9-9 |
| 333 | 17-Feb-79 | Wales | 5N | H Parc des Princess, Paris | W | 14-13 |
| 334 | 3-Mar-79 | England | 5N | A Twickenham, London | L | 6-7 |
| 335 | 17-Mar-79 | Scotland | 5N | H Parc des Princess, Paris | W | 21-17 |
| 336 | 7-Jul-79 | New Zealand | Int-T | A Lancaster Park Oval, Christchurch | L | 9-23 |
| 337 | 14-Jul-79 | New Zealand | Int-T | A Eden Park, Auckland | W | 24-19 |
| 338 | 2-Dec-79 | Romania | FIRA | H Stade de Sapiac, Montauban | W | 30-12 |
| 339 | 19-Jan-80 | Wales | 5N | A National Stadium, Cardiff | L | 9-18 |
| 340 | 2-Feb-80 | England | 5N | H Parc des Princess, Paris | L | 13-17 |
| 341 | 16-Feb-80 | Scotland | 5N | A Murrayfield, Edinburgh | L | 14-22 |
| 342 | 1-Mar-80 | Ireland | 5N | H Parc des Princess, Paris | W | 19-18 |
| 343 | 8-Nov-80 | South Africa | Int-T | A Loftus Versfeld Stadium, Pretoria | L | 15-37 |
| 344 | 23-Nov-80 | Romania | FIRA | A Stadionul Giuleşti-V Stănescu, Bucharest | L | 0-15 |
| 345 | 17-Jan-81 | Scotland | 5N | H Parc des Princess, Paris | W | 16-9 |
| 346 | 7-Feb-81 | Ireland | 5N | A Lansdowne Road, Dublin | W | 19-13 |
| 347 | 7-Mar-81 | Wales | 5N | H Parc des Princess, Paris | W | 19-15 |
| 348 | 21-Mar-81 | England | 5N | A Twickenham, London | W | 16-12 |
| 349 | 5-Jul-81 | Australia | Int-T | A Ballymore Oval, Brisbane | L | 15-17 |
| 350 | 11-Jul-81 | Australia | Int-T | A Cricket Ground, Sydney | L | 14-24 |
| 351 | 1-Nov-81 | Romania | FIRA | H Stade de L'Egassiairal, Narbonne | W | 17-9 |
| 352 | 14-Nov-81 | New Zealand | Int | H Stade Municipal de Toulouse, Toulouse | L | 9-13 |
| 353 | 21-Nov-81 | New Zealand | Int | H Parc des Princess, Paris | L | 6-18 |
| 354 | 6-Feb-82 | Wales | 5N | A National Stadium, Cardiff | L | 12-22 |
| 355 | 20-Feb-82 | England | 5N | H Parc des Princess, Paris | L | 15-27 |
| 356 | 6-Mar-82 | Scotland | 5N | A Murrayfield, Edinburgh | L | 7-16 |
| 357 | 20-Mar-82 | Ireland | 5N | H Parc des Princess, Paris | W | 22-9 |
| 358 | 31-Oct-82 | Romania | FIRA | A Stadionul Dinamo, Bucharest | L | 9-13 |
| 359 | 14-Nov-82 | Argentina | Int | H Stade Municipal de Toulouse, Toulouse | W | 25-12 |
| 360 | 20-Nov-82 | Argentina | Int | H Parc des Princess, Paris | W | 13-6 |

| No | Date | Opponents | Tmt | Match Venue | Result | |
|-----|----------|-------------|-------|------------------------------------------|---|-------|
| 361 | 15-Jan-83 | England | 5N | A Twickenham, London | W | 19-15 |
| 362 | 5-Feb-83 | Scotland | 5N | H Parc des Princess, Paris | W | 19-15 |
| 363 | 19-Feb-83 | Ireland | 5N | A Lansdowne Road, Dublin | L | 16-22 |
| 364 | 19-Mar-83 | Wales | 5N | H Parc des Princess, Paris | W | 16-9 |
| 365 | 13-Nov-83 | Australia | Int | H Stade Marcel Michelin, Clermont Ferrand | D | 15-15 |
| 366 | 19-Nov-83 | Australia | Int | H Parc des Princess, Paris | W | 15-6 |
| 367 | 4-Dec-83 | Romania | FIRA | H Stade Ernest Wallon, Toulouse | W | 26-15 |
| 368 | 21-Jan-84 | Ireland | 5N | H Parc des Princess, Paris | W | 25-12 |
| 369 | 18-Feb-84 | Wales | 5N | A National Stadium, Cardiff | W | 21-16 |
| 370 | 3-Mar-84 | England | 5N | H Parc des Princess, Paris | W | 32-18 |
| 371 | 17-Mar-84 | Scotland | 5N | A Murrayfield, Edinburgh | L | 12-21 |
| 372 | 16-Jun-84 | New Zealand | Int-T | A Lancaster Park Oval, Christchurch | L | 9-10 |
| 373 | 23-Jun-84 | New Zealand | Int-T | A Eden Park, Auckland | L | 18-31 |
| 374 | 10-Nov-84 | Romania | FIRA | A Stadionul 23 August, Bucharest | W | 18-3 |
| 375 | 2-Feb-85 | England | 5N | A Twickenham, London | D | 9-9 |
| 376 | 16-Feb-85 | Scotland | 5N | H Parc des Princess, Paris | W | 11-3 |
| 377 | 2-Mar-85 | Ireland | 5N | A Lansdowne Road, Dublin | D | 15-15 |
| 378 | 30-Mar-85 | Wales | 5N | H Parc des Princess, Paris | W | 14-3 |
| 379 | 22-Jun-85 | Argentina | Int-T | A Ferro Carril Oeste Stadium, B Aires | L | 16-24 |
| 380 | 29-Jun-85 | Argentina | Int-T | A Ferro Carril Oeste Stadium, B Aires | W | 23-15 |
| 381 | 18-Jan-86 | Scotland | 5N | A Murrayfield, Edinburgh | L | 17-18 |
| 382 | 1-Feb-86 | Ireland | 5N | H Parc des Princess, Paris | W | 29-9 |
| 383 | 1-Mar-86 | Wales | 5N | A National Stadium, Cardiff | W | 23-15 |
| 384 | 15-Mar-86 | England | 5N | H Parc des Princess, Paris | W | 29-10 |
| 385 | 12-Apr-86 | Romania | FIRA | H Stade Nord Lille Métropole | W | 25-13 |
| 386 | 31-May-86 | Argentina | Int-T | A Vélez Sarsfield Stadium, Buenos Aires | L | 13-15 |
| 387 | 7-Jun-86 | Argentina | Int-T | A Vélez Sarsfield Stadium, Buenos Aires | W | 22-9 |
| 388 | 21-Jun-86 | Australia | Int-T | A Cricket Ground, Sydney | L | 14-27 |
| 389 | 28-Jun-86 | New Zealand | Int-T | A Lancaster Park Oval, Christchurch | L | 9-18 |
| 390 | 25-Oct-86 | Romania | FIRA | A Stadionul Giuleşti-V Stănescu, Bucharest | W | 20-3 |
| 391 | 8-Nov-86 | New Zealand | Int | H Stade Municipal de Toulouse, Toulouse | L | 7-19 |
| 392 | 15-Nov-86 | New Zealand | Int | H Stade de la Beaujoire, Nantes | W | 16-3 |
| 393 | 7-Feb-87 | Wales | 5N | H Parc des Princess, Paris | W | 16-9 |
| 394 | 21-Feb-87 | England | 5N | A Twickenham, London | W | 19-15 |
| 395 | 7-Mar-87 | Scotland | 5N | H Parc des Princess, Paris | W | 28-22 |
| 396 | 21-Mar-87 | Ireland | 5N | A Lansdowne Road, Dublin | W | 19-13 |
| 397 | 23-May-87 | Scotland | WCp | N Lancaster Park Oval, Christchurch | D | 20-20 |
| 398 | 28-May-87 | Romania | WCp | N Athletic Park, Wellington | W | 55-12 |
| 399 | 2-Jun-87 | Zimbabwe | WCp | N Eden Park, Auckland | W | 70-12 |
| 400 | 7-Jun-87 | Fiji | WCqf | N Eden Park, Auckland | W | 31-16 |

| No | Date | Opponents | Tmt | | Match Venue | | Result | |
|-----|------------|--------------|--------|---|------------------------------------------|---|---|--------|
| 401 | 13-Jun-87 | Australia | WCsf | A | Concord Oval, Sydney | | W | 30-24 |
| 402 | 20-Jun-87 | New Zealand | WCf | A | Eden Park, Auckland | | L | 9-29 |
| 403 | 11-Nov-87 | Romania | FIRA | H | Stade Armandie, Agen | | W | 49-3 |
| 404 | 16-Jan-88 | England | 5N | H | Parc des Princess, Paris | | W | 10-9 |
| 405 | 6-Feb-88 | Scotland | 5N | A | Murrayfield, Edinburgh | | L | 12-23 |
| 406 | 20-Feb-88 | Ireland | 5N | H | Parc des Princess, Paris | | W | 25-6 |
| 407 | 19-Mar-88 | Wales | 5N | A | National Stadium, Cardiff | | W | 10-9 |
| 408 | 18-Jun-88 | Argentina | Int-T | A | Vélez Sarsfield Stadium, Buenos Aires | | W | 18-15 |
| 409 | 25-Jun-88 | Argentina | Int-T | A | Vélez Sarsfield Stadium, Buenos Aires | | L | 6-18 |
| 410 | 5-Nov-88 | Argentina | Int | H | Stade de la Beaujoire, Nantes | | W | 29-9 |
| 411 | 11-Nov-88 | Argentina | Int | H | Stade Nord Lille Métropole | | W | 28-18 |
| 412 | 26-Nov-88 | Romania | FIRA | A | Stadionul Giuleşti-V Stănescu, Bucharest | | W | 16-12 |
| 413 | 21-Jan-89 | Ireland | 5N | A | Lansdowne Road, Dublin | | W | 26-21 |
| 414 | 18-Feb-89 | Wales | 5N | H | Parc des Princess, Paris | | W | 31-12 |
| 415 | 4-Mar-89 | England | 5N | A | Twickenham, London | | L | 0-11 |
| 416 | 18-Mar-89 | Scotland | 5N | H | Parc des Princess, Paris | | W | 19-3 |
| 417 | 17-Jun-89 | New Zealand | Int-T | A | Lancaster Park Oval, Christchurch | | L | 17-25 |
| 418 | 1-Jul-89 | New Zealand | Int-T | A | Eden Park, Auckland | | L | 20-34 |
| 419 | 4-Oct-89 | Lions XV | Int | H | Parc des Princess, Paris | | L | 27-29 |
| 420 | 4-Nov-89 | Australia | BIC | H | Stade de la Meinau, Strasbourg | | L | 15-32 |
| 421 | 11-Nov-89 | Australia | BIC | H | Stade Nord Lille Métropole | | W | 25-19 |
| 422 | 20-Jan-90 | Wales | 5N | A | National Stadium, Cardiff | | W | 29-19 |
| 423 | 3-Feb-90 | England | 5N | H | Parc des Princess, Paris | | L | 7-26 |
| 424 | 17-Feb-90 | Scotland | 5N | A | Murrayfield, Edinburgh | | L | 0-21 |
| 425 | 3-Mar-90 | Ireland | 5N | H | Parc des Princess, Paris | | W | 31-12 |
| 426 | 24-May-90 | Romania | FIRA | H | Stade Jacques Fouroux, Auch | | L | 6-12 |
| 427 | 9-Jun-90 | Australia | BIC-T | A | Football Stadium, Sydney | | L | 9-21 |
| 428 | 24-Jun-90 | Australia | BIC-T | A | Ballymore Oval, Brisbane | | L | 31-48 |
| 429 | 30-Jun-90 | Australia | BIC-T | A | Football Stadium, Sydney | | W | 28-19 |
| 430 | 3-Nov-90 | New Zealand | Int | H | Stade de la Beaujoire, Nantes | | L | 3-24 |
| 431 | 10-Nov-90 | New Zealand | Int | H | Parc des Princess, Paris | | L | 12-30 |
| 432 | 19-Jan-91 | Scotland | 5N | H | Parc des Princess, Paris | | W | 15-9 |
| 433 | 2-Feb-91 | Ireland | 5N | A | Lansdowne Road, Dublin | | W | 21-13 |
| 434 | 2-Mar-91 | Wales | 5N | H | Parc des Princess, Paris | | W | 36-3 |
| 435 | 16-Mar-91 | England | 5N | A | Twickenham, London | | L | 19-21 |
| 436 | 22-Jun-91 | Romania | FIRA | A | Stadionul 23 August, Bucharest | | W | 33-21 |
| 437 | 13-Jul-91 | United States | Int-T | A | Observatory Park, Denver, Colorado | | W | 41-9 |
| 438 | 20-Jul-91 | United States | Int-T | A | Colorado Springs | | W | 10-3 |
| 439 | 4-Sep-91 | Wales | Int | A | National Stadium, Cardiff | | W | 22-9 |
| 440 | 4-Oct-91 | Romania | WCp | H | Stade de la Méditerranée, Béziers | | W | 30-3 |

FRANCE

| No | Date | Opponents | Tmt | Match Venue | Result | |
|---|---|---|---|---|---|---|
| 441 | 8-Oct-91 | Fiji | WCp | H Stade Lesdiguières, Grenoble | W | 33-9 |
| 442 | 13-Oct-91 | Canada | WCp | H Stade Armandie, Agen | W | 19-13 |
| 443 | 19-Oct-91 | England | WCqf | H Parc des Princess, Paris | L | 10-19 |
| 444 | 1-Feb-92 | Wales | 5N | A National Stadium, Cardiff | W | 12-9 |
| 445 | 15-Feb-92 | England | 5N | H Parc des Princess, Paris | L | 13-31 |
| 446 | 7-Mar-92 | Scotland | 5N | A Murrayfield, Edinburgh | L | 6-10 |
| 447 | 21-Mar-92 | Ireland | 5N | H Parc des Princess, Paris | W | 44-12 |
| 448 | 28-May-92 | Romania | FIRA | H Stade Jules Deschaseaux, Le Havre | W | 25-6 |
| 449 | 4-Jul-92 | Argentina | Int-T | A Vélez Sarsfield Stadium, Buenos Aires | W | 27-12 |
| 450 | 11-Jul-92 | Argentina | Int-T | A Vélez Sarsfield Stadium, Buenos Aires | W | 33-9 |
| 451 | 17-Oct-92 | South Africa | Int | H Stade de Gerland, Lyon | L | 15-20 |
| 452 | 24-Oct-92 | South Africa | Int | H Parc des Princess, Paris | W | 29-16 |
| 453 | 14-Nov-92 | Argentina | Int | H Stade de la Beaujoire, Nantes | L | 20-24 |
| 454 | 16-Jan-93 | England | 5N | A Twickenham, London | L | 15-16 |
| 455 | 6-Feb-93 | Scotland | 5N | H Parc des Princess, Paris | W | 11-3 |
| 456 | 20-Feb-93 | Ireland | 5N | A Lansdowne Road, Dublin | W | 21-6 |
| 457 | 20-Mar-93 | Wales | 5N | H Parc des Princess, Paris | W | 26-10 |
| 458 | 20-May-93 | Romania | Int | A Stadionul Dinamo, Bucharest | W | 37-20 |
| 459 | 26-Jun-93 | South Africa | Int-T | A Kings Park Stadium, Durban | D | 20-20 |
| 460 | 3-Jul-93 | South Africa | Int-T | A Ellis Park, Johannesburg | W | 18-17 |
| 461 | 17-Oct-93 | Romania | FIRA | H Stade Parc Municipal des Sports, Brive | W | 51-0 |
| 462 | 30-Oct-93 | Australia | BIC | H Stade du Parc Lescure, Bordeaux | W | 16-13 |
| 463 | 6-Nov-93 | Australia | BIC | H Parc des Princess, Paris | L | 3-24 |
| 464 | 15-Jan-94 | Ireland | 5N | H Parc des Princess, Paris | W | 35-15 |
| 465 | 19-Feb-94 | Wales | 5N | A National Stadium, Cardiff | L | 15-24 |
| 466 | 5-Mar-94 | England | 5N | H Parc des Princess, Paris | L | 14-18 |
| 467 | 19-Mar-94 | Scotland | 5N | A Murrayfield, Edinburgh | W | 20-12 |
| 468 | 4-Jun-94 | Canada | Int-T | A Twin Elms Rugby Park, Nepean, Ontario | L | 16-18 |
| 469 | 26-Jun-94 | New Zealand | Int-T | A Lancaster Park Oval, Christchurch | W | 22-8 |
| 470 | 3-Jul-94 | New Zealand | Int-T | A Eden Park, Auckland | W | 23-20 |
| 471 | 17-Dec-94 | Canada | Int | H Stade Leo Lagrange, Besançon | W | 28-9 |
| 472 | 21-Jan-95 | Wales | 5N | H Parc des Princess, Paris | W | 21-9 |
| 473 | 4-Feb-95 | England | 5N | A Twickenham, London | L | 10-31 |
| 474 | 18-Feb-95 | Scotland | 5N | H Parc des Princess, Paris | L | 21-23 |
| 475 | 4-Mar-95 | Ireland | 5N | A Lansdowne Road, Dublin | W | 25-7 |
| 476 | 8-Apr-95 | Romania | Int | A Stadionul 23 August, Bucharest | W | 24-15 |
| 477 | 26-May-95 | Tonga | WCp | N Loftus Versfeld Stadium, Pretoria | W | 38-10 |
| 478 | 30-May-95 | Côte d'Ivoire | WCp | N Olympia Park, Rustenburg | W | 54-18 |
| 479 | 3-Jun-95 | Scotland | WCp | N Loftus Versfeld Stadium, Pretoria | W | 22-19 |
| 480 | 10-Jun-95 | Ireland | WCqf | N Kings Park Stadium, Durban | W | 36-12 |

| No | Date | Opponents | Tmt | | Match Venue | | Result |
|-----|------------|--------------|-------|---|---------------------------------------------|---|--------|
| 481 | 17-Jun-95 | South Africa | WCsf | A | Kings Park Stadium, Durban | L | 15-19 |
| 482 | 22-Jun-95 | England | WC34 | N | Loftus Versfeld Stadium, Pretoria | W | 19-9 |
| 483 | 14-Oct-95 | Italy | LTC | N | Ferro Carril Oeste Stadium, B Aires | W | 34-22 |
| 484 | 17-Oct-95 | Romania | LTC | N | Estadio Monumental José Fierro, Tucumán | W | 52-8 |
| 485 | 21-Oct-95 | Argentina | LTC | A | Ferro Carril Oeste Stadium, B Aires | W | 47-12 |
| 486 | 11-Nov-95 | New Zealand | Int | H | Stade Municipal de Toulouse, Toulouse | W | 22-15 |
| 487 | 18-Nov-95 | New Zealand | Int | H | Parc des Princess, Paris | L | 12-37 |
| 488 | 20-Jan-96 | England | 5N | H | Parc des Princess, Paris | W | 15-12 |
| 489 | 3-Feb-96 | Scotland | 5N | A | Murrayfield, Edinburgh | L | 14-19 |
| 490 | 17-Feb-96 | Ireland | 5N | H | Parc des Princess, Paris | W | 45-10 |
| 491 | 16-Mar-96 | Wales | 5N | A | National Stadium, Cardiff | L | 15-16 |
| 492 | 20-Apr-96 | Romania | Int | H | Stade Jean Alric, Aurillac | W | 64-12 |
| 493 | 22-Jun-96 | Argentina | Int-T | A | Ferro Carril Oeste Stadium, B Aires | W | 34-27 |
| 494 | 29-Jun-96 | Argentina | Int-T | A | Ferro Carril Oeste Stadium, B Aires | W | 34-15 |
| 495 | 25-Sep-96 | Wales | Int | A | National Stadium, Cardiff | W | 40-33 |
| 496 | 30-Nov-96 | South Africa | Int | H | Stade du Parc Lescure, Bordeaux | L | 12-22 |
| 497 | 7-Dec-96 | South Africa | Int | H | Parc des Princess, Paris | L | 12-13 |
| 498 | 18-Jan-97 | Ireland | 5N | A | Lansdowne Road, Dublin | W | 32-15 |
| 499 | 15-Feb-97 | Wales | 5N | H | Parc des Princess, Paris | W | 27-22 |
| 500 | 1-Mar-97 | England | 5N | A | Twickenham, London | W | 23-20 |
| 501 | 15-Mar-97 | Scotland | 5N | H | Parc des Princess, Paris | W | 47-20 |
| 502 | 22-Mar-97 | Italy | FIRA | H | Stade Lesdiguières, Grenoble | L | 32-40 |
| 503 | 1-Jun-97 | Romania | Int | A | Stadionul Dinamo, Bucharest | W | 51-20 |
| 504 | 21-Jun-97 | Australia | BIC-T | A | Football Stadium, Sydney | L | 15-29 |
| 505 | 28-Jun-97 | Australia | BIC-T | A | Ballymore Oval, Brisbane | L | 19-26 |
| 506 | 18-Oct-97 | Italy | LTC | H | Stade Jacques Fouroux, Auch | W | 30-19 |
| 507 | 22-Oct-97 | Romania | LTC | H | Stade Antoine Béguère, Lourdes | W | 39-3 |
| 508 | 26-Oct-97 | Argentina | LTC | H | Stade Maurice Trélut, Tarbes | W | 32-27 |
| 509 | 15-Nov-97 | South Africa | Int | H | Stade de Gerland, Lyon | L | 32-36 |
| 510 | 22-Nov-97 | South Africa | Int | H | Parc des Princess, Paris | L | 10-52 |
| 511 | 7-Feb-98 | England | 5N | H | Stade de France, Paris | W | 24-17 |
| 512 | 21-Feb-98 | Scotland | 5N | A | Murrayfield, Edinburgh | W | 51-16 |
| 513 | 7-Mar-98 | Ireland | 5N | H | Stade de France, Paris | W | 18-16 |
| 514 | 5-Apr-98 | Wales | 5N | N | Wembley Stadium, London | W | 51-0 |
| 515 | 13-Jun-98 | Argentina | Int-T | A | Vélez Sarsfield Stadium, Buenos Aires | W | 35-18 |
| 516 | 20-Jun-98 | Argentina | Int-T | A | Vélez Sarsfield Stadium, Buenos Aires | W | 37-12 |
| 517 | 27-Jun-98 | Fiji | Int-T | A | National Stadium, Suva | W | 34-9 |
| 518 | 14-Nov-98 | Argentina | Int | H | Stade de la Beaujoire, Nantes | W | 34-14 |
| 519 | 21-Nov-98 | Australia | BIC | H | Stade de France, Paris | L | 21-32 |
| 520 | 6-Feb-99 | Ireland | 5N | A | Lansdowne Road, Dublin | W | 10-9 |

| No | Date | Opponents | Tmt | | Match Venue | Result | |
|----|------|-----------|-----|---|-------------|--------|---|
| 521 | 6-Mar-99 | Wales | 5N | H | Stade de France, Paris | L | 33-34 |
| 522 | 20-Mar-99 | England | 5N | A | Twickenham, London | L | 10-21 |
| 523 | 10-Apr-99 | Scotland | 5N | H | Stade de France, Paris | L | 22-36 |
| 524 | 3-Jun-99 | Romania | Int | H | Stade Pierre-Antoine, Castres | W | 62-8 |
| 525 | 12-Jun-99 | Samoa | Int-T | A | Apia Park, Apia | W | 39-22 |
| 526 | 16-Jun-99 | Tonga | Int-T | A | Teufaiva Sport Stadium, Nuku'alofa | L | 16-20 |
| 527 | 26-Jun-99 | New Zealand | Int-T | A | Athletic Park, Wellington | L | 7-54 |
| 528 | 28-Aug-99 | Wales | Int | A | Millennium Stadium, Cardiff | L | 23-34 |
| 529 | 2-Oct-99 | Canada | WCp | H | Stade de la Méditerranée, Béziers | W | 33-20 |
| 530 | 8-Oct-99 | Namibia | WCp | H | Stade du Parc Lescure, Bordeaux | W | 47-13 |
| 531 | 16-Oct-99 | Fiji | WCp | H | Stade Municipal de Toulouse, Toulouse | W | 28-19 |
| 532 | 24-Oct-99 | Argentina | Wcqf | N | Lansdowne Road, Dublin | W | 47-26 |
| 533 | 31-Oct-99 | New Zealand | WCsf | N | Twickenham, London | W | 43-31 |
| 534 | 6-Nov-99 | Australia | WCf | N | Millennium Stadium, Cardiff | L | 12-35 |
| 535 | 5-Feb-00 | Wales | 6N | A | Millennium Stadium, Cardiff | W | 36-3 |
| 536 | 19-Feb-00 | England | 6N | H | Stade de France, Paris | L | 9-15 |
| 537 | 4-Mar-00 | Scotland | 6N | A | Murrayfield, Edinburgh | W | 28-16 |
| 538 | 19-Mar-00 | Ireland | 6N | H | Stade de France, Paris | L | 25-27 |
| 539 | 1-Apr-00 | Italy | 6N | H | Stade de France, Paris | W | 42-31 |
| 540 | 28-May-00 | Romania | Int | A | Stadionul Dinamo, Bucharest | W | 67-20 |
| 541 | 4-Nov-00 | Australia | BIC | H | Stade de France, Paris | L | 13-18 |
| 542 | 11-Nov-00 | New Zealand | DGT | H | Stade de France, Paris | L | 26-39 |
| 543 | 18-Nov-00 | New Zealand | Int | H | Stade Vélodrome, Marseille | W | 42-33 |
| 544 | 4-Feb-01 | Scotland | 6N | H | Stade de France, Paris | W | 16-6 |
| 545 | 17-Feb-01 | Ireland | 6N | A | Lansdowne Road, Dublin | L | 15-22 |
| 546 | 3-Mar-01 | Italy | 6N | A | Stadio Flaminio, Rome | W | 30-19 |
| 547 | 17-Mar-01 | Wales | 6N | H | Stade de France, Paris | L | 35-43 |
| 548 | 7-Apr-01 | England | 6N | A | Twickenham, London | L | 19-48 |
| 549 | 16-Jun-01 | South Africa | Int-T | A | Ellis Park, Johannesburg | W | 32-23 |
| 550 | 23-Jun-01 | South Africa | Int-T | A | ABSA Stadium, Durban | L | 15-20 |
| 551 | 30-Jun-01 | New Zealand | DGT-T | A | Westpac Trust Stadium, Wellington | L | 12-37 |
| 552 | 10-Nov-01 | South Africa | Int | H | Stade de France, Paris | W | 20-10 |
| 553 | 17-Nov-01 | Australia | BIC | H | Stade Vélodrome, Marseille | W | 14-13 |
| 554 | 24-Nov-01 | Fiji | Int | H | Stade Geoffroy-Guichard, St Étienne | W | 77-10 |
| 555 | 2-Feb-02 | Italy | 6N | H | Stade de France, Paris | W | 33-12 |
| 556 | 16-Feb-02 | Wales | 6N | A | Millennium Stadium, Cardiff | W | 37-33 |
| 557 | 2-Mar-02 | England | 6N | H | Stade de France, Paris | W | 20-15 |
| 558 | 23-Mar-02 | Scotland | 6N | A | Murrayfield, Edinburgh | W | 22-10 |
| 559 | 6-Apr-02 | Ireland | 6N | H | Stade de France, Paris | W | 44-5 |
| 560 | 15-Jun-02 | Argentina | Int-T | A | Vélez Sarsfield Stadium, Buenos Aires | L | 27-28 |

| No | Date | Opponents | Tmt | | Match Venue | Result | |
|----|------|-----------|-----|---|-------------|--------|---|
| 561 | 22-Jun-02 | Australia | BIC-T | A | Colonial Stadium, Melbourne | L | 17-29 |
| 562 | 29-Jun-02 | Australia | BIC-T | A | Stadium Australia, Sydney | L | 25-31 |
| 563 | 9-Nov-02 | South Africa | Int | H | Stade Vélodrome, Marseille | W | 30-10 |
| 564 | 16-Nov-02 | New Zealand | DGT | H | Stade de France, Paris | D | 20-20 |
| 565 | 23-Nov-02 | Canada | Int | H | Stade de France, Paris | W | 35-3 |
| 566 | 15-Feb-03 | England | 6N | A | Twickenham, London | L | 17-25 |
| 567 | 23-Feb-03 | Scotland | 6N | H | Stade de France, Paris | W | 38-3 |
| 568 | 8-Mar-03 | Ireland | 6N | A | Lansdowne Road, Dublin | L | 12-15 |
| 569 | 23-Mar-03 | Italy | 6N | A | Stadio Flaminio, Rome | W | 53-27 |
| 570 | 29-Mar-03 | Wales | 6N | H | Stade de France, Paris | W | 33-5 |
| 571 | 14-Jun-03 | Argentina | Int-T | A | Vélez Sarsfield Stadium, Buenos Aires | L | 6-10 |
| 572 | 20-Jun-03 | Argentina | Int-T | A | Vélez Sarsfield Stadium, Buenos Aires | L | 32-33 |
| 573 | 28-Jun-03 | New Zealand | DGT-T | A | Jade Stadium, Christchurch | L | 23-31 |
| 574 | 22-Aug-03 | Romania | Int | II | Stade Félix Bollaert, Lens | W | 56-8 |
| 575 | 30-Aug-03 | England | Int | H | Stade Vélodrome, Marseille | W | 17-16 |
| 576 | 6-Sep-03 | England | Int | A | Twickenham, London | L | 14-45 |
| 577 | 11-Oct-03 | Fiji | WCp | N | Suncorp Stadium, Brisbane | W | 61-18 |
| 578 | 18-Oct-03 | Japan | WCp | N | Dairy Farmers Stadium, Townsville | W | 51-29 |
| 579 | 25-Oct-03 | Scotland | WCp | N | Telstra Stadium, Sydney | W | 51-9 |
| 580 | 31-Oct-03 | United States | WCp | N | WIN Stadium, Wollongong | W | 41-14 |
| 581 | 9-Nov-03 | Ireland | WCqf | N | Telstra Dome, Melbourne | W | 43-21 |
| 582 | 16-Nov-03 | England | WCsf | N | Telstra Stadium, Sydney | L | 7-24 |
| 583 | 20-Nov-03 | New Zealand | WC34 | N | Telstra Stadium, Sydney | L | 13-40 |
| 584 | 14-Feb-04 | Ireland | 6N | H | Stade de France, Paris | W | 35-17 |
| 585 | 21-Feb-04 | Italy | 6N | H | Stade de France, Paris | W | 25-0 |
| 586 | 7-Mar-04 | Wales | 6N | A | Millennium Stadium, Cardiff | W | 29-22 |
| 587 | 21-Mar-04 | Scotland | 6N | A | Murrayfield, Edinburgh | W | 31-0 |
| 588 | 27-Mar-04 | England | 6N | H | Stade de France, Paris | W | 24-21 |
| 589 | 3-Jul-04 | United States | Int-T | A | Rentschler Field, Hartford, Connecticut | W | 39-31 |
| 590 | 10-Jul-04 | Canada | Int-T | A | York Stadium, Toronto | W | 47-13 |
| 591 | 13-Nov-04 | Australia | BIC | H | Stade de France, Paris | W | 27-14 |
| 592 | 20-Nov-04 | Argentina | Int | H | Stade Vélodrome, Marseille | L | 14-24 |
| 593 | 27-Nov-04 | New Zealand | DGT | H | Stade de France, Paris | L | 6-45 |
| 594 | 5-Feb-05 | Scotland | 6N | H | Stade de France, Paris | W | 16-9 |
| 595 | 13-Feb-05 | England | 6N | A | Twickenham, London | W | 18-17 |
| 596 | 26-Feb-05 | Wales | 6N | H | Stade de France, Paris | L | 18-24 |
| 597 | 12-Mar-05 | Ireland | 6N | A | Lansdowne Road, Dublin | W | 26-19 |
| 598 | 19-Mar-05 | Italy | 6N | A | Stadio Flaminio, Rome | W | 56-13 |
| 599 | 18-Jun-05 | South Africa | Int-T | A | The ABSA Stadium, Durban | D | 30-30 |
| 600 | 25-Jun-05 | South Africa | Int-T | A | EPRFU Stadium, Port Elizabeth | L | 13-27 |

# FRANCE

| No | Date | Opponents | Tmt | Match Venue | | Result |
|-----|-----------|-------------|--------|--------------------------------------|---|--------|
| 601 | 2-Jul-05 | Australia | BIC-T | A Suncorp Stadium, Brisbane | L | 31-37 |
| 602 | 5-Nov-05 | Australia | BIC | H Stade Vélodrome, Marseille | W | 26-16 |
| 603 | 12-Nov-05 | Canada | Int | H Stade de la Beaujoire, Nantes | W | 50-6 |
| 604 | 19-Nov-05 | Tonga | Int | H Stade Municipal de Toulouse, Toulouse | W | 43-8 |
| 605 | 26-Nov-05 | South Africa | Int | H Stade de France, Paris | W | 26-20 |
| 606 | 5-Feb-06 | Scotland | 6N | A Murrayfield, Edinburgh | L | 16-20 |
| 607 | 11-Feb-06 | Ireland | 6N | H Stade de France, Paris | W | 43-31 |
| 608 | 25-Feb-06 | Italy | 6N | H Stade de France, Paris | W | 37-12 |
| 609 | 12-Mar-06 | England | 6N | H Stade de France, Paris | W | 31-6 |
| 610 | 18-Mar-06 | Wales | 6N | A Millennium Stadium, Cardiff | W | 21-16 |
| 611 | 17-Jun-06 | Romania | Int | A Stadionul Cotroceni, Bucharest | W | 62-14 |
| 612 | 24-Jun-06 | South Africa | Int-T | A Newlands Stadium, Cape Town | W | 36-26 |
| 613 | 11-Nov-06 | New Zealand | DGT | H Stade de Gerland, Lyon | L | 3-47 |
| 614 | 18-Nov-06 | New Zealand | Int | H Stade de France, Paris | L | 11-23 |
| 615 | 25-Nov-06 | Argentina | Int | H Stade de France, Paris | W | 27-26 |
| 616 | 3-Feb-07 | Italy | 6N-GG | A Stadio Flaminio, Rome | W | 39-3 |
| 617 | 11-Feb-07 | Ireland | 6N | A Croke Park, Dublin | W | 20-17 |
| 618 | 24-Feb-07 | Wales | 6N | H Stade de France, Paris | W | 32-21 |
| 619 | 11-Mar-07 | England | 6N | A Twickenham, London | L | 18-26 |
| 620 | 17-Mar-07 | Scotland | 6N | H Stade de France, Paris | W | 46-19 |
| 621 | 2-Jun-07 | New Zealand | DGT-T | A Eden Park, Auckland | L | 11-42 |
| 622 | 9-Jun-07 | New Zealand | Int-T | A Westpac Stadium, Wellington | L | 10-61 |
| 623 | 11-Aug-07 | England | Int | A Twickenham, London | W | 21-15 |
| 624 | 18-Aug-07 | England | Int | H Stade Vélodrome, Marseille | W | 22-9 |
| 625 | 26-Aug-07 | Wales | Int | A Millennium Stadium, Cardiff | W | 34-7 |
| 626 | 7-Sep-07 | Argentina | WCp | H Stade de France, Paris | L | 12-17 |
| 627 | 16-Sep-07 | Namibia | WCp | H Stade Municipal de Toulouse, Toulouse | W | 87-10 |
| 628 | 21-Sep-07 | Ireland | WCp | H Stade de France, Paris | W | 25-3 |
| 629 | 30-Sep-07 | Georgia | WCp | H Stade Vélodrome, Marseille | W | 64-7 |
| 630 | 6-Oct-07 | New Zealand | WCqf | N Millennium Stadium, Cardiff | W | 20-18 |
| 631 | 13-Oct-07 | England | WCsf | H Stade de France, Paris | L | 9-14 |
| 632 | 19-Oct-07 | Argentina | WC34 | H Parc des Princess, Paris | L | 10-34 |
| 633 | 3-Feb-08 | Scotland | 6N | A Murrayfield, Edinburgh | W | 27-6 |
| 634 | 9-Feb-08 | Ireland | 6N | H Stade de France, Paris | W | 26-21 |
| 635 | 23-Feb-08 | England | 6N | H Stade de France, Paris | L | 13-24 |
| 636 | 9-Mar-08 | Italy | 6N-GG | H Stade de France, Paris | W | 25-13 |
| 637 | 15-Mar-08 | Wales | 6N | A Millennium Stadium, Cardiff | L | 12-29 |
| 638 | 28-Jun-08 | Australia | BIC-T | A ANZ Stadium, Sydney | L | 13-34 |
| 639 | 5-Jul-08 | Australia | BIC-T | A Suncorp Stadium, Brisbane | L | 10-40 |
| 640 | 8-Nov-08 | Argentina | Int | H Stade Vélodrome, Marseille | W | 12-6 |

81

| No | Date | Opponents | Tmt | | Match Venue | Result | |
|----|------|-----------|-----|---|-------------|--------|---|
| 641 | 15-Nov-08 | Pacific Islands | Int | H | Stade Auguste Bonal, Montbéliard | W | 42-17 |
| 642 | 22-Nov-08 | Australia | BIC | H | Stade de France, Paris | L | 13-18 |
| 643 | 7-Feb-09 | Ireland | 6N | A | Croke Park, Dublin | L | 21-30 |
| 644 | 14-Feb-09 | Scotland | 6N | H | Stade de France, Paris | W | 22-13 |
| 645 | 27-Feb-09 | Wales | 6N | H | Stade de France, Paris | W | 21-16 |
| 646 | 15-Mar-09 | England | 6N | A | Twickenham, London | L | 10-34 |
| 647 | 21-Mar-09 | Italy | 6N-GG | A | Stadio Flaminio, Rome | W | 50-8 |
| 648 | 13-Jun-09 | New Zealand | DGT-T | A | Carisbrook, Dunedin | W | 27-22 |
| 649 | 20-Jun-09 | New Zealand | DGT-T | A | Westpac Stadium, Wellington | L | 10-14 |
| 650 | 27-Jun-09 | Australia | BIC-T | A | ANZ Stadium, Sydney | L | 6-22 |
| 651 | 13-Nov-09 | South Africa | Int | H | Stade Municipal de Toulouse, Toulouse | W | 20-13 |
| 652 | 21-Nov-09 | Samoa | Int | H | Stade de France, Paris | W | 43-5 |
| 653 | 28-Nov-09 | New Zealand | DGT | H | Stade Vélodrome, Marseille | L | 12-39 |
| 654 | 7-Feb-10 | Scotland | 6N | A | Murrayfield, Edinburgh | W | 18-9 |
| 655 | 13-Feb-10 | Ireland | 6N | H | Stade de France, Paris | W | 33-10 |
| 656 | 26-Feb-10 | Wales | 6N | A | Millennium Stadium, Cardiff | W | 26-20 |
| 657 | 14-Mar-10 | Italy | 6N-GG | H | Stade de France, Paris | W | 46-20 |
| 658 | 20-Mar-10 | England | 6N | H | Stade de France, Paris | W | 12-10 |
| 659 | 12-Jun-10 | South Africa | Int-T | A | Newlands Stadium, Cape Town | L | 17-42 |
| 660 | 26-Jun-10 | Argentina | Int | A | Vélez Sarsfield Stadium, Buenos Aires | L | 13-41 |
| 661 | 13-Nov-10 | Fiji | Int-T | H | Stade de la Beaujoire, Nantes | W | 34-12 |
| 662 | 20-Nov-10 | Argentina | Int | H | Stade de la Mosson, Montpellier | W | 15-9 |
| 663 | 27-Nov-10 | Australia | BIC | H | Stade de France, Paris | L | 16-59 |
| 664 | 5-Feb-11 | Scotland | 6N | H | Stade de France, Paris | W | 34-21 |
| 665 | 13-Feb-11 | Ireland | 6N | A | Aviva Stadium, Dublin | W | 25-22 |
| 666 | 26-Feb-11 | England | 6N | A | Twickenham, London | L | 9-17 |
| 667 | 12-Mar-11 | Italy | 6N-GG | A | Stadio Flaminio, Rome | L | 21-22 |
| 668 | 19-Mar-11 | Wales | 6N | H | Stade de France, Paris | W | 28-9 |
| 669 | 13-Aug-11 | Ireland | Int | H | Stade Chaban-Delmas, Bordeaux | W | 19-12 |
| 670 | 20-Aug-11 | Ireland | Int | A | Aviva Stadium, Dublin | W | 26-22 |
| 671 | 10-Sep-11 | Japan | WCp | N | North Harbour Stadium, Albany | W | 47-21 |
| 672 | 18-Sep-11 | Canada | WCp | N | McLean Park, Napier | W | 46-19 |
| 673 | 24-Sep-11 | New Zealand | WCp | A | Eden Park, Auckland | L | 17-37 |
| 674 | 1-Oct-11 | Tonga | WCp | N | Wellington Regional Stadium, Wellington | L | 14-19 |
| 675 | 8-Oct-11 | England | WCqf | N | Eden Park, Auckland | W | 19-12 |
| 676 | 15-Oct-11 | Wales | WCsf | N | Eden Park, Auckland | W | 9-8 |
| 677 | 21-Oct-11 | New Zealand | WCf | A | Eden Park, Auckland | L | 7-8 |
| 678 | 4-Feb-12 | Italy | 6N-GG | H | Stade de France, Paris | W | 30-12 |
| 679 | 26-Feb-12 | Scotland | 6N | A | Murrayfield, Edinburgh | W | 23-17 |
| 680 | 4-Mar-12 | Ireland | 6N | H | Stade de France, Paris | D | 17-17 |

| No | Date | Opponents | Tmt | | Match Venue | | Result |
|----|------|-----------|-----|---|-------------|---|--------|
| 681 | 11-Mar-12 | England | 6N | H | Stade de France, Paris | L | 22-24 |
| 682 | 17-Mar- | Wales | 6N | A | Millennium Stadium, Cardiff | L | 9-16 |
| 683 | 1216-Jun-12 | Argentina | Int-T | A | Estadio Olimpico Château Carreras,Córdoba | L | 20-23 |
| 684 | 23-Jun-12 | Argentina | Int-T | A | Estadio Monumental José Fierro, Tucumán | W | 49-10 |
| 685 | 10-Nov-12 | Australia | BIC | H | Stade de France, Paris | W | 33-6 |
| 686 | 17-Nov-12 | Argentina | Int | H | Grand Stade, Lille Métropole | W | 39-22 |
| 687 | 24-Nov-12 | Samoa | Int | H | Stade de France, Paris | W | 22-14 |
| 688 | 3-Feb-13 | Italy | 6N-GG | A | Stadio Olimpico, Rome | L | 18-23 |
| 689 | 9-Feb-13 | Wales | 6N | H | Stade de France, Paris | L | 6-16 |
| 690 | 23-Feb-13 | England | 6N | A | Twickenham, London | L | 13-23 |
| 691 | 9-Mar-13 | Ireland | 6N | A | Aviva Stadium, Dublin | D | 13-13 |
| 692 | 16-Mar-13 | Scotland | 6N | H | Stade de France, Paris | W | 23-16 |
| 693 | 8-Jun-13 | New Zealand | DGT-T | A | Eden Park, Auckland | L | 13-23 |
| 694 | 15-Jun-13 | New Zealand | DGT-T | A | AMI Stadium, Addington | L | 0-30 |
| 695 | 22-Jun-13 | New Zealand | DGT-T | A | Yarrow Stadium, New Plymouth | L | 9-24 |
| 696 | 9-Nov-13 | New Zealand | DGT | H | Stade de France, Paris | L | 19-26 |
| 697 | 16-Nov-13 | Tonga | Int | H | Stade Océane, Le Havre | W | 38-18 |
| 698 | 23-Nov-13 | South Africa | Int | H | Stade de France, Paris | L | 10-19 |
| 699 | 1-Feb-14 | England | 6N | H | Stade de France, Paris | W | 26-24 |
| 700 | 9-Feb-14 | Italy | 6N-GG | H | Stade de France, Paris | W | 30-10 |
| 701 | 21-Feb-14 | Wales | 6N | A | Millennium Stadium, Cardiff | L | 6-27 |
| 702 | 8-Mar-14 | Scotland | 6N | A | Murrayfield, Edinburgh | W | 19-17 |
| 703 | 15-Mar-14 | Ireland | 6N | H | Stade de France, Paris | L | 20-22 |
| 704 | 7-Jun-14 | Australia | BIC-T | A | Suncorp Stadium, Brisbane | L | 23-50 |
| 705 | 14-Jun-14 | Australia | BIC-T | A | Etihad Stadium, Docklands, Melbourne | L | 0-6 |
| 706 | 21-Jun-14 | Australia | BIC-T | A | Football Stadium, Sydney | L | 13-39 |
| 707 | 8-Nov-14 | Fiji | Int | H | Stade Vélodrome, Marseille | W | 40-15 |
| 708 | 15-Nov-14 | Australia | BIC | H | Stade de France, Paris | W | 29-26 |
| 709 | 22-Nov-14 | Argentina | Int | H | Stade de France, Paris | L | 13-18 |
| 710 | 7-Feb-15 | Scotland | 6N | H | Stade de France, Paris | W | 15-8 |
| 711 | 14-Feb-15 | Ireland | 6N | A | Aviva Stadium, Dublin | L | 11-18 |
| 712 | 28-Feb-15 | Wales | 6N | H | Stade de France, Paris | L | 13-20 |
| 713 | 15-Mar-15 | Italy | 6N-GG | A | Stadio Olimpico, Rome | W | 29-0 |
| 714 | 21-Mar-15 | England | 6N | A | Twickenham, London | L | 35-55 |
| 715 | 15-Aug-15 | England | Int | A | Twickenham, London | L | 14-19 |
| 716 | 22-Aug-15 | England | Int | H | Stade de France, Paris | W | 25-20 |
| 717 | 5-Sep-15 | Scotland | Int | H | Stade de France, Paris | W | 19-16 |
| 718 | 19-Sep-15 | Italy | WCp | N | Twickenham, London | W | 32-10 |
| 719 | 23-Sep-15 | Romania | WCp | N | Olympic Stadium, London | W | 38-11 |
| 720 | 1-Oct-15 | Canada | WCp | N | Stadium MK, Milton Keynes | W | 41-18 |

| | Date | Opponents | Tmt | | Match Venue | Result | |
|---|---|---|---|---|---|---|---|
| **721** | 11-Oct-15 | Ireland | WCp | N | Millennium Stadium, Cardiff | L | 9-24 |
| **722** | 17-Oct-15 | New Zealand | WCqf | N | Millennium Stadium, Cardiff | L | 13-62 |

# IRELAND

The Irish Rugby Football Union, formed in 1874, resulted from the unification of the Irish Football Union and the North of Ireland Union. A year later, the Irish played their first International match against England at the Kennington Oval in London, which they lost by seven points to nil. The next nine matches also ended in defeat for the Irish, and even after forty-four games, to the end of the 1893 season, the men in green had won only five times. There was, however, a dramatic turnaround in 1894 when Ireland won its first Triple Crown by defeating the other three Home Nations. The achievement was repeated five years later, in 1899.

Apart from winning the Four Nations Championship in 1935, and only sharing the title six times, the Irish team's performance was very mediocre during the first forty-seven years of the twentieth century. In that lean period the Irish also lost all seven matches against the three touring Southern Hemisphere teams, losing once to Australia and three times to both New Zealand and South Africa. The tide then changed, and the four seasons from 1948 to 1951 turned out to be very successful for the Irish team. In 1948 they won their first Grand Slam and followed it with a third Triple Crown in 1949. A loss in Paris that year prevented Ireland from winning back-to-back Grand Slams, and a draw in Cardiff in 1951 also denied the Irish a second Grand Slam.

In 1958 Ireland secured their first win over Southern Hemisphere opposition when they defeated Australia by 9 points to 6, but losses to the other two touring sides continued when they were beaten twice by New Zealand and three times by South Africa between 1951 and 1963. The third of those defeats by the

Springboks took place in Cape Town on Ireland's first tour to the Southern Hemisphere.

During the same period, the Irish performed miserably in the Five Nations Championship, gaining only the occasional win each year and suffering some indignity in 1960 when they lost all four Championship matches. Things improved in 1965 when the Irish team narrowly lost a Triple Crown decider to Wales in Cardiff in March, having drawn with France in Dublin earlier in the campaign. They defeated South Africa for the first time at Lansdowne Road, a month later, in April.

In January 1967, Ireland defeated Australia, again at Lansdowne Road, and four months later became the first Home Nations team to win in the Southern Hemisphere, when they beat Australia at the Cricket Ground in Sydney. The following year was also a good one for Ireland with just one defeat in the Five Nations and a fourth successive win, on home ground, against the Wallabies in October. In 1969 Ireland won in Paris for the first time in ten years but were denied a Grand Slam in Cardiff in the final game of the Championship. Three years later, in 1972, they missed an opportunity of a Grand Slam yet again, when, having won both their away games, the Five Nations Championship was not completed owing to unrest in Northern Ireland (both Scotland and Wales refused to travel to Dublin for security reasons).

A Championship title in 1974 was followed by a series of poor Irish performances to the end of 1978 when they mustered only four wins in twenty-one matches. Things improved for the team on their tour to Australia in June 1979, when they defeated the home side in both Internationals, staged in Brisbane and Sydney.

In 1982 Ireland won the Triple Crown for the first time in thirty-three years, a feat they repeated in 1985 (on that occasion a draw against France denied them that elusive second Grand Slam). Following losses to Australia at the quarter-final stage in both the 1987 and the 1991 World Cup, Ireland's performances throughout the 1990s were disappointing, especially during the period from 1996 to 1998 when the Irish team managed just six wins in twenty-four matches, with four of these being against the weaker Tier 2/3 sides namely Canada, Georgia, Romania and the United States.

The new millennium, however, hailed a marked improvement for the Irish, especially during the period 2004 to 2007, when they won three Triple Crowns. This success gave the whole of Ireland high expectations for the 2007 World Cup, but unfortunately hopes were dashed when the team was eliminated at the pool stage by Argentina and France. Two years later, in 2009, the Irish rallied and that elusive second Grand Slam was finally won, bridging a sixty-one-year gap since their only other success in 1948.

The success continued into the autumn of that year with a drawn game against Australia and a win against South Africa, but 2010 proved to be less fruitful when Ireland managed only five wins in eleven matches.

Three wins from five in the 2011 Six Nations Championship and four defeats in the August warm-up games did not inspire much confidence as the team prepared for the World Cup in New Zealand later that year, but the team rose to the occasion and fully deserved their win against Australia to top their pool. Unfortunately, high expectations were dashed yet again when they were beaten three weeks later by an inspired Welsh team in the quarter-final.

A mediocre period followed with only three wins from ten matches in 2012 and four wins from ten games in 2013. Fortunes, however, changed in the 2014 Six Nations Championship when the Irish claimed their first title, apart from the 2009 Grand Slam, since 1985. The good form continued on their Argentinian tour in June with a 2-0 series win over the host nation, and it reached a peak during the autumn Internationals when Ireland defeated both South Africa and Australia. Ireland had thus achieved a remarkable record of nine wins from ten matches in 2014, which included seven in a row. By winning the first three matches in the 2015 Six Nations Championship, the Irish had now achieved ten consecutive wins. The run came to an end when they lost to Wales in the fourth game of the Championship, but in winning the fifth match against Scotland, Ireland claimed the title, on points difference, from both England and Wales for the second successive year.

Ireland finished top of their pool in the 2015 Rugby World Cup, winning all four matches. It was a different story in the quarter-final however, when they were well beaten by an inspired Argentinian side who won by 43 points to 20.

# IRELAND

## HEAD TO HEAD RESULTS TO 31 OCTOBER 2015

|                        | P   | W   | D  | L   | %     | F    | A    |
|------------------------|-----|-----|----|-----|-------|------|------|
| **v TIER 1 Teams**     |     |     |    |     |       |      |      |
| v Argentina            | 16  | 10  | 0  | 6   | 62.5  | 351  | 326  |
| v Australia            | 32  | 10  | 1  | 21  | 32.8  | 453  | 657  |
| v England *            | 130 | 47  | 8  | 75  | 39.2  | 1069 | 1505 |
| v France               | 94  | 32  | 7  | 55  | 37.8  | 1108 | 1517 |
| v Italy                | 25  | 21  | 0  | 4   | 84.0  | 788  | 391  |
| v New Zealand          | 28  | 0   | 1  | 27  | 1.8   | 310  | 812  |
| v Scotland * / **      | 131 | 60  | 5  | 65  | 48.1  | 1440 | 1355 |
| v South Africa         | 22  | 5   | 1  | 16  | 25.0  | 277  | 432  |
| v Wales *              | 123 | 50  | 6  | 67  | 43.1  | 1365 | 1461 |
| **Sub-Total**          | **601** | **235** | **29** | **336** | **41.6** | **7161** | **8456** |
| **v TIER 2/3 Group**   |     |     |    |     |       |      |      |
| v Canada               | 7   | 6   | 1  | 0   | 92.9  | 276  | 84   |
| v Fiji                 | 3   | 3   | 0  | 0   | 100.0 | 149  | 31   |
| v Japan                | 5   | 5   | 0  | 0   | 100.0 | 251  | 83   |
| v Romania              | 9   | 9   | 0  | 0   | 100.0 | 390  | 102  |
| v Samoa                | 6   | 5   | 0  | 1   | 83.3  | 209  | 103  |
| v Tonga                | 2   | 2   | 0  | 0   | 100.0 | 72   | 28   |
| v United States        | 8   | 8   | 0  | 0   | 100.0 | 306  | 82   |
| v Georgia              | 4   | 4   | 0  | 0   | 100.0 | 196  | 31   |
| v Namibia              | 4   | 2   | 0  | 2   | 50.00 | 117  | 65   |
| v Russia               | 2   | 2   | 0  | 0   | 100.0 | 97   | 15   |
| v Uruguay              | 0   | 0   | 0  | 0   | 0.0   | 0    | 0    |
| **Sub-Total**          | **50** | **46** | **1** | **3** | **93.0** | **2063** | **624** |
| **v Other Teams**      |     |     |    |     |       |      |      |
| v Zimbabwe             | 1   | 1   | 0  | 0   | 100.0 | 55   | 11   |
| v New Zealand Natives *| 1   | 0   | 0  | 1   | 0.0   | -    | -    |
| v Pacific Islanders    | 1   | 1   | 0  | 0   | 100.0 | 61   | 17   |
| v President's XV       | 1   | 0   | 1  | 0   | 50.0  | 18   | 18   |
| **Sub-Total**          | **4** | **2** | **1** | **1** | **62.5** | **134** | **46** |
| **All Internationals** | **655** | **283** | **31** | **340** | **45.6** | **9358** | **9126** |

* excludes points scored before the introduction of the modern points system
** excludes the abandoned match on 21 February 1885 (Ireland 0 Scotland 1)

| No | Date | Opponents | Tmt | | Match Venue | Result | |
|----|------|-----------|-----|---|-------------|--------|---|
| 1 | 15-Feb-75 | England | Int | A | Kennington Oval, London | L | 0-7 |
| 2 | 13-Dec-75 | England | Int | H | Leinster CC, Rathmines, Dublin | L | 0-4 |
| 3 | 5-Feb-77 | England | Int | A | Kennington Oval, London | L | 0-8 |
| 4 | 19-Feb-77 | Scotland | Int | H | Ormeau, Belfast | L | 0-20 |
| 5 | 11-Mar-78 | England | Int | H | Lansdowne Road, Dublin | L | 0-7 |
| 6 | 17-Feb-79 | Scotland | Int | H | Ormeau, Belfast | L | 0-7 |
| 7 | 24-Mar-79 | England | Int | A | Kennington Oval, London | L | 0-11 |
| 8 | 30-Jan-80 | England | Int | H | Lansdowne Road, Dublin | L | 1-4 |
| 9 | 14-Feb-80 | Scotland | Int | A | Hamilton Crescent, Glasgow | L | 0-11 |
| 10 | 5-Feb-81 | England | Int | A | Whalley Range, Manchester | L | 0-8 |
| 11 | 19-Feb-81 | Scotland | Int | H | Ormeau, Belfast | W | 3-1 |
| 12 | 28-Jan-82 | Wales | Int | H | Lansdowne Road, Dublin | L | 0-8 |
| 13 | 6-Feb-82 | England | Int | H | Lansdowne Road, Dublin | D | 2-2 |
| 14 | 18-Feb-82 | Scotland | Int | A | Hamilton Crescent, Glasgow | L | 0-2 |
| 15 | 5-Feb-83 | England | 4N | A | Whalley Range, Manchester | L | 1-6 |
| 16 | 17-Feb-83 | Scotland | 4N | H | Ormeau, Belfast | L | 0-4 |
| 17 | 4-Feb-84 | England | 4N | H | Lansdowne Road, Dublin | L | 0-3 |
| 18 | 16-Feb-84 | Scotland | 4N | A | Raeburn Place, Edinburgh | L | 1-8 |
| 19 | 12-Apr-84 | Wales | 4N | A | Arms Park, Cardiff | L | 0-5 |
| 20 | 7-Feb-85 | England | 4N | A | Whalley Range, Manchester | L | 1-2 |
| 21 | 21-Feb-85 | Scotland | 4N | H | Ormeau, Belfast (abandoned) | A | 0-1 |
| 22 | 7-Mar-85 | Scotland | 4N | A | Raeburn Place, Edinburgh | L | 0-5 |
| 23 | 6-Feb-86 | England | 4N | H | Lansdowne Road, Dublin | L | 0-1 |
| 24 | 20-Feb-86 | Scotland | 4N | A | Raeburn Place, Edinburgh | L | 0-14 |
| 25 | 5-Feb-87 | England | 4N | H | Lansdowne Road, Dublin | W | 6-0 |
| 26 | 19-Feb-87 | Scotland | 4N | H | Ormeau, Belfast | L | 0-8 |
| 27 | 12-Mar-87 | Wales | 4N | N | Upper Park, Birkenhead Park | L | 3-4 |
| 28 | 3-Mar-88 | Wales | 4N | H | Lansdowne Road, Dublin | W | 7-0 |
| 29 | 10-Mar-88 | Scotland | 4N | A | Raeburn Place, Edinburgh | L | 0-3 |
| 30 | 1-Dec-88 | N Z Natives | Int | H | Lansdowne Road, Dublin | L | 4-13 |
| 31 | 16-Feb-89 | Scotland | 4N | H | Ormeau, Belfast | L | 0-3 |
| 32 | 2-Mar-89 | Wales | 4N | A | St Helen's, Swansea | W | 2-0 |
| 33 | 22-Feb-90 | Scotland | 4N | A | Raeburn Place, Edinburgh | L | 0-5 |
| 34 | 1-Mar-90 | Wales | 4N | H | Lansdowne Road, Dublin | D | 3-3 |
| 35 | 15-Mar-90 | England | 4N | A | Rectory Field, Blackheath | L | 0-3 |
| 36 | 7-Feb-91 | England | 4N | H | Lansdowne Road, Dublin | L | 0-9 |
| 37 | 21-Feb-91 | Scotland | 4N | H | Ballynafeigh, Belfast | L | 0-14 |
| 38 | 7-Mar-91 | Wales | 4N | A | Stradey Park, Llanelli | L | 4-6 |
| 39 | 6-Feb-92 | England | 4N | A | Whalley Range, Manchester | L | 0-7 |
| 40 | 20-Feb-92 | Scotland | 4N | A | Raeburn Place, Edinburgh | L | 0-2 |

| No | Date | Opponents | Tmt | Match Venue | Result | |
|----|------|-----------|-----|-------------|--------|---|
| 41 | 5-Mar-92 | Wales | 4N | H Lansdowne Road, Dublin | W | 9-0 |
| 42 | 4-Feb-93 | England | 4N | H Lansdowne Road, Dublin | L | 0-4 |
| 43 | 18-Feb-93 | Scotland | 4N | H Ballynafeigh, Belfast | D | 0-0 |
| 44 | 11-Mar-93 | Wales | 4N | A Stradey Park, Llanelli | L | 0-2 |
| 45 | 3-Feb-94 | England | 4N | A Rectory Field, Blackheath | W | 7-5 |
| 46 | 24-Feb-94 | Scotland | 4N | H Lansdowne Road, Dublin | W | 5-0 |
| 47 | 10-Mar-94 | Wales | 4N | H Ballynafeigh, Belfast | W | 3-0 |
| 48 | 2-Feb-95 | England | 4N | H Lansdowne Road, Dublin | L | 3-6 |
| 49 | 2-Mar-95 | Scotland | 4N | A Raeburn Place, Edinburgh | L | 0-6 |
| 50 | 16-Mar-95 | Wales | 4N | A Arms Park, Cardiff | L | 3-5 |
| 51 | 1-Feb-96 | England | 4N | A Meanwood Road, Leeds | W | 10-4 |
| 52 | 15-Feb-96 | Scotland | 4N | H Lansdowne Road, Dublin | D | 0-0 |
| 53 | 14-Mar-96 | Wales | 4N | H Lansdowne Road, Dublin | W | 8-4 |
| 54 | 6-Feb-97 | England | 4N | H Lansdowne Road, Dublin | W | 13-9 |
| 55 | 20-Feb-97 | Scotland | 4N | A Powderhall, Edinburgh | L | 3-8 |
| 56 | 5-Feb-98 | England | 4N | A Athletic Ground, Richmond | W | 9-6 |
| 57 | 19-Feb-98 | Scotland | 4N | H Balmoral Showgrounds, Belfast | L | 0-8 |
| 58 | 19-Mar-98 | Wales | 4N | H Thomond Park, Limerick | L | 3-11 |
| 59 | 4-Feb-99 | England | 4N | H Lansdowne Road, Dublin | W | 6-0 |
| 60 | 18-Feb-99 | Scotland | 4N | A Inverleith, Edinburgh | W | 9-3 |
| 61 | 18-Mar-99 | Wales | 4N | A Arms Park, Cardiff | W | 3-0 |
| 62 | 3-Feb-00 | England | 4N | A Athletic Ground, Richmond | L | 4-15 |
| 63 | 24-Feb-00 | Scotland | 4N | H Lansdowne Road, Dublin | D | 0-0 |
| 64 | 17-Mar-00 | Wales | 4N | H Balmoral Showgrounds, Belfast | L | 0-3 |
| 65 | 9-Feb-01 | England | 4N | H Lansdowne Road, Dublin | W | 10-6 |
| 66 | 23-Feb-01 | Scotland | 4N | A Inverleith, Edinburgh | L | 5-9 |
| 67 | 16-Mar-01 | Wales | 4N | A St Helen's, Swansea | L | 9-10 |
| 68 | 8-Feb-02 | England | 4N | A Welford Road, Leicester | L | 3-6 |
| 69 | 22-Feb-02 | Scotland | 4N | H Balmoral Showgrounds, Belfast | W | 5-0 |
| 70 | 8-Mar-02 | Wales | 4N | H Lansdowne Road, Dublin | L | 0-15 |
| 71 | 14-Feb-03 | England | 4N | H Lansdowne Road, Dublin | W | 6-0 |
| 72 | 28-Feb-03 | Scotland | 4N | A Inverleith, Edinburgh | L | 0-3 |
| 73 | 14-Mar-03 | Wales | 4N | A Arms Park, Cardiff | L | 0-18 |
| 74 | 13-Feb-04 | England | 4N | A Rectory Field, Blackheath | L | 0-19 |
| 75 | 27-Feb-04 | Scotland | 4N | H Lansdowne Road, Dublin | L | 3-19 |
| 76 | 12-Mar-04 | Wales | 4N | H Balmoral Showgrounds, Belfast | W | 14-12 |
| 77 | 11-Feb-05 | England | 4N | H Mardyke, Cork | W | 17-3 |
| 78 | 25-Feb-05 | Scotland | 4N | A Inverleith, Edinburgh | W | 11-5 |
| 79 | 11-Mar-05 | Wales | 4N | A St Helen's, Swansea | L | 3-10 |
| 80 | 25-Nov-05 | New Zealand | Int | H Lansdowne Road, Dublin | L | 0-15 |

| No | Date | Opponents | Tmt | | Match Venue | Result | |
|----|------|-----------|-----|---|-------------|--------|---|
| 81 | 10-Feb-06 | England | 4N | A | Welford Road, Leicester | W | 16-6 |
| 82 | 24-Feb-06 | Scotland | 4N | H | Lansdowne Road, Dublin | L | 6-13 |
| 83 | 10-Mar-06 | Wales | 4N | H | Balmoral Showgrounds, Belfast | W | 11-6 |
| 84 | 24-Nov-06 | South Africa | Int | H | Balmoral Showgrounds, Belfast | L | 12-15 |
| 85 | 9-Feb-07 | England | 4N | H | Lansdowne Road, Dublin | W | 17-9 |
| 86 | 23-Feb-07 | Scotland | 4N | A | Inverleith, Edinburgh | L | 3-15 |
| 87 | 9-Mar-07 | Wales | 4N | A | Arms Park, Cardiff | L | 0-29 |
| 88 | 8-Feb-08 | England | 4N | A | Athletic Ground, Richmond | L | 3-13 |
| 89 | 29-Feb-08 | Scotland | 4N | H | Lansdowne Road, Dublin | W | 16-11 |
| 90 | 14-Mar-08 | Wales | 4N | H | Balmoral Showgrounds, Belfast | L | 5-11 |
| 91 | 13-Feb-09 | England | 4N | H | Lansdowne Road, Dublin | L | 5-11 |
| 92 | 27-Feb-09 | Scotland | 4N | A | Inverleith, Edinburgh | L | 3-9 |
| 93 | 13-Mar-09 | Wales | 4N | A | St Helen's, Swansea | L | 5-18 |
| 94 | 20-Mar-09 | France | Int | H | Lansdowne Road, Dublin | W | 19-8 |
| 95 | 12-Feb-10 | England | 5N | A | Twickenham, London | D | 0-0 |
| 96 | 26-Feb-10 | Scotland | 5N | H | Balmoral Showgrounds, Belfast | L | 0-14 |
| 97 | 12-Mar-10 | Wales | 5N | H | Lansdowne Road, Dublin | L | 3-19 |
| 98 | 28-Mar-10 | France | 5N | A | Parc des Princess, Paris | W | 8-3 |
| 99 | 11-Feb-11 | England | 5N | H | Lansdowne Road, Dublin | W | 3-0 |
| 100 | 25-Feb-11 | Scotland | 5N | A | Inverleith, Edinburgh | W | 16-10 |
| 101 | 11-Mar-11 | Wales | 5N | A | Arms Park, Cardiff | L | 0-16 |
| 102 | 25-Mar-11 | France | 5N | H | Mardyke, Cork | W | 25-5 |
| 103 | 1-Jan-12 | France | 5N | A | Parc des Princess, Paris | W | 11-6 |
| 104 | 10-Feb-12 | England | 5N | A | Twickenham, London | L | 0-15 |
| 105 | 24-Feb-12 | Scotland | 5N | H | Lansdowne Road, Dublin | W | 10-8 |
| 106 | 9-Mar-12 | Wales | 5N | H | Balmoral Showgrounds, Belfast | W | 12-5 |
| 107 | 30-Nov-12 | South Africa | Int | H | Lansdowne Road, Dublin | L | 0-38 |
| 108 | 8-Feb-13 | England | 5N | H | Lansdowne Road, Dublin | L | 4-15 |
| 109 | 22-Feb-13 | Scotland | 5N | A | Inverleith, Edinburgh | L | 14-29 |
| 110 | 8-Mar-13 | Wales | 5N | A | St Helen's, Swansea | L | 13-16 |
| 111 | 24-Mar-13 | France | 5N | H | Mardyke, Cork | W | 24-0 |
| 112 | 1-Jan-14 | France | 5N | A | Parc des Princess, Paris | W | 8-6 |
| 113 | 14-Feb-14 | England | 5N | A | Twickenham, London | L | 12-17 |
| 114 | 28-Feb-14 | Scotland | 5N | H | Lansdowne Road, Dublin | W | 6-0 |
| 115 | 14-Mar-14 | Wales | 5N | H | Balmoral Showgrounds, Belfast | L | 3-11 |
| 116 | 14-Feb-20 | England | 5N | H | Lansdowne Road, Dublin | L | 11-14 |
| 117 | 28-Feb-20 | Scotland | 5N | A | Inverleith, Edinburgh | L | 0-19 |
| 118 | 13-Mar-20 | Wales | 5N | A | Arms Park, Cardiff | L | 4-28 |
| 119 | 3-Apr-20 | France | 5N | H | Lansdowne Road, Dublin | L | 7-15 |
| 120 | 12-Feb-21 | England | 5N | A | Twickenham, London | L | 0-15 |

| No | Date | Opponents | Tmt | Match Venue | Result | |
|----|------|-----------|-----|-------------|--------|---|
| 121 | 26-Feb-21 | Scotland | 5N | H Lansdowne Road, Dublin | W | 9-8 |
| 122 | 12-Mar-21 | Wales | 5N | H Balmoral Showgrounds, Belfast | L | 0-6 |
| 123 | 9-Apr-21 | France | 5N | A Stade Colombes, Paris | L | 10-20 |
| 124 | 11-Feb-22 | England | 5N | H Lansdowne Road, Dublin | L | 3-12 |
| 125 | 25-Feb-22 | Scotland | 5N | A Inverleith, Edinburgh | L | 3-6 |
| 126 | 11-Mar-22 | Wales | 5N | A St Helen's, Swansea | L | 5-11 |
| 127 | 8-Apr-22 | France | 5N | H Lansdowne Road, Dublin | W | 8-3 |
| 128 | 10-Feb-23 | England | 5N | A Welford Road, Leicester | L | 5-23 |
| 129 | 24-Feb-23 | Scotland | 5N | H Lansdowne Road, Dublin | L | 3-13 |
| 130 | 10-Mar-23 | Wales | 5N | H Lansdowne Road, Dublin | W | 5-4 |
| 131 | 14-Apr-23 | France | 5N | A Stade Colombes, Paris | L | 8-14 |
| 132 | 26-Jan-24 | France | 5N | H Lansdowne Road, Dublin | W | 6-0 |
| 133 | 9-Feb-24 | England | 5N | H Lansdowne Road, Dublin | L | 3-14 |
| 134 | 23-Feb-24 | Scotland | 5N | A Inverleith, Edinburgh | L | 8-13 |
| 135 | 8-Mar-24 | Wales | 5N | A Arms Park, Cardiff | W | 13-10 |
| 136 | 1-Nov-24 | New Zealand | Int | H Lansdowne Road, Dublin | L | 0-6 |
| 137 | 1-Jan-25 | France | 5N | A Stade Colombes, Paris | W | 9-3 |
| 138 | 14-Feb-25 | England | 5N | A Twickenham, London | D | 6-6 |
| 139 | 28-Feb-25 | Scotland | 5N | H Lansdowne Road, Dublin | L | 8-14 |
| 140 | 14-Mar-25 | Wales | 5N | H Ravenhill, Belfast | W | 19-3 |
| 141 | 23-Jan-26 | France | 5N | H Ravenhill, Belfast | W | 11-0 |
| 142 | 13-Feb-26 | England | 5N | H Lansdowne Road, Dublin | W | 19-15 |
| 143 | 27-Feb-26 | Scotland | 5N | A Murrayfield, Edinburgh | W | 3-0 |
| 144 | 13-Mar-26 | Wales | 5N | A St Helen's, Swansea | L | 8-11 |
| 145 | 1-Jan-27 | France | 5N | A Stade Colombes, Paris | W | 8-3 |
| 146 | 12-Feb-27 | England | 5N | A Twickenham, London | L | 6-8 |
| 147 | 26-Feb-27 | Scotland | 5N | H Lansdowne Road, Dublin | W | 6-0 |
| 148 | 12-Mar-27 | Wales | 5N | H Lansdowne Road, Dublin | W | 19-9 |
| 149 | 12-Nov-27 | Australia | Int | H Lansdowne Road, Dublin | L | 3-5 |
| 150 | 28-Jan-28 | France | 5N | H Ravenhill, Belfast | W | 12-8 |
| 151 | 11-Feb-28 | England | 5N | H Lansdowne Road, Dublin | L | 6-7 |
| 152 | 25-Feb-28 | Scotland | 5N | A Murrayfield, Edinburgh | W | 13-5 |
| 153 | 10-Mar-28 | Wales | 5N | A Arms Park, Cardiff | W | 13-10 |
| 154 | 31-Dec-28 | France | 5N | A Stade Colombes, Paris | W | 6-0 |
| 155 | 9-Feb-29 | England | 5N | A Twickenham, London | W | 6-5 |
| 156 | 23-Feb-29 | Scotland | 5N | H Lansdowne Road, Dublin | L | 7-16 |
| 157 | 9-Mar-29 | Wales | 5N | H Ravenhill, Belfast | D | 5-5 |
| 158 | 25-Jan-30 | France | 5N | H Ravenhill, Belfast | L | 0-5 |
| 159 | 8-Feb-30 | England | 5N | H Lansdowne Road, Dublin | W | 4-3 |
| 160 | 22-Feb-30 | Scotland | 5N | A Murrayfield, Edinburgh | W | 14-11 |

| No | Date | Opponents | Tmt | | Match Venue | Result | |
|---|---|---|---|---|---|---|---|
| 161 | 8-Mar-30 | Wales | 5N | A | St Helen's, Swansea | L | 7-12 |
| 162 | 1-Jan-31 | France | 5N | A | Stade Colombes, Paris | L | 0-3 |
| 163 | 14-Feb-31 | England | 5N | A | Twickenham, London | W | 6-5 |
| 164 | 28-Feb-31 | Scotland | 5N | H | Lansdowne Road, Dublin | W | 8-5 |
| 165 | 14-Mar-31 | Wales | 5N | H | Ravenhill, Belfast | L | 3-15 |
| 166 | 19-Dec-31 | South Africa | Int | H | Lansdowne Road, Dublin | L | 3-8 |
| 167 | 13-Feb-32 | England | 4N | H | Lansdowne Road, Dublin | L | 8-11 |
| 168 | 27-Feb-32 | Scotland | 4N | A | Murrayfield, Edinburgh | W | 20-8 |
| 169 | 12-Mar-32 | Wales | 4N | A | Arms Park, Cardiff | W | 12-10 |
| 170 | 11-Feb-33 | England | 4N | A | Twickenham, London | L | 6-17 |
| 171 | 11-Mar-33 | Wales | 4N | H | Ravenhill, Belfast | W | 10-5 |
| 172 | 1-Apr-33 | Scotland | 4N | H | Lansdowne Road, Dublin | L | 6-8 |
| 173 | 10-Feb-34 | England | 4N | H | Lansdowne Road, Dublin | L | 3-13 |
| 174 | 24-Feb-34 | Scotland | 4N | A | Murrayfield, Edinburgh | L | 9-16 |
| 175 | 10-Mar-34 | Wales | 4N | A | St Helen's, Swansea | L | 0-13 |
| 176 | 9-Feb-35 | England | 4N | A | Twickenham, London | L | 3-14 |
| 177 | 23-Feb-35 | Scotland | 4N | H | Lansdowne Road, Dublin | W | 12-5 |
| 178 | 9-Mar-35 | Wales | 4N | H | Ravenhill, Belfast | W | 9-3 |
| 179 | 7-Dec-35 | New Zealand | Int | H | Lansdowne Road, Dublin | L | 9-17 |
| 180 | 8-Feb-36 | England | 4N | H | Lansdowne Road, Dublin | W | 6-3 |
| 181 | 22-Feb-36 | Scotland | 4N | A | Murrayfield, Edinburgh | W | 10-4 |
| 182 | 14-Mar-36 | Wales | 4N | A | Arms Park, Cardiff | L | 0-3 |
| 183 | 13-Feb-37 | England | 4N | A | Twickenham, London | L | 8-9 |
| 184 | 27-Feb-37 | Scotland | 4N | H | Lansdowne Road, Dublin | W | 11-4 |
| 185 | 3-Apr-37 | Wales | 4N | H | Ravenhill, Belfast | W | 5-3 |
| 186 | 12-Feb-38 | England | 4N | H | Lansdowne Road, Dublin | L | 14-36 |
| 187 | 26-Feb-38 | Scotland | 4N | A | Murrayfield, Edinburgh | L | 14-23 |
| 188 | 12-Mar-38 | Wales | 4N | A | St Helen's, Swansea | L | 5-11 |
| 189 | 11-Feb-39 | England | 4N | A | Twickenham, London | W | 5-0 |
| 190 | 25-Feb-39 | Scotland | 4N | H | Lansdowne Road, Dublin | W | 12-3 |
| 191 | 11-Mar-39 | Wales | 4N | H | Ravenhill, Belfast | L | 0-7 |
| 192 | 25-Jan-47 | France | 5N | H | Lansdowne Road, Dublin | L | 8-12 |
| 193 | 8-Feb-47 | England | 5N | H | Lansdowne Road, Dublin | W | 22-0 |
| 194 | 22-Feb-47 | Scotland | 5N | A | Murrayfield, Edinburgh | W | 3-0 |
| 195 | 29-Mar-47 | Wales | 5N | A | St Helen's, Swansea | L | 0-6 |
| 196 | 6-Dec-47 | Australia | Int | H | Lansdowne Road, Dublin | L | 3-16 |
| 197 | 1-Jan-48 | France | 5N | A | Stade Colombes, Paris | W | 13-6 |
| 198 | 14-Feb-48 | England | 5N | A | Twickenham, London | W | 11-10 |
| 199 | 28-Feb-48 | Scotland | 5N | H | Lansdowne Road, Dublin | W | 6-0 |
| 200 | 13-Mar-48 | Wales | 5N | H | Ravenhill, Belfast | W | 6-3 |

| No | Date | Opponents | Tmt | Match Venue | Result | |
|----|------|-----------|-----|-------------|--------|---|
| 201 | 29-Jan-49 | France | 5N | H Lansdowne Road, Dublin | L | 9-16 |
| 202 | 12-Feb-49 | England | 5N | H Lansdowne Road, Dublin | W | 14-5 |
| 203 | 26-Feb-49 | Scotland | 5N | A Murrayfield, Edinburgh | W | 13-3 |
| 204 | 12-Mar-49 | Wales | 5N | A St Helen's, Swansea | W | 5-0 |
| 205 | 28-Jan-50 | France | 5N | A Stade Colombes, Paris | D | 3-3 |
| 206 | 11-Feb-50 | England | 5N | A Twickenham, London | L | 0-3 |
| 207 | 25-Feb-50 | Scotland | 5N | H Lansdowne Road, Dublin | W | 21-0 |
| 208 | 11-Mar-50 | Wales | 5N | H Ravenhill, Belfast | L | 3-6 |
| 209 | 27-Jan-51 | France | 5N | H Lansdowne Road, Dublin | W | 9-8 |
| 210 | 10-Feb-51 | England | 5N | H Lansdowne Road, Dublin | W | 3-0 |
| 211 | 24-Feb-51 | Scotland | 5N | A Murrayfield, Edinburgh | W | 6-5 |
| 212 | 10-Mar-51 | Wales | 5N | A Arms Park, Cardiff | D | 3-3 |
| 213 | 8-Dec-51 | South Africa | Int | H Lansdowne Road, Dublin | L | 5-17 |
| 214 | 26-Jan-52 | France | 5N | A Stade Colombes, Paris | W | 11-8 |
| 215 | 23-Feb-52 | Scotland | 5N | H Lansdowne Road, Dublin | W | 12-8 |
| 216 | 8-Mar-52 | Wales | 5N | H Lansdowne Road, Dublin | L | 3-14 |
| 217 | 29-Mar-52 | England | 5N | A Twickenham, London | L | 0-3 |
| 218 | 24-Jan-53 | France | 5N | H Ravenhill, Belfast | W | 16-3 |
| 219 | 14-Feb-53 | England | 5N | H Lansdowne Road, Dublin | D | 9-9 |
| 220 | 28-Feb-53 | Scotland | 5N | A Murrayfield, Edinburgh | W | 26-8 |
| 221 | 14-Mar-53 | Wales | 5N | A St Helen's, Swansea | L | 3-5 |
| 222 | 9-Jan-54 | New Zealand | Int | H Lansdowne Road, Dublin | L | 3-14 |
| 223 | 23-Jan-54 | France | 5N | A Stade Colombes, Paris | L | 0-8 |
| 224 | 13-Feb-54 | England | 5N | A Twickenham, London | L | 3-14 |
| 225 | 27-Feb-54 | Scotland | 5N | H Ravenhill, Belfast | W | 6-0 |
| 226 | 13-Mar-54 | Wales | 5N | H Lansdowne Road, Dublin | L | 9-12 |
| 227 | 22-Jan-55 | France | 5N | H Lansdowne Road, Dublin | L | 3-5 |
| 228 | 12-Feb-55 | England | 5N | H Lansdowne Road, Dublin | D | 6-6 |
| 229 | 26-Feb-55 | Scotland | 5N | A Murrayfield, Edinburgh | L | 3-12 |
| 230 | 12-Mar-55 | Wales | 5N | A Arms Park, Cardiff | L | 3-21 |
| 231 | 28-Jan-56 | France | 5N | A Stade Colombes, Paris | L | 8-14 |
| 232 | 11-Feb-56 | England | 5N | A Twickenham, London | L | 0-20 |
| 233 | 25-Feb-56 | Scotland | 5N | H Lansdowne Road, Dublin | W | 14-10 |
| 234 | 10-Mar-56 | Wales | 5N | H Lansdowne Road, Dublin | W | 11-3 |
| 235 | 26-Jan-57 | France | 5N | H Lansdowne Road, Dublin | W | 11-6 |
| 236 | 9-Feb-57 | England | 5N | H Lansdowne Road, Dublin | L | 0-6 |
| 237 | 23-Feb-57 | Scotland | 5N | A Murrayfield, Edinburgh | W | 5-3 |
| 238 | 9-Mar-57 | Wales | 5N | A Arms Park, Cardiff | L | 5-6 |
| 239 | 18-Jan-58 | Australia | Int | H Lansdowne Road, Dublin | W | 9-6 |
| 240 | 8-Feb-58 | England | 5N | A Twickenham, London | L | 0-6 |

| No | Date | Opponents | Tmt | | Match Venue | Result | |
|----|------|-----------|-----|---|-------------|--------|--|
| 241 | 1-Mar-58 | Scotland | 5N | H | Lansdowne Road, Dublin | W | 12-6 |
| 242 | 15-Mar-58 | Wales | 5N | H | Lansdowne Road, Dublin | L | 6-9 |
| 243 | 19-Apr-58 | France | 5N | A | Stade Colombes, Paris | L | 6-11 |
| 244 | 14-Feb-59 | England | 5N | H | Lansdowne Road, Dublin | L | 0-3 |
| 245 | 28-Feb-59 | Scotland | 5N | A | Murrayfield, Edinburgh | W | 8-3 |
| 246 | 14-Mar-59 | Wales | 5N | A | Arms Park, Cardiff | L | 6-8 |
| 247 | 18-Apr-59 | France | 5N | H | Lansdowne Road, Dublin | W | 9-5 |
| 248 | 13-Feb-60 | England | 5N | A | Twickenham, London | L | 5-8 |
| 249 | 27-Feb-60 | Scotland | 5N | H | Lansdowne Road, Dublin | L | 5-6 |
| 250 | 12-Mar-60 | Wales | 5N | H | Lansdowne Road, Dublin | L | 9-10 |
| 251 | 9-Apr-60 | France | 5N | A | Stade Colombes, Paris | L | 6-23 |
| 252 | 17-Dec-60 | South Africa | Int | H | Lansdowne Road, Dublin | L | 3-8 |
| 253 | 11-Feb-61 | England | 5N | H | Lansdowne Road, Dublin | W | 11-8 |
| 254 | 25-Feb-61 | Scotland | 5N | A | Murrayfield, Edinburgh | L | 8-16 |
| 255 | 11-Mar-61 | Wales | 5N | A | Arms Park, Cardiff | L | 0-9 |
| 256 | 15-Apr-61 | France | 5N | H | Lansdowne Road, Dublin | L | 3-15 |
| 257 | 13-May-61 | South Africa | Int-T | A | Newlands Stadium, Cape Town | L | 8-24 |
| 258 | 10-Feb-62 | England | 5N | A | Twickenham, London | L | 0-16 |
| 259 | 24-Feb-62 | Scotland | 5N | H | Lansdowne Road, Dublin | L | 6-20 |
| 260 | 14-Apr-62 | France | 5N | A | Stade Colombes, Paris | L | 0-11 |
| 261 | 17-Nov-62 | Wales | 5N | H | Lansdowne Road, Dublin | D | 3-3 |
| 262 | 26-Jan-63 | France | 5N | H | Lansdowne Road, Dublin | L | 5-24 |
| 263 | 9-Feb-63 | England | 5N | H | Lansdowne Road, Dublin | D | 0-0 |
| 264 | 23-Feb-63 | Scotland | 5N | A | Murrayfield, Edinburgh | L | 0-3 |
| 265 | 9-Mar-63 | Wales | 5N | A | Arms Park, Cardiff | W | 14-6 |
| 266 | 7-Dec-63 | New Zealand | Int | H | Lansdowne Road, Dublin | L | 5-6 |
| 267 | 8-Feb-64 | England | 5N | A | Twickenham, London | W | 18-5 |
| 268 | 22-Feb-64 | Scotland | 5N | H | Lansdowne Road, Dublin | L | 3-6 |
| 269 | 7-Mar-64 | Wales | 5N | H | Lansdowne Road, Dublin | L | 6-15 |
| 270 | 11-Apr-64 | France | 5N | A | Stade Colombes, Paris | L | 6-27 |
| 271 | 23-Jan-65 | France | 5N | H | Lansdowne Road, Dublin | D | 3-3 |
| 272 | 13-Feb-65 | England | 5N | H | Lansdowne Road, Dublin | W | 5-0 |
| 273 | 27-Feb-65 | Scotland | 5N | A | Murrayfield, Edinburgh | W | 16-6 |
| 274 | 13-Mar-65 | Wales | 5N | A | Arms Park, Cardiff | L | 8-14 |
| 275 | 10-Apr-65 | South Africa | Int | H | Lansdowne Road, Dublin | W | 9-6 |
| 276 | 29-Jan-66 | France | 5N | A | Stade Colombes, Paris | L | 6-11 |
| 277 | 12-Feb-66 | England | 5N | A | Twickenham, London | D | 6-6 |
| 278 | 26-Feb-66 | Scotland | 5N | H | Lansdowne Road, Dublin | L | 3-11 |
| 279 | 12-Mar-66 | Wales | 5N | H | Lansdowne Road, Dublin | W | 9-6 |
| 280 | 21-Jan-67 | Australia | Int | H | Lansdowne Road, Dublin | W | 15-8 |

| No | Date | Opponents | Tmt | | Match Venue | | Result |
|----|------|-----------|-----|---|-------------|---|--------|
| 281 | 11-Feb-67 | England | 5N | H | Lansdowne Road, Dublin | L | 3-8 |
| 282 | 25-Feb-67 | Scotland | 5N | A | Murrayfield, Edinburgh | W | 5-3 |
| 283 | 11-Mar-67 | Wales | 5N | A | Arms Park, Cardiff | W | 3-0 |
| 284 | 15-Apr-67 | France | 5N | H | Lansdowne Road, Dublin | L | 6-11 |
| 285 | 13-May-67 | Australia | Int-T | A | Cricket Ground, Sydney | W | 11-5 |
| 286 | 27-Jan-68 | France | 5N | A | Stade Colombes, Paris | L | 6-16 |
| 287 | 10-Feb-68 | England | 5N | A | Twickenham, London | D | 9-9 |
| 288 | 24-Feb-68 | Scotland | 5N | H | Lansdowne Road, Dublin | W | 14-6 |
| 289 | 9-Mar-68 | Wales | 5N | H | Lansdowne Road, Dublin | W | 9-6 |
| 290 | 26-Oct-68 | Australia | Int | H | Lansdowne Road, Dublin | W | 10-3 |
| 291 | 25-Jan-69 | France | 5N | H | Lansdowne Road, Dublin | W | 17-9 |
| 292 | 8-Feb-69 | England | 5N | H | Lansdowne Road, Dublin | W | 17-15 |
| 293 | 22-Feb-69 | Scotland | 5N | A | Murrayfield, Edinburgh | W | 16-0 |
| 294 | 8-Mar-69 | Wales | 5N | A | National Stadium, Cardiff | L | 11-24 |
| 295 | 10-Jan-70 | South Africa | Int | H | Lansdowne Road, Dublin | D | 8-8 |
| 296 | 24-Jan-70 | France | 5N | A | Stade Colombes, Paris | L | 0-8 |
| 297 | 14-Feb-70 | England | 5N | A | Twickenham, London | L | 3-9 |
| 298 | 28-Feb-70 | Scotland | 5N | H | Lansdowne Road, Dublin | W | 16-11 |
| 299 | 14-Mar-70 | Wales | 5N | H | Lansdowne Road, Dublin | W | 14-0 |
| 300 | 30-Jan-71 | France | 5N | H | Lansdowne Road, Dublin | D | 9-9 |
| 301 | 13-Feb-71 | England | 5N | H | Lansdowne Road, Dublin | L | 6-9 |
| 302 | 27-Feb-71 | Scotland | 5N | A | Murrayfield, Edinburgh | W | 17-5 |
| 303 | 13-Mar-71 | Wales | 5N | A | National Stadium, Cardiff | L | 9-23 |
| 304 | 29-Jan-72 | France | 5N | A | Stade Colombes, Paris | W | 14-9 |
| 305 | 12-Feb-72 | England | 5N | A | Twickenham, London | W | 16-12 |
| 306 | 29-Apr-72 | France | Int | H | Lansdowne Road, Dublin | W | 24-14 |
| 307 | 20-Jan-73 | New Zealand | Int | H | Lansdowne Road, Dublin | D | 10-10 |
| 308 | 10-Feb-73 | England | 5N | H | Lansdowne Road, Dublin | W | 18-9 |
| 309 | 24-Feb-73 | Scotland | 5N | A | Murrayfield, Edinburgh | L | 14-19 |
| 310 | 10-Mar-73 | Wales | 5N | A | National Stadium, Cardiff | L | 12-16 |
| 311 | 14-Apr-73 | France | 5N | H | Lansdowne Road, Dublin | W | 6-4 |
| 312 | 19-Jan-74 | France | 5N | A | Parc des Princess, Paris | L | 6-9 |
| 313 | 2-Feb-74 | Wales | 5N | H | Lansdowne Road, Dublin | D | 9-9 |
| 314 | 16-Feb-74 | England | 5N | A | Twickenham, London | W | 26-21 |
| 315 | 2-Mar-74 | Scotland | 5N | H | Lansdowne Road, Dublin | W | 9-6 |
| 316 | 7-Sep-74 | President's XV | Int | H | Lansdowne Road, Dublin | D | 18-18 |
| 317 | 23-Nov-74 | New Zealand | Int | H | Lansdowne Road, Dublin | L | 6-15 |
| 318 | 18-Jan-75 | England | 5N | H | Lansdowne Road, Dublin | W | 12-9 |
| 319 | 1-Feb-75 | Scotland | 5N | A | Murrayfield, Edinburgh | L | 13-20 |
| 320 | 1-Mar-75 | France | 5N | H | Lansdowne Road, Dublin | W | 25-6 |

| No | Date | Opponents | Tmt | | Match Venue | Result | |
|-----|-----------|-------------|-------|---|----------------------------|---|-------|
| 321 | 15-Mar-75 | Wales | 5N | A | National Stadium, Cardiff | L | 4-32 |
| 322 | 17-Jan-76 | Australia | Int | H | Lansdowne Road, Dublin | L | 10-20 |
| 323 | 7-Feb-76 | France | 5N | A | Parc des Princess, Paris | L | 3-26 |
| 324 | 21-Feb-76 | Wales | 5N | H | Lansdowne Road, Dublin | L | 9-34 |
| 325 | 6-Mar-76 | England | 5N | A | Twickenham, London | W | 13-12 |
| 326 | 20-Mar-76 | Scotland | 5N | H | Lansdowne Road, Dublin | L | 6-15 |
| 327 | 5-Jun-76 | New Zealand | Int-T | A | Athletic Park, Wellington | L | 3-11 |
| 328 | 15-Jan-77 | Wales | 5N | A | National Stadium, Cardiff | L | 9-25 |
| 329 | 5-Feb-77 | England | 5N | H | Lansdowne Road, Dublin | L | 0-4 |
| 330 | 19-Feb-77 | Scotland | 5N | A | Murrayfield, Edinburgh | L | 18-21 |
| 331 | 19-Mar-77 | France | 5N | H | Lansdowne Road, Dublin | L | 6-15 |
| 332 | 21-Jan-78 | Scotland | 5N | H | Lansdowne Road, Dublin | W | 12-9 |
| 333 | 18-Feb-78 | France | 5N | A | Parc des Princess, Paris | L | 9-10 |
| 334 | 4-Mar-78 | Wales | 5N | H | Lansdowne Road, Dublin | L | 16-20 |
| 335 | 18-Mar-78 | England | 5N | A | Twickenham, London | L | 9-15 |
| 336 | 4-Nov-78 | New Zealand | Int | H | Lansdowne Road, Dublin | L | 6-10 |
| 337 | 20-Jan-79 | France | 5N | H | Lansdowne Road, Dublin | D | 9-9 |
| 338 | 3-Feb-79 | Wales | 5N | A | National Stadium, Cardiff | L | 21-24 |
| 339 | 17-Feb-79 | England | 5N | H | Lansdowne Road, Dublin | W | 12-7 |
| 340 | 3-Mar-79 | Scotland | 5N | A | Murrayfield, Edinburgh | D | 11-11 |
| 341 | 3-Jun-79 | Australia | Int-T | A | Ballymore Oval, Brisbane | W | 27-12 |
| 342 | 16-Jun-79 | Australia | Int-T | A | Cricket Ground, Sydney | W | 9-3 |
| 343 | 19-Jan-80 | England | 5N | A | Twickenham, London | L | 9-24 |
| 344 | 2-Feb-80 | Scotland | 5N | H | Lansdowne Road, Dublin | W | 22-15 |
| 345 | 1-Mar-80 | France | 5N | A | Parc des Princess, Paris | L | 18-19 |
| 346 | 15-Mar-80 | Wales | 5N | H | Lansdowne Road, Dublin | W | 21-7 |
| 347 | 7-Feb-81 | France | 5N | H | Lansdowne Road, Dublin | L | 13-19 |
| 348 | 21-Feb-81 | Wales | 5N | A | National Stadium, Cardiff | L | 8-9 |
| 349 | 7-Mar-81 | England | 5N | H | Lansdowne Road, Dublin | L | 6-10 |
| 350 | 21-Mar-81 | Scotland | 5N | A | Murrayfield, Edinburgh | L | 9-10 |
| 351 | 30-May-81 | South Africa | Int-T | A | Newlands Stadium, Cape Town | L | 15-23 |
| 352 | 6-Jun-81 | South Africa | Int-T | A | Kings Park Stadium, Durban | L | 10-12 |
| 353 | 21-Nov-81 | Australia | Int | H | Lansdowne Road, Dublin | L | 12-16 |
| 354 | 23-Jan-82 | Wales | 5N | H | Lansdowne Road, Dublin | W | 20-12 |
| 355 | 6-Feb-82 | England | 5N | A | Twickenham, London | W | 16-15 |
| 356 | 20-Feb-82 | Scotland | 5N | H | Lansdowne Road, Dublin | W | 21-12 |
| 357 | 20-Mar-82 | France | 5N | A | Parc des Princess, Paris | L | 9-22 |
| 358 | 15-Jan-83 | Scotland | 5N | A | Murrayfield, Edinburgh | W | 15-13 |
| 359 | 19-Feb-83 | France | 5N | H | Lansdowne Road, Dublin | W | 22-16 |
| 360 | 5-Mar-83 | Wales | 5N | A | National Stadium, Cardiff | L | 9-23 |

| No | Date | Opponents | Tmt | Match Venue | | Result | |
|----|------|-----------|-----|-------------|---|--------|---|
| 361 | 19-Mar-83 | England | 5N | H | Lansdowne Road, Dublin | W | 25-15 |
| 362 | 21-Jan-84 | France | 5N | A | Parc des Princess, Paris | L | 12-25 |
| 363 | 4-Feb-84 | Wales | 5N | H | Lansdowne Road, Dublin | L | 9-18 |
| 364 | 18-Feb-84 | England | 5N | A | Twickenham, London | L | 9-12 |
| 365 | 3-Mar-84 | Scotland | 5N | H | Lansdowne Road, Dublin | L | 9-32 |
| 366 | 10-Nov-84 | Australia | Int | H | Lansdowne Road, Dublin | L | 9-16 |
| 367 | 2-Feb-85 | Scotland | 5N | A | Murrayfield, Edinburgh | W | 18-15 |
| 368 | 2-Mar-85 | France | 5N | H | Lansdowne Road, Dublin | D | 15-15 |
| 369 | 16-Mar-85 | Wales | 5N | A | National Stadium, Cardiff | W | 21-9 |
| 370 | 30-Mar-85 | England | 5N | H | Lansdowne Road, Dublin | W | 13-10 |
| 371 | 1-Feb-86 | France | 5N | A | Parc des Princess, Paris | L | 9-29 |
| 372 | 15-Feb-86 | Wales | 5N | H | Lansdowne Road, Dublin | L | 12-19 |
| 373 | 1-Mar-86 | England | 5N | A | Twickenham, London | L | 20-25 |
| 374 | 15-Mar-86 | Scotland | 5N | H | Lansdowne Road, Dublin | L | 9-10 |
| 375 | 1-Nov-86 | Romania | Int | H | Lansdowne Road, Dublin | W | 60-0 |
| 376 | 7-Feb-87 | England | 5N | H | Lansdowne Road, Dublin | W | 17-0 |
| 377 | 21-Feb-87 | Scotland | 5N | A | Murrayfield, Edinburgh | L | 12-16 |
| 378 | 21-Mar-87 | France | 5N | H | Lansdowne Road, Dublin | L | 13-19 |
| 379 | 4-Apr-87 | Wales | 5N | A | National Stadium, Cardiff | W | 15-11 |
| 380 | 25-May-87 | Wales | WCp | N | Athletic Park, Wellington | L | 6-13 |
| 381 | 30-May-87 | Canada | WCp | N | Carisbrook, Dunedin | W | 46-19 |
| 382 | 3-Jun-87 | Tonga | WCp | N | Ballymore Oval, Brisbane | W | 32-9 |
| 383 | 7-Jun-87 | Australia | WCp | A | Concord Oval, Sydney | L | 15-33 |
| 384 | 16-Jan-88 | Scotland | 5N | H | Lansdowne Road, Dublin | W | 22-18 |
| 385 | 20-Feb-88 | France | 5N | A | Parc des Princess, Paris | L | 6-25 |
| 386 | 5-Mar-88 | Wales | 5N | H | Lansdowne Road, Dublin | L | 9-12 |
| 387 | 19-Mar-88 | England | 5N | A | Twickenham, London | L | 3-35 |
| 388 | 23-Apr-88 | England | MT | H | Lansdowne Road, Dublin | L | 10-21 |
| 389 | 29-Oct-88 | Western Samoa | Int | H | Lansdowne Road, Dublin | W | 49-22 |
| 390 | 31-Dec-88 | Italy | Int | H | Lansdowne Road, Dublin | W | 31-15 |
| 391 | 21-Jan-89 | France | 5N | H | Lansdowne Road, Dublin | L | 21-26 |
| 392 | 4-Feb-89 | Wales | 5N | A | National Stadium, Cardiff | W | 19-13 |
| 393 | 18-Feb-89 | England | 5N-MT | H | Lansdowne Road, Dublin | L | 3-16 |
| 394 | 4-Mar-89 | Scotland | 5N-CQ | A | Murrayfield, Edinburgh | L | 21-37 |
| 395 | 18-Nov-89 | New Zealand | Int | H | Lansdowne Road, Dublin | L | 6-23 |
| 396 | 20-Jan-90 | England | 5N-MT | A | Twickenham, London | L | 0-23 |
| 397 | 3-Feb-90 | Scotland | 5N-CQ | H | Lansdowne Road, Dublin | L | 10-13 |
| 398 | 3-Mar-90 | France | 5N | A | Parc des Princess, Paris | L | 12-31 |
| 399 | 24-Mar-90 | Wales | 5N | H | Lansdowne Road, Dublin | W | 14-8 |
| 400 | 27-Oct-90 | Argentina | Int | H | Lansdowne Road, Dublin | W | 20-18 |

| No | Date | Opponents | Tmt | | Match Venue | Result | |
|----|------|-----------|-----|--|-------------|--------|--|
| 401 | 2-Feb-91 | France | 5N | H | Lansdowne Road, Dublin | L | 13-21 |
| 402 | 16-Feb-91 | Wales | 5N | A | National Stadium, Cardiff | D | 21-21 |
| 403 | 2-Mar-91 | England | 5N-MT | H | Lansdowne Road, Dublin | L | 7-16 |
| 404 | 16-Mar-91 | Scotland | 5N-CQ | A | Murrayfield, Edinburgh | L | 25-28 |
| 405 | 20-Jul-91 | Namibia | Int-T | A | South West Stadium, Windhoek | L | 6-15 |
| 406 | 27-Jul-91 | Namibia | Int-T | A | South West Stadium, Windhoek | L | 15-26 |
| 407 | 6-Oct-91 | Zimbabwe | WCp | H | Lansdowne Road, Dublin | W | 55-11 |
| 408 | 9-Oct-91 | Japan | WCp | H | Lansdowne Road, Dublin | W | 32-16 |
| 409 | 12-Oct-91 | Scotland | WCp | A | Murrayfield, Edinburgh | L | 15-24 |
| 410 | 20-Oct-91 | Australia | WCq | H | Lansdowne Road, Dublin | L | 18-19 |
| 411 | 18-Jan-92 | Wales | 5N | H | Lansdowne Road, Dublin | L | 15-16 |
| 412 | 1-Feb-92 | England | 5N-MT | A | Twickenham, London | L | 9-38 |
| 413 | 15-Feb-92 | Scotland | 5N-CQ | H | Lansdowne Road, Dublin | L | 10-18 |
| 414 | 21-Mar-92 | France | 5N | A | Parc des Princess, Paris | L | 12-44 |
| 415 | 30-May-92 | New Zealand | Int-T | A | Carisbrook, Dunedin | L | 21-24 |
| 416 | 6-Jun-92 | New Zealand | Int-T | A | Athletic Park, Wellington | L | 6-59 |
| 417 | 31-Oct-92 | Australia | Int | H | Lansdowne Road, Dublin | L | 17-42 |
| 418 | 16-Jan-93 | Scotland | 5N-CQ | A | Murrayfield, Edinburgh | L | 3-15 |
| 419 | 20-Feb-93 | France | 5N | H | Lansdowne Road, Dublin | L | 6-21 |
| 420 | 6-Mar-93 | Wales | 5N | A | National Stadium, Cardiff | W | 19-14 |
| 421 | 20-Mar-93 | England | 5N-MT | H | Lansdowne Road, Dublin | W | 17-3 |
| 422 | 13-Nov-93 | Romania | Int | H | Lansdowne Road, Dublin | W | 25-3 |
| 423 | 15-Jan-94 | France | 5N | A | Parc des Princess, Paris | L | 15-35 |
| 424 | 5-Feb-94 | Wales | 5N | H | Lansdowne Road, Dublin | L | 15-17 |
| 425 | 19-Feb-94 | England | 5N-MT | A | Twickenham, London | W | 13-12 |
| 426 | 5-Mar-94 | Scotland | 5N-CQ | H | Lansdowne Road, Dublin | D | 6-6 |
| 427 | 5-Jun-94 | Australia | Int-T | A | Ballymore Oval, Brisbane | L | 13-33 |
| 428 | 11-Jun-94 | Australia | Int-T | A | Football Stadium, Sydney | L | 18-32 |
| 429 | 5-Nov-94 | United States | Int | H | Lansdowne Road, Dublin | W | 26-15 |
| 430 | 21-Jan-95 | England | 5N-MT | H | Lansdowne Road, Dublin | L | 8-20 |
| 431 | 4-Feb-95 | Scotland | 5N-CQ | A | Murrayfield, Edinburgh | L | 13-26 |
| 432 | 4-Mar-95 | France | 5N | H | Lansdowne Road, Dublin | L | 7-25 |
| 433 | 18-Mar-95 | Wales | 5N | A | National Stadium, Cardiff | W | 16-12 |
| 434 | 6-May-95 | Italy | Int | A | Stadio Comunale di Monigo, Treviso | L | 12-22 |
| 435 | 27-May-95 | New Zealand | WCp | N | Ellis Park, Johannesburg | L | 19-43 |
| 436 | 31-May-95 | Japan | WCp | N | Free State Stadium, Bloemfontein | W | 50-28 |
| 437 | 4-Jun-95 | Wales | WCp | N | Ellis Park, Johannesburg | W | 24-23 |
| 438 | 10-Jun-95 | France | WCqf | N | Kings Park Stadium, Durban | L | 12-36 |
| 439 | 18-Nov-95 | Fiji | Int | H | Lansdowne Road, Dublin | W | 44-8 |
| 440 | 6-Jan-96 | United States | Int-T | A | Life College Stadium, Atlanta, Georgia | W | 25-18 |

| No | Date | Opponents | Tmt | | Match Venue | | Result |
|-----|------------|---------------|--------|---|----------------------------------------|---|--------|
| 441 | 20-Jan-96 | Scotland | 5N-CQ | H | Lansdowne Road, Dublin | L | 10-16 |
| 442 | 17-Feb-96 | France | 5N | A | Parc des Princess, Paris | L | 10-45 |
| 443 | 2-Mar-96 | Wales | 5N | H | Lansdowne Road, Dublin | W | 30-17 |
| 444 | 16-Mar-96 | England | 5N-MT | A | Twickenham, London | L | 15-28 |
| 445 | 12-Nov-96 | Western Samoa | Int | H | Lansdowne Road, Dublin | L | 25-40 |
| 446 | 23-Nov-96 | Australia | Int | H | Lansdowne Road, Dublin | L | 12-22 |
| 447 | 4-Jan-97 | Italy | Int | H | Lansdowne Road, Dublin | L | 29-37 |
| 448 | 18-Jan-97 | France | 5N | H | Lansdowne Road, Dublin | L | 15-32 |
| 449 | 1-Feb-97 | Wales | 5N | A | National Stadium, Cardiff | W | 26-25 |
| 450 | 15-Feb-97 | England | 5N-MT | H | Lansdowne Road, Dublin | L | 6-46 |
| 451 | 1-Mar-97 | Scotland | 5N-CQ | A | Murrayfield, Edinburgh | L | 10-38 |
| 452 | 15-Nov-97 | New Zealand | Int | H | Lansdowne Road, Dublin | L | 15-63 |
| 453 | 30-Nov-97 | Canada | Int | H | Lansdowne Road, Dublin | W | 33-11 |
| 454 | 20-Dec-97 | Italy | Int | A | Stadio Renato Dall'Ara, Bologna | L | 22-37 |
| 455 | 7-Feb-98 | Scotland | 5N-CQ | H | Lansdowne Road, Dublin | L | 16-17 |
| 456 | 7-Mar-98 | France | 5N | A | Stade de France, Paris | L | 16-18 |
| 457 | 21-Mar-98 | Wales | 5N | H | Lansdowne Road, Dublin | L | 21-30 |
| 458 | 4-Apr-98 | England | 5N-MT | A | Twickenham, London | L | 17-35 |
| 459 | 13-Jun-98 | South Africa | Int-T | A | Free State Stadium, Bloemfontein | L | 13-37 |
| 460 | 20-Jun-98 | South Africa | Int-T | A | Minolta Loftus Stadium, Pretoria | L | 0-33 |
| 461 | 14-Nov-98 | Georgia | WCQ | H | Lansdowne Road, Dublin | W | 70-0 |
| 462 | 21-Nov-98 | Romania | WCQ | H | Lansdowne Road, Dublin | W | 53-35 |
| 463 | 28-Nov-98 | South Africa | Int | H | Lansdowne Road, Dublin | L | 13-27 |
| 464 | 6-Feb-99 | France | 5N | H | Lansdowne Road, Dublin | L | 9-10 |
| 465 | 20-Feb-99 | Wales | 5N | N | Wembley Stadium, London | W | 29-23 |
| 466 | 6-Mar-99 | England | 5N-MT | H | Lansdowne Road, Dublin | L | 15-27 |
| 467 | 20-Mar-99 | Scotland | 5N-CQ | A | Murrayfield, Edinburgh | L | 13-30 |
| 468 | 10-Apr-99 | Italy | Int | H | Lansdowne Road, Dublin | W | 39-30 |
| 469 | 12-Jun-99 | Australia | LC-T | A | Ballymore Oval, Brisbane | L | 10-46 |
| 470 | 19-Jun-99 | Australia | LC-T | A | Subiaco Oval, Perth | L | 26-32 |
| 471 | 28-Aug-99 | Argentina | Int | H | Lansdowne Road, Dublin | W | 32-24 |
| 472 | 2-Oct-99 | United States | WCp | H | Lansdowne Road, Dublin | W | 53-8 |
| 473 | 10-Oct-99 | Australia | WCp | H | Lansdowne Road, Dublin | L | 3-23 |
| 474 | 15-Oct-99 | Romania | WCp | H | Lansdowne Road, Dublin | W | 44-14 |
| 475 | 20-Oct-99 | Argentina | QFpo | N | Stade Félix Bollaert, Lens | L | 24-28 |
| 476 | 5-Feb-00 | England | 6N-MT | A | Twickenham, London | L | 18-50 |
| 477 | 19-Feb-00 | Scotland | 6N-CQ | H | Lansdowne Road, Dublin | W | 44-22 |
| 478 | 4-Mar-00 | Italy | 6N | H | Lansdowne Road, Dublin | W | 60-13 |
| 479 | 19-Mar-00 | France | 6N | A | Stade de France, Paris | W | 27-25 |
| 480 | 1-Apr-00 | Wales | 6N | H | Lansdowne Road, Dublin | L | 19-23 |

| No | Date | Opponents | Tmt | | Match Venue | Result | |
|---|---|---|---|---|---|---|---|
| 481 | 3-Jun-00 | Argentina | Int-T | A | Ferro Carril Oeste Stadium, B Aires | L | 23-34 |
| 482 | 10-Jun-00 | United States | Int-T | A | Singer Family Park, Manchester, NH | W | 83-3 |
| 483 | 17-Jun-00 | Canada | Int-T | A | Fletcher's Fields, Markham, Toronto | D | 27-27 |
| 484 | 11-Nov-00 | Japan | Int | H | Lansdowne Road, Dublin | W | 78-9 |
| 485 | 19-Nov-00 | South Africa | Int | H | Lansdowne Road, Dublin | L | 18-28 |
| 486 | 3-Feb-01 | Italy | 6N | A | Stadio Flaminio, Rome | W | 41-22 |
| 487 | 17-Feb-01 | France | 6N | H | Lansdowne Road, Dublin | W | 22-15 |
| 488 | 2-Jun-01 | Romania | Int | A | Stadionul Dinamo, Bucharest | W | 37-3 |
| 489 | 22-Sep-01 | Scotland | 6N-CQ | A | Murrayfield, Edinburgh | L | 10-32 |
| 490 | 13-Oct-01 | Wales | 6N | A | Millennium Stadium, Cardiff | W | 36-6 |
| 491 | 20-Oct-01 | England | 6N-MT | H | Lansdowne Road, Dublin | W | 20-14 |
| 492 | 11-Nov-01 | Samoa | Int | H | Lansdowne Road, Dublin | W | 35-8 |
| 493 | 17-Nov-01 | New Zealand | Int | H | Lansdowne Road, Dublin | L | 29-40 |
| 494 | 3-Feb-02 | Wales | 6N | H | Lansdowne Road, Dublin | W | 54-10 |
| 495 | 16-Feb-02 | England | 6N-MT | A | Twickenham, London | L | 11-45 |
| 496 | 2-Mar-02 | Scotland | 6N-CQ | H | Lansdowne Road, Dublin | W | 43-22 |
| 497 | 23-Mar-02 | Italy | 6N | H | Lansdowne Road, Dublin | W | 32-17 |
| 498 | 6-Apr-02 | France | 6N | A | Stade de France, Paris | L | 5-44 |
| 499 | 15-Jun-02 | New Zealand | Int-T | A | Carisbrook, Dunedin | L | 6-15 |
| 500 | 22-Jun-02 | New Zealand | Int-T | A | Eden Park, Auckland | L | 8-40 |
| 501 | 7-Sep-02 | Romania | Int | H | Thomond Park, Limerick | W | 39-8 |
| 502 | 21-Sep-02 | Russia | WCQ | A | Central Stadium, Krasnoyarsk | W | 35-3 |
| 503 | 28-Sep-02 | Georgia | WCQ | H | Lansdowne Road, Dublin | W | 63-14 |
| 504 | 9-Nov-02 | Australia | LC | H | Lansdowne Road, Dublin | W | 18-9 |
| 505 | 17-Nov-02 | Fiji | Int | H | Lansdowne Road, Dublin | W | 64-17 |
| 506 | 23-Nov-02 | Argentina | Int | H | Lansdowne Road, Dublin | W | 16-7 |
| 507 | 16-Feb-03 | Scotland | 6N-CQ | A | Murrayfield, Edinburgh | W | 36-6 |
| 508 | 22-Feb-03 | Italy | 6N | A | Stadio Flaminio, Rome | W | 37-13 |
| 509 | 8-Mar-03 | France | 6N | H | Lansdowne Road, Dublin | W | 15-12 |
| 510 | 22-Mar-03 | Wales | 6N | A | Millennium Stadium, Cardiff | W | 25-24 |
| 511 | 30-Mar-03 | England | 6N-MT | H | Lansdowne Road, Dublin | L | 6-42 |
| 512 | 7-Jun-03 | Australia | LC-T | A | Subiaco Oval, Perth | L | 16-45 |
| 513 | 14-Jun-03 | Tonga | Int-T | A | Teufaiva Sport Stadium, Nuku'alofa | W | 40-19 |
| 514 | 20-Jun-03 | Samoa | Int-T | A | Apia Park, Apia | W | 40-14 |
| 515 | 16-Aug-03 | Wales | Int | H | Lansdowne Road, Dublin | W | 35-12 |
| 516 | 30-Aug-03 | Italy | Int | H | Thomond Park, Limerick | W | 61-6 |
| 517 | 6-Sep-03 | Scotland | Int | A | Murrayfield, Edinburgh | W | 29-10 |
| 518 | 11-Oct-03 | Romania | WCp | N | Central Coast Stadium, Gosford, NSW | W | 45-17 |
| 519 | 19-Oct-03 | Namibia | WCp | N | Aussie Stadium, Sydney | W | 64-7 |
| 520 | 26-Oct-03 | Argentina | WCp | N | Adelaide Oval, Adelaide | W | 16-15 |

| No | Date | Opponents | Tmt | | Match Venue | Result | |
|-----|-----------|----------------|--------|---|--------------------------------------------|---|-------|
| 521 | 1-Nov-03 | Australia | WCp | A | Telstra Dome, Melbourne | L | 16-17 |
| 522 | 9-Nov-03 | France | WCq | N | Telstra Dome, Melbourne | L | 21-43 |
| 523 | 14-Feb-04 | France | 6N | A | Stade de France, Paris | L | 17-35 |
| 524 | 22-Feb-04 | Wales | 6N | H | Lansdowne Road, Dublin | W | 36-15 |
| 525 | 6-Mar-04 | England | 6N-MT | A | Twickenham, London | W | 19-13 |
| 526 | 20-Mar-04 | Italy | 6N | H | Lansdowne Road, Dublin | W | 19-3 |
| 527 | 27-Mar-04 | Scotland | 6N-CQ | H | Lansdowne Road, Dublin | W | 37-16 |
| 528 | 12-Jun-04 | South Africa | Int-T | A | Vodacom Park Stadium, Bloemfontein | L | 17-31 |
| 529 | 19-Jun-04 | South Africa | Int-T | A | Newlands Stadium, Cape Town | L | 17-26 |
| 530 | 13-Nov-04 | South Africa | Int | H | Lansdowne Road, Dublin | W | 17-12 |
| 531 | 20-Nov-04 | United States | Int | H | Lansdowne Road, Dublin | W | 55-6 |
| 532 | 27-Nov-04 | Argentina | Int | H | Lansdowne Road, Dublin | W | 21-19 |
| 533 | 6-Feb-05 | Italy | 6N | A | Stadio Flaminio, Rome | W | 28-17 |
| 534 | 12-Feb-05 | Scotland | 6N-CQ | A | Murrayfield, Edinburgh | W | 40-13 |
| 535 | 27-Feb-05 | England | 6N-MT | H | Lansdowne Road, Dublin | W | 19-13 |
| 536 | 12-Mar-05 | France | 6N | H | Lansdowne Road, Dublin | L | 19-26 |
| 537 | 19-Mar-05 | Wales | 6N | A | Millennium Stadium, Cardiff | L | 20-32 |
| 538 | 12-Jun-05 | Japan | Int-T | A | Nagai Stadium, Osaka | W | 44-12 |
| 539 | 19-Jun-05 | Japan | Int-T | A | Prince Chichibu Memorial Ground, Tokyo | W | 47-18 |
| 540 | 12-Nov-05 | New Zealand | Int | H | Lansdowne Road, Dublin | L | 7-45 |
| 541 | 19-Nov-05 | Australia | LC | H | Lansdowne Road, Dublin | L | 14-30 |
| 542 | 26-Nov-05 | Romania | Int | H | Lansdowne Road, Dublin | W | 43-12 |
| 543 | 4-Feb-06 | Italy | 6N | H | Lansdowne Road, Dublin | W | 26-16 |
| 544 | 11-Feb-06 | France | 6N | A | Stade de France, Paris | L | 31-43 |
| 545 | 26-Feb-06 | Wales | 6N | H | Lansdowne Road, Dublin | W | 31-5 |
| 546 | 11-Mar-06 | Scotland | 6N-CQ | H | Lansdowne Road, Dublin | W | 15-9 |
| 547 | 18-Mar-06 | England | 6N-MT | A | Twickenham, London | W | 28-24 |
| 548 | 10-Jun-06 | New Zealand | Int-T | A | Waikato Stadium, Hamilton | L | 23-34 |
| 549 | 17-Jun-06 | New Zealand | Int-T | A | Eden Park, Auckland | L | 17-27 |
| 550 | 24-Jun-06 | Australia | LC-T | A | Subiaco Oval, Perth | L | 15-37 |
| 551 | 11-Nov-06 | South Africa | Int | H | Lansdowne Road, Dublin | W | 32-15 |
| 552 | 19-Nov-06 | Australia | LC | H | Lansdowne Road, Dublin | W | 21-6 |
| 553 | 26-Nov-06 | Pacific Islands | Int | H | Lansdowne Road, Dublin | W | 61-17 |
| 554 | 4-Feb-07 | Wales | 6N | A | Millennium Stadium, Cardiff | W | 19-9 |
| 555 | 11-Feb-07 | France | 6N | H | Croke Park, Dublin | L | 17-20 |
| 556 | 24-Feb-07 | England | 6N-MT | H | Croke Park, Dublin | W | 43-13 |
| 557 | 10-Mar-07 | Scotland | 6N-CQ | A | Murrayfield, Edinburgh | W | 19-18 |
| 558 | 17-Mar-07 | Italy | 6N | A | Stadio Flaminio, Rome | W | 51-24 |
| 559 | 26-May-07 | Argentina | Int-T | A | Estadio Brig General E. López, Santa Fe | L | 20-22 |
| 560 | 2-Jun-07 | Argentina | Int-T | A | Vélez Sarsfield Stadium, Buenos Aires | L | 0-16 |

| No | Date | Opponents | Tmt | | Match Venue | Result | |
|----|------|-----------|-----|---|-------------|--------|---|
| 561 | 11-Aug-07 | Scotland | Int | A | Murrayfield, Edinburgh | L | 21-31 |
| 562 | 24-Aug-07 | Italy | Int | H | Ravenhill, Belfast | W | 23-20 |
| 563 | 9-Sep-07 | Namibia | WCp | N | Stade Chaban-Delmas, Bordeaux | W | 32-17 |
| 564 | 15-Sep-07 | Georgia | WCp | N | Stade Chaban-Delmas, Bordeaux | W | 14-10 |
| 565 | 21-Sep-07 | France | WCp | A | Stade de France, Paris | L | 3-25 |
| 566 | 30-Sep-07 | Argentina | WCp | N | Parc des Princess, Paris | L | 15-30 |
| 567 | 2-Feb-08 | Italy | 6N | H | Croke Park, Dublin | W | 16-11 |
| 568 | 9-Feb-08 | France | 6N | A | Stade de France, Paris | L | 21-26 |
| 569 | 23-Feb-08 | Scotland | 6N-CQ | H | Croke Park, Dublin | W | 34-13 |
| 570 | 8-Mar-08 | Wales | 6N | H | Croke Park, Dublin | L | 12-16 |
| 571 | 15-Mar-08 | England | 6N-MT | A | Twickenham, London | L | 10-33 |
| 572 | 7-Jun-08 | New Zealand | Int-T | A | Westpac Stadium, Wellington | L | 11-21 |
| 573 | 14-Jun-08 | Australia | LC-T | A | Telstra Dome, Melbourne | L | 12-18 |
| 574 | 8-Nov-08 | Canada | Int | H | Thomond Park, Limerick | W | 55-0 |
| 575 | 15-Nov-08 | New Zealand | Int | H | Croke Park, Dublin | L | 3-22 |
| 576 | 22-Nov-08 | Argentina | Int | H | Croke Park, Dublin | W | 17-3 |
| 577 | 7-Feb-09 | France | 6N | H | Croke Park, Dublin | W | 30-21 |
| 578 | 15-Feb-09 | Italy | 6N | A | Stadio Flaminio, Rome | W | 38-9 |
| 579 | 28-Feb-09 | England | 6N-MT | H | Croke Park, Dublin | W | 14-13 |
| 580 | 14-Mar-09 | Scotland | 6N-CQ | A | Murrayfield, Edinburgh | W | 22-15 |
| 581 | 21-Mar-09 | Wales | 6N | A | Millennium Stadium, Cardiff | W | 17-15 |
| 582 | 23-May-09 | Canada | Int-T | A | Thunderbird Stadium, Vancouver | W | 25-6 |
| 583 | 31-May-09 | United States | Int-T | A | Buck Shaw Stadium, Santa Clara | W | 27-10 |
| 584 | 15-Nov-09 | Australia | LC | H | Croke Park, Dublin | D | 20-20 |
| 585 | 21-Nov-09 | Fiji | Int | H | RDS Showgrounds, Dublin | W | 41-6 |
| 586 | 28-Nov-09 | South Africa | Int | H | Croke Park, Dublin | W | 15-10 |
| 587 | 6-Feb-10 | Italy | 6N | H | Croke Park, Dublin | W | 29-11 |
| 588 | 13-Feb-10 | France | 6N | A | Stade de France, Paris | L | 10-33 |
| 589 | 27-Feb-10 | England | 6N-MT | A | Twickenham, London | W | 20-16 |
| 590 | 13-Mar-10 | Wales | 6N | H | Croke Park, Dublin | W | 27-12 |
| 591 | 20-Mar-10 | Scotland | 6N-CQ | H | Croke Park, Dublin | L | 20-23 |
| 592 | 12-Jun-10 | New Zealand | Int-T | A | Yarrow Stadium, New Plymouth | L | 28-66 |
| 593 | 26-Jun-10 | Australia | LC-T | A | Suncorp Stadium, Brisbane | L | 15-22 |
| 594 | 6-Nov-10 | South Africa | Int | H | Aviva Stadium, Dublin | L | 21-23 |
| 595 | 13-Nov-10 | Samoa | Int | H | Aviva Stadium, Dublin | W | 20-10 |
| 596 | 20-Nov-10 | New Zealand | Int | H | Aviva Stadium, Dublin | L | 18-38 |
| 597 | 28-Nov-10 | Argentina | Int | H | Aviva Stadium, Dublin | W | 29-9 |
| 598 | 5-Feb-11 | Italy | 6N | A | Stadio Flaminio, Rome | W | 13-11 |
| 599 | 13-Feb-11 | France | 6N | H | Aviva Stadium, Dublin | L | 22-25 |
| 600 | 27-Feb-11 | Scotland | 6N-CQ | A | Murrayfield, Edinburgh | W | 21-18 |

| No | Date | Opponents | Tmt | | Match Venue | Result | |
|----|------|-----------|-----|---|-------------|--------|---|
| 601 | 12-Mar-11 | Wales | 6N | A | Millennium Stadium, Cardiff | L | 13-19 |
| 602 | 19-Mar-11 | England | 6N-MT | H | Aviva Stadium, Dublin | W | 24-8 |
| 603 | 6-Aug-11 | Scotland | Int | A | Murrayfield, Edinburgh | L | 6-10 |
| 604 | 13-Aug-11 | France | Int | A | Stade Chaban-Delmas, Bordeaux | L | 12-19 |
| 605 | 20-Aug-11 | France | Int | H | Aviva Stadium, Dublin | L | 22-26 |
| 606 | 27-Aug-11 | England | Int | H | Aviva Stadium, Dublin | L | 9-20 |
| 607 | 11-Sep-11 | United States | WCp | N | Stadium Taranaki, New Plymouth | W | 22-10 |
| 608 | 17-Sep-11 | Australia | WCp | N | Eden Park, Auckland | W | 15-6 |
| 609 | 25-Sep-11 | Russia | WCp | N | Rotorua International Stadium, Rotorua | W | 62-12 |
| 610 | 2-Oct-11 | Italy | WCp | N | Otago Stadium, Dunedin | W | 36-6 |
| 611 | 9-Oct-11 | Wales | WCq | N | Wellington Regional Stadium, Wellington | L | 10-22 |
| 612 | 5-Feb-12 | Wales | 6N | H | Aviva Stadium, Dublin | L | 21-23 |
| 613 | 25-Feb-12 | Italy | 6N | H | Aviva Stadium, Dublin | W | 42-10 |
| 614 | 4-Mar-12 | France | 6N | A | Stade de France, Paris | D | 17-17 |
| 615 | 10-Mar-12 | Scotland | 6N-CQ | H | Aviva Stadium, Dublin | W | 32-14 |
| 616 | 17-Mar-12 | England | 6N-MT | A | Twickenham, London | L | 9-30 |
| 617 | 9-Jun-12 | New Zealand | Int-T | A | Eden Park, Auckland | L | 10-42 |
| 618 | 16-Jun-12 | New Zealand | Int-T | A | Rugby League Park, Christchurch | L | 19-22 |
| 619 | 23-Jun-12 | New Zealand | Int-T | A | Waikato Stadium, Hamilton | L | 0-60 |
| 620 | 10-Nov-12 | South Africa | Int | H | Aviva Stadium, Dublin | L | 12-16 |
| 621 | 24-Nov-12 | Argentina | ABC | H | Aviva Stadium, Dublin | W | 46-24 |
| 622 | 2-Feb-13 | Wales | 6N | A | Millennium Stadium, Cardiff | W | 30-22 |
| 623 | 10-Feb-13 | England | 6N-MT | H | Aviva Stadium, Dublin | L | 6-12 |
| 624 | 24-Feb-13 | Scotland | 6N-CQ | A | Murrayfield, Edinburgh | L | 8-12 |
| 625 | 9-Mar-13 | France | 6N | H | Aviva Stadium, Dublin | D | 13-13 |
| 626 | 16-Mar-13 | Italy | 6N | A | Stadio Olimpico, Rome | L | 15-22 |
| 627 | 8-Jun-13 | United States | Int-T | A | BBVA Compass Stadium, Houston | W | 15-12 |
| 628 | 15-Jun-13 | Canada | Int-T | A | BMO Stadium, Toronto | W | 40-14 |
| 629 | 9-Nov-13 | Samoa | Int | H | Aviva Stadium, Dublin | W | 40-9 |
| 630 | 16-Nov-13 | Australia | LC | H | Aviva Stadium, Dublin | L | 15-32 |
| 631 | 24-Nov-13 | New Zealand | Int | H | Aviva Stadium, Dublin | L | 22-24 |
| 632 | 2-Feb-14 | Scotland | 6N-CQ | H | Aviva Stadium, Dublin | W | 28-6 |
| 633 | 8-Feb-14 | Wales | 6N | H | Aviva Stadium, Dublin | W | 26-3 |
| 634 | 22-Feb-14 | England | 6N-MT | A | Twickenham, London | L | 10-13 |
| 635 | 8-Mar-14 | Italy | 6N | H | Aviva Stadium, Dublin | W | 46-7 |
| 636 | 15-Mar-14 | France | 6N | A | Stade de France, Paris | W | 22-20 |
| 637 | 7-Jun-14 | Argentina | ABC-T | A | Estadio Centenario, Resistencia | W | 29-17 |
| 638 | 14-Jun-14 | Argentina | ABC-T | A | Estadio Monumental José Fierro, Tucumán | W | 23-17 |
| 639 | 8-Nov-14 | South Africa | Int | H | Aviva Stadium, Dublin | W | 29-15 |
| 640 | 16-Nov-14 | Georgia | Int | H | Aviva Stadium, Dublin | W | 49-7 |

| No | Date | Opponents | Tmt | | Match Venue | | Result | |
|---|---|---|---|---|---|---|---|---|
| 641 | 22-Nov-14 | Australia | LC | H | Aviva Stadium, Dublin | | W | 26-23 |
| 642 | 7-Feb-15 | Italy | 6N | A | Stadio Olimpico, Rome | | W | 26-3 |
| 643 | 14-Feb-15 | France | 6N | H | Aviva Stadium, Dublin | | W | 18-11 |
| 644 | 1-Mar-15 | England | 6N-MT | H | Aviva Stadium, Dublin | | W | 19-9 |
| 645 | 14-Mar-15 | Wales | 6N | A | Millennium Stadium, Cardiff | | L | 16-23 |
| 646 | 21-Mar-15 | Scotland | 6N-CQ | A | Murrayfield, Edinburgh | | W | 40-10 |
| 647 | 8-Aug-15 | Wales | Int | A | Millennium Stadium, Cardiff | | W | 35-21 |
| 648 | 15-Aug-15 | Scotland | Int | H | Aviva Stadium, Dublin | | W | 28-22 |
| 649 | 29-Aug-15 | Wales | Int | H | Aviva Stadium, Dublin | | L | 10-16 |
| 650 | 5-Sep-15 | England | Int | A | Twickenham, London | | L | 13-21 |
| 651 | 19-Sep-15 | Canada | WCp | N | Millennium Stadium, Cardiff | | W | 50-7 |
| 652 | 27-Sep-15 | Romania | WCp | N | Wembley Stadium, London | | W | 44-10 |
| 653 | 4-Oct-15 | Italy | WCp | N | Olympic Stadium, London | | W | 16-9 |
| 654 | 11-Oct-15 | France | WCp | N | Millennium Stadium, Cardiff | | W | 24-9 |
| 655 | 18-Oct-15 | Argentina | WCqf | N | Millennium Stadium, Cardiff | | L | 20-43 |

# ITALY

On 25 July 1911, a 'Propaganda Committee' was formed to promote the game of rugby in Italy and, over a decade later, in 1928, the Federazione Italiana Rugby was formed.

The following year, Italy played its first International match, against Spain in Barcelona, and lost by 9 points to nil. In 1932 the Fédération Internationale de Rugby Amateur, better known as FIRA, was founded, and an association consisting of Italy, France, Romania, Czechoslovakia, Spain and Germany was created two years later.

The FIRA European Trophy tournament (FET) was staged between 1936 and 1938, with France winning the trophy in all three years, and the Italian team finishing in second place in 1937. The French team also won the first two FIRA European Cup (FEC) competitions held between 1952 and 1954, with Italy finishing runners-up in both years.

A third FIRA tournament, known as the Nations Cup, was inaugurated in 1965. France once again dominated this competition by winning eight out of the nine titles before the tournament's demise in 1973. Italy's best achievement during that period came in the first season, 1965-66, when they finished in second place.

In 1974, a new FIRA Championship was launched to provide an alternative European international competition to the Five Nations Championship. The tournament ran until 1997, with the French playing all their matches, except for games against Romania and Italy in 1997, as France 'A'. The French team won thirteen titles during that period, with the Romanians winning four times. Italy surprised everyone by winning the title in the final competition, held between 1995 and 1997, beating a full French side in the process.

The FIRA Championship was finally replaced three years later, in 2000, by the European Nations Cup (ENC), a tournament that currently runs in tandem with the Six Nations Championship. The Italians did not enter the ENC that year because they were invited to join the newly formed Six Nations Championship. Italy also competed in the two Latin Cup tournaments, the first held in Argentina in October 1995 and the second hosted by France in October 1997. The four nations taking part were Italy, Romania, France and Argentina, and the Italian team's performance was disappointing, winning just two matches out of the six they played over the two years.

Italy's first International against a major nation was in 1978 when they faced Argentina in Rovigo. They won that match comfortably by 19 points to 6, but it was another five years before they faced another major nation: Australia, also in Rovigo. On that occasion they were well beaten by 29 points to 7. The Italians lost again to Australia in Brisbane three years later, in 1986. In 1987 Italy lost both their matches against New Zealand and Argentina at the pool stage of the inaugural World Cup, and three more defeats to the top teams followed, with losses to Australia and Ireland in December 1988 and to Argentina in Buenos Aires in June 1989.

Throughout the 1990s, Italy had ambitions to play in an expanded Five Nations Championship, but it wasn't until the second half of the decade that they were able to achieve wins against the teams competing in that tournament. Wins against Ireland in 1995, against France and Ireland (twice) in 1997, and against Scotland in 1998 strengthened the Italians' case for entry to the Five Nations Championship, and in 2000 they were finally invited to join the tournament which was renamed the Six Nations Championship.

However, the 1990s didn't prove to be a successful decade for the 'Azzuri' as they were known, in the World Cup tournaments: in 1991 they lost to both England and New Zealand in the pool games. They fared slightly better in 1995, losing narrowly to England by 27 points to 20, before beating Argentina in their final pool match. In the 1999 World Cup, Italy lost all three pool games: firstly to England, then to Tonga and finally, in a devastating match against New Zealand, the Italians were overrun, scoring just 3 points to New Zealand's 101. Their World Cup record improved a little in 2003 and 2007 when they won two pool games out of four in each competition.

In thirty-six Internationals contested between the beginning of 2008 to March 2011, Italy suffered thirty defeats, including a sequence of thirteen straight losses. Going into the 2011 Rugby World Cup with that kind of record, it was not surprising that the team failed to qualify for the quarter-finals, and only won two pool games from four (against Russia and the United States). The Italians also lost four of the five matches in the 2012 Six Nations Championship, winning only the final game of the tournament against Scotland in Rome. There was an improvement in the 2013 Six Nations Championship, when they achieved two victories in the Championship for only the second time since their entry in 2000. They defeated France at home in their opening game of the campaign, and then went on to secure a first-ever Championship win against Ireland in the final match, also in Rome.

Italy's poor form returned when they lost all five matches in the 2014 Six Nations Championship. This was followed by three further defeats to Tier 2 teams: Fiji, Samoa and Japan, in June. The team's dismal results meant that they had suffered nine losses in a row, all in the space of seven months. The sequence was finally broken in November 2014 when they defeated

Samoa by 24 points to 13. The Azzuri have not had a happy time in the Six Nations Championships, having won on only twelve occassions and drawn once in eighty matches played: a success rate of 15.6% over the sixteen seasons to 2015.

Drawn in the same pool as France and Ireland in the 2015 Rugby World Cup it was no surprise that Italy failed to qualify for the quarter-finals. However they did run Ireland close in their 16 points to 9 defeat.

# ITALY

## HEAD TO HEAD RESULTS TO 31 OCTOBER 2015

| | P | W | D | L | % | F | A |
|---|---|---|---|---|---|---|---|
| **v TIER 1 Teams** | | | | | | | |
| v Argentina | 20 | 5 | 1 | 14 | 27.5 | 344 | 496 |
| v Australia | 16 | 0 | 0 | 16 | 0.0 | 217 | 565 |
| v England | 21 | 0 | 0 | 21 | 0.0 | 266 | 842 |
| v France | 37 | 3 | 0 | 34 | 8.1 | 392 | 1101 |
| v Ireland | 25 | 4 | 0 | 21 | 16.0 | 391 | 788 |
| v New Zealand | 12 | 0 | 0 | 12 | 0.0 | 118 | 686 |
| v Scotland | 25 | 8 | 0 | 17 | 32.0 | 435 | 588 |
| v South Africa | 12 | 0 | 0 | 12 | 0.0 | 145 | 599 |
| v Wales | 23 | 2 | 1 | 20 | 10.9 | 386 | 748 |
| **Sub-Total** | **191** | **22** | **2** | **167** | **12.0** | **2694** | **6413** |
| **v TIER 2/3 Group** | | | | | | | |
| v Canada | 8 | 6 | 0 | 2 | 75.0 | 226 | 110 |
| v Fiji | 10 | 5 | 0 | 5 | 50.0 | 244 | 243 |
| v Japan | 6 | 5 | 0 | 1 | 83.3 | 199 | 90 |
| v Romania | 42 | 23 | 3 | 16 | 58.3 | 609 | 634 |
| v Samoa | 7 | 2 | 0 | 5 | 28.6 | 109 | 175 |
| v Tonga | 4 | 3 | 0 | 1 | 75.0 | 137 | 63 |
| v United States | 4 | 4 | 0 | 0 | 100.0 | 130 | 54 |
| v Georgia | 1 | 1 | 0 | 0 | 100.0 | 31 | 22 |
| v Namibia | 3 | 1 | 0 | 2 | 33.3 | 75 | 74 |
| v Russia | 4 | 4 | 0 | 0 | 100.0 | 198 | 61 |
| v Uruguay | 3 | 3 | 0 | 0 | 100.0 | 92 | 25 |
| **Sub-Total** | **92** | **57** | **3** | **32** | **63.6** | **2050** | **1551** |
| **v Tier 3 Selection** | | | | | | | |
| v Czechoslovakia * | 11 | 9 | 1 | 1 | 86.4 | 162 | 54 |
| v Portugal | 12 | 10 | 1 | 1 | 87.5 | 333 | 71 |
| v Spain | 27 | 23 | 1 | 3 | 87.0 | 581 | 187 |
| v USSR ** | 14 | 4 | 1 | 9 | 32.1 | 171 | 165 |
| v W. Germany *** | 14 | 13 | 1 | 0 | 96.4 | 226 | 69 |
| **Sub-Total** | **78** | **59** | **5** | **14** | **78.8** | **1473** | **546** |
| **v Other Teams** | | | | | | | |
| v France 'A' | 30 | 1 | 1 | 28 | 5.0 | 289 | 751 |
| v Various Teams | 71 | 39 | 3 | 29 | 57.0 | 1418 | 927 |
| **All Internationals** | **462** | **178** | **14** | **270** | **40.0** | **7924** | **10188** |

* 1933-77      ** 1978-91      *** 1952-82

| No | Date | Opponents | Tmt | Match Venue | Result | |
|----|------|-----------|-----|-------------|--------|---|
| 1 | 20-May-29 | Spain | Int | A Estadi Olimpic de Montjuïc, Barcelona | L | 0-9 |
| 2 | 29-May-30 | Spain | Int | H Arena Civica, Milan | W | 3-0 |
| 3 | 12-Feb-33 | Czechoslovakia | Int | H Arena Civica, Milan | W | 7-3 |
| 4 | 16-Apr-33 | Czechoslovakia | Int | A Great Strahov Stadium, Prague | W | 12-3 |
| 5 | 14-Apr-34 | Catalonia | Int | A Estadi Olimpic de Montjuïc, Barcelona | D | 5-5 |
| 6 | 26-Dec-34 | Romania | Int | H Arena Civica, Milan | W | 7-0 |
| 7 | 24-Mar-35 | Catalonia | Int | H Stadio Luigi Ferraris, Genova | W | 5-3 |
| 8 | 22-Apr-35 | France XV | Int | H Stadio Nazionale del Roma, Rome | L | 6-44 |
| 9 | 14-May-36 | Germany (pOG) | FET | A Berlin | L | 8-19 |
| 10 | 17-May-36 | Romania (pOG) | FET | N Berlin | W | 8-7 |
| 11 | 1-Jan-37 | Germany | Int | H Arena Civica, Milan | L | 3-6 |
| 12 | 25-Apr-37 | Romania | Int | A Stadionul Dinamo, Bucharest | D | 0-0 |
| 13 | 10-Oct-37 | Belgium | FET | N Stade Sébastien, Charléty, Paris | W | 45-0 |
| 14 | 14-Oct-37 | Germany | FET | N Stade Sébastien, Charléty, Paris | W | 9-7 |
| 15 | 17-Oct-37 | France | FET | A Parc des Princess, Paris | L | 5-43 |
| 16 | 6-Mar-38 | Germany | Int | A Stuttgart | L | 0-10 |
| 17 | 11-Feb-39 | Germany | Int | H Arena Civica, Milan | L | 3-12 |
| 18 | 29-Apr-39 | Romania | Int | H Stadio Testaccio, Rome | W | 3-0 |
| 19 | 14-Apr-40 | Romania | Int | A Stadionul Dinamo, Bucharest | L | 0-3 |
| 20 | 5-May-40 | Germany | Int | A Stuttgart | W | 4-0 |
| 21 | 2-May-42 | Romania | Int | H Arena Civica, Milan | W | 22-3 |
| 22 | 28-Mar-48 | France XV | Int | H Stadio Mario Battaglini, Rovigo | L | 6-39 |
| 23 | 23-May-48 | Czechoslovakia | Int | H Stadio Comunale Ennio Tardini, Parma | W | 17-0 |
| 24 | 27-Mar-49 | France XV | Int | A Stade Vélodrome, Marseille | L | 0-27 |
| 25 | 22-May-49 | Czechoslovakia | Int | A Great Strahov Stadium, Prague | L | 6-14 |
| 26 | 6-May-51 | Spain | Int | H Stadio Flaminio, Rome | W | 12-0 |
| 27 | 13-Apr-52 | Spain | FEC | A Estadi Olimpic de Montjuïc, Barcelona | W | 6-0 |
| 28 | 27-Apr-52 | West Germany | FEC | H Stadio Plebiscito, Padova | W | 14-6 |
| 29 | 17-May-52 | France | FEC | H Arena Civica, Milan | L | 8-17 |
| 30 | 26-Apr-53 | France | Int | A Stade de Gerland, Lyon | L | 8-22 |
| 31 | 17-May-53 | West Germany | Int | A Hanover | W | 21-3 |
| 32 | 24-May-53 | Romania | Int | A Stadionul Republicii, Bucharest | W | 16-14 |
| 33 | 19-Apr-54 | Spain | FEC | H Naples | W | 16-6 |
| 34 | 24-Apr-54 | France | FEC | H Stadio Olimpico, Rome | L | 12-39 |
| 35 | 13-Mar-55 | West Germany | Int | H Arena Civica, Milan | W | 24-8 |
| 36 | 10-Apr-55 | France | Int | A Stade Lesdiguières, Grenoble | L | 0-24 |
| 37 | 18-Jul-55 | Spain | MED | A Estadi Olimpic de Montjuïc, Barcelona | W | 8-0 |
| 38 | 21-Jul-55 | France XV | MED | N Estadi Olimpic de Montjuïc, Barcelona | L | 8-16 |
| 39 | 11-Dec-55 | Czechoslovakia | Int | H Stadio Flaminio, Rome | W | 17-6 |
| 40 | 25-Mar-56 | West Germany | Int | A Fritz Grunebaum-Sportpark, Heidelburg | W | 12-3 |

| No | Date | Opponents | Tmt | Match Venue | Result | |
|----|------|-----------|-----|-------------|--------|---|
| 41 | 2-Apr-56 | France | Int | H Stadio Silvio Appiani, Padova | L | 3-16 |
| 42 | 29-Apr-56 | Czechoslovakia | Int | A Great Strahov Stadium, Prague | W | 19-9 |
| 43 | 21-Apr-57 | France | Int | A Stade Armandie, Agen | L | 6-38 |
| 44 | 7-Dec-57 | West Germany | Int | H Arena Civica, Milan | W | 8-0 |
| 45 | 7-Apr-58 | France | Int | H Stadio Arturo Collana, Naples | L | 3-11 |
| 46 | 7-Dec-58 | Romania | Int | H Stadio Santa Maria Goretti, Catania | W | 6-3 |
| 47 | 29-Mar-59 | France | Int | A Stade Marcel Saupin, Nantes | L | 0-22 |
| 48 | 10-Apr-60 | West Germany | Int | A Hanover | W | 11-5 |
| 49 | 17-Apr-60 | France | Int | H Stadio Omobono Tenni, Treviso | L | 0-26 |
| 50 | 15-Jan-61 | West Germany | Int | H Stadio Comunale Beltrametti, Piacenza | W | 19-0 |
| 51 | 2-Apr-61 | France | Int | A Stade Municipal, Chambéry | L | 0-17 |
| 52 | 22-Apr-62 | France | Int | H Stadio Mompiano, Brescia | L | 3-6 |
| 53 | 27-May-62 | West Germany | Int | A Berlin | W | 13-11 |
| 54 | 10-Jun-62 | Romania | Int | A Stadionul 23 August, Bucharest | L | 6-14 |
| 55 | 14-Apr-63 | France | Int | A Stade Lesdiguières, Grenoble | L | 12-14 |
| 56 | 22-Mar-64 | West Germany | Int | H Stadio Renato Dall'Ara, Bologna | W | 17-3 |
| 57 | 29-Mar-64 | France | Int | H Stadio Comunale, Ennio Tardini, Parma | L | 3-12 |
| 58 | 18-Apr-65 | France | Int | A Stade de la Croix du Prince, Pau | L | 0-21 |
| 59 | 8-Dec-65 | Czechoslovakia | FIRA | H Stadio Comunale Carlo Montano, Livorno | W | 11-0 |
| 60 | 9-Apr-66 | France | FIRA | H Naples | L | 0-21 |
| 61 | 30-Oct-66 | West Germany | FIRA | A Berlin | D | 3-3 |
| 62 | 6-Nov-66 | Romania | FIRA | H Stadio Tommaso Fattori, L'Aquila | W | 3-0 |
| 63 | 26-Mar-67 | France | FIRA | A Stade Félix Mayol, Toulon | L | 13-60 |
| 64 | 7-May-67 | Portugal | FIRA | H Stadio Luigi Ferraris, Genova | W | 6-3 |
| 65 | 14-May-67 | Romania | FIRA | A Stadionul Republicii, Bucharest | L | 3-24 |
| 66 | 12-May-68 | Portugal | Int | A Estádio Universitário de Lisboa, Lisbon | W | 17-3 |
| 67 | 3-Nov-68 | West Germany | Int | H Stadio Pierluigi Penzo, Venice | W | 22-14 |
| 68 | 29-Dec-68 | Yugoslavia | FIRA | H Stadio San Dona di Piave, Venice | W | 22-3 |
| 69 | 2-Mar-69 | Bulgaria | FIRA | A Sofia | W | 17-0 |
| 70 | 4-May-69 | Spain | FIRA | H Stadio Tommaso Fattori, L'Aquila | W | 12-5 |
| 71 | 10-May-69 | Belgium | FIRA | A Stade Roi Baudouin, Brussels | W | 30-0 |
| 72 | 9-Nov-69 | France XV | FIRA | H Stadio Santa Maria Goretti, Catania | L | 8-22 |
| 73 | 26-Apr-70 | Czechoslovakia | FIRA | A Stadion Krč, Prague | W | 11-3 |
| 74 | 24-May-70 | Madagascar | Int-T | A Mahamasina Stadium, Antananarivo | W | 17-9 |
| 75 | 31-May-70 | Madagascar | Int-T | A Mahamasina Stadium, Antananarivo | W | 9-6 |
| 76 | 25-Oct-70 | Romania | FIRA | H Stadio Mario Battaglini, Rovigo | L | 3-14 |
| 77 | 21-Feb-71 | Morocco | FIRA | H Stadio San Paulo, Naples | L | 6-8 |
| 78 | 28-Feb-71 | France XV | FIRA | A Stade du Ray, Nice | L | 13-37 |
| 79 | 11-Apr-71 | Romania | FIRA | A Stadionul Dinamo, Bucharest | L | 6-32 |
| 80 | 20-Feb-72 | Portugal | FIRA | H Stadio Plebiscito, Padova | D | 0-0 |

| No | Date | Opponents | Tmt | | Match Venue | Result | |
|----|------|-----------|-----|---|-------------|--------|---|
| 81 | 2-Apr-72 | Portugal | FIRA | A | Estádio Universitário de Lisboa, Lisbon | W | 15-7 |
| 82 | 14-May-72 | Spain | FIRA | A | Campo Ciudad Universitaria, Madrid | L | 0-10 |
| 83 | 21-May-72 | Spain | FIRA | H | Stadio Gino Pistoni-Ivrea,Turin | D | 6-6 |
| 84 | 26-Nov-72 | Yugoslavia | FIRA | H | Stadio P. Perucca, St Vincent, Aosta | W | 13-12 |
| 85 | 25-Feb-73 | Portugal | FIRA | A | Estadio Sérgio Conceição, Coimbra | L | 6-9 |
| 86 | 16-Jun-73 | Rhodesia | Int-T | A | Police Ground, Salisbury | L | 4-42 |
| 87 | 20-Jun-73 | W. Transvaal | Int-T | A | Olën Park, Potchefstroom | L | 6-32 |
| 88 | 23-Jun-73 | Border | Int-T | A | Basil Kenyon Stadium, East London | L | 12-25 |
| 89 | 27-Jun-73 | N.E Transvaal | Int-T | A | Cradock RC ,Cradock, Eastern Cape | L | 12-31 |
| 90 | 30-Jun-73 | Natal | Int-T | A | Kings Park Stadium, Durban | L | 3-23 |
| 91 | 4-Jul-73 | S.E Transvaal | Int-T | A | Johann van Riebeeck Stad, Witbank | L | 12-39 |
| 92 | 7-Jul-73 | SA Africans | Int-T | A | Boet Erasmus Stadium, Port Elizabeth | W | 24-4 |
| 93 | 9-Jul-73 | N. Free State | Int-T | A | North West Stadium, Welkom | L | 11-12 |
| 94 | 11-Jul-73 | Transvaal 'B' | Int-T | A | Ellis Park, Johannesburg | L | 24-28 |
| 95 | 4-Nov-73 | Czechoslovakia | FIRA | H | Stadio Mario Battaglini, Rovigo | D | 3-3 |
| 96 | 11-Nov-73 | Yugoslavia | FIRA | A | Stadion Maksimir, Zagreb | W | 25-7 |
| 97 | 21-Nov-73 | Australia XV | Int | H | Stadio Tommaso Fattori, L'Aquila | L | 21-59 |
| 98 | 10-Feb-74 | Portugal | FIRA | A | Estádio Universitário de Lisboa, Lisbon | W | 11-3 |
| 99 | 15-Mar-74 | Middlesex | Int-T | A | Stoop Memorial Ground, London | L | 12-28 |
| 100 | 17-Mar-74 | Sussex | Int-T | A | Withdean Stadium, Brighton | L | 7-16 |
| 101 | 20-Mar-74 | Oxfordshire | Int-T | A | Iffley Road, Oxford | L | 6-30 |
| 102 | 5-May-74 | West Germany | FIRA | H | Stadio Comunale Rho, Rho | W | 16-10 |
| 103 | 15-May-74 | SA Africans | Int | H | Stadio Mompiano, Brescia | W | 25-10 |
| 104 | 15-Feb-75 | France XV | FIRA | H | Stadio Flaminio, Rome | L | 9-16 |
| 105 | 6-Apr-75 | Spain | FIRA | A | Campo Ciudad Universitaria, Madrid | W | 19-3 |
| 106 | 27-Apr-75 | Romania | FIRA | A | Dinamo Stadion, Bucharest | D | 3-3 |
| 107 | 10-May-75 | Czechoslovakia | FIRA | H | Stadio Oreste Granillo, Reggio di Calabria | W | 49-9 |
| 108 | 13-Sep-75 | England U 23 | Int | A | County Ground, Gosforth | L | 13-29 |
| 109 | 25-Oct-75 | Poland | FIRA | H | Stadio Comunale di Monigo, Treviso | W | 28-13 |
| 110 | 23-Nov-75 | Netherlands | FIRA | A | Sports Park Berg and Bos, Apeldoorn | W | 24-0 |
| 111 | 20-Dec-75 | Spain | FIRA | A | Campo Ciudad Universitaria, Madrid | W | 19-6 |
| 112 | 7-Feb-76 | France XV | FIRA | H | Arena Civica, Milan | L | 11-23 |
| 113 | 24-Apr-76 | Romania | FIRA | H | Stadio Comunale, Ennio Tardini, Parma | W | 13-12 |
| 114 | 21-Oct-76 | Japan | Int | H | Stadio Silvio Appiani, Padova | W | 25-3 |
| 115 | 4-Nov-76 | Australia XV | Int | H | Arena Civica, Milan | L | 15-16 |
| 116 | 27-Nov-76 | Spain | FIRA | H | Stadio Flaminio, Rome | W | 17-4 |
| 117 | 6-Feb-77 | France XV | FIRA | A | Stade Lesdiguières, Grenoble | L | 3-10 |
| 118 | 6-Mar-77 | Morocco | FIRA | A | COC Stadium, Casablanca | L | 9-10 |
| 119 | 2-Apr-77 | Poland | FIRA | H | Stadio Santa Maria Goretti, Catania | W | 29-3 |
| 120 | 1-May-77 | Romania | FIRA | A | Stadionul Dinamo, Bucharest | L | 0-69 |

| No | Date | Opponents | Tmt | | Match Venue | Result | |
|----|------|-----------|-----|---|-------------|--------|---|
| 121 | 23-Oct-77 | Poland | FIRA | A | Skra Stadium, Warsaw | L | 6-12 |
| 122 | 29-Oct-77 | Czechoslovakia | FIRA | A | Stadion Krč, Prague | W | 10-4 |
| 123 | 26-Nov-77 | Romania | FIRA | H | Stadio Oreste Granillo, Reggio di Calabria | D | 10-10 |
| 124 | 17-Dec-77 | Spain | FIRA | A | Campo Ciudad Universitaria, Madrid | L | 3-10 |
| 125 | 4-Feb-78 | France XV | FIRA | H | Stadio Tommaso Fattori, L'Aquila | L | 9-31 |
| 126 | 24-Oct-78 | Argentina | Int | H | Stadio Mario Battaglini, Rovigo | W | 19-6 |
| 127 | 18-Nov-78 | USSR | FIRA | H | Stadio Flaminio, Rome | L | 9-11 |
| 128 | 17-Dec-78 | Spain | FIRA | H | Stadio Comunale di Monigo, Treviso | W | 35-3 |
| 129 | 18-Feb-79 | France XV | FIRA | H | Stadio Plebiscito, Padova | L | 9-15 |
| 130 | 14-Apr-79 | Poland | FIRA | H | Stadio Tommaso Fattori, L'Aquila | W | 18-3 |
| 131 | 22-Apr-79 | Romania | FIRA | A | Stadionul Parcul Copilului, Bucharest | L | 0-44 |
| 132 | 16-May-79 | England U 23 | Int | H | Stadio Mompiano, Brescia | D | 6-6 |
| 133 | 18-Sep-79 | Spain | MED | N | Makarska Stadium, Makaraska, Yugoslavia | W | 16-9 |
| 134 | 20-Sep-79 | Morocco | MED | N | Makarska Stadium, Makaraska, Yugoslavia | W | 10-7 |
| 135 | 22-Sep-79 | France XV | MED | N | Makarska Stadium, Makaraska, Yugoslavia | L | 12-38 |
| 136 | 30-Sep-79 | Poland | FIRA | A | Sochaczew, Poland | W | 13-3 |
| 137 | 28-Oct-79 | USSR | FIRA | A | Fili Stadion, Moscow | L | 0-9 |
| 138 | 28-Nov-79 | NZ XV | Int | H | Stadio Mario Battaglini, Rovigo | L | 12-18 |
| 139 | 22-Dec-79 | Morocco | FIRA | H | Stadio Santa Colomba, Benevento | W | 34-6 |
| 140 | 17-Feb-80 | France XV | FIRA | A | Stade Marcel Michelin, Clermont Ferrand | L | 9-46 |
| 141 | 13-Apr-80 | Romania | FIRA | H | Stadio Tommaso Fattori, L'Aquila | W | 24-17 |
| 142 | 14-Jun-80 | Fiji | Int-T | A | National Stadium, Suva | L | 3-16 |
| 143 | 5-Jul-80 | Jnr All Blacks | Int-T | A | Eden Park, Auckland | L | 13-30 |
| 144 | 6-Jul-80 | Cook Islands | Int-T | A | National Stadium, Avarua, Rarotonga | L | 6-15 |
| 145 | 5-Oct-80 | Poland | FIRA | H | Stadio Mario Battaglini, Rovigo | W | 37-12 |
| 146 | 2-Nov-80 | U S S R | FIRA | H | Stadio Mario Battaglini, Rovigo | L | 3-4 |
| 147 | 21-Dec-80 | Spain | FIRA | A | Campo Ciudad Universitaria, Madrid | W | 18-13 |
| 148 | 8-Mar-81 | France XV | FIRA | H | Stadio Mario Battaglini, Rovigo | L | 9-17 |
| 149 | 12-Apr-81 | Romania | FIRA | A | Stadionul Municipal, Brăilla | L | 9-35 |
| 150 | 25-Oct-81 | U S S R | FIRA | A | Nauka Stadion, Moscow | D | 12-12 |
| 151 | 29-Nov-81 | West Germany | FIRA | H | Stadio Mario Battaglini, Rovigo | W | 23-0 |
| 152 | 21-Feb-82 | France XV | FIRA | A | Stade Albert Domec, Carcassonne | L | 19-25 |
| 153 | 11-Apr-82 | Romania | FIRA | H | Stadio Mario Battaglini, Rovigo | W | 21-15 |
| 154 | 22-May-82 | England U 23 | Int | H | Stadio Plebiscito, Padova | W | 12-7 |
| 155 | 7-Nov-82 | West Germany | FIRA | A | Hanover | W | 23-3 |
| 156 | 19-Dec-82 | Morocco | FIRA | A | COC Stadium, Casablanca | W | 13-3 |
| 157 | 6-Feb-83 | France XV | FIRA | H | Stadio Mario Battaglini, Rovigo | D | 6-6 |
| 158 | 10-Apr-83 | Romania | FIRA | A | Stadionul Municipal Gloria, Buzău | L | 6-13 |
| 159 | 22-May-83 | U S S R | FIRA | H | Stadio Santa Maria Goretti, Catania | W | 12-10 |
| 160 | 25-Jun-83 | Canada | Int-T | A | Swanguard Stadium, Burnaby Lake, BC | L | 13-19 |

| No | Date | Opponents | Tmt | | Match Venue | Result | |
|-----|-----------|------------|-------|---|--------------------------------------------------|---|------|
| 161 | 1-Jul-83 | Canada | Int-T | A | Varsity Stadium, Stanley Park, Toronto | W | 37-9 |
| 162 | 7-Sep-83 | Spain | MED | N | COC Stadium, Casablanca | W | 27-9 |
| 163 | 10-Sep-83 | Morocco | MED | A | COC Stadium, Casablanca | W | 15-9 |
| 164 | 13-Sep-83 | France XV | MED | N | COC Stadium, Casablanca | L | 12-26 |
| 165 | 22-Oct-83 | Australia | Int | H | Stadio Mario Battaglini, Rovigo | L | 7-29 |
| 166 | 30-Oct-83 | U S S R | FIRA | A | Spartak Stadium, Kiev | L | 7-16 |
| 167 | 19-Feb-84 | France XV | FIRA | A | Stade Municipal, Chalon-sur-Saone | L | 16-38 |
| 168 | 18-Mar-84 | Morocco | FIRA | H | Stadio Comunale Beltrametti, Piacenza | W | 27-0 |
| 169 | 22-Apr-84 | Romania | FIRA | H | Stadio Tommaso Fattori, L'Aquila | W | 12-6 |
| 170 | 20-Oct-84 | Tunisia | FIRA | A | Stade Mustapha Ben Jannet, Monastir | W | 20-6 |
| 171 | 18-Nov-84 | U S S R | FIRA | H | Stadio Tommaso Fattori, L'Aquila | W | 13-12 |
| 172 | 3-Mar-85 | France XV | FIRA | H | Stadio Comunale di Monigo, Treviso | L | 9-22 |
| 173 | 14-Apr-85 | Romania | FIRA | A | Stadionul Municipal, Brasov | L | 6-7 |
| 174 | 17-Apr-85 | England B | Int | A | Twickenham, London | L | 9-21 |
| 175 | 18-May-85 | Spain | FIRA | H | Stadio Danilo Martelli, Mantova | W | 22-13 |
| 176 | 22-Jun-85 | Zimbabwe | Int-T | A | Hartsfield Rugby Ground, Bulawayo | W | 25-6 |
| 177 | 30-Jun-85 | Zimbabwe | Int-T | A | Police Ground, Harare | W | 12-10 |
| 178 | 10-Nov-85 | U S S R | FIRA | A | Fili Stadion, Moscow | L | 13-15 |
| 179 | 7-Dec-85 | Romania | FIRA | H | Stadio Tommaso Fattori, L'Aquila | W | 19-3 |
| 180 | 8-Feb-86 | Tunisia | FIRA | H | Stadio Mario Battaglini, Rovigo | W | 18-4 |
| 181 | 15-Feb-86 | France XV | FIRA | A | Union Sportif Annecy Rugby, Annecy | L | 0-18 |
| 182 | 13-Apr-86 | Portugal | FIRA | H | Stadio Jesi Arriva, Jesi | W | 26-24 |
| 183 | 10-May-86 | England XV | Int | H | Stadio Olimpico, Rome | D | 15-15 |
| 184 | 1-Jun-86 | Australia | Int-T | A | Ballymore Oval, Brisbane | L | 18-39 |
| 185 | 18-Oct-86 | Tunisia | FIRA | A | Stade Africain de Menzel, Bourghiba | W | 22-9 |
| 186 | 16-Nov-86 | U S S R | FIRA | H | Stadio Luigi Ferraris, Genova | L | 14-16 |
| 187 | 18-Jan-87 | Portugal | FIRA | A | Estádio Universitário de Lisboa, Lisbon | W | 41-3 |
| 188 | 22-Feb-87 | France XV | FIRA | H | Stadio Plebiscito, Padova | L | 6-22 |
| 189 | 12-Apr-87 | Romania | FIRA | A | Stadionul 1 Mai, Constanta | L | 3-9 |
| 190 | 22-May-87 | New Zealand | WCp | A | Eden Park, Auckland | L | 6-70 |
| 191 | 28-May-87 | Argentina | WCp | N | Lancaster Park Oval, Christchurch | L | 16-25 |
| 192 | 31-May-87 | Fiji | WCp | A | Carisbrook, Dunedin | W | 18-15 |
| 193 | 7-Nov-87 | U S S R | FIRA | A | Stadionul Republican Chişinău, Moldova | L | 9-12 |
| 194 | 5-Dec-87 | Spain | FIRA | A | Estadi Olímpic Lluís Companys, Barcelona | W | 13-0 |
| 195 | 7-Feb-88 | France XV | FIRA | A | Stade Louis II, Monte Carlo | L | 9-19 |
| 196 | 2-Apr-88 | Romania | FIRA | H | Stadio San Siro, Milan | L | 3-12 |
| 197 | 5-Nov-88 | U S S R | FIRA | H | Stadio Comunale di Monigo, Treviso | L | 12-18 |
| 198 | 3-Dec-88 | Australia | Int | H | Stadio Flaminio, Rome | L | 6-55 |
| 199 | 31-Dec-88 | Ireland | Int | A | Lansdowne Road, Dublin | L | 15-31 |
| 200 | 19-Feb-89 | France XV | FIRA | H | Stadio Mompiano, Brescia | L | 12-40 |

| No | Date | Opponents | Tmt | | Match Venue | Result | |
|---|---|---|---|---|---|---|---|
| 201 | 15-Apr-89 | Romania | FIRA | A | Stadionul Dinamo, Bucharest | L | 4-28 |
| 202 | 2-Jun-89 | Spain | FIRA | H | Stadio Tommaso Fattori, L'Aquila | W | 33-19 |
| 203 | 24-Jun-89 | Argentina | Int-T | A | Vélez Sarsfield Stadium, Buenos Aires | L | 16-21 |
| 204 | 30-Sep-89 | Zimbabwe | Int | H | Stadio Comunale di Monigo, Treviso | W | 33-9 |
| 205 | 5-Nov-89 | U S S R | FIRA | A | Fili Stadion, Moscow | L | 12-15 |
| 206 | 18-Feb-90 | France XV | FIRA | A | Stade Municipal, Albi | L | 12-22 |
| 207 | 7-Apr-90 | Poland | FIRA | H | Naples | W | 34-3 |
| 208 | 14-Apr-90 | Romania | FIRA | H | Frascati Rugby Stadium, Rome | L | 9-16 |
| 209 | 30-Sep-90 | Spain (WCQ) | FIRA | H | Stadio Mario Battaglini, Rovigo | W | 30-6 |
| 210 | 3-Oct-90 | Netherlands | WCQ | H | Stadio Comunale di Monigo, Treviso | W | 24-11 |
| 211 | 7-Oct-90 | Romania | WCQ | H | Stadio Plebiscito, Padova | W | 29-21 |
| 212 | 24-Nov-90 | U S S R | FIRA | H | Stadio Mario Battaglini, Rovigo | W | 34-12 |
| 213 | 2-Mar-91 | France XV | FIRA | H | Stadio Flaminio, Rome | L | 9-15 |
| 214 | 21-Apr-91 | Romania | FIRA | A | Stadionul Dinamo, Bucharest | W | 21-18 |
| 215 | 15-Jun-91 | Namibia | Int-T | A | South West Stadium, Windhoek | L | 7-17 |
| 216 | 22-Jun-91 | Namibia | Int-T | A | South West Stadium, Windhoek | L | 19-33 |
| 217 | 5-Oct-91 | United States | WCp | N | Cross Green, Otley, Yorkshire | W | 30-9 |
| 218 | 8-Oct-91 | England | WCP | A | Twickenham, London | L | 6-36 |
| 219 | 13-Oct-91 | New Zealand | WCp | N | Welford Road, Leicester | L | 21-31 |
| 220 | 3-Nov-91 | C I S | FIRA | A | Fili Stadion, Moscow | W | 21-3 |
| 221 | 9-Feb-92 | Spain | FIRA | A | Campo Ciudad Universitaria, Madrid | W | 22-21 |
| 222 | 16-Feb-92 | France Espoirs | FIRA | A | Stade Maurice Trélut, Tarbes | L | 18-21 |
| 223 | 18-Apr-92 | Romania | FIRA | H | Stadio Mario Battaglini, Rovigo | W | 39-13 |
| 224 | 1-Oct-92 | Romania | FIRA | H | Stadio Flaminio, Rome | W | 22-3 |
| 225 | 19-Dec-92 | Scotland A | Int | A | The Greenyards, Melrose | L | 17-22 |
| 226 | 14-Feb-93 | Spain | FIRA | A | Campo Ciudad Universitaria, Madrid | W | 52-0 |
| 227 | 20-Feb-93 | France XV | Int | H | Stadio Comunale di Monigo, Treviso | L | 12-14 |
| 228 | 17-Apr-93 | Portugal | FIRA | A | Estádio Universitário de Coimbra, Coimbra | W | 33-11 |
| 229 | 17-Jun-93 | Croatia | MED | N | Stade Aimé Giral, Perpignan | W | 76-11 |
| 230 | 19-Jun-93 | Morocco | MED | N | Stade Albert Domec, Carcassonne | W | 70-9 |
| 231 | 21-Jun-93 | Spain | MED | N | Stade Aimé Giral, Perpignan | W | 38-6 |
| 232 | 25-Jun-93 | France XV | MED | A | Stade Méditerranée, Béziers | L | 6-31 |
| 233 | 6-Nov-93 | Russia | FIRA | A | Fili Stadion, Moscow | W | 30-19 |
| 234 | 11-Nov-93 | France XV | FIRA | H | Stadio Comunale di Monigo, Treviso | W | 16-9 |
| 235 | 18-Dec-93 | Scotland A | Int | H | Stadio Mario Battaglini, Rovigo | W | 18-15 |
| 236 | 7-May-94 | Spain | FIRA | H | Stadio Comunale Sergio Lanfrachi, Parma | W | 62-15 |
| 237 | 14-May-94 | Romania | FIRA | A | Stadionul Dinamo, Bucharest | L | 12-26 |
| 238 | 18-May-94 | Czech Republic | WCQ | H | Stadio Luigi Zaffanella, Viadana | W | 104-8 |
| 239 | 21-May-94 | Netherlands | WCQ | H | Centro Sportivo San Michele, Calvisano | W | 63-9 |
| 240 | 18-Jun-94 | Australia | Int-T | A | Ballymore Oval, Brisbane | L | 20-23 |

| No | Date | Opponents | Tmt | Match Venue | Result | |
|-----|-----------|----------------|------|-------------------------------------------|---|-------|
| 241 | 25-Jun-94 | Australia | Int-T A | Olympic Park Stadium, Melbourne | L | 7-20 |
| 242 | 1-Oct-94 | Romania | WCQ H | Stadio Santa Maria Goretti, Catania | W | 24-6 |
| 243 | 12-Oct-94 | Wales | WCQ A | National Stadium, Cardiff | L | 19-29 |
| 244 | 4-Dec-94 | France XV | Int A | Stade Bourillot, Dijon | L | 9-14 |
| 245 | 7-Jan-95 | Scotland A | Int A | McDiarmid Park, Perth | L | 16-18 |
| 246 | 6-May-95 | Ireland | Int H | Stadio Comunale di Monigo, Treviso | W | 22-12 |
| 247 | 27-May-95 | Western Samoa | WCp N | Basil Kenyon Stadium, East London | L | 18-42 |
| 248 | 31-May-95 | England | WCp N | Kings Park Stadium, Durban | L | 20-27 |
| 249 | 4-Jun-95 | Argentina | WCp N | Basil Kenyon Stadium, East London | W | 31-25 |
| 250 | 14-Oct-95 | France | LTC N | Ferro Carril Oeste Stadium, B Aires | L | 22-34 |
| 251 | 17-Oct-95 | Argentina | LTC A | Estadio Monumental José Fierro, Tucumán | L | 6-26 |
| 252 | 21-Oct-95 | Romania LTC | FIRA N | Ferro Carril Oeste Stadium, B Aires | W | 40-3 |
| 253 | 28-Oct-95 | New Zealand | Int H | Stadio Renato Dall'Ara, Bologna | L | 6-70 |
| 254 | 12-Nov-95 | South Africa | Int H | Stadio Olimpico, Rome | L | 21-40 |
| 255 | 16-Jan-96 | Wales | Int A | National Stadium, Cardiff | L | 26-31 |
| 256 | 2-Mar-96 | Portugal | FIRA A | Estádio Universitário de Lisboa, Lisbon | W | 64-3 |
| 257 | 5-Oct-96 | Wales | Int H | Stadio Olimpico, Rome | L | 22-31 |
| 258 | 23-Oct-96 | Australia | Int H | Stadio Plebiscito, Padova | L | 18-40 |
| 259 | 23-Nov-96 | England | Int A | Twickenham, London | L | 21-54 |
| 260 | 14-Dec-96 | Scotland | Int A | Murrayfield, Edinburgh | L | 22-29 |
| 261 | 4-Jan-97 | Ireland | Int A | Lansdowne Road, Dublin | W | 37-29 |
| 262 | 22-Mar-97 | France | FIRA A | Stade Lesdiguières, Grenoble | W | 40-32 |
| 263 | 18-Oct-97 | France | LTC A | Stade Jacques Fouroux, Auch | L | 19-30 |
| 264 | 22-Oct-97 | Argentina | LTC N | Stade Antoine Béguère, Lourdes | D | 18-18 |
| 265 | 26-Oct-97 | Romania | LTC N | Stade Maurice Trélut, Tarbes | W | 55-32 |
| 266 | 8-Nov-97 | South Africa | Int H | Stadio Renato Dall'Ara, Bologna | L | 31-62 |
| 267 | 20-Dec-97 | Ireland | Int H | Stadio Renato Dall'Ara, Bologna | W | 37-22 |
| 268 | 24-Jan-98 | Scotland | Int H | Stadio Comunale di Monigo, Treviso | W | 25-21 |
| 269 | 7-Feb-98 | Wales | Int A | Stradey Park, Llanelli | L | 20-23 |
| 270 | 18-Apr-98 | Russia | WCQ A | Central Stadium, Krasnoyarsk | W | 48-18 |
| 271 | 7-Nov-98 | Argentina | Int H | Stadio Comunale Beltrametti, Piacenza | W | 23-19 |
| 272 | 18-Nov-98 | Netherlands | WCQ N | McAlpine Stadium, Huddersfield | W | 67-7 |
| 273 | 22-Nov-98 | England | WCQ A | McAlpine Stadium, Huddersfield | L | 15-23 |
| 274 | 30-Jan-99 | France XV | Int H | Stadio Luigi Ferraris, Genova | L | 24-49 |
| 275 | 6-Mar-99 | Scotland | Int A | Murrayfield, Edinburgh | L | 12-30 |
| 276 | 20-Mar-99 | Wales | Int H | Stadio Comunale di Monigo, Treviso | L | 21-60 |
| 277 | 10-Apr-99 | Ireland | Int A | Lansdowne Road, Dublin | L | 30-39 |
| 278 | 12-Jun-99 | South Africa | Int-T A | Telkom Park Stadium, Port Elizabeth | L | 3-74 |
| 279 | 19-Jun-99 | South Africa | Int-T A | Kings Park Stadium, Durban | L | 0-101 |
| 280 | 22-Aug-99 | Uruguay | Int H | Stadio Tommaso Fattori, L'Aquila | W | 49-17 |

| No | Date | Opponents | Tmt | Match Venue | Result | |
|----|------|-----------|-----|-------------|--------|---|
| 281 | 26-Aug-99 | Spain | Int | H Stadio Tommaso Fattori, L'Aquila | W | 42-11 |
| 282 | 28-Aug-99 | Fiji | Int | H Stadio Tommaso Fattori, L'Aquila | L | 32-50 |
| 283 | 2-Oct-99 | England | WCp | A Twickenham, London | L | 7-67 |
| 284 | 10-Oct-99 | Tonga | WCp | N Welford Road, Leicester | L | 25-28 |
| 285 | 14-Oct-99 | New Zealand | WCp | N McAlpine Stadium, Huddersfield | L | 3-101 |
| 286 | 5-Feb-00 | Scotland | 6N | H Stadio Flaminio, Rome | W | 34-20 |
| 287 | 19-Feb-00 | Wales | 6N | A Millennium Stadium, Cardiff | L | 16-47 |
| 288 | 4-Mar-00 | Ireland | 6N | A Lansdowne Road, Dublin | L | 13-60 |
| 289 | 18-Mar-00 | England | 6N | H Stadio Flaminio, Rome | L | 12-59 |
| 290 | 1-Apr-00 | France | 6N | A Stade de France, Paris | L | 31-42 |
| 291 | 8-Jul-00 | Samoa | Int-T | A Apia Park, Apia | L | 24-43 |
| 292 | 15-Jul-00 | Fiji | Int-T | A Churchill Park, Lautoka | L | 9-43 |
| 293 | 11-Nov-00 | Canada | Int | H Stadio Mario Battaglini, Rovigo | L | 17-22 |
| 294 | 18 Nov 00 | Romania | Int | H Stadio Santa Columba, Benevento | W | 37-17 |
| 295 | 25-Nov-00 | New Zealand | Int | H Stadio Luigi Ferraris, Genova | L | 19-56 |
| 296 | 3-Feb-01 | Ireland | 6N | H Stadio Flaminio, Rome | L | 22-41 |
| 297 | 17-Feb-01 | England | 6N | A Twickenham, London | L | 23-80 |
| 298 | 3-Mar-01 | France | 6N | H Stadio Flaminio, Rome | L | 19-30 |
| 299 | 17-Mar-01 | Scotland | 6N | A Murrayfield, Edinburgh | L | 19-23 |
| 300 | 8-Apr-01 | Wales | 6N | H Stadio Flaminio, Rome | L | 23-33 |
| 301 | 23-Jun-01 | Namibia | Int-T | A South West Stadium, Windhoek | W | 49-24 |
| 302 | 30-Jun-01 | South Africa | Int-T | A Telkom Park Stadium, Port Elizabeth | L | 14-60 |
| 303 | 7-Jul-01 | Uruguay | Int-T | A Estadio Gran Parque Central, Montevideo | W | 14-3 |
| 304 | 14-Jul-01 | Argentina | Int-T | A Ferro Carril Oeste Stadium, B Aires | L | 17-38 |
| 305 | 10-Nov-01 | Fiji | Int | H Stadio Comunale di Monigo, Treviso | W | 66-10 |
| 306 | 17-Nov-01 | South Africa | Int | H Stadio Luigi Ferraris, Genova | L | 26-54 |
| 307 | 24-Nov-01 | Samoa | Int | H Stadio Tommaso Fattori, L'Aquila | L | 9-17 |
| 308 | 2-Feb-02 | France | 6N | A Stade de France, Paris | L | 12-33 |
| 309 | 16-Feb-02 | Scotland | 6N | H Stadio Flaminio, Rome | L | 12-29 |
| 310 | 2-Mar-02 | Wales | 6N | A Millennium Stadium, Cardiff | L | 20-44 |
| 311 | 23-Mar-02 | Ireland | 6N | A Lansdowne Road, Dublin | L | 17-32 |
| 312 | 7-Apr-02 | England | 6N | H Stadio Flaminio, Rome | L | 9-45 |
| 313 | 8-Jun-02 | New Zealand | Int-T | A Waikato Stadium, Hamilton | L | 10-64 |
| 314 | 22-Sep-02 | Spain | WCQ | A Campo de Pepe Rojo, Valladolid | W | 50-3 |
| 315 | 28-Sep-02 | Romania | WCQ | H Stadio Comunale Sergio Lanfrachi, Parma | W | 25-17 |
| 316 | 16-Nov-02 | Argentina | Int | H Stadio Flaminio, Rome | L | 6-36 |
| 317 | 23-Nov-02 | Australia | Int | H Stadio Luigi Ferraris, Genova | L | 3-34 |
| 318 | 15-Feb-03 | Wales | 6N | H Stadio Flaminio, Rome | W | 30-22 |
| 319 | 22-Feb-03 | Ireland | 6N | H Stadio Flaminio, Rome | L | 13-37 |
| 320 | 9-Mar-03 | England | 6N | A Twickenham, London | L | 5-40 |

| No | Date | Opponents | Tmt | | Match Venue | Result | |
|-----|-----------|---------------|-------|---|------------------------------------------------|---|-------|
| 321 | 23-Mar-03 | France | 6N | H | Stadio Flaminio, Rome | L | 27-53 |
| 322 | 29-Mar-03 | Scotland | 6N | A | Murrayfield, Edinburgh | L | 25-33 |
| 323 | 23-Aug-03 | Scotland | Int | A | Murrayfield, Edinburgh | L | 15-47 |
| 324 | 30-Aug-03 | Ireland | Int | A | Thomond Park, Limerick | L | 6-61 |
| 325 | 6-Sep-03 | Georgia | Int | H | Stadio Comunale Censin Bosia, Asti | W | 31-22 |
| 326 | 11-Oct-03 | New Zealand | WCp | N | Telstra Dome, Melbourne | L | 7-70 |
| 327 | 15-Oct-03 | Tonga | WCp | N | Canberra Stadium, Canberra | W | 36-12 |
| 328 | 21-Oct-03 | Canada | WCp | N | Canberra Stadium, Canberra | W | 19-14 |
| 329 | 25-Oct-03 | Wales | WCp | N | Canberra Stadium, Canberra | L | 15-27 |
| 330 | 15-Feb-04 | England | 6N | H | Stadio Flaminio, Rome | L | 9-50 |
| 331 | 21-Feb-04 | France | 6N | A | Stade de France, Paris | L | 0-25 |
| 332 | 6-Mar-04 | Scotland | 6N | H | Stadio Flaminio, Rome | W | 20-14 |
| 333 | 20-Mar-04 | Ireland | 6N | A | Lansdowne Road, Dublin | L | 3-19 |
| 334 | 27-Mar-04 | Wales | 6N | A | Millennium Stadium, Cardiff | L | 10-44 |
| 335 | 26-Jun-04 | Romania | Int | A | Lia Manoliu Stadium, Bucharest | L | 24-25 |
| 336 | 4-Jul-04 | Japan | Int-T | A | Prince Chichibu Memorial Ground, Tokyo | W | 32-19 |
| 337 | 6-Nov-04 | Canada | Int | H | Stadio Tommaso Fattori, L'Aquila | W | 51-6 |
| 338 | 13-Nov-04 | New Zealand | Int | H | Stadio Flaminio, Rome | L | 10-59 |
| 339 | 27-Nov-04 | United States | Int | H | Stadio Lamarmora, Biella-in-Piedmont | W | 43-25 |
| 340 | 6-Feb-05 | Ireland | 6N | H | Stadio Flaminio, Rome | L | 17-28 |
| 341 | 12-Feb-05 | Wales | 6N | H | Stadio Flaminio, Rome | L | 8-38 |
| 342 | 26-Feb-05 | Scotland | 6N | A | Murrayfield, Edinburgh | L | 10-18 |
| 343 | 12-Mar-05 | England | 6N | A | Twickenham, London | L | 7-39 |
| 344 | 19-Mar-05 | France | 6N | H | Stadio Flaminio, Rome | L | 13-56 |
| 345 | 11-Jun-05 | Argentina | Int-T | A | Estadio Padre Ernesto Martearena, Salta | L | 21-35 |
| 346 | 17-Jun-05 | Argentina | Int-T | A | Estadio Olimpico Château Carreras, Córdoba | W | 30-29 |
| 347 | 25-Jun-05 | Australia | Int-T | A | Telstra Dome, Melbourne | L | 21-69 |
| 348 | 12-Nov-05 | Tonga | Int | H | Stadio Lungobisenzio, Prato | W | 48-0 |
| 349 | 19-Nov-05 | Argentina | Int | H | Stadio Luigi Ferraris, Genova | L | 22-39 |
| 350 | 26-Nov-05 | Fiji | Int | H | Stadio Brianteo, Monza, Milan | W | 23-8 |
| 351 | 4-Feb-06 | Ireland | 6N | A | Lansdowne Road, Dublin | L | 16-26 |
| 352 | 11-Feb-06 | England | 6N | H | Stadio Flaminio, Rome | L | 16-31 |
| 353 | 25-Feb-06 | France | 6N | A | Stade de France, Paris | L | 12-37 |
| 354 | 11-Mar-06 | Wales | 6N | A | Millennium Stadium, Cardiff | D | 18-18 |
| 355 | 18-Mar-06 | Scotland | 6N | H | Stadio Flaminio, Rome | L | 10-13 |
| 356 | 11-Jun-06 | Japan | Int-T | A | Prince Chichibu Memorial Ground, Tokyo | W | 52-6 |
| 357 | 17-Jun-06 | Fiji | Int-T | A | Churchill Park, Lautoka | L | 18-29 |
| 358 | 7-Oct-06 | Portugal | WCQ | H | Stadio Tommaso Fattori, L'Aquila | W | 83-0 |
| 359 | 14-Oct-06 | Russia | WCQ | A | Slava Stadion, Moscow | W | 67-7 |
| 360 | 11-Nov-06 | Australia | Int | H | Stadio Flaminio, Rome | L | 18-25 |

| No | Date | Opponents | Tmt | | Match Venue | Result | |
|----|------|-----------|-----|---|-------------|--------|---|
| 361 | 18-Nov-06 | Argentina | Int | H | Stadio Flaminio, Rome | L | 16-23 |
| 362 | 25-Nov-06 | Canada | Int | H | Stadio Comprensoriale, Fontanafredda | W | 41-6 |
| 363 | 3-Feb-07 | France | 6N-GG | H | Stadio Flaminio, Rome | L | 3-39 |
| 364 | 10-Feb-07 | England | 6N | A | Twickenham, London | L | 7-20 |
| 365 | 24-Feb-07 | Scotland | 6N | A | Murrayfield, Edinburgh | W | 37-17 |
| 366 | 10-Mar-07 | Wales | 6N | H | Stadio Flaminio, Rome | W | 23-20 |
| 367 | 17-Mar-07 | Ireland | 6N | H | Stadio Flaminio, Rome | L | 24-51 |
| 368 | 2-Jun-07 | Uruguay | Int-T | A | Estadio Gran Parque Central, Montevideo | W | 29-5 |
| 369 | 9-Jun-07 | Argentina | Int-T | A | Estadio Malvinas Argentinas, Mendoza | L | 6-24 |
| 370 | 18-Aug-07 | Japan | Int | H | Stadio P. Perucca, St Vincent, Aosta | W | 36-12 |
| 371 | 24-Aug-07 | Ireland | Int | A | Ravenhill, Belfast | L | 20-23 |
| 372 | 8-Sep-07 | New Zealand | WCp | N | Stade Vélodrome, Marseille | L | 14-76 |
| 373 | 12-Sep-07 | Romania | WCp | N | Stade Vélodrome, Marseille | W | 24-18 |
| 374 | 19-Sep-07 | Portugal | WCp | N | Parc des Princess, Paris | W | 31-5 |
| 375 | 29-Sep-07 | Scotland | WCp | N | Stade Geoffroy-Guichard, Saint Étienne | L | 16-18 |
| 376 | 2-Feb-08 | Ireland | 6N | A | Croke Park, Dublin | L | 11-16 |
| 377 | 10-Feb-08 | England | 6N | H | Stadio Flaminio, Rome | L | 19-23 |
| 378 | 23-Feb-08 | Wales | 6N | A | Millennium Stadium, Cardiff | L | 8-47 |
| 379 | 9-Mar-08 | France | 6N-GG | A | Stade de France, Paris | L | 13-25 |
| 380 | 15-Mar-08 | Scotland | 6N | H | Stadio Flaminio, Rome | W | 23-20 |
| 381 | 21-Jun-08 | South Africa | Int-T | A | Newlands Stadium, Cape Town | L | 0-26 |
| 382 | 28-Jun-08 | Argentina | Int-T | A | Estadio Olimpico Château Carreras, Córdoba | W | 13-12 |
| 383 | 8-Nov-08 | Australia | Int | H | Stadio Euganeo, Padova | L | 20-30 |
| 384 | 15-Nov-08 | Argentina | Int | H | Stadio Olimpico di Torino, Turin | L | 14-22 |
| 385 | 22-Nov-08 | Pacific Islands | Int | H | Stadio Giglio, Reggio Emilia | L | 17-25 |
| 386 | 7-Feb-09 | England | 6N | A | Twickenham, London | L | 11-36 |
| 387 | 15-Feb-09 | Ireland | 6N | H | Stadio Flaminio, Rome | L | 9-38 |
| 388 | 28-Feb-09 | Scotland | 6N | A | Murrayfield, Edinburgh | L | 6-26 |
| 389 | 14-Mar-09 | Wales | 6N | H | Stadio Flaminio, Rome | L | 15-20 |
| 390 | 21-Mar-09 | France | 6N-GG | H | Stadio Flaminio, Rome | L | 8-50 |
| 391 | 13-Jun-09 | Australia | Int-T | A | Canberra Stadium, Canberrra | L | 8-31 |
| 392 | 20-Jun-09 | Australia | Int-T | A | Etihad Stadium, Docklands, Melbourne | L | 12-34 |
| 393 | 27-Jun-09 | New Zealand | Int-T | A | AMI Stadium, Christchurch | L | 6-27 |
| 394 | 14-Nov-09 | New Zealand | Int | H | Stadio San Siro, Milan | L | 6-20 |
| 395 | 21-Nov-09 | South Africa | Int | H | Stadio Friuli, Udine | L | 10-32 |
| 396 | 28-Nov-09 | Samoa | Int | H | Stadio Cino e Lillo del Duca, Ascoli Piceno | W | 24-6 |
| 397 | 6-Feb-10 | Ireland | 6N | A | Croke Park, Dublin | L | 11-29 |
| 398 | 14-Feb-10 | England | 6N | H | Stadio Flaminio, Rome | L | 12-17 |
| 399 | 27-Feb-10 | Scotland | 6N | H | Stadio Flaminio, Rome | W | 16-12 |
| 400 | 14-Mar-10 | France | 6N-GG | A | Stade de France, Paris | L | 20-46 |

| No | Date | Opponents | Tmt | | Match Venue | Result | |
|-----|---------|--------------|--------|---|-------------------------------------------------|---|-------|
| 401 | 20-Mar-10 | Wales | 6N | A | Millennium Stadium, Cardiff | L | 10-33 |
| 402 | 19-Jun-10 | South Africa | Int-T | A | Johann van Riebeeck Stadium, Witbank | L | 13-29 |
| 403 | 26-Jun-10 | South Africa | Int-T | A | Buffalo City Stadium, East London | L | 11-55 |
| 404 | 13-Nov-10 | Argentina | Int | H | Stadio Marc'Antonio Bentegodi, Verona | L | 16-22 |
| 405 | 20-Nov-10 | Australia | Int | H | Stadio Artemio Franchi, Florence | L | 14-32 |
| 406 | 27-Nov-10 | Fiji | Int | H | Stadio Alberto Braglia, Modena | W | 24-16 |
| 407 | 5-Feb-11 | Ireland | 6N | H | Stadio Flaminio, Rome | L | 11-13 |
| 408 | 12-Feb-11 | England | 6N | A | Twickenham, London | L | 13-59 |
| 409 | 26-Feb-11 | Wales | 6N | H | Stadio Flaminio, Rome | L | 16-24 |
| 410 | 12-Mar-11 | France | 6N-GG | H | Stadio Flaminio, Rome | W | 22-21 |
| 411 | 19-Mar-11 | Scotland | 6N | A | Murrayfield, Edinburgh | L | 8-21 |
| 412 | 13-Aug-11 | Japan | Int | H | Stadio Dino Manuzzi, Cesana, Trieste | W | 31-24 |
| 413 | 20-Aug-11 | Scotland | Int | A | Murrayfield, Edinburgh | L | 12-23 |
| 414 | 11-Sep-11 | Australia | WCp | N | North Harbour Stadium, Albany | L | 6-32 |
| 415 | 20-Sep-11 | Russia | WCp | N | Trafalgar Park, Nelson | W | 53-17 |
| 416 | 27-Sep-11 | United States | WCp | N | Trafalgar Park, Nelson | W | 27-10 |
| 417 | 2-Oct-11 | Ireland | WCp | N | Otago Stadium, Dunedin | L | 6-36 |
| 418 | 4-Feb-12 | France | 6N-GG | A | Stade de France, Paris | L | 12-30 |
| 419 | 11-Feb-12 | England | 6N | H | Stadio Olimpico, Rome | L | 15-19 |
| 420 | 25-Feb-12 | Ireland | 6N | A | Aviva Stadium, Dublin | L | 10-42 |
| 421 | 10-Mar-12 | Wales | 6N | A | Millennium Stadium, Cardiff | L | 3-24 |
| 422 | 17-Mar-12 | Scotland | 6N | H | Stadio Olimpico, Rome | W | 13-6 |
| 423 | 9-Jun-12 | Argentina | Int-T | A | Estadio S. Juan del Bicentenario, San Juan | L | 22-37 |
| 424 | 15-Jun-12 | Canada | Int-T | A | BMO Stadium, Toronto | W | 25-16 |
| 425 | 23-Jun-12 | United States | Int-T | A | BBVA Compass Stadium, Houston | W | 30-10 |
| 426 | 10-Nov-12 | Tonga | Int-T | H | Stadio Mario Rigamonti, Brescia | W | 28-23 |
| 427 | 17-Nov-12 | New Zealand | Int-T | H | Stadio Olimpico, Rome | L | 10-42 |
| 428 | 24-Nov-12 | Australia | Int | H | Stadio Artemio Franchi, Florence | L | 19-22 |
| 429 | 3-Feb-13 | France | 6N-GG | H | Stadio Olimpico, Rome | W | 23-18 |
| 430 | 9-Feb-13 | Scotland | 6N | A | Murrayfield, Edinburgh | L | 10-34 |
| 431 | 23-Feb-13 | Wales | 6N | H | Stadio Olimpico, Rome | L | 9-26 |
| 432 | 10-Mar-13 | England | 6N | A | Twickenham, London | L | 11-18 |
| 433 | 16-Mar-13 | Ireland | 6N | H | Stadio Olimpico, Rome | W | 22-15 |
| 434 | 8-Jun-13 | South Africa | quad | A | Kings Park Stadium, Durban | L | 10-44 |
| 435 | 15-Jun-13 | Samoa | quad | N | Mbombela Stadium, Nelspruit | L | 10-39 |
| 436 | 22-Jun-13 | Scotland | quad | N | Loftus Versfeld Stadium, Pretoria | L | 29-30 |
| 437 | 9-Nov-13 | Australia | Int | H | Stadio Olimpico di Torino, Turin | L | 20-50 |
| 438 | 16-Nov-13 | Fiji | Int | H | Stadio Giovanni Zini, Cremona | W | 37-31 |
| 439 | 23-Nov-13 | Argentina | Int | A | Stadio Olimpico, Rome | L | 14-19 |
| 440 | 1-Feb-14 | Wales | 6N | A | Millennium Stadium, Cardiff | L | 15-23 |

| No | Date | Opponents | Tmt | | Match Venue | Result | |
|----|------|-----------|-----|---|-------------|--------|---|
| 441 | 9-Feb-14 | France | 6N-GG | A | Stade de France, Paris | L | 10-30 |
| 442 | 22-Feb-14 | Scotland | 6N | H | Stadio Olimpico, Rome | L | 20-21 |
| 443 | 8-Mar-14 | Ireland | 6N | A | Aviva Stadium, Dublin | L | 7-46 |
| 444 | 15-Mar-14 | England | 6N | H | Stadio Olimpico, Rome | L | 11-52 |
| 445 | 7-Jun-14 | Fiji | Int-T | A | National Stadium, Suva | L | 14-25 |
| 446 | 14-Jun-14 | Samoa | Int-T | A | Apia Park, Apia | L | 0-15 |
| 447 | 21-Jun-14 | Japan | Int-T | A | Prince Chichibu Memorial Ground, Tokyo | L | 23-26 |
| 448 | 8-Nov-14 | Samoa | Int | H | Stadio Cino el Lillo del Duca, Ascoli Piceno | W | 24-13 |
| 449 | 14-Nov-14 | Argentina | Int | H | Stadio Luigi Ferraris, Genova | L | 18-20 |
| 450 | 22-Nov-14 | South Africa | Int | H | Stadio Euganeo, Padova | L | 6-22 |
| 451 | 7-Feb-15 | Ireland | 6N | H | Stadio Olimpico, Rome | L | 3-26 |
| 452 | 14-Feb-15 | England | 6N | A | Twickenham, London | L | 17-47 |
| 453 | 28-Feb-15 | Scotland | 6N | A | Murrayfield, Edinburgh | W | 22-19 |
| 454 | 15-Mar-15 | France | 6N-GG | H | Stadio Olimpico, Rome | L | 0-29 |
| 455 | 28-Mar-15 | Wales | 6N | H | Stadio Olimpico, Rome | L | 20-61 |
| 456 | 22-Aug-15 | Scotland | Int | H | Stadio Olimpico di Torino, Turin | L | 12-16 |
| 457 | 29-Aug-15 | Scotland | Int | A | Murrayfield, Edinburgh | L | 7-48 |
| 458 | 5-Sep-15 | Wales | Int | A | Millennium Stadium, Cardiff | L | 19-23 |
| 459 | 19-Sep-15 | France | WCp | N | Twickenham, London | L | 10-32 |
| 460 | 26-Sep-15 | Canada | WCp | N | Elland Road, Leeds | W | 23-18 |
| 461 | 4-Oct-15 | Ireland | WCp | N | Olympic Stadium, London | L | 9-16 |
| 462 | 11-Oct-15 | Romania | WCp | N | Sandy Park, Exeter | W | 32-22 |

# NEW ZEALAND

The New Zealand Rugby Football Union was founded in Wellington on 16 April 1892, at a meeting of the ten Provincial Unions, which had been formed over the previous twelve years. Despite the fact that New Zealand representative sides had toured Australia in 1884, 1893 and 1897, it was only on the 1903 tour that New Zealand actually played their first International against Australia in Sydney, which they won by 22 points to 3. In 1904, New Zealand defeated the visiting Great Britain team by 9 points to 3 and four years later they won a three-match series against the touring Anglo-Welsh team. It was during their first overseas tour of Britain, Ireland, France and the USA, in 1905-06, that the team became known as the All Blacks, and they certainly made an impression: they won thirty-four out of thirty-five games during that first tour, losing only to Wales by a try to nil. There were more triumphs to come in the following years, and on the 1924-25 Northern Hemisphere tour they won all thirty-two games, including the four International matches. Facing up to their Antipodean neighbours on twelve occasions between 1907 and 1914, New Zealand lost to the Australian team just twice.

After the First World War, in 1921, the All Blacks faced South Africa for the first time. The three-match series, played in New Zealand, was halved when the third International ended in a draw. Then, in 1928, it was South Africa's turn to host New Zealand and that four-match series was also shared, with two wins apiece. A 3-1 series win in 1930, against the touring Lions, was followed by a 2-1 series win in Australia in 1932. The team began to slip a little on the 1935-36 tour of the Northern Hemisphere when they won just two of the four Tests played against the Home Nations (losing to both Wales and England). The All Blacks also lost a home Test series 2-1 to the Springboks in 1937, but recovered to win the 1938 series in Australia, 3-0. They went on to beat the Wallabies four times in a row after the Second World War, only to suffer six successive defeats in 1949, when they lost two home Internationals to Australia and four Internationals on tour to South Africa.

The next decade was far more successful for the All Blacks, since they won both the 1950 and the 1959 Test series against the touring Lions, and also the 1956 series against the touring Springboks. In all, they lost a mere seven matches out of thirty during those ten years, two of which were against Wales and France on the 1953-54 Northern Hemisphere tour. The 1960s proved to be an amazing decade for New Zealand: in the period 1961 to 1969 they lost just two Internationals out of a total of thirty-eight played, and between 1961 and 1964 they achieved a run of seventeen games without defeat. Then from September 1965 to the end of 1969, the All Blacks remarkably topped their previous record with a sequence of seventeen wins in a row.

The start of the 1970s saw a dramatic reversal of form for the All Blacks when they lost an away series to South Africa 3-1, followed by a historic first-ever home series loss to the Lions, a year later, in 1971. Yet another 3-1 series loss to the Springboks in 1976 was a bitter pill to swallow and it wasn't until the following year that the All Blacks returned to their winning ways with a 3-1 home series win against the Lions. On their 1978 Northern Hemisphere tour they achieved a first-ever 'grand slam' of four wins against the four Home Nations. Home series wins against South Africa in 1981 and Australia in 1982 were followed by an incredible 4-0 series win against the touring Lions in 1983, and another 2-1 series win away to Australia in 1984. Just three defeats in eleven matches during 1985 and 1986 made New Zealand firm favourites to win the inaugural World Cup in 1987 and they did not disappoint their supporters: the team won all six games, which included a comprehensive 29 points to 9 win against France in the final in Auckland. Between May 1987 and August 1990, New Zealand were undefeated for twenty-three matches and from April 1995 to June 1998 they lost only three times in thirty-six games.

The All Blacks maintained their remarkable sequence of wins at the start of the new millennium with a run of eleven consecutive wins in 2003, fifteen in a row between August 2005 and August 2006 and a further fifteen in a row between September 2009 and September 2010. Another phenomenal run of sixteen wins began in September 2011, which extended to twenty matches without defeat but ended disappointingly for the All Blacks when they surprisingly lost to England at Twickenham in December 2012. However, within that run, they did win the 2011 World Cup, on home territory, after a gap of twenty-four years since their previous success in 1987. The final against France turned out to be much closer than expected, with only one point separating the teams at the end.

The New Zealanders dominated the Tri Nations Championship, launched in 1996. The competition was contested sixteen times to 2011 and during that period they won the title ten times, achieving a 100% record in four of the tournaments.

In 2012 Argentina finally entered the Tri Nations competition, which was renamed the Rugby Championship, and in the first two years of its existence the All Blacks won all twelve Internationals. In the calendar year 2013, New Zealand played fourteen Internationals and won every one of them. With a 3-0 series win against England in June 2014, they extended their run of wins to a world-record equalling sequence of seventeen matches. This came to an end, however, when they drew with Australia in August of that year.

The All Blacks' unbeaten sequence reached twenty-two before they lost the final match of the 2014 Rugby Championship to South Africa in Johannesburg in October. This meant that New Zealand had only been defeated once in three years (to England in December 2012), in forty-three matches between September 2011 and September 2014. Despite the loss to the Springboks in October 2014, New Zealand still retained the title they had held for the first two years of the competition. The All Blacks then finished the year with a successful autumn tour of the United Kingdom, recording three wins against England, Scotland and Wales.

New Zealand, winners of the Rugby Championship in the first three years (2012 to 2014), relinquished the title in 2015 when they were beaten by Australia, in Sydney, in the final game of the tournament, which was reduced due to World Cup commitments to three matches. However, they avenged that defeat a week later when they won in Auckland and retained the Bledisloe Cup. This trophy is awarded each year to the winner of a single game or a series of matches between New Zealand and Australia. The Cup has been contested fifty-six times between 1931 and 2015 and the All Blacks have been title holders on forty-four occasions.

In the 2015 World Cup, New Zealand cruised through the pool matches, before demolishing France by 62 points to 13 in the quarter-final. The semi-final against South Africa, however, was quite the opposite. In that enthralling battle, the All Blacks finally emerged winners by 20 points to 18.

By defeating Australia 34 points to 17, in the final, New Zealand became the first nation to retain the Webb Ellis Cup and the first team to win the trophy three times.

# NEW ZEALAND

## HEAD TO HEAD RESULTS TO 31 OCTOBER 2015

| | P | W | D | L | % | F | A |
|---|---|---|---|---|---|---|---|
| **v TIER 1 Teams** | | | | | | | |
| v Argentina | 22 | 21 | 1 | 0 | 97.7 | 881 | 294 |
| v Australia | 155 | 106 | 7 | 42 | 70.6 | 3160 | 2160 |
| v England | 40 | 32 | 1 | 7 | 81.3 | 969 | 560 |
| v France | 56 | 43 | 1 | 12 | 77.7 | 1407 | 726 |
| v Ireland | 28 | 27 | 1 | 0 | 98.2 | 812 | 310 |
| v Italy | 12 | 12 | 0 | 0 | 100.0 | 686 | 118 |
| v Scotland | 30 | 28 | 2 | 0 | 96.7 | 900 | 332 |
| v South Africa | 91 | 53 | 3 | 35 | 59.4 | 1765 | 1430 |
| v Wales | 30 | 27 | 0 | 3 | 90.0 | 916 | 307 |
| v Lions | 35 | 27 | 2 | 6 | 80.0 | 570 | 337 |
| **Sub-Total** | **499** | **376** | **18** | **105** | **77.2** | **12066** | **6574** |
| **v TIER 2/3 Group** | | | | | | | |
| v Canada | 5 | 5 | 0 | 0 | 100.0 | 313 | 54 |
| v Fiji | 5 | 5 | 0 | 0 | 100.0 | 364 | 50 |
| v Japan | 3 | 3 | 0 | 0 | 100.0 | 282 | 30 |
| v Romania | 2 | 2 | 0 | 0 | 100.0 | 99 | 14 |
| v Samoa | 6 | 6 | 0 | 0 | 100.0 | 333 | 72 |
| v Tonga | 4 | 4 | 0 | 0 | 100.0 | 279 | 26 |
| v United States | 3 | 3 | 0 | 0 | 100.0 | 171 | 15 |
| v Georgia | 0 | 0 | 0 | 0 | 0.0 | 0 | 0 |
| v Namibia | 0 | 0 | 0 | 0 | 0.0 | 0 | 0 |
| v Russia | 0 | 0 | 0 | 0 | 0.0 | 0 | 0 |
| v Uruguay | 0 | 0 | 0 | 0 | 0.0 | 0 | 0 |
| **Sub-Total** | **31** | **31** | **0** | **0** | **100.0** | **1989** | **294** |
| **v Other Teams** | | | | | | | |
| v Anglo-Welsh | 3 | 2 | 1 | 0 | 66.7 | 64 | 8 |
| v Pacific Islanders | 1 | 1 | 0 | 0 | 100.0 | 41 | 26 |
| v Portugal | 1 | 1 | 0 | 0 | 100.0 | 108 | 13 |
| v World XV | 3 | 2 | 0 | 1 | 66.7 | 94 | 69 |
| **Sub-Total** | **8** | **6** | **1** | **1** | **81.3** | **307** | **116** |
| **All Internationals** | **538** | **413** | **19** | **106** | **78.5** | **14362** | **6984** |

| No | Date | Opponents | Tmt | | Match Venue | Result | |
|----|------|-----------|-----|---|-------------|--------|---|
| 1 | 15-Aug-03 | Australia | Int-T | A | Cricket Ground, Sydney | W | 22-3 |
| 2 | 13-Aug-04 | Lions | Int | H | Athletic Park, Wellington | W | 9-3 |
| 3 | 2-Sep-05 | Australia | Int | H | Tahuna Park, Dunedin | W | 14-3 |
| 4 | 18-Nov-05 | Scotland | Int-T | A | Inverleith, Edinburgh | W | 12-7 |
| 5 | 25-Nov-05 | Ireland | Int-T | A | Lansdowne Road, Dublin | W | 15-0 |
| 6 | 2-Dec-05 | England | Int-T | A | Crystal Palace, London | W | 15-0 |
| 7 | 16-Dec-05 | Wales | Int-T | A | Arms Park, Cardiff | L | 0-3 |
| 8 | 1-Jan-06 | France | Int-T | A | Parc des Princess, Paris | W | 38-8 |
| 9 | 20-Jul-07 | Australia | Int-T | A | Cricket Ground, Sydney | W | 26-6 |
| 10 | 3-Aug-07 | Australia | Int-T | A | The Gabba Cricket Ground, Brisbane | W | 14-5 |
| 11 | 10-Aug-07 | Australia | Int-T | A | Cricket Ground, Sydney | D | 5-5 |
| 12 | 6-Jun-08 | Anglo-Welsh | Int | H | Carisbrook, Dunedin | W | 32-5 |
| 13 | 27-Jun-08 | Anglo-Welsh | Int | H | Athletic Park, Wellington | D | 3-3 |
| 14 | 25-Jul-08 | Anglo-Welsh | Int | H | Potter's Park, Auckland | W | 29-0 |
| 15 | 25-Jun-10 | Australia | Int-T | A | Cricket Ground, Sydney | W | 6-0 |
| 16 | 27-Jun-10 | Australia | Int-T | A | Cricket Ground, Sydney | L | 0-11 |
| 17 | 2-Jul-10 | Australia | Int-T | A | Cricket Ground, Sydney | W | 28-13 |
| 18 | 6-Sep-13 | Australia | Int | H | Athletic Park, Wellington | W | 30-5 |
| 19 | 13-Sep-13 | Australia | Int | H | Carisbrook, Dunedin | W | 25-13 |
| 20 | 20-Sep-13 | Australia | Int | H | Lancaster Park Oval, Christchurch | L | 5-16 |
| 21 | 15-Nov-13 | United States | Int-T | A | St Ignatius, California Field, Berkeley | W | 51-3 |
| 22 | 18-Jul-14 | Australia | Int-T | A | Sports Ground, Sydney | W | 5-0 |
| 23 | 1-Aug-14 | Australia | Int-T | A | The Gabba Cricket Ground, Brisbane | W | 17-0 |
| 24 | 15-Aug-14 | Australia | Int-T | A | Sports Ground, Sydney | W | 22-7 |
| 25 | 13-Aug-21 | South Africa | Int | H | Carisbrook, Dunedin | W | 13-5 |
| 26 | 27-Aug-21 | South Africa | Int | H | Eden Park, Auckland | L | 5-9 |
| 27 | 17-Sep-21 | South Africa | Int | H | Athletic Park, Wellington | D | 0-0 |
| 28 | 1-Nov-24 | Ireland | Int-T | A | Lansdowne Road, Dublin | W | 6-0 |
| 29 | 29-Nov-24 | Wales | Int-T | A | St Helen's, Swansea | W | 19-0 |
| 30 | 3-Jan-25 | England | Int-T | A | Twickenham, London | W | 17-11 |
| 31 | 18-Jan-25 | France | Int-T | A | Stade des Ponts, Jumeaux, Toulouse | W | 30-6 |
| 32 | 30-Jun-28 | South Africa | Int-T | A | Kingsmead Ground, Durban | L | 0-17 |
| 33 | 21-Jul-28 | South Africa | Int-T | A | Ellis Park, Johannesburg | W | 7-6 |
| 34 | 18-Aug-28 | South Africa | Int-T | A | Crusaders Ground, Port Elizabeth | L | 6-11 |
| 35 | 1-Sep-28 | South Africa | Int-T | A | Newlands Stadium, Cape Town | W | 13-5 |
| 36 | 6-Jul-29 | Australia | Int-T | A | Cricket Ground, Sydney | L | 8-9 |
| 37 | 20-Jul-29 | Australia | Int-T | A | Exhibition Ground, Brisbane | L | 9-17 |
| 38 | 27-Jul-29 | Australia | Int-T | A | Cricket Ground, Sydney | L | 13-15 |
| 39 | 21-Jun-30 | Lions | Int | H | Carisbrook, Dunedin | L | 3-6 |
| 40 | 5-Jul-30 | Lions | Int | H | Lancaster Park Oval, Christchurch | W | 13-10 |

| No | Date | Opponents | Tmt | | Match Venue | Result | |
|----|------|-----------|-----|---|-------------|--------|---|
| 41 | 26-Jul-30 | Lions | Int | H | Eden Park, Auckland | W | 15-10 |
| 42 | 9-Aug-30 | Lions | Int | H | Athletic Park, Wellington | W | 22-8 |
| 43 | 12-Sep-31 | Australia | Bled | H | Eden Park, Auckland | W | 20-13 |
| 44 | 2-Jul-32 | Australia | Bled-T | A | Cricket Ground, Sydney | L | 17-22 |
| 45 | 16-Jul-32 | Australia | Bled-T | A | Exhibition Ground, Brisbane | W | 21-3 |
| 46 | 23-Jul-32 | Australia | Bled-T | A | Cricket Ground, Sydney | W | 21-13 |
| 47 | 11-Aug-34 | Australia | Bled-T | A | Cricket Ground, Sydney | L | 11-25 |
| 48 | 25-Aug-34 | Australia | Bled-T | A | Cricket Ground, Sydney | D | 3-3 |
| 49 | 23-Nov-35 | Scotland | Int-T | A | Murrayfield, Edinburgh | W | 18-8 |
| 50 | 7-Dec-35 | Ireland | Int-T | A | Lansdowne Road, Dublin | W | 17-9 |
| 51 | 21-Dec-35 | Wales | Int-T | A | Arms Park, Cardiff | L | 12-13 |
| 52 | 4-Jan-36 | England | Int-T | A | Twickenham, London | L | 0-13 |
| 53 | 5-Sep-36 | Australia | Bled | H | Athletic Park, Wellington | W | 11-6 |
| 54 | 12-Sep-36 | Australia | Bled | H | Carisbrook, Dunedin | W | 38-13 |
| 55 | 14-Aug-37 | South Africa | Int | H | Athletic Park, Wellington | W | 13-7 |
| 56 | 4-Sep-37 | South Africa | Int | H | Lancaster Park Oval, Christchurch | L | 6-13 |
| 57 | 25-Sep-37 | South Africa | Int | H | Eden Park, Auckland | L | 6-17 |
| 58 | 23-Jul-38 | Australia | Bled-T | A | Cricket Ground, Sydney | W | 24-9 |
| 59 | 6-Aug-38 | Australia | Bled-T | A | Exhibition Ground, Brisbane | W | 20-14 |
| 60 | 13-Aug-38 | Australia | Bled-T | A | Cricket Ground, Sydney | W | 14-6 |
| 61 | 14-Sep-46 | Australia | Bled | H | Carisbrook, Dunedin | W | 31-8 |
| 62 | 28-Sep-46 | Australia | Bled | H | Eden Park, Auckland | W | 14-10 |
| 63 | 14-Jun-47 | Australia | Bled-T | A | Exhibition Ground, Brisbane | W | 13-5 |
| 64 | 28-Jun-47 | Australia | Bled-T | A | Cricket Ground, Sydney | W | 27-14 |
| 65 | 16-Jul-49 | South Africa | Int-T | A | Newlands Stadium, Cape Town | L | 11-15 |
| 66 | 13-Aug-49 | South Africa | Int-T | A | Ellis Park, Johannesburg | L | 6-12 |
| 67 | 3-Sep-49 | Australia | Bled | H | Athletic Park, Wellington | L | 6-11 |
| 68 | 3-Sep-49 | South Africa | Int-T | A | Kingsmead Ground, Durban | L | 3-9 |
| 69 | 17-Sep-49 | South Africa | Int-T | A | Crusaders Ground, Port Elizabeth | L | 8-11 |
| 70 | 24-Sep-49 | Australia | Bled | H | Eden Park, Auckland | L | 9-16 |
| 71 | 27-May-50 | Lions | Int | H | Carisbrook, Dunedin | D | 9-9 |
| 72 | 10-Jun-50 | Lions | Int | H | Lancaster Park Oval, Christchurch | W | 8-0 |
| 73 | 1-Jul-50 | Lions | Int | H | Athletic Park, Wellington | W | 6-3 |
| 74 | 29-Jul-50 | Lions | Int | H | Eden Park, Auckland | W | 11-8 |
| 75 | 23-Jun-51 | Australia | Bled-T | A | Cricket Ground, Sydney | W | 8-0 |
| 76 | 7-Jul-51 | Australia | Bled-T | A | Cricket Ground, Sydney | W | 17-11 |
| 77 | 21-Jul-51 | Australia | Bled-T | A | The Gabba Cricket Ground, Brisbane | W | 16-6 |
| 78 | 6-Sep-52 | Australia | Bled | H | Lancaster Park Oval, Christchurch | L | 9-14 |
| 79 | 13-Sep-52 | Australia | Bled | H | Athletic Park, Wellington | W | 15-8 |
| 80 | 19-Dec-53 | Wales | Int-T | A | Arms Park, Cardiff | L | 8-13 |

| No | Date | Opponents | Tmt | | Match Venue | Result | |
|----|------|-----------|-----|---|-------------|--------|---|
| 81 | 9-Jan-54 | Ireland | Int-T | A | Lansdowne Road, Dublin | W | 14-3 |
| 82 | 30-Jan-54 | England | Int-T | A | Twickenham, London | W | 5-0 |
| 83 | 13-Feb-54 | Scotland | Int-T | A | Murrayfield, Edinburgh | W | 3-0 |
| 84 | 27-Feb-54 | France | Int-T | A | Stade Colombes, Paris | L | 0-3 |
| 85 | 20-Aug-55 | Australia | Bled | H | Athletic Park, Wellington | W | 16-8 |
| 86 | 3-Sep-55 | Australia | Bled | H | Carisbrook, Dunedin | W | 8-0 |
| 87 | 17-Sep-55 | Australia | Bled | H | Eden Park, Auckland | L | 3-8 |
| 88 | 14-Jul-56 | South Africa | Int | H | Carisbrook, Dunedin | W | 10-6 |
| 89 | 4-Aug-56 | South Africa | Int | H | Athletic Park, Wellington | L | 3-8 |
| 90 | 18-Aug-56 | South Africa | Int | H | Lancaster Park Oval, Christchurch | W | 17-10 |
| 91 | 1-Sep-56 | South Africa | Int | H | Eden Park, Auckland | W | 11-5 |
| 92 | 25-May-57 | Australia | Bled-T | A | Cricket Ground, Sydney | W | 25-11 |
| 93 | 1-Jun-57 | Australia | Bled-T | A | Exhibition Ground, Brisbane | W | 22-9 |
| 94 | 23-Aug-58 | Australia | Bled | H | Athletic Park, Wellington | W | 25-3 |
| 95 | 6-Sep-58 | Australia | Bled | H | Lancaster Park Oval, Christchurch | L | 3-6 |
| 96 | 20-Sep-58 | Australia | Bled | H | Epsom Showgrounds, Auckland | W | 17-8 |
| 97 | 18-Jul-59 | Lions | Int | H | Carisbrook, Dunedin | W | 18-17 |
| 98 | 15-Aug-59 | Lions | Int | H | Athletic Park, Wellington | W | 11-8 |
| 99 | 29-Aug-59 | Lions | Int | H | Lancaster Park Oval, Christchurch | W | 22-8 |
| 100 | 19-Sep-59 | Lions | Int | H | Eden Park, Auckland | L | 6-9 |
| 101 | 25-Jun-60 | South Africa | Int-T | A | Ellis Park, Johannesburg | L | 0-13 |
| 102 | 23-Jul-60 | South Africa | Int-T | A | Newlands Stadium, Cape Town | W | 11-3 |
| 103 | 13-Aug-60 | South Africa | Int-T | A | Free State Stadium, Bloemfontein | D | 11-11 |
| 104 | 27-Aug-60 | South Africa | Int-T | A | Boet Erasmus Stadium, Port Elizabeth | L | 3-8 |
| 105 | 22-Jul-61 | France | Int | H | Eden Park, Auckland | W | 13-6 |
| 106 | 5-Aug-61 | France | Int | H | Athletic Park, Wellington | W | 5-3 |
| 107 | 19-Aug-61 | France | Int | H | Lancaster Park Oval, Christchurch | W | 32-3 |
| 108 | 26-May-62 | Australia | Bled-T | A | Exhibition Ground, Brisbane | W | 20-6 |
| 109 | 4-Jun-62 | Australia | Bled-T | A | Cricket Ground, Sydney | W | 14-5 |
| 110 | 25-Aug-62 | Australia | Bled | H | Athletic Park, Wellington | D | 9-9 |
| 111 | 8-Sep-62 | Australia | Bled | H | Carisbrook, Dunedin | W | 3-0 |
| 112 | 22-Sep-62 | Australia | Bled | H | Eden Park, Auckland | W | 16-8 |
| 113 | 25-May-63 | England | Int | H | Eden Park, Auckland | W | 21-11 |
| 114 | 1-Jun-63 | England | Int | H | Lancaster Park Oval, Christchurch | W | 9-6 |
| 115 | 7-Dec-63 | Ireland | Int-T | A | Lansdowne Road, Dublin | W | 6-5 |
| 116 | 21-Dec-63 | Wales | Int-T | A | Arms Park, Cardiff | W | 6-0 |
| 117 | 4-Jan-64 | England | Int-T | A | Twickenham, London | W | 14-0 |
| 118 | 18-Jan-64 | Scotland | Int-T | A | Murrayfield, Edinburgh | D | 0-0 |
| 119 | 8-Feb-64 | France | Int-T | A | Stade Colombes, Paris | W | 12-3 |
| 120 | 15-Aug-64 | Australia | Bled | H | Carisbrook, Dunedin | W | 14-9 |

| No | Date | Opponents | Tmt | Match Venue | Result | |
|----|------|-----------|-----|-------------|--------|---|
| 121 | 22-Aug-64 | Australia | Bled | H Lancaster Park Oval, Christchurch | W | 18-3 |
| 122 | 29-Aug-64 | Australia | Bled | H Athletic Park, Wellington | L | 5-20 |
| 123 | 31-Jul-65 | South Africa | Int | H Athletic Park, Wellington | W | 6-3 |
| 124 | 21-Aug-65 | South Africa | Int | H Carisbrook, Dunedin | W | 13-0 |
| 125 | 4-Sep-65 | South Africa | Int | H Lancaster Park Oval, Christchurch | L | 16-19 |
| 126 | 18-Sep-65 | South Africa | Int | H Eden Park, Auckland | W | 20-3 |
| 127 | 16-Jul-66 | Lions | Int | H Carisbrook, Dunedin | W | 20-3 |
| 128 | 6-Aug-66 | Lions | Int | H Athletic Park, Wellington | W | 16-12 |
| 129 | 27-Aug-66 | Lions | Int | H Lancaster Park Oval, Christchurch | W | 19-6 |
| 130 | 10-Sep-66 | Lions | Int | H Eden Park, Auckland | W | 24-11 |
| 131 | 19-Aug-67 | Australia | Bled | H Athletic Park, Wellington | W | 29-9 |
| 132 | 4-Nov-67 | England | Int-T | A Twickenham, London | W | 23-11 |
| 133 | 11-Nov-67 | Wales | Int-T | A Arms Park, Cardiff | W | 13-6 |
| 134 | 25-Nov-67 | France | Int-T | A Stade Colombes, Paris | W | 21-15 |
| 135 | 2-Dec-67 | Scotland | Int-T | A Murrayfield, Edinburgh | W | 14-3 |
| 136 | 15-Jun-68 | Australia | Bled-T | A Cricket Ground, Sydney | W | 27-11 |
| 137 | 22-Jun-68 | Australia | Bled-T | A Ballymore Oval, Brisbane | W | 19-18 |
| 138 | 13-Jul-68 | France | Int | H Lancaster Park Oval, Christchurch | W | 12-9 |
| 139 | 27-Jul-68 | France | Int | H Athletic Park, Wellington | W | 9-3 |
| 140 | 10-Aug-68 | France | Int | H Eden Park, Auckland | W | 19-12 |
| 141 | 31-May-69 | Wales | Int | H Lancaster Park Oval, Christchurch | W | 19-0 |
| 142 | 14-Jun-69 | Wales | Int | H Eden Park, Auckland | W | 33-12 |
| 143 | 25-Jul-70 | South Africa | Int-T | A Loftus Versfeld Stadium, Pretoria | L | 6-17 |
| 144 | 8-Aug-70 | South Africa | Int-T | A Newlands Stadium, Cape Town | W | 9-8 |
| 145 | 29-Aug-70 | South Africa | Int-T | A Boet Erasmus Stadium, Port Elizabeth | L | 3-14 |
| 146 | 12-Sep-70 | South Africa | Int-T | A Ellis Park, Johannesburg | L | 17-20 |
| 147 | 26-Jun-71 | Lions | Int | H Carisbrook, Dunedin | L | 3-9 |
| 148 | 10-Jul-71 | Lions | Int | H Lancaster Park Oval, Christchurch | W | 22-12 |
| 149 | 31-Jul-71 | Lions | Int | H Athletic Park, Wellington | L | 3-13 |
| 150 | 14-Aug-71 | Lions | Int | H Eden Park, Auckland | D | 14-14 |
| 151 | 19-Aug-72 | Australia | Bled | H Athletic Park, Wellington | W | 29-6 |
| 152 | 2-Sep-72 | Australia | Bled | H Lancaster Park Oval, Christchurch | W | 30-17 |
| 153 | 16-Sep-72 | Australia | Bled | H Eden Park, Auckland | W | 38-3 |
| 154 | 2-Dec-72 | Wales | Int-T | A National Stadium, Cardiff | W | 19-16 |
| 155 | 16-Dec-72 | Scotland | Int-T | A Murrayfield, Edinburgh | W | 14-9 |
| 156 | 6-Jan-73 | England | Int-T | A Twickenham, London | W | 9-0 |
| 157 | 20-Jan-73 | Ireland | Int-T | A Lansdowne Road, Dublin | D | 10-10 |
| 158 | 10-Feb-73 | France | Int-T | A Parc des Princess, Paris | L | 6-13 |
| 159 | 15-Sep-73 | England | Int | H Eden Park, Auckland | L | 10-16 |
| 160 | 25-May-74 | Australia | Bled-T | A Cricket Ground, Sydney | W | 11-6 |

| No | Date | Opponents | Tmt | | Match Venue | Result | |
|----|------|-----------|-----|---|-------------|--------|---|
| 161 | 1-Jun-74 | Australia | Bled-T | A | Ballymore Oval, Brisbane | D | 16-16 |
| 162 | 8-Jun-74 | Australia | Bled-T | A | Cricket Ground, Sydney | W | 16-6 |
| 163 | 23-Nov-74 | Ireland | Int-T | A | Lansdowne Road, Dublin | W | 15-6 |
| 164 | 14-Jun-75 | Scotland | Int | H | Eden Park, Auckland | W | 24-0 |
| 165 | 5-Jun-76 | Ireland | Int | H | Athletic Park, Wellington | W | 11-3 |
| 166 | 24-Jul-76 | South Africa | Int-T | A | Kings Park Stadium, Durban | L | 7-16 |
| 167 | 14-Aug-76 | South Africa | Int-T | A | Free State Stadium, Bloemfontein | W | 15-9 |
| 168 | 4-Sep-76 | South Africa | Int-T | A | Newlands Stadium, Cape Town | L | 10-15 |
| 169 | 18-Sep-76 | South Africa | Int-T | A | Ellis Park, Johannesburg | L | 14-15 |
| 170 | 18-Jun-77 | Lions | Int | H | Athletic Park, Wellington | W | 16-12 |
| 171 | 9-Jul-77 | Lions | Int | H | Lancaster Park Oval, Christchurch | L | 9-13 |
| 172 | 30-Jul-77 | Lions | Int | H | Carisbrook, Dunedin | W | 19-7 |
| 173 | 13-Aug-77 | Lions | Int | H | Eden Park, Auckland | W | 10-9 |
| 174 | 11-Nov-77 | France | Int-T | A | Stade Municipal de Toulouse, Toulouse | L | 13-18 |
| 175 | 19-Nov-77 | France | Int-T | A | Parc des Princess, Paris | W | 15-3 |
| 176 | 19-Aug-78 | Australia | Bled | H | Athletic Park, Wellington | W | 13-12 |
| 177 | 26-Aug-78 | Australia | Bled | H | Lancaster Park Oval, Christchurch | W | 22-6 |
| 178 | 9-Sep-78 | Australia | Bled | H | Eden Park, Auckland | L | 16-30 |
| 179 | 4-Nov-78 | Ireland | Int-T | A | Lansdowne Road, Dublin | W | 10-6 |
| 180 | 11-Nov-78 | Wales | Int-T | A | National Stadium, Cardiff | W | 13-12 |
| 181 | 25-Nov-78 | England | Int-T | A | Twickenham, London | W | 16-6 |
| 182 | 9-Dec-78 | Scotland | Int-T | A | Murrayfield, Edinburgh | W | 18-9 |
| 183 | 7-Jul-79 | France | Int | H | Lancaster Park Oval, Christchurch | W | 23-9 |
| 184 | 14-Jul-79 | France | Int | H | Eden Park, Auckland | L | 19-24 |
| 185 | 28-Jul-79 | Australia | Bled-T | A | Cricket Ground, Sydney | L | 6-12 |
| 186 | 10-Nov-79 | Scotland | Int-T | A | Murrayfield, Edinburgh | W | 20-6 |
| 187 | 24-Nov-79 | England | Int-T | A | Twickenham, London | W | 10-9 |
| 188 | 21-Jun-80 | Australia | Bled-T | A | Cricket Ground, Sydney | L | 9-13 |
| 189 | 28-Jun-80 | Australia | Bled-T | A | Ballymore Oval, Brisbane | W | 12-9 |
| 190 | 12-Jul-80 | Australia | Bled-T | A | Cricket Ground, Sydney | L | 10-26 |
| 191 | 1-Nov-81 | Wales | Int-T | A | National Stadium, Cardiff | W | 23-3 |
| 192 | 13-Jun-81 | Scotland | Int | H | Carisbrook, Dunedin | W | 11-4 |
| 193 | 20-Jun-81 | Scotland | Int | H | Eden Park, Auckland | W | 40-15 |
| 194 | 15-Aug-81 | South Africa | Int | H | Lancaster Park Oval, Christchurch | W | 14-9 |
| 195 | 29-Aug-81 | South Africa | Int | H | Athletic Park, Wellington | L | 12-24 |
| 196 | 12-Sep-81 | South Africa | Tmt | H | Eden Park, Auckland | W | 25-22 |
| 197 | 24-Oct-81 | Romania | Int-T | A | Stadionul 23 August, Bucharest | W | 14-6 |
| 198 | 14-Nov-81 | France | Int-T | A | Stade Municipal de Toulouse, Toulouse | W | 13-9 |
| 199 | 21-Nov-81 | France | Int-T | A | Parc des Princess, Paris | W | 18-6 |
| 200 | 14-Aug-82 | Australia | Bled | H | Lancaster Park Oval, Christchurch | W | 23-16 |

| No | Date | Opponents | Tmt | | Match Venue | Result | |
|----|------|-----------|-----|---|-------------|--------|---|
| 201 | 28-Aug-82 | Australia | Bled | H | Athletic Park, Wellington | L | 16-19 |
| 202 | 11-Sep-82 | Australia | Bled | H | Eden Park, Auckland | W | 33-18 |
| 203 | 4-Jun-83 | Lions | Int | H | Lancaster Park Oval, Christchurch | W | 16-12 |
| 204 | 18-Jun-83 | Lions | Int | H | Athletic Park, Wellington | W | 9-0 |
| 205 | 2-Jul-83 | Lions | Int | H | Carisbrook, Dunedin | W | 15-8 |
| 206 | 16-Jul-83 | Lions | Int | H | Eden Park, Auckland | W | 38-6 |
| 207 | 20-Aug-83 | Australia | Bled-T | A | Cricket Ground, Sydney | W | 18-8 |
| 208 | 12-Nov-83 | Scotland | Int-T | A | Murrayfield, Edinburgh | D | 25-25 |
| 209 | 19-Nov-83 | England | Int-T | A | Twickenham, London | L | 9-15 |
| 210 | 16-Jun-84 | France | Int | H | Lancaster Park Oval, Christchurch | W | 10-9 |
| 211 | 23-Jun-84 | France | Int | H | Eden Park, Auckland | W | 31-18 |
| 212 | 21-Jul-84 | Australia | Bled-T | A | Cricket Ground, Sydney | L | 9-16 |
| 213 | 4-Aug-84 | Australia | Bled-T | A | Ballymore Oval, Brisbane | W | 19-15 |
| 214 | 18-Aug-84 | Australia | Bled-T | A | Cricket Ground, Sydney | W | 25-24 |
| 215 | 1-Jun-85 | England | Int | H | Lancaster Park Oval, Christchurch | W | 18-13 |
| 216 | 8-Jun-85 | England | Int | H | Athletic Park, Wellington | W | 42-15 |
| 217 | 29-Jun-85 | Australia | Bled | H | Eden Park, Auckland | W | 10-9 |
| 218 | 26-Oct-85 | Argentina | Int-T | A | Ferro Carril Oeste Stadium, B Aires | W | 33-20 |
| 219 | 2-Nov-85 | Argentina | Int-T | A | Ferro Carril Oeste Stadium, B Aires | D | 21-21 |
| 220 | 28-Jun-86 | France | Int | H | Lancaster Park Oval, Christchurch | W | 18-9 |
| 221 | 9-Aug-86 | Australia | Bled | H | Athletic Park, Wellington | L | 12-13 |
| 222 | 23-Aug-86 | Australia | Bled | H | Carisbrook, Dunedin | W | 13-12 |
| 223 | 6-Sep-86 | Australia | Bled | H | Eden Park, Auckland | L | 9-22 |
| 224 | 8-Nov-86 | France | Int-T | A | Stade Municipal de Toulouse, Toulouse | W | 19-7 |
| 225 | 15-Nov-86 | France | Int-T | A | Stade de la Beaujoire, Nantes | L | 3-16 |
| 226 | 22-May-87 | Italy | WCp | H | Eden Park, Auckland | W | 70-6 |
| 227 | 27-May-87 | Fiji | WCp | H | Lancaster Park Oval, Christchurch | W | 74-13 |
| 228 | 1-Jun-87 | Argentina | WCp | H | Athletic Park, Wellington | W | 46-15 |
| 229 | 6-Jun-87 | Scotland | WCqf | H | Lancaster Park Oval, Christchurch | W | 30-3 |
| 230 | 14-Jun-87 | Wales | WCsf | N | Ballymore Oval, Brisbane | W | 49-6 |
| 231 | 20-Jun-87 | France | WCf | H | Eden Park, Auckland | W | 29-9 |
| 232 | 25-Jul-87 | Australia | Bled-T | A | Concord Oval, Sydney | W | 30-16 |
| 233 | 23-May-88 | Wales | Int | H | Lancaster Park Oval, Christchurch | W | 52-3 |
| 234 | 11-Jun-88 | Wales | Int | H | Eden Park, Auckland | W | 54-9 |
| 235 | 3-Jul-88 | Australia | Bled-T | A | Concord Oval, Sydney | W | 32-7 |
| 236 | 16-Jul-88 | Australia | Bled-T | A | Ballymore Oval, Brisbane | D | 19-19 |
| 237 | 30-Jul-88 | Australia | Bled-T | A | Concord Oval, Sydney | W | 30-9 |
| 238 | 17-Jun-89 | France | Int | H | Lancaster Park Oval, Christchurch | W | 25-17 |
| 239 | 1-Jul-89 | France | Int | H | Eden Park, Auckland | W | 34-20 |
| 240 | 15-Jul-89 | Argentina | Int | H | Carisbrook, Dunedin | W | 60-9 |

| No | Date | Opponents | Tmt | | Match Venue | Result | |
|-----|------|-----------|-----|---|-------------|--------|---|
| 241 | 29-Jul-89 | Argentina | Int | H | Athletic Park, Wellington | W | 49-12 |
| 242 | 5-Aug-89 | Australia | Bled | H | Eden Park, Auckland | W | 24-12 |
| 243 | 4-Nov-89 | Wales | Int-T | A | National Stadium, Cardiff | W | 34-9 |
| 244 | 18-Nov-89 | Ireland | Int-T | A | Lansdowne Road, Dublin | W | 23-6 |
| 245 | 16-Jun-90 | Scotland | Int | H | Carisbrook, Dunedin | W | 31-16 |
| 246 | 23-Jun-90 | Scotland | Int | H | Eden Park, Auckland | W | 21-18 |
| 247 | 21-Jul-90 | Australia | Bled | H | Lancaster Park Oval, Christchurch | W | 21-6 |
| 248 | 4-Aug-90 | Australia | Bled | H | Eden Park, Auckland | W | 27-17 |
| 249 | 18-Aug-90 | Australia | Bled | H | Athletic Park, Wellington | L | 9-21 |
| 250 | 3-Nov-90 | France | Int-T | A | Stade de la Beaujoire, Nantes | W | 24-3 |
| 251 | 10-Nov-90 | France | Int-T | A | Parc des Princess, Paris | W | 30-12 |
| 252 | 6-Jul-91 | Argentina | Int-T | A | Vélez Sarsfield Stadium, Buenos Aires | W | 28-14 |
| 253 | 13-Jul-91 | Argentina | Int-T | A | Vélez Sarsfield Stadium, Buenos Aires | W | 36-6 |
| 254 | 10-Aug-91 | Australia | Bled-T | A | Football Stadium, Sydney | L | 12-21 |
| 255 | 24-Aug-91 | Australia | Bled | H | Eden Park, Auckland | W | 6-3 |
| 256 | 3-Oct-91 | England | WCp | A | Twickenham, London | W | 18-12 |
| 257 | 8-Oct-91 | United States | WCp | N | Kingsholm, Gloucester | W | 46-6 |
| 258 | 13-Oct-91 | Italy | WCp | N | Welford Road, Leicester | W | 31-21 |
| 259 | 20-Oct-91 | Canada | WCqf | N | Stade Nord Lille Métropole | W | 29-13 |
| 260 | 27-Oct-91 | Australia | WCsf | N | Lansdowne Road, Dublin | L | 6-16 |
| 261 | 30-Oct-91 | Scotland | WC34 | N | National Stadium, Cardiff | W | 13-6 |
| 262 | 18-Apr-92 | World XV | Int | H | Lancaster Park Oval, Christchurch | L | 14-28 |
| 263 | 22-Apr-92 | World XV | Int | H | Athletic Park, Wellington | W | 54-26 |
| 264 | 25-Apr-92 | World XV | Int | H | Eden Park, Auckland | W | 26-15 |
| 265 | 30-May-92 | Ireland | Int | H | Carisbrook, Dunedin | W | 24-21 |
| 266 | 6-Jun-92 | Ireland | Int | H | Athletic Park, Wellington | W | 59-6 |
| 267 | 4-Jul-92 | Australia | Bled-T | A | Football Stadium, Sydney | L | 15-16 |
| 268 | 19-Jul-92 | Australia | Bled-T | A | Ballymore Oval, Brisbane | L | 17-19 |
| 269 | 25-Jul-92 | Australia | Bled-T | A | Football Stadium, Sydney | W | 26-23 |
| 270 | 15-Aug-92 | South Africa | Int-T | A | Ellis Park, Johannesburg | W | 27-24 |
| 271 | 12-Jun-93 | Lions | Int | H | Lancaster Park Oval, Christchurch | W | 20-18 |
| 272 | 26-Jun-93 | Lions | Int | H | Athletic Park, Wellington | L | 7-20 |
| 273 | 3-Jul-93 | Lions | Int | H | Eden Park, Auckland | W | 30-13 |
| 274 | 17-Jul-93 | Australia | Bled | H | Carisbrook, Dunedin | W | 25-10 |
| 275 | 31-Jul-93 | Western Samoa | Int | H | Eden Park, Auckland | W | 35-13 |
| 276 | 20-Nov-93 | Scotland | Int-T | A | Murrayfield, Edinburgh | W | 51-15 |
| 277 | 27-Nov-93 | England | Int-T | A | Twickenham, London | L | 9-15 |
| 278 | 26-Jun-94 | France | Int | H | Lancaster Park Oval, Christchurch | L | 8-22 |
| 279 | 3-Jul-94 | France | Int | H | Eden Park, Auckland | L | 20-23 |
| 280 | 9-Jul-94 | South Africa | Int | H | Carisbrook, Dunedin | W | 22-14 |

| No | Date | Opponents | Tmt | | Match Venue | Result | |
|----|------|-----------|-----|---|-------------|--------|---|
| 281 | 23-Jul-94 | South Africa | Int | H | Athletic Park, Wellington | W | 13-9 |
| 282 | 6-Aug-94 | South Africa | Int | H | Eden Park, Auckland | D | 18-18 |
| 283 | 17-Aug-94 | Australia | Bled-T | A | Football Stadium, Sydney | L | 16-20 |
| 284 | 22-Apr-95 | Canada | Int | H | Eden Park, Auckland | W | 73-7 |
| 285 | 27-May-95 | Ireland | WCp | N | Ellis Park, Johannesburg | W | 43-19 |
| 286 | 31-May-95 | Wales | WCp | N | Ellis Park, Johannesburg | W | 34-9 |
| 287 | 4-Jun-95 | Japan | WCp | N | Free State Stadium, Bloemfontein | W | 145-17 |
| 288 | 11-Jun-95 | Scotland | WCqf | N | Loftus Versfeld Stadium, Pretoria | W | 48-30 |
| 289 | 18-Jun-95 | England | WCsf | N | Newlands Stadium, Cape Town | W | 45-29 |
| 290 | 24-Jun-95 | South Africa | WCf | A | Ellis Park, Johannesburg ( a-e-t ) | L | 12-15 |
| 291 | 22-Jul-95 | Australia | Bled | H | Eden Park, Auckland | W | 28-16 |
| 292 | 29-Jul-95 | Australia | Bled-T | A | Football Stadium, Sydney | W | 34-23 |
| 293 | 28-Oct-95 | Italy | Int-T | A | Stadio Renato Dall'Ara, Bologna | W | 70-6 |
| 294 | 11 Nov 95 | France | Int-T | A | Stade Municipal de Toulouse, Toulouse | L | 15-22 |
| 295 | 18-Nov-95 | France | Int-T | A | Parc des Princess, Paris | W | 37-12 |
| 296 | 7-Jun-96 | Western Samoa | Int | H | McLean Park, Napier | W | 51-10 |
| 297 | 15-Jun-96 | Scotland | Int | H | Carisbrook, Dunedin | W | 62-31 |
| 298 | 22-Jun-96 | Scotland | Int | H | Eden Park, Auckland | W | 36-12 |
| 299 | 6-Jul-96 | Australia | TN-B | H | Athletic Park, Wellington | W | 43-6 |
| 300 | 20-Jul-96 | South Africa | TN | H | Lancaster Park Oval, Christchurch | W | 15-11 |
| 301 | 27-Jul-96 | Australia | TN-B | A | Suncorp Stadium, Brisbane | W | 32-25 |
| 302 | 10-Aug-96 | South Africa | TN | A | Norwich Park, Newlands, Cape Town | W | 29-18 |
| 303 | 17-Aug-96 | South Africa | Int-T | A | Kings Park Stadium, Durban | W | 23-19 |
| 304 | 24-Aug-96 | South Africa | Int-T | A | Loftus Versfeld Stadium, Pretoria | W | 33-26 |
| 305 | 31-Aug-96 | South Africa | Int-T | A | Ellis Park, Johannesburg | L | 22-32 |
| 306 | 14-Jun-97 | Fiji | Int | H | North Harbour Stadium, Albany | W | 71-5 |
| 307 | 21-Jun-97 | Argentina | Int | H | Athletic Park, Wellington | W | 93-8 |
| 308 | 28-Jun-97 | Argentina | Int | H | Rugby Park, Hamilton | W | 62-10 |
| 309 | 5-Jul-97 | Australia | Bled | H | Lancaster Park Oval, Christchurch | W | 30-13 |
| 310 | 19-Jul-97 | South Africa | TN | A | Ellis Park, Johannesburg | W | 35-32 |
| 311 | 26-Jul-97 | Australia | TN-B | A | Cricket Ground, Melbourne | W | 33-18 |
| 312 | 9-Aug-97 | South Africa | TN | H | Eden Park, Auckland | W | 55-35 |
| 313 | 16-Aug-97 | Australia | TN-B | H | Carisbrook, Dunedin | W | 36-24 |
| 314 | 15-Nov-97 | Ireland | Int-T | A | Lansdowne Road, Dublin | W | 63-15 |
| 315 | 22-Nov-97 | England | Int-T | A | Old Trafford, Manchester | W | 25-8 |
| 316 | 29-Nov-97 | Wales | Int-T | N | Wembley Stadium, London | W | 42-7 |
| 317 | 6-Dec-97 | England | Int-T | A | Twickenham, London | D | 26-26 |
| 318 | 20-Jun-98 | England | Int | H | Carisbrook, Dunedin | W | 64-22 |
| 319 | 27-Jun-98 | England | Int | H | Eden Park, Auckland | W | 40-10 |
| 320 | 11-Jul-98 | Australia | TN-B | A | Cricket Ground, Melbourne | L | 16-24 |

| No | Date | Opponents | Tmt | | Match Venue | Result | |
|----|------|-----------|-----|---|-------------|--------|---|
| 321 | 25-Jul-98 | South Africa | TN | H | Athletic Park, Wellington | L | 3-13 |
| 322 | 1-Aug-98 | Australia | TN-B | H | Jade Stadium, Christchurch | L | 23-27 |
| 323 | 15-Aug-98 | South Africa | TN | A | Kings Park Stadium, Durban | L | 23-24 |
| 324 | 29-Aug-98 | Australia | Bled-T | A | Football Stadium, Sydney | L | 14-19 |
| 325 | 18-Jun-99 | Samoa | Int | H | North Harbour Stadium, Albany | W | 71-13 |
| 326 | 26-Jun-99 | France | Int | H | Athletic Park, Wellington | W | 54-7 |
| 327 | 10-Jul-99 | South Africa | TN | H | Carisbrook, Dunedin | W | 28-0 |
| 328 | 24-Jul-99 | Australia | TN-B | H | Eden Park, Auckland | W | 34-15 |
| 329 | 7-Aug-99 | South Africa | TN | A | Minolta Loftus Stadium, Pretoria | W | 34-18 |
| 330 | 28-Aug-99 | Australia | TN-B | A | Stadium Australia, Sydney | L | 7-28 |
| 331 | 3-Oct-99 | Tonga | WCp | N | Ashton Gate, Bristol | W | 45-9 |
| 332 | 9-Oct-99 | England | WCp | A | Twickenham, London | W | 30-16 |
| 333 | 14-Oct-99 | Italy | WCp | N | McAlpine Stadium, Huddersfield | W | 101-3 |
| 334 | 24-Oct-99 | Scotland | WCqf | A | Murrayfield, Edinburgh | W | 30-18 |
| 335 | 31-Oct-99 | France | WCsf | N | Twickenham, London | L | 31-43 |
| 336 | 4-Nov-99 | South Africa | WC34 | N | Millennium Stadium, Cardiff | L | 18-22 |
| 337 | 16-Jun-00 | Tonga | Int | H | North Harbour Stadium, Albany | W | 102-0 |
| 338 | 24-Jun-00 | Scotland | Int | H | Carisbrook, Dunedin | W | 69-20 |
| 339 | 1-Jul-00 | Scotland | Int | H | Eden Park, Auckland | W | 48-14 |
| 340 | 15-Jul-00 | Australia | TN-B | A | Stadium Australia, Sydney | W | 39-35 |
| 341 | 22-Jul-00 | South Africa | TN | H | Jade Stadium, Christchurch | W | 25-12 |
| 342 | 5-Aug-00 | Australia | TN-B | H | Westpac Trust Stadium, Wellington | L | 23-24 |
| 343 | 19-Aug-00 | South Africa | TN | A | Ellis Park, Johannesburg | L | 40-46 |
| 344 | 11-Nov-00 | France | DGT-T | A | Stade de France, Paris | W | 39-26 |
| 345 | 18-Nov-00 | France | Int-T | A | Stade Vélodrome, Marseille | L | 33-42 |
| 346 | 25-Nov-00 | Italy | Int-T | A | Stadio Luigi Ferraris, Genova | W | 56-19 |
| 347 | 16-Jun-01 | Samoa | Int | H | North Harbour Stadium, Albany | W | 50-6 |
| 348 | 23-Jun-01 | Argentina | Int | H | Jade Stadium, Christchurch | W | 67-19 |
| 349 | 30-Jun-01 | France | DGT | H | Westpac Trust Stadium, Wellington | W | 37-12 |
| 350 | 21-Jul-01 | South Africa | TN | A | Fedsure Park, Newlands, Cape Town | W | 12-3 |
| 351 | 11-Aug-01 | Australia | TN-B | H | Carisbrook, Dunedin | L | 15-23 |
| 352 | 25-Aug-01 | South Africa | TN | H | Eden Park, Auckland | W | 26-15 |
| 353 | 1-Sep-01 | Australia | TN-B | A | Stadium Australia, Sydney | L | 26-29 |
| 354 | 17-Nov-01 | Ireland | Int-T | A | Lansdowne Road, Dublin | W | 40-29 |
| 355 | 24-Nov-01 | Scotland | Int-T | A | Murrayfield, Edinburgh | W | 37-6 |
| 356 | 1-Dec-01 | Argentina | Int-T | A | Estadio Monumental A V Liberti, B Aires | W | 24-20 |
| 357 | 8-Jun-02 | Italy | Int | H | Waikato Stadium, Hamilton | W | 64-10 |
| 358 | 15-Jun-02 | Ireland | Int | H | Carisbrook, Dunedin | W | 15-6 |
| 359 | 22-Jun-02 | Ireland | Int | H | Eden Park, Auckland | W | 40-8 |
| 360 | 29-Jun-02 | Fiji | Int | H | Westpac Trust Stadium, Wellington | W | 68-18 |

| No | Date | Opponents | Tmt | | Match Venue | Result | |
|---|---|---|---|---|---|---|---|
| 361 | 13-Jul-02 | Australia | TN-B | H | Jade Stadium, Christchurch | W | 12-6 |
| 362 | 20-Jul-02 | South Africa | TN | H | Westpac Trust Stadium, Wellington | W | 41-20 |
| 363 | 3-Aug-02 | Australia | TN-B | A | Telstra Stadium, Sydney | L | 14-16 |
| 364 | 10-Aug-02 | South Africa | TN | A | ABSA Stadium, Durban | W | 30-23 |
| 365 | 9-Nov-02 | England | Int-T | A | Twickenham, London | L | 28-31 |
| 366 | 16-Nov-02 | France | DGT-T | A | Stade de France, Paris | D | 20-20 |
| 367 | 23-Nov-02 | Wales | Int-T | A | Millennium Stadium, Cardiff | W | 43-17 |
| 368 | 14-Jun-03 | England | Int | H | Westpac Trust Stadium, Wellington | L | 13-15 |
| 369 | 21-Jun-03 | Wales | Int | H | Waikato Stadium, Hamilton | W | 55-3 |
| 370 | 28-Jun-03 | France | DGT | H | Jade Stadium, Christchurch | W | 31-23 |
| 371 | 19-Jul-03 | South Africa | TN | A | Securicor Loftus Stadium, Pretoria | W | 52-16 |
| 372 | 26-Jul-03 | Australia | TN-B | A | Telstra Stadium, Sydney | W | 50-21 |
| 373 | 9-Aug-03 | South Africa | TN | H | Carisbrook, Dunedin | W | 19-11 |
| 374 | 16-Aug-03 | Australia | TN-B | H | Eden Park, Auckland | W | 21-17 |
| 375 | 11-Oct-03 | Italy | WCp | N | Telstra Dome, Melbourne | W | 70-7 |
| 376 | 17-Oct-03 | Canada | WCp | N | Telstra Dome, Melbourne | W | 68-6 |
| 377 | 24-Oct-03 | Tonga | WCp | N | Suncorp Stadium, Brisbane | W | 91-7 |
| 378 | 2-Nov-03 | Wales | WCp | N | Telstra Stadium, Sydney | W | 53-37 |
| 379 | 8-Nov-03 | South Africa | WCqf | N | Telstra Dome, Melbourne | W | 29-9 |
| 380 | 15-Nov-03 | Australia | WCsf | A | Telstra Stadium, Sydney | L | 10-22 |
| 381 | 20-Nov-03 | France | WC34 | N | Telstra Stadium, Sydney | W | 40-13 |
| 382 | 12-Jun-04 | England | Int | H | Carisbrook, Dunedin | W | 36-3 |
| 383 | 19-Jun-04 | England | Int | H | Eden Park, Auckland | W | 36-12 |
| 384 | 26-Jun-04 | Argentina | Int | H | Waikato Stadium, Hamilton | W | 41-7 |
| 385 | 10-Jul-04 | Pacific Islands | Int | H | North Harbour Stadium, Albany | W | 41-26 |
| 386 | 17-Jul-04 | Australia | TN-B | H | Westpac Stadium, Wellington | W | 16-7 |
| 387 | 24-Jul-04 | South Africa | TN | H | Jade Stadium, Christchurch | W | 23-21 |
| 388 | 7-Aug-04 | Australia | TN-B | A | Telstra Stadium, Sydney | L | 18-23 |
| 389 | 14-Aug-04 | South Africa | TN-F | A | Ellis Park, Johannesburg | L | 26-40 |
| 390 | 13-Nov-04 | Italy | Int-T | A | Stadio Flaminio, Rome | W | 59-10 |
| 391 | 20-Nov-04 | Wales | Int-T | A | Millennium Stadium, Cardiff | W | 26-25 |
| 392 | 27-Nov-04 | France | DGT-T | A | Stade de France, Paris | W | 45-6 |
| 393 | 10-Jun-05 | Fiji | Int | H | North Harbour Stadium, Albany | W | 91-0 |
| 394 | 25-Jun-05 | Lions | Int | H | Jade Stadium, Christchurch | W | 21-3 |
| 395 | 2-Jul-05 | Lions | Int | H | Westpac Stadium, Wellington | W | 48-18 |
| 396 | 9-Jul-05 | Lions | Int | H | Eden Park, Auckland | W | 38-19 |
| 397 | 6-Aug-05 | South Africa | TN | A | Newlands Stadium, Cape Town | L | 16-22 |
| 398 | 13-Aug-05 | Australia | TN-B | A | Telstra Stadium, Sydney | W | 30-13 |
| 399 | 27-Aug-05 | South Africa | TN | H | Carisbrook, Dunedin | W | 31-27 |
| 400 | 3-Sep-05 | Australia | TN-B | H | Eden Park, Auckland | W | 34-24 |

| No | Date | Opponents | Tmt | | Match Venue | | Result |
|---|---|---|---|---|---|---|---|
| 401 | 5-Nov-05 | Wales | Int-T | A | Millennium Stadium, Cardiff | W | 41-3 |
| 402 | 12-Nov-05 | Ireland | Int-T | A | Lansdowne Road, Dublin | W | 45-7 |
| 403 | 19-Nov-05 | England | Int-T | A | Twickenham, London | W | 23-19 |
| 404 | 26-Nov-05 | Scotland | Int-T | A | Murrayfield, Edinburgh | W | 29-10 |
| 405 | 10-Jun-06 | Ireland | Int | H | Waikato Stadium, Hamilton | W | 34-23 |
| 406 | 17-Jun-06 | Ireland | Int | H | Eden Park, Auckland | W | 27-17 |
| 407 | 24-Jun-06 | Argentina | Int-T | A | Vélez Sarsfield Stadium, Buenos Aires | W | 25-19 |
| 408 | 8-Jul-06 | Australia | TN-B | H | Jade Stadium, Christchurch | W | 32-12 |
| 409 | 22-Jul-06 | South Africa | TN-F | H | Westpac Stadium, Wellington | W | 35-17 |
| 410 | 29-Jul-06 | Australia | TN-B | A | Suncorp Stadium, Brisbane | W | 13-9 |
| 411 | 19-Aug-06 | Australia | TN-B | H | Eden Park, Auckland | W | 34-27 |
| 412 | 26-Aug-06 | South Africa | TN-F | A | Loftus Versfeld Stadium, Pretoria | W | 45-26 |
| 413 | 2-Sep-06 | South Africa | TN-F | A | Royal Bafokeng Sports Palace, Rustenburg | L | 20-21 |
| 414 | 5-Nov-06 | England | Int-T | A | Twickenham, London | W | 41-20 |
| 415 | 11-Nov-06 | France | DGT-T | A | Stade de Gerland, Lyon | W | 47-3 |
| 416 | 18-Nov-06 | France | Int-T | A | Stade de France, Paris | W | 23-11 |
| 417 | 25-Nov-06 | Wales | Int-T | A | Millennium Stadium, Cardiff | W | 45-10 |
| 418 | 2-Jun-07 | France | DGT | H | Eden Park, Auckland | W | 42-11 |
| 419 | 9-Jun-07 | France | Int | H | Westpac Stadium, Wellington | W | 61-10 |
| 420 | 16-Jun-07 | Canada | Int | H | Waikato Stadium, Hamilton | W | 64-13 |
| 421 | 23-Jun-07 | South Africa | TN-F | A | The ABSA Stadium, Durban | W | 26-21 |
| 422 | 30-Jun-07 | Australia | TN-B | A | Cricket Ground, Melbourne | L | 15-20 |
| 423 | 14-Jul-07 | South Africa | TN-F | H | Jade Stadium, Christchurch | W | 33-6 |
| 424 | 21-Jul-07 | Australia | TN-B | H | Eden Park, Auckland | W | 26-12 |
| 425 | 8-Sep-07 | Italy | WCp | N | Stade Vélodrome, Marseille | W | 76-14 |
| 426 | 15-Sep-07 | Portugal | WCp | N | Stade de Gerland, Lyon | W | 108-13 |
| 427 | 23-Sep-07 | Scotland | WCp | A | Murrayfield, Edinburgh | W | 40-0 |
| 428 | 29-Sep-07 | Romania | WCp | N | Stade Municipal de Toulouse, Toulouse | W | 85-8 |
| 429 | 6-Oct-07 | France | WCqf | N | Millennium Stadium, Cardiff | L | 18-20 |
| 430 | 7-Jun-08 | Ireland | Int | H | Westpac Stadium, Wellington | W | 21-11 |
| 431 | 14-Jun-08 | England | Int | H | Eden Park, Auckland | W | 37-20 |
| 432 | 21-Jun-08 | England | Int | H | AMI Stadium, Christchurch | W | 44-12 |
| 433 | 5-Jul-08 | South Africa | TN-F | H | Westpac Stadium, Wellington | W | 19-8 |
| 434 | 12-Jul-08 | South Africa | TN-F | H | Carisbrook, Dunedin | L | 28-30 |
| 435 | 26-Jul-08 | Australia | TN-B | A | ANZ Stadium, Sydney | L | 19-34 |
| 436 | 2-Aug-08 | Australia | TN-B | H | Eden Park, Auckland | W | 39-10 |
| 437 | 16-Aug-08 | South Africa | TN-F | A | Newlands Stadium, Cape Town | W | 19-0 |
| 438 | 3-Sep-08 | Samoa | Int | H | Yarrow Stadium, New Plymouth | W | 101-14 |
| 439 | 13-Sep-08 | Australia | TN-B | A | Suncorp Stadium, Brisbane | W | 28-24 |
| 440 | 1-Nov-08 | Australia | Bled | N | So Kon Po Stadium, Hong Kong | W | 19-14 |

| No | Date | Opponents | Tmt | | Match Venue | Result | |
|---|---|---|---|---|---|---|---|
| 441 | 8-Nov-08 | Scotland | Int-T | A | Murrayfield, Edinburgh | W | 32-6 |
| 442 | 15-Nov-08 | Ireland | Int-T | A | Croke Park, Dublin | W | 22-3 |
| 443 | 22-Nov-08 | Wales | Int-T | A | Millennium Stadium, Cardiff | W | 29-9 |
| 444 | 29-Nov-08 | England | EHS-T | A | Twickenham, London | W | 32-6 |
| 445 | 13-Jun-09 | France | DGT | H | Carisbrook, Dunedin | L | 22-27 |
| 446 | 20-Jun-09 | France | DGT | H | Westpac Stadium, Wellington | W | 14-10 |
| 447 | 27-Jun-09 | Italy | Int | H | AMI Stadium, Christchurch | W | 27-6 |
| 448 | 18-Jul-09 | Australia | TN-B | H | Eden Park, Auckland | W | 22-16 |
| 449 | 25-Jul-09 | South Africa | TN-F | A | Vodacom Park Stadium, Bloemfontein | L | 19-28 |
| 450 | 1-Aug-09 | South Africa | TN-F | A | ABSA Stadium, Durban | L | 19-31 |
| 451 | 22-Aug-09 | Australia | TN-B | A | ANZ Stadium, Sydney | W | 19-18 |
| 452 | 12-Sep-09 | South Africa | TN-F | H | Waikato Stadium, Hamilton | L | 29-32 |
| 453 | 19-Sep-09 | Australia | TN-B | H | Westpac Stadium, Wellington | W | 33-6 |
| 454 | 31-Oct-09 | Australia | Bled | N | National Olympic Stadium, Tokyo | W | 32-19 |
| 455 | 7-Nov-09 | Wales | Int-T | A | Millennium Stadium, Cardiff | W | 19-12 |
| 456 | 14-Nov-09 | Italy | Int-T | A | Stadio San Siro, Milan | W | 20-6 |
| 457 | 21-Nov-09 | England | EHS-T | A | Twickenham, London | W | 19-6 |
| 458 | 28-Nov-09 | France | DGT-T | A | Stade Vélodrome, Marseille | W | 39-12 |
| 459 | 12-Jun-10 | Ireland | Int | H | Yarrow Stadium, New Plymouth | W | 66-28 |
| 460 | 19-Jun-10 | Wales | Int | H | Carisbrook, Dunedin | W | 42-9 |
| 461 | 26-Jun-10 | Wales | Int | H | Waikato Stadium, Hamilton | W | 29-10 |
| 462 | 10-Jul-10 | South Africa | TN-F | H | Eden Park, Auckland | W | 32-12 |
| 463 | 17-Jul-10 | South Africa | TN-F | H | Westpac Stadium, Wellington | W | 31-17 |
| 464 | 31-Jul-10 | Australia | TN-B | A | Etihad Stadium, Docklands, Melbourne | W | 49-28 |
| 465 | 7-Aug-10 | Australia | TN-B | H | AMI Stadium, Christchurch | W | 20-10 |
| 466 | 21-Aug-10 | South Africa | TN-F | A | FNB Stadium, Soweto, Johannesburg | W | 29-22 |
| 467 | 11-Sep-10 | Australia | TN-B | A | ANZ Stadium, Sydney | W | 23-22 |
| 468 | 30-Oct-10 | Australia | Bled | N | So Kon Po Stadium, Hong Kong | L | 24-26 |
| 469 | 6-Nov-10 | England | EHS-T | A | Twickenham, London | W | 26-16 |
| 470 | 13-Nov-10 | Scotland | Int-T | A | Murrayfield, Edinburgh | W | 49-3 |
| 471 | 20-Nov-10 | Ireland | Int-T | A | Aviva Stadium, Dublin | W | 38-18 |
| 472 | 27-Nov-10 | Wales | Int-T | A | Millennium Stadium, Cardiff | W | 37-25 |
| 473 | 22-Jul-11 | Fiji | Int | H | Carisbrook, Dunedin | W | 60-14 |
| 474 | 30-Jul-11 | South Africa | TN-F | H | Westpac Stadium, Wellington | W | 40-7 |
| 475 | 5-Aug-11 | Australia | TN-B | H | Eden Park, Auckland | W | 30-14 |
| 476 | 20-Aug-11 | South Africa | TN-F | A | Nelson Mandela Bay Stad, Port Elizabeth | L | 5-18 |
| 477 | 27-Aug-11 | Australia | TN-B | A | Suncorp Stadium, Brisbane | L | 20-25 |
| 478 | 9-Sep-11 | Tonga | WCp | H | Eden Park, Auckland | W | 41-10 |
| 479 | 16-Sep-11 | Japan | WCp | H | Waikato Stadium, Hamilton | W | 83-7 |
| 480 | 24-Sep-11 | France | WCp | H | Eden Park, Auckland | W | 37-17 |

| No | Date | Opponents | Tmt | | Match Venue | | Result |
|---|---|---|---|---|---|---|---|
| 481 | 2-Oct-11 | Canada | WCp | H | Wellington Regional Stadium, Wellington | W | 79-15 |
| 482 | 9-Oct-11 | Argentina | WCqf | H | Eden Park, Auckland | W | 33-10 |
| 483 | 16-Oct-11 | Australia | WCsf | H | Eden Park, Auckland | W | 20-6 |
| 484 | 23-Oct-11 | France | WCf | H | Eden Park, Auckland | W | 8-7 |
| 485 | 9-Jun-12 | Ireland | Int | H | Eden Park, Auckland | W | 42-10 |
| 486 | 16-Jun-12 | Ireland | Int | H | Rugby League Park, Christchurch | W | 22-19 |
| 487 | 23-Jun-12 | Ireland | Int | H | Waikato Stadium, Hamilton | W | 60-0 |
| 488 | 18-Aug-12 | Australia | RC-B | A | ANZ Stadium, Sydney | W | 27-19 |
| 489 | 25-Aug-12 | Australia | RC-B | H | Eden Park, Auckland | W | 22-0 |
| 490 | 8-Sep-12 | Argentina | RC | H | Westpac Stadium, Wellington | W | 21-5 |
| 491 | 15-Sep-12 | South Africa | RC-F | H | Forsyth Barr Stadium, Dunedin | W | 21-11 |
| 492 | 29-Sep-12 | Argentina | RC | A | Estadio Ciudad de la Plata, La Plata | W | 54-15 |
| 493 | 6-Oct-12 | South Africa | RC-F | A | FNB Stadium, Soweto, Johannesburg | W | 32-16 |
| 494 | 20-Oct-12 | Australia | Bled-T | A | Suncorp Stadium, Brisbane | D | 18-18 |
| 495 | 11-Nov-12 | Scotland | Int-T | A | Murrayfield, Edinburgh | W | 51-22 |
| 496 | 17-Nov-12 | Italy | Int-T | A | Stadio Olimpico, Rome | W | 42-10 |
| 497 | 24-Nov-12 | Wales | Int-T | A | Millennium Stadium, Cardiff | W | 33-10 |
| 498 | 1-Dec-12 | England | EHS-T | A | Twickenham, London | L | 21-38 |
| 499 | 8-Jun-13 | France | DGT | H | Eden Park, Auckland | W | 23-13 |
| 500 | 15-Jun-13 | France | DGT | H | AMI Stadium, Addington | W | 30-0 |
| 501 | 22-Jun-13 | France | DGT | H | Yarrow Stadium, New Plymouth | W | 24-9 |
| 502 | 17-Aug-13 | Australia | RC-B | A | ANZ Stadium, Sydney | W | 47-29 |
| 503 | 24-Aug-13 | Australia | RC-B | H | Westpac Stadium, Wellington | W | 27-16 |
| 504 | 7-Sep-13 | Argentina | RC | H | Waikato Stadium, Hamilton | W | 28-13 |
| 505 | 14-Sep-13 | South Africa | RC-F | H | Eden Park, Auckland | W | 29-15 |
| 506 | 28-Sep-13 | Argentina | RC | A | Estadio Ciudad de la Plata, La Plata | W | 33-15 |
| 507 | 5-Oct-13 | South Africa | RC-F | A | Ellis Park, Johannesburg | W | 38-27 |
| 508 | 19-Oct-13 | Australia | Bled | H | Forsyth Barr Stadium, Dunedin | W | 41-33 |
| 509 | 2-Nov-13 | Japan | Int-T | A | Prince Chichibu Memorial Ground, Tokyo | W | 54-6 |
| 510 | 9-Nov-13 | France | DGT-T | A | Stade de France, Paris | W | 26-19 |
| 511 | 16-Nov-13 | England | EHS-T | A | Twickenham, London | W | 30-22 |
| 512 | 24-Nov-13 | Ireland | Int-T | A | Aviva Stadium, Dublin | W | 24-22 |
| 513 | 7-Jun-14 | England | EHS | H | Eden Park, Auckland | W | 20-15 |
| 514 | 14-Jun-14 | England | EHS | H | Forsyth Barr Stadium, Dunedin | W | 28-27 |
| 515 | 21-Jun-14 | England | EHS | H | Waikato Stadium, Hamilton | W | 36-13 |
| 516 | 16-Aug-14 | Australia | RC-B | A | ANZ Stadium, Sydney | D | 12-12 |
| 517 | 23-Aug-14 | Australia | RC-B | H | Eden Park, Auckland | W | 51-20 |
| 518 | 6-Sep-14 | Argentina | RC | H | McLean Park, Napier | W | 28-9 |
| 519 | 13-Sep-14 | South Africa | RC-F | H | Westpac Stadium, Wellington | W | 14-10 |
| 520 | 27-Sep-14 | Argentina | RC | A | Estadio Ciudad de la Plata, La Plata | W | 34-13 |

| No | Date | Opponents | Tmt | | Match Venue | | Result |
|----|------|-----------|-----|---|-------------|---|--------|
| 521 | 4-Oct-14 | South Africa | RC-F | A | Ellis Park, Johannesburg | L | 25-27 |
| 522 | 11-Oct-14 | Australia | RC-B | A | Suncorp Stadium, Brisbane | W | 29-28 |
| 523 | 1-Nov-14 | United States | Int-T | A | Soldier Field, Chicago | W | 74-6 |
| 524 | 8-Nov-14 | England | EHS-T | A | Twickenham, London | W | 24-21 |
| 525 | 15-Nov-14 | Scotland | Int-T | A | Murrayfield, Edinburgh | W | 24-16 |
| 526 | 22-Nov-14 | Wales | Int-T | A | Millennium Stadium, Cardiff | W | 34-16 |
| 527 | 8-Jul-15 | Samoa | Int-T | A | Apia Park, Apia | W | 25-16 |
| 528 | 17-Jul-15 | Argentina | RC | H | Rugby League Park, Christchurch | W | 39-18 |
| 529 | 25-Jul-15 | South Africa | RC-F | A | Ellis Park, Johannesburg | W | 27-20 |
| 530 | 8-Aug-15 | Australia | RC-B | A | Stadium Australia, Sydney | L | 19-27 |
| 531 | 15-Aug-15 | Australia | Bled | H | Eden Park, Auckland | W | 41-13 |
| 532 | 20-Sep-15 | Argentina | WCp | N | Wembley Stadium, London | W | 26-16 |
| 533 | 24-Sep-15 | Namibia | WCp | N | Olympic Stadium, London | W | 58-14 |
| 534 | 2-Oct-15 | Georgia | WCp | N | Millennium Stadium, Cardiff | W | 43-10 |
| 535 | 9-Oct-15 | Tonga | WCp | N | St James' Park, Newcastle | W | 47-9 |
| 536 | 17-Oct-15 | France | WCqf | N | Millennium Stadium, Cardiff | W | 62-13 |
| 537 | 24-Oct-15 | South Africa | WCsf | N | Twickenham, London | W | 20-18 |
| 538 | 31-Oct-15 | Australia | WCf | N | Twickenham, London | W | 34-17 |

# SCOTLAND

On 25 March 1871, the *Glasgow Herald* reported that a rugby match would take place between Scotland and England. The newspaper noted that the rules of Rugby school would be used, with some minor alterations. With twenty players each side, the match was played at Raeburn Place in Edinburgh on a pitch measuring 120 yards by 55 yards. Two days later, the first rugby International took place and Scotland won by one goal and one try to one try. In 1883 Scotland finished runners-up in the inaugural Home Nations Championship, losing only to Triple Crown winners England.

Scotland finally won the Championship four years later, in 1887, in a three nations tournament that had excluded England because of their refusal to join the IRB in 1888. In the eleven-year period between 1882 and 1892 Scotland played 29 matches and lost just five times, but despite this fine run, they managed to win only one Triple Crown, in 1891. However, their record improved as they won four more Triple Crowns between 1895 and 1907 and, after a gap of eighteen years, they won a sixth Triple Crown in the 1925 Five Nations Championship. In addition, having beaten France earlier, they secured their first Grand Slam. The team's final match in that campaign was the inaugural game held at Murrayfield in Edinburgh.

The next Triple Crown success for Scotland came in 1933, but it was followed by a relatively uneventful period for the team between 1934 and 1937 as they won only three games out of thirteen, before finally winning the Triple Crown again in 1938.

The fortunes of the Scottish side were very disappointing in the four years after the Second World War and the team lost eleven games out of the first seventeen played. Their losing streak continued between February 1951 and February 1955, when Scotland suffered seventeen defeats in succession, including a 44 points to nil trouncing by the touring Springboks. There was a slight improvement from 1955 to 1963, but still no win against England.

That eventually came in 1964 when Scotland finally triumphed over the English side in March and, to the surprise of many, had earlier held New Zealand to a scoreless draw. The second half of the decade produced some stunning results for Scotland: not only did they defeat South Africa in 1965 and 1969 (thus ending five defeats in a row since their historic win in 1906), they also beat Australia in the two games played in 1966 and 1968. Unfortunately, Scotland failed to complete a hat-trick of wins over Southern Hemisphere opposition, losing to New Zealand in 1967.

The barren years of the 1970s and early 1980s came to an unexpected end in 1984, when Scotland achieved a second Grand Slam, a result that bridged a gap of fifty-nine years since their first Grand Slam in 1925. And there was more to come: six years later, in 1990, the Scots repeated their 1984 achievement when they gained a third Grand Slam at the expense of England (who were themselves seeking a Grand Slam).

Scotland's good form continued in the 1991 World Cup when they won their pool group and the quarter-final against Western Samoa by 28 points to 6, to reach the semi-final, only to lose by 9 points to 6 to England. Scottish success was not forthcoming in the next four World Cups when they lost each time at the quarter-final stage: to New Zealand in 1995 in a high-scoring match by 48 points to 30 and again to the All Blacks in 1999 by 30 points to 18; to hosts Australia in 2003 by 33 points to 16; and to Argentina by 19 points to 13 at the Stade de France in Paris in 2007.

With the advent of the Six Nations Championship in 2000,

the Scottish team failed to impress in the first twelve years of the competition: they performed so poorly that they were landed with the 'wooden spoon' (finishing in sixth place), in 2004 and again in 2007. Finishing in fifth place in each year from 2008 to 2011 wasn't much better. On the credit side, however, Scotland defeated Australia in Murrayfield in 2009, and Argentina twice on their 2010 Southern Hemisphere tour. They also beat South Africa in Murrayfield later that autumn.

The Scottish team failed to reach the quarter-final stage of a World Cup for the first time in 2011, losing to both Argentina and England in the pool matches. Things got even worse in the 2012 Six Nations Championship when Scotland lost all five matches again and with it gained a third wooden spoon in that tournament. This was followed, however, by a successful summer tour where Scotland defeated Australia away from home for the first time since 1982, winning by 9 points to 6 in a rain-lashed Newcastle to retain the Hopetoun Cup, before defeating Fiji by 37 points to 25 at Churchill Park, Lautoka, and concluding the tour with a victory over Samoa at Apia Park, Apia, by 17 points to 16.

There was a marked improvement in the 2013 Championship when the Scottish team won two home games against Italy and Ireland to finish in third place (a position they also held in 2001 and 2006).

A sole win in Rome in the 2014 Six Nations Championship, however, relegated Scotland back to fifth place in the table, before a stirring autumn where they defeated Argentina by 41 points to 31 and pushed New Zealand close in a 24 point to 16 loss at Murrayfield, before concluding the series with a 37 points to 12 win over Tonga at Rugby Park, Kilmarnock, which was notable as the first International to be played on an artificial surface.

However, five defeats in the 2015 Championship plunged the Scots to their fourth wooden spoon in sixteen years of the competition. In eighty Six Nations Championships, Scotland have won only nineteen games and drawn one: a record of less than 25%.

In the 2015 Rugby World Cup the Scots' only defeat in the pool was against South Africa. Qualifying as pool runners-up, they were very unlucky to lose at the quarter-final stage to Australia, by 35 points to 34.

# SCOTLAND

## HEAD TO HEAD RESULTS TO 31 OCTOBER 2015

|  | P | W | D | L | % | F | A |
|---|---|---|---|---|---|---|---|
| **v TIER 1 Teams** | | | | | | | |
| v Argentina | 15 | 6 | 0 | 9 | 40.0 | 309 | 268 |
| v Australia | 29 | 9 | 0 | 20 | 31.0 | 364 | 706 |
| v England * | 133 | 42 | 18 | 73 | 38.3 | 1132 | 1547 |
| v France | 89 | 34 | 3 | 52 | 39.9 | 1073 | 1262 |
| v Ireland * / ** | 131 | 65 | 5 | 60 | 51.9 | 1355 | 1440 |
| v Italy | 25 | 17 | 0 | 8 | 68.0 | 588 | 435 |
| v New Zealand | 30 | 0 | 2 | 28 | 3.3 | 332 | 900 |
| v South Africa | 26 | 5 | 0 | 21 | 19.2 | 286 | 686 |
| v Wales * | 120 | 48 | 3 | 69 | 41.2 | 1211 | 1584 |
| **Sub-Total** | **598** | **226** | **31** | **340** | **40.5** | **6650** | **8828** |
| **v TIER 2/3 Group** | | | | | | | |
| v Canada | 4 | 3 | 0 | 1 | 75.0 | 105 | 49 |
| v Fiji | 6 | 5 | 0 | 1 | 83.3 | 182 | 145 |
| v Japan | 5 | 5 | 0 | 0 | 100.0 | 266 | 55 |
| v Romania | 13 | 11 | 0 | 2 | 84.6 | 475 | 192 |
| v Samoa | 10 | 8 | 1 | 1 | 85.0 | 254 | 155 |
| v Tonga | 4 | 3 | 0 | 1 | 75.0 | 136 | 58 |
| v United States | 5 | 5 | 0 | 0 | 100.0 | 220 | 66 |
| v Georgia | 1 | 1 | 0 | 0 | 100.0 | 15 | 6 |
| v Namibia | 0 | 0 | 0 | 0 | 0.0 | 0.0 | 0 |
| v Russia | 0 | 0 | 0 | 0 | 0.0 | 0.0 | 0 |
| v Uruguay | 1 | 1 | 0 | 0 | 100.0 | 43 | 12 |
| **Sub-Total** | **49** | **42** | **1** | **6** | **86.7** | **1696** | **738** |
| **v Other Teams** | | | | | | | |
| v Côte d'Ivoire | 1 | 1 | 0 | 0 | 100.0 | 89 | 0 |
| v Pacific Islanders | 1 | 1 | 0 | 0 | 100.0 | 34 | 22 |
| v Portugal | 1 | 1 | 0 | 0 | 100.0 | 56 | 10 |
| v President's XV | 1 | 1 | 0 | 0 | 100.0 | 27 | 16 |
| v Spain | 1 | 1 | 0 | 0 | 100.0 | 48 | 0 |
| v Zimbabwe | 2 | 2 | 0 | 0 | 100.0 | 111 | 33 |
| **Sub-Total** | **7** | **7** | **0** | **0** | **100.0** | **365** | **81** |
| **All Internationals** | **654** | **275** | **32** | **346** | **44.6** | **8711** | **9647** |

\* excludes points scored before the introduction of the modern points system
\** excludes the abandoned match on 21 February 1885 (Ireland 0 Scotland 1)

| No | Date | Opponents | Tmt | | Match Venue | Result | |
|----|------|-----------|-----|---|-------------|--------|---|
| 1 | 27-Mar-71 | England | Int | H | Raeburn Place, Edinburgh | W | 4-1 |
| 2 | 5-Feb-72 | England | Int | A | Kennington Oval, London | L | 3-8 |
| 3 | 3-Mar-73 | England | Int | H | Hamilton Crescent, Glasgow | D | 0-0 |
| 4 | 23-Feb-74 | England | Int | A | Kennington Oval, London | L | 1-3 |
| 5 | 8-Mar-75 | England | Int | H | Raeburn Place, Edinburgh | D | 0-0 |
| 6 | 6-Mar-76 | England | Int | A | Kennington Oval, London | L | 0-4 |
| 7 | 19-Feb-77 | Ireland | Int | A | Ormeau, Belfast | W | 20-0 |
| 8 | 5-Mar-77 | England | Int | H | Raeburn Place, Edinburgh | W | 3-0 |
| 9 | 4-Mar-78 | England | Int | A | Kennington Oval, London | D | 0-0 |
| 10 | 17-Feb-79 | Ireland | Int | A | Ormeau, Belfast | W | 7-0 |
| 11 | 10-Mar-79 | England | CC | H | Raeburn Place, Edinburgh | D | 3-3 |
| 12 | 14-Feb-80 | Ireland | Int | H | Hamilton Crescent, Glasgow | W | 11-0 |
| 13 | 28-Feb-80 | England | CC | A | Whalley Range, Manchester | L | 3-9 |
| 14 | 19-Feb-81 | Ireland | Int | A | Ormeau, Belfast | L | 1-3 |
| 15 | 19-Mar-81 | England | CC | H | Raeburn Place, Edinburgh | D | 4-4 |
| 16 | 18-Feb-82 | Ireland | Int | H | Hamilton Crescent, Glasgow | W | 2-0 |
| 17 | 4-Mar-82 | England | CC | A | Whalley Range, Manchester | W | 2-0 |
| 18 | 8-Jan-83 | Wales | 4N | H | Raeburn Place, Edinburgh | W | 9-3 |
| 19 | 17-Feb-83 | Ireland | Int | A | Ormeau, Belfast | W | 4-0 |
| 20 | 3-Mar-83 | England | 4N-CC | H | Raeburn Place, Edinburgh | L | 1-2 |
| 21 | 12-Jan-84 | Wales | 4N | A | Rodney Parade, Newport | W | 4-0 |
| 22 | 16-Feb-84 | Ireland | 4N | H | Raeburn Place, Edinburgh | W | 8-1 |
| 23 | 1-Mar-84 | England | 4N-CC | A | Rectory Field, Blackheath | L | 1-3 |
| 24 | 10-Jan-85 | Wales | 4N | H | Hamilton Crescent, Glasgow | D | 0-0 |
| 25 | 21-Feb-85 | Ireland | 4N | A | Ormeau, Belfast (abandoned) | a | 1-0 |
| 26 | 7-Mar-85 | Ireland | 4N | H | Raeburn Place, Edinburgh | W | 5-0 |
| 27 | 9-Jan-86 | Wales | 4N | A | Arms Park, Cardiff | W | 7-0 |
| 28 | 20-Feb-86 | Ireland | 4N | H | Raeburn Place, Edinburgh | W | 14-0 |
| 29 | 13-Mar-86 | England | 4N-CC | H | Raeburn Place, Edinburgh | D | 0-0 |
| 30 | 19-Feb-87 | Ireland | 4N | A | Ormeau, Belfast | W | 8-0 |
| 31 | 26-Feb-87 | Wales | 4N | H | Raeburn Place, Edinburgh | W | 20-0 |
| 32 | 5-Mar-87 | England | 4N-CC | A | Whalley Range, Manchester | D | 1-1 |
| 33 | 4-Feb-88 | Wales | 4N | A | Rodney Parade, Newport | L | 0-1 |
| 34 | 10-Mar-88 | Ireland | 4N | H | Raeburn Place, Edinburgh | W | 3-0 |
| 35 | 2-Feb-89 | Wales | 4N | H | Raeburn Place, Edinburgh | W | 2-0 |
| 36 | 16-Feb-89 | Ireland | 4N | A | Ormeau, Belfast | W | 3-0 |
| 37 | 1-Feb-90 | Wales | 4N | A | Arms Park, Cardiff | W | 5-1 |
| 38 | 22-Feb-90 | Ireland | 4N | H | Raeburn Place, Edinburgh | W | 5-0 |
| 39 | 1-Mar-90 | England | 4N-CC | H | Raeburn Place, Edinburgh | L | 0-6 |
| 40 | 7-Feb-91 | Wales | 4N | H | Raeburn Place, Edinburgh | W | 15-0 |

| No | Date | Opponents | Tmt | | Match Venue | Result | |
|----|------|-----------|-----|---|-------------|--------|---|
| 41 | 21-Feb-91 | Ireland | 4N | A | Ballynafeigh, Belfast | W | 14-0 |
| 42 | 7-Mar-91 | England | 4N-CC | A | Athletic Ground, Richmond | W | 9-3 |
| 43 | 6-Feb-92 | Wales | 4N | A | St Helen's, Swansea | W | 7-2 |
| 44 | 20-Feb-92 | Ireland | 4N | H | Raeburn Place, Edinburgh | W | 2-0 |
| 45 | 5-Mar-92 | England | 4N-CC | H | Raeburn Place, Edinburgh | L | 0-5 |
| 46 | 4-Feb-93 | Wales | 4N | H | Raeburn Place, Edinburgh | L | 0-9 |
| 47 | 18-Feb-93 | Ireland | 4N | A | Ballynafeigh, Belfast | D | 0-0 |
| 48 | 4-Mar-93 | England | 4N-CC | A | Headingley, Leeds | W | 8-0 |
| 49 | 3-Feb-94 | Wales | 4N | A | Rodney Parade, Newport | L | 0-7 |
| 50 | 24-Feb-94 | Ireland | 4N | A | Lansdowne Road, Dublin | L | 0-5 |
| 51 | 17-Mar-94 | England | 4N-CC | H | Raeburn Place, Edinburgh | W | 6-0 |
| 52 | 26-Jan-95 | Wales | 4N | H | Raeburn Place, Edinburgh | W | 5-4 |
| 53 | 2-Mar-95 | Ireland | 4N | H | Raeburn Place, Edinburgh | W | 6-0 |
| 54 | 9-Mar-95 | England | 4N-CC | A | Athletic Ground, Richmond | W | 6-3 |
| 55 | 25-Jan-96 | Wales | 4N | A | Arms Park, Cardiff | L | 0-6 |
| 56 | 15-Feb-96 | Ireland | 4N | A | Lansdowne Road, Dublin | D | 0-0 |
| 57 | 14-Mar-96 | England | 4N-CC | H | Old Hampden Park, Glasgow | W | 11-0 |
| 58 | 20-Feb-97 | Ireland | 4N | H | Powderhall, Edinburgh | W | 8-3 |
| 59 | 13-Mar-97 | England | 4N-CC | A | Fallowfield, Manchester | L | 3-12 |
| 60 | 19-Feb-98 | Ireland | 4N | A | Balmoral Showgrounds, Belfast | W | 8-0 |
| 61 | 12-Mar-98 | England | 4N-CC | H | Powderhall, Edinburgh | D | 3-3 |
| 62 | 18-Feb-99 | Ireland | 4N | H | Inverleith, Edinburgh | L | 3-9 |
| 63 | 4-Mar-99 | Wales | 4N | H | Inverleith, Edinburgh | W | 21-10 |
| 64 | 11-Mar-99 | England | 4N-CC | A | Rectory Field, Blackheath | W | 5-0 |
| 65 | 27-Jan-00 | Wales | 4N | A | St Helen's, Swansea | L | 3-12 |
| 66 | 24-Feb-00 | Ireland | 4N | A | Lansdowne Road, Dublin | D | 0-0 |
| 67 | 10-Mar-00 | England | 4N-CC | H | Inverleith, Edinburgh | D | 0-0 |
| 68 | 9-Feb-01 | Wales | 4N | H | Inverleith, Edinburgh | W | 18-8 |
| 69 | 23-Feb-01 | Ireland | 4N | H | Inverleith, Edinburgh | W | 9-5 |
| 70 | 9-Mar-01 | England | 4N-CC | A | Rectory Field, Blackheath | W | 18-3 |
| 71 | 1-Feb-02 | Wales | 4N | A | Arms Park, Cardiff | L | 5-14 |
| 72 | 22-Feb-02 | Ireland | 4N | A | Balmoral Showgrounds, Belfast | L | 0-5 |
| 73 | 15-Mar-02 | England | 4N-CC | H | Inverleith, Edinburgh | L | 3-6 |
| 74 | 7-Feb-03 | Wales | 4N | H | Inverleith, Edinburgh | W | 6-0 |
| 75 | 28-Feb-03 | Ireland | 4N | H | Inverleith, Edinburgh | W | 3-0 |
| 76 | 21-Mar-03 | England | 4N-CC | A | Athletic Ground, Richmond | W | 10-6 |
| 77 | 6-Feb-04 | Wales | 4N | A | St Helen's, Swansea | L | 3-21 |
| 78 | 27-Feb-04 | Ireland | 4N | A | Lansdowne Road, Dublin | W | 19-3 |
| 79 | 19-Mar-04 | England | 4N-CC | H | Inverleith, Edinburgh | W | 6-3 |
| 80 | 4-Feb-05 | Wales | 4N | H | Inverleith, Edinburgh | L | 3-6 |

| No | Date | Opponents | Tmt | | Match Venue | Result | |
|----|------|-----------|-----|--|-------------|--------|--|
| 81 | 25-Feb-05 | Ireland | 4N | H | Inverleith, Edinburgh | L | 5-11 |
| 82 | 18-Mar-05 | England | 4N-CC | A | Athletic Ground, Richmond | W | 8-0 |
| 83 | 18-Nov-05 | New Zealand | Int | H | Inverleith, Edinburgh | L | 7-12 |
| 84 | 3-Feb-06 | Wales | 4N | A | Arms Park, Cardiff, | L | 3-9 |
| 85 | 24-Feb-06 | Ireland | 4N | A | Lansdowne Road, Dublin | W | 13-6 |
| 86 | 17-Mar-06 | England | 4N-CC | H | Inverleith, Edinburgh | L | 3-9 |
| 87 | 17-Nov-06 | South Africa | Int | H | Hampden Park, Glasgow | W | 6-0 |
| 88 | 2-Feb-07 | Wales | 4N | H | Inverleith, Edinburgh | W | 6-3 |
| 89 | 23-Feb-07 | Ireland | 4N | H | Inverleith, Edinburgh | W | 15-3 |
| 90 | 16-Mar-07 | England | 4N-CC | A | Rectory Field, Blackheath | W | 8-3 |
| 91 | 1-Feb-08 | Wales | 4N | A | St Helen's, Swansea | L | 5-6 |
| 92 | 29-Feb-08 | Ireland | 4N | A | Lansdowne Road, Dublin | L | 11-16 |
| 93 | 21-Mar-08 | England | 4N-CC | H | Inverleith, Edinburgh | W | 16-10 |
| 94 | 6-Feb-09 | Wales | 4N | H | Inverleith, Edinburgh | L | 3-5 |
| 95 | 27-Feb-09 | Ireland | 4N | H | Inverleith, Edinburgh | W | 9-3 |
| 96 | 20-Mar-09 | England | 4N-CC | A | Athletic Ground, Richmond | W | 18-8 |
| 97 | 22-Jan-10 | France | 5N | H | Inverleith, Edinburgh | W | 27-0 |
| 98 | 5-Feb-10 | Wales | 5N | A | Arms Park, Cardiff | L | 0-14 |
| 99 | 26-Feb-10 | Ireland | 5N | A | Balmoral Showgrounds, Belfast | W | 14-0 |
| 100 | 19-Mar-10 | England | 5N-CC | H | Inverleith, Edinburgh | L | 5-14 |
| 101 | 2-Jan-11 | France | 5N | A | Stade Colombes, Paris | L | 15-16 |
| 102 | 4-Feb-11 | Wales | 5N | H | Inverleith, Edinburgh | L | 10-32 |
| 103 | 25-Feb-11 | Ireland | 5N | H | Inverleith, Edinburgh | L | 10-16 |
| 104 | 18-Mar-11 | England | 5N-CC | A | Twickenham, London | L | 8-13 |
| 105 | 20-Jan-12 | France | 5N | H | Inverleith, Edinburgh | W | 31-3 |
| 106 | 3-Feb-12 | Wales | 5N | A | St Helen's, Swansea | L | 6-21 |
| 107 | 24-Feb-12 | Ireland | 5N | A | Lansdowne Road, Dublin | L | 8-10 |
| 108 | 16-Mar-12 | England | 5N-CC | H | Inverleith, Edinburgh | W | 8-3 |
| 109 | 23-Nov-12 | South Africa | Int | H | Inverleith, Edinburgh | L | 0-16 |
| 110 | 1-Jan-13 | France | 5N | A | Parc des Princess, Paris | W | 21-3 |
| 111 | 1-Feb-13 | Wales | 5N | H | Inverleith, Edinburgh | L | 0-8 |
| 112 | 22-Feb-13 | Ireland | 5N | H | Inverleith, Edinburgh | W | 29-14 |
| 113 | 15-Mar-13 | England | 5N-CC | A | Twickenham, London | L | 0-3 |
| 114 | 7-Feb-14 | Wales | 5N | A | Arms Park, Cardiff | L | 5-24 |
| 115 | 28-Feb-14 | Ireland | 5N | A | Lansdowne Road, Dublin | L | 0-6 |
| 116 | 21-Mar-14 | England | 5N-CC | H | Inverleith, Edinburgh | L | 15-16 |
| 117 | 1-Jan-20 | France | 5N | A | Parc des Princess, Paris | W | 5-0 |
| 118 | 7-Feb-20 | Wales | 5N | H | Inverleith, Edinburgh | W | 9-5 |
| 119 | 28-Feb-20 | Ireland | 5N | H | Inverleith, Edinburgh | W | 19-0 |
| 120 | 20-Mar-20 | England | 5N-CC | A | Twickenham, London | L | 4-13 |

| No | Date | Opponents | Tmt | | Match Venue | Result | |
|----|------|-----------|-----|---|-------------|--------|---|
| 121 | 22-Jan-21 | France | 5N | H | Inverleith, Edinburgh | L | 0-3 |
| 122 | 5-Feb-21 | Wales | 5N | A | St Helen's, Swansea | W | 14-8 |
| 123 | 26-Feb-21 | Ireland | 5N | A | Lansdowne Road, Dublin | L | 8-9 |
| 124 | 19-Mar-21 | England | 5N-CC | H | Inverleith, Edinburgh | L | 0-18 |
| 125 | 2-Jan-22 | France | 5N | A | Stade Colombes, Paris | D | 3-3 |
| 126 | 4-Feb-22 | Wales | 5N | H | Inverleith, Edinburgh | D | 9-9 |
| 127 | 25-Feb-22 | Ireland | 5N | H | Inverleith, Edinburgh | W | 6-3 |
| 128 | 18-Mar-22 | England | 5N-CC | A | Twickenham, London | L | 5-11 |
| 129 | 20-Jan-23 | France | 5N | H | Inverleith, Edinburgh | W | 16-3 |
| 130 | 3-Feb-23 | Wales | 5N | A | Arms Park, Cardiff | W | 11-8 |
| 131 | 24-Feb-23 | Ireland | 5N | A | Lansdowne Road, Dublin | W | 13-3 |
| 132 | 17-Mar-23 | England | 5N-CC | H | Inverleith, Edinburgh | L | 6-8 |
| 133 | 1-Jan-24 | France | 5N | A | Stade Pershing, Vincennes, Paris | L | 10-12 |
| 134 | 2-Feb-24 | Wales | 5N | H | Inverleith, Edinburgh | W | 35 10 |
| 135 | 23-Feb-24 | Ireland | 5N | H | Inverleith, Edinburgh | W | 13-8 |
| 136 | 15-Mar-24 | England | 5N-CC | A | Twickenham, London | L | 0-19 |
| 137 | 24-Jan-25 | France | 5N | H | Inverleith, Edinburgh | W | 25-4 |
| 138 | 7-Feb-25 | Wales | 5N | A | St Helen's, Swansea | W | 24-14 |
| 139 | 28-Feb-25 | Ireland | 5N | A | Lansdowne Road, Dublin | W | 14-8 |
| 140 | 21-Mar-25 | England | 5N-CC | H | Murrayfield, Edinburgh | W | 14-11 |
| 141 | 2-Jan-26 | France | 5N | A | Stade Colombes, Paris | W | 20-6 |
| 142 | 6-Feb-26 | Wales | 5N | H | Murrayfield, Edinburgh | W | 8-5 |
| 143 | 27-Feb-26 | Ireland | 5N | H | Murrayfield, Edinburgh | L | 0-3 |
| 144 | 20-Mar-26 | England | 5N-CC | A | Twickenham, London | W | 17-9 |
| 145 | 22-Jan-27 | France | 5N | H | Murrayfield, Edinburgh | W | 23-6 |
| 146 | 5-Feb-27 | Wales | 5N | A | Arms Park, Cardiff | W | 5-0 |
| 147 | 26-Feb-27 | Ireland | 5N | A | Lansdowne Road, Dublin | L | 0-6 |
| 148 | 19-Mar-27 | England | 5N-CC | H | Murrayfield, Edinburgh | W | 21-13 |
| 149 | 17-Dec-27 | Australia | Int | H | Murrayfield, Edinburgh | W | 10-8 |
| 150 | 2-Jan-28 | France | 5N | A | Stade Colombes, Paris | W | 15-6 |
| 151 | 4-Feb-28 | Wales | 5N | H | Murrayfield, Edinburgh | L | 0-13 |
| 152 | 25-Feb-28 | Ireland | 5N | H | Murrayfield, Edinburgh | L | 5-13 |
| 153 | 17-Mar-28 | England | 5N-CC | A | Twickenham, London | L | 0-6 |
| 154 | 19-Jan-29 | France | 5N | H | Murrayfield, Edinburgh | W | 6-3 |
| 155 | 2-Feb-29 | Wales | 5N | A | St Helen's, Swansea | L | 7-14 |
| 156 | 23-Feb-29 | Ireland | 5N | A | Lansdowne Road, Dublin | W | 16-7 |
| 157 | 16-Mar-29 | England | 5N-CC | H | Murrayfield, Edinburgh | W | 12-6 |
| 158 | 1-Jan-30 | France | 5N | A | Stade Colombes, Paris | L | 3-7 |
| 159 | 1-Feb-30 | Wales | 5N | H | Murrayfield, Edinburgh | W | 12-9 |
| 160 | 22-Feb-30 | Ireland | 5N | H | Murrayfield, Edinburgh | L | 11-14 |

| No | Date | Opponents | Tmt | | Match Venue | Result | |
|-----|-----------|--------------|--------|---|------------------------|---|-------|
| 161 | 15-Mar-30 | England | 5N-CC | A | Twickenham, London | D | 0-0 |
| 162 | 24-Jan-31 | France | 5N | H | Murrayfield, Edinburgh | W | 6-4 |
| 163 | 7-Feb-31 | Wales | 5N | A | Arms Park, Cardiff | L | 8-13 |
| 164 | 28-Feb-31 | Ireland | 5N | A | Lansdowne Road, Dublin | L | 5-8 |
| 165 | 21-Mar-31 | England | 5N-CC | H | Murrayfield, Edinburgh | W | 28-19 |
| 166 | 16-Jan-32 | South Africa | Int | H | Murrayfield, Edinburgh | L | 3-6 |
| 167 | 6-Feb-32 | Wales | 4N | H | Murrayfield, Edinburgh | L | 0-6 |
| 168 | 27-Feb-32 | Ireland | 4N | H | Murrayfield, Edinburgh | L | 8-20 |
| 169 | 19-Mar-32 | England | 4N-CC | A | Twickenham, London | L | 3-16 |
| 170 | 4-Feb-33 | Wales | 4N | A | St Helen's, Swansea | W | 11-3 |
| 171 | 18-Mar-33 | England | 4N-CC | H | Murrayfield, Edinburgh | W | 3-0 |
| 172 | 1-Apr-33 | Ireland | 4N | A | Lansdowne Road, Dublin | W | 8-6 |
| 173 | 3-Feb-34 | Wales | 4N | H | Murrayfield, Edinburgh | L | 6-13 |
| 174 | 24-Feb-34 | Ireland | 4N | H | Murrayfield, Edinburgh | W | 16-9 |
| 175 | 17-Mar-34 | England | 4N-CC | A | Twickenham, London | L | 3-6 |
| 176 | 2-Feb-35 | Wales | 4N | A | Arms Park, Cardiff | L | 6-10 |
| 177 | 23-Feb-35 | Ireland | 4N | A | Lansdowne Road, Dublin | L | 5-12 |
| 178 | 16-Mar-35 | England | 4N-CC | H | Murrayfield, Edinburgh | W | 10-7 |
| 179 | 23-Nov-35 | New Zealand | Int | H | Murrayfield, Edinburgh | L | 8-18 |
| 180 | 1-Feb-36 | Wales | 4N | H | Murrayfield, Edinburgh | L | 3-13 |
| 181 | 22-Feb-36 | Ireland | 4N | H | Murrayfield, Edinburgh | L | 4-10 |
| 182 | 21-Mar-36 | England | 4N-CC | A | Twickenham, London | L | 8-9 |
| 183 | 6-Feb-37 | Wales | 4N | A | St Helen's, Swansea | W | 13-6 |
| 184 | 27-Feb-37 | Ireland | 4N | A | Lansdowne Road, Dublin | L | 4-11 |
| 185 | 20-Mar-37 | England | 4N-CC | H | Murrayfield, Edinburgh | L | 3-6 |
| 186 | 5-Feb-38 | Wales | 4N | H | Murrayfield, Edinburgh | W | 8-6 |
| 187 | 26-Feb-38 | Ireland | 4N | H | Murrayfield, Edinburgh | W | 23-14 |
| 188 | 19-Mar-38 | England | 4N-CC | A | Twickenham, London | W | 21-16 |
| 189 | 4-Feb-39 | Wales | 4N | A | Arms Park, Cardiff | L | 3-11 |
| 190 | 25-Feb-39 | Ireland | 4N | A | Lansdowne Road, Dublin | L | 3-12 |
| 191 | 18-Mar-39 | England | 4N-CC | H | Murrayfield, Edinburgh | L | 6-9 |
| 192 | 1-Jan-47 | France | 5N | A | Stade Colombes, Paris | L | 3-8 |
| 193 | 1-Feb-47 | Wales | 5N | H | Murrayfield, Edinburgh | L | 8-22 |
| 194 | 22-Feb-47 | Ireland | 5N | H | Murrayfield, Edinburgh | L | 0-3 |
| 195 | 15-Mar-47 | England | 5N-CC | A | Twickenham, London | L | 5-24 |
| 196 | 22-Nov-47 | Australia | Int | H | Murrayfield, Edinburgh | L | 7-16 |
| 197 | 24-Jan-48 | France | 5N | H | Murrayfield, Edinburgh | W | 9-8 |
| 198 | 7-Feb-48 | Wales | 5N | A | Arms Park, Cardiff | L | 0-14 |
| 199 | 28-Feb-48 | Ireland | 5N | A | Lansdowne Road, Dublin | L | 0-6 |
| 200 | 20-Mar-48 | England | 5N-CC | H | Murrayfield, Edinburgh | W | 6-3 |

| No | Date | Opponents | Tmt | | Match Venue | Result | |
|----|------|-----------|-----|---|-------------|--------|---|
| 201 | 15-Jan-49 | France | 5N | A | Stade Colombes, Paris | W | 8-0 |
| 202 | 5-Feb-49 | Wales | 5N | H | Murrayfield, Edinburgh | W | 6-5 |
| 203 | 26-Feb-49 | Ireland | 5N | H | Murrayfield, Edinburgh | L | 3-13 |
| 204 | 19-Mar-49 | England | 5N-CC | A | Twickenham, London | L | 3-19 |
| 205 | 14-Jan-50 | France | 5N | H | Murrayfield, Edinburgh | W | 8-5 |
| 206 | 4-Feb-50 | Wales | 5N | A | St Helen's, Swansea | L | 0-12 |
| 207 | 25-Feb-50 | Ireland | 5N | A | Lansdowne Road, Dublin | L | 0-21 |
| 208 | 18-Mar-50 | England | 5N-CC | H | Murrayfield, Edinburgh | W | 13-11 |
| 209 | 13-Jan-51 | France | 5N | A | Stade Colombes, Paris | L | 12-14 |
| 210 | 3-Feb-51 | Wales | 5N | H | Murrayfield, Edinburgh | W | 19-0 |
| 211 | 24-Feb-51 | Ireland | 5N | H | Murrayfield, Edinburgh | L | 5-6 |
| 212 | 17-Mar-51 | England | 5N-CC | A | Twickenham, London | L | 3-5 |
| 213 | 24-Nov-51 | South Africa | Int | H | Murrayfield, Edinburgh | L | 0-44 |
| 214 | 12-Jan-52 | France | 5N | H | Murrayfield, Edinburgh | L | 11-13 |
| 215 | 2-Feb-52 | Wales | 5N | A | Arms Park, Cardiff | L | 0-11 |
| 216 | 23-Feb-52 | Ireland | 5N | A | Lansdowne Road, Dublin | L | 8-12 |
| 217 | 15-Mar-52 | England | 5N-CC | H | Murrayfield, Edinburgh | L | 3-19 |
| 218 | 10-Jan-53 | France | 5N | A | Stade Colombes, Paris | L | 5-11 |
| 219 | 7-Feb-53 | Wales | 5N | H | Murrayfield, Edinburgh | L | 0-12 |
| 220 | 28-Feb-53 | Ireland | 5N | H | Murrayfield, Edinburgh | L | 8-26 |
| 221 | 21-Mar-53 | England | 5N-CC | A | Twickenham, London | L | 8-26 |
| 222 | 9-Jan-54 | France | 5N | H | Murrayfield, Edinburgh | L | 0-3 |
| 223 | 13-Feb-54 | New Zealand | Int | H | Murrayfield, Edinburgh | L | 0-3 |
| 224 | 27-Feb-54 | Ireland | 5N | A | Ravenhill, Belfast | L | 0-6 |
| 225 | 20-Mar-54 | England | 5N-CC | H | Murrayfield, Edinburgh | L | 3-13 |
| 226 | 10-Apr-54 | Wales | 5N | A | St Helen's, Swansea | L | 3-15 |
| 227 | 8-Jan-55 | France | 5N | A | Stade Colombes, Paris | L | 0-15 |
| 228 | 5-Feb-55 | Wales | 5N | H | Murrayfield, Edinburgh | W | 14-8 |
| 229 | 26-Feb-55 | Ireland | 5N | H | Murrayfield, Edinburgh | W | 12-3 |
| 230 | 19-Mar-55 | England | 5N-CC | A | Twickenham, London | L | 6-9 |
| 231 | 14-Jan-56 | France | 5N | H | Murrayfield, Edinburgh | W | 12-0 |
| 232 | 4-Feb-56 | Wales | 5N | A | Arms Park, Cardiff | L | 3-9 |
| 233 | 25-Feb-56 | Ireland | 5N | A | Lansdowne Road, Dublin | L | 10-14 |
| 234 | 17-Mar-56 | England | 5N-CC | H | Murrayfield, Edinburgh | L | 6-11 |
| 235 | 12-Jan-57 | France | 5N | A | Stade Colombes, Paris | W | 6-0 |
| 236 | 2-Feb-57 | Wales | 5N | H | Murrayfield, Edinburgh | W | 9-6 |
| 237 | 23-Feb-57 | Ireland | 5N | H | Murrayfield, Edinburgh | L | 3-5 |
| 238 | 16-Mar-57 | England | 5N-CC | A | Twickenham, London | L | 3-16 |
| 239 | 11-Jan-58 | France | 5N | H | Murrayfield, Edinburgh | W | 11-9 |
| 240 | 1-Feb-58 | Wales | 5N | A | Arms Park, Cardiff | L | 3-8 |

| No | Date | Opponents | Tmt | | Match Venue | | Result |
|----|------|-----------|-----|---|-------------|---|--------|
| 241 | 15-Feb-58 | Australia | Int | H | Murrayfield, Edinburgh | W | 12-8 |
| 242 | 1-Mar-58 | Ireland | 5N | A | Lansdowne Road, Dublin | L | 6-12 |
| 243 | 15-Mar-58 | England | 5N-CC | H | Murrayfield, Edinburgh | D | 3-3 |
| 244 | 10-Jan-59 | France | 5N | A | Stade Colombes, Paris | L | 0-9 |
| 245 | 7-Feb-59 | Wales | 5N | H | Murrayfield, Edinburgh | W | 6-5 |
| 246 | 28-Feb-59 | Ireland | 5N | H | Murrayfield, Edinburgh | L | 3-8 |
| 247 | 21-Mar-59 | England | 5N-CC | A | Twickenham, London | D | 3-3 |
| 248 | 9-Jan-60 | France | 5N | H | Murrayfield, Edinburgh | L | 11-13 |
| 249 | 6-Feb-60 | Wales | 5N | A | Arms Park, Cardiff | L | 0-8 |
| 250 | 27-Feb-60 | Ireland | 5N | A | Lansdowne Road, Dublin | W | 6-5 |
| 251 | 19-Mar-60 | England | 5N-CC | H | Murrayfield, Edinburgh | L | 12-21 |
| 252 | 30-Apr-60 | South Africa | Int-T | A | Boet Erasmus Stadium, Port Elizabeth | L | 10-18 |
| 253 | 7-Jan-61 | France | 5N | A | Stade Colombes, Paris | L | 0-11 |
| 254 | 21-Jan-61 | South Africa | Int | H | Murrayfield, Edinburgh | L | 5-12 |
| 255 | 11-Feb-61 | Wales | 5N | H | Murrayfield, Edinburgh | W | 3-0 |
| 256 | 25-Feb-61 | Ireland | 5N | H | Murrayfield, Edinburgh | W | 16-8 |
| 257 | 18-Mar-61 | England | 5N-CC | A | Twickenham, London | L | 0-6 |
| 258 | 13-Jan-62 | France | 5N | H | Murrayfield, Edinburgh | L | 3-11 |
| 259 | 3-Feb-62 | Wales | 5N | A | Arms Park, Cardiff | W | 8-3 |
| 260 | 24-Feb-62 | Ireland | 5N | A | Lansdowne Road, Dublin | W | 20-6 |
| 261 | 17-Mar-62 | England | 5N-CC | H | Murrayfield, Edinburgh | D | 3-3 |
| 262 | 12-Jan-63 | France | 5N | A | Stade Colombes, Paris | W | 11-6 |
| 263 | 2-Feb-63 | Wales | 5N | H | Murrayfield, Edinburgh | L | 0-6 |
| 264 | 23-Feb-63 | Ireland | 5N | H | Murrayfield, Edinburgh | W | 3-0 |
| 265 | 16-Mar-63 | England | 5N-CC | A | Twickenham, London | L | 8-10 |
| 266 | 4-Jan-64 | France | 5N | H | Murrayfield, Edinburgh | W | 10-0 |
| 267 | 18-Jan-64 | New Zealand | Int | H | Murrayfield, Edinburgh | D | 0-0 |
| 268 | 1-Feb-64 | Wales | 5N | A | Arms Park, Cardiff | L | 3-11 |
| 269 | 22-Feb-64 | Ireland | 5N | A | Lansdowne Road, Dublin | W | 6-3 |
| 270 | 21-Mar-64 | England | 5N-CC | H | Murrayfield, Edinburgh | W | 15-6 |
| 271 | 9-Jan-65 | France | 5N | A | Stade Colombes, Paris | L | 8-16 |
| 272 | 6-Feb-65 | Wales | 5N | H | Murrayfield, Edinburgh | L | 12-14 |
| 273 | 27-Feb-65 | Ireland | 5N | H | Murrayfield, Edinburgh | L | 6-16 |
| 274 | 20-Mar-65 | England | 5N-CC | A | Twickenham, London | D | 3-3 |
| 275 | 17-Apr-65 | South Africa | Int | H | Murrayfield, Edinburgh | W | 8-5 |
| 276 | 15-Jan-66 | France | 5N | H | Murrayfield, Edinburgh | D | 3-3 |
| 277 | 5-Feb-66 | Wales | 5N | A | Arms Park, Cardiff | L | 3-8 |
| 278 | 26-Feb-66 | Ireland | 5N | A | Lansdowne Road, Dublin | W | 11-3 |
| 279 | 19-Mar-66 | England | 5N-CC | H | Murrayfield, Edinburgh | W | 6-3 |
| 280 | 17-Dec-66 | Australia | Int | H | Murrayfield, Edinburgh | W | 11-5 |

| No | Date | Opponents | Tmt | | Match Venue | Result | |
|----|------|-----------|-----|---|-------------|--------|---|
| 281 | 14-Jan-67 | France | 5N | A | Stade Colombes, Paris | W | 9-8 |
| 282 | 4-Feb-67 | Wales | 5N | H | Murrayfield, Edinburgh | W | 11-5 |
| 283 | 25-Feb-67 | Ireland | 5N | H | Murrayfield, Edinburgh | L | 3-5 |
| 284 | 18-Mar-67 | England | 5N-CC | A | Twickenham, London | L | 14-27 |
| 285 | 2-Dec-67 | New Zealand | Int | H | Murrayfield, Edinburgh | L | 3-14 |
| 286 | 13-Jan-68 | France | 5N | H | Murrayfield, Edinburgh | L | 6-8 |
| 287 | 3-Feb-68 | Wales | 5N | A | Arms Park, Cardiff | L | 0-5 |
| 288 | 24-Feb-68 | Ireland | 5N | A | Lansdowne Road, Dublin | L | 6-14 |
| 289 | 16-Mar-68 | England | 5N-CC | H | Murrayfield, Edinburgh | L | 6-8 |
| 290 | 2-Nov-68 | Australia | Int | H | Murrayfield, Edinburgh | W | 9-3 |
| 291 | 11-Jan-69 | France | 5N | A | Stade Colombes, Paris | W | 6-3 |
| 292 | 1-Feb-69 | Wales | 5N | H | Murrayfield, Edinburgh | L | 3-17 |
| 293 | 22-Feb-69 | Ireland | 5N | H | Murrayfield, Edinburgh | L | 0-16 |
| 294 | 15-Mar-69 | England | 5N-CC | A | Twickenham, London | L | 3-8 |
| 295 | 6-Dec-69 | South Africa | Int | H | Murrayfield, Edinburgh | W | 6-3 |
| 296 | 10-Jan-70 | France | 5N | H | Murrayfield, Edinburgh | L | 9-11 |
| 297 | 7-Feb-70 | Wales | 5N | A | National Stadium, Cardiff | L | 9-18 |
| 298 | 28-Feb-70 | Ireland | 5N | A | Lansdowne Road, Dublin | L | 11-16 |
| 299 | 21-Mar-70 | England | 5N-CC | H | Murrayfield, Edinburgh | W | 14-5 |
| 300 | 6-Jun-70 | Australia | Int-T | A | Cricket Ground, Sydney | L | 3-23 |
| 301 | 16-Jan-71 | France | 5N | A | Stade Colombes, Paris | L | 8-13 |
| 302 | 6-Feb-71 | Wales | 5N | H | Murrayfield, Edinburgh | L | 18-19 |
| 303 | 27-Feb-71 | Ireland | 5N | H | Murrayfield, Edinburgh | L | 5-17 |
| 304 | 20-Mar-71 | England | 5N-CC | A | Twickenham, London | W | 16-15 |
| 305 | 27-Mar-71 | England | Int-C | H | Murrayfield, Edinburgh | W | 26-6 |
| 306 | 15-Jan-72 | France | 5N | H | Murrayfield, Edinburgh | W | 20-9 |
| 307 | 5-Feb-72 | Wales | 5N | A | National Stadium, Cardiff | L | 12-35 |
| 308 | 18-Mar-72 | England | 5N-CC | H | Murrayfield, Edinburgh | W | 23-9 |
| 309 | 16-Dec-72 | New Zealand | Int | H | Murrayfield, Edinburgh | L | 9-14 |
| 310 | 13-Jan-73 | France | 5N | A | Parc des Princess, Paris | L | 13-16 |
| 311 | 3-Feb-73 | Wales | 5N | H | Murrayfield, Edinburgh | W | 10-9 |
| 312 | 24-Feb-73 | Ireland | 5N | H | Murrayfield, Edinburgh | W | 19-14 |
| 313 | 17-Mar-73 | England | 5N-CC | A | Twickenham, London | L | 13-20 |
| 314 | 31-Mar-73 | President's XV | Int-C | H | Murrayfield, Edinburgh | W | 27-16 |
| 315 | 19-Jan-74 | Wales | 5N | A | National Stadium, Cardiff | L | 0-6 |
| 316 | 2-Feb-74 | England | 5N-CC | H | Murrayfield, Edinburgh | W | 16-14 |
| 317 | 2-Mar-74 | Ireland | 5N | A | Lansdowne Road, Dublin | L | 6-9 |
| 318 | 16-Mar-74 | France | 5N | H | Murrayfield, Edinburgh | W | 19-6 |
| 319 | 1-Feb-75 | Ireland | 5N | H | Murrayfield, Edinburgh | W | 20-13 |
| 320 | 15-Feb-75 | France | 5N | A | Parc des Princess, Paris | L | 9-10 |

| No | Date | Opponents | Tmt | | Match Venue | Result | |
|---|---|---|---|---|---|---|---|
| 321 | 1-Mar-75 | Wales | 5N | H | Murrayfield, Edinburgh | W | 12-10 |
| 322 | 15-Mar-75 | England | 5N-CC | A | Twickenham, London | L | 6-7 |
| 323 | 14-Jun-75 | New Zealand | Int-T | A | Eden Park, Auckland | L | 0-24 |
| 324 | 6-Dec-75 | Australia | Int | H | Murrayfield, Edinburgh | W | 10-3 |
| 325 | 10-Jan-76 | France | 5N | H | Murrayfield, Edinburgh | L | 6-13 |
| 326 | 7-Feb-76 | Wales | 5N | A | National Stadium, Cardiff | L | 6-28 |
| 327 | 21-Feb-76 | England | 5N-CC | H | Murrayfield, Edinburgh | W | 22-12 |
| 328 | 20-Mar-76 | Ireland | 5N | A | Lansdowne Road, Dublin | W | 15-6 |
| 329 | 15-Jan-77 | England | 5N-CC | A | Twickenham, London | L | 6-26 |
| 330 | 19-Feb-77 | Ireland | 5N | H | Murrayfield, Edinburgh | W | 21-18 |
| 331 | 5-Mar-77 | France | 5N | A | Parc des Princess, Paris | L | 3-23 |
| 332 | 19-Mar-77 | Wales | 5N | H | Murrayfield, Edinburgh | L | 9-18 |
| 333 | 21-Jan-78 | Ireland | 5N | A | Lansdowne Road, Dublin | L | 9-12 |
| 334 | 4-Feb-78 | France | 5N | H | Murrayfield, Edinburgh | L | 16-19 |
| 335 | 18-Feb-78 | Wales | 5N | A | National Stadium, Cardiff | L | 14-22 |
| 336 | 4-Mar-78 | England | 5N-CC | H | Murrayfield, Edinburgh | L | 0-15 |
| 337 | 9-Dec-78 | New Zealand | Int | H | Murrayfield, Edinburgh | L | 9-18 |
| 338 | 20-Jan-79 | Wales | 5N | H | Murrayfield, Edinburgh | L | 13-19 |
| 339 | 3-Feb-79 | England | 5N-CC | A | Twickenham, London | D | 7-7 |
| 340 | 3-Mar-79 | Ireland | 5N | H | Murrayfield, Edinburgh | D | 11-11 |
| 341 | 17-Mar-79 | France | 5N | A | Parc des Princess, Paris | L | 17-21 |
| 342 | 10-Nov-79 | New Zealand | Int | H | Murrayfield, Edinburgh | L | 6-20 |
| 343 | 2-Feb-80 | Ireland | 5N | A | Lansdowne Road, Dublin | L | 15-22 |
| 344 | 16-Feb-80 | France | 5N | H | Murrayfield, Edinburgh | W | 22-14 |
| 345 | 1-Mar-80 | Wales | 5N | A | National Stadium, Cardiff | L | 6-17 |
| 346 | 15-Mar-80 | England | 5N-CC | H | Murrayfield, Edinburgh | L | 18-30 |
| 347 | 17-Jan-81 | France | 5N | A | Parc des Princess, Paris | L | 9-16 |
| 348 | 7-Feb-81 | Wales | 5N | H | Murrayfield, Edinburgh | W | 15-6 |
| 349 | 21-Feb-81 | England | 5N-CC | A | Twickenham, London | L | 17-23 |
| 350 | 21-Mar-81 | Ireland | 5N | H | Murrayfield, Edinburgh | W | 10-9 |
| 351 | 13-Jun-81 | New Zealand | Int-T | A | Carisbrook, Dunedin | L | 4-11 |
| 352 | 20-Jun-81 | New Zealand | Int-T | A | Eden Park, Auckland | L | 15-40 |
| 353 | 26-Sep-81 | Romania | Int | H | Murrayfield, Edinburgh | W | 12-6 |
| 354 | 19-Dec-81 | Australia | Int | H | Murrayfield, Edinburgh | W | 24-15 |
| 355 | 16-Jan-82 | England | 5N-CC | H | Murrayfield, Edinburgh | D | 9-9 |
| 356 | 20-Feb-82 | Ireland | 5N | A | Lansdowne Road, Dublin | L | 12-21 |
| 357 | 6-Mar-82 | France | 5N | H | Murrayfield, Edinburgh | W | 16-7 |
| 358 | 20-Mar-82 | Wales | 5N | A | National Stadium, Cardiff | W | 34-18 |
| 359 | 4-Jul-82 | Australia | Int-T | A | Ballymore Oval, Brisbane | W | 12-7 |
| 360 | 10-Jul-82 | Australia | Int-T | A | Cricket Ground, Sydney | L | 9-33 |

| No | Date | Opponents | Tmt | | Match Venue | Result | |
|----|------|-----------|-----|---|-------------|--------|---|
| 361 | 15-Jan-83 | Ireland | 5N | H | Murrayfield, Edinburgh | L | 13-15 |
| 362 | 5-Feb-83 | France | 5N | A | Parc des Princess, Paris | L | 15-19 |
| 363 | 19-Feb-83 | Wales | 5N | H | Murrayfield, Edinburgh | L | 15-19 |
| 364 | 5-Mar-83 | England | 5N-CC | A | Twickenham, London | W | 22-12 |
| 365 | 12-Nov-83 | New Zealand | Int | H | Murrayfield, Edinburgh | D | 25-25 |
| 366 | 21-Jan-84 | Wales | 5N | A | National Stadium, Cardiff | W | 15-9 |
| 367 | 4-Feb-84 | England | 5N-CC | H | Murrayfield, Edinburgh | W | 18-6 |
| 368 | 3-Mar-84 | Ireland | 5N | A | Lansdowne Road, Dublin | W | 32-9 |
| 369 | 17-Mar-84 | France | 5N | H | Murrayfield, Edinburgh | W | 21-12 |
| 370 | 12-May-84 | Romania | Int | A | Stadionul 23 August, Bucharest | L | 22-28 |
| 371 | 8-Dec-84 | Australia | Int | H | Murrayfield, Edinburgh | L | 12-37 |
| 372 | 2-Feb-85 | Ireland | 5N | H | Murrayfield, Edinburgh | L | 15-18 |
| 373 | 16-Feb-85 | France | 5N | A | Parc des Princess, Paris | L | 3-11 |
| 374 | 2-Mar-85 | Wales | 5N | H | Murrayfield, Edinburgh | L | 21-25 |
| 375 | 16-Mar-85 | England | 5N-CC | A | Twickenham, London | L | 7-10 |
| 376 | 18-Jan-86 | France | 5N | H | Murrayfield, Edinburgh | W | 18-17 |
| 377 | 1-Feb-86 | Wales | 5N | A | National Stadium, Cardiff | L | 15-22 |
| 378 | 15-Feb-86 | England | 5N-CC | H | Murrayfield, Edinburgh | W | 33-6 |
| 379 | 15-Mar-86 | Ireland | 5N | A | Lansdowne Road, Dublin | W | 10-9 |
| 380 | 29-Mar-86 | Romania | Int | A | Stadionul 23 August, Bucharest | W | 33-18 |
| 381 | 21-Feb-87 | Ireland | 5N | H | Murrayfield, Edinburgh | W | 16-12 |
| 382 | 7-Mar-87 | France | 5N | A | Parc des Princess, Paris | L | 22-28 |
| 383 | 21-Mar-87 | Wales | 5N | H | Murrayfield, Edinburgh | W | 21-15 |
| 384 | 4-Apr-87 | England | 5N-CC | A | Twickenham, London | L | 12-21 |
| 385 | 23-May-87 | France | WCp | N | Lancaster Park Oval, Christchurch | D | 20-20 |
| 386 | 30-May-87 | Zimbabwe | WCp | N | Athletic Park, Wellington | W | 60-21 |
| 387 | 2-Jun-87 | Romania | WCp | N | Carisbrook, Dunedin | W | 55-28 |
| 388 | 6-Jun-87 | New Zealand | WCqf | A | Lancaster Park Oval, Christchurch | L | 3-30 |
| 389 | 16-Jan-88 | Ireland | 5N | A | Lansdowne Road, Dublin | L | 18-22 |
| 390 | 6-Feb-88 | France | 5N | H | Murrayfield, Edinburgh | W | 23-12 |
| 391 | 20-Feb-88 | Wales | 5N | A | National Stadium, Cardiff | L | 20-25 |
| 392 | 5-Mar-88 | England | 5N-CC | H | Murrayfield, Edinburgh | L | 6-9 |
| 393 | 19-Nov-88 | Australia | Int | H | Murrayfield, Edinburgh | L | 13-32 |
| 394 | 21-Jan-89 | Wales | 5N | H | Murrayfield, Edinburgh | W | 23-7 |
| 395 | 4-Feb-89 | England | 5N-CC | A | Twickenham, London | D | 12-12 |
| 396 | 4-Mar-89 | Ireland | 5N-CQ | H | Murrayfield, Edinburgh | W | 37-21 |
| 397 | 18-Mar-89 | France | 5N | A | Parc des Princess, Paris | L | 3-19 |
| 398 | 28-Oct-89 | Fiji | Int | H | Murrayfield, Edinburgh | W | 38-17 |
| 399 | 9-Dec-89 | Romania | Int | H | Murrayfield, Edinburgh | W | 32-0 |
| 400 | 3-Feb-90 | Ireland | 5N-CQ | A | Lansdowne Road, Dublin | W | 13-10 |

| No | Date | Opponents | Tmt | | Match Venue | Result | |
|----|------|-----------|-----|---|-------------|--------|---|
| 401 | 17-Feb-90 | France | 5N | H | Murrayfield, Edinburgh | W | 21-0 |
| 402 | 3-Mar-90 | Wales | 5N | A | National Stadium, Cardiff | W | 13-9 |
| 403 | 17-Mar-90 | England | 5N-CC | H | Murrayfield, Edinburgh | W | 13-7 |
| 404 | 16-Jun-90 | New Zealand | Int-T | A | Carisbrook, Dunedin | L | 16-31 |
| 405 | 23-Jun-90 | New Zealand | Int-T | A | Eden Park, Auckland | L | 18-21 |
| 406 | 10-Nov-90 | Argentina | Int | H | Murrayfield, Edinburgh | W | 49-3 |
| 407 | 19-Jan-91 | France | 5N | A | Parc des Princess, Paris | L | 9-15 |
| 408 | 2-Feb-91 | Wales | 5N | H | Murrayfield, Edinburgh | W | 32-12 |
| 409 | 16-Feb-91 | England | 5N-CC | A | Twickenham, London | L | 12-21 |
| 410 | 16-Mar-91 | Ireland | 5N-CQ | H | Murrayfield, Edinburgh | W | 28-25 |
| 411 | 31-Aug-91 | Romania | Int | A | Stadionul 23 August, Bucharest | L | 12-18 |
| 412 | 5-Oct-91 | Japan | WCp | H | Murrayfield, Edinburgh | W | 47-9 |
| 413 | 9-Oct-91 | Zimbabwe | WCp | H | Murrayfield, Edinburgh | W | 51-12 |
| 414 | 12-Oct-91 | Ireland | WCp | H | Murrayfield, Edinburgh | W | 24-15 |
| 415 | 19-Oct-91 | Western Samoa | WCqf | H | Murrayfield, Edinburgh | W | 28-6 |
| 416 | 26-Oct-91 | England | WCsf | H | Murrayfield, Edinburgh | L | 6-9 |
| 417 | 30-Oct-91 | New Zealand | WC34 | N | National Stadium, Cardiff | L | 6-13 |
| 418 | 18-Jan-92 | England | 5N-CC | H | Murrayfield, Edinburgh | L | 7-25 |
| 419 | 15-Feb-92 | Ireland | 5N-CQ | A | Lansdowne Road, Dublin | W | 18-10 |
| 420 | 7-Mar-92 | France | 5N | H | Murrayfield, Edinburgh | W | 10-6 |
| 421 | 21-Mar-92 | Wales | 5N | A | National Stadium, Cardiff | L | 12-15 |
| 422 | 13-Jun-92 | Australia | Int-T | A | Football Stadium, Sydney | L | 12-27 |
| 423 | 21-Jun-92 | Australia | Int-T | A | Ballymore Oval, Brisbane | L | 13-37 |
| 424 | 16-Jan-93 | Ireland | 5N-CQ | H | Murrayfield, Edinburgh | W | 15-3 |
| 425 | 6-Feb-93 | France | 5N | A | Parc des Princess, Paris | L | 3-11 |
| 426 | 20-Feb-93 | Wales | 5N | H | Murrayfield, Edinburgh | W | 20-0 |
| 427 | 6-Mar-93 | England | 5N-CC | A | Twickenham, London | L | 12-26 |
| 428 | 20-Nov-93 | New Zealand | Int | H | Murrayfield, Edinburgh | L | 15-51 |
| 429 | 15-Jan-94 | Wales | 5N | A | National Stadium, Cardiff | L | 6-29 |
| 430 | 5-Feb-94 | England | 5N-CC | H | Murrayfield, Edinburgh | L | 14-15 |
| 431 | 5-Mar-94 | Ireland | 5N-CQ | A | Lansdowne Road, Dublin | D | 6-6 |
| 432 | 19-Mar-94 | France | 5N | H | Murrayfield, Edinburgh | L | 12-20 |
| 433 | 4-Jun-94 | Argentina | Int-T | A | Ferro Carril Oeste Stadium, B Aires | L | 15-16 |
| 434 | 11-Jun-94 | Argentina | Int-T | A | Ferro Carril Oeste Stadium, B Aires | L | 17-19 |
| 435 | 19-Nov-94 | South Africa | Int | H | Murrayfield, Edinburgh | L | 10-34 |
| 436 | 21-Jan-95 | Canada | Int | H | Murrayfield, Edinburgh | W | 22-6 |
| 437 | 4-Feb-95 | Ireland | 5N-CQ | H | Murrayfield, Edinburgh | W | 26-13 |
| 438 | 18-Feb-95 | France | 5N | A | Parc des Princess, Paris | W | 23-21 |
| 439 | 4-Mar-95 | Wales | 5N | H | Murrayfield, Edinburgh | W | 26-13 |
| 440 | 18-Mar-95 | England | 5N-CC | A | Twickenham, London | L | 12-24 |

| No | Date | Opponents | Tmt | | Match Venue | Result | |
|----|------|-----------|-----|---|-------------|--------|---|
| 441 | 22-Apr-95 | Romania | Int | H | Murrayfield, Edinburgh | W | 49-16 |
| 442 | 26-May-95 | Côte d'Ivoire | WCp | N | Olympia Park, Rustenburg | W | 89-0 |
| 443 | 30-May-95 | Tonga | WCp | N | Loftus Versfeld Stadium, Pretoria | W | 41-5 |
| 444 | 3-Jun-95 | France | WCp | N | Loftus Versfeld Stadium, Pretoria | L | 19-22 |
| 445 | 11-Jun-95 | New Zealand | WCqf | N | Loftus Versfeld Stadium, Pretoria | L | 30-48 |
| 446 | 18-Nov-95 | Western Samoa | Int | H | Murrayfield, Edinburgh | D | 15-15 |
| 447 | 20-Jan-96 | Ireland | 5N-CQ | A | Lansdowne Road, Dublin | W | 16-10 |
| 448 | 3-Feb-96 | France | 5N | H | Murrayfield, Edinburgh | W | 19-14 |
| 449 | 17-Feb-96 | Wales | 5N | A | National Stadium, Cardiff | W | 16-14 |
| 450 | 2-Mar-96 | England | 5N-CC | H | Murrayfield, Edinburgh | L | 9-18 |
| 451 | 15-Jun-96 | New Zealand | Int-T | A | Carisbrook, Dunedin | L | 31-62 |
| 452 | 22-Jun-96 | New Zealand | Int-T | A | Eden Park, Auckland | L | 12-36 |
| 453 | 9-Nov-96 | Australia | Int | H | Murrayfield, Edinburgh | L | 19-29 |
| 454 | 14-Dec-96 | Italy | Int | H | Murrayfield, Edinburgh | W | 29-22 |
| 455 | 18-Jan-97 | Wales | 5N | H | Murrayfield, Edinburgh | L | 19-34 |
| 456 | 1-Feb-97 | England | 5N-CC | A | Twickenham, London | L | 13-41 |
| 457 | 1-Mar-97 | Ireland | 5N-CQ | H | Murrayfield, Edinburgh | W | 38-10 |
| 458 | 15-Mar-97 | France | 5N | A | Parc des Princess, Paris | L | 20-47 |
| 459 | 22-Nov-97 | Australia | Int | H | Murrayfield, Edinburgh | L | 8-37 |
| 460 | 6-Dec-97 | South Africa | Int | H | Murrayfield, Edinburgh | L | 10-68 |
| 461 | 24-Jan-98 | Italy | Int | A | Stadio Comunale di Monigo, Treviso | L | 21-25 |
| 462 | 7-Feb-98 | Ireland | 5N-CQ | A | Lansdowne Road, Dublin | W | 17-16 |
| 463 | 21-Feb-98 | France | 5N | H | Murrayfield, Edinburgh | L | 16-51 |
| 464 | 7-Mar-98 | Wales | 5N | N | Wembley Stadium, London | L | 13-19 |
| 465 | 22-Mar-98 | England | 5N-CC | H | Murrayfield, Edinburgh | L | 20-34 |
| 466 | 26-May-98 | Fiji | Int-T | A | National Stadium, Suva | L | 26-51 |
| 467 | 13-Jun-98 | Australia | HT-T | A | Football Stadium, Sydney | L | 3-45 |
| 468 | 20-Jun-98 | Australia | HT-T | A | Ballymore Oval, Brisbane | L | 11-33 |
| 469 | 21-Nov-98 | South Africa | Int | H | Murrayfield, Edinburgh | L | 10-35 |
| 470 | 6-Feb-99 | Wales | 5N | H | Murrayfield, Edinburgh | W | 33-20 |
| 471 | 20-Feb-99 | England | 5N-CC | A | Twickenham, London | L | 21-24 |
| 472 | 6-Mar-99 | Italy | Int | H | Murrayfield, Edinburgh | W | 30-12 |
| 473 | 20-Mar-99 | Ireland | 5N-CQ | H | Murrayfield, Edinburgh | W | 30-13 |
| 474 | 10-Apr-99 | France | 5N | A | Stade de France, Paris | W | 36-22 |
| 475 | 21-Aug-99 | Argentina | Int | H | Murrayfield, Edinburgh | L | 22-31 |
| 476 | 28-Aug-99 | Romania | Int | H | Hampden Park, Glasgow | W | 60-19 |
| 477 | 3-Oct-99 | South Africa | WCp | H | Murrayfield, Edinburgh | L | 29-46 |
| 478 | 8-Oct-99 | Uruguay | WCp | H | Murrayfield, Edinburgh | W | 43-12 |
| 479 | 16-Oct-99 | Spain | WCp | H | Murrayfield, Edinburgh | W | 48-0 |
| 480 | 20-Oct-99 | Samoa | QFpo | H | Murrayfield, Edinburgh | W | 35-20 |

| No | Date | Opponents | Tmt | | Match Venue | Result | |
|---|---|---|---|---|---|---|---|
| 481 | 24-Oct-99 | New Zealand | WCqf | H | Murrayfield, Edinburgh | L | 18-30 |
| 482 | 5-Feb-00 | Italy | 6N | A | Stadio Flaminio, Rome | L | 20-34 |
| 483 | 19-Feb-00 | Ireland | 6N-CQ | A | Lansdowne Road, Dublin | L | 22-44 |
| 484 | 4-Mar-00 | France | 6N | H | Murrayfield, Edinburgh | L | 16-28 |
| 485 | 18-Mar-00 | Wales | 6N | A | Millennium Stadium, Cardiff | L | 18-26 |
| 486 | 2-Apr-00 | England | 6N-CC | H | Murrayfield, Edinburgh | W | 19-13 |
| 487 | 24-Jun-00 | New Zealand | Int-T | A | Carisbrook, Dunedin | L | 20-69 |
| 488 | 1-Jul-00 | New Zealand | Int-T | A | Eden Park, Auckland | L | 14-48 |
| 489 | 4-Nov-00 | United States | Int | H | Murrayfield, Edinburgh | W | 53-6 |
| 490 | 11-Nov-00 | Australia | HT | H | Murrayfield, Edinburgh | L | 9-30 |
| 491 | 18-Nov-00 | Samoa | Int | H | Murrayfield, Edinburgh | W | 31-8 |
| 492 | 4-Feb-01 | France | 6N | A | Stade de France, Paris | L | 6-16 |
| 493 | 17-Feb-01 | Wales | 6N | H | Murrayfield, Edinburgh | D | 28-28 |
| 494 | 3-Mar-01 | England | 6N-CC | A | Twickenham, London | L | 3-43 |
| 495 | 17-Mar-01 | Italy | 6N | H | Murrayfield, Edinburgh | W | 23-19 |
| 496 | 22-Sep-01 | Ireland | 6N-CQ | H | Murrayfield, Edinburgh | W | 32-10 |
| 497 | 10-Nov-01 | Tonga | Int | H | Murrayfield, Edinburgh | W | 43-20 |
| 498 | 18-Nov-01 | Argentina | Int | H | Murrayfield, Edinburgh | L | 16-25 |
| 499 | 24-Nov-01 | New Zealand | Int | H | Murrayfield, Edinburgh | L | 6-37 |
| 500 | 2-Feb-02 | England | 6N-CC | H | Murrayfield, Edinburgh | L | 3-29 |
| 501 | 16-Feb-02 | Italy | 6N | A | Stadio Flaminio, Rome | W | 29-12 |
| 502 | 2-Mar-02 | Ireland | 6N-CQ | A | Lansdowne Road, Dublin | L | 22-43 |
| 503 | 23-Mar-02 | France | 6N | H | Murrayfield, Edinburgh | L | 10-22 |
| 504 | 6-Apr-02 | Wales | 6N | A | Millennium Stadium, Cardiff | W | 27-22 |
| 505 | 15-Jun-02 | Canada | Int-T | A | Thunderbird Stadium, Vancouver | L | 23-26 |
| 506 | 22-Jun-02 | United States | Int-T | A | Boxer Stadium, San Francisco | W | 65-23 |
| 507 | 9-Nov-02 | Romania | Int | H | Murrayfield, Edinburgh | W | 37-10 |
| 508 | 16-Nov-02 | South Africa | Int | H | Murrayfield, Edinburgh | W | 21-6 |
| 509 | 24-Nov-02 | Fiji | Int | H | Murrayfield, Edinburgh | W | 36-22 |
| 510 | 16-Feb-03 | Ireland | 6N-CQ | H | Murrayfield, Edinburgh | L | 6-36 |
| 511 | 23-Feb-03 | France | 6N | A | Stade de France, Paris | L | 3-38 |
| 512 | 8-Mar-03 | Wales | 6N | H | Murrayfield, Edinburgh | W | 30-22 |
| 513 | 22-Mar-03 | England | 6N-CC | A | Twickenham, London | L | 9-40 |
| 514 | 29-Mar-03 | Italy | 6N | H | Murrayfield, Edinburgh | W | 33-25 |
| 515 | 7-Jun-03 | South Africa | Int-T | A | ABSA Stadium, Durban | L | 25-29 |
| 516 | 14-Jun-03 | South Africa | Int-T | A | Ellis Park, Johannesburg | L | 19-28 |
| 517 | 23-Aug-03 | Italy | Int | H | Murrayfield, Edinburgh | W | 47-15 |
| 518 | 30-Aug-03 | Wales | Int | A | Millennium Stadium, Cardiff | L | 9-23 |
| 519 | 6-Sep-03 | Ireland | Int | H | Murrayfield, Edinburgh | L | 10-29 |
| 520 | 12-Oct-03 | Japan | WCp | N | Dairy Farmers Stadium, Townsville | W | 32-11 |

| No | Date | Opponents | Tmt | Match Venue | | Result |
|----|------|-----------|-----|-------------|---|--------|
| 521 | 20-Oct-03 | United States | WCp | N | Suncorp Stadium, Brisbane | W | 39-15 |
| 522 | 25-Oct-03 | France | WCp | N | Telstra Stadium, Sydney | L | 9-51 |
| 523 | 1-Nov-03 | Fiji | WCp | N | Aussie Stadium, Sydney | W | 22-20 |
| 524 | 8-Nov-03 | Australia | WCqf | A | Suncorp Stadium, Brisbane | L | 16-33 |
| 525 | 14-Feb-04 | Wales | 6N | A | Millennium Stadium, Cardiff | L | 10-23 |
| 526 | 21-Feb-04 | England | 6N-CC | H | Murrayfield, Edinburgh | L | 13-35 |
| 527 | 6-Mar-04 | Italy | 6N | A | Stadio Flaminio, Rome | L | 14-20 |
| 528 | 21-Mar-04 | France | 6N | H | Murrayfield, Edinburgh | L | 0-31 |
| 529 | 27-Mar-04 | Ireland | 6N-CQ | A | Lansdowne Road, Dublin | L | 16-37 |
| 530 | 4-Jun-04 | Samoa | Int-T | N | Westpac Trust Stadium, Wellington | W | 38-3 |
| 531 | 13-Jun-04 | Australia | HT-T | A | Telstra Dome, Melbourne | L | 15-35 |
| 532 | 19-Jun-04 | Australia | HT-T | A | Telstra Stadium, Sydney | L | 13-34 |
| 533 | 6-Nov-04 | Australia | HT | H | Murrayfield, Edinburgh | L | 14-31 |
| 534 | 13-Nov-04 | Japan | Int | H | McDiarmid Park, Perth | W | 100-8 |
| 535 | 20-Nov-04 | Australia | HT | H | Hampden Park, Glasgow | L | 17-31 |
| 536 | 27-Nov-04 | South Africa | Int | H | Murrayfield, Edinburgh | L | 10-45 |
| 537 | 5-Feb-05 | France | 6N | A | Stade de France, Paris | L | 9-16 |
| 538 | 12-Feb-05 | Ireland | 6N-CQ | H | Murrayfield, Edinburgh | L | 13-40 |
| 539 | 26-Feb-05 | Italy | 6N | H | Murrayfield, Edinburgh | W | 18-10 |
| 540 | 13-Mar-05 | Wales | 6N | H | Murrayfield, Edinburgh | L | 22-46 |
| 541 | 19-Mar-05 | England | 6N-CC | A | Twickenham, London | L | 22-43 |
| 542 | 5-Jun-05 | Romania | Int | A | Stadionul Dinamo, Bucharest | W | 39-19 |
| 543 | 12-Nov-05 | Argentina | Int | H | Murrayfield, Edinburgh | L | 19-23 |
| 544 | 20-Nov-05 | Samoa | Int | H | Murrayfield, Edinburgh | W | 18-11 |
| 545 | 26-Nov-05 | New Zealand | Int | H | Murrayfield, Edinburgh | L | 10-29 |
| 546 | 5-Feb-06 | France | 6N | H | Murrayfield, Edinburgh | W | 20-16 |
| 547 | 12-Feb-06 | Wales | 6N | A | Millennium Stadium, Cardiff | L | 18-28 |
| 548 | 25-Feb-06 | England | 6N-CC | H | Murrayfield, Edinburgh | W | 18-12 |
| 549 | 11-Mar-06 | Ireland | 6N-CQ | A | Lansdowne Road, Dublin | L | 9-15 |
| 550 | 18-Mar-06 | Italy | 6N | A | Stadio Flaminio, Rome | W | 13-10 |
| 551 | 10-Jun-06 | South Africa | Int-T | A | The ABSA Stadium, Durban | L | 16-36 |
| 552 | 17-Jun-06 | South Africa | Int-T | A | EPRFU Stadium, Port Elizabeth | L | 15-29 |
| 553 | 11-Nov-06 | Romania | Int | H | Murrayfield, Edinburgh | W | 48-6 |
| 554 | 18-Nov-06 | Pacific Islands | Int | H | Murrayfield, Edinburgh | W | 34-22 |
| 555 | 25-Nov-06 | Australia | HT | H | Murrayfield, Edinburgh | L | 15-44 |
| 556 | 3-Feb-07 | England | 6N-CC | A | Twickenham, London | L | 20-42 |
| 557 | 10-Feb-07 | Wales | 6N | H | Murrayfield, Edinburgh | W | 21-9 |
| 558 | 24-Feb-07 | Italy | 6N | H | Murrayfield, Edinburgh | L | 17-37 |
| 559 | 10-Mar-07 | Ireland | 6N-CQ | H | Murrayfield, Edinburgh | L | 18-19 |
| 560 | 17-Mar-07 | France | 6N | A | Stade de France, Paris | L | 19-46 |

| No | Date | Opponents | Tmt | | Match Venue | Result | |
|-----|------|-----------|-----|---|-------------|--------|---|
| 561 | 11-Aug-07 | Ireland | Int | H | Murrayfield, Edinburgh | W | 31-21 |
| 562 | 25-Aug-07 | South Africa | Int | H | Murrayfield, Edinburgh | L | 3-27 |
| 563 | 9-Sep-07 | Portugal | WCp | N | Stade Geoffroy Guichard, Saint Étienne | W | 56-10 |
| 564 | 18-Sep-07 | Romania | WCp | H | Murrayfield, Edinburgh | W | 42-0 |
| 565 | 23-Sep-07 | New Zealand | WCp | H | Murrayfield, Edinburgh | L | 0-40 |
| 566 | 29-Sep-07 | Italy | WCp | N | Stade Geoffroy Guichard, Saint Étienne | W | 18-16 |
| 567 | 7-Oct-07 | Argentina | WCqf | N | Stade de France, Paris | L | 13-19 |
| 568 | 3-Feb-08 | France | 6N | H | Murrayfield, Edinburgh | L | 6-27 |
| 569 | 9-Feb-08 | Wales | 6N | A | Millennium Stadium, Cardiff | L | 15-30 |
| 570 | 23-Feb-08 | Ireland | 6N-CQ | A | Croke Park, Dublin | L | 13-34 |
| 571 | 8-Mar-08 | England | 6N-CC | H | Murrayfield, Edinburgh | W | 15-9 |
| 572 | 15-Mar-08 | Italy | 6N | A | Stadio Flaminio, Rome | L | 20-23 |
| 573 | 7-Jun-08 | Argentina | Int-T | A | Stadio Gigante de Arroyito, Rosario | L | 15-21 |
| 574 | 14-Jun-08 | Argentina | Int-T | A | Vélez Sarsfield Stadium, Buenos Aires | W | 26-14 |
| 575 | 8-Nov-08 | New Zealand | Int | H | Murrayfield, Edinburgh | L | 6-32 |
| 576 | 15-Nov-08 | South Africa | Int | H | Murrayfield, Edinburgh | L | 10-14 |
| 577 | 22-Nov-08 | Canada | DHT | H | Pittodrie Stadium, Aberdeen | W | 41-0 |
| 578 | 8-Feb-09 | Wales | 6N | H | Murrayfield, Edinburgh | L | 13-26 |
| 579 | 14-Feb-09 | France | 6N | A | Stade de France, Paris | L | 13-22 |
| 580 | 28-Feb-09 | Italy | 6N | H | Murrayfield, Edinburgh | W | 26-6 |
| 581 | 14-Mar-09 | Ireland | 6N-CQ | H | Murrayfield, Edinburgh | L | 15-22 |
| 582 | 21-Mar-09 | England | 6N-CC | A | Twickenham, London | L | 12-26 |
| 583 | 14-Nov-09 | Fiji | Int | H | Murrayfield, Edinburgh | W | 23-10 |
| 584 | 21-Nov-09 | Australia | HT | H | Murrayfield, Edinburgh | W | 9-8 |
| 585 | 28-Nov-09 | Argentina | Int | H | Murrayfield, Edinburgh | L | 6-9 |
| 586 | 7-Feb-10 | France | 6N | H | Murrayfield, Edinburgh | L | 9-18 |
| 587 | 13-Feb-10 | Wales | 6N | A | Millennium Stadium, Cardiff | L | 24-31 |
| 588 | 27-Feb-10 | Italy | 6N | A | Stadio Flaminio, Rome | L | 12-16 |
| 589 | 13-Mar-10 | England | 6N-CC | H | Murrayfield, Edinburgh | D | 15-15 |
| 590 | 20-Mar-10 | Ireland | 6N-CQ | A | Croke Park, Dublin | W | 23-20 |
| 591 | 12-Jun-10 | Argentina | Int-T | A | Estadio Monumental José Fierro, Tucumán | W | 24-16 |
| 592 | 19-Jun-10 | Argentina | Int-T | A | Estadio José Maria Minella, Mar del Plata | W | 13-9 |
| 593 | 13-Nov-10 | New Zealand | Int | H | Murrayfield, Edinburgh | L | 3-49 |
| 594 | 20-Nov-10 | South Africa | Int | H | Murrayfield, Edinburgh | W | 21-17 |
| 595 | 27-Nov-10 | Samoa | Int | H | Pittodrie Stadium, Aberdeen | W | 19-16 |
| 596 | 5-Feb-11 | France | 6N | A | Stade de France, Paris | L | 21-34 |
| 597 | 12-Feb-11 | Wales | 6N | H | Murrayfield, Edinburgh | L | 6-24 |
| 598 | 27-Feb-11 | Ireland | 6N-CQ | H | Murrayfield, Edinburgh | L | 18-21 |
| 599 | 13-Mar-11 | England | 6N-CC | A | Twickenham, London | L | 16-22 |
| 600 | 19-Mar-11 | Italy | 6N | H | Murrayfield, Edinburgh | W | 21-8 |

| No | Date | Opponents | Tmt | | Match Venue | Result | |
|----|------|-----------|-----|---|-------------|--------|---|
| 601 | 6-Aug-11 | Ireland | Int | H | Murrayfield, Edinburgh | W | 10-6 |
| 602 | 20-Aug-11 | Italy | Int | H | Murrayfield, Edinburgh | W | 23-12 |
| 603 | 10-Sep-11 | Romania | WCp | N | Rugby Park Stadium, Invercargill | W | 34-24 |
| 604 | 14-Sep-11 | Georgia | WCp | N | Rugby Park Stadium, Invercargill | W | 15-6 |
| 605 | 25-Sep-11 | Argentina | WCp | N | Wellington Regional Stadium, Wellington | L | 12-13 |
| 606 | 1-Oct-11 | England | WCp | N | Eden Park, Auckland | L | 12-16 |
| 607 | 4-Feb-12 | England | 6N-CC | H | Murrayfield, Edinburgh | L | 6-13 |
| 608 | 12-Feb-12 | Wales | 6N | A | Millennium Stadium, Cardiff | L | 13-27 |
| 609 | 25-Feb-12 | France | 6N | H | Murrayfield, Edinburgh | L | 17-23 |
| 610 | 10-Mar-12 | Ireland | 6N-CQ | A | Aviva Stadium, Dublin | L | 14-32 |
| 611 | 17-Mar-12 | Italy | 6N | A | Stadio Olimpico, Rome | L | 6-13 |
| 612 | 5-Jun-12 | Australia | HT-T | A | Ausgrid Stadium, Newcastle, NSW | W | 9-6 |
| 613 | 16-Jun-12 | Fiji | Int-T | A | Churchill Park, Lautoka | W | 37-25 |
| 614 | 23-Jun-12 | Samoa | Int T | A | Apia Park, Apia | W | 17-16 |
| 615 | 11-Nov-12 | New Zealand | Int | H | Murrayfield, Edinburgh | L | 22-51 |
| 616 | 17-Nov-12 | South Africa | Int | H | Murrayfield, Edinburgh | L | 10-21 |
| 617 | 24-Nov-12 | Tonga | Int | H | Murrayfield, Edinburgh | L | 15-21 |
| 618 | 2-Feb-13 | England | 6N-CC | A | Twickenham, London | L | 18-38 |
| 619 | 9-Feb-13 | Italy | 6N | H | Murrayfield, Edinburgh | W | 34-10 |
| 620 | 24-Feb-13 | Ireland | 6N-CQ | H | Murrayfield, Edinburgh | W | 12-8 |
| 621 | 9-Mar-13 | Wales | 6N | H | Murrayfield, Edinburgh | L | 18-28 |
| 622 | 16-Mar-13 | France | 6N | A | Stade de France, Paris | L | 16-23 |
| 623 | 8-Jun-13 | Samoa | quad | N | Kings Park Stadium, Durban | L | 17-27 |
| 624 | 15-Jun-13 | South Africa | quad | A | Mbombela Stadium, Nelspruit | L | 17-30 |
| 625 | 22-Jun-13 | Italy | quad | N | Loftus Versfeld Stadium, Pretoria | W | 30-29 |
| 626 | 9-Nov-13 | Japan | Int | H | Murrayfield, Edinburgh | W | 42-17 |
| 627 | 16-Nov-13 | South Africa | Int | H | Murrayfield, Edinburgh | L | 0-28 |
| 628 | 23-Nov-13 | Australia | HT | A | Murrayfield, Edinburgh | L | 15-21 |
| 629 | 2-Feb-14 | Ireland | 6N-CQ | A | Aviva Stadium, Dublin | L | 6-28 |
| 630 | 8-Feb-14 | England | 6N-CC | H | Murrayfield, Edinburgh | L | 0-20 |
| 631 | 22-Feb-14 | Italy | 6N | A | Stadio Olimpico, Rome | W | 21-20 |
| 632 | 8-Mar-14 | France | 6N | H | Murrayfield, Edinburgh | L | 17-19 |
| 633 | 15-Mar-14 | Wales | 6N | A | Millennium Stadium, Cardiff | L | 3-51 |
| 634 | 7-Jun-14 | United States | Int-T | A | BBVA Compass Stadium, Houston | W | 24-6 |
| 635 | 14-Jun-14 | Canada | DHT-T | A | BMO Stadium, Toronto | W | 19-17 |
| 636 | 21-Jun-14 | Argentina | Int-T | A | Estadio Olimpico Ch. Carreras, Córdoba | W | 21-19 |
| 637 | 28-Jun-14 | South Africa | Int-T | A | Nelson Mandela Bay Stad, Port Elizabeth | L | 6-55 |
| 638 | 8-Nov-14 | Argentina | Int | H | Murrayfield, Edinburgh | W | 41-31 |
| 639 | 15-Nov-14 | New Zealand | Int | H | Murrayfield, Edinburgh | L | 16-24 |
| 640 | 22-Nov-14 | Tonga | Int | H | Rugby Park, Kilmarnock | W | 37-12 |

| No | Date | Opponents | Tmt | | Match Venue | | Result |
|----|------|-----------|-----|---|-------------|---|--------|
| 641 | 7-Feb-15 | France | 6N | A | Stade de France, Paris | L | 8-15 |
| 642 | 15-Feb-15 | Wales | 6N | H | Murrayfield, Edinburgh | L | 23-26 |
| 643 | 28-Feb-15 | Italy | 6N | H | Murrayfield, Edinburgh | L | 19-22 |
| 644 | 14-Mar-15 | England | 6N-CC | A | Twickenham, London | L | 13-25 |
| 645 | 21-Mar-15 | Ireland | 6N-CQ | H | Murrayfield, Edinburgh | L | 10-40 |
| 646 | 15-Aug-15 | Ireland | Int | A | Aviva Stadium, Dublin | L | 22-28 |
| 647 | 22-Aug-15 | Italy | Int | A | Stadio Olimpico di Torino, Turin | W | 16-12 |
| 648 | 29-Aug-15 | Italy | Int | H | Murrayfield, Edinburgh | W | 48-7 |
| 649 | 5-Sep-15 | France | Int | A | Stade de France, Paris | L | 16-19 |
| 650 | 23-Sep-15 | Japan | WCp | N | Kingsholm, Gloucester | W | 45-10 |
| 651 | 27-Sep-15 | United States | WCp | N | Elland Road, Leeds | W | 39-16 |
| 652 | 3-Oct-15 | South Africa | WCp | N | St James' Park, Newcastle | L | 16-34 |
| 653 | 10-Oct-15 | Samoa | WCp | N | St James' Park, Newcastle | W | 36-33 |
| 654 | 18-Oct-15 | Australia | WCqf | N | Twickenham, London | L | 34-35 |

# SOUTH AFRICA

The South African Rugby Union was formed in Kimberley in 1889. Two years later, a team drawn from the four Home Nations, known at the time as 'Great Britain' but later as the Lions, toured South Africa and won all three Internationals. A second tour followed in 1896 and on that occasion the South Africans won their very first International in the fourth match of the series. In 1903 they were even more successful, winning the third match against the touring Great Britain team after drawing the first two. A tour of Britain and Ireland was arranged in 1906, and the team, now known as the Springboks, lost their first International to Scotland, before beating Ireland and Wales and drawing with England. The Great Britain tour of South Africa in 1910 brought more success for the Springboks as they won the three-match series, 2-1. The second South African tour of the Northern Hemisphere in 1912-13 was an outstanding one for the Springboks, because they won all five International matches against the Home Nations and France.

In 1921 South Africa toured New Zealand for the first time and shared the three-match series with a win apiece and a drawn third match. The Lions name was adopted by the 1924 British and Irish touring team, and on that tour the Lions lost the four-match series 3-0, with one test drawn. The Springboks squared up against the visiting New Zealand team in 1928 and the result was a closely contested series that ended in two wins apiece. Three years later, on a 1931-32 tour of Britain and Ireland, the third Springboks won all four Internationals against the Home Nations.

In 1933, Australia faced the Springboks on their first visit to South Africa and lost a five-match series 3-2. Four years later, in 1937, the South Africans toured Australia and New Zealand and won 2-1 in a three match series against the All Blacks. They also triumphed 2-0 in the series against the Wallabies. The Springboks' winning streak continued the following year as they won a three-match series against the touring Lions, 2-1.

After the Second World War the Springboks hit a purple patch, winning ten games in a row, including a 4-0 clean sweep against New Zealand in the 1949 home series and ultimately achieving a 'grand slam' of five victories over the Home Nations and France on their 1951-52 tour. Next came a 3-1 home series win over Australia in 1953 and a drawn series against the touring Lions in 1955. The sequence was finally broken when the All Blacks gained their revenge and won the 1956 series 3-1. However, the Springboks came back again with a series win against the touring All Blacks in 1960, four wins against the Home Nations on their 1960-61 tour, and a series win against the touring Lions in 1962. In another twist, the Springboks hit their most mediocre run to date as they lost seven games in a row between 1964 and 1965, which included a 3-1 series defeat to New Zealand.

The South Africans soon recovered and recorded a 3-0 series win against the touring Lions in 1968, a 2-0 series win in France, also in 1968, and a 4-0 series win against Australia in 1969. However, this success was soon followed by a disastrous four match mini-tour of Britain and Ireland, when they lost to both Scotland and England in December 1969 and could muster only draws against Ireland and Wales in the following month.

Although massive anti-apartheid demonstrations dominated the 1970s, South Africa rode the storm with two 3-1 home series wins against New Zealand in 1970 and 1976, a 3-0 away series win against Australia in 1971, and four wins in a row against France in 1974-75. Indeed the only blemish on that decade of success was the series loss to the unbeaten Lions on tour in 1974, which was later avenged with a 3-1 home series win against the Lions in 1980.

The Springboks played very few matches against the major nations during the 1980s, but when the apartheid system was dismantled, the team was finally readmitted to international rugby in 1992. And what a comeback it was: having missed the 1987 and the 1991 World Cup competitions, the South Africans stormed back, triumphing in extra time with a 15 points to 12 win over the All Blacks in the final of the 1995 World Cup. It was a victory that was even sweeter since it took place on home ground in Johannesburg. Despite this success, the Springboks' performance level over the next two years slipped a little, but by August 1997 they were back on track, and during the next fifteen months they won seventeen Internationals in a row, an impressive record that they currently share with New Zealand. The South African performance in the next two World Cup tournaments was, by their standard, less stellar, as they lost to Australia in the semi-final in 1999 and to the All Blacks in the quarter-final in 2003, before finally turning it around and securing the coveted trophy for a second time in 2007.

South Africa entered the 2011 World Cup as title holders and, despite strong resistance from both Wales and Samoa, they topped the pool. However, they were eventually forced to relinquish the title in the quarter-final when they lost to Australia by 11 points to 9.

The Springboks have not fared so well in the Tri Nations Championship, launched in 1996 and contested annually with Australia and New Zealand: in sixteen years of the competition, the All Blacks have dominated, with ten title wins to South Africa's three (1998, 2004 and 2009). With the admission of Argentina in 2012, the tournament was replaced by a new competition known as the Rugby Championship. The Springboks have encountered mixed results in that tournament: they finished in third place in 2012, before registering a slight improvement in 2013 when they moved up to second place. As before, it was New Zealand, title winners in both those years, which dominated: the All Blacks won all twelve matches, compared to South Africa's six.

The Springboks were much more successful on both their 2012 and 2013 Northern Hemisphere autumn tours. In 2012 they defeated Ireland, Scotland and England, and in 2013 they overcame Wales, Scotland and France. In the 2014 summer Internationals they recorded a 2-0 series win against the touring Welsh team and a thumping 55 points to 6 win at home to Scotland. The South African team also finished runners-up in the 2014 Rugby Championship, defeating New Zealand in the final match. However, South Africa's performance in the 2014 autumn series of games was, by their high standards, very disappointing: they lost to both Ireland and Wales and managed only a narrow win, by 31 points to 28, against England.

South African pride was severely dented in the reduced 2015 Rugby Championship when the Springboks lost all three Internationals: in particular, their 37 points to 25 loss to Argentina in the final match, in Durban. They did however redeem themselves by reversing that result a week later, in Buenos Aires, when they defeated the Pumas in a non-championship game by 26 points to 12.

Despite a sensational loss to Japan in their first match of the 2015 World Cup campaign, South Africa still emerged as easy winners of the pool. They narrowly overcame Wales in a closely contested quarter-final before losing to New Zealand in an extremely physical semi-final. The Springboks had some consolation in the play-off for third place when they comfortably defeated Argentina by 24 points to 13.

# SOUTH AFRICA

## HEAD TO HEAD RESULTS TO 31 OCTOBER 2015

|  | P | W | D | L | % | F | A |
|---|---|---|---|---|---|---|---|
| **v TIER 1 Teams** | | | | | | | |
| v Argentina | 22 | 20 | 1 | 1 | 93.2 | 803 | 423 |
| v Australia | 81 | 45 | 1 | 35 | 56.2 | 1572 | 1415 |
| v England | 37 | 23 | 2 | 12 | 64.9 | 780 | 592 |
| v France | 39 | 22 | 6 | 11 | 64.1 | 783 | 578 |
| v Ireland | 22 | 16 | 1 | 5 | 75.0 | 432 | 277 |
| v Italy | 12 | 12 | 0 | 0 | 100.0 | 599 | 145 |
| v New Zealand | 91 | 35 | 3 | 53 | 40.1 | 1430 | 1765 |
| v Scotland | 26 | 21 | 0 | 5 | 80.8 | 686 | 286 |
| v Wales | 31 | 28 | 1 | 2 | 91.9 | 837 | 459 |
| v Lions | 46 | 23 | 6 | 17 | 56.5 | 600 | 516 |
| **Sub-Total** | **407** | **245** | **21** | **141** | **62.8** | **8522** | **6456** |
| **v TIER 2/3 Group** | | | | | | | |
| v Canada | 2 | 2 | 0 | 0 | 100.0 | 71 | 18 |
| v Fiji | 3 | 3 | 0 | 0 | 100.0 | 129 | 41 |
| v Japan | 1 | 0 | 0 | 1 | 0.0 | 32 | 34 |
| v Romania | 1 | 1 | 0 | 0 | 100.0 | 21 | 8 |
| v Samoa | 9 | 9 | 0 | 0 | 100.0 | 431 | 99 |
| v Tonga | 2 | 2 | 0 | 0 | 100.0 | 104 | 35 |
| v United States | 4 | 4 | 0 | 0 | 100.0 | 209 | 42 |
| v Georgia | 1 | 1 | 0 | 0 | 100.0 | 46 | 19 |
| v Namibia | 2 | 2 | 0 | 0 | 100.0 | 192 | 13 |
| v Russia | 0 | 0 | 0 | 0 | 0.0 | 0 | 0 |
| v Uruguay | 3 | 3 | 0 | 0 | 100.0 | 245 | 12 |
| **Sub-Total** | **28** | **27** | **0** | **1** | **96.4** | **1480** | **321** |
| **v Other Teams** | | | | | | | |
| v N Z Cavaliers | 4 | 3 | 0 | 1 | 75.0 | 96 | 62 |
| v Pacific Islanders | 1 | 1 | 0 | 0 | 100.0 | 38 | 24 |
| v South America | 8 | 7 | 0 | 1 | 87.5 | 210 | 114 |
| v Spain | 1 | 1 | 0 | 0 | 100.0 | 47 | 3 |
| v World XV | 3 | 3 | 0 | 0 | 100.0 | 87 | 59 |
| **Sub-Total** | **17** | **15** | **0** | **2** | **88.2** | **478** | **262** |
| **All Internationals** | **452** | **287** | **21** | **144** | **65.8** | **10480** | **7039** |

| No | Date | Opponents | Tmt | | Match Venue | | Result | |
|----|------|-----------|-----|---|-------------|---|--------|---|
| 1 | 30-Jul-91 | Lions | Int | H | Crusaders Ground, Port Elizabeth | | L | 0-4 |
| 2 | 29-Aug-91 | Lions | Int | H | Eclectic Cricket Ground, Kimberley | | L | 0-3 |
| 3 | 5-Sep-91 | Lions | Int | H | Newlands Stadium, Cape Town | | L | 0-4 |
| 4 | 30-Jul-96 | Lions | Int | H | Crusaders Ground, Port Elizabeth | | L | 0-8 |
| 5 | 22-Aug-96 | Lions | Int | H | The Wanderers Ground, Johannesburg | | L | 8-17 |
| 6 | 29-Aug-96 | Lions | Int | H | The Kimberley Athletics Club, Kimberley | | L | 3-9 |
| 7 | 5-Sep-96 | Lions | Int | H | Newlands Stadium, Cape Town | | W | 5-0 |
| 8 | 26-Aug-03 | Lions | Int | H | The Wanderers Ground, Johannesburg | | D | 10-10 |
| 9 | 5-Sep-03 | Lions | Int | H | The Kimberley Athletics Club, Kimberley | | D | 0-0 |
| 10 | 12-Sep-03 | Lions | Int | H | Newlands Stadium, Cape Town | | W | 8-0 |
| 11 | 17-Nov-06 | Scotland | Int-T | A | Hampden Park, Glasgow | | L | 0-6 |
| 12 | 24-Nov-06 | Ireland | Int-T | A | Balmoral Showgrounds, Belfast | | W | 15-12 |
| 13 | 1-Dec-06 | Wales | Int-T | A | St Helen's, Swansea | | W | 11-0 |
| 14 | 8-Dec-06 | England | Int-T | A | Crystal Palace, London | | D | 3-3 |
| 15 | 6-Aug-10 | Lions | Int | H | The Wanderers Ground, Johannesburg | | W | 14-10 |
| 16 | 27-Aug-10 | Lions | Int | H | Crusaders Ground, Port Elizabeth | | L | 3-8 |
| 17 | 3-Sep-10 | Lions | Int | H | Newlands Stadium, Cape Town | | W | 21-5 |
| 18 | 23-Nov-12 | Scotland | Int-T | A | Inverleith, Edinburgh | | W | 16-0 |
| 19 | 30-Nov-12 | Ireland | Int-T | A | Lansdowne Road, Dublin | | W | 38-0 |
| 20 | 14-Dec-12 | Wales | Int-T | A | Arms Park, Cardiff | | W | 3-0 |
| 21 | 4-Jan-13 | England | Int-T | A | Twickenham, London | | W | 9-3 |
| 22 | 11-Jan-13 | France | Int-T | A | Route du Médoc, Le Bouscat, Bordeaux | | W | 38-5 |
| 23 | 13-Aug-21 | New Zealand | Int-T | A | Carisbrook, Dunedin | | L | 5-13 |
| 24 | 27-Aug-21 | New Zealand | Int-T | A | Eden Park, Auckland | | W | 9-5 |
| 25 | 17-Sep-21 | New Zealand | Int-T | A | Athletic Park, Wellington | | D | 0-0 |
| 26 | 16-Aug-24 | Lions | Int | H | Kingsmead Ground, Durban | | W | 7-3 |
| 27 | 23-Aug-24 | Lions | Int | H | The Wanderers Ground, Johannesburg | | W | 17-0 |
| 28 | 13-Sep-24 | Lions | Int | H | Crusaders Ground, Port Elizabeth | | D | 3-3 |
| 29 | 20-Sep-24 | Lions | Int | H | Newlands Stadium, Cape Town | | W | 16-9 |
| 30 | 30-Jun-28 | New Zealand | Int | H | Kingsmead Ground, Durban | | W | 17-0 |
| 31 | 21-Jul-28 | New Zealand | Int | H | Ellis Park, Johannesburg | | L | 6-7 |
| 32 | 18-Aug-28 | New Zealand | Int | H | Crusaders Ground, Port Elizabeth | | W | 11-6 |
| 33 | 1-Sep-28 | New Zealand | Int | H | Newlands Stadium, Cape Town | | L | 5-13 |
| 34 | 5-Dec-31 | Wales | Int-T | A | St Helen's, Swansea | | W | 8-3 |
| 35 | 19-Dec-31 | Ireland | Int-T | A | Lansdowne Road, Dublin | | W | 8-3 |
| 36 | 2-Jan-32 | England | Int-T | A | Twickenham, London | | W | 7-0 |
| 37 | 16-Jan-32 | Scotland | Int-T | A | Murrayfield, Edinburgh | | W | 6-3 |
| 38 | 8-Jul-33 | Australia | Int | H | Newlands Stadium, Cape Town | | W | 17-3 |
| 39 | 22-Jul-33 | Australia | Int | H | Kingsmead Ground, Durban | | L | 6-21 |
| 40 | 12-Aug-33 | Australia | Int | H | Ellis Park, Johannesburg | | W | 12-3 |

| No | Date | Opponents | Tmt | | Match Venue | Result | |
|----|------|-----------|-----|---|-------------|--------|---|
| 41 | 26-Aug-33 | Australia | Int | H | Crusaders Ground, Port Elizabeth | W | 11-0 |
| 42 | 2-Sep-33 | Australia | Int | H | Springbok Park, Bloemfontein | L | 4-15 |
| 43 | 26-Jun-37 | Australia | Int-T | A | Cricket Ground, Sydney | W | 9-5 |
| 44 | 17-Jul-37 | Australia | Int-T | A | Cricket Ground, Sydney | W | 26-17 |
| 45 | 14-Aug-37 | New Zealand | Int-T | A | Athletic Park, Wellington | L | 7-13 |
| 46 | 4-Sep-37 | New Zealand | Int-T | A | Lancaster Park Oval, Christchurch | W | 13-6 |
| 47 | 25-Sep-37 | New Zealand | Int-T | A | Eden Park, Auckland | W | 17-6 |
| 48 | 6-Aug-38 | Lions | Int | H | Ellis Park, Johannesburg | W | 26-12 |
| 49 | 3-Sep-38 | Lions | Int | H | Crusaders Ground, Port Elizabeth | W | 19-3 |
| 50 | 10-Sep-38 | Lions | Int | H | Newlands Stadium, Cape Town | L | 16-21 |
| 51 | 16-Jul-49 | New Zealand | Int | H | Newlands Stadium, Cape Town | W | 15-11 |
| 52 | 13-Aug-49 | New Zealand | Int | H | Ellis Park, Johannesburg | W | 12-6 |
| 53 | 3-Sep-49 | New Zealand | Int | H | Kingsmead Ground, Durban | W | 9-3 |
| 54 | 17-Sep-49 | New Zealand | Int | H | Crusaders Ground, Port Elizabeth | W | 11-8 |
| 55 | 24-Nov-51 | Scotland | Int-T | A | Murrayfield, Edinburgh | W | 44-0 |
| 56 | 8-Dec-51 | Ireland | Int-T | A | Lansdowne Road, Dublin | W | 17-5 |
| 57 | 22-Dec-51 | Wales | Int-T | A | Arms Park, Cardiff | W | 6-3 |
| 58 | 5-Jan-52 | England | Int-T | A | Twickenham, London | W | 8-3 |
| 59 | 16-Feb-52 | France | Int-T | A | Stade Colombes, Paris | W | 25-3 |
| 60 | 22-Aug-53 | Australia | Int | H | Ellis Park, Johannesburg | W | 25-3 |
| 61 | 5-Sep-53 | Australia | Int | H | Newlands Stadium, Cape Town | L | 14-18 |
| 62 | 19-Sep-53 | Australia | Int | H | Kingsmead Ground, Durban | W | 18-8 |
| 63 | 26-Sep-53 | Australia | Int | H | Crusaders Ground, Port Elizabeth | W | 22-9 |
| 64 | 6-Aug-55 | Lions | Int | H | Ellis Park, Johannesburg | L | 22-23 |
| 65 | 20-Aug-55 | Lions | Int | H | Newlands Stadium, Cape Town | W | 25-9 |
| 66 | 3-Sep-55 | Lions | Int | H | Loftus Versfeld Stadium, Pretoria | L | 6-9 |
| 67 | 24-Sep-55 | Lions | Int | H | Crusaders Ground, Port Elizabeth | W | 22-8 |
| 68 | 26-May-56 | Australia | Int-T | A | Cricket Ground, Sydney | W | 9-0 |
| 69 | 2-Jun-56 | Australia | Int-T | A | Exhibition Ground, Brisbane | W | 9-0 |
| 70 | 14-Jul-56 | New Zealand | Int-T | A | Carisbrook, Dunedin | L | 6-10 |
| 71 | 4-Aug-56 | New Zealand | Int-T | A | Athletic Park, Wellington | W | 8-3 |
| 72 | 18-Aug-56 | New Zealand | Int-T | A | Lancaster Park Oval, Christchurch | L | 10-17 |
| 73 | 1-Sep-56 | New Zealand | Int-T | A | Eden Park, Auckland | L | 5-11 |
| 74 | 26-Jul-58 | France | Int | H | Newlands Stadium, Cape Town | D | 3-3 |
| 75 | 16-Aug-58 | France | Int | H | Ellis Park, Johannesburg | L | 5-9 |
| 76 | 30-Apr-60 | Scotland | Tmt | H | Boet Erasmus Stadium, Port Elizabeth | W | 18-10 |
| 77 | 25-Jun-60 | New Zealand | Int | H | Ellis Park, Johannesburg | W | 13-0 |
| 78 | 23-Jul-60 | New Zealand | Int | H | Newlands Stadium, Cape Town | L | 3-11 |
| 79 | 13-Aug-60 | New Zealand | Int | H | Free State Stadium, Bloemfontein | D | 11-11 |
| 80 | 27-Aug-60 | New Zealand | Int | H | Boet Erasmus Stadium, Port Elizabeth | W | 8-3 |

| No | Date | Opponents | Tmt | | Match Venue | Result | |
|----|------|-----------|-----|---|-------------|--------|---|
| 81 | 3-Dec-60 | Wales | Int-T | A | Arms Park, Cardiff | W | 3-0 |
| 82 | 17-Dec-60 | Ireland | Int-T | A | Lansdowne Road, Dublin | W | 8-3 |
| 83 | 7-Jan-61 | England | Int-T | A | Twickenham, London | W | 5-0 |
| 84 | 21-Jan-61 | Scotland | Int-T | A | Murrayfield, Edinburgh | W | 12-5 |
| 85 | 18-Feb-61 | France | Int-T | A | Stade Colombes, Paris | D | 0-0 |
| 86 | 13-May-61 | Ireland | Int | H | Newlands Stadium, Cape Town | W | 24-8 |
| 87 | 5-Aug-61 | Australia | Int | H | Ellis Park, Johannesburg | W | 28-3 |
| 88 | 12-Aug-61 | Australia | Int | H | Boet Erasmus Stadium, Port Elizabeth | W | 23-11 |
| 89 | 23-Jun-62 | Lions | Int | H | Ellis Park, Johannesburg | D | 3-3 |
| 90 | 21-Jul-62 | Lions | Int | H | Kings Park Stadium, Durban | W | 3-0 |
| 91 | 4-Aug-62 | Lions | Int | H | Newlands Stadium, Cape Town | W | 8-3 |
| 92 | 25-Aug-62 | Lions | Int | H | Free State Stadium, Bloemfontein | W | 34-14 |
| 93 | 13-Jul-63 | Australia | Int | H | Loftus Versfeld Stadium, Pretoria | W | 14-3 |
| 94 | 10-Aug-63 | Australia | Int | H | Newlands Stadium, Cape Town | L | 5-9 |
| 95 | 24-Aug-63 | Australia | Int | H | Ellis Park, Johannesburg | L | 9-11 |
| 96 | 7-Sep-63 | Australia | Int | H | Boet Erasmus Stadium, Port Elizabeth | W | 22-6 |
| 97 | 23-May-64 | Wales | Int | H | Kings Park Stadium, Durban | W | 24-3 |
| 98 | 25-Jul-64 | France | Int | H | P A M Brink Stadium, Springs | L | 6-8 |
| 99 | 10-Apr-65 | Ireland | Int-T | A | Lansdowne Road, Dublin | L | 6-9 |
| 100 | 17-Apr-65 | Scotland | Int-T | A | Murrayfield, Edinburgh | L | 5-8 |
| 101 | 19-Jun-65 | Australia | Int-T | A | Cricket Ground, Sydney | L | 11-18 |
| 102 | 26-Jun-65 | Australia | Int-T | A | Lang Park, Brisbane | L | 8-12 |
| 103 | 31-Jul-65 | New Zealand | Int-T | A | Athletic Park, Wellington | L | 3-6 |
| 104 | 21-Aug-65 | New Zealand | Int-T | A | Carisbrook, Dunedin | L | 0-13 |
| 105 | 4-Sep-65 | New Zealand | Int-T | A | Lancaster Park Oval, Christchurch | W | 19-16 |
| 106 | 18-Sep-65 | New Zealand | Int-T | A | Eden Park, Auckland | L | 3-20 |
| 107 | 15-Jul-67 | France | Int | H | Kings Park Stadium, Durban | W | 26-3 |
| 108 | 22-Jul-67 | France | Int | H | Free State Stadium, Bloemfontein | W | 16-3 |
| 109 | 29-Jul-67 | France | Int | H | Ellis Park, Johannesburg | L | 14-19 |
| 110 | 12-Aug-67 | France | Int | H | Newlands Stadium, Cape Town | D | 6-6 |
| 111 | 8-Jun-68 | Lions | Int | H | Loftus Versfeld Stadium, Pretoria | W | 25-20 |
| 112 | 22-Jun-68 | Lions | Int | H | Boet Erasmus Stadium, Port Elizabeth | D | 6-6 |
| 113 | 13-Jul-68 | Lions | Int | H | Newlands Stadium, Cape Town | W | 11-6 |
| 114 | 27-Jul-68 | Lions | Int | H | Ellis Park, Johannesburg | W | 19-6 |
| 115 | 9-Nov-68 | France | Int-T | A | Stade du Parc Lescure, Bordeaux | W | 12-9 |
| 116 | 16-Nov-68 | France | Int-T | A | Stade Colombes, Paris | W | 16-11 |
| 117 | 2-Aug-69 | Australia | Int | H | Ellis Park, Johannesburg | W | 30-11 |
| 118 | 16-Aug-69 | Australia | Int | H | Kings Park Stadium, Durban | W | 16-9 |
| 119 | 6-Sep-69 | Australia | Int | H | Newlands Stadium, Cape Town | W | 11-3 |
| 120 | 20-Sep-69 | Australia | Int | H | Free State Stadium, Bloemfontein | W | 19-8 |

| No | Date | Opponents | Tmt | | Match Venue | | Result |
|----|------|-----------|-----|---|-------------|---|--------|
| 121 | 6-Dec-69 | Scotland | Int-T | A | Murrayfield, Edinburgh | L | 3-6 |
| 122 | 20-Dec-69 | England | Int-T | A | Twickenham, London | L | 8-11 |
| 123 | 10-Jan-70 | Ireland | Int-T | A | Lansdowne Road, Dublin | D | 8-8 |
| 124 | 24-Jan-70 | Wales | Int-T | A | National Stadium, Cardiff | D | 6-6 |
| 125 | 25-Jul-70 | New Zealand | Int | H | Loftus Versfeld Stadium, Pretoria | W | 17-6 |
| 126 | 8-Aug-70 | New Zealand | Int | H | Newlands Stadium, Cape Town | L | 8-9 |
| 127 | 29-Aug-70 | New Zealand | Int | H | Boet Erasmus Stadium, Port Elizabeth | W | 14-3 |
| 128 | 12-Sep-70 | New Zealand | Int | H | Ellis Park, Johannesburg | W | 20-17 |
| 129 | 12-Jun-71 | France | Int | H | Free State Stadium, Bloemfontein | W | 22-9 |
| 130 | 19-Jun-71 | France | Int | H | Kings Park Stadium, Durban | D | 8-8 |
| 131 | 17-Jul-71 | Australia | Int-T | A | Cricket Ground, Sydney | W | 19-11 |
| 132 | 31-Jul-71 | Australia | Int-T | A | Exhibition Ground, Brisbane | W | 14-6 |
| 133 | 7-Aug-71 | Australia | Int-T | A | Cricket Ground, Sydney | W | 18-6 |
| 134 | 3-Jun-72 | England | Int | H | Ellis Park, Johannesburg | L | 9-18 |
| 135 | 8-Jun-74 | Lions | Int | H | Newlands Stadium, Cape Town | L | 3-12 |
| 136 | 22-Jun-74 | Lions | Int | H | Loftus Versfeld Stadium, Pretoria | L | 9-28 |
| 137 | 13-Jul-74 | Lions | Int | H | Boet Erasmus Stadium, Port Elizabeth | L | 9-26 |
| 138 | 27-Jul-74 | Lions | Int | H | Ellis Park, Johannesburg | D | 13-13 |
| 139 | 23-Nov-74 | France | Int-T | A | Stade Municipal de Toulouse, Toulouse | W | 13-4 |
| 140 | 30-Nov-74 | France | Int-T | A | Parc de Princes, Paris | W | 10-8 |
| 141 | 21-Jun-75 | France | Int | H | Free State Stadium, Bloemfontein | W | 38-25 |
| 142 | 28-Jun-75 | France | Int | H | Loftus Versfeld Stadium, Pretoria | W | 33-18 |
| 143 | 24-Jul-76 | New Zealand | Int | H | Kings Park Stadium, Durban | W | 16-7 |
| 144 | 14-Aug-76 | New Zealand | Int | H | Free State Stadium, Bloemfontein | L | 9-15 |
| 145 | 4-Sep-76 | New Zealand | Int | H | Newlands Stadium, Cape Town | W | 15-10 |
| 146 | 18-Sep-76 | New Zealand | Int | H | Ellis Park, Johannesburg | W | 15-14 |
| 147 | 27-Aug-77 | World XV | Int | H | Loftus Versfeld Stadium, Pretoria | W | 45-24 |
| 148 | 26-Apr-80 | South America | Int | H | The Wanderers Ground, Johannesburg | W | 24-9 |
| 149 | 3-May-80 | South America | Int | H | Kings Park Stadium, Durban | W | 18-9 |
| 150 | 31-May-80 | Lions | Int | H | Newlands Stadium, Cape Town | W | 26-22 |
| 151 | 14-Jun-80 | Lions | Int | H | Free State Stadium, Bloemfontein | W | 26-19 |
| 152 | 28-Jun-80 | Lions | Int | H | Boet Erasmus Stadium, Port Elizabeth | W | 12-10 |
| 153 | 12-Jul-80 | Lions | Int | H | Loftus Versfeld Stadium, Pretoria | L | 13-17 |
| 154 | 18-Oct-80 | South America | Int-T | A | Wanderers Club Ground, Montevideo | W | 22-13 |
| 155 | 25-Oct-80 | South America | Int-T | A | Prince of Wales Country Club, Santiago | W | 30-16 |
| 156 | 8-Nov-80 | France | Tmt | H | Loftus Versfeld Stadium, Pretoria | W | 37-15 |
| 157 | 30-May-81 | Ireland | Int | H | Newlands Stadium, Cape Town | W | 23-15 |
| 158 | 6-Jun-81 | Ireland | Int | H | Kings Park Stadium, Durban | W | 12-10 |
| 159 | 15-Aug-81 | New Zealand | Int-T | A | Lancaster Park Oval, Christchurch | L | 9-14 |
| 160 | 29-Aug-81 | New Zealand | Int-T | A | Athletic Park, Wellington | W | 24-12 |

| No | Date | Opponents | Tmt | | Match Venue | Result | |
|----|------|-----------|-----|---|-------------|--------|---|
| 161 | 12-Sep-81 | New Zealand | Int-T | A | Eden Park, Auckland | L | 22-25 |
| 162 | 25-Sep-81 | United States | Int-T | A | Owl Creek Polo Field, Glenville, New York | W | 38-7 |
| 163 | 27-Mar-82 | South America | Int | H | Loftus Versfeld Stadium, Pretoria | W | 50-18 |
| 164 | 3-Apr-82 | South America | Int | H | Free State Stadium, Bloemfontein | L | 12-21 |
| 165 | 2-Jun-84 | England | Int | H | Boet Erasmus Stadium, Port Elizabeth | W | 33-15 |
| 166 | 9-Jun-84 | England | Int | H | Ellis Park, Johannesburg | W | 35-9 |
| 167 | 20-Oct-84 | South America | Int | H | Loftus Versfeld Stadium, Pretoria | W | 32-15 |
| 168 | 27-Oct-84 | South America | Int | H | Newlands Stadium, Cape Town | W | 22-13 |
| 169 | 10-May-86 | NZ Cavaliers | Int | H | Newlands Stadium, Cape Town | W | 21-15 |
| 170 | 17-May-86 | NZ Cavaliers | Int | H | Kings Park Stadium, Durban | L | 18-19 |
| 171 | 24-May-86 | NZ Cavaliers | Int | H | Loftus Versfeld Stadium, Pretoria | W | 33-18 |
| 172 | 31-May-86 | NZ Cavaliers | Int | H | Ellis Park, Johannesburg | W | 24-10 |
| 173 | 26-Aug-89 | World XV | Int | H | Newlands Stadium, Cape Town | W | 20-19 |
| 174 | 2-Sep-89 | World XV | Int | H | Ellis Park, Johannesburg | W | 22-16 |
| 175 | 15-Aug-92 | New Zealand | Int | H | Ellis Park, Johannesburg | L | 24-27 |
| 176 | 22-Aug-92 | Australia | Int | H | Newlands Stadium, Cape Town | L | 3-26 |
| 177 | 17-Oct-92 | France | Int-T | A | Stade de Gerland, Lyon | W | 20-15 |
| 178 | 24-Oct-92 | France | Int-T | A | Parc de Princes, Paris | L | 16-29 |
| 179 | 14-Nov-92 | England | Int-T | A | Twickenham, London | L | 16-33 |
| 180 | 26-Jun-93 | France | Int | H | Kings Park Stadium, Durban | D | 20-20 |
| 181 | 3-Jul-93 | France | Int | H | Ellis Park, Johannesburg | L | 17-18 |
| 182 | 31-Jul-93 | Australia | Int-T | A | Football Stadium, Sydney | W | 19-12 |
| 183 | 14-Aug-93 | Australia | Int-T | A | Ballymore Oval, Brisbane | L | 20-28 |
| 184 | 21-Aug-93 | Australia | Int-T | A | Football Stadium, Sydney | L | 12-19 |
| 185 | 6-Nov-93 | Argentina | Int-T | A | Ferro Carril Oeste Stadium, B Aires | W | 29-26 |
| 186 | 13-Nov-93 | Argentina | Int-T | A | Ferro Carril Oeste Stadium, B Aires | W | 52-23 |
| 187 | 4-Jun-94 | England | Int | H | Loftus Versfeld Stadium, Pretoria | L | 15-32 |
| 188 | 11-Jun-94 | England | Int | H | Newlands Stadium, Cape Town | W | 27-9 |
| 189 | 9-Jul-94 | New Zealand | Int-T | A | Carisbrook, Dunedin | L | 14-22 |
| 190 | 23-Jul-94 | New Zealand | Int-T | A | Athletic Park, Wellington | L | 9-13 |
| 191 | 6-Aug-94 | New Zealand | Int-T | A | Eden Park, Auckland | D | 18-18 |
| 192 | 8-Oct-94 | Argentina | Int | H | Boet Erasmus Stadium, Port Elizabeth | W | 42-22 |
| 193 | 15-Oct-94 | Argentina | Int | H | Ellis Park, Johannesburg | W | 46-26 |
| 194 | 19-Nov-94 | Scotland | Int-T | A | Murrayfield, Edinburgh | W | 34-10 |
| 195 | 26-Nov-94 | Wales | Int-T | A | National Stadium, Cardiff | W | 20-12 |
| 196 | 13-Apr-95 | Western Samoa | Int | H | Ellis Park, Johannesburg | W | 60-8 |
| 197 | 25-May-95 | Australia | WCp | H | Newlands Stadium, Cape Town | W | 27-18 |
| 198 | 30-May-95 | Romania | WCp | H | Newlands Stadium, Cape Town | W | 21-8 |
| 199 | 3-Jun-95 | Canada | WCp | H | Boet Erasmus Stadium, Port Elizabeth | W | 20-0 |
| 200 | 10-Jun-95 | Western Samoa | WCqf | H | Ellis Park, Johannesburg | W | 42-14 |

| No | Date | Opponents | Tmt | | Match Venue | Result | |
|----|------|-----------|-----|---|-------------|--------|---|
| 201 | 17-Jun-95 | France | WCsf | H | Kings Park Stadium, Durban | W | 19-15 |
| 202 | 24-Jun-95 | New Zealand | WCf | H | Ellis Park, Johannesburg ( a-e-t ) | W | 15-12 |
| 203 | 2-Sep-95 | Wales | Int | H | Ellis Park, Johannesburg | W | 40-11 |
| 204 | 12-Nov-95 | Italy | Int-T | A | Stadio Olimpico, Rome | W | 40-21 |
| 205 | 18-Nov-95 | England | Int-T | A | Twickenham, London | W | 24-14 |
| 206 | 2-Jul-96 | Fiji | Int | H | Loftus Versfeld Stadium, Pretoria | W | 43-18 |
| 207 | 13-Jul-96 | Australia | TN | A | Football Stadium, Sydney | L | 16-21 |
| 208 | 20-Jul-96 | New Zealand | TN | A | Lancaster Park Oval, Christchurch | L | 11-15 |
| 209 | 3-Aug-96 | Australia | TN | H | Free State Stadium, Bloemfontein | W | 25-19 |
| 210 | 10-Aug-96 | New Zealand | TN | H | Norwich Park, Newlands, Cape Town | L | 18-29 |
| 211 | 17-Aug-96 | New Zealand | Int | H | Kings Park Stadium, Durban | L | 19-23 |
| 212 | 24-Aug-96 | New Zealand | Int | H | Loftus Versfeld Stadium, Pretoria | L | 26-33 |
| 213 | 31-Aug-96 | New Zealand | Int | H | Ellis Park, Johannesburg | W | 32-22 |
| 214 | 9-Nov-96 | Argentina | Int-T | A | Ferro Carril Oeste Stadium, B Aires | W | 46-15 |
| 215 | 16-Nov-96 | Argentina | Int-T | A | Ferro Carril Oeste Stadium, B Aires | W | 44-21 |
| 216 | 30-Nov-96 | France | Int-T | A | Stade du Parc Lescure, Bordeaux | W | 22-12 |
| 217 | 7-Dec-96 | France | Int-T | A | Parc de Princes, Paris | W | 13-12 |
| 218 | 15-Dec-96 | Wales | Int-T | A | National Stadium, Cardiff | W | 37-20 |
| 219 | 10-Jun-97 | Tonga | Int | H | Norwich Park, Newlands, Cape Town | W | 74-10 |
| 220 | 21-Jun-97 | Lions | Int | H | Norwich Park, Newlands, Cape Town | L | 16-25 |
| 221 | 28-Jun-97 | Lions | Int | H | Kings Park Stadium, Durban | L | 15-18 |
| 222 | 5-Jul-97 | Lions | Int | H | Ellis Park, Johannesburg | W | 35-16 |
| 223 | 19-Jul-97 | New Zealand | TN | H | Ellis Park, Johannesburg | L | 32-35 |
| 224 | 2-Aug-97 | Australia | TN | A | Suncorp Stadium, Lang Park, Brisbane | L | 20-32 |
| 225 | 9-Aug-97 | New Zealand | TN | A | Eden Park, Auckland | L | 35-55 |
| 226 | 23-Aug-97 | Australia | TN | H | Loftus Versfeld Stadium, Pretoria | W | 61-22 |
| 227 | 8-Nov-97 | Italy | Int-T | A | Stadio Renato Dall'Ara, Bologna | W | 62-31 |
| 228 | 15-Nov-97 | France | Int-T | A | Stade de Gerland, Lyon | W | 36-32 |
| 229 | 22-Nov-97 | France | Int-T | A | Parc de Princes, Paris | W | 52-10 |
| 230 | 29-Nov-97 | England | Int-T | A | Twickenham, London | W | 29-11 |
| 231 | 6-Dec-97 | Scotland | Int-T | A | Murrayfield, Edinburgh | W | 68-10 |
| 232 | 13-Jun-98 | Ireland | Int | H | Free State Stadium, Bloemfontein | W | 37-13 |
| 233 | 20-Jun-98 | Ireland | Int | H | Minolta Loftus Stadium, Pretoria | W | 33-0 |
| 234 | 27-Jun-98 | Wales | Int | H | Minolta Loftus Stadium, Pretoria | W | 96-13 |
| 235 | 4-Jul-98 | England | Int | H | Norwich Park, Newlands, Cape Town | W | 18-0 |
| 236 | 18-Jul-98 | Australia | TN | A | Subiaco Oval, Perth | W | 14-13 |
| 237 | 25-Jul-98 | New Zealand | TN | A | Athletic Park, Wellington | W | 13-3 |
| 238 | 15-Aug-98 | New Zealand | TN | H | Kings Park Stadium, Durban | W | 24-23 |
| 239 | 22-Aug-98 | Australia | TN | H | Ellis Park, Johannesburg | W | 29-15 |
| 240 | 14-Nov-98 | Wales | Int-T | N | Wembley Stadium, London | W | 28-20 |

| No | Date | Opponents | Tmt | | Match Venue | Result | |
|----|------|-----------|-----|---|-------------|--------|---|
| 241 | 21-Nov-98 | Scotland | Int-T | A | Murrayfield, Edinburgh | W | 35-10 |
| 242 | 28-Nov-98 | Ireland | Int-T | A | Lansdowne Road, Dublin | W | 27-13 |
| 243 | 5-Dec-98 | England | Int-T | A | Twickenham, London | L | 7-13 |
| 244 | 12-Jun-99 | Italy | Int | H | Telkom Park Stadium, Port Elizabeth | W | 74-3 |
| 245 | 19-Jun-99 | Italy | Int | H | Kings Park Stadium, Durban | W | 101-0 |
| 246 | 26-Jun-99 | Wales | Int-T | A | Millennium Stadium, Cardiff | L | 19-29 |
| 247 | 10-Jul-99 | New Zealand | TN | A | Carisbrook, Dunedin | L | 0-28 |
| 248 | 17-Jul-99 | Australia | TN | A | Suncorp Stadium, Brisbane | L | 6-32 |
| 249 | 7-Aug-99 | New Zealand | TN | H | Minolta Loftus Stadium, Pretoria | L | 18-34 |
| 250 | 14-Aug-99 | Australia | TN | H | Norwich Park, Newlands, Cape Town | W | 10-9 |
| 251 | 3-Oct-99 | Scotland | WCp | A | Murrayfield, Edinburgh | W | 46-29 |
| 252 | 10-Oct-99 | Spain | WCp | N | Murrayfield, Edinburgh | W | 47-3 |
| 253 | 15-Oct-99 | Uruguay | WCp | N | Hampden Park, Glasgow | W | 39-3 |
| 254 | 24-Oct-99 | England | WCqf | N | Stade de France, Paris | W | 44-21 |
| 255 | 30-Oct-99 | Australia | WCsf | N | Twickenham, London | L | 21-27 |
| 256 | 4-Nov-99 | New Zealand | WC34 | N | Millennium Stadium, Cardiff | W | 22-18 |
| 257 | 10-Jun-00 | Canada | Int | H | Waverley Park, East London | W | 51-18 |
| 258 | 17-Jun-00 | England | Int | H | Minolta Loftus Stadium, Pretoria | W | 18-13 |
| 259 | 24-Jun-00 | England | Int | H | Free State Stadium, Bloemfontein | L | 22-27 |
| 260 | 8-Jul-00 | Australia | MCP T | A | Colonial Stadium, Melbourne | L | 23-44 |
| 261 | 22-Jul-00 | New Zealand | TN | A | Jade Stadium, Christchurch | L | 12-25 |
| 262 | 29-Jul-00 | Australia | TN | A | Stadium Australia, Sydney | L | 6-26 |
| 263 | 19-Aug-00 | New Zealand | TN | H | Ellis Park, Johannesburg | W | 46-40 |
| 264 | 26-Aug-00 | Australia | TN | H | ABSA Stadium, Durban | L | 18-19 |
| 265 | 12-Nov-00 | Argentina | Int-T | A | Estadio Monumental A V Liberti, B Aires | W | 37-33 |
| 266 | 19-Nov-00 | Ireland | Int-T | A | Lansdowne Road, Dublin | W | 28-18 |
| 267 | 26-Nov-00 | Wales | Int-T | A | Millennium Stadium, Cardiff | W | 23-13 |
| 268 | 2-Dec-00 | England | Int-T | A | Twickenham, London | L | 17-25 |
| 269 | 16-Jun-01 | France | Int | H | Ellis Park, Johannesburg | L | 23-32 |
| 270 | 23-Jun-01 | France | Int | H | ABSA Stadium, Durban | W | 20-15 |
| 271 | 30-Jun-01 | Italy | Int | H | Telkom Park Stadium, Port Elizabeth | W | 60-14 |
| 272 | 21-Jul-01 | New Zealand | TN | H | Fedsure Park, Newlands, Cape Town | L | 3-12 |
| 273 | 28-Jul-01 | Australia | TN | H | Minolta Loftus Stadium, Pretoria | W | 20-15 |
| 274 | 18-Aug-01 | Australia | TN | A | Subiaco Oval, Perth | D | 14-14 |
| 275 | 25-Aug-01 | New Zealand | TN | A | Eden Park, Auckland | L | 15-26 |
| 276 | 10-Nov-01 | France | Int-T | A | Stade de France, Paris | L | 10-20 |
| 277 | 17-Nov-01 | Italy | Int-T | A | Stadio Luigi Ferraris, Genova | W | 54-26 |
| 278 | 24-Nov-01 | England | Int-T | A | Twickenham, London | L | 9-29 |
| 279 | 1-Dec-01 | United States | Int-T | A | Robertson Stadium, Houston | W | 43-20 |
| 280 | 8-Jun-02 | Wales | Int | H | Vodacom Park Stadium, Bloemfontein | W | 34-19 |

| No | Date | Opponents | Tmt | Match Venue | Result |
|----|------|-----------|-----|-------------|--------|
| 281 | 15-Jun-02 | Wales | Int | H Newlands Stadium, Cape Town | W 19-8 |
| 282 | 29-Jun-02 | Argentina | Int | H P A M Brink Stadium, Springs | W 49-29 |
| 283 | 6-Jul-02 | Samoa | Int | H Minolta Loftus Stadium, Pretoria | W 60-18 |
| 284 | 20-Jul-02 | New Zealand | TN | A Westpac Trust Stadium, Wellington | L 20-41 |
| 285 | 27-Jul-02 | Australia | TN | A The Gabba Cricket Ground, Brisbane | L 27-38 |
| 286 | 10-Aug-02 | New Zealand | TN | H ABSA Stadium, Durban | L 23-30 |
| 287 | 17-Aug-02 | Australia | TN-M | H Ellis Park, Johannesburg | W 33-31 |
| 288 | 9-Nov-02 | France | Int-T | A Stade Vélodrome, Marseille | L 10-30 |
| 289 | 16-Nov-02 | Scotland | Int-T | A Murrayfield, Edinburgh | L 6-21 |
| 290 | 23-Nov-02 | England | Int-T | A Twickenham, London | L 3-53 |
| 291 | 7-Jun-03 | Scotland | Int | H ABSA Stadium, Durban | W 29-25 |
| 292 | 14-Jun-03 | Scotland | Int | H Ellis Park, Johannesburg | W 28-19 |
| 293 | 28-Jun-03 | Argentina | Int | H EPRFU Stadium, Port Elizabeth | W 26-25 |
| 294 | 12-Jul-03 | Australia | TN | H Newlands Stadium, Cape Town | W 26-22 |
| 295 | 19-Jul-03 | New Zealand | TN | H Securicor Loftus Stadium, Pretoria | L 16-52 |
| 296 | 2-Aug-03 | Australia | TN | A Suncorp Stadium, Brisbane | L 9-29 |
| 297 | 9-Aug-03 | New Zealand | TN | A Carisbrook, Dunedin | L 11-19 |
| 298 | 11-Oct-03 | Uruguay | WCp | N Subiaco Oval, Perth | W 72-6 |
| 299 | 18-Oct-03 | England | WCp | N Subiaco Oval, Perth | L 6-25 |
| 300 | 24-Oct-03 | Georgia | WCp | N Aussie Stadium, Sydney | W 46-19 |
| 301 | 1-Nov-03 | Samoa | WCp | N Suncorp Stadium, Brisbane | W 60-10 |
| 302 | 8-Nov-03 | New Zealand | WCq | N Telstra Dome, Melbourne | L 9-29 |
| 303 | 12-Jun-04 | Ireland | Int | H Vodacom Park Stadium, Bloemfontein | W 31-17 |
| 304 | 19-Jun-04 | Ireland | Int | H Newlands Stadium, Cape Town | W 26-17 |
| 305 | 26-Jun-04 | Wales | Int | H Securicor Loftus Stadium, Pretoria | W 53-18 |
| 306 | 17-Jul-04 | Pacific Islands | Int | N Express Advocate Stadium, Gosford, NSW | W 38-24 |
| 307 | 24-Jul-04 | New Zealand | TN | A Jade Stadium, Christchurch | L 21-23 |
| 308 | 31-Jul-04 | Australia | TN | A Subiaco Oval, Perth | L 26-30 |
| 309 | 14-Aug-04 | New Zealand | TN-F | H Ellis Park, Johannesburg | W 40-26 |
| 310 | 21-Aug-04 | Australia | TN | H ABSA Stadium, Durban | W 23-19 |
| 311 | 6-Nov-04 | Wales | Int-T | A Millennium Stadium, Cardiff | W 38-36 |
| 312 | 13-Nov-04 | Ireland | Int-T | A Lansdowne Road, Dublin | L 12-17 |
| 313 | 20-Nov-04 | England | Int-T | A Twickenham, London | L 16-32 |
| 314 | 27-Nov-04 | Scotland | Int-T | A Murrayfield, Edinburgh | W 45-10 |
| 315 | 4-Dec-04 | Argentina | Int-T | A Velez Sarsfield Stadium, Buenos Aires | W 39-7 |
| 316 | 11-Jun-05 | Uruguay | Int | H ABSA Stadium, East London | W 134-3 |
| 317 | 18-Jun-05 | France | Int | H The ABSA Stadium, Durban | D 30-30 |
| 318 | 25-Jun-05 | France | Int | H EPRFU Stadium, Port Elizabeth | W 27-13 |
| 319 | 9-Jul-05 | Australia | MCP-T | A Telstra Stadium, Sydney | L 12-30 |
| 320 | 23-Jul-05 | Australia | MCP | H Ellis Park, Johannesburg | W 33-20 |

| No | Date | Opponents | Tmt | | Match Venue | Result | |
|----|------|-----------|-----|---|-------------|--------|---|
| 321 | 30-Jul-05 | Australia | TN | H | Securicor Loftus Stadium, Pretoria | W | 22-16 |
| 322 | 6-Aug-05 | New Zealand | TN | H | Newlands Stadium, Cape Town | W | 22-16 |
| 323 | 20-Aug-05 | Australia | TN | A | Subiaco Oval, Perth | W | 22-19 |
| 324 | 27-Aug-05 | New Zealand | TN | A | Carisbrook, Dunedin | L | 27-31 |
| 325 | 5-Nov-05 | Argentina | Int-T | A | Vélez Sarsfield Stadium, Buenos Aires | W | 34-23 |
| 326 | 19-Nov-05 | Wales | Int-T | A | Millennium Stadium, Cardiff | W | 33-16 |
| 327 | 26-Nov-05 | France | Int-T | A | Stade de France, Paris | L | 20-26 |
| 328 | 10-Jun-06 | Scotland | Int | H | The ABSA Stadium, Durban | W | 36-16 |
| 329 | 17-Jun-06 | Scotland | Int | H | EPRFU Stadium, Port Elizabeth | W | 29-15 |
| 330 | 24-Jun-06 | France | Int | H | Newlands Stadium, Cape Town | L | 26-36 |
| 331 | 15-Jul-06 | Australia | TN-M | A | Suncorp Stadium, Brisbane | L | 0-49 |
| 332 | 22-Jul-06 | New Zealand | TN-F | A | Westpac Stadium, Wellington | L | 17-35 |
| 333 | 5-Aug-06 | Australia | TN-M | A | Telstra Stadium, Sydney | L | 18-20 |
| 334 | 26-Aug-06 | New Zealand | TN-F | H | Loftus Versfeld Stadium, Pretoria | L | 26-45 |
| 335 | 2-Sep-06 | New Zealand | TN-F | H | Royal Bafokeng Sports Palace, Rustenburg | W | 21-20 |
| 336 | 9-Sep-06 | Australia | TN-M | H | Ellis Park, Johannesburg | W | 24-16 |
| 337 | 11-Nov-06 | Ireland | Int-T | A | Lansdowne Road, Dublin | L | 15-32 |
| 338 | 18-Nov-06 | England | Int-T | A | Twickenham, London | L | 21-23 |
| 339 | 25-Nov-06 | England | Int-T | A | Twickenham, London | W | 25-14 |
| 340 | 26-May-07 | England | Int | H | Vodacom Park Stadium, Bloemfontein | W | 58-10 |
| 341 | 2-Jun-07 | England | Int | H | Loftus Versfeld Stadium, Pretoria | W | 55-22 |
| 342 | 9-Jun-07 | Samoa | Int | H | Royal Bafokeng Sports Palace, Rustenburg | W | 35-8 |
| 343 | 16-Jun-07 | Australia | TN-M | H | Ellis Park, Johannesburg | W | 22-19 |
| 344 | 23-Jun-07 | New Zealand | TNa-F | H | The ABSA Stadium, Durban | L | 21-26 |
| 345 | 7-Jul-07 | Australia | TN-M | A | Telstra Stadium, Sydney | L | 17-25 |
| 346 | 14-Jul-07 | New Zealand | TN-F | A | Jade Stadium, Christchurch | L | 6-33 |
| 347 | 15-Aug-07 | Namibia | Int | H | Newlands Stadium, Cape Town | W | 105-13 |
| 348 | 25-Aug-07 | Scotland | Int-T | A | Murrayfield, Edinburgh | W | 27-3 |
| 349 | 9-Sep-07 | Samoa | WCp | N | Parc de Princes, Paris | W | 59-7 |
| 350 | 14-Sep-07 | England | WCp | N | Stade de France, Paris | W | 36-0 |
| 351 | 22-Sep-07 | Tonga | WCp | N | Stade Félix Bolleart, Lens | W | 30-25 |
| 352 | 30-Sep-07 | United States | WCp | N | Stade de la Mosson, Montpellier | W | 64-15 |
| 353 | 7-Oct-07 | Fiji | WCqf | N | Stade Vélodrome, Marseille | W | 37-20 |
| 354 | 14-Oct-07 | Argentina | WCsf | N | Stade de France, Paris | W | 37-13 |
| 355 | 20-Oct-07 | England | WCf | N | Stade de France, Paris | W | 15-6 |
| 356 | 24-Nov-07 | Wales | PWC-T | A | Millennium Stadium, Cardiff | W | 34-12 |
| 357 | 7-Jun-08 | Wales | PWC | H | Vodacom Park Stadium, Bloemfontein | W | 43-17 |
| 358 | 14-Jun-08 | Wales | PWC | H | Loftus Versfeld Stadium, Pretoria | W | 37-21 |
| 359 | 21-Jun-08 | Italy | Int | H | Newlands Stadium, Cape Town | W | 26-0 |
| 360 | 5-Jul-08 | New Zealand | TN-F | A | Westpac Stadium, Wellington | L | 8-19 |

| No | Date | Opponents | Tmt | | Match Venue | Result | |
|----|------|-----------|-----|---|-------------|--------|---|
| 361 | 12-Jul-08 | New Zealand | TN-F | A | Carisbrook, Dunedin | W | 30-28 |
| 362 | 19-Jul-08 | Australia | TN-M | A | Subiaco Oval, Perth | L | 9-16 |
| 363 | 9-Aug-08 | Argentina | Int | H | Coca Cola Park, Johannesburg | W | 63-9 |
| 364 | 16-Aug-08 | New Zealand | TN-F | H | Newlands Stadium, Cape Town | L | 0-19 |
| 365 | 23-Aug-08 | Australia | TN-M | H | The ABSA Stadium, Durban | L | 15-27 |
| 366 | 30-Aug-08 | Australia | TN-M | H | Coca Cola Park, Johannesburg | W | 53-8 |
| 367 | 8-Nov-08 | Wales | PWC-T | A | Millennium Stadium, Cardiff | W | 20-15 |
| 368 | 15-Nov-08 | Scotland | Int-T | A | Murrayfield, Edinburgh | W | 14-10 |
| 369 | 22-Nov-08 | England | Int-T | A | Twickenham, London | W | 42-6 |
| 370 | 20-Jun-09 | Lions | LSA | H | The ABSA Stadium, Durban | W | 26-21 |
| 371 | 27-Jun-09 | Lions | LSA | H | Loftus Versfeld Stadium, Pretoria | W | 28-25 |
| 372 | 4-Jul-09 | Lions | LSA | H | Coca Cola Park, Johannesburg | L | 9-28 |
| 373 | 25-Jul-09 | New Zealand | TN-F | H | Vodacom Park Stadium, Bloemfontein | W | 28-19 |
| 374 | 1-Aug-09 | New Zealand | TN-F | H | The ABSA Stadium, Durban | W | 31-19 |
| 375 | 8-Aug-09 | Australia | TN-M | H | Newlands Stadium, Cape Town | W | 29-17 |
| 376 | 29-Aug-09 | Australia | TN-M | A | Subiaco Oval, Perth | W | 32-25 |
| 377 | 5-Sep-09 | Australia | TN-M | A | Suncorp Stadium, Brisbane | L | 6-21 |
| 378 | 12-Sep-09 | New Zealand | TN-F | A | Waikato Stadium, Hamilton | W | 32-29 |
| 379 | 13-Nov-09 | France | Int-T | A | Stade Municipal de Toulouse, Toulouse | L | 13-20 |
| 380 | 21-Nov-09 | Italy | Int-T | A | Stadio Friuli, Udine | W | 32-10 |
| 381 | 28-Nov-09 | Ireland | Int-T | A | Croke Park, Dublin | L | 10-15 |
| 382 | 5-Jun-10 | Wales | PWC-T | A | Millennium Stadium, Cardiff | W | 34-31 |
| 383 | 12-Jun-10 | France | Int | H | Newlands Stadium, Cape Town | W | 42-17 |
| 384 | 19-Jun-10 | Italy | Int | H | Johann van Riebeeck Stadium, Witbank | W | 29-13 |
| 385 | 26-Jun-10 | Italy | Int | H | Buffalo City Stadium, East London | W | 55-11 |
| 386 | 10-Jul-10 | New Zealand | TN-F | A | Eden Park, Auckland | L | 12-32 |
| 387 | 17-Jul-10 | New Zealand | TN-F | A | Westpac Stadium, Wellngton | L | 17-31 |
| 388 | 24-Jul-10 | Australia | TN-M | A | Suncorp Stadium, Brisbane | L | 13-30 |
| 389 | 21-Aug-10 | New Zealand | TN-F | H | FNB Stadium, Soweto, Johannesburg | L | 22-29 |
| 390 | 28-Aug-10 | Australia | TN-M | H | Loftus Versfeld Stadium, Pretoria | W | 44-31 |
| 391 | 4-Sep-10 | Australia | TN-M | H | Vodacom Park Stadium, Bloemfontein | L | 39-41 |
| 392 | 6-Nov-10 | Ireland | Int-T | A | Aviva Stadium, Dublin | W | 23-21 |
| 393 | 13-Nov-10 | Wales | PWC-T | A | Millennium Stadium, Cardiff | W | 29-25 |
| 394 | 20-Nov-10 | Scotland | Int-T | A | Murrayfield, Edinburgh | L | 17-21 |
| 395 | 27-Nov-10 | England | Int-T | A | Twickenham, London | W | 21-11 |
| 396 | 23-Jul-11 | Australia | TN-M | A | ANZ Stadium, Sydney | L | 20-39 |
| 397 | 30-Jul-11 | New Zealand | TN-F | A | Westpac Stadium, Wellngton | L | 7-40 |
| 398 | 13-Aug-11 | Australia | TN-M | H | Kings Park Stadium, Durban | L | 9-14 |
| 399 | 20-Aug-11 | New Zealand | TN-F | H | Nelson Mandela Bay Stad., Port Elizabeth | W | 18-5 |
| 400 | 11-Sep-11 | Wales | WCp | N | Wellington Regional Stadium, Wellington | W | 17-16 |

| No | Date | Opponents | Tmt | Match Venue | | Result | |
|----|------|-----------|-----|-------------|---|--------|---|
| 401 | 17-Sep-11 | Fiji | WCp | N | Wellington Regional Stadium, Wellington | W | 49-3 |
| 402 | 22-Sep-11 | Namibia | WCp | N | North Harbour Stadium, Albany | W | 87-0 |
| 403 | 30-Sep-11 | Samoa | WCp | N | North Harbour Stadium, Albany | W | 13-5 |
| 404 | 9-Oct-11 | Australia | WCqf | N | Wellington Regional Stadium, Wellington | L | 9-11 |
| 405 | 9-Jun-12 | England | Int | H | Kings Park Stadium, Durban | W | 22-17 |
| 406 | 16-Jun-12 | England | Int | H | Ellis Park, Johannesburg | W | 36-27 |
| 407 | 23-Jun-12 | England | Int | H | Nelson Mandela Bay Stad., Port Elizabeth | D | 14-14 |
| 408 | 18-Aug-12 | Argentina | RC | H | Newlands Stadium, Cape Town | W | 27-6 |
| 409 | 25-Aug-12 | Argentina | RC | A | Estadio Malvinas Argentinas, Mendoza | D | 16-16 |
| 410 | 8-Sep-12 | Australia | RC-M | A | Patersons Stadium, Perth | L | 19-26 |
| 411 | 15-Sep-12 | New Zealand | RC-F | A | Forsyth Barr Stadium, Dunedin | L | 11-21 |
| 412 | 29-Sep-12 | Australia | RC-M | H | Loftus Versfeld Stadium, Pretoria | W | 31-8 |
| 413 | 6-Oct-12 | New Zealand | RC-F | H | FNB Stadium, Soweto, Johannesburg | L | 16-32 |
| 414 | 10-Nov-12 | Ireland | Int-T | A | Aviva Stadium, Dublin | W | 16-12 |
| 415 | 17-Nov-12 | Scotland | Int-T | A | Murrayfield, Edinburgh | W | 21-10 |
| 416 | 24-Nov-12 | England | Int-T | A | Twickenham, London | W | 16-15 |
| 417 | 8-Jun-13 | Italy | quad | H | Growthpoint Kings Park, Durban | W | 44-10 |
| 418 | 15-Jun-13 | Scotland | quad | H | Mbombela Stadium, Nelspruit | W | 30-17 |
| 419 | 22-Jun-13 | Samoa | quad | H | Loftus Versfeld Stadium, Pretoria | W | 56-23 |
| 420 | 17-Aug-13 | Argentina | RC | H | FNB Stadium, Soweto, Johannesburg | W | 73-13 |
| 421 | 24-Aug-13 | Argentina | RC | A | Estadio Malvinas Argentinas, Mendoza | W | 22-17 |
| 422 | 7-Sep-13 | Australia | RC-M | A | Suncorp Stadium, Brisbane | W | 38-12 |
| 423 | 14-Sep-13 | New Zealand | RC-F | A | Eden Park, Auckland | L | 15-29 |
| 424 | 28-Sep-13 | Australia | RC-M | H | Newlands Stadium, Cape Town | W | 28-8 |
| 425 | 5-Oct-13 | New Zealand | RC-F | H | Ellis Park, Johannesburg | L | 27-38 |
| 426 | 9-Nov-13 | Wales | PWC-T | A | Millennium Stadium, Cardiff | W | 24-15 |
| 427 | 16-Nov-13 | Scotland | Int-T | A | Murrayfield, Edinburgh | W | 28-0 |
| 428 | 23-Nov-13 | France | Int-T | A | Stade de France, Paris | W | 19-10 |
| 429 | 14-Jun-14 | Wales | PWC | H | Kings Park Stadium, Durban | W | 38-16 |
| 430 | 21-Jun-14 | Wales | PWC | H | Mbombela Stadium, Nelspruit | W | 31-30 |
| 431 | 28-Jun-14 | Scotland | Int | H | Nelson Mandela Bay Stad., Port Elizabeth | W | 55-6 |
| 432 | 16-Aug-14 | Argentina | RC | H | Loftus Versfeld Stadium, Pretoria | W | 13-6 |
| 433 | 23-Aug-14 | Argentina | RC | A | Estadio Padre Ernesto Martearena, Salta | W | 33-31 |
| 434 | 6-Sep-14 | Australia | RC-M | A | Patersons Stadium, Perth | L | 23-24 |
| 435 | 13-Sep-14 | New Zealand | RC-F | A | Westpac Stadium, Wellngton | L | 10-14 |
| 436 | 27-Sep-14 | Australia | RC-M | H | Newlands Stadium, Cape Town | W | 28-10 |
| 437 | 4-Oct-14 | New Zealand | RC-F | H | Ellis Park, Johannesburg | W | 27-25 |
| 438 | 8-Nov-14 | Ireland | Int-T | A | Aviva Stadium, Dublin | L | 15-29 |
| 439 | 15-Nov-14 | England | Int-T | A | Twickenham, London | W | 31-28 |
| 440 | 22-Nov-14 | Italy | Int-T | A | Stadio Euganeo, Padova | W | 22-6 |

| No | Date | Opponents | Tmt | | Match Venue | Result | |
|---|---|---|---|---|---|---|---|
| 441 | 29-Nov-14 | Wales | PWC-T | A | Millennium Stadium, Cardiff | L | 6-12 |
| 442 | 18-Jul-15 | Australia | RC-M | A | Suncorp Stadium, Brisbane | L | 20-24 |
| 443 | 25-Jul-15 | New Zealand | RC-F | H | Ellis Park, Johannesburg | L | 20-27 |
| 444 | 8-Aug-15 | Argentina | RC | H | Kings Park Stadium, Durban | L | 25-37 |
| 445 | 15-Aug-15 | Argentina | RC | A | Vélez Sarsfield Stadium, Buenos Aires | W | 26-12 |
| 446 | 19-Sep-15 | Japan | WCp | N | Brighton Community Stadium, Brighton | L | 32-34 |
| 447 | 26-Sep-15 | Samoa | WCp | N | Villa Park, Birmingham | W | 46-6 |
| 448 | 3-Oct-15 | Scotland | WCp | N | St James' Park, Newcastle | W | 34-16 |
| 449 | 7-Oct-15 | United States | WCp | N | Olympic Stadium, London | W | 64-0 |
| 450 | 17-Oct-15 | Wales | WCqf | N | Twickenham, London | W | 23-19 |
| 451 | 24-Oct-15 | New Zealand | WCsf | N | Twickenham, London | L | 18-20 |
| 452 | 31-Oct-15 | Argentina | WC34 | N | Olympic Stadium, London | W | 24-13 |

# WALES

The first International played by Wales, which ended in a defeat to England, was held at Mr. Richardson's Field, Blackheath on 18 February 1881. Three weeks later, on 12 March 1881, delegates representing eleven rugby clubs met at the Castle Hotel in Neath and the Welsh Rugby Union was formed. The first Home Nations Championship was staged in 1883. Wales lost both games, and another decade passed before the Welsh team finally won the Championship and with it the first of twenty Triple Crowns. The start of the twentieth century heralded a 'Welsh Golden Era'. Between 1900 and 1911, Wales played forty-three matches, won thirty-five, drew one, and lost only seven. They also won six Triple Crowns and three Grand Slams during that period, and recorded twenty-two consecutive home wins against the Home Nations and France (who had entered the Championship in 1910). Wales also defeated New Zealand in 1905 and Australia in 1908, but lost to South Africa in 1906. In 1911 Wales won the first Five Nations Grand Slam, but it took them another thirty-nine years to repeat that feat, when they won the Grand Slam for a second time in 1950.

After the First World War, Welsh rugby declined somewhat but there was a significant resurgence during the 1930s and Wales had some famous victories (defeating New Zealand for a second time in 1935), but also some disappointing defeats (a third loss to South Africa in 1931). Between 1950 and 1956 Wales played thirty matches and won twenty-two; these included two Grand Slams and a third victory over New Zealand in 1953.

With the exception of a Triple Crown victory in 1965, the 1960s proved to be a mediocre decade for the team, in comparison with the previous decade. However, the years 1969 to 1979 ushered in a 'Second Golden Era' for Wales, when the team won the Championship outright six times, including six Triple Crowns, four of which were won in consecutive years between 1976 and 1979, and three Grand Slams. During that memorable period Wales played forty-three Five Nations Championship games, winning thirty-three, drawing three and losing only seven. This winning streak also included a sequence of twenty-two home Championship games without defeat, which was extended to twenty-seven in 1982.

In contrast, Wales fared poorly against the Southern Hemisphere major nations, losing four times to the All Blacks, drawing against the Springboks, and winning three of five games against Australia.

The 1980s again proved to be a disappointing anti-climax for the Welsh team as they suffered twenty defeats out of forty matches up to the beginning of the World Cup in 1987. The team did, however, derive some comfort in that 1987 World Cup by securing third place, and followed it with a Triple Crown in 1988. The next three years leading up to the second World Cup in 1991, would be witness to the worse sequence of results in Welsh rugby history. In twenty-four matches played between late March 1988 and early October 1991, Wales recorded only four wins, two of which were against Namibia, an emerging rugby nation. Those wins were of little consolation as the Welsh suffered three heavy defeats: two to the All Blacks on their summer tour of New Zealand in 1988, and one to the Wallabies in Brisbane in 1991. Worse was to follow when Wales, beaten by Western Samoa in Cardiff at the pool stage, failed to qualify for the quarter-final of the 1991 World Cup.

Mixed fortunes continued for the Welsh team when, after winning the 1994 Five Nations Championship, they failed to reach the quarter-final of the 1995 World Cup in South Africa, losing by one point to Ireland at the pool stage. In 1999, the year that Wales hosted the fourth World Cup, the home team strung together ten straight victories, including a first-ever win over South Africa in the opening match at the newly built Millennium Stadium in Cardiff. The Welsh qualified for the quarter-final after a gap of twelve long years, but were well beaten at that stage by Australia, the eventual winners of the trophy. Wales also qualified for the quarter-final of the 2003 World Cup, losing to England the eventual winners of the competition.

A roller-coaster of results occurred during the first decade of the new millennium. After finishing in fourth place in both the inaugural year of the Six Nations Championship in 2000 and also in 2001, Wales finished fifth in 2002, then hit rock bottom by finishing in sixth place in 2003, fourth again in 2004, only to amazingly win the Grand Slam in 2005. In both the 2006 and 2007 competition Wales finished back in fifth place yet again, before bouncing back and gaining their tenth Grand Slam in 2008. However, a year before that 2008 Grand Slam there had been further disappointment for the Welsh team in the 2007 World Cup held in France, when they failed to qualify for the quarter-final for the third time in a World Cup competition after losing to Fiji at the pool stage.

The 2008 success did not continue and in each of the three seasons, 2009 to 2011, Wales finished in fourth place in the Six Nations Championship, with only Scotland and Italy below them in the table. Things looked bleak as the 2011 World Cup loomed. The Welsh performance in that tournament surprised everyone when they reached the semi-final, only to lose by one point to France. Although they had lost that game, there was a sense that there was a renewed energy on the Welsh side: and they went on to win an eleventh Grand Slam in 2012. Three Grand Slams in the space of eight years (between 2005 and 2012) recalled the great

Welsh team of the 1970s, which had also won three Grand Slams in eight years (between 1971 and 1978).

In 2013, Wales again topped the Six Nations table with four wins, denying England a Grand Slam in the final Championship match, but they failed in their bid to win three titles in succession when they lost both their away matches in the 2014 Six Nations campaign to finish in third place. On tour in June 2014, the Welsh team lost both Internationals to South Africa, but gained revenge in the November series when they defeated the Springboks (for only the second time) by 12 points to 6.

Despite the recent success against Northern Hemisphere opponents, the Welsh team has fared very badly against Australia, New Zealand and South Africa. Since the start of the new millennium, the Welsh team has lost forty-four times in forty-eight matches against the three Southern Hemisphere giants. In the 2015 Six Nations Championship, despite winning four matches, Wales finished in third place again when the team lost on points difference to both England and the title winners, Ireland.

Wales were drawn in an extremely competitive pool in the 2015 Rugby World Cup which contained England, Australia, Fiji and Uruguay. Although beaten by Australia, they qualified for the last eight by winning the other three matches. The team however bowed out in the quarter-final when they lost to South Africa by 23 points to 19 in a closely fought match.

# WALES

## HEAD TO HEAD RESULTS TO 31 OCTOBER 2015

| | P | W | D | L | % | F | A |
|---|---|---|---|---|---|---|---|
| **v TIER 1 Teams** | | | | | | | |
| v Argentina | 15 | 10 | 0 | 5 | 66.7 | 428 | 350 |
| v Australia | 39 | 10 | 1 | 28 | 26.9 | 596 | 912 |
| v England * | 127 | 57 | 12 | 58 | 49.6 | 1484 | 1621 |
| v France | 93 | 47 | 3 | 43 | 52.1 | 1384 | 1338 |
| v Ireland * | 123 | 67 | 6 | 50 | 56.9 | 1461 | 1365 |
| v Italy | 23 | 20 | 1 | 2 | 89.1 | 748 | 386 |
| v New Zealand | 30 | 3 | 0 | 27 | 10.0 | 307 | 916 |
| v Scotland * | 120 | 69 | 3 | 48 | 58.8 | 1584 | 1211 |
| v South Africa | 31 | 2 | 1 | 28 | 8.1 | 459 | 837 |
| **Sub-Total** | **601** | **285** | **27** | **289** | **49.7** | **8451** | **8936** |
| **v TIER 2/3 Group** | | | | | | | |
| v Canada | 12 | 11 | 0 | 1 | 91.7 | 460 | 207 |
| v Fiji | 11 | 9 | 1 | 1 | 86.4 | 329 | 145 |
| v Japan | 9 | 8 | 0 | 1 | 88.9 | 493 | 129 |
| v Romania | 8 | 6 | 0 | 2 | 75.0 | 342 | 96 |
| v Samoa | 9 | 5 | 0 | 4 | 55.6 | 216 | 163 |
| v Tonga | 7 | 7 | 0 | 0 | 100.0 | 203 | 78 |
| v United States | 7 | 7 | 0 | 0 | 100.0 | 305 | 86 |
| v Georgia | 0 | 0 | 0 | 0 | 0.0 | 0 | 0 |
| v Namibia | 4 | 4 | 0 | 0 | 100.0 | 171 | 69 |
| v Uruguay | 1 | 1 | 0 | 0 | 100.0 | 54 | 9 |
| **Sub-Total** | **68** | **58** | **1** | **9** | **86.0** | **2573** | **982** |
| **v Other Teams** | | | | | | | |
| v Barbarians | 4 | 2 | 0 | 2 | 50.0 | 113 | 93 |
| v N Z Services | 1 | 0 | 0 | 1 | 0.0 | 3 | 6 |
| v New Zealand Natives* | 1 | 1 | 0 | 0 | 100.0 | - | - |
| v Pacific Islanders | 1 | 1 | 0 | 0 | 100.0 | 38 | 20 |
| v Portugal | 1 | 1 | 0 | 0 | 100.0 | 102 | 11 |
| v Spain | 1 | 1 | 0 | 0 | 100.0 | 54 | 0 |
| v Zimbabwe | 3 | 3 | 0 | 0 | 100.0 | 126 | 38 |
| **Sub-Total** | **12** | **9** | **0** | **3** | **75.0** | **436** | **168** |
| **All Internationals** | **681** | **352** | **28** | **301** | **53.7** | **11460** | **10086** |

* excludes points scored before the introduction of the modern points system

| No | Date | Opponents | Tmt | | Match Venue | Result | |
|----|------|-----------|-----|---|-------------|--------|---|
| 1 | 19-Feb-81 | England | Int | A | Richardson's Field, Blackheath | L | 0-30 |
| 2 | 28-Jan-82 | Ireland | Int | A | Lansdowne Road, Dublin | W | 8-0 |
| 3 | 16-Dec-82 | England | 4N | H | St Helen's, Swansea | L | 0-10 |
| 4 | 8-Jan-83 | Scotland | 4N | A | Raeburn Place, Edinburgh | L | 3-9 |
| 5 | 5-Jan-84 | England | 4N | A | Cardigan Fields, Leeds | L | 3-5 |
| 6 | 12-Jan-84 | Scotland | 4N | H | Rodney Parade, Newport | L | 0-4 |
| 7 | 12-Apr-84 | Ireland | 4N | H | Arms Park, Cardiff | W | 5-0 |
| 8 | 3-Jan-85 | England | 4N | H | St Helen's, Swansea | L | 4-7 |
| 9 | 10-Jan-85 | Scotland | 4N | A | Hamilton Crescent, Glasgow | D | 0-0 |
| 10 | 2-Jan-86 | England | 4N | A | Rectory Field, Blackheath | L | 3-5 |
| 11 | 9-Jan-86 | Scotland | 4N | H | Arms Park, Cardiff | L | 0-7 |
| 12 | 8-Jan-87 | England | 4N | H | Stradey Park, Llanelli | D | 0-0 |
| 13 | 26-Feb-87 | Scotland | 4N | A | Raeburn Place, Edinburgh | L | 0-20 |
| 14 | 12-Mar-87 | Ireland | 4N | N | Upper Park, Birkenhead Park | W | 4-3 |
| 15 | 4-Feb-88 | Scotland | 4N | H | Rodney Parade, Newport | W | 1-0 |
| 16 | 3-Mar-88 | Ireland | 4N | A | Lansdowne Road, Dublin | L | 0-7 |
| 17 | 22-Dec-88 | N Z Natives | Int | H | St Helen's, Swansea | W | 5-0 |
| 18 | 2-Feb-89 | Scotland | 4N | A | Raeburn Place, Edinburgh | L | 0-2 |
| 19 | 2-Mar-89 | Ireland | 4N | H | St Helen's, Swansea | L | 0-2 |
| 20 | 1-Feb-90 | Scotland | 4N | H | Arms Park, Cardiff | L | 1-5 |
| 21 | 15-Feb-90 | England | 4N | A | Crown Flatt, Dewsbury | W | 1-0 |
| 22 | 1-Mar-90 | Ireland | 4N | A | Lansdowne Road, Dublin | D | 3-3 |
| 23 | 3-Jan-91 | England | 4N | H | Rodney Parade, Newport | L | 3-7 |
| 24 | 7-Feb-91 | Scotland | 4N | A | Raeburn Place, Edinburgh | L | 0-15 |
| 25 | 7-Mar-91 | Ireland | 4N | H | Stradey Park, Llanelli | W | 6-4 |
| 26 | 2-Jan-92 | England | 4N | A | Rectory Field, Blackheath | L | 0-17 |
| 27 | 6-Feb-92 | Scotland | 4N | H | St Helen's, Swansea | L | 2-7 |
| 28 | 5-Mar-92 | Ireland | 4N | A | Lansdowne Road, Dublin | L | 0-9 |
| 29 | 7-Jan-93 | England | 4N | H | Arms Park, Cardiff | W | 12-11 |
| 30 | 4-Feb-93 | Scotland | 4N | A | Raeburn Place, Edinburgh | W | 9-0 |
| 31 | 11-Mar-93 | Ireland | 4N | H | Stradey Park, Llanelli | W | 2-0 |
| 32 | 6-Jan-94 | England | 4N | A | Upper Park, Birkenhead Park | L | 3-24 |
| 33 | 3-Feb-94 | Scotland | 4N | H | Rodney Parade, Newport | W | 7-0 |
| 34 | 10-Mar-94 | Ireland | 4N | A | Ballynafeigh, Belfast | L | 0-3 |
| 35 | 5-Jan-95 | England | 4N | H | St Helen's, Swansea | L | 6-14 |
| 36 | 26-Jan-95 | Scotland | 4N | A | Raeburn Place, Edinburgh | L | 4-5 |
| 37 | 16-Mar-95 | Ireland | 4N | H | Arms Park, Cardiff | W | 5-3 |
| 38 | 4-Jan-96 | England | 4N | A | Rectory Field, Blackheath | L | 0-25 |
| 39 | 25-Jan-96 | Scotland | 4N | H | Arms Park, Cardiff | W | 6-0 |
| 40 | 14-Mar-96 | Ireland | 4N | A | Lansdowne Road, Dublin | L | 4-8 |

| No | Date | Opponents | Tmt | | Match Venue | Result | |
|----|------|-----------|-----|---|-------------|--------|---|
| 41 | 9-Jan-97 | England | 4N | H | Rodney Parade, Newport | W | 11-0 |
| 42 | 19-Mar-98 | Ireland | 4N | A | Thomond Park, Limerick | W | 11-3 |
| 43 | 2-Apr-98 | England | 4N | A | Rectory Field, Blackheath | L | 7-14 |
| 44 | 7-Jan-99 | England | 4N | H | St Helen's, Swansea | W | 26-3 |
| 45 | 4-Mar-99 | Scotland | 4N | A | Inverleith, Edinburgh | L | 10-21 |
| 46 | 18-Mar-99 | Ireland | 4N | H | Arms Park, Cardiff | L | 0-3 |
| 47 | 6-Jan-00 | England | 4N | A | Kingsholm, Gloucester | W | 13-3 |
| 48 | 27-Jan-00 | Scotland | 4N | H | St Helen's, Swansea | W | 12-3 |
| 49 | 17-Mar-00 | Ireland | 4N | A | Balmoral Showgrounds, Belfast | W | 3-0 |
| 50 | 5-Jan-01 | England | 4N | H | Arms Park, Cardiff | W | 13-0 |
| 51 | 9-Feb-01 | Scotland | 4N | A | Inverleith, Edinburgh | L | 8-18 |
| 52 | 16-Mar-01 | Ireland | 4N | H | St Helen's, Swansea | W | 10-9 |
| 53 | 11-Jan-02 | England | 4N | A | Rectory Field, Blackheath | W | 9-8 |
| 54 | 1-Feb-02 | Scotland | 4N | H | Arms Park, Cardiff | W | 14-5 |
| 55 | 8-Mar-02 | Ireland | 4N | A | Lansdowne Road, Dublin | W | 15-0 |
| 56 | 10-Jan-03 | England | 4N | H | St Helen's, Swansea | W | 21-5 |
| 57 | 7-Feb-03 | Scotland | 4N | A | Inverleith, Edinburgh | L | 0-6 |
| 58 | 14-Mar-03 | Ireland | 4N | H | Arms Park, Cardiff | W | 18-0 |
| 59 | 9-Jan-04 | England | 4N | A | Welford Road, Leicester | D | 14-14 |
| 60 | 6-Feb-04 | Scotland | 4N | H | St Helen's, Swansea | W | 21-3 |
| 61 | 12-Mar-04 | Ireland | 4N | A | Balmoral Showgrounds, Belfast | L | 12-14 |
| 62 | 14-Jan-05 | England | 4N | H | Arms Park, Cardiff | W | 25-0 |
| 63 | 4-Feb-05 | Scotland | 4N | A | Inverleith, Edinburgh | W | 6-3 |
| 64 | 11-Mar-05 | Ireland | 4N | H | St Helen's, Swansea | W | 10-3 |
| 65 | 16-Dec-05 | New Zealand | Int | H | Arms Park, Cardiff | W | 3-0 |
| 66 | 13-Jan-06 | England | 4N | A | Athletic Ground, Richmond | W | 16-3 |
| 67 | 3-Feb-06 | Scotland | 4N | H | Arms Park, Cardiff | W | 9-3 |
| 68 | 10-Mar-06 | Ireland | 4N | A | Balmoral Showgrounds, Belfast | L | 6-11 |
| 69 | 1-Dec-06 | South Africa | Int | H | St Helen's, Swansea | L | 0-11 |
| 70 | 12-Jan-07 | England | 4N | H | St Helen's, Swansea | W | 22-0 |
| 71 | 2-Feb-07 | Scotland | 4N | A | Inverleith, Edinburgh | L | 3-6 |
| 72 | 9-Mar-07 | Ireland | 4N | H | Arms Park, Cardiff | W | 29-0 |
| 73 | 18-Jan-08 | England | 4N | A | Ashton Gate, Bristol | W | 28-18 |
| 74 | 1-Feb-08 | Scotland | 4N | H | St Helen's, Swansea | W | 6-5 |
| 75 | 2-Mar-08 | France | Int | H | Arms Park, Cardiff | W | 36-4 |
| 76 | 14-Mar-08 | Ireland | 4N | A | Balmoral Showgrounds, Belfast | W | 11-5 |
| 77 | 12-Dec-08 | Australia | Int | H | Arms Park, Cardiff | W | 9-6 |
| 78 | 16-Jan-09 | England | 4N | H | Arms Park, Cardiff | W | 8-0 |
| 79 | 6-Feb-09 | Scotland | 4N | A | Inverleith, Edinburgh | W | 5-3 |
| 80 | 23-Feb-09 | France | Int | A | Stade Colombes, Paris | W | 47-5 |

| No | Date | Opponents | Tmt | | Match Venue | Result | |
|----|------|-----------|-----|---|-------------|--------|---|
| 81 | 13-Mar-09 | Ireland | 4N | H | St Helen's, Swansea | W | 18-5 |
| 82 | 1-Jan-10 | France | 5N | H | St Helen's, Swansea | W | 49-14 |
| 83 | 15-Jan-10 | England | 5N | A | Twickenham, London | L | 6-11 |
| 84 | 5-Feb-10 | Scotland | 5N | H | Arms Park, Cardiff | W | 14-0 |
| 85 | 12-Mar-10 | Ireland | 5N | A | Lansdowne Road, Dublin | W | 19-3 |
| 86 | 21-Jan-11 | England | 5N | H | St Helen's, Swansea | W | 15-11 |
| 87 | 4-Feb-11 | Scotland | 5N | A | Inverleith, Edinburgh | W | 32-10 |
| 88 | 28-Feb-11 | France | 5N | A | Parc des Princess, Paris | W | 15-0 |
| 89 | 11-Mar-11 | Ireland | 5N | H | Arms Park, Cardiff | W | 16-0 |
| 90 | 20-Jan-12 | England | 5N | A | Twickenham, London | L | 0-8 |
| 91 | 3-Feb-12 | Scotland | 5N | H | St Helen's, Swansea | W | 21-6 |
| 92 | 9-Mar-12 | Ireland | 5N | A | Balmoral Showgrounds, Belfast | L | 5-12 |
| 93 | 25-Mar-12 | France | 5N | H | Rodney Parade, Newport | W | 14-8 |
| 94 | 14-Dec-12 | South Africa | Int | H | Arms Park, Cardiff | L | 0-3 |
| 95 | 18-Jan-13 | England | 5N | H | Arms Park, Cardiff | L | 0-12 |
| 96 | 1-Feb-13 | Scotland | 5N | A | Inverleith, Edinburgh | W | 8-0 |
| 97 | 27-Feb-13 | France | 5N | A | Parc des Princess, Paris | W | 11-8 |
| 98 | 8-Mar-13 | Ireland | 5N | H | St Helen's, Swansea | W | 16-13 |
| 99 | 17-Jan-14 | England | 5N | A | Twickenham, London | L | 9-10 |
| 100 | 7-Feb-14 | Scotland | 5N | H | Arms Park, Cardiff | W | 24-5 |
| 101 | 2-Mar-14 | France | 5N | H | St Helen's, Swansea | W | 31-0 |
| 102 | 14-Mar-14 | Ireland | 5N | A | Balmoral Showgrounds, Belfast | W | 11-3 |
| 103 | 21-Apr-19 | NZ Army | Int | H | St Helen's, Swansea | L | 3-6 |
| 104 | 17-Jan-20 | England | 5N | H | St Helen's, Swansea | W | 19-5 |
| 105 | 7-Feb-20 | Scotland | 5N | A | Inverleith, Edinburgh | L | 5-9 |
| 106 | 17-Feb-20 | France | 5N | A | Stade Colombes, Paris | W | 6-5 |
| 107 | 13-Mar-20 | Ireland | 5N | H | Arms Park, Cardiff | W | 28-4 |
| 108 | 15-Jan-21 | England | 5N | A | Twickenham, London | L | 3-18 |
| 109 | 5-Feb-21 | Scotland | 5N | H | St Helen's, Swansea | L | 8-14 |
| 110 | 26-Feb-21 | France | 5N | H | Arms Park, Cardiff | W | 12-4 |
| 111 | 12-Mar-21 | Ireland | 5N | A | Balmoral Showgrounds, Belfast | W | 6-0 |
| 112 | 21-Jan-22 | England | 5N | H | Arms Park, Cardiff | W | 28-6 |
| 113 | 4-Feb-22 | Scotland | 5N | A | Inverleith, Edinburgh | D | 9-9 |
| 114 | 11-Mar-22 | Ireland | 5N | H | St Helen's, Swansea | W | 11-5 |
| 115 | 23-Mar-22 | France | 5N | A | Stade Colombes, Paris | W | 11-3 |
| 116 | 20-Jan-23 | England | 5N | A | Twickenham, London | L | 3-7 |
| 117 | 3-Feb-23 | Scotland | 5N | H | Arms Park, Cardiff | L | 8-11 |
| 118 | 24-Feb-23 | France | 5N | H | St Helen's, Swansea | W | 16-8 |
| 119 | 10-Mar-23 | Ireland | 5N | A | Lansdowne Road, Dublin | L | 4-5 |
| 120 | 19-Jan-24 | England | 5N | H | St Helen's, Swansea | L | 9-17 |

WALES

| No | Date | Opponents | Tmt | | Match Venue | Result | |
|----|------|-----------|-----|---|-------------|--------|---|
| 121 | 2-Feb-24 | Scotland | 5N | A | Inverleith, Edinburgh | L | 10-35 |
| 122 | 8-Mar-24 | Ireland | 5N | H | Arms Park, Cardiff | L | 10-13 |
| 123 | 27-Mar-24 | France | 5N | A | Stade Colombes, Paris | W | 10-6 |
| 124 | 29-Nov-24 | New Zealand | Int | H | St Helen's, Swansea | L | 0-19 |
| 125 | 17-Jan-25 | England | 5N | A | Twickenham, London | L | 6-12 |
| 126 | 7-Feb-25 | Scotland | 5N | H | St Helen's, Swansea | L | 14-24 |
| 127 | 28-Feb-25 | France | 5N | H | Arms Park, Cardiff | W | 11-5 |
| 128 | 14-Mar-25 | Ireland | 5N | A | Ravenhill, Belfast | L | 3-19 |
| 129 | 16-Jan-26 | England | 5N | H | Arms Park, Cardiff | D | 3-3 |
| 130 | 6-Feb-26 | Scotland | 5N | A | Murrayfield, Edinburgh | L | 5-8 |
| 131 | 13-Mar-26 | Ireland | 5N | H | St Helen's, Swansea | W | 11-8 |
| 132 | 5-Apr-26 | France | 5N | A | Stade Colombes, Paris | W | 7-5 |
| 133 | 15-Jan-27 | England | 5N | A | Twickenham, London | L | 9-11 |
| 134 | 5-Feb-27 | Scotland | 5N | H | Arms Park, Cardiff | L | 0-5 |
| 135 | 26-Feb-27 | France | 5N | H | St Helen's, Swansea | W | 25-7 |
| 136 | 12-Mar-27 | Ireland | 5N | A | Lansdowne Road, Dublin | L | 9-19 |
| 137 | 26-Nov-27 | Australia | Int | H | Arms Park, Cardiff | L | 8-18 |
| 138 | 21-Jan-28 | England | 5N | H | St Helen's, Swansea | L | 8-10 |
| 139 | 4-Feb-28 | Scotland | 5N | A | Murrayfield, Edinburgh | W | 13-0 |
| 140 | 10-Mar-28 | Ireland | 5N | H | Arms Park, Cardiff | L | 10-13 |
| 141 | 9-Apr-28 | France | 5N | A | Stade Colombes, Paris | L | 3-8 |
| 142 | 19-Jan-29 | England | 5N | A | Twickenham, London | L | 3-8 |
| 143 | 2-Feb-29 | Scotland | 5N | H | St Helen's, Swansea | W | 14-7 |
| 144 | 23-Feb-29 | France | 5N | H | Arms Park, Cardiff | W | 8-3 |
| 145 | 9-Mar-29 | Ireland | 5N | A | Ravenhill, Belfast | D | 5-5 |
| 146 | 18-Jan-30 | England | 5N | H | Arms Park, Cardiff | L | 3-11 |
| 147 | 1-Feb-30 | Scotland | 5N | A | Murrayfield, Edinburgh | L | 9-12 |
| 148 | 8-Mar-30 | Ireland | 5N | H | St Helen's, Swansea | W | 12-7 |
| 149 | 21-Apr-30 | France | 5N | A | Stade Colombes, Paris | W | 11-0 |
| 150 | 17-Jan-31 | England | 5N | A | Twickenham, London | D | 11-11 |
| 151 | 7-Feb-31 | Scotland | 5N | H | Arms Park, Cardiff | W | 13-8 |
| 152 | 28-Feb-31 | France | 5N | H | St Helen's, Swansea | W | 35-3 |
| 153 | 14-Mar-31 | Ireland | 5N | A | Ravenhill, Belfast | W | 15-3 |
| 154 | 5-Dec-31 | South Africa | Int | H | St Helen's, Swansea | L | 3-8 |
| 155 | 16-Jan-32 | England | 4N | H | St Helen's, Swansea | W | 12-5 |
| 156 | 6-Feb-32 | Scotland | 4N | A | Murrayfield, Edinburgh | W | 6-0 |
| 157 | 12-Mar-32 | Ireland | 4N | H | Arms Park, Cardiff | L | 10-12 |
| 158 | 21-Jan-33 | England | 4N | A | Twickenham, London | W | 7-3 |
| 159 | 4-Feb-33 | Scotland | 4N | H | St Helen's, Swansea | L | 3-11 |
| 160 | 11-Mar-33 | Ireland | 4N | A | Ravenhill, Belfast | L | 5-10 |

| No | Date | Opponents | Tmt | Match Venue | | Result | |
|---|---|---|---|---|---|---|---|
| 161 | 20-Jan-34 | England | 4N | H | Arms Park, Cardiff | L | 0-9 |
| 162 | 3-Feb-34 | Scotland | 4N | A | Murrayfield, Edinburgh | W | 13-6 |
| 163 | 10-Mar-34 | Ireland | 4N | H | St Helen's, Swansea | W | 13-0 |
| 164 | 19-Jan-35 | England | 4N | A | Twickenham, London | D | 3-3 |
| 165 | 2-Feb-35 | Scotland | 4N | H | Arms Park, Cardiff | W | 10-6 |
| 166 | 9-Mar-35 | Ireland | 4N | A | Ravenhill, Belfast | L | 3-9 |
| 167 | 21-Dec-35 | New Zealand | Int | H | Arms Park, Cardiff | W | 13-12 |
| 168 | 18-Jan-36 | England | 4N | H | St Helen's, Swansea | D | 0-0 |
| 169 | 1-Feb-36 | Scotland | 4N | A | Murrayfield, Edinburgh | W | 13-3 |
| 170 | 14-Mar-36 | Ireland | 4N | H | Arms Park, Cardiff | W | 3-0 |
| 171 | 16-Jan-37 | England | 4N | A | Twickenham, London | L | 3-4 |
| 172 | 6-Feb-37 | Scotland | 4N | H | St Helen's, Swansea | L | 6-13 |
| 173 | 3-Apr-37 | Ireland | 4N | A | Ravenhill, Belfast | L | 3-5 |
| 174 | 15-Jan-38 | England | 4N | H | Arms Park, Cardiff | W | 14-8 |
| 175 | 5-Feb-38 | Scotland | 4N | A | Murrayfield, Edinburgh | L | 6-8 |
| 176 | 12-Mar-38 | Ireland | 4N | H | St Helen's, Swansea | W | 11-5 |
| 177 | 21-Jan-39 | England | 4N | A | Twickenham, London | L | 0-3 |
| 178 | 4-Feb-39 | Scotland | 4N | H | Arms Park, Cardiff | W | 11-3 |
| 179 | 11-Mar-39 | Ireland | 4N | A | Ravenhill, Belfast | W | 7-0 |
| 180 | 18-Jan-47 | England | 5N | H | Arms Park, Cardiff | L | 6-9 |
| 181 | 1-Feb-47 | Scotland | 5N | A | Murrayfield, Edinburgh | W | 22-8 |
| 182 | 22-Mar-47 | France | 5N | A | Stade Colombes, Paris | W | 3-0 |
| 183 | 29-Mar-47 | Ireland | 5N | H | St Helen's, Swansea | W | 6-0 |
| 184 | 20-Dec-47 | Australia | Int | H | Arms Park, Cardiff | W | 6-0 |
| 185 | 17-Jan-48 | England | 5N | A | Twickenham, London | D | 3-3 |
| 186 | 7-Feb-48 | Scotland | 5N | H | Arms Park, Cardiff | W | 14-0 |
| 187 | 21-Feb-48 | France | 5N | H | St Helen's, Swansea | L | 3-11 |
| 188 | 13-Mar-48 | Ireland | 5N | A | Ravenhill, Belfast | L | 3-6 |
| 189 | 15-Jan-49 | England | 5N | H | Arms Park, Cardiff | W | 9-3 |
| 190 | 5-Feb-49 | Scotland | 5N | A | Murrayfield, Edinburgh | L | 5-6 |
| 191 | 12-Mar-49 | Ireland | 5N | H | St Helen's, Swansea | L | 0-5 |
| 192 | 26-Mar-49 | France | 5N | A | Stade Colombes, Paris | L | 3-5 |
| 193 | 21-Jan-50 | England | 5N | A | Twickenham, London | W | 11-5 |
| 194 | 4-Feb-50 | Scotland | 5N | H | St Helen's, Swansea | W | 12-0 |
| 195 | 11-Mar-50 | Ireland | 5N | A | Ravenhill, Belfast | W | 6-3 |
| 196 | 25-Mar-50 | France | 5N | H | Arms Park, Cardiff | W | 21-0 |
| 197 | 20-Jan-51 | England | 5N | H | St Helen's, Swansea | W | 23-5 |
| 198 | 3-Feb-51 | Scotland | 5N | A | Murrayfield, Edinburgh | L | 0-19 |
| 199 | 10-Mar-51 | Ireland | 5N | H | Arms Park, Cardiff | D | 3-3 |
| 200 | 7-Apr-51 | France | 5N | A | Stade Colombes, Paris | L | 3-8 |

| No | Date | Opponents | Tmt | | Match Venue | Result | |
|----|------|-----------|-----|---|-------------|--------|---|
| 201 | 22-Dec-51 | South Africa | Int | H | Arms Park, Cardiff | L | 3-6 |
| 202 | 19-Jan-52 | England | 5N | A | Twickenham, London | W | 8-6 |
| 203 | 2-Feb-52 | Scotland | 5N | H | Arms Park, Cardiff | W | 11-0 |
| 204 | 8-Mar-52 | Ireland | 5N | A | Lansdowne Road, Dublin | W | 14-3 |
| 205 | 22-Mar-52 | France | 5N | H | St Helen's, Swansea | W | 9-5 |
| 206 | 17-Jan-53 | England | 5N | H | Arms Park, Cardiff | L | 3-8 |
| 207 | 7-Feb-53 | Scotland | 5N | A | Murrayfield, Edinburgh | W | 12-0 |
| 208 | 14-Mar-53 | Ireland | 5N | H | St Helen's, Swansea | W | 5-3 |
| 209 | 28-Mar-53 | France | 5N | A | Stade Colombes, Paris | W | 6-3 |
| 210 | 19-Dec-53 | New Zealand | Int | H | Arms Park, Cardiff | W | 13-8 |
| 211 | 16-Jan-54 | England | 5N | A | Twickenham, London | L | 6-9 |
| 212 | 13-Mar-54 | Ireland | 5N | A | Lansdowne Road, Dublin | W | 12-9 |
| 213 | 27-Mar-54 | France | 5N | H | Arms Park, Cardiff | W | 19-13 |
| 214 | 10-Apr-54 | Scotland | 5N | H | St Helen's, Swansea | W | 15-3 |
| 215 | 22-Jan-55 | England | 5N | H | Arms Park, Cardiff | W | 3-0 |
| 216 | 5-Feb-55 | Scotland | 5N | A | Murrayfield, Edinburgh | L | 8-14 |
| 217 | 12-Mar-55 | Ireland | 5N | H | Arms Park, Cardiff | W | 21-3 |
| 218 | 26-Mar-55 | France | 5N | A | Stade Colombes, Paris | W | 16-11 |
| 219 | 21-Jan-56 | England | 5N | A | Twickenham, London | W | 8-3 |
| 220 | 4-Feb-56 | Scotland | 5N | H | Arms Park, Cardiff | W | 9-3 |
| 221 | 10-Mar-56 | Ireland | 5N | A | Lansdowne Road, Dublin | L | 3-11 |
| 222 | 24-Mar-56 | France | 5N | H | Arms Park, Cardiff | W | 5-3 |
| 223 | 19-Jan-57 | England | 5N | H | Arms Park, Cardiff | L | 0-3 |
| 224 | 2-Feb-57 | Scotland | 5N | A | Murrayfield, Edinburgh | L | 6-9 |
| 225 | 9-Mar-57 | Ireland | 5N | H | Arms Park, Cardiff | W | 6-5 |
| 226 | 23-Mar-57 | France | 5N | A | Stade Colombes, Paris | W | 19-13 |
| 227 | 4-Jan-58 | Australia | Int | H | Arms Park, Cardiff | W | 9-3 |
| 228 | 18-Jan-58 | England | 5N | A | Twickenham, London | D | 3-3 |
| 229 | 1-Feb-58 | Scotland | 5N | H | Arms Park, Cardiff | W | 8-3 |
| 230 | 15-Mar-58 | Ireland | 5N | A | Lansdowne Road, Dublin | W | 9-6 |
| 231 | 29-Mar-58 | France | 5N | H | Arms Park, Cardiff | L | 6-16 |
| 232 | 17-Jan-59 | England | 5N | H | Arms Park, Cardiff | W | 5-0 |
| 233 | 7-Feb-59 | Scotland | 5N | A | Murrayfield, Edinburgh | L | 5-6 |
| 234 | 14-Mar-59 | Ireland | 5N | H | Arms Park, Cardiff | W | 8-6 |
| 235 | 4-Apr-59 | France | 5N | A | Stade Colombes, Paris | L | 3-11 |
| 236 | 16-Jan-60 | England | 5N | A | Twickenham, London | L | 6-14 |
| 237 | 6-Feb-60 | Scotland | 5N | H | Arms Park, Cardiff | W | 8-0 |
| 238 | 12-Mar-60 | Ireland | 5N | A | Lansdowne Road, Dublin | W | 10-9 |
| 239 | 26-Mar-60 | France | 5N | H | Arms Park, Cardiff | L | 8-16 |
| 240 | 3-Dec-60 | South Africa | Int | H | Arms Park, Cardiff | L | 0-3 |

| No | Date | Opponents | Tmt | Match Venue | Result | |
|---|---|---|---|---|---|---|
| 241 | 21-Jan-61 | England | 5N | H | Arms Park, Cardiff | W | 6-3 |
| 242 | 11-Feb-61 | Scotland | 5N | A | Murrayfield, Edinburgh | L | 0-3 |
| 243 | 11-Mar-61 | Ireland | 5N | H | Arms Park, Cardiff | W | 9-0 |
| 244 | 25-Mar-61 | France | 5N | A | Stade Colombes, Paris | L | 6-8 |
| 245 | 20-Jan-62 | England | 5N | A | Twickenham, London | D | 0-0 |
| 246 | 3-Feb-62 | Scotland | 5N | H | Arms Park, Cardiff | L | 3-8 |
| 247 | 24-Mar-62 | France | 5N | H | Arms Park, Cardiff | W | 3-0 |
| 248 | 17-Nov-62 | Ireland | 5N | A | Lansdowne Road, Dublin | D | 3-3 |
| 249 | 19-Jan-63 | England | 5N | H | Arms Park, Cardiff | L | 6-13 |
| 250 | 2-Feb-63 | Scotland | 5N | A | Murrayfield, Edinburgh | W | 6-0 |
| 251 | 9-Mar-63 | Ireland | 5N | H | Arms Park, Cardiff | L | 6-14 |
| 252 | 23-Mar-63 | France | 5N | A | Stade Colombes, Paris | L | 3-5 |
| 253 | 21-Dec-63 | New Zealand | Int | H | Arms Park, Cardiff | L | 0-6 |
| 254 | 18-Jan-64 | England | 5N | A | Twickenham, London | D | 6-6 |
| 255 | 1-Feb-64 | Scotland | 5N | H | Arms Park, Cardiff | W | 11-3 |
| 256 | 7-Mar-64 | Ireland | 5N | A | Lansdowne Road, Dublin | W | 15-6 |
| 257 | 21-Mar-64 | France | 5N | H | Arms Park, Cardiff | D | 11-11 |
| 258 | 23-May-64 | South Africa | Int-T | A | Kings Park Stadium, Durban | L | 3-24 |
| 259 | 16-Jan-65 | England | 5N | H | Arms Park, Cardiff | W | 14-3 |
| 260 | 6-Feb-65 | Scotland | 5N | A | Murrayfield, Edinburgh | W | 14-12 |
| 261 | 13-Mar-65 | Ireland | 5N | H | Arms Park, Cardiff | W | 14-8 |
| 262 | 27-Mar-65 | France | 5N | A | Stade Colombes, Paris | L | 13-22 |
| 263 | 15-Jan-66 | England | 5N | A | Twickenham, London | W | 11-6 |
| 264 | 5-Feb-66 | Scotland | 5N | H | Arms Park, Cardiff | W | 8-3 |
| 265 | 12-Mar-66 | Ireland | 5N | A | Lansdowne Road, Dublin | L | 6-9 |
| 266 | 26-Mar-66 | France | 5N | H | Arms Park, Cardiff | W | 9-8 |
| 267 | 3-Dec-66 | Australia | Int | H | Arms Park, Cardiff | L | 11-14 |
| 268 | 4-Feb-67 | Scotland | 5N | A | Murrayfield, Edinburgh | L | 5-11 |
| 269 | 11-Mar-67 | Ireland | 5N | H | Arms Park, Cardiff | L | 0-3 |
| 270 | 1-Apr-67 | France | 5N | A | Stade Colombes, Paris | L | 14-20 |
| 271 | 15-Apr-67 | England | 5N | H | Arms Park, Cardiff | W | 34-21 |
| 272 | 11-Nov-67 | New Zealand | Int | H | Arms Park, Cardiff | L | 6-13 |
| 273 | 20-Jan-68 | England | 5N | A | Twickenham, London | D | 11-11 |
| 274 | 3-Feb-68 | Scotland | 5N | H | Arms Park, Cardiff | W | 5-0 |
| 275 | 9-Mar-68 | Ireland | 5N | A | Lansdowne Road, Dublin | L | 6-9 |
| 276 | 23-Mar-68 | France | 5N | H | Arms Park, Cardiff | L | 9-14 |
| 277 | 1-Feb-69 | Scotland | 5N | A | Murrayfield, Edinburgh | W | 17-3 |
| 278 | 8-Mar-69 | Ireland | 5N | H | National Stadium, Cardiff | W | 24-11 |
| 279 | 22-Mar-69 | France | 5N | A | Stade Colombes, Paris | D | 8-8 |
| 280 | 12-Apr-69 | England | 5N | H | National Stadium, Cardiff | W | 30-9 |

| No | Date | Opponents | Tmt | | Match Venue | | Result |
|----|------|-----------|-----|---|-------------|---|--------|
| 281 | 31-May-69 | New Zealand | Int-T | A | Lancaster Park Oval, Christchurch | L | 0-19 |
| 282 | 14-Jun-69 | New Zealand | Int-T | A | Eden Park, Auckland | L | 12-33 |
| 283 | 21-Jun-69 | Australia | Int-T | A | Cricket Ground, Sydney | W | 19-16 |
| 284 | 24-Jan-70 | South Africa | Int | H | National Stadium, Cardiff | D | 6-6 |
| 285 | 7-Feb-70 | Scotland | 5N | H | National Stadium, Cardiff | W | 18-9 |
| 286 | 28-Feb-70 | England | 5N | A | Twickenham, London | W | 17-13 |
| 287 | 14-Mar-70 | Ireland | 5N | A | Lansdowne Road, Dublin | L | 0-14 |
| 288 | 4-Apr-70 | France | 5N | H | National Stadium, Cardiff | W | 11-6 |
| 289 | 16-Jan-71 | England | 5N | H | National Stadium, Cardiff | W | 22-6 |
| 290 | 6-Feb-71 | Scotland | 5N | A | Murrayfield, Edinburgh | W | 19-18 |
| 291 | 13-Mar-71 | Ireland | 5N | H | National Stadium, Cardiff | W | 23-9 |
| 292 | 27-Mar-71 | France | 5N | A | Stade Colombes, Paris | W | 9-5 |
| 293 | 15-Jan-72 | England | 5N | A | Twickenham, London | W | 12-3 |
| 294 | 5-Feb-72 | Scotland | 5N | H | National Stadium, Cardiff | W | 35-12 |
| 295 | 25-Mar-72 | France | 5N | H | National Stadium, Cardiff | W | 20-6 |
| 296 | 2-Dec-72 | New Zealand | Int | H | National Stadium, Cardiff | L | 16-19 |
| 297 | 20-Jan-73 | England | 5N | H | National Stadium, Cardiff | W | 25-9 |
| 298 | 3-Feb-73 | Scotland | 5N | A | Murrayfield, Edinburgh | L | 9-10 |
| 299 | 10-Mar-73 | Ireland | 5N | H | National Stadium, Cardiff | W | 16-12 |
| 300 | 24-Mar-73 | France | 5N | A | Parc des Princess, Paris | L | 3-12 |
| 301 | 10-Nov-73 | Australia | Int | H | National Stadium, Cardiff | W | 24-0 |
| 302 | 19-Jan-74 | Scotland | 5N | H | National Stadium, Cardiff | W | 6-0 |
| 303 | 2-Feb-74 | Ireland | 5N | A | Lansdowne Road, Dublin | D | 9-9 |
| 304 | 16-Feb-74 | France | 5N | H | National Stadium, Cardiff | D | 16-16 |
| 305 | 16-Mar-74 | England | 5N | A | Twickenham, London | L | 12-16 |
| 306 | 18-Jan-75 | France | 5N | A | Parc des Princess, Paris | W | 25-10 |
| 307 | 15-Feb-75 | England | 5N | H | National Stadium, Cardiff | W | 20-4 |
| 308 | 1-Mar-75 | Scotland | 5N | A | Murrayfield, Edinburgh | L | 10-12 |
| 309 | 15-Mar-75 | Ireland | 5N | H | National Stadium, Cardiff | W | 32-4 |
| 310 | 20-Dec-75 | Australia | Int | H | National Stadium, Cardiff | W | 28-3 |
| 311 | 17-Jan-76 | England | 5N | A | Twickenham, London | W | 21-9 |
| 312 | 7-Feb-76 | Scotland | 5N | H | National Stadium, Cardiff | W | 28-6 |
| 313 | 21-Feb-76 | Ireland | 5N | A | Lansdowne Road, Dublin | W | 34-9 |
| 314 | 6-Mar-76 | France | 5N | H | National Stadium, Cardiff | W | 19-13 |
| 315 | 15-Jan-77 | Ireland | 5N | H | National Stadium, Cardiff | W | 25-9 |
| 316 | 5-Feb-77 | France | 5N | A | Parc des Princess, Paris | L | 9-16 |
| 317 | 5-Mar-77 | England | 5N | H | National Stadium, Cardiff | W | 14-9 |
| 318 | 19-Mar-77 | Scotland | 5N | A | Murrayfield, Edinburgh | W | 18-9 |
| 319 | 4-Feb-78 | England | 5N | A | Twickenham, London | W | 9-6 |
| 320 | 18-Feb-78 | Scotland | 5N | H | National Stadium, Cardiff | W | 22-14 |

| No | Date | Opponents | Tmt | | Match Venue | Result | |
|-----|------------|-------------|-------|---|------------------------------|---|-------|
| 321 | 4-Mar-78 | Ireland | 5N | A | Lansdowne Road, Dublin | W | 20-16 |
| 322 | 18-Mar-78 | France | 5N | H | National Stadium, Cardiff | W | 16-7 |
| 323 | 11-Jun-78 | Australia | Int-T | A | Ballymore Oval, Brisbane | L | 8-18 |
| 324 | 17-Jun-78 | Australia | Int-T | A | Cricket Ground, Sydney | L | 17-19 |
| 325 | 11-Nov-78 | New Zealand | Int | H | National Stadium, Cardiff | L | 12-13 |
| 326 | 20-Jan-79 | Scotland | 5N | A | Murrayfield, Edinburgh | W | 19-13 |
| 327 | 3-Feb-79 | Ireland | 5N | H | National Stadium, Cardiff | W | 24-21 |
| 328 | 17-Feb-79 | France | 5N | A | Parc des Princess, Paris | L | 13-14 |
| 329 | 17-Mar-79 | England | 5N | H | National Stadium, Cardiff | W | 27-3 |
| 330 | 19-Jan-80 | France | 5N | H | National Stadium, Cardiff | W | 18-9 |
| 331 | 16-Feb-80 | England | 5N | A | Twickenham, London | L | 8-9 |
| 332 | 1-Mar-80 | Scotland | 5N | H | National Stadium, Cardiff | W | 17-6 |
| 333 | 15-Mar-80 | Ireland | 5N | A | Lansdowne Road, Dublin | L | 7-21 |
| 334 | 1-Nov-80 | New Zealand | Int | H | National Stadium, Cardiff | L | 3-23 |
| 335 | 17-Jan-81 | England | 5N | H | National Stadium, Cardiff | W | 21-19 |
| 336 | 7-Feb-81 | Scotland | 5N | A | Murrayfield, Edinburgh | L | 6-15 |
| 337 | 21-Feb-81 | Ireland | 5N | H | National Stadium, Cardiff | W | 9-8 |
| 338 | 7-Mar-81 | France | 5N | A | Parc des Princess, Paris | L | 15-19 |
| 339 | 5-Dec-81 | Australia | Int | H | National Stadium, Cardiff | W | 18-13 |
| 340 | 23-Jan-82 | Ireland | 5N | A | Lansdowne Road, Dublin | L | 12-20 |
| 341 | 6-Feb-82 | France | 5N | H | National Stadium, Cardiff | W | 22-12 |
| 342 | 6-Mar-82 | England | 5N | A | Twickenham, London | L | 7-17 |
| 343 | 20-Mar-82 | Scotland | 5N | H | National Stadium, Cardiff | L | 18-34 |
| 344 | 5-Feb-83 | England | 5N | H | National Stadium, Cardiff | D | 13-13 |
| 345 | 19-Feb-83 | Scotland | 5N | A | Murrayfield, Edinburgh | W | 19-15 |
| 346 | 5-Mar-83 | Ireland | 5N | H | National Stadium, Cardiff | W | 23-9 |
| 347 | 19-Mar-83 | France | 5N | A | Parc des Princess, Paris | L | 9-16 |
| 348 | 12-Nov-83 | Romania | Int | A | Stadionul 23 August, Bucharest | L | 6-24 |
| 349 | 21-Jan-84 | Scotland | 5N | H | National Stadium, Cardiff | L | 9-15 |
| 350 | 4-Feb-84 | Ireland | 5N | A | Lansdowne Road, Dublin | W | 18-9 |
| 351 | 18-Feb-84 | France | 5N | H | National Stadium, Cardiff | L | 16-21 |
| 352 | 17-Mar-84 | England | 5N | A | Twickenham, London | W | 24-15 |
| 353 | 24-Nov-84 | Australia | Int | H | National Stadium, Cardiff | L | 9-28 |
| 354 | 2-Mar-85 | Scotland | 5N | A | Murrayfield, Edinburgh | W | 25-21 |
| 355 | 16-Mar-85 | Ireland | 5N | H | National Stadium, Cardiff | L | 9-21 |
| 356 | 30-Mar-85 | France | 5N | A | Parc des Princess, Paris | L | 3-14 |
| 357 | 20-Apr-85 | England | 5N | H | National Stadium, Cardiff | W | 24-15 |
| 358 | 9-Nov-85 | Fiji | Int | H | National Stadium, Cardiff | W | 40-3 |
| 359 | 18-Jan-86 | England | 5N | A | Twickenham, London | L | 18-21 |
| 360 | 1-Feb-86 | Scotland | 5N | H | National Stadium, Cardiff | W | 22-15 |

| No | Date | Opponents | Tmt | | Match Venue | Result | |
|----|------|-----------|-----|---|-------------|--------|---|
| 361 | 15-Feb-86 | Ireland | 5N | A | Lansdowne Road, Dublin | W | 19-12 |
| 362 | 1-Mar-86 | France | 5N | H | National Stadium, Cardiff | L | 15-23 |
| 363 | 31-May-86 | Fiji | Int-T | A | National Stadium, Suva | W | 22-15 |
| 364 | 12-Jun-86 | Tonga | Int-T | A | Teufaiva Sport Stadium, Nuku'alofa | W | 15-7 |
| 365 | 14-Jun-86 | Western Samoa | Int-T | A | Apia Park, Apia | W | 32-14 |
| 366 | 7-Feb-87 | France | 5N | A | Parc des Princess, Paris | L | 9-16 |
| 367 | 7-Mar-87 | England | 5N | H | National Stadium, Cardiff | W | 19-12 |
| 368 | 21-Mar-87 | Scotland | 5N | A | Murrayfield, Edinburgh | L | 15-21 |
| 369 | 4-Apr-87 | Ireland | 5N | H | National Stadium, Cardiff | L | 11-15 |
| 370 | 25-May-87 | Ireland | WCp | N | Athletic Park, Wellington | W | 13-6 |
| 371 | 29-May-87 | Tonga | WCp | N | Showgrounds Oval, Palmerston North | W | 29-16 |
| 372 | 3-Jun-87 | Canada | WCp | N | Rugby Park Stadium, Invercargill | W | 40-9 |
| 373 | 8-Jun-87 | England | WCqf | N | Ballymore Oval, Brisbane | W | 16-3 |
| 374 | 14-Jun-87 | New Zealand | WCsf | N | Ballymore Oval, Brisbane | L | 6-49 |
| 375 | 18-Jun-87 | Australia | WC34 | N | Rotorua International Stadium, Rotorua | W | 22-21 |
| 376 | 7-Nov-87 | United States | Int | H | National Stadium, Cardiff | W | 46-0 |
| 377 | 6-Feb-88 | England | 5N | A | Twickenham, London | W | 11-3 |
| 378 | 20-Feb-88 | Scotland | 5N | H | National Stadium, Cardiff | W | 25-20 |
| 379 | 5-Mar-88 | Ireland | 5N | A | Lansdowne Road, Dublin | W | 12-9 |
| 380 | 19-Mar-88 | France | 5N | H | National Stadium, Cardiff | L | 9-10 |
| 381 | 28-May-88 | New Zealand | Int-T | A | Lancaster Park Oval, Christchurch | L | 3-52 |
| 382 | 11-Jun-88 | New Zealand | Int-T | A | Eden Park, Auckland | L | 9-54 |
| 383 | 12-Nov-88 | Western Samoa | Int | H | National Stadium, Cardiff | W | 28-6 |
| 384 | 10-Dec-88 | Romania | Int | H | National Stadium, Cardiff | L | 9-15 |
| 385 | 21-Jan-89 | Scotland | 5N | A | Murrayfield, Edinburgh | L | 7-23 |
| 386 | 4-Feb-89 | Ireland | 5N | H | National Stadium, Cardiff | L | 13-19 |
| 387 | 18-Feb-89 | France | 5N | A | Parc des Princess, Paris | L | 12-31 |
| 388 | 18-Mar-89 | England | 5N | H | National Stadium, Cardiff | W | 12-9 |
| 389 | 4-Nov-89 | New Zealand | Int | H | National Stadium, Cardiff | L | 9-34 |
| 390 | 20-Jan-90 | France | 5N | H | National Stadium, Cardiff | L | 19-29 |
| 391 | 17-Feb-90 | England | 5N | A | Twickenham, London | L | 6-34 |
| 392 | 3-Mar-90 | Scotland | 5N | H | National Stadium, Cardiff | L | 9-13 |
| 393 | 24-Mar-90 | Ireland | 5N | A | Lansdowne Road, Dublin | L | 8-14 |
| 394 | 2-Jun-90 | Namibia | Int-T | A | South-West Stadium, Windhoek | W | 18-9 |
| 395 | 9-Jun-90 | Namibia | Int-T | A | South-West Stadium, Windhoek | W | 34-30 |
| 396 | 6-Oct-90 | Barbarians | Int | H | National Stadium, Cardiff | L | 24-31 |
| 397 | 19-Jan-91 | England | 5N | H | National Stadium, Cardiff | L | 6-25 |
| 398 | 2-Feb-91 | Scotland | 5N | A | Murrayfield, Edinburgh | L | 12-32 |
| 399 | 16-Feb-91 | Ireland | 5N | H | National Stadium, Cardiff | D | 21-21 |
| 400 | 2-Mar-91 | France | 5N | A | Parc des Princess, Paris | L | 3-36 |

| No | Date | Opponents | Tmt | Match Venue | Result | |
|-----|----------|-----------|-------|-------------|--------|------|
| 401 | 22-Jul-91 | Australia | Int-T | A Ballymore Oval, Brisbane | L | 6-63 |
| 402 | 4-Sep-91 | France | Int | H National Stadium, Cardiff | L | 9-22 |
| 403 | 6-Oct-91 | Western Samoa | WCp | H National Stadium, Cardiff | L | 13-16 |
| 404 | 9-Oct-91 | Argentina | WCp | H National Stadium, Cardiff | W | 16-7 |
| 405 | 12-Oct-91 | Australia | WCp | H National Stadium, Cardiff | L | 3-38 |
| 406 | 18-Jan-92 | Ireland | 5N | A Lansdowne Road, Dublin | W | 16-15 |
| 407 | 1-Feb-92 | France | 5N | H National Stadium, Cardiff | L | 9-12 |
| 408 | 7-Mar-92 | England | 5N | A Twickenham, London | L | 0-24 |
| 409 | 21-Mar-92 | Scotland | 5N | H National Stadium, Cardiff | W | 15-12 |
| 410 | 21-Nov-92 | Australia | Int | H National Stadium, Cardiff | L | 6-23 |
| 411 | 6-Feb-93 | England | 5N | H National Stadium, Cardiff | W | 10-9 |
| 412 | 20-Feb-93 | Scotland | 5N | A Murrayfield, Edinburgh | L | 0-20 |
| 413 | 6-Mar-93 | Ireland | 5N | H National Stadium, Cardiff | L | 14-19 |
| 414 | 20-Mar-93 | France | 5N | A Parc des Princess, Paris | L | 10-26 |
| 415 | 22-May-93 | Zimbabwe | Int-T | A Hartsfield Rugby Ground, Bulawayo | W | 35-14 |
| 416 | 29-May-93 | Zimbabwe | Int-T | A Police Ground, Harare | W | 42-13 |
| 417 | 5-Jun-93 | Namibia | Int-T | A South West Stadium, Windhoek | W | 38-23 |
| 418 | 16-Oct-93 | Japan | Int | H National Stadium, Cardiff | W | 55-5 |
| 419 | 10-Nov-93 | Canada | Int | H National Stadium, Cardiff | L | 24-26 |
| 420 | 15-Jan-94 | Scotland | 5N | H National Stadium, Cardiff | W | 29-6 |
| 421 | 5-Feb-94 | Ireland | 5N | A Lansdowne Road, Dublin | W | 17-15 |
| 422 | 19-Feb-94 | France | 5N | H National Stadium, Cardiff | W | 24-15 |
| 423 | 19-Mar-94 | England | 5N | A Twickenham, London | L | 8-15 |
| 424 | 18-May-94 | Portugal | WCQ | A Estádio Universitário de Lisboa, Lisbon | W | 102-11 |
| 425 | 21-May-94 | Spain | WCQ | A Campo Ciudad Universitaria, Madrid | W | 54-0 |
| 426 | 11-Jun-94 | Canada | Int-T | A Fletcher's Field, Markham, Toronto | W | 33-15 |
| 427 | 18-Jun-94 | Fiji | Int-T | A National Stadium, Suva | W | 23-8 |
| 428 | 22-Jun-94 | Tonga | Int-T | A Teufaiva Sport Stadium, Nuku'alofa | W | 18-9 |
| 429 | 25-Jun-94 | Western Samoa | Int-T | A Chanel College, Moamoa, Apia | L | 9-34 |
| 430 | 17-Sep-94 | Romania | WCQ | A Stadionul 23 August, Bucharest | W | 16-9 |
| 431 | 12-Oct-94 | Italy | WCQ | H National Stadium, Cardiff | W | 29-19 |
| 432 | 26-Nov-94 | South Africa | Int | H National Stadium, Cardiff | L | 12-20 |
| 433 | 21-Jan-95 | France | 5N | A Parc des Princess, Paris | L | 9-21 |
| 434 | 18-Feb-95 | England | 5N | H National Stadium, Cardiff | L | 9-23 |
| 435 | 4-Mar-95 | Scotland | 5N | A Murrayfield, Edinburgh | L | 13-26 |
| 436 | 18-Mar-95 | Ireland | 5N | H National Stadium, Cardiff | L | 12-16 |
| 437 | 27-May-95 | Japan | WCp | N Free State Stadium, Bloemfontein | W | 57-10 |
| 438 | 31-May-95 | New Zealand | WCp | N Ellis Park, Johannesburg | L | 9-34 |
| 439 | 4-Jun-95 | Ireland | WCp | N Ellis Park, Johannesburg | L | 23-24 |
| 440 | 2-Sep-95 | South Africa | Int-T | A Ellis Park, Johannesburg | L | 11-40 |

| No | Date | Opponents | Tmt | | Match Venue | Result | |
|----|------|-----------|-----|---|-------------|--------|---|
| 441 | 11-Nov-95 | Fiji | Int | H | National Stadium, Cardiff | W | 19-15 |
| 442 | 16-Jan-96 | Italy | Int | H | National Stadium, Cardiff | W | 31-26 |
| 443 | 3-Feb-96 | England | 5N | A | Twickenham, London | L | 15-21 |
| 444 | 17-Feb-96 | Scotland | 5N | H | National Stadium, Cardiff | L | 14-16 |
| 445 | 2-Mar-96 | Ireland | 5N | A | Lansdowne Road, Dublin | L | 17-30 |
| 446 | 16-Mar-96 | France | 5N | H | National Stadium, Cardiff | W | 16-15 |
| 447 | 9-Jun-96 | Australia | Int-T | A | Ballymore Oval, Brisbane | L | 25-56 |
| 448 | 22-Jun-96 | Australia | Int-T | A | Football Stadium, Sydney | L | 3-42 |
| 449 | 24-Aug-96 | Barbarians | Int | H | National Stadium, Cardiff | W | 31-10 |
| 450 | 25-Sep-96 | France | Int | H | National Stadium, Cardiff | L | 33-40 |
| 451 | 5-Oct-96 | Italy | Int | A | Stadio Olimpico, Rome | W | 31-22 |
| 452 | 1-Dec-96 | Australia | Int | H | National Stadium, Cardiff | L | 19-28 |
| 453 | 15-Dec-96 | South Africa | Int | H | National Stadium, Cardiff | L | 20-37 |
| 454 | 11-Jan-97 | United States | Int | H | National Stadium, Cardiff | W | 34-14 |
| 455 | 18-Jan-97 | Scotland | 5N | A | Murrayfield, Edinburgh | W | 34-19 |
| 456 | 1-Feb-97 | Ireland | 5N | H | National Stadium, Cardiff | L | 25-26 |
| 457 | 15-Feb-97 | France | 5N | A | Parc des Princess, Paris | L | 22-27 |
| 458 | 15-Mar-97 | England | 5N | H | National Stadium, Cardiff | L | 13-34 |
| 459 | 5-Jul-97 | United States | Int-T | A | Brook's Field, Wilmington, North Carolina | W | 30-20 |
| 460 | 12-Jul-97 | United States | Int-T | A | Boxer Stadium, San Francisco | W | 28-23 |
| 461 | 19-Jul-97 | Canada | Int-T | A | Fletcher's Field, Markham, Toronto | W | 28-25 |
| 462 | 30-Aug-97 | Romania | Int | H | The Racecourse, Wrexham | W | 70-21 |
| 463 | 16-Nov-97 | Tonga | Int | H | St Helen's, Swansea | W | 46-12 |
| 464 | 29-Nov-97 | New Zealand | Int | N | Wembley Stadium, London | L | 7-42 |
| 465 | 7-Feb-98 | Italy | Int | H | Stradey Park, Llanelli | W | 23-20 |
| 466 | 21-Feb-98 | England | 5N | A | Twickenham, London | L | 26-60 |
| 467 | 7-Mar-98 | Scotland | 5N | N | Wembley Stadium, London | W | 19-13 |
| 468 | 21-Mar-98 | Ireland | 5N | A | Lansdowne Road, Dublin | W | 30-21 |
| 469 | 5-Apr-98 | France | 5N | N | Wembley Stadium, London | L | 0-51 |
| 470 | 6-Jun-98 | Zimbabwe | Int-T | A | National Sports Stadium, Harare | W | 49-11 |
| 471 | 27-Jun-98 | South Africa | Int-T | A | Minolta Loftus Stadium, Pretoria | L | 13-96 |
| 472 | 14-Nov-98 | South Africa | Int | N | Wembley Stadium, London | L | 20-28 |
| 473 | 21-Nov-98 | Argentina | Int | H | Stradey Park, Llanelli | W | 43-30 |
| 474 | 6-Feb-99 | Scotland | 5N | A | Murrayfield, Edinburgh | L | 20-33 |
| 475 | 20-Feb-99 | Ireland | 5N | N | Wembley Stadium, London | L | 23-29 |
| 476 | 6-Mar-99 | France | 5N | A | Stade de France, Paris | W | 34-33 |
| 477 | 20-Mar-99 | Italy | Int | A | Stadio Comunale di Monigo, Treviso | W | 60-21 |
| 478 | 11-Apr-99 | England | 5N | N | Wembley Stadium, London | W | 32-31 |
| 479 | 5-Jun-99 | Argentina | Int-T | A | Ferro Carril Oeste Stadium, B Aires | W | 36-26 |
| 480 | 12-Jun-99 | Argentina | Int-T | A | Ferro Carril Oeste Stadium, B Aires | W | 23-16 |

| No | Date | Opponents | Tmt | | Match Venue | Result | |
|---|---|---|---|---|---|---|---|
| 481 | 26-Jun-99 | South Africa | Int | H | Millennium Stadium, Cardiff | W | 29-19 |
| 482 | 21-Aug-99 | Canada | Int | H | Millennium Stadium, Cardiff | W | 33-19 |
| 483 | 28-Aug-99 | France | Int | H | Millennium Stadium, Cardiff | W | 34-23 |
| 484 | 1-Oct-99 | Argentina | WCp | H | Millennium Stadium, Cardiff | W | 23-18 |
| 485 | 9-Oct-99 | Japan | WCp | H | Millennium Stadium, Cardiff | W | 64-15 |
| 486 | 14-Oct-99 | Samoa | WCp | H | Millennium Stadium, Cardiff | L | 31-38 |
| 487 | 23-Oct-99 | Australia | WCqf | H | Millennium Stadium, Cardiff | L | 9-24 |
| 488 | 5-Feb-00 | France | 6N | H | Millennium Stadium, Cardiff | L | 3-36 |
| 489 | 19-Feb-00 | Italy | 6N | H | Millennium Stadium, Cardiff | W | 47-16 |
| 490 | 4-Mar-00 | England | 6N | A | Twickenham, London | L | 12-46 |
| 491 | 18-Mar-00 | Scotland | 6N | H | Millennium Stadium, Cardiff | W | 26-18 |
| 492 | 1-Apr-00 | Ireland | 6N | A | Lansdowne Road, Dublin | W | 23-19 |
| 493 | 11-Nov-00 | Samoa | Int | H | Millennium Stadium, Cardiff | W | 50-6 |
| 494 | 18-Nov-00 | United States | Int | H | Millennium Stadium, Cardiff | W | 42-11 |
| 495 | 26-Nov-00 | South Africa | Int | H | Millennium Stadium, Cardiff | L | 13-23 |
| 496 | 3-Feb-01 | England | 6N | H | Millennium Stadium, Cardiff | L | 15-44 |
| 497 | 17-Feb-01 | Scotland | 6N | A | Murrayfield, Edinburgh | D | 28-28 |
| 498 | 17-Mar-01 | France | 6N | A | Stade de France, Paris | W | 43-35 |
| 499 | 8-Apr-01 | Italy | 6N | A | Stadio Flaminio, Rome | W | 33-23 |
| 500 | 10-Jun-01 | Japan | Int-T | A | Hanazono Stadium, Osaka | W | 64-10 |
| 501 | 17-Jun-01 | Japan | Int-T | A | Prince Chichibu Memorial Ground, Tokyo | W | 53-30 |
| 502 | 19-Sep-01 | Romania | Int | H | Millennium Stadium, Cardiff | W | 81-9 |
| 503 | 13-Oct-01 | Ireland | 6N | H | Millennium Stadium, Cardiff | L | 6-36 |
| 504 | 10-Nov-01 | Argentina | Int | H | Millennium Stadium, Cardiff | L | 16-30 |
| 505 | 17-Nov-01 | Tonga | Int | H | Millennium Stadium, Cardiff | W | 51-7 |
| 506 | 25-Nov-01 | Australia | Int | H | Millennium Stadium, Cardiff | L | 13-21 |
| 507 | 3-Feb-02 | Ireland | 6N | A | Lansdowne Road, Dublin | L | 10-54 |
| 508 | 16-Feb-02 | France | 6N | H | Millennium Stadium, Cardiff | L | 33-37 |
| 509 | 2-Mar-02 | Italy | 6N | H | Millennium Stadium, Cardiff | W | 44-20 |
| 510 | 23-Mar-02 | England | 6N | A | Twickenham, London | L | 10-50 |
| 511 | 6-Apr-02 | Scotland | 6N | H | Millennium Stadium, Cardiff | L | 22-27 |
| 512 | 8-Jun-02 | South Africa | Int-T | A | Vodacom Park Stadium, Bloemfontein | L | 19-34 |
| 513 | 15-Jun-02 | South Africa | Int-T | A | Newlands Stadium, Cape Town | L | 8-19 |
| 514 | 1-Nov-02 | Romania | Int | H | The Racecourse, Wrexham | W | 40-3 |
| 515 | 9-Nov-02 | Fiji | Int | H | Millennium Stadium, Cardiff | W | 58-14 |
| 516 | 16-Nov-02 | Canada | Int | H | Millennium Stadium, Cardiff | W | 32-21 |
| 517 | 23-Nov-02 | New Zealand | Int | H | Millennium Stadium, Cardiff | L | 17-43 |
| 518 | 15-Feb-03 | Italy | 6N | A | Stadio Flaminio, Rome | L | 22-30 |
| 519 | 22-Feb-03 | England | 6N | H | Millennium Stadium, Cardiff | L | 9-26 |
| 520 | 8-Mar-03 | Scotland | 6N | A | Murrayfield, Edinburgh | L | 22-30 |

| No | Date | Opponents | Tmt | | Match Venue | Result | |
|-----|-----------|--------------|-------|---|------------------------------------------|---|-------|
| 521 | 22-Mar-03 | Ireland | 6N | H | Millennium Stadium, Cardiff | L | 24-25 |
| 522 | 29-Mar-03 | France | 6N | A | Stade de France, Paris | L | 5-33 |
| 523 | 14-Jun-03 | Australia | Int-T | A | Telstra Stadium, Sydney | L | 10-30 |
| 524 | 21-Jun-03 | New Zealand | Int-T | A | Waikato Stadium, Hamilton | L | 3-55 |
| 525 | 16-Aug-03 | Ireland | Int | A | Lansdowne Road, Dublin | L | 12-35 |
| 526 | 23-Aug-03 | England | Int | H | Millennium Stadium, Cardiff | L | 9-43 |
| 527 | 27-Aug-03 | Romania | Int | H | The Racecourse, Wrexham | W | 54-8 |
| 528 | 30-Aug-03 | Scotland | Int | H | Millennium Stadium, Cardiff | W | 23-9 |
| 529 | 12-Oct-03 | Canada | WCp | N | Telstra Dome, Melbourne | W | 41-10 |
| 530 | 19-Oct-03 | Tonga | WCp | N | Canberra Stadium, Canberra | W | 27-20 |
| 531 | 25-Oct-03 | Italy | WCp | N | Canberra Stadium, Canberra | W | 27-15 |
| 532 | 2-Nov-03 | New Zealand | WCp | N | Telstra Stadium, Sydney | L | 37-53 |
| 533 | 9-Nov-03 | England | WCqf | N | Suncorp Stadium, Brisbane | L | 17-28 |
| 534 | 14-Feb-04 | Scotland | 6N | H | Millennium Stadium, Cardiff | W | 23-10 |
| 535 | 22-Feb-04 | Ireland | 6N | A | Lansdowne Road, Dublin | L | 15-36 |
| 536 | 7-Mar-04 | France | 6N | H | Millennium Stadium, Cardiff | L | 22-29 |
| 537 | 20-Mar-04 | England | 6N | A | Twickenham, London | L | 21-31 |
| 538 | 27-Mar-04 | Italy | 6N | H | Millennium Stadium, Cardiff | W | 44-10 |
| 539 | 12-Jun-04 | Argentina | Int-T | A | Estadio Monumental José Fierro, Tucumán | L | 44-50 |
| 540 | 19-Jun-04 | Argentina | Int-T | A | Vélez Sarsfield Stadium, Buenos Aires | W | 35-20 |
| 541 | 26-Jun-04 | South Africa | Int-T | A | Securicor Loftus Stadium, Pretoria | L | 18-53 |
| 542 | 6-Nov-04 | South Africa | Int | H | Millennium Stadium, Cardiff | L | 36-38 |
| 543 | 12-Nov-04 | Romania | Int | H | Millennium Stadium, Cardiff | W | 66-7 |
| 544 | 20-Nov-04 | New Zealand | Int | H | Millennium Stadium, Cardiff | L | 25-26 |
| 545 | 26-Nov-04 | Japan | Int | H | Millennium Stadium, Cardiff | W | 98-0 |
| 546 | 5-Feb-05 | England | 6N | H | Millennium Stadium, Cardiff | W | 11-9 |
| 547 | 12-Feb-05 | Italy | 6N | A | Stadio Flaminio, Rome | W | 38-8 |
| 548 | 26-Feb-05 | France | 6N | A | Stade de France, Paris | W | 24-18 |
| 549 | 13-Mar-05 | Scotland | 6N | A | Murrayfield, Edinburgh | W | 46-22 |
| 550 | 19-Mar-05 | Ireland | 6N | H | Millennium Stadium, Cardiff | W | 32-20 |
| 551 | 4-Jun-05 | United States | Int-T | A | Rentschler Field, Hartford, Connecticut | W | 77-3 |
| 552 | 11-Jun-05 | Canada | Int-T | A | York Stadium, Toronto | W | 60-3 |
| 553 | 5-Nov-05 | New Zealand | Int | H | Millennium Stadium, Cardiff | L | 3-41 |
| 554 | 9-Nov-05 | Fiji | Int | H | Millennium Stadium, Cardiff | W | 11-10 |
| 555 | 19-Nov-05 | South Africa | Int | H | Millennium Stadium, Cardiff | L | 16-33 |
| 556 | 26-Nov-05 | Australia | Int | H | Millennium Stadium, Cardiff | W | 24-22 |
| 557 | 4-Feb-06 | England | 6N | A | Twickenham, London | L | 13-47 |
| 558 | 12-Feb-06 | Scotland | 6N | H | Millennium Stadium, Cardiff | W | 28-18 |
| 559 | 26-Feb-06 | Ireland | 6N | A | Lansdowne Road, Dublin | L | 5-31 |
| 560 | 11-Mar-06 | Italy | 6N | H | Millennium Stadium, Cardiff | D | 18-18 |

| No | Date | Opponents | Tmt | | Match Venue | Result | |
|-----|------|-----------|-----|---|------------|--------|---|
| 561 | 18-Mar-06 | France | 6N | H | Millennium Stadium, Cardiff | L | 16-21 |
| 562 | 11-Jun-06 | Argentina | Int-T | A | Estadio Raúl Conti, Puerto Madryn | L | 25-27 |
| 563 | 17-Jun-06 | Argentina | Int-T | A | Vélez Sarsfield Stadium, Buenos Aires | L | 27-45 |
| 564 | 4-Nov-06 | Australia | Int | H | Millennium Stadium, Cardiff | D | 29-29 |
| 565 | 11-Nov-06 | Pacific Islands | Int | H | Millennium Stadium, Cardiff | W | 38-20 |
| 566 | 17-Nov-06 | Canada | Int | H | Millennium Stadium, Cardiff | W | 61-26 |
| 567 | 25-Nov-06 | New Zealand | Int | H | Millennium Stadium, Cardiff | L | 10-45 |
| 568 | 4-Feb-07 | Ireland | 6N | H | Millennium Stadium, Cardiff | L | 9-19 |
| 569 | 10-Feb-07 | Scotland | 6N | A | Murrayfield, Edinburgh | L | 9-21 |
| 570 | 24-Feb-07 | France | 6N | A | Stade de France, Paris | L | 21-32 |
| 571 | 10-Mar-07 | Italy | 6N | A | Stadio Flaminio, Rome | L | 20-23 |
| 572 | 17-Mar-07 | England | 6N | H | Millennium Stadium, Cardiff | W | 27-18 |
| 573 | 26-May-07 | Australia | JBT-T | A | Telstra Stadium, Sydney | L | 23-29 |
| 574 | 2-Jun-07 | Australia | JBT-T | A | Suncorp Stadium, Brisbane | L | 0-31 |
| 575 | 4-Aug-07 | England | Int | A | Twickenham, London | L | 5-62 |
| 576 | 18-Aug-07 | Argentina | Int | H | Millennium Stadium, Cardiff | W | 27-20 |
| 577 | 26-Aug-07 | France | Int | H | Millennium Stadium, Cardiff | L | 7-34 |
| 578 | 9-Sep-07 | Canada | WCp | N | Stade de la Beaujoire, Nantes | W | 42-17 |
| 579 | 15-Sep-07 | Australia | WCp | H | Millennium Stadium, Cardiff | L | 20-32 |
| 580 | 20-Sep-07 | Japan | WCp | H | Millennium Stadium, Cardiff | W | 72-18 |
| 581 | 29-Sep-07 | Fiji | WCp | N | Stade de la Beaujoire, Nantes | L | 34-38 |
| 582 | 24-Nov-07 | South Africa | PWC | H | Millennium Stadium, Cardiff | L | 12-34 |
| 583 | 2-Feb-08 | England | 6N | A | Twickenham, London | W | 26-19 |
| 584 | 9-Feb-08 | Scotland | 6N | H | Millennium Stadium, Cardiff | W | 30-15 |
| 585 | 23-Feb-08 | Italy | 6N | H | Millennium Stadium, Cardiff | W | 47-8 |
| 586 | 8-Mar-08 | Ireland | 6N | A | Croke Park, Dublin | W | 16-12 |
| 587 | 15-Mar-08 | France | 6N | H | Millennium Stadium, Cardiff | W | 29-12 |
| 588 | 7-Jun-08 | South Africa | PWC-T | A | Vodacom Park Stadium, Bloemfontein | L | 17-43 |
| 589 | 14-Jun-08 | South Africa | PWC-T | A | Loftus Versfeld Stadium, Pretoria | L | 21-37 |
| 590 | 8-Nov-08 | South Africa | PWC | H | Millennium Stadium, Cardiff | L | 15-20 |
| 591 | 14-Nov-08 | Canada | Int | H | Millennium Stadium, Cardiff | W | 34-13 |
| 592 | 22-Nov-08 | New Zealand | Int | H | Millennium Stadium, Cardiff | L | 9-29 |
| 593 | 29-Nov-08 | Australia | JBT | H | Millennium Stadium, Cardiff | W | 21-18 |
| 594 | 8-Feb-09 | Scotland | 6N | A | Murrayfield, Edinburgh | W | 26-13 |
| 595 | 14-Feb-09 | England | 6N | H | Millennium Stadium, Cardiff | W | 23-15 |
| 596 | 27-Feb-09 | France | 6N | A | Stade de France, Paris | L | 16-21 |
| 597 | 14-Mar-09 | Italy | 6N | A | Stadio Flaminio, Rome | W | 20-15 |
| 598 | 21-Mar-09 | Ireland | 6N | H | Millennium Stadium, Cardiff | L | 15-17 |
| 599 | 30-May-09 | Canada | Int-T | A | York Stadium, Toronto | W | 32-23 |
| 600 | 6-Jun-09 | United States | Int-T | A | Toyota Park Stadium, Chicago | W | 48-15 |

| No | Date | Opponents | Tmt | | Match Venue | | Result | |
|-----|-----------|--------------|-------|---|---------------------------------------------|---|--------|-------|
| 601 | 7-Nov-09 | New Zealand | Int | H | Millennium Stadium, Cardiff | | L | 12-19 |
| 602 | 13-Nov-09 | Samoa | Int | H | Millennium Stadium, Cardiff | | W | 17-13 |
| 603 | 21-Nov-09 | Argentina | Int | H | Millennium Stadium, Cardiff | | W | 33-16 |
| 604 | 28-Nov-09 | Australia | JBT | H | Millennium Stadium, Cardiff | | L | 12-33 |
| 605 | 6-Feb-10 | England | 6N | A | Twickenham, London | | L | 17-30 |
| 606 | 13-Feb-10 | Scotland | 6N | H | Millennium Stadium, Cardiff | | W | 31-24 |
| 607 | 26-Feb-10 | France | 6N | H | Millennium Stadium, Cardiff | | L | 20-26 |
| 608 | 13-Mar-10 | Ireland | 6N | A | Croke Park, Dublin | | L | 12-27 |
| 609 | 20-Mar-10 | Italy | 6N | H | Millennium Stadium, Cardiff | | W | 33-10 |
| 610 | 5-Jun-10 | South Africa | PWC | H | Millennium Stadium, Cardiff | | L | 31-34 |
| 611 | 19-Jun-10 | New Zealand | Int-T | A | Carisbrook, Dunedin | | L | 9-42 |
| 612 | 26-Jun-10 | New Zealand | Int-T | A | Waikato Stadium, Hamilton | | L | 10-29 |
| 613 | 6-Nov-10 | Australia | JBT | H | Millennium Stadium, Cardiff | | L | 16-25 |
| 614 | 13-Nov-10 | South Africa | PWC | H | Millennium Stadium, Cardiff | | L | 25-29 |
| 615 | 19-Nov-10 | Fiji | Int | H | Millennium Stadium, Cardiff | | D | 16-16 |
| 616 | 27-Nov-10 | New Zealand | Int | H | Millennium Stadium, Cardiff | | L | 25-37 |
| 617 | 4-Feb-11 | England | 6N | H | Millennium Stadium, Cardiff | | L | 19-26 |
| 618 | 12-Feb-11 | Scotland | 6N | A | Murrayfield, Edinburgh | | W | 24-6 |
| 619 | 26-Feb-11 | Italy | 6N | A | Stadio Flaminio, Rome | | W | 24-16 |
| 620 | 12-Mar-11 | Ireland | 6N | H | Millennium Stadium, Cardiff | | W | 19-13 |
| 621 | 19-Mar-11 | France | 6N | A | Stade de France, Paris | | L | 9-28 |
| 622 | 4-Jun-11 | Barbarians | Int | H | Millennium Stadium, Cardiff | | L | 28-31 |
| 623 | 6-Aug-11 | England | Int | A | Twickenham, London | | L | 19-23 |
| 624 | 13-Aug-11 | England | Int | H | Millennium Stadium, Cardiff | | W | 19-9 |
| 625 | 20-Aug-11 | Argentina | Int | H | Millennium Stadium, Cardiff | | W | 28-13 |
| 626 | 11-Sep-11 | South Africa | WCp | N | Wellington Regional Stadium, Wellington | | L | 16-17 |
| 627 | 18-Sep-11 | Samoa | WCp | N | Waikato Stadium, Hamilton | | W | 17-10 |
| 628 | 26-Sep-11 | Namibia | WCp | N | Stadium Taranaki, New Plymouth | | W | 81-7 |
| 629 | 2-Oct-11 | Fiji | WCp | N | Waikato Stadium, Hamilton | | W | 66-0 |
| 630 | 8-Oct-11 | Ireland | WCqf | N | Wellington Regional Stadium, Wellington | | W | 22-10 |
| 631 | 15-Oct-11 | France | WCsf | N | Eden Park, Auckland | | L | 8-9 |
| 632 | 21-Oct-11 | Australia | WC34 | N | Eden Park, Auckland | | L | 18-21 |
| 633 | 3-Dec-11 | Australia | JBT | H | Millennium Stadium, Cardiff | | L | 18-24 |
| 634 | 5-Feb-12 | Ireland | 6N | A | Aviva Stadium, Dublin | | W | 23-21 |
| 635 | 12-Feb-12 | Scotland | 6N | H | Millennium Stadium, Cardiff | | W | 27-13 |
| 636 | 25-Feb-12 | England | 6N | A | Twickenham, London | | W | 19-12 |
| 637 | 10-Mar-12 | Italy | 6N | H | Millennium Stadium, Cardiff | | W | 24-3 |
| 638 | 17-Mar-12 | France | 6N | H | Millennium Stadium, Cardiff | | W | 16-9 |
| 639 | 2-Jun-12 | Barbarians | Int | H | Millennium Stadium, Cardiff | | W | 30-21 |
| 640 | 9-Jun-12 | Australia | JBT-T | A | Suncorp Stadium, Brisbane | | L | 19-27 |

| No | Date | Opponents | Tmt | | Match Venue | Result | |
|-----|------|-----------|-----|---|-------------|--------|---|
| 641 | 16-Jun-12 | Australia | JBT-T | A | Etihad Stadium, Docklands, Melbourne | L | 23-25 |
| 642 | 23-Jun-12 | Australia | JBT-T | A | Football Stadium, Sydney | L | 19-20 |
| 643 | 10-Nov-12 | Argentina | Int | H | Millennium Stadium, Cardiff | L | 12-26 |
| 644 | 16-Nov-12 | Samoa | Int | H | Millennium Stadium, Cardiff | L | 19-26 |
| 645 | 24-Nov-12 | New Zealand | Int | H | Millennium Stadium, Cardiff | L | 10-33 |
| 646 | 1-Dec-12 | Australia | JBT | H | Millennium Stadium, Cardiff | L | 12-14 |
| 647 | 2-Feb-13 | Ireland | 6N | H | Millennium Stadium, Cardiff | L | 22-30 |
| 648 | 9-Feb-13 | France | 6N | A | Stade de France, Paris | W | 16-6 |
| 649 | 23-Feb-13 | Italy | 6N | A | Stadio Olimpico, Rome | W | 26-9 |
| 650 | 9-Mar-13 | Scotland | 6N | A | Murrayfield, Edinburgh | W | 28-18 |
| 651 | 16-Mar-13 | England | 6N | H | Millennium Stadium, Cardiff | W | 30-3 |
| 652 | 8-Jun-13 | Japan | Int-T | A | Hanazono Stadium, Osaka | W | 22-18 |
| 653 | 15-Jun-13 | Japan | Int-T | A | Prince Chichibu Memorial Ground, Tokyo | L | 8-23 |
| 654 | 9-Nov-13 | South Africa | PWC | H | Millennium Stadium, Cardiff | L | 15-24 |
| 655 | 16-Nov-13 | Argentina | Int | H | Millennium Stadium, Cardiff | W | 40-6 |
| 656 | 22-Nov-13 | Tonga | Int | H | Millennium Stadium, Cardiff | W | 17-7 |
| 657 | 30-Nov-13 | Australia | JBT | H | Millennium Stadium, Cardiff | L | 26-30 |
| 658 | 1-Feb-14 | Italy | 6N | H | Millennium Stadium, Cardiff | W | 23-15 |
| 659 | 8-Feb-14 | Ireland | 6N | A | Aviva Stadium, Dublin | L | 3-26 |
| 660 | 21-Feb-14 | France | 6N | H | Millennium Stadium, Cardiff | W | 27-6 |
| 661 | 9-Mar-14 | England | 6N | A | Twickenham, London | L | 18-29 |
| 662 | 15-Mar-14 | Scotland | 6N | H | Millennium Stadium, Cardiff | W | 51-3 |
| 663 | 14-Jun-14 | South Africa | PWC-T | A | Kings Park Stadium, Durban | L | 16-38 |
| 664 | 21-Jun-14 | South Africa | PWC-T | A | Mbombela Stadium, Nelspruit | L | 30-31 |
| 665 | 8-Nov-14 | Australia | JBT | H | Millennium Stadium, Cardiff | L | 28-33 |
| 666 | 15-Nov-14 | Fiji | Int | H | Millennium Stadium, Cardiff | W | 17-13 |
| 667 | 22-Nov-14 | New Zealand | Int | H | Millennium Stadium, Cardiff | L | 16-34 |
| 668 | 29-Nov-14 | South Africa | PWC | H | Millennium Stadium, Cardiff | W | 12-6 |
| 669 | 6-Feb-15 | England | 6N | H | Millennium Stadium, Cardiff | L | 16-21 |
| 670 | 15-Feb-15 | Scotland | 6N | A | Murrayfield, Edinburgh | W | 26-23 |
| 671 | 28-Feb-15 | France | 6N | A | Stade de France, Paris | W | 20-13 |
| 672 | 14-Mar-15 | Ireland | 6N | H | Millennium Stadium, Cardiff | W | 23-16 |
| 673 | 21-Mar-15 | Italy | 6N | A | Stadio Olimpico, Rome | W | 61-20 |
| 674 | 8-Aug-15 | Ireland | Int | H | Millennium Stadium, Cardiff | L | 21-35 |
| 675 | 29-Aug-15 | Ireland | Int | A | Aviva Stadium, Dublin | W | 16-10 |
| 676 | 5-Sep-15 | Italy | Int | H | Millennium Stadium, Cardiff | W | 23-19 |
| 677 | 20-Sep-15 | Uruguay | WCp | H | Millennium Stadium, Cardiff | W | 54-9 |
| 678 | 26-Sep-15 | England | WCp | N | Twickenham, London | W | 28-25 |
| 679 | 1-Oct-15 | Fiji | WCp | H | Millennium Stadium, Cardiff | W | 23-13 |
| 680 | 10-Oct-15 | Australia | WCp | N | Twickenham, London | L | 6-15 |
| 681 | 17-Oct-15 | South Africa | WCqf | N | Twickenham, London | L | 19-23 |

An England shirt from the first Test match, played at Raeburn Place in Edinburgh on 27 March 1871. Scotland won by one goal and one try to one try.

The first eighteen 'All Blacks' from New Zealand who toured New South Wales in 1884, winning eight matches without defeat.

'The Calcutta Cup match at Raeburn Place, 1886' by WH Overend and LP Smythe.
The match ended in a 0-0 draw.

The pioneer 'Lions' on route to New Zealand and Australia in 1888.

The first ever Test match between the 'Lions' and South Africa, in Port Elizabeth, in 1891. The Lions won 4-0.

Scotland versus England at Raeburn Place, Edinburgh, 1892.
England won 5-0.

Half-time at Cardiff in 1922 during a Wales-England Five Nations encounter.
Wales went on to win 28-6.

The first post-war Calcutta Cup match, played at Twickenham in 1947.
England won 24-5.

Action from Ireland v England in the 1973 Five Nations – a match that took place at the height of 'The Troubles' and was crucial in keeping the tournament alive.

The iconic figure of Willie John McBride, captain of the undefeated Lions in South Africa in 1974.

Gareth Edwards of Wales, considered by many as the greatest player ever.

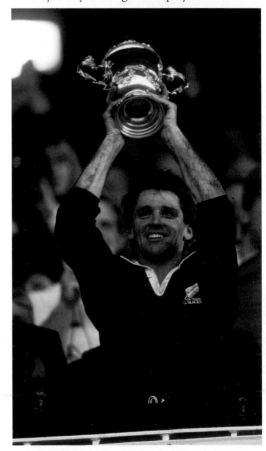

David Kirk of New Zealand lifts
the inaugural Rugby World Cup
in 1987 after defeating France
29-9 in Auckland.

Scotland captain David Sole leads his players out to play England in a Grand Slam decider at Murrayfield in 1990. Scotland won 13-7.

Nick Farr-Jones and David Campese share a smile as they raise the William Webb Ellis trophy after defeating England 12-6 in 1991 Rugby World Cup final.

Jonah Lomu almost single-handedly changed rugby's profile around the world after his dominant display for New Zealand in a 45-29 win over England in the semi-final of the 1995 Rugby World Cup in South Africa.

South Africa's François Pienaar receives the World Cup from Nelson Mandela after the Springboks' dramatic 15-12 win over New Zealand in the 1995 final at Ellis Park, Johannesburg.

John Eales celebrates with the William Webb Ellis trophy after Australia become the first side to win the Rugby World Cup twice following their 35-12 victory over France at the Millennium Stadium in Wales.

Fly-half Diego Dominguez of Italy gets the ball away during the opening game of the newly formed Six Nations Championship in 2000. Italy marked the historic occasion with a victory over 1999 Five Nations champions Scotland, winning 34-20.

Jonny Wilkinson's metronomic boot helped England dominate world rugby for several years on their road to glory at the 2003 Rugby World Cup. Here his drop-goal sealed the trophy for his team as they defeat tournament hosts Australia 20-17 in Sydney.

Considered by many pundits as the game's greatest-ever fly-half, New Zealand's Dan Carter played what has been dubbed 'the most complete performance by a 10' against the Lions in the Second Test of the 2005 series. Carter scored two tries, four conversions and five penalties in the 48-18 victory for the All Blacks.

Canada's Luke Tait rises to win a lineout against Australia in Bordeaux during their Pool B match at the 2007 Rugby World Cup. The Wallabies won 37-6.

Springbok captain John Smit and his team celebrate with the William Webb Ellis Trophy after defeating England 15-6 in the 2007 Rugby World Cup final in Paris.

The Samoan players challenge the All Blacks at Yarrow Stadium, New Plymouth, in 2008 with their traditional pre-match 'Siva Tau'. New Zealand more than met the ferocity of the challenge by going on to win 101-14.

After Ireland defeated Wales 17-15 at the Millennium Stadium to clinch the 2009 Six Nations (and with it the Grand Slam), Brian O'Driscoll is congratulated by legend Jack Kyle, who had been part of Ireland's only other Grand Slam-winning side – sixty-one years earlier, in 1948.

6 NATIONS CHAMPIONS

France captain Thierry Dusautoir lifts the Six Nations trophy after his side completed the Grand Slam by beating England 12-10 at the Stade de France in 2010.

Despite being the single most successful team on the planet (in any sport) and dominating the world game, New Zealand have underperformed, by their standards, in the Rugby World Cup. Richie McCaw's class of 2011 did not disappoint, however, raising the William Webb Ellis trophy after a nerve-jangling 8-7 victory over France at Eden Park.

Adriaan Strauss of South Africa is tackled by Gonzalo Camacho of Argentina as the Pumas make their debut in the newly formed Rugby Championship in 2012. South Africa won this encounter, at Newlands Stadium in Cape Town, 27-6.

England captain Chris Robshaw punches the air after his team's spectacular triumph over New Zealand at Twickenham in December 2012. England defeated the world champions 38-21.

Leigh Halfpenny of Wales kicks a penalty against England at the Millennium Stadium during the 2013 Six Nations. Wales won 30-3 to secure the title, their fourth since the tournament's inception in 2000.

The greatest rivalry in world rugby? New Zealand take on South Africa in Auckland during the 2013 Rugby Championship. The All Blacks emerged victorious, 29-15, extending their winning record at Eden Park to more than 17 years and 32 Test matches in a row.

Karne Hesketh of Japan scores the match-winning try against South Africa during the 2015 World Cup Pool B match at the Brighton Community Stadium, to secure the biggest upset in the tournament's history.

New Zealand's record-breaking captain, Richie McCaw, raises the World Cup for the second time as his side become the first team in the tournament's history to defend their crown and to claim the title on three times.

# THE MINOR NATIONS

## TIER 2,3 TEAMS

# CANADA

The Canadian Rugby Football Union (CRU) was established in 1884, but was disbanded just before the First World War. The Rugby Union of Canada was then formed in 1929 and was followed by a tour of Japan in 1932. Most of the players on this tour were from British Columbia and the team lost both Internationals, the first in Osaka, by 9 points to 8, and the second in Tokyo, by 38 points to 5.

In the years that followed, the Canadian team seldom toured internationally, but they did visit the UK in 1962 with a team that was again made up of many players from British Columbia. During that tour, they drew with the Barbarians 3 points all, before losing by 8 points to nil to a Welsh under-23 side. In 1965, the Rugby Union of Canada was renamed the Canadian Rugby Union, and a year later the team, nicknamed the 'Canucks', lost by 19 points to 8 to the Lions who were returning from their tour of Australia and New Zealand.

Canada, along with fifteen other countries, was invited to compete in the 1987 World Cup. The team finished in third place in their pool behind Wales and Ireland. They performed better in the 1991 tournament and qualified for the quarter-finals by beating Fiji and Romania and finishing in second place to France in the pool. Two years later, the Canadians scored a famous victory against Wales in Cardiff in November 1993, and this was followed by an equally impressive home win over France the following year, in June 1994.

To date Canada has been successful on seven occasions in sixty-seven matches against Tier 1 teams, having beaten Italy twice in 1983 and in 2000, Argentina twice in 1990 and Scotland once in

2002, in addition to the two wins against Wales and France. As quarter-finalists in the World Cup in 1991, Canada automatically qualified for the 1995 competition, but finished only in third place in a tough pool that contained holders Australia, and hosts and eventual winners, South Africa. Canada had to qualify for the next five World Cup tournaments and on each occasion failed to make it to the quarter-final stage.

The Canucks were very successful in the Pacific Rim tournament held between 1996 and 2001, having won three titles in succession: in 1996, 1997 and 1998. They also performed well in the Pan American Championship by finishing runners-up to Argentina in four of the five competitions held between 1995 and 2003. Canada also competed in all nine Churchill Cup tournaments held between 2003 and 2011.

The Canadians have a good record against their main Tier 2 and 3 group rivals and have won 71 out of the 125 matches played to date. To the end of October 2015, the Canadians have played a total of 234 international matches, and of these have won 95, drawn 5, and lost 134. They have defeated nearest rivals, the United States, 38 times in 54 games played, and are currently in 18th place in the World Rugby rankings table.

# CANADA

## HEAD TO HEAD RESULTS TO 31 OCTOBER 2015

|  | P | W | D | L | % | F | A |
|---|---|---|---|---|---|---|---|
| **v TIER 1 Teams** | | | | | | | |
| v Argentina | 8 | 2 | 0 | 6 | 25.0 | 137 | 262 |
| v Australia | 6 | 0 | 0 | 6 | 0.0 | 60 | 283 |
| v England | 6 | 0 | 0 | 6 | 0.0 | 73 | 273 |
| v France | 9 | 1 | 0 | 8 | 11.1 | 119 | 315 |
| v Ireland | 7 | 0 | 1 | 6 | 7.1 | 84 | 276 |
| v Italy | 8 | 2 | 0 | 6 | 25.0 | 110 | 226 |
| v New Zealand | 5 | 0 | 0 | 5 | 0.0 | 54 | 313 |
| v Scotland | 4 | 1 | 0 | 3 | 25.0 | 49 | 105 |
| v South Africa | 2 | 0 | 0 | 2 | 0.0 | 18 | 71 |
| v Wales | 12 | 1 | 0 | 11 | 8.3 | 207 | 460 |
| **Sub-Total** | **67** | **7** | **1** | **59** | **11.2** | **911** | **2584** |
| **v TIER 2/3 Group** | | | | | | | |
| v Fiji | 10 | 3 | 0 | 7 | 30.0 | 191 | 314 |
| v Japan | 24 | 8 | 2 | 14 | 37.5 | 559 | 586 |
| v Romania | 6 | 2 | 0 | 4 | 33.3 | 117 | 92 |
| v Samoa | 5 | 0 | 0 | 5 | 0.0 | 80 | 144 |
| v Tonga | 8 | 5 | 0 | 3 | 62.5 | 193 | 155 |
| v United States | 54 | 38 | 1 | 15 | 71.3 | 1262 | 810 |
| v Georgia | 5 | 3 | 0 | 2 | 60.0 | 119 | 78 |
| v Namibia | 2 | 2 | 0 | 0 | 100.0 | 89 | 24 |
| v Russia | 3 | 3 | 0 | 0 | 100.0 | 91 | 27 |
| v Uruguay | 8 | 7 | 0 | 1 | 87.5 | 247 | 108 |
| **Sub-Total** | **125** | **71** | **3** | **51** | **58.0** | **2948** | **2338** |
| **v Tier 3 Selection** | | | | | | | |
| v Hong Kong | 6 | 5 | 0 | 1 | 83.3 | 182 | 99 |
| v Portugal | 4 | 4 | 0 | 0 | 100.0 | 138 | 53 |
| v Spain | 1 | 1 | 0 | 0 | 100.0 | 60 | 22 |
| **Sub-Total** | **11** | **10** | **0** | **1** | **90.9** | **380** | **174** |
| v Tier 1 XV teams | 14 | 3 | 0 | 11 | 21.4 | 163 | 422 |
| v Other Teams | 17 | 4 | 1 | 12 | 26.5 | 307 | 422 |
| **All Internationals** | **234** | **95** | **5** | **134** | **41.7** | **4709** | **5940** |

# FIJI

Although rugby was first played on Viti Levu island in 1884, the Fiji Rugby Football Union was not officially formed until 1913. Two years later, the Fiji Native Rugby Union was established, and later on that year became affiliated to the Fiji RFU.

On 18 August 1924, the Fijians played their first International match against Western Samoa in Apia, which they won by six points to nil. They continued their tour by visiting Tonga to play three Internationals against the home side. A win, a draw and a defeat in Nuku'alofa meant that the series was shared. They returned via Apia to play the final match against Western Samoa on 19 September 1924, which they lost by 9 points to 3.

The Fijian team toured Australia in 1952 and 1954 and on each occasion shared the two-Test series, 1-1. In 1963 the Fiji RFU was renamed Fiji Rugby Union and a year later the Fijians, on their first European tour, lost by 28 points to 22 to a Wales XV and by 21 points to 3 to France.

The Fijians have contested seven of the eight World Cup competitions held to date, the only exception being the 1995 tournament when they failed to qualify. In the first World Cup in 1987 they reached the quarter-final before bowing out to France, and in 1999, in a sudden death play-off for a quarter-final place, Fiji lost a high-scoring game against England by 45 points to 24. In 2003, a narrow 22 points to 20 defeat to Scotland in the final pool game deprived them of a quarter-final place, but in 2007 they finally reached the quarter-final for the second time by beating Wales by 38 points to 34 in a pulsating match. South Africa, the eventual champions, won the quarter-final encounter by 37 points to 20.

In 1982 the South Pacific Championship was established and held annually until 1997 (except on one occasion, in 1989). The Fijians won three titles out of the fifteen tournaments staged. They also won three titles in the Pacific Tri Nations Series held between 1998 and 2005, and were twice winners (in 2013 and 2015), of the IRB Pacific Nations Cup competition.

The Fijians have beaten Tier 1 teams ten times: their victories include five wins against Italy, a home win against Scotland in 1998, and two away wins against Australia in 1952 and 1954. The remaining two victories occurred in the 1987 World Cup game against Argentina, and in the aforementioned 2007 World Cup match against Wales.

Fiji has played 177 matches against Tier 2 and 3 group rivals and has won 117 of them. To the end of October 2015, the Fijians have played 318 international matches and of these have won 153, drawn 10, and lost 155. They have beaten their great rivals Samoa 26 times in 49 games and Tonga 59 times in 88 games. Fiji is currently ranked 11th in the World Rugby rankings table.

# FIJI

## HEAD TO HEAD RESULTS TO 31 OCTOBER 2015

|  | P | W | D | L | % | F | A |
|---|---|---|---|---|---|---|---|
| **v TIER 1 Teams** | | | | | | | |
| v Argentina | 4 | 1 | 0 | 3 | 25.0 | 96 | 130 |
| v Australia | 20 | 2 | 1 | 17 | 12.5 | 234 | 574 |
| v England | 6 | 0 | 0 | 6 | 0.0 | 94 | 245 |
| v France | 9 | 0 | 0 | 9 | 0.0 | 111 | 359 |
| v Ireland | 3 | 0 | 0 | 3 | 0.0 | 31 | 149 |
| v Italy | 10 | 5 | 0 | 5 | 50.0 | 243 | 244 |
| v New Zealand | 5 | 0 | 0 | 5 | 0.00 | 50 | 364 |
| v Scotland | 6 | 1 | 0 | 5 | 16.7 | 145 | 182 |
| v South Africa | 3 | 0 | 0 | 3 | 0.00 | 41 | 129 |
| v Wales | 11 | 1 | 1 | 9 | 13.6 | 145 | 329 |
| **Sub-Total** | **77** | **10** | **2** | **65** | **14.3** | **1190** | **2705** |
| **v TIER 2/3 Group** | | | | | | | |
| v Canada | 10 | 7 | 0 | 3 | 70.0 | 314 | 191 |
| v Japan | 16 | 13 | 0 | 3 | 81.3 | 429 | 287 |
| v Romania | 3 | 2 | 0 | 1 | 66.7 | 70 | 42 |
| v Samoa | 49 | 26 | 3 | 20 | 56.1 | 951 | 864 |
| v Tonga | 88 | 59 | 3 | 26 | 68.7 | 1724 | 1163 |
| v United States | 6 | 5 | 0 | 1 | 83.3 | 143 | 97 |
| v Georgia | 1 | 1 | 0 | 0 | 100.0 | 24 | 19 |
| v Namibia | 2 | 2 | 0 | 0 | 100.0 | 116 | 43 |
| v Russia | 0 | 0 | 0 | 0 | 0.0 | 0 | 0 |
| v Uruguay | 2 | 2 | 0 | 0 | 100.0 | 86 | 39 |
| **Sub-Total** | **177** | **117** | **6** | **54** | **67.8** | **3857** | **2745** |
| **v Tier 3 Selection** | | | | | | | |
| v Portugal | 2 | 2 | 0 | 0 | 100.0 | 62 | 30 |
| v Spain | 1 | 1 | 0 | 0 | 100.0 | 39 | 20 |
| **Sub-Total** | **3** | **3** | **0** | **0** | **100.0** | **101** | **50** |
| v New Zealand Maori | 29 | 7 | 2 | 20 | 27.6 | 383 | 517 |
| v Tier 1 XV teams | 16 | 0 | 0 | 16 | 0.0 | 137 | 449 |
| v Other Teams | 16 | 16 | 0 | 0 | 100.0 | 1095 | 110 |
| **All Internationals** | **318** | **153** | **10** | **155** | **49.7** | **6763** | **6576** |

# GEORGIA

The first rugby session in Georgia was held at Tblisi in 1959 and five years later, in 1964, the Georgia Rugby Union was founded and became part of the Soviet Union's rugby federation. During that Soviet period, Georgia regularly supplied players to the USSR national side, until May 1991, when the Independent Georgian Rugby Union was established. On achieving independence in 1992, they became an official affiliate of the International Rugby Board (IRB).

Georgia's first International, against Zimbabwe, took place in Kutaisi, the country's second largest city, on 12 September 1989, and the home team won it by 16 points to 3. The following year, the Georgians made a return visit to Zimbabwe and drew the two Test series. Throughout the 1990s all their games were played against European opposition, until March 1999 when they faced Tonga in a match over two legs to decide who would gain entry to the 1999 World Cup in Wales. They lost the first game in Nuku'alofa by 37 points to 6, but, despite winning the return leg by 28 points to 27, it was not enough to qualify for the finals. However, the Georgians did contest the next four World Cup tournaments. In Australia in 2003, they lost all four pool games, but fared slightly better in both the 2007 and the 2011 World Cup competitions, winning one of their four pool games on each occasion. In the 2015 World Cup Georgia achieved their best performance in the competition by defeating both Tonga and Romania to finish in third place in the pool behind New Zealand and Argentina.

The Georgian team's performance in European competition has been more impressive: in their first season in the 1992-94 FIRA Trophy competition they won the Division 3 Pool 'A' title and followed it with a second place in Division 2 Pool 1 in the 1995-97 season. In 2000 the tournament was revamped and renamed the European Nations Cup (ENC), and Georgia, now in Division 1, continued to improve by finishing as runners-up to Romania in that first year and went on to win the title in 2001. Known as the 'Lelos', they won two further titles in the 2007-08 and 2008-10 seasons.

Georgia also won the ENC Division 1 competition, renamed Six Nations 'B' Championship, in its first two seasons, 2011-12, and 2013-14. The Georgians competed in four IRB Nations Cup competitions between 2007 and 2011, finishing in second place in 2008 and in 2011. They also competed in the first three Tbilisi Cup competitions held in 2013, 2014 and 2015.

Georgia's best sequence of seven wins, which started on 20 November 2010, was finally ended by the South African Kings in the IRB Nations Cup on 10 June 2011. The same winning sequence was repeated between November 2013 and June 2014 and again between November 2014 and June 2015. Their worst run of seven losses occurred between March 2003 and February 2004.

In 68 Internationals against Tier 2 and 3 group rivals, the Georgians have won 41 times. They have played fifteen times against Tier 1 teams, but have yet to win. To the end of October 2015, the Lelos have played 184 international matches, and of these have won 110, drawn 6, and lost 68. They are currently in 14th place in the World Rugby rankings table.

# GEORGIA

## HEAD TO HEAD RESULTS TO 31 OCTOBER 2015

|                      | P   | W   | D   | L   | %     | F    | A    |
|----------------------|-----|-----|-----|-----|-------|------|------|
| **v TIER 1 Teams**   |     |     |     |     |       |      |      |
| v Argentina          | 4   | 0   | 0   | 4   | 0.0   | 37   | 141  |
| v Australia          | 0   | 0   | 0   | 0   | 0.0   | 0    | 0    |
| v England            | 2   | 0   | 0   | 2   | 0.0   | 16   | 125  |
| v France             | 1   | 0   | 0   | 1   | 0.0   | 7    | 64   |
| v Ireland            | 4   | 0   | 0   | 4   | 0.0   | 31   | 196  |
| v Italy              | 1   | 0   | 0   | 1   | 0.0   | 22   | 31   |
| v New Zealand        | 1   | 0   | 0   | 1   | 0.0   | 10   | 43   |
| v Scotland           | 1   | 0   | 0   | 1   | 0.0   | 6    | 15   |
| v South Africa       | 1   | 0   | 0   | 1   | 0.0   | 19   | 46   |
| v Wales              | 0   | 0   | 0   | 0   | 0.0   | 0    | 0    |
| **Sub-Total**        | 15  | 0   | 0   | 15  | 0.0   | 148  | 661  |
| **v TIER 2/3 Group** |     |     |     |     |       |      |      |
| v Canada             | 5   | 2   | 0   | 3   | 40.0  | 78   | 119  |
| v Fiji               | 1   | 0   | 0   | 1   | 0.0   | 19   | 24   |
| v Japan              | 4   | 1   | 0   | 3   | 25.0  | 74   | 94   |
| v Romania            | 19  | 10  | 1   | 8   | 55.3  | 347  | 339  |
| v Samoa              | 2   | 1   | 0   | 1   | 50.0  | 25   | 61   |
| v Tonga              | 4   | 2   | 0   | 2   | 50.0  | 60   | 97   |
| v United States      | 4   | 1   | 0   | 3   | 25.0  | 75   | 109  |
| v Namibia            | 5   | 4   | 0   | 1   | 80.0  | 112  | 73   |
| v Russia             | 19  | 17  | 1   | 1   | 92.1  | 476  | 224  |
| v Uruguay            | 5   | 3   | 0   | 2   | 60.0  | 85   | 72   |
| **Sub-Total**        | 68  | 41  | 2   | 25  | 61.8  | 1351 | 1212 |
| **v Tier 3 Selection** |   |     |     |     |       |      |      |
| v Czech Republic     | 8   | 8   | 0   | 0   | 100.0 | 310  | 58   |
| v Germany            | 4   | 4   | 0   | 0   | 100.0 | 193  | 19   |
| v Netherlands        | 4   | 3   | 0   | 1   | 75.0  | 164  | 64   |
| v Portugal           | 19  | 13  | 2   | 4   | 73.7  | 440  | 265  |
| v Spain              | 16  | 12  | 1   | 3   | 78.1  | 509  | 253  |
| v Ukraine            | 9   | 9   | 0   | 0   | 100.0 | 281  | 63   |
| **Sub-Total**        | 60  | 49  | 3   | 8   | 84.2  | 1897 | 722  |
| **v Other Teams**    | 41  | 20  | 1   | 20  | 50.0  | 790  | 813  |
| **All Internationals** | 184 | 110 | 6 | 68  | 61.4  | 4186 | 3408 |

# JAPAN

Rugby was introduced to Japan at Keio University in Minato, Tokyo, in 1899, and in 1926 the Japanese Rugby Football Union (JRFU) was founded. In 1930, in their first match, a touring Japanese team drew 3 points all with British Columbia in Vancouver, and two years later, on 31 January 1932, they played their first International against Canada in Osaka, which they won by 9 points to 8. They also won the second match in Tokyo eleven days later, by 38 points to 5.

Nicknamed the 'Cherry Blossoms', they had to wait until the 1970s before meeting Tier 1 teams. They met France in 1973, Australia twice in 1975, and Italy in 1976, all away from home, and on each occasion it resulted in a defeat for the touring team.

The Japanese competed in all seven World Cup competitions between 1987 and 2011 but failed to qualify for the quarter-finals on each occasion. In twenty four matches played, their only win was in 1991, when they defeated Zimbabwe by 52 points to 8. Japan's next best performance in the World Cup was their two drawn games, both against Canada, in 2007 and 2011. The heaviest defeat came in the 1995 World Cup when they were soundly beaten by 145 points to 17 by a strong New Zealand team.

Japan's performance in the 2015 Rugby World Cup however was sensational, when they defeated South Africa in the first pool game, and followed it with wins over Samoa and the United States, to finish in third place. In fact Japan is the only team in the history of the tournament to have achieved three pool wins and failed to qualify for the quarter final stage

The Japanese have won four times in forty-two Internationals against Tier 1 teams. Their first win was achieved in Tokyo in

September 1998 when they beat Argentina by 44 points to 29. The second success came in June 2013 when they triumphed over Wales in Osaka by 23 points to 8, the third victory came in June 2014, when they defeated Italy in Tokyo by 26 points to 23, and the fourth was against South Africa in the 2015 World Cup. The Cherry Blossoms have now faced all ten Tier 1 countries.

While the Japanese team's record in Internationals has been rather poor, they have a more impressive record in Asian competitions. In nineteen Asian Championships held between 1969 and 2004, the Japanese have won the title fourteen times, and have been runners-up to South Korea the remaining five times. They also won the Asia Nations Series in 2007, and have been crowned champions in all seven of the current Asia Five Nations Championships staged between 2008 and 2014. Japan also won the 2015 tournament which was renamed the Asian Rugby Championship.

The Japanese have played in all ten IRB Pacific Cup competitions held between 2006 to 2015, winning the title in 2011 and the North American section of the competition in 2014. Between 15 November 2013 and 15 November 2014, Japan recorded eleven successive wins before losing to Georgia in the final match of the year on 23 November 2014.

To the end of October 2015, the Cherry Blossoms have played a total of 320 international matches and of these have won 135, drawn 9, and lost 176. The team has played Tier 2 and 3 group rivals 111 times and has won on 50 occasions. Japan is currently in 10th place in the World Rugby rankings table.

# JAPAN

## HEAD TO HEAD RESULTS TO 31 OCTOBER 2015

| | P | W | D | L | % | F | A |
|---|---|---|---|---|---|---|---|
| **v TIER 1 Teams** | | | | | | | |
| v Argentina | 5 | 1 | 0 | 4 | 20.0 | 139 | 205 |
| v Australia | 4 | 0 | 0 | 4 | 0.0 | 58 | 220 |
| v England | 1 | 0 | 0 | 1 | 0.0 | 7 | 60 |
| v France | 3 | 0 | 0 | 3 | 0.0 | 68 | 128 |
| v Ireland | 5 | 0 | 0 | 5 | 0.0 | 83 | 251 |
| v Italy | 6 | 1 | 0 | 5 | 16.7 | 90 | 199 |
| v New Zealand | 3 | 0 | 0 | 3 | 0.0 | 30 | 282 |
| v Scotland | 5 | 0 | 0 | 5 | 0.0 | 55 | 266 |
| v South Africa | 1 | 1 | 0 | 0 | 100.0 | 34 | 32 |
| v Wales | 9 | 1 | 0 | 8 | 11.1 | 129 | 493 |
| **Sub-Total** | **42** | **4** | **0** | **38** | **9.5** | **693** | **2136** |
| **v TIER 2/3 Group** | | | | | | | |
| v Canada | 24 | 14 | 2 | 8 | 62.5 | 586 | 559 |
| v Fiji | 16 | 3 | 0 | 13 | 18.7 | 287 | 429 |
| v Romania | 5 | 4 | 0 | 1 | 80.0 | 119 | 98 |
| v Samoa | 15 | 4 | 0 | 11 | 26.7 | 273 | 482 |
| v Tonga | 16 | 7 | 0 | 9 | 43.7 | 379 | 440 |
| v United States | 23 | 9 | 1 | 13 | 41.3 | 526 | 655 |
| v Georgia | 4 | 3 | 0 | 1 | 75.0 | 94 | 74 |
| v Namibia | 0 | 0 | 0 | 0 | 0.0 | 0 | 0 |
| v Russia | 5 | 4 | 0 | 1 | 80.0 | 237 | 90 |
| v Uruguay | 3 | 2 | 0 | 1 | 66.7 | 88 | 32 |
| **Sub-Total** | **111** | **50** | **3** | **58** | **46.4** | **2589** | **2859** |
| **v Tier 3 Selection** | | | | | | | |
| v Hong Kong | 24 | 20 | 0 | 4 | 83.3 | 1030 | 333 |
| v Kazakhstan | 5 | 5 | 0 | 0 | 100.0 | 418 | 23 |
| v South Korea | 32 | 25 | 1 | 6 | 79.7 | 1342 | 475 |
| v Spain | 3 | 3 | 0 | 0 | 100.0 | 114 | 43 |
| **Sub-Total** | **64** | **53** | **1** | **10** | **83.6** | **2904** | **874** |
| v Tier 1 XV teams | 23 | 1 | 0 | 22 | 4.3 | 254 | 1058 |
| v Other Teams | 80 | 27 | 5 | 48 | 36.9 | 2466 | 2107 |
| **All Internationals** | **320** | **135** | **9** | **176** | **43.6** | **8906** | **9034** |

# NAMIBIA

Rugby was first played in Namibia, then known as South-West Africa, in 1916, having been introduced to the game by South African soldiers who had invaded the German-run colony during the First World War.

Namibia gained its independence in 1990 and the Namibia Rugby Union was formed in March of that year. The Namibians joined the IRB in the same month and played their first International against Zimbabwe in Windhoek on 24 March. They won that match comfortably by 33 points to 18, and followed it with a resounding 86 points to 9 win against Portugal on 21 April 1990. However, the team lost the next two matches to the touring Welsh side in June of that year – but bounced back with an amazing period of fourteen straight wins in a sequence stretching from July 1990 to June 1993. During that incredible run, the Namibians had home wins against Italy (twice) in June 1991, and Ireland (twice) in July 1991. The team's winning streak was brought to an end when they lost to Wales by 38 points to 23 in June 1993.

The Namibians competed in all the World Cup competitions between 1999 and 2015 but struggled against the opposition, losing all nineteen matches played in the five tournaments: including eleven games by more than fifty points. Their heaviest defeat came in 2003 when they lost by 142 points to nil to host nation, Australia. Nicknamed the 'Welwitschias', they have been successful in competitions on the African continent, winning the Confederation of African Rugby Championship (CAR), held between 2000 and 2005, in both 2002 and 2004. The tournament was renamed the Africa Cup in 2006 and the Namibian team won the title for the third time in the 2008-09 season. Namibia withdrew from that competition the following year to concentrate on the much more demanding IRB Nations Cup, which was first held in 2006. The team first entered that tournament in 2007, but had to wait until 2010 before their second invitation, and on that occasion they won the cup, defeating both Georgia and the then tournament hosts, Romania, en route to the final. The following year however they finished a disappointing fourth out of six. Those two wins and a further two wins against Russia in July 2015 remain their only victories against Tier 2 and Tier 3 group rivals in 23 matches played.

Namibia's four wins against Tier 1 countries are confined to the ones achieved against Italy and Ireland in 1991. In July 2014, the Namibians qualified for the 2015 World Cup when they won the Africa Cup for the fourth time on points difference from Zimbabwe and Kenya. They also retained the Cup in 2015.

To the end of October 2015, the Namibians have played 131 Internationals and of these have won 74, drawn 2, and lost 55. They are currently in 20th place in the World Rugby ratings table.

# NAMIBIA

## HEAD TO HEAD RESULTS TO 31 OCTOBER 2015

|  | P | W | D | L | % | F | A |
|---|---|---|---|---|---|---|---|
| **v TIER 1 Teams** | | | | | | | |
| v Argentina | 3 | 0 | 0 | 3 | 0.0 | 36 | 194 |
| v Australia | 1 | 0 | 0 | 1 | 0.0 | 0 | 142 |
| v England | 0 | 0 | 0 | 0 | 0.0 | 0 | 0 |
| v France | 2 | 0 | 0 | 2 | 0.0 | 23 | 134 |
| v Ireland | 4 | 2 | 0 | 2 | 50.0 | 65 | 117 |
| v Italy | 3 | 2 | 0 | 1 | 66.7 | 74 | 75 |
| v New Zealand | 1 | 0 | 0 | 1 | 0.0 | 14 | 58 |
| v Scotland | 0 | 0 | 0 | 0 | 0.0 | 0 | 0 |
| v South Africa | 2 | 0 | 0 | 2 | 0.0 | 13 | 192 |
| v Wales | 4 | 0 | 0 | 4 | 0.0 | 69 | 171 |
| **Sub-Total** | **20** | **4** | **0** | **16** | **20.0** | **294** | **1083** |
| **v TIER 2/3 Group** | | | | | | | |
| v Canada | 2 | 0 | 0 | 2 | 0.0 | 24 | 89 |
| v Fiji | 2 | 0 | 0 | 2 | 0.0 | 43 | 116 |
| v Japan | 0 | 0 | 0 | 0 | 0.0 | 0 | 0 |
| v Romania | 5 | 1 | 0 | 4 | 20.0 | 58 | 138 |
| v Samoa | 2 | 0 | 0 | 2 | 0.0 | 25 | 89 |
| v Tonga | 2 | 0 | 0 | 2 | 0.0 | 35 | 55 |
| v United States | 0 | 0 | 0 | 0 | 0.0 | 0 | 0 |
| v Georgia | 5 | 1 | 0 | 4 | 20.0 | 73 | 112 |
| v Russia | 4 | 2 | 0 | 2 | 50.0 | 111 | 85 |
| v Uruguay | 1 | 0 | 0 | 1 | 0.0 | 12 | 23 |
| **Sub-Total** | **23** | **4** | **0** | **19** | **17.4** | **381** | **707** |
| **v Tier 3 Selection** | | | | | | | |
| v Côte d'Ivoire | 4 | 2 | 1 | 1 | 62.5 | 101 | 50 |
| v Kenya | 9 | 7 | 0 | 2 | 77.8 | 428 | 155 |
| v Madagascar | 4 | 3 | 0 | 1 | 75.0 | 310 | 84 |
| v Morocco | 7 | 4 | 1 | 2 | 64.3 | 133 | 137 |
| v Portugal | 7 | 5 | 0 | 2 | 71.4 | 229 | 125 |
| v Tunisia | 9 | 6 | 0 | 3 | 66.7 | 197 | 152 |
| v Zimbabwe | 28 | 26 | 0 | 2 | 92.9 | 1023 | 557 |
| **Sub-Total** | **68** | **53** | **2** | **13** | **79.4** | **2421** | **1260** |
| **v Other Teams** | **20** | **13** | **0** | **7** | **65.0** | **741** | **378** |
| **All Internationals** | **131** | **74** | **2** | **55** | **57.2** | **3837** | **3428** |

# ROMANIA

Rugby was first brought to Romania when students, returning from their studies in Paris, formed Stadiul Roman, in addition to seventeen other clubs in Bucharest, in 1913. Although the Romanian Rugby Championship was contested in 1914, it was five years before the national side played its first International – against the United States in Stade Colombes, Paris, in June 1919. They lost that match by 21 points to nil.

In 1931, the governing body for rugby union in Romania, Federația Română de Rugby (FRR), was formed and a year later Romania became one of the nine founder members of the Fédération Internationale de Rugby Amateur (FIRA).

During the period 1919 to 1936, the Romanians played their opening eleven matches away from home, and it wasn't until 25 April 1937 that they finally played a home International against Italy in Bucharest, which ended scoreless. The Romanians were one of three teams to enter both the 1920 Antwerp Olympic Games and the 1924 Paris Olympic Games. They lost heavily to both a France XV and to the United States in the 1924 Games.

The team, nicknamed the 'Oaks', first entered the FIRA tournament in 1935 and are the only team to have played in all the competitions ever since. Of the eight FIRA Nations Cups held between 1965 and 1973, they won the title in 1968-69 and were runners-up to France on six occasions.

The Romanians were also four-time winners in the FIRA Trophy competition, held between 1974 and 1996, and runners-up to France on five occasions. During that time, the Oaks were arguably the top team in Europe, outside the Five Nations sides.

Romania won the European Nations Cup three times between 2000 and 2010 and finished in second place twice. The Romanians were also runners-up to Georgia in both the 2011-12 and the 2013-14 season of the ENC competition (which is now known as the Six Nations 'B' Championship).

Except for the 2006 tournament, Romania played in nine of the ten IRB Nations Cup competitions held between 2006 and 2015, winning in 2012, 2013 and 2015, and gaining second place in 2010 and 2014.

The Oaks have played in all eight World Cup competitions since their invitation to the 1987 tournament, the same year they joined the IRB. Unfortunately, they failed to progress further than the pool stage on each occasion. Their World Cup record currently stands at six wins in twenty-eight games played. They have played 73 matches against Tier 2 and 3 group rivals, winning on 38 occasions. They have beaten Tier 1 teams 28 times in 141 games, which includes 16 wins against Italy, 8 wins against France, and two each against Wales and Scotland. The away wins against Wales in 1988 and against France in 1990 remain their most memorable victories.

To the end of October 2015, the Oaks have played 418 international matches and of these have won 234, drawn 12, and lost 172; 108 of these defeats were against Tier 1 teams. Romania is currently in 17th place in the World Rugby rankings table.

# ROMANIA

## HEAD TO HEAD RESULTS TO 31 OCTOBER 2015

| | P | W | D | L | % | F | A |
|---|---|---|---|---|---|---|---|
| **v TIER 1 Teams** | | | | | | | |
| v Argentina | 8 | 0 | 0 | 8 | 0.0 | 97 | 317 |
| v Australia | 3 | 0 | 0 | 3 | 0.0 | 20 | 189 |
| v England | 5 | 0 | 0 | 5 | 0.0 | 24 | 335 |
| v France | 50 | 8 | 2 | 40 | 18.0 | 462 | 1315 |
| v Ireland | 9 | 0 | 0 | 9 | 0.0 | 102 | 390 |
| v Italy | 42 | 16 | 3 | 23 | 41.7 | 634 | 609 |
| v New Zealand | 2 | 0 | 0 | 2 | 0.0 | 14 | 99 |
| v Scotland | 13 | 2 | 0 | 11 | 15.4 | 192 | 475 |
| v South Africa | 1 | 0 | 0 | 1 | 0.0 | 8 | 21 |
| v Wales | 8 | 2 | 0 | 6 | 25.0 | 96 | 342 |
| **Sub-Total** | **141** | **28** | **5** | **108** | **21.6** | **1649** | **4092** |
| **v TIER 2/3 Group** | | | | | | | |
| v Canada | 6 | 4 | 0 | 2 | 66.7 | 92 | 117 |
| v Fiji | 3 | 1 | 0 | 2 | 33.3 | 42 | 70 |
| v Japan | 5 | 1 | 0 | 4 | 20.0 | 98 | 119 |
| v Samoa | 1 | 1 | 0 | 0 | 100.0 | 32 | 24 |
| v Tonga | 2 | 1 | 0 | 1 | 50.0 | 35 | 39 |
| v United States | 7 | 1 | 0 | 6 | 14.3 | 76 | 189 |
| v Georgia | 19 | 8 | 1 | 10 | 44.7 | 339 | 347 |
| v Namibia | 5 | 4 | 0 | 1 | 80.0 | 138 | 58 |
| v Russia | 19 | 12 | 1 | 6 | 65.8 | 460 | 284 |
| v Uruguay | 6 | 5 | 1 | 0 | 91.7 | 150 | 75 |
| **Sub-Total** | **73** | **38** | **3** | **32** | **54.1** | **1462** | **1322** |
| **v Tier 3 Selection** | | | | | | | |
| v Netherlands | 7 | 7 | 0 | 0 | 100.0 | 296 | 46 |
| v Poland | 16 | 14 | 0 | 2 | 87.5 | 514 | 143 |
| v Portugal | 22 | 19 | 0 | 3 | 86.4 | 683 | 213 |
| v Spain | 33 | 31 | 0 | 2 | 93.9 | 997 | 320 |
| v Ukraine | 7 | 7 | 0 | 0 | 100.0 | 400 | 43 |
| v USSR * | 15 | 12 | 0 | 3 | 80.0 | 251 | 153 |
| **Sub-Total** | **100** | **90** | **0** | **10** | **90.0** | **3141** | **918** |
| **v Other Teams** | **104** | **78** | **4** | **22** | **76.9** | **2928** | **1256** |
| **All Internationals** | **418** | **234** | **12** | **172** | **57.4** | **9180** | **7588** |

* 1976-90

# RUSSIA

The first official rugby match in the USSR took place in Moscow in 1923, but the Rugby Union of the Soviet Union was founded much later, in 1936. The national side did not play its first International until 1974, and all subsequent matches over the next two years were against eastern European teams. In 1977, the USSR was invited to play in Division 2 of the Fédération Internationale de Amateur (FIRA) tournament. By winning the title at the first attempt, the team was then promoted to Division 1. The Soviets performed reasonably well at the top level for the next six years and excelled in the 1984-85 season when they finished runners-up to France, ahead of both Romania and Italy. They also repeated that feat the following three seasons, in 1985-87, 1987-89 and 1989-90.

With the break up of the USSR in 1991, the Russian national team was born. It was administered by the Rugby Union of Russia (RUR), which subsequently became affiliated to the IRB. The Russians played their first match against Belgium on 11 October 1992, in the FIRA 1992-94 tournament, and although the team was depleted owing to the loss of a large number of players (who, following the break up of USSR, were now playing for the independent states), they still won that match by 17 points to 11. However, this loss of experienced players had a longer term effect on the team's performance and Russia was placed in Division 2 of the newly structured European Nations Cup in 2000.

Despite this, as immediate champions of that division the Russians were promoted to Division 1 in 2001, and were placed more or less in mid-table for the next six years. Success returned in 2007-08 and 2008-10 when they finished in second place to Georgia in both seasons. The Russians competed in ENC Division 1, renamed Six Nations 'B' in the 2011-12 and 2013-14 seasons.

They also competed in the IRB Nations Cup in 2006, 2008, 2009, 2012, 2013 and 2014, and by invitation in the Churchill Cup in 2010 and 2011. The then-USSR was invited to play in the first World Cup in 1987, but declined to take part on political grounds, not least the continued IRB membership of apartheid South Africa. In both the 1995 and 1999 World Cups, the Russian team failed to qualify, and was expelled from qualifying for the 2003 tournament for fielding ineligible players.

A loss to Portugal in the European qualifying rounds deprived them of a place in the 2007 World Cup, but they finally made it to the next World Cup in New Zealand in 2011. Disappointingly, they lost all four matches and finished bottom in a tough pool that consisted of Australia, Italy, Ireland and the United States.

The Russians have never beaten a Tier 1 team in all seven of their attempts, but they have defeated Tier 2 and 3 group rivals on 14 occasions in 63 matches. They failed to qualify for the 2015 World Cup when they lost on aggregate to Uruguay in a two-match play-off.

To the end of October 2015, the Russians have played 172 international matches, and of these have won 86, drawn 3, and lost 83. Russia is currently in 22nd place in the World Rugby rankings table.

# RUSSIA

## HEAD TO HEAD RESULTS TO 31 OCTOBER 2015

|  | P | W | D | L | % | F | A |
|---|---|---|---|---|---|---|---|
| **v TIER 1 Teams** | | | | | | | |
| v Australia | 1 | 0 | 0 | 1 | 0.0 | 22 | 68 |
| v Ireland | 2 | 0 | 0 | 2 | 0.0 | 15 | 97 |
| v Italy | 4 | 0 | 0 | 4 | 0.0 | 61 | 198 |
| **Sub-Total** | **7** | **0** | **0** | **7** | **0.0** | **98** | **363** |
| **v TIER 2/3 Group** | | | | | | | |
| v Canada | 3 | 0 | 0 | 3 | 0.0 | 27 | 91 |
| v Fiji | 0 | 0 | 0 | 0 | 0.0 | 0 | 0 |
| v Japan | 5 | 1 | 0 | 4 | 20.0 | 90 | 237 |
| v Romania | 19 | 6 | 1 | 12 | 34.2 | 284 | 460 |
| v Samoa | 0 | 0 | 0 | 0 | 0.0 | 0 | 0 |
| v Tonga | 0 | 0 | 0 | 0 | 0.0 | 0 | 0 |
| v United States | 6 | 0 | 0 | 6 | 0.0 | 97 | 193 |
| v Georgia | 19 | 1 | 1 | 17 | 7.9 | 224 | 476 |
| v Namibia | 4 | 2 | 0 | 2 | 50.0 | 85 | 111 |
| v Uruguay | 7 | 4 | 0 | 3 | 57.1 | 160 | 151 |
| **Sub-Total** | **63** | **14** | **2** | **47** | **23.8** | **967** | **1719** |
| **v Tier 3 Selection** | | | | | | | |
| v Belgium | 4 | 4 | 0 | 0 | 100.0 | 126 | 78 |
| v Czech Republic | 8 | 6 | 0 | 2 | 75.0 | 309 | 104 |
| v Denmark | 3 | 3 | 0 | 0 | 100.0 | 191 | 28 |
| v Germany | 7 | 7 | 0 | 0 | 100.0 | 352 | 79 |
| v Hong Kong | 2 | 2 | 0 | 0 | 100.0 | 70 | 37 |
| v Morocco | 3 | 2 | 0 | 1 | 66.7 | 44 | 46 |
| v Netherlands | 4 | 4 | 0 | 0 | 100.0 | 208 | 39 |
| v Poland | 4 | 4 | 0 | 0 | 100.0 | 201 | 59 |
| v Portugal | 17 | 11 | 1 | 5 | 67.7 | 442 | 329 |
| v Spain | 18 | 15 | 0 | 3 | 83.3 | 572 | 415 |
| v Tunisia | 2 | 2 | 0 | 0 | 100.0 | 57 | 41 |
| v Ukraine | 9 | 9 | 0 | 0 | 100.0 | 439 | 115 |
| **Sub-Total** | **81** | **69** | **1** | **11** | **85.8** | **3011** | **1370** |
| **v Other Teams** | **21** | **3** | **0** | **18** | **14.3** | **353** | **719** |
| **All Internationals** | **172** | **86** | **3** | **83** | **50.9** | **4429** | **4171** |

# SAMOA

The Marist Brothers religious order brought rugby to Western Samoa in 1920 and the Western Samoa Rugby Union was formed in 1924. Later that year, on 18 August, they lost their first International to Fiji on home ground in Apia, by 6 points to nil. A month later, on 19 September, Western Samoa gained revenge by defeating Fiji by 9 points to 3. In their third game at home, again against Fiji in 1928, they lost by 9 points to 8. The next match, in Apia in 1932, was against Tonga, and the Western Samoan team lost by 15 points to 9. However, they defeated Tonga in their next match in 1947, by 5 points to 3.

Nearly forty years elapsed before Western Samoans finally faced opponents from outside the South Pacific islands, in a match against Wales on 14 June 1986, which the Welsh won by 32 points to 14. This led to a return visit to Wales in 1988. Western Samoa lost the two Internationals on that tour: the first to Ireland by 49 points to 22, and the second to their hosts, Wales, by 28 points to 6.

The three Pacific Island teams met so regularly during the 1950s, 1960s and 1970s that in 1982 the South Pacific Championship was formed. Western Samoa won the inaugural competition, and also triumphed in 1985, but unlike Fiji and Tonga, the team was not invited to compete in the first World Cup in 1987. However, they have subsequently competed in all seven of the other World Cup tournaments.

Western Samoa caused a sensation in the 1991 World Cup when the team reached the quarter-final stage by eliminating both Wales and Argentina in the pool games. They repeated that feat in the 1995 World Cup when they beat Italy and Argentina again at the pool stage, only to lose to eventual winners South Africa in the last eight. The team, renamed Samoa in 1997, defeated hosts Wales yet again in the Millennium Stadium in the 1999 World Cup, but lost to Scotland in the play-off, required to secure a place in the quarter-final. The Samoans have not emerged from the pool stage in subsequent World Cup competitions.

Samoa have beaten Tier 1 teams 15 times in 66 games played, and Tier 2 and 3 group rivals 77 times in 140 games played. On the domestic front, the Samoans has been very successful, winning ten titles in the South Pacific Championship held between 1982 and 1997, and four titles in the Pacific Tri Nations Series staged between 1998 and 2005. Samoa also won the IRB Pacific Nations Cup in 2010 and 2012, and the Pacific section of that tournament in 2014.

To the end of October 2015, the Samoans have played 214 Internationals, and of these have won 97 of them, drawn 8 and lost 109. They have beaten local rivals, Tonga, 32 times out of 60 games played, and Fiji 20 times in 49 internationals. Samoa is currently in 15th place in the World Rugby rankings table.

# SAMOA

## HEAD TO HEAD RESULTS TO 31 OCTOBER 2015

| | P | W | D | L | % | F | A |
|---|---|---|---|---|---|---|---|
| **v TIER 1 Teams** | | | | | | | |
| v Argentina | 4 | 3 | 0 | 1 | 75.0 | 111 | 82 |
| v Australia | 5 | 1 | 0 | 4 | 20.0 | 58 | 204 |
| v England | 7 | 0 | 0 | 7 | 0.0 | 100 | 244 |
| v France | 3 | 0 | 0 | 3 | 0.0 | 41 | 104 |
| v Ireland | 6 | 1 | 0 | 5 | 16.7 | 103 | 209 |
| v Italy | 7 | 5 | 0 | 2 | 71.4 | 175 | 109 |
| v New Zealand | 6 | 0 | 0 | 6 | 0.0 | 72 | 333 |
| v Scotland | 10 | 1 | 1 | 8 | 15.0 | 155 | 254 |
| v South Africa | 9 | 0 | 0 | 9 | 0.0 | 99 | 431 |
| v Wales | 9 | 4 | 0 | 5 | 44.4 | 163 | 216 |
| **Sub-Total** | **66** | **15** | **1** | **50** | **23.5** | **1077** | **2186** |
| **v TIER 2/3 Group** | | | | | | | |
| v Canada | 5 | 5 | 0 | 0 | 100.0 | 144 | 80 |
| v Fiji | 49 | 20 | 3 | 26 | 43.9 | 864 | 951 |
| v Japan | 15 | 11 | 0 | 4 | 73.3 | 482 | 273 |
| v Romania | 1 | 0 | 0 | 1 | 0.0 | 24 | 32 |
| v Tonga | 60 | 32 | 4 | 24 | 56.7 | 1040 | 872 |
| v United States | 5 | 5 | 0 | 0 | 100.0 | 117 | 85 |
| v Georgia | 2 | 1 | 0 | 1 | 50.0 | 61 | 25 |
| v Namibia | 2 | 2 | 0 | 0 | 100.0 | 89 | 25 |
| v Russia | 0 | 0 | 0 | 0 | 0.0 | 0 | 0 |
| v Uruguay | 1 | 1 | 0 | 0 | 100.0 | 60 | 13 |
| **Sub-Total** | **140** | **77** | **7** | **56** | **57.5** | **2881** | **2356** |
| **v Tier 3 Selection** | | | | | | | |
| v Belgium | 1 | 1 | 0 | 0 | 100.0 | 37 | 8 |
| v South Korea | 1 | 1 | 0 | 0 | 100.0 | 74 | 7 |
| v Papua New Guinea | 2 | 2 | 0 | 0 | 100.0 | 188 | 19 |
| **Sub-Total** | **4** | **4** | **0** | **0** | **100.0** | **299** | **34** |
| **v Other Teams** | **4** | **1** | **0** | **3** | **25.0** | **74** | **67** |
| **All Internationals** | **214** | **97** | **8** | **109** | **47.2** | **4331** | **4643** |

# TONGA

Rugby was introduced to Tonga in the early part of the twentieth century. Following the formation of the Tonga Rugby Football Union in late 1923, the team (nicknamed 'The Sea Eagles') won their first match at home, in Nuku'alofa, in August 1924 by defeating neighbours Fiji by 9 points to 6. With the exception of one match against Western Samoa in 1932, Tonga's only opponent was Fiji, whom they played a further sixteen times between September 1924 and July 1947, before facing Western Samoa again in August 1947.

Most of the Sea Eagles' games in the 1960s were against old rivals Fiji and Western Samoa, but in 1973 they toured Australia and gained a memorable 16 points to 11 win against their hosts in the second International. The Tongans lost heavily to a Scottish XV and to a Welsh XV on their first tour to the Northern Hemisphere in 1974, but redeemed themselves admirably by beating Canada by 40 points to 14 on their return journey home.

Tonga has contested seven of the eight World Cup competitions held to date, the only exception being the 1991 tournament when the team failed to qualify. Despite their involvement, they have never progressed beyond the pool stages, winning only seven matches out of twenty-five played. The Sea Eagles' most notable victory came in the 2011 World Cup when they defeated France by 19 points to 14, recalling an earlier home win against the French in June 1999. A previous World Cup win against Italy, also in 1999, meant that their 2011 triumph was the fourth against Tier 1 teams. This record was increased to five when the Tongans defeated Scotland in Edinburgh in November 2012.

When it comes to wins, Tonga has never had more than four in a row, but sequences of losses have been rather more commonplace: twelve consecutive defeats between October 2003 and November 2005 probably represents the lowest point in their history. Tonga has also been less successful than both Fiji and Samoa in the domestic tournaments, winning only two titles out of fifteen (in 1983 and 1986) in the South Pacific Championship held between 1982 and 1997, and registering no victories at all in the Pacific Tri Nations Series staged between 1998 and 2005. The Sea Eagles did achieve some success when they beat both their South Sea rivals in the IRB Pacific Nations Cup in 2011.

The Tongans have played 188 Internationals against Tier 2 and 3 group rivals, and of these have won 74, drawn 7, and lost 107. Their record against Tier 1 countries remains at 5 wins in 36 matches played.

To the end of October 2015, the Sea Eagles have played 259 international matches and of these have won 99, drawn 7, and lost 153. Against their Pacific rivals, they have beaten Fiji only 26 times in 88 matches played, and Samoa only 24 times in 60 matches. Tonga is currently in 13th place in the World Rugby rankings table.

# TONGA

## HEAD TO HEAD RESULTS TO 31 OCTOBER 2015

| | P | W | D | L | % | F | A |
|---|---|---|---|---|---|---|---|
| **v TIER 1 Teams** | | | | | | | |
| v Argentina | 1 | 0 | 0 | 1 | 0.0 | 16 | 45 |
| v Australia | 4 | 1 | 0 | 3 | 25.0 | 42 | 167 |
| v England | 2 | 0 | 0 | 2 | 0.0 | 30 | 137 |
| v France | 5 | 2 | 0 | 3 | 40.0 | 75 | 149 |
| v Ireland | 2 | 0 | 0 | 2 | 0.0 | 28 | 72 |
| v Italy | 4 | 1 | 0 | 3 | 25.0 | 63 | 137 |
| v New Zealand | 5 | 0 | 0 | 5 | 0.0 | 35 | 326 |
| v Scotland | 4 | 1 | 0 | 3 | 25.0 | 58 | 136 |
| v South Africa | 2 | 0 | 0 | 2 | 0.0 | 35 | 104 |
| v Wales | 7 | 0 | 0 | 7 | 0.0 | 78 | 203 |
| **Sub-Total** | **36** | **5** | **0** | **31** | **13.9** | **460** | **1476** |
| **v TIER 2/3 Group** | | | | | | | |
| v Canada | 8 | 3 | 0 | 5 | 37.5 | 155 | 193 |
| v Fiji | 88 | 26 | 3 | 59 | 31.2 | 1163 | 1724 |
| v Japan | 16 | 9 | 0 | 7 | 56.2 | 440 | 379 |
| v Romania | 2 | 1 | 0 | 1 | 50.0 | 39 | 35 |
| v Samoa | 60 | 24 | 4 | 32 | 43.3 | 872 | 1040 |
| v United States | 8 | 7 | 0 | 1 | 87.5 | 221 | 117 |
| v Georgia | 4 | 2 | 0 | 2 | 50.0 | 97 | 60 |
| v Namibia | 2 | 2 | 0 | 0 | 100.0 | 55 | 35 |
| v Russia | 0 | 0 | 0 | 0 | 0.0 | 0 | 0 |
| v Uruguay | 0 | 0 | 0 | 0 | 0.0 | 0 | 0 |
| **Sub-Total** | **188** | **74** | **7** | **107** | **41.2** | **3042** | **3583** |
| **v Tier 3 Selection** | | | | | | | |
| v Cook Islands | 3 | 3 | 0 | 0 | 100.0 | 235 | 22 |
| v South Korea | 6 | 6 | 0 | 0 | 100.0 | 464 | 66 |
| v New Zealand Maori | 12 | 4 | 0 | 8 | 33.3 | 165 | 319 |
| v Papua New Guinea | 2 | 2 | 0 | 0 | 100.0 | 131 | 26 |
| **Sub-Total** | **23** | **15** | **0** | **8** | **65.2** | **995** | **433** |
| **v Other Teams** | **12** | **5** | **0** | **7** | **41.7** | **218** | **345** |
| **All Internationals** | **259** | **99** | **7** | **153** | **39.6** | **4715** | **5837** |

# UNITED STATES

The first rugby match recorded in the United States occurred on 14 May 1874, when Harvard University hosted a team from McGill University, Montreal. The national team then played its first International in 1912, losing by 12 points to 8 against Australia.

The United States' first International win was against Romania in 1919, and a year later, at the Antwerp Olympics, the US team won the rugby Gold Medal. Nicknamed 'The Eagles', the team surprised the world at the next Olympic Games, held in Paris in 1924, when they defeated the host nation, France, in the final and won a second Gold Medal. Because Rugby has not featured in subsequent Olympics, the USA remains the holders.

The Eagles have competed in seven of the eight World Cup competitions held to date, the only exception being the 1995 tournament when they failed to qualify for the finals. In twenty-five matches played in the World Cup, the USA has won only three times: twice against Japan in 1987 and 2003, and once against Russia in 2011.

There were also few triumphs for the Eagles in the five Pacific Rim championships, held annually between 1996 and 2001. However, some success came their way in 2003 when they finished runners-up to Argentina, ahead of both Canada and Uruguay, in the Pan American Championships, which was staged five times between 1995 and 2003. It was also in 2003 that the Eagles won four International matches in a row, for the first time, when they defeated Japan, Canada, and Spain twice. They also gained four successive wins between November 2009 and November 2010. On the other side of the coin, the US team suffered a run of ten consecutive losses between May 2007 and June 2008. Four of those losses, to England, Tonga, Samoa and South Africa, occurred in the 2007 World Cup in France.

The Eagles have also competed in all nine Churchill Cup tournaments, held between 2003 and 2011. Their best result in that competition was in 2005 when they won the plate competition as runners-up to England 'A'. In March 2014, the United States qualified for the 2015 World Cup by holding Uruguay to a draw in Montevideo and defeating them in Atlanta a week later.

With the exception of their win against France in 1924, the United States have never beaten any of the Tier 1 teams in the 59 matches played, and have won only 57 times in the 127 internationals played against Tier 2 and 3 group rivals.

To the end of October 2015, the Eagles have played 221 Internationals, and of these have won 71 games, drawn 3, and lost 147. They are currently in 16th place in the World Rugby rankings table.

# UNITED STATES

## HEAD TO HEAD RESULTS TO 31 OCTOBER 2015

|  | P | W | D | L | % | F | A |
|---|---|---|---|---|---|---|---|
| **v TIER 1 Teams** | | | | | | | |
| v Argentina | 8 | 0 | 0 | 8 | 0.0 | 119 | 247 |
| v Australia | 8 | 0 | 0 | 8 | 0.0 | 78 | 368 |
| v England | 5 | 0 | 0 | 5 | 0.0 | 52 | 253 |
| v France | 7 | 1 | 0 | 6 | 14.3 | 93 | 181 |
| v Ireland | 8 | 0 | 0 | 8 | 0.0 | 82 | 306 |
| v Italy | 4 | 0 | 0 | 4 | 0.0 | 54 | 130 |
| v New Zealand | 3 | 0 | 0 | 3 | 0.0 | 15 | 171 |
| v Scotland | 5 | 0 | 0 | 5 | 0.0 | 66 | 220 |
| v South Africa | 4 | 0 | 0 | 4 | 0.0 | 42 | 209 |
| v Wales | 7 | 0 | 0 | 7 | 0.0 | 86 | 305 |
| **Sub-Total** | **59** | **1** | **0** | **58** | **1.7** | **687** | **2390** |
| **v TIER 2/3 Group** | | | | | | | |
| v Canada | 54 | 15 | 1 | 38 | 28.7 | 810 | 1262 |
| v Fiji | 6 | 1 | 0 | 5 | 16.7 | 97 | 143 |
| v Japan | 23 | 13 | 1 | 9 | 58.7 | 655 | 526 |
| v Romania | 7 | 6 | 0 | 1 | 85.7 | 189 | 76 |
| v Samoa | 5 | 0 | 0 | 5 | 0.0 | 85 | 117 |
| v Tonga | 8 | 1 | 0 | 7 | 12.5 | 117 | 221 |
| v Georgia | 4 | 3 | 0 | 1 | 75.0 | 109 | 75 |
| v Namibia | 0 | 0 | 0 | 0 | 0.0 | 0 | 0 |
| v Russia | 6 | 6 | 0 | 0 | 100.0 | 193 | 97 |
| v Uruguay | 14 | 12 | 1 | 1 | 89.3 | 438 | 211 |
| **Sub-Total** | **127** | **57** | **3** | **67** | **46.1** | **2693** | **2728** |
| **v Tier 3 Selection** | | | | | | | |
| v Hong Kong | 7 | 3 | 0 | 4 | 42.9 | 152 | 191 |
| v Portugal | 2 | 2 | 0 | 0 | 100.0 | 83 | 22 |
| v Spain | 3 | 3 | 0 | 0 | 100.0 | 169 | 29 |
| **Sub-Total** | **12** | **8** | **0** | **4** | **66.7** | **404** | **242** |
| **v Tier 1 XV teams** | **8** | **1** | **0** | **7** | **12.5** | **84** | **272** |
| **v Other Teams** | **15** | **4** | **0** | **11** | **26.7** | **358** | **479** |
| **All Internationals** | **221** | **71** | **3** | **147** | **32.8** | **4226** | **6111** |

# URUGUAY

It is generally accepted that rugby was introduced to Uruguay in the early twentieth century through the network of schools run by the Christian Brothers religious order. The Uruguayan Rugby Union, known as Unión de Rugby del Uruguay, was then formed in January 1951. Nine months later, the first South American Championship was staged: Uruguay lost heavily to the Argentinians but defeated both Chile and Brazil and finished as runners-up. In the second Championship, held in 1958, Uruguay lost to both Argentina and Chile and finished in third place ahead of Peru, who lost all three of their matches. In August 1960, the Uruguayan team played a France XV, their first match against a Northern Hemisphere side, and lost by 59 points to nil.

Throughout the 1960s all Uruguay's matches were against fellow South American sides, and only once during the 1970s, when they lost to a touring New Zealand XV in 1976, did they face a nation outside the continent. The Uruguayans played only four matches against non-South American teams during the 1980s, losing to a France XV in 1985, Spain in 1987, winning against Belgium in 1988 and losing to the United States in 1989. It was in 1989 that the Uruguayan Union joined the IRB. This development opened up opportunities to play against teams outside South America.

A loss to Canada and a win against Spain in 1995 paved the way for Uruguay's first fixtures overseas, with a visit to North America in 1996. Nicknamed 'Los Teros' (the Lapwings), they lost on two occasions on that tour: first to Canada and then to the USA. They hosted both countries in return matches in 1998, only to lose both games again. On the domestic front, however, Uruguay has come second only to Argentina as the dominant team in South America.

The highlight of the 1990s occurred when Uruguay qualified for the 1999 World Cup in Wales and by defeating Spain, Los Teros finished third in a pool of four teams. In 2003, they again qualified for the World Cup and finished fourth in a pool of five after defeating Georgia. Uruguay failed to qualify for either the 2007 World Cup or the 2011 World Cup, but qualified for the 2015 World Cup by winning, on aggregate, a two-legged play-off against Russia in October 2014.

Throughout the 2000s, Uruguay has been involved in many tournaments, such as the Pan American Championship, the Intercontinental Cup, the IRB Nations Cup (in 2008, 2009, 2012 and 2014), and the Tblisi Cup in 2013 and 2015.

The Uruguayans have an excellent record in the South American Championship. In thirty-seven tournaments, to 2015, they have been runners-up to Argentina on twenty-seven occasions and won the tournament in 1981 and again in 2014 (on both occasions, Argentina did not enter the competition).

In their 58 attempts, most of which have been against Argentina, they have failed to beat a Tier 1 team and have had only 9 wins in 50 International matches against Tier 2 and 3 group rivals.

To the end of October 2015, Los Teros have played 235 Internationals and of these have won 103, drawn 4, and lost 128. They are currently in 19th place in the World Rugby rankings table.

# URUGUAY

## HEAD TO HEAD RESULTS TO 31 OCTOBER 2015

| | P | W | D | L | % | F | A |
|---|---|---|---|---|---|---|---|
| **v TIER 1 Teams** | | | | | | | |
| v Argentina | 40 | 0 | 0 | 40 | 0.0 | 405 | 1702 |
| v Argentina XV | 7 | 1 | 0 | 6 | 14.3 | 81 | 344 |
| v Australia | 1 | 0 | 0 | 1 | 0.0 | 3 | 65 |
| v England | 2 | 0 | 0 | 2 | 0.0 | 16 | 171 |
| v France 'A' | 2 | 0 | 0 | 2 | 0.0 | 6 | 93 |
| v Italy | 3 | 0 | 0 | 3 | 0.0 | 25 | 92 |
| v New Zealand XV | 1 | 0 | 0 | 1 | 0.0 | 3 | 64 |
| v Scotland | 1 | 0 | 0 | 1 | 0.0 | 12 | 43 |
| v South Africa | 3 | 0 | 0 | 3 | 0.0 | 12 | 245 |
| v Wales | 1 | 0 | 0 | 1 | 0.0 | 9 | 54 |
| **Sub-Total** | **58** | **1** | **0** | **57** | **1.8** | **563** | **2716** |
| **v TIER 2/3 Group** | | | | | | | |
| v Canada | 8 | 1 | 0 | 7 | 12.5 | 108 | 247 |
| v Fiji | 2 | 0 | 0 | 2 | 0.0 | 39 | 86 |
| v Fiji XV | 3 | 0 | 0 | 3 | 0.0 | 47 | 96 |
| v Japan | 3 | 1 | 0 | 2 | 33.3 | 32 | 88 |
| v Romania | 6 | 0 | 1 | 5 | 8.3 | 75 | 150 |
| v Samoa | 1 | 0 | 0 | 1 | 0.0 | 13 | 60 |
| v United States | 14 | 1 | 1 | 12 | 10.7 | 211 | 438 |
| v Georgia | 5 | 2 | 0 | 3 | 40.0 | 72 | 85 |
| v Namibia | 1 | 1 | 0 | 0 | 100.0 | 23 | 12 |
| v Russia | 7 | 3 | 0 | 4 | 42.9 | 151 | 160 |
| **Sub-Total** | **50** | **9** | **2** | **39** | **20.0** | **771** | **1422** |
| **v Tier 3 Selection** | | | | | | | |
| v Belgium | 1 | 1 | 0 | 0 | 100.0 | 39 | 13 |
| v Brazil | 21 | 19 | 0 | 2 | 90.5 | 760 | 171 |
| v Chile | 46 | 34 | 1 | 11 | 75.0 | 1060 | 709 |
| v Morocco | 2 | 1 | 0 | 1 | 50.0 | 36 | 24 |
| v Paraguay | 24 | 23 | 1 | 0 | 97.9 | 1217 | 204 |
| v Portugal | 10 | 7 | 0 | 3 | 70.0 | 234 | 142 |
| v Spain | 8 | 4 | 0 | 4 | 50.0 | 155 | 109 |
| v Venezuela | 1 | 1 | 0 | 0 | 100.0 | 92 | 8 |
| **Sub-Total** | **113** | **90** | **2** | **21** | **80.5** | **3593** | **1380** |
| **v Other Teams** | **14** | **3** | **0** | **11** | **21.4** | **169** | **464** |
| **All Internationals** | **235** | **103** | **4** | **128** | **44.7** | **5096** | **5982** |

# RUGBY WORLD CUPS

## 1987-2015

| | |
|---|---|
| 1987 | NEW ZEALAND & AUSTRALIA |
| 1991 | ENGLAND |
| 1995 | SOUTH AFRICA |
| 1999 | WALES |
| 2003 | AUSTRALIA |
| 2007 | FRANCE |
| 2011 | NEW ZEALAND |
| 2015 | ENGLAND |

## POOL STAGES

### Pool

| | | | | | | |
|---|---|---|---|---|---|---|
| 3 | 22 May | New Zealand | 70 | Italy | 6 | Eden Park, Auckland |
| 4 | 23 May | Scotland | 20 | France | 20 | Lancaster Park Oval, Christchurch |
| 4 | 23 May | Romania | 21 | Zimbabwe | 20 | Eden Park, Auckland |
| 1 | 23 May | Australia | 19 | England | 6 | Concord Oval, Sydney |
| 2 | 24 May | Canada | 37 | Tonga | 4 | McLean Park, Napier |
| 3 | 24 May | Fiji | 28 | Argentina | 9 | Rugby Park, Hamilton |
| 1 | 24 May | United States | 21 | Japan | 18 | Ballymore Oval, Brisbane |
| 2 | 25 May | Wales | 13 | Ireland | 6 | Athletic Park, Wellington |
| 3 | 27 May | New Zealand | 74 | Fiji | 13 | Lancaster Park Oval, Christchurch |
| 3 | 28 May | Argentina | 25 | Italy | 16 | Lancaster Park Oval, Christchurch |
| 4 | 28 May | France | 55 | Romania | 12 | Athletic Park, Wellington |
| 2 | 29 May | Wales | 29 | Tonga | 16 | Showgrounds Oval, Palmerston N. |
| 2 | 30 May | Ireland | 46 | Canada | 19 | Carisbrook, Dunedin |
| 4 | 30 May | Scotland | 60 | Zimbabwe | 21 | Athletic Park, Wellington |
| 1 | 30 May | England | 60 | Japan | 7 | Concord Oval, Sydney |
| 3 | 31 May | Italy | 18 | Fiji | 15 | Carisbrook, Dunedin |
| 1 | 31 May | Australia | 47 | United States | 12 | Ballymore Oval, Brisbane |
| 3 | 1 June | New Zealand | 46 | Argentina | 15 | Athletic Park, Wellington |
| 4 | 2 June | Scotland | 55 | Romania | 28 | Carisbrook, Dunedin |
| 4 | 2 June | France | 70 | Zimbabwe | 12 | Eden Park, Auckland |
| 2 | 3 June | Wales | 40 | Canada | 9 | Rugby Park Stadium, Invercargill |
| 2 | 3 June | Ireland | 32 | Tonga | 9 | Ballymore Oval, Brisbane |
| 1 | 3 June | Australia | 42 | Japan | 23 | Concord Oval, Sydney |
| 1 | 3 June | England | 34 | United States | 6 | Concord Oval, Sydney |

### QUARTER-FINALS

| | | | | | |
|---|---|---|---|---|---|
| 6 June | New Zealand | 30 | Scotland | 3 | Lancaster Park Oval, Christchurch |
| 7 June | France | 31 | Fiji | 16 | Eden Park, Auckland |
| 7 June | Australia | 33 | Ireland | 15 | Concord Oval, Sydney |
| 8 June | Wales | 16 | England | 3 | Ballymore Oval, Brisbane |

### SEMI-FINALS

| | | | | | |
|---|---|---|---|---|---|
| 13 June | Australia | 24 | France | 30 | Concord Oval, Sydney |
| 14 June | New Zealand | 49 | Wales | 6 | Ballymore Oval, Brisbane |

### BRONZE

| | | | | | |
|---|---|---|---|---|---|
| 18 June | Wales | 22 | Australia | 21 | Rotorua Internat. Stadium, Rotorua |

### FINAL

| | | | | | |
|---|---|---|---|---|---|
| 20 June | New Zealand | 29 | France | 9 | Eden Park, Auckland |

## POOL STAGES

**POOL 1**

| | P | W | D | L | For | Against | PTS |
|---|---|---|---|---|---|---|---|
| Australia | 3 | 3 | 0 | 0 | 108 | 41 | 6 |
| England | 3 | 2 | 0 | 1 | 100 | 32 | 4 |
| United States | 3 | 1 | 0 | 2 | 39 | 99 | 2 |
| Japan | 3 | 0 | 0 | 3 | 48 | 123 | 0 |

**POOL 2**

| | P | W | D | L | For | Against | PTS |
|---|---|---|---|---|---|---|---|
| Wales | 3 | 3 | 0 | 0 | 82 | 31 | 6 |
| Ireland | 3 | 2 | 0 | 1 | 84 | 41 | 4 |
| Canada | 3 | 1 | 0 | 2 | 65 | 90 | 2 |
| Tonga | 3 | 0 | 0 | 3 | 29 | 98 | 0 |

**POOL 3**

| | P | W | D | L | For | Against | PTS |
|---|---|---|---|---|---|---|---|
| New Zealand | 3 | 3 | 0 | 0 | 190 | 34 | 6 |
| Fiji | 3 | 1 | 0 | 2 | 56 | 101 | 2 |
| Argentina | 3 | 1 | 0 | 2 | 49 | 90 | 2 |
| Italy | 3 | 1 | 0 | 2 | 40 | 110 | 2 |

**POOL 4**

| | P | W | D | L | For | Against | PTS |
|---|---|---|---|---|---|---|---|
| France | 3 | 2 | 1 | 0 | 145 | 44 | 5 |
| Scotland | 3 | 2 | 1 | 0 | 135 | 69 | 5 |
| Romania | 3 | 1 | 0 | 2 | 61 | 130 | 2 |
| Zimbabwe | 3 | 0 | 0 | 3 | 53 | 151 | 0 |

## POOL STAGES
### Pool

| | | | | | | |
|---|---|---|---|---|---|---|
| A | 3 Oct. | England | 12 | New Zealand | 18 | Twickenham, London |
| C | 4 Oct. | Australia | 32 | Argentina | 19 | Stradey Park, Llanelli |
| D | 4 Oct. | France | 30 | Romania | 3 | Stade de la Méditerranée, Béziers |
| A | 5 Oct. | Italy | 30 | United States | 9 | Cross Green, Otley |
| B | 5 Oct. | Scotland | 47 | Japan | 9 | Murrayfield, Edinburgh |
| D | 5 Oct. | Canada | 13 | Fiji | 3 | Stade Jean Dauger, Bayonne |
| C | 6 Oct. | Wales | 13 | W. Samoa | 16 | National Stadium, Cardiff |
| B | 6 Oct. | Ireland | 55 | Zimbabwe | 11 | Lansdowne Road, Dublin |
| A | 8 Oct. | New Zealand | 46 | United States | 6 | Kingsholm, Gloucester |
| A | 8 Oct. | England | 36 | Italy | 6 | Twickenham, London |
| D | 8 Oct. | France | 33 | Fiji | 9 | Stade Lesdiguières, Grenoble |
| C | 9 Oct. | Australia | 9 | W. Samoa | 3 | Pontypool Park, Pontypool |
| B | 9 Oct. | Ireland | 32 | Japan | 16 | Lansdowne Road, Dublin |
| B | 9 Oct. | Scotland | 51 | Zimbabwe | 12 | Murrayfield, Edinburgh |
| D | 9 Oct. | Canada | 19 | Romania | 11 | Stade Ernest -Wallon, Toulouse |
| C | 9 Oct. | Wales | 16 | Argentina | 7 | National Stadium, Cardiff |
| A | 11 Oct. | England | 37 | United States | 9 | Twickenham, London |
| B | 12 Oct. | Scotland | 24 | Ireland | 15 | Murrayfield, Edinburgh |
| C | 12 Oct. | Wales | 3 | Australia | 38 | National Stadium, Cardiff |
| D | 12 Oct. | Romania | 17 | Fiji | 15 | Parc Municipal des Sports, Brive |
| C | 13 Oct. | W Samoa | 35 | Argentina | 12 | Sardis Road, Pontypridd |
| A | 13 Oct. | New Zealand | 31 | Italy | 21 | Welford Road, Leicester |
| D | 13 Oct. | France | 19 | Canada | 13 | Stade Armandie, Agen |
| B | 14 Oct. | Japan | 52 | Zimbabwe | 6 | Ravenhill, Belfast |

### QUARTER-FINALS

| | | | | | |
|---|---|---|---|---|---|
| 19 Oct. | Scotland | 28 | W. Samoa | 6 | Murrayfield, Edinburgh |
| 19 Oct. | France | 10 | England | 19 | Parc des Princess, Paris |
| 20 Oct. | New Zealand | 29 | Canada | 13 | Stade Lille-Métropole, Villeneuve |
| 20 Oct. | Ireland | 18 | Australia | 19 | Lansdowne Road, Dublin |

### SEMI-FINALS

| | | | | | |
|---|---|---|---|---|---|
| 26 Oct. | Scotland | 6 | England | 9 | Murrayfield, Edinburgh |
| 27 Oct. | Australia | 16 | New Zealand | 6 | Lansdowne Road, Dublin |

### BRONZE

| | | | | | |
|---|---|---|---|---|---|
| 30 Oct. | New Zealand | 13 | Scotland | 6 | National Stadium, Cardiff |

### FINAL

| | | | | | |
|---|---|---|---|---|---|
| 2 Nov. | England | 6 | Australia | 12 | Twickenham, London |

**POOL STAGES**

**POOL A**

| | P | W | D | L | For | Against | PTS |
|---|---|---|---|---|---|---|---|
| New Zealand | 3 | 3 | 0 | 0 | 95 | 39 | 9 |
| England | 3 | 2 | 0 | 1 | 85 | 33 | 7 |
| Italy | 3 | 1 | 0 | 2 | 57 | 76 | 5 |
| United States | 3 | 0 | 0 | 3 | 24 | 113 | 3 |

**POOL B**

| | P | W | D | L | For | Against | PTS |
|---|---|---|---|---|---|---|---|
| Scotland | 3 | 3 | 0 | 0 | 122 | 36 | 9 |
| Ireland | 3 | 2 | 0 | 1 | 102 | 51 | 7 |
| Japan | 3 | 1 | 0 | 2 | 77 | 87 | 5 |
| Zimbabwe | 3 | 0 | 0 | 3 | 31 | 158 | 3 |

**POOL C**

| | P | W | D | L | For | Against | PTS |
|---|---|---|---|---|---|---|---|
| Australia | 3 | 3 | 0 | 0 | 79 | 25 | 9 |
| W. Samoa | 3 | 2 | 0 | 1 | 54 | 34 | 7 |
| Wales | 3 | 1 | 0 | 2 | 32 | 61 | 5 |
| Argentina | 3 | 0 | 0 | 3 | 38 | 83 | 3 |

**POOL D**

| | P | W | D | L | For | Against | PTS |
|---|---|---|---|---|---|---|---|
| France | 3 | 3 | 0 | 0 | 82 | 25 | 9 |
| Canada | 3 | 2 | 0 | 1 | 45 | 33 | 7 |
| Romania | 3 | 1 | 0 | 2 | 31 | 64 | 5 |
| Fiji | 3 | 0 | 0 | 3 | 27 | 63 | 3 |

## POOL STAGES
### Pool

| | | | | | | |
|---|---|---|---|---|---|---|
| A | 25 May | South Africa | 27 | Australia | 18 | Newlands Stadium, Cape Town |
| D | 26 May | Scotland | 89 | Côte d'Ivoire | 0 | Olympia Park, Rustenburg |
| D | 26 May | France | 38 | Tonga | 10 | Loftus Versfeld Stadium, Pretoria |
| A | 26 May | Canada | 34 | Romania | 3 | Boet Erasmus Stadium, Port Elizabeth |
| B | 27 May | W Samoa | 42 | Italy | 18 | Basil Kenyon Stadium, East London |
| C | 27 May | Wales | 57 | Japan | 10 | Free State Stadium, Bloemfontein |
| B | 27 May | England | 24 | Argentina | 18 | Kings Park Stadium, Durban |
| C | 27 May | New Zealand | 43 | Ireland | 19 | Ellis Park, Johannesburg |
| B | 30 May | W Samoa | 32 | Argentina | 26 | Basil Kenyon Stadium, East London |
| A | 30 May | South Africa | 21 | Romania | 8 | Newlands Stadium, Cape Town |
| D | 30 May | France | 54 | Côte d'Ivoire | 18 | Olympia Park, Rustenburg |
| D | 30 May | Scotland | 41 | Tonga | 5 | Loftus Versfeld Stadium, Pretoria |
| A | 31 May | Australia | 27 | Canada | 11 | Boet Erasmus Stadium, Port Elizabeth |
| C | 31 May | Ireland | 50 | Japan | 28 | Free State Stadium, Bloemfontein |
| B | 31 May | England | 27 | Italy | 20 | Kings Park Stadium, Durban |
| C | 31 May | New Zealand | 34 | Wales | 9 | Ellis Park, Johannesburg |
| D | 3 June | Tonga | 29 | Côte d'Ivoire | 11 | Olympia Park, Rustenburg |
| A | 3 June | Australia | 42 | Romania | 3 | Danie Craven Stadium, Stellenbosch |
| D | 3 June | France | 22 | Scotland | 19 | Loftus Versfeld Stadium, Pretoria |
| A | 3 June | South Africa | 20 | Canada | 0 | Boet Erasmus Stadium, Port Elizabeth |
| B | 4 June | Italy | 31 | Argentina | 25 | Basil Kenyon Stadium, East London |
| C | 4 June | New Zealand | 145 | Japan | 17 | Free State Stadium, Bloemfontein |
| C | 4 June | Ireland | 24 | Wales | 23 | Ellis Park, Johannesburg |
| B | 4 June | England | 44 | W Samoa | 22 | Kings Park Stadium, Durban |

### QUARTER-FINALS

| | | | | | | |
|---|---|---|---|---|---|---|
| | 10 June | South Africa | 42 | W. Samoa | 14 | Ellis Park, Johannesburg |
| | 10 June | France | 36 | Ireland | 12 | Kings Park Stadium, Durban |
| | 11 June | England | 25 | Australia | 22 | Newlands Stadium, Cape Town |
| | 11 June | New Zealand | 48 | Scotland | 30 | Loftus Versfeld, Pretoria |

### SEMI-FINALS

| | | | | | | |
|---|---|---|---|---|---|---|
| | 17 June | South Africa | 19 | France | 15 | Kings Park Stadium, Durban |
| | 18 June | New Zealand | 45 | England | 29 | Newlands Stadium, Cape Town |

### BRONZE

| | | | | | | |
|---|---|---|---|---|---|---|
| | 22 June | France | 19 | England | 9 | Loftus Versfeld Stadium, Pretoria |

### FINAL

| | | | | | | |
|---|---|---|---|---|---|---|
| | 24 June | South Africa | 15 | New Zealand | 12 | Ellis Park, Johannesburg (a e t) |

## POOL STAGES

| POOL A | | P | W | D | L | For | Against | PTS |
|---|---|---|---|---|---|---|---|---|
| | South Africa | 3 | 3 | 0 | 0 | 68 | 26 | 9 |
| | Australia | 3 | 2 | 0 | 1 | 87 | 41 | 7 |
| | Canada | 3 | 1 | 0 | 2 | 45 | 50 | 5 |
| | Romania | 3 | 0 | 0 | 3 | 14 | 97 | 3 |

| POOL B | | P | W | D | L | For | Against | PTS |
|---|---|---|---|---|---|---|---|---|
| | England | 3 | 3 | 0 | 0 | 95 | 60 | 9 |
| | W. Samoa | 3 | 2 | 0 | 1 | 96 | 88 | 7 |
| | Italy | 3 | 1 | 0 | 2 | 69 | 94 | 5 |
| | Argentina | 3 | 0 | 0 | 3 | 69 | 87 | 3 |

| POOL C | | P | W | D | L | For | Against | PTS |
|---|---|---|---|---|---|---|---|---|
| | New Zealand | 3 | 3 | 0 | 0 | 222 | 45 | 9 |
| | Ireland | 3 | 2 | 0 | 1 | 93 | 94 | 7 |
| | Wales | 3 | 1 | 0 | 2 | 89 | 68 | 5 |
| | Japan | 3 | 0 | 0 | 3 | 55 | 252 | 3 |

| POOL D | | P | W | D | L | For | Against | PTS |
|---|---|---|---|---|---|---|---|---|
| | France | 3 | 3 | 0 | 0 | 114 | 47 | 9 |
| | Scotland | 3 | 2 | 0 | 1 | 149 | 27 | 7 |
| | Tonga | 3 | 1 | 0 | 2 | 44 | 90 | 5 |
| | Côte d'Ivoire | 3 | 0 | 0 | 3 | 29 | 172 | 3 |

## POOL STAGES
**Pool**

| | | | | | | |
|---|---|---|---|---|---|---|
| 4 | 1 Oct. | Wales | 23 | Argentina | 18 | Millennium Stadium, Cardiff |
| 3 | 1 Oct. | Fiji | 67 | Namibia | 18 | Stade de la Méditerranée, Béziers |
| 3 | 2 Oct. | France | 33 | Canada | 20 | Stade de la Méditerranée, Béziers |
| 1 | 2 Oct. | Uruguay | 27 | Spain | 15 | Netherdale, Galashiels |
| 2 | 2 Oct. | England | 67 | Italy | 7 | Twickenham, London |
| 5 | 2 Oct. | Ireland | 53 | United States | 8 | Lansdowne Road, Dublin |
| 4 | 3 Oct. | Samoa | 43 | Japan | 9 | Racecourse Ground, Wrexham |
| 2 | 3 Oct. | New Zealand | 45 | Tonga | 9 | Ashdon Gate, Bristol |
| 1 | 3 Oct. | Scotland | 29 | South Africa | 46 | Murrayfield, Edinburgh |
| 5 | 3 Oct. | Australia | 57 | Romania | 9 | Ravenhill, Belfast |
| 1 | 8 Oct. | Scotland | 43 | Uruguay | 12 | Murrayfield, Edinburgh |
| 3 | 8 Oct. | France | 47 | Namibia | 13 | Stade Municipal du Parc Lescure, Bordeaux |
| 3 | 9 Oct. | Fiji | 38 | Canada | 22 | Stade Municipal du Parc Lescure, Bordeaux |
| 4 | 9 Oct. | Wales | 64 | Japan | 15 | Millennium Stadium, Cardiff |
| 2 | 9 Oct. | England | 16 | New Zealand | 30 | Twickenham, London |
| 5 | 9 Oct. | Romania | 27 | United States | 25 | Lansdowne Road, Dublin |
| 4 | 10 Oct. | Argentina | 32 | Samoa | 16 | Stradey Park, Llanelli |
| 5 | 10 Oct. | Ireland | 3 | Australia | 23 | Lansdowne Road, Dublin |
| 1 | 10 Oct. | South Africa | 47 | Spain | 3 | Murrayfield, Edinburgh |
| 2 | 10 Oct. | Tonga | 28 | Italy | 25 | Welford Road, Leicester |
| 2 | 14 Oct. | New Zealand | 101 | Italy | 3 | McAlpine Stadium, Huddersfield |
| 4 | 14 Oct. | Wales | 31 | Samoa | 38 | Millennium Stadium, Cardiff |
| 5 | 14 Oct. | Australia | 55 | United States | 19 | Thomond Park, Limerick |
| 3 | 14 Oct. | Canada | 72 | Namibia | 11 | Stade Municipal de Toulouse, Toulouse |
| 2 | 15 Oct. | England | 101 | Tonga | 10 | Twickenham, London |
| 1 | 15 Oct. | South Africa | 39 | Uruguay | 3 | Hampden Park, Glasgow |
| 5 | 15 Oct. | Ireland | 44 | Romania | 14 | Lansdowne Road, Dublin |
| 3 | 16 Oct. | France | 28 | Fiji | 19 | Stade Municipal de Toulouse, Toulouse |
| 1 | 16 Oct. | Scotland | 48 | Spain | 0 | Murrayfield, Edinburgh |
| 4 | 16 Oct. | Argentina | 33 | Japan | 12 | Millennium Stadium, Cardiff |

## QUARTER-FINAL PLAY-OFFS

| | | | | | |
|---|---|---|---|---|---|
| 20 Oct. | England | 45 | Fiji | 24 | Twickenham, London |
| 20 Oct. | Scotland | 35 | Samoa | 20 | Murrayfield, Edinburgh |
| 20 Oct. | Argentina | 28 | Ireland | 24 | Stade Félix Bollaert, Lens |

## QUARTER-FINALS

| | | | | | |
|---|---|---|---|---|---|
| 23 Oct. | Wales | 9 | Australia | 24 | Millennium Stadium, Cardiff |
| 24 Oct. | South Africa | 44 | England | 21 | Stade de France, Paris |
| 24 Oct. | Scotland | 18 | New Zealand | 30 | Murrayfield, Edinburgh |
| 24 Oct. | France | 47 | Argentina | 26 | Lansdowne Road, Dublin |

## SEMI-FINALS

| | | | | | |
|---|---|---|---|---|---|
| 30 Oct. | Australia | 27 | South Africa | 21 | Twickenham, London (a e t) |
| 31 Oct. | France | 43 | New Zealand | 31 | Twickenham, London |

## BRONZE

| | | | | | |
|---|---|---|---|---|---|
| 4 Nov. | South Africa | 22 | New Zealand | 18 | Millennium Stadium, Cardiff |

## FINAL

| | | | | | |
|---|---|---|---|---|---|
| 6 Nov. | Australia | 35 | France | 12 | Millennium Stadium, Cardiff |

## POOL STAGES

**POOL 1**

| | P | W | D | L | For | Against | PTS |
|---|---|---|---|---|---|---|---|
| South Africa | 3 | 3 | 0 | 0 | 132 | 35 | 6 |
| Scotland | 3 | 2 | 0 | 1 | 120 | 58 | 4 |
| Uruguay | 3 | 1 | 0 | 2 | 42 | 97 | 2 |
| Spain | 3 | 0 | 0 | 3 | 18 | 122 | 0 |

**POOL 2**

| | P | W | D | L | For | Against | PTS |
|---|---|---|---|---|---|---|---|
| New Zealand | 3 | 3 | 0 | 0 | 176 | 28 | 6 |
| England | 3 | 2 | 0 | 1 | 184 | 47 | 4 |
| Tonga | 3 | 1 | 0 | 2 | 47 | 171 | 2 |
| Italy | 3 | 0 | 0 | 3 | 35 | 196 | 0 |

**POOL 3**

| | P | W | D | L | For | Against | PTS |
|---|---|---|---|---|---|---|---|
| France | 3 | 3 | 0 | 0 | 108 | 52 | 6 |
| Fiji | 3 | 2 | 0 | 1 | 124 | 68 | 4 |
| Canada | 3 | 1 | 0 | 2 | 114 | 82 | 2 |
| Namibia | 3 | 0 | 0 | 3 | 42 | 186 | 4 |

**POOL 4**

| | P | W | D | L | For | Against | PTS |
|---|---|---|---|---|---|---|---|
| Wales | 3 | 2 | 0 | 1 | 118 | 71 | 4 |
| Samoa | 3 | 2 | 0 | 1 | 97 | 72 | 4 |
| Argentina | 3 | 2 | 0 | 1 | 83 | 51 | 4 |
| Japan | 3 | 0 | 0 | 3 | 36 | 140 | 0 |

**POOL 5**

| | P | W | D | L | For | Against | PTS |
|---|---|---|---|---|---|---|---|
| Australia | 3 | 3 | 0 | 0 | 135 | 31 | 6 |
| Ireland | 3 | 2 | 0 | 1 | 100 | 45 | 4 |
| Romania | 3 | 1 | 0 | 2 | 50 | 126 | 2 |
| United States | 3 | 0 | 0 | 3 | 52 | 135 | 0 |

## POOL STAGES

| | | | | | | |
|---|---|---|---|---|---|---|
| A | 10 Oct. | Australia | 24 | Argentina | 8 | Telstra Stadium, Sydney |
| D | 11 Oct. | New Zealand | 70 | Italy | 7 | Telstra Dome, Melbourne |
| A | 11 Oct. | Ireland | 45 | Romania | 17 | Central Coast Stadium, Gosford, NSW |
| B | 11 Oct. | France | 61 | Fiji | 18 | Suncorp Stadium, Brisbane |
| C | 11 Oct. | South Africa | 72 | Uruguay | 6 | Subiaco Oval, Perth |
| D | 12 Oct. | Wales | 41 | Canada | 10 | Telstra Dome, Melbourne |
| B | 12 Oct. | Scotland | 32 | Japan | 11 | Dairy Farmers Stadium, Townsville |
| C | 12 Oct. | England | 84 | Georgia | 6 | Subiaco Oval, Perth |
| A | 14 Oct. | Argentina | 67 | Namibia | 14 | Central Coast Stadium, Gosford, NSW |
| B | 14 Oct. | Fiji | 19 | United States | 18 | Suncorp Stadium, Brisbane |
| D | 15 Oct. | Italy | 36 | Tonga | 12 | Canberra Stadium, Canberra |
| C | 15 Oct. | Samoa | 60 | Uruguay | 13 | Subiaco Oval, Perth |
| D | 17 Oct. | New Zealand | 68 | Canada | 6 | Telstra Dome, Melbourne |
| A | 18 Oct. | Australia | 90 | Romania | 8 | Suncorp Stadium, Brisbane |
| B | 18 Oct. | France | 51 | Japan | 29 | Dairy Farmers Stadium, Townsville |
| C | 18 Oct. | England | 25 | South Africa | 6 | Subiaco Oval, Perth |
| D | 19 Oct. | Wales | 27 | Tonga | 20 | Canberra Stadium, Canberra |
| A | 19 Oct. | Ireland | 64 | Namibia | 7 | Aussie Stadium, Sydney |
| C | 19 Oct. | Samoa | 48 | Georgia | 9 | Subiaco Oval, Perth |
| B | 20 Oct. | Scotland | 39 | United States | 15 | Suncorp Stadium, Brisbane |
| D | 21 Oct. | Italy | 19 | Canada | 14 | Canberra Stadium, Canberra |
| A | 22 Oct. | Argentina | 50 | Romania | 3 | Aussie Stadium, Sydney |
| B | 23 Oct. | Fiji | 41 | Japan | 13 | Dairy Farmers Stadium, Townsville |
| D | 24 Oct. | New Zealand | 91 | Tonga | 7 | Suncorp Stadium, Brisbane |
| C | 24 Oct. | South Africa | 46 | Georgia | 19 | Aussie Stadium, Sydney |
| A | 25 Oct. | Australia | 142 | Namibia | 0 | Adelaide Oval, Adelaide |
| D | 25 Oct. | Wales | 27 | Italy | 15 | Canberra Stadium, Canberra |
| B | 25 Oct. | France | 51 | Scotland | 9 | Telstra Stadium, Sydney |
| A | 26 Oct. | Ireland | 16 | Argentina | 15 | Adelaide Oval, Adelaide |
| C | 26 Oct. | England | 35 | Samoa | 22 | Telstra Dome, Melbourne |
| B | 27 Oct. | United States | 39 | Japan | 26 | Central Coast Stadium, Gosford, NSW |
| C | 28 Oct. | Uruguay | 24 | Georgia | 12 | Aussie Stadium, Sydney |
| D | 29 Oct. | Canada | 24 | Tonga | 7 | WIN Stadium, Wollongong |
| A | 30 Oct. | Romania | 37 | Namibia | 7 | Aurora Stadium, Launceston |
| B | 31 Oct. | France | 41 | United States | 14 | WIN Stadium, Wollongong |
| B | 1 Nov. | Scotland | 22 | Fiji | 20 | Aussie Stadium, Sydney |
| C | 1 Nov. | South Africa | 60 | Samoa | 10 | Suncorp Stadium, Brisbane |
| A | 1 Nov. | Australia | 17 | Ireland | 16 | Telstra Dome, Melbourne |
| C | 2 Nov. | England | 111 | Uruguay | 13 | Suncorp Stadium, Brisbane |
| D | 2 Nov. | New Zealand | 53 | Wales | 37 | Telstra Stadium, Sydney |

## POOL STAGES

### POOL A

| | | P | W | D | L | For | Against | Bonus | PTS |
|---|---|---|---|---|---|---|---|---|---|
| | Australia | 4 | 4 | 0 | 0 | 273 | 32 | 2 | 18 |
| | Ireland | 4 | 3 | 0 | 1 | 141 | 56 | 3 | 15 |
| | Argentina | 4 | 2 | 0 | 2 | 140 | 57 | 3 | 11 |
| | Romania | 4 | 1 | 0 | 3 | 65 | 192 | 1 | 5 |
| | Namibia | 4 | 0 | 0 | 4 | 28 | 310 | 0 | 0 |

### POOL B

| | | P | W | D | L | For | Against | Bonus | PTS |
|---|---|---|---|---|---|---|---|---|---|
| | France | 4 | 4 | 0 | 0 | 204 | 70 | 4 | 20 |
| | Scotland | 4 | 3 | 0 | 1 | 102 | 97 | 2 | 14 |
| | Fiji | 4 | 2 | 0 | 2 | 98 | 114 | 2 | 10 |
| | United States | 4 | 1 | 0 | 3 | 86 | 125 | 2 | 6 |
| | Japan | 4 | 0 | 0 | 4 | 79 | 163 | 0 | 0 |

### POOL C

| | | P | W | D | L | For | Against | Bonus | PTS |
|---|---|---|---|---|---|---|---|---|---|
| | England | 4 | 4 | 0 | 0 | 255 | 47 | 3 | 19 |
| | South Africa | 4 | 3 | 0 | 1 | 184 | 60 | 3 | 15 |
| | Samoa | 4 | 2 | 0 | 2 | 138 | 117 | 2 | 10 |
| | Uruguay | 4 | 1 | 0 | 3 | 56 | 255 | 0 | 4 |
| | Georgia | 4 | 0 | 0 | 4 | 46 | 200 | 0 | 0 |

### POOL D

| | | P | W | D | L | For | Against | Bonus | PTS |
|---|---|---|---|---|---|---|---|---|---|
| | New Zealand | 4 | 4 | 0 | 0 | 282 | 57 | 4 | 20 |
| | Wales | 4 | 3 | 0 | 1 | 132 | 98 | 2 | 14 |
| | Italy | 4 | 2 | 0 | 2 | 77 | 123 | 0 | 8 |
| | Canada | 4 | 1 | 0 | 3 | 54 | 135 | 1 | 5 |
| | Tonga | 4 | 0 | 0 | 4 | 46 | 178 | 1 | 1 |

## QUARTER-FINALS

| 8 Nov. | New Zealand | 29 | South Africa | 9 | Telstra Dome, Melbourne |
| 8 Nov. | Australia | 33 | Scotland | 16 | Suncorp Stadium, Sydney |
| 9 Nov. | France | 43 | Ireland | 21 | Telstra Dome, Melbourne |
| 9 Nov. | England | 28 | Wales | 17 | Suncorp Stadium, Sydney |

## SEMI-FINALS

| 15 Nov. | Australia | 22 | New Zealand | 10 | Telstra Stadium, Sydney |
| 16 Nov. | England | 24 | France | 7 | Telstra Stadium, Sydney |

## BRONZE

| 20 Nov. | New Zealand | 40 | France | 13 | Telstra Stadium, Sydney |

## FINAL

| 22 Nov. | Australia | 17 | England | 20 | Telstra Stadium, Sydney (a e t) |

## POOL STAGES

| D | 7 Sep. | France | 12 | Argentina | 17 | Stade de France, Paris |
|---|--------|--------|----|-----------|----|------------------------|
| C | 8 Sep. | New Zealand | 76 | Italy | 14 | Stade Vélodrome, Marseille |
| B | 8 Sep. | Australia | 91 | Japan | 3 | Stade de Gerland, Lyon |
| A | 8 Sep. | England | 28 | United States | 10 | Stade Félix Bollaert, Lens |
| B | 9 Sep. | Wales | 42 | Canada | 17 | Stade de la Beaujoire, Nantes |
| A | 9 Sep. | South Africa | 59 | Samoa | 7 | Parc des Princess, Paris |
| C | 9 Sep. | Scotland | 56 | Portugal | 10 | Stade Geoffroy-Guichard, Saint Étienne |
| D | 9 Sep. | Ireland | 32 | Namibia | 17 | Stade Chaban-Delmas, Bordeaux |
| D | 11 Sep. | Argentina | 33 | Georgia | 3 | Stade de Gerland, Lyon |
| A | 12 Sep. | Tonga | 25 | United States | 15 | Stade de la Mosson, Montpellier |
| B | 12 Sep. | Fiji | 35 | Japan | 31 | Stade Municipal de Toulouse, Toulouse |
| C | 12 Sep. | Italy | 24 | Romania | 18 | Stade Vélodrome, Marseille |
| A | 14 Sep. | South Africa | 36 | England | 0 | Stade de France, Paris |
| C | 15 Sep. | New Zealand | 108 | Portugal | 13 | Stade de Gerland, Lyon |
| B | 15 Sep. | Wales | 20 | Australia | 32 | Millennium Stadium, Cardiff |
| D | 15 Sep. | Ireland | 14 | Georgia | 10 | Stade Chaban-Delmas, Bordeaux |
| B | 16 Sep. | Fiji | 29 | Canada | 16 | Millennium Stadium, Cardiff |
| A | 16 Sep. | Tonga | 19 | Samoa | 15 | Stade de la Mosson, Montpelier |
| D | 16 Sep. | France | 87 | Namibia | 10 | Stade Municipal de Toulouse, Toulouse |
| C | 18 Sep. | Scotland | 42 | Romania | 0 | Murrayfield, Edinburgh |
| C | 19 Sep. | Italy | 31 | Portugal | 5 | Parc des Princess, Paris |
| B | 20 Sep. | Wales | 72 | Japan | 18 | Millennium Stadium, Cardiff |
| D | 21 Sep. | France | 25 | Ireland | 3 | Stade de France, Paris |
| A | 22 Sep. | South Africa | 30 | Tonga | 25 | Stade Félix Bollaert, Lens |
| A | 22 Sep. | England | 44 | Samoa | 22 | Stade de la Beaujoire, Nantes |
| D | 22 Sep. | Argentina | 63 | Namibia | 3 | Stade Vélodrome, Marseille |
| B | 23 Sep. | Australia | 55 | Fiji | 12 | Stade de la Mosson, Montpelier |
| C | 23 Sep. | Scotland | 0 | New Zealand | 40 | Murrayfield, Edinburgh |
| B | 25 Sep. | Canada | 12 | Japan | 12 | Stade Chaban-Delmas, Bordeaux |
| C | 25 Sep. | Romania | 14 | Portugal | 10 | Stade Municipal de Toulouse, Toulouse |
| D | 26 Sep. | Georgia | 30 | Namibia | 0 | Stade Félix Bollaert, Lens |
| A | 26 Sep. | Samoa | 25 | United States | 21 | Stade Geoffroy-Guichard, Saint Étienne |
| A | 28 Sep. | England | 36 | Tonga | 20 | Parc des Princess, Paris |
| C | 29 Sep. | New Zealand | 85 | Romania | 8 | Stade Municipal de Toulouse, Toulouse |
| B | 29 Sep. | Australia | 37 | Canada | 6 | Stade Chaban-Delmas, Bordeaux |
| B | 29 Sep. | Fiji | 38 | Wales | 34 | Stade de la Beaujoire, Nantes |
| C | 29 Sep. | Scotland | 18 | Italy | 16 | Stade Geoffroy-Guichard, Saint Étienne |
| D | 30 Sep. | France | 64 | Georgia | 7 | Stade Vélodrome, Marseille |
| D | 30 Sep. | Argentina | 30 | Ireland | 15 | Parc des Princess, Paris |
| A | 30 Sep. | South Africa | 64 | United States | 15 | Stade de la Mosson, Montpellier |

## POOL STAGES

### POOL A

| | | P | W | D | L | For | Against | Bonus | PTS |
|---|---|---|---|---|---|---|---|---|---|
| | South Africa | 4 | 4 | 0 | 0 | 189 | 47 | 3 | 19 |
| | England | 4 | 3 | 0 | 1 | 108 | 88 | 2 | 14 |
| | Tonga | 4 | 2 | 0 | 2 | 89 | 96 | 1 | 9 |
| | Samoa | 4 | 1 | 0 | 3 | 69 | 143 | 1 | 5 |
| | United States | 4 | 0 | 0 | 4 | 61 | 142 | 1 | 1 |

### POOL B

| | | P | W | D | L | For | Against | Bonus | PTS |
|---|---|---|---|---|---|---|---|---|---|
| | Australia | 4 | 4 | 0 | 0 | 215 | 41 | 4 | 20 |
| | Fiji | 4 | 3 | 0 | 1 | 114 | 136 | 3 | 15 |
| | Wales | 4 | 2 | 0 | 2 | 168 | 105 | 4 | 12 |
| | Japan | 4 | 0 | 1 | 3 | 64 | 210 | 1 | 3 |
| | Canada | 4 | 0 | 1 | 3 | 51 | 120 | 0 | 2 |

### POOL C

| | | P | W | D | L | For | Against | Bonus | PTS |
|---|---|---|---|---|---|---|---|---|---|
| | New Zealand | 4 | 4 | 0 | 0 | 309 | 35 | 4 | 20 |
| | Scotland | 4 | 3 | 0 | 1 | 116 | 66 | 2 | 14 |
| | Italy | 4 | 2 | 0 | 2 | 85 | 117 | 1 | 9 |
| | Romania | 4 | 1 | 0 | 3 | 40 | 161 | 1 | 5 |
| | Portugal | 4 | 0 | 0 | 4 | 38 | 209 | 1 | 1 |

### POOL D

| | | P | W | D | L | For | Against | Bonus | PTS |
|---|---|---|---|---|---|---|---|---|---|
| | Argentina | 4 | 4 | 0 | 0 | 143 | 33 | 2 | 18 |
| | France | 4 | 3 | 0 | 1 | 188 | 37 | 3 | 15 |
| | Ireland | 4 | 2 | 0 | 2 | 64 | 82 | 1 | 9 |
| | Georgia | 4 | 1 | 0 | 3 | 50 | 111 | 1 | 5 |
| | Namibia | 4 | 0 | 0 | 4 | 30 | 212 | 0 | 0 |

## QUARTER-FINALS

| 6 Oct. | England | 12 | Australia | 10 | Stade Vélodrome, Marseille |
|---|---|---|---|---|---|
| 6 Oct. | France | 20 | New Zealand | 18 | Millennium Stadium, Cardiff |
| 7 Oct. | South Africa | 37 | Fiji | 20 | Stade Vélodrome, Marseille |
| 7 Oct. | Argentina | 19 | Scotland | 13 | Stade de France, Paris |

## SEMI-FINALS

| 13 Oct. | France | 9 | England | 14 | Stade de France, Paris |
|---|---|---|---|---|---|
| 14 Oct. | South Africa | 37 | Argentina | 13 | Stade de France, Paris |

## BRONZE

| 19 Oct. | France | 10 | Argentina | 34 | Parc des Princes, Paris |
|---|---|---|---|---|---|

## FINAL

| 20 Oct. | South Africa | 15 | England | 6 | Stade de France, Paris |
|---|---|---|---|---|---|

## POOL STAGES

| | | | | | | |
|---|---|---|---|---|---|---|
| A | 9 Sep. | New Zealand | 41 | Tonga | 10 | Eden Park, Auckland |
| B | 10 Sep. | Scotland | 34 | Romania | 24 | Rugby Park Stadium, Invercargill |
| D | 10 Sep. | Fiji | 49 | Namibia | 25 | Rotorua International Stadium, Rotorua |
| A | 10 Sep. | France | 47 | Japan | 21 | North Harbour Stadium, Albany |
| B | 10 Sep. | Argentina | 9 | England | 13 | Otago Stadium, Dunedin |
| C | 11 Sep. | Australia | 32 | Italy | 6 | North Harbour Stadium, Albany |
| C | 11 Sep. | Ireland | 22 | United States | 10 | Stadium Taranaki, New Plymouth |
| D | 11 Sep. | South Africa | 17 | Wales | 16 | Wellington Regional Stadium, Wellington |
| D | 14 Sep. | Samoa | 49 | Namibia | 12 | Rotorua International Stadium, Rotorua |
| A | 14 Sep. | Tonga | 20 | Canada | 25 | Northland Events Centre, Whangarei |
| B | 14 Sep. | Scotland | 15 | Georgia | 6 | Rugby Park Stadium, Invercargill |
| C | 15 Sep. | Russia | 6 | United States | 13 | Stadium Taranaki, New Plymouth |
| A | 16 Sep. | New Zealand | 83 | Japan | 7 | Waikato Stadium, Hamilton |
| B | 17 Sep. | Argentina | 43 | Romania | 8 | Rugby Park Stadium, Invercargill |
| D | 17 Sep. | South Africa | 49 | Fiji | 3 | Wellington Regional Stadium, Wellington |
| C | 17 Sep. | Australia | 6 | Ireland | 15 | Eden Park, Auckland |
| D | 18 Sep. | Wales | 17 | Samoa | 10 | Waikato Stadium, Hamilton |
| B | 18 Sep. | England | 41 | Georgia | 10 | Otago Stadium, Dunedin |
| A | 18 Sep. | France | 46 | Canada | 19 | McLean Park, Napier |
| C | 20 Sep. | Italy | 53 | Russia | 17 | Trafalgar Park, Nelson |
| A | 21 Sep. | Tonga | 31 | Japan | 18 | Northland Events Centre, Whangarei |
| D | 22 Sep. | South Africa | 87 | Namibia | 0 | North Harbour Stadium, Albany |
| C | 23 Sep. | Australia | 67 | United States | 5 | Wellington Regional Stadium, Wellington |
| B | 24 Sep. | England | 67 | Romania | 3 | Otago Stadium, Dunedin |
| A | 24 Sep. | New Zealand | 37 | France | 17 | Eden Park, Auckland |
| D | 25 Sep. | Fiji | 7 | Samoa | 27 | Eden Park, Auckland |
| C | 25 Sep. | Ireland | 62 | Russia | 12 | Rotorua International Stadium, Rotorua |
| B | 25 Sep. | Argentina | 13 | Scotland | 12 | Wellington Regional Stadium, Wellington |
| D | 26 Sep. | Wales | 81 | Namibia | 7 | Stadium Taranaki, New Plymouth |
| A | 27 Sep. | Canada | 23 | Japan | 23 | McLean Park, Napier |
| C | 27 Sep. | Italy | 27 | United States | 10 | Trafalgar Park, Nelson |
| B | 28 Sep. | Georgia | 25 | Romania | 9 | Arena Manawatu, Palmerston North |
| D | 30 Sep. | South Africa | 13 | Samoa | 5 | North Harbour Stadium, Albany |
| C | 1 Oct. | Australia | 68 | Russia | 22 | Trafalgar Park, Nelson |
| A | 1 Oct. | France | 14 | Tonga | 19 | Wellington Regional Stadium, Wellington |
| B | 1 Oct. | England | 16 | Scotland | 12 | Eden Park, Auckland |
| B | 2 Oct. | Argentina | 25 | Georgia | 7 | Arena Manawatu, Palmerston North |
| A | 2 Oct. | New Zealand | 79 | Canada | 15 | Wellington Regional Stadium, Wellington |
| D | 2 Oct. | Wales | 66 | Fiji | 0 | Waikato Stadium, Hamilton |
| C | 2 Oct. | Ireland | 36 | Italy | 6 | Otago Stadium, Dunedin |

## POOL STAGES

### POOL A

| | P | W | D | L | For | Against | Bonus | PTS |
|---|---|---|---|---|---|---|---|---|
| New Zealand | 4 | 4 | 0 | 0 | 240 | 49 | 4 | 20 |
| France | 4 | 2 | 0 | 2 | 124 | 96 | 3 | 11 |
| Tonga | 4 | 2 | 0 | 2 | 80 | 98 | 1 | 9 |
| Canada | 4 | 1 | 1 | 2 | 82 | 168 | 0 | 6 |
| Japan | 4 | 0 | 1 | 3 | 69 | 184 | 0 | 2 |

### POOL B

| | P | W | D | L | For | Against | Bonus | PTS |
|---|---|---|---|---|---|---|---|---|
| England | 4 | 4 | 0 | 0 | 137 | 34 | 2 | 18 |
| Argentina | 4 | 3 | 0 | 1 | 90 | 40 | 2 | 14 |
| Scotland | 4 | 2 | 0 | 2 | 73 | 59 | 3 | 11 |
| Georgia | 4 | 1 | 0 | 3 | 48 | 90 | 0 | 4 |
| Romania | 4 | 0 | 0 | 4 | 44 | 189 | 0 | 0 |

### POOL C

| | P | W | D | L | For | Against | Bonus | PTS |
|---|---|---|---|---|---|---|---|---|
| Ireland | 4 | 4 | 0 | 0 | 135 | 34 | 1 | 17 |
| Australia | 4 | 3 | 0 | 1 | 173 | 48 | 3 | 15 |
| Italy | 4 | 2 | 0 | 2 | 92 | 95 | 2 | 10 |
| United States | 4 | 1 | 0 | 3 | 38 | 122 | 0 | 4 |
| Russia | 4 | 0 | 0 | 4 | 57 | 196 | 1 | 1 |

### POOL D

| | P | W | D | L | For | Against | Bonus | PTS |
|---|---|---|---|---|---|---|---|---|
| South Africa | 4 | 4 | 0 | 0 | 166 | 24 | 2 | 18 |
| Wales | 4 | 3 | 0 | 1 | 180 | 34 | 3 | 15 |
| Samoa | 4 | 2 | 0 | 2 | 91 | 49 | 2 | 10 |
| Fiji | 4 | 1 | 0 | 3 | 59 | 167 | 1 | 5 |
| Namibia | 4 | 0 | 0 | 4 | 44 | 266 | 0 | 0 |

## QUARTER-FINALS

| 8 Oct. | Ireland | 10 | Wales | 22 | Wellington Reg'l Stadium, Wellington |
|---|---|---|---|---|---|
| 8 Oct. | England | 12 | France | 19 | Eden Park, Auckland |
| 9 Oct. | South Africa | 9 | Australia | 11 | Wellington Reg'l Stadium, Wellington |
| 9 Oct. | New Zealand | 33 | Argentina | 10 | Eden Park, Auckland |

## SEMI-FINALS

| 15 Oct. | Wales | 8 | France | 9 | Eden Park, Auckland |
|---|---|---|---|---|---|
| 16 Oct. | New Zealand | 20 | Australia | 6 | Eden Park, Auckland |

## BRONZE

| 21 Oct. | Wales | 18 | Australia | 21 | Eden Park, Auckland |
|---|---|---|---|---|---|

## FINAL

| 23 Oct. | New Zealand | 8 | France | 7 | Eden Park, Auckland |
|---|---|---|---|---|---|

## POOL STAGES

| | | | | | | |
|---|---|---|---|---|---|---|
| A | 18 Sep. | England | 35 | Fiji | 11 | Twickenham, London |
| C | 19 Sep. | Tonga | 10 | Georgia | 17 | Kingsholm, Gloucester |
| D | 19 Sep. | Ireland | 50 | Canada | 7 | Millennium Stadium, Cardiff |
| D | 19 Sep. | France | 32 | Italy | 10 | Twickenham, London |
| B | 19 Sep. | South Africa | 32 | Japan | 34 | Brighton Community Stadium |
| B | 20 Sep. | Samoa | 25 | United States | 16 | Brighton Community Stadium |
| A | 20 Sep. | Wales | 54 | Uruguay | 9 | Millennium Stadium, Cardiff |
| C | 20 Sep. | New Zealand | 26 | Argentina | 16 | Wembley Stadium, London |
| B | 23 Sep. | Scotland | 45 | Japan | 10 | Kingsholm, Gloucester |
| A | 23 Sep. | Australia | 28 | Fiji | 13 | Millennium Stadium, Cardiff |
| D | 23 Sep. | France | 38 | Romania | 11 | Olympic Stadium, London |
| C | 24 Sep. | New Zealand | 58 | Namibia | 14 | Olympic Stadium, London |
| C | 25 Sep. | Argentina | 54 | Georgia | 9 | Kingsholm, Gloucester |
| D | 26 Sep. | Italy | 23 | Canada | 18 | Elland Road, Leeds |
| B | 26 Sep. | South Africa | 46 | Samoa | 6 | Villa Park, Birmingham |
| A | 26 Sep. | England | 25 | Wales | 28 | Twickenham, London |
| A | 27 Sep. | Australia | 65 | Uruguay | 3 | Villa Park, Birmingham |
| B | 27 Sep. | Scotland | 39 | United States | 16 | Elland Road, Leeds |
| D | 27 Sep. | Ireland | 44 | Romania | 10 | Wembley Stadium, London |
| C | 29 Sep. | Tonga | 35 | Namibia | 21 | Sandy Park, Exeter |
| D | 1 Oct. | France | 41 | Canada | 18 | Stadium MK, Milton Keynes |
| A | 1 Oct. | Wales | 23 | Fiji | 13 | Millennium Stadium, Cardiff |
| C | 2 Oct. | New Zealand | 43 | Georgia | 10 | Millennium Stadium, Cardiff |
| B | 3 Oct. | Samoa | 5 | Japan | 26 | Stadium MK, Milton Keynes |
| B | 3 Oct. | South Africa | 34 | Scotland | 16 | St James' Park, Newcastle |
| A | 3 Oct. | England | 13 | Australia | 33 | Twickenham, London |
| C | 4 Oct. | Argentina | 45 | Tonga | 16 | Leicester City Stadium, Leicester |
| D | 4 Oct. | Ireland | 16 | Italy | 9 | Olympic Stadium, London |
| D | 6 Oct. | Canada | 15 | Romania | 17 | Leicester City Stadium, Leicester |
| A | 6 Oct. | Fiji | 47 | Uruguay | 15 | Stadium MK, Milton Keynes |
| B | 7 Oct. | South Africa | 64 | United States | 0 | Olympic Stadium, London |
| C | 7 Oct. | Namibia | 16 | Georgia | 17 | Sandy Park, Exeter |
| C | 9 Oct. | New Zealand | 47 | Tonga | 9 | St James' Park, Newcastle |
| B | 10 Oct. | Samoa | 33 | Scotland | 36 | St James' Park, Newcastle |
| A | 10 Oct. | Australia | 15 | Wales | 6 | Twickenham, London |
| A | 10 Oct. | England | 60 | Uruguay | 3 | Manchester City Stadium, Manchester |
| C | 11 Oct. | Argentina | 64 | Namibia | 19 | Leicester City Stadium, Leicester |
| D | 11 Oct. | Italy | 32 | Romania | 22 | Sandy Park, Exeter |
| B | 11 Oct. | United States | 18 | Japan | 28 | Kingsholm, Gloucester |
| D | 11 Oct. | Ireland | 24 | France | 9 | Millennium Stadium, Cardiff |

## POOL STAGES

### POOL A

| | P | W | D | L | For | Against | Bonus | PTS |
|---|---|---|---|---|---|---|---|---|
| Australia | 4 | 4 | 0 | 0 | 141 | 35 | 1 | 17 |
| Wales | 4 | 3 | 0 | 1 | 111 | 62 | 1 | 13 |
| England | 4 | 2 | 0 | 2 | 133 | 75 | 3 | 11 |
| Fiji | 4 | 1 | 0 | 3 | 84 | 101 | 1 | 5 |
| Uruguay | 4 | 0 | 0 | 4 | 30 | 226 | 0 | 0 |

### POOL B

| | P | W | D | L | For | Against | Bonus | PTS |
|---|---|---|---|---|---|---|---|---|
| South Africa | 4 | 3 | 0 | 1 | 176 | 56 | 4 | 16 |
| Scotland | 4 | 3 | 0 | 1 | 136 | 93 | 2 | 14 |
| Japan | 4 | 3 | 0 | 1 | 98 | 100 | 0 | 12 |
| Samoa | 4 | 1 | 0 | 3 | 69 | 124 | 2 | 6 |
| United States | 4 | 0 | 0 | 4 | 50 | 156 | 0 | 0 |

### POOL C

| | P | W | D | L | For | Against | Bonus | PTS |
|---|---|---|---|---|---|---|---|---|
| New Zealand | 4 | 4 | 0 | 0 | 174 | 149 | 3 | 19 |
| Argentina | 4 | 3 | 0 | 1 | 179 | 70 | 3 | 15 |
| Georgia | 4 | 2 | 0 | 2 | 53 | 123 | 0 | 8 |
| Tonga | 4 | 1 | 0 | 3 | 70 | 130 | 2 | 6 |
| Namibia | 4 | 0 | 0 | 4 | 70 | 174 | 1 | 1 |

### POOL D

| | P | W | D | L | For | Against | Bonus | PTS |
|---|---|---|---|---|---|---|---|---|
| Ireland | 4 | 4 | 0 | 0 | 134 | 35 | 2 | 18 |
| France | 4 | 3 | 0 | 1 | 120 | 63 | 2 | 14 |
| Italy | 4 | 2 | 0 | 2 | 74 | 88 | 2 | 10 |
| Romania | 4 | 1 | 0 | 3 | 60 | 129 | 0 | 4 |
| Canada | 4 | 0 | 0 | 4 | 58 | 131 | 2 | 2 |

## QUARTER-FINALS

| 17 Oct. | South Africa | 23 | Wales | 19 | Twickenham, London |
|---|---|---|---|---|---|
| 17 Oct. | New Zealand | 62 | France | 13 | Millennium Stadium, Cardiff |
| 18 Oct. | Ireland | 20 | Argentina | 43 | Millennium Stadium, Cardiff |
| 18 Oct. | Australia | 35 | Scotland | 34 | Twickenham, London |

## SEMI-FINALS

| 24 Oct. | South Africa | 18 | New Zealand | 20 | Twickenham, London |
|---|---|---|---|---|---|
| 25 Oct. | Argentina | 15 | Australia | 29 | Twickenham, London |

## BRONZE

| 30 Oct. | South Africa | 24 | Argentina | 13 | Olympic Stadium, London |
|---|---|---|---|---|---|

## FINAL

| 31 Oct. | New Zealand | 34 | Australia | 17 | Twickenham, London |
|---|---|---|---|---|---|

# RUGBY TRIVIA

# RUGBY TRIVIA

## IN THE BEGINNING

When William Webb Ellis decided to pick up the ball in a football match at Rugby school in 1823, the sport of rugby was born. In those early days there were many interpretations of the rules, and even the dimensions of the ball varied enormously in shape and size. That was until Richard Linden, an apprentice working for shoemaker William Gilbert, hit upon the idea of creating a standard leather ball that could be inflated with a pig's bladder. Gilbert displayed his ball in 1851 at the Great Exhibition in London and, amazingly, the Gilbert manufactured ball is still used to this day.

## THE EARLY DAYS IN THE NORTHERN HEMISPHERE

The rules of rugby in the first half of the nineteenth century were anything but uniform and were adopted to reflect local influences. In fact, Rugby school started to discuss the standardisation of rules with university students from other schools during the 1830s and the 1840s. The basic rules of rugby, therefore, developed gradually by word of mouth. The main feature of those early rules was that by taking the ball across the opposing team's line, your team earned a try at goal, hence the word 'try'. Points were awarded only for a successful kick at goal.

The first set of rules actually written down was in 1845. These defined the concept of off-side and also confirmed the definition of the try, which would be followed by a kick at goal. Hacking was permitted, as was kicking an opposing player nearest the ball or within a scrummage. During the mid-1850s, rugby was rapidly spreading from the schools and universities to the towns. A

Liverpool team played its first match in 1857, and the Manchester club was born three years later, in 1860. Richmond football club, founded in 1861, took up rugby a year later but declined to become a founder member of the Football Association (FA) in 1863. Blackheath was another staunch English rugby club, founded in 1858.

The rugby tradition was also taken up in the Edinburgh and Glasgow areas in the 1850s. It is generally accepted that the game arrived at the Edinburgh Academy in 1854 via the Crombie brothers, and within three years it had reached Merchiston Castle School and the Royal Academy in Edinburgh. Soon after, in 1858, fixtures were being arranged by these schools. Rugby football soon spread to Wales, when students at Lampeter College, played the game in 1850. University connections also helped to spread the word across the Irish Sea, when rugby was introduced to students in Trinity College, Dublin in 1854. The Trinity Club, nowadays known as Dublin University, claims to be the oldest existing rugby club in the world. In France, the first rugby club was Le Havre, formed in 1872 by a group of British wine merchants who worked in the area surrounding the port.

## THE EARLY DAYS IN THE SOUTHERN HEMISPHERE

Canon George Ogilvie emigrated from England to South Africa in 1858 and three years later, in 1861, he became headmaster at a leading private school and introduced rugby football to his pupils. The rules adopted were the ones then used at Winchester public school, the Canon's alma mater.

Rugby was introduced to New Zealand in 1870 by Charles John Monro who learnt the sport whilst studying at Christ's College Finchley in north London. At the age of 19, he returned home to Nelson on the South Island, and was successful in persuading the local club to switch from football to rugby. He then arranged a match between the converted Nelson club and Nelson College on 14 May 1870, and on 12 September 1870, he organised a match between the Nelson club and Wellington on the North Island (by bringing the home team by steamer across the Cook Straits). Nelson won the game.

Sydney University Football Club, believed to have been founded in 1863, began playing rugby matches in 1865. The first officially recorded game was between Sydney University and its near neighbours, Sydney Football Club. The match took place on 19 August 1865.

Rugby Union also reached South America in the 1870s when the first match was played in Argentina in 1873.

## RUGBY UNION AT THE OLYMPIC GAMES

Rugby was played at four Olympic Games between 1900 and 1924. Three teams participated at the Paris Games in 1900. France was represented by a team from Paris, Great Britain by Moseley Wanderers, and Germany by Eintracht Frankfurt. Host nation France won the Gold Medal by defeating Great Britain by 27 points to 8 and then Germany by 27 points to 17 in the final.

Only two teams turned up for the 1908 Games held in London. Great Britain, the host nation, nominated Cornwall as County champions to compete against Australia, who were touring Britain at the time. Australia won the Gold Medal by beating Cornwall by 32 points to 3, but it was not recognised as a full International match. The Wallabies, however, did play two Internationals on that tour, beating England but losing to Wales. They also lost to three Welsh clubs: Llanelli, Swansea and Cardiff.

Only two teams entered the 1920 Olympics in Antwerp, with the United States taking the Gold Medal by defeating France by 8 point to nil. As was the case in 1908, this match was again not classified as a rugby International. Three teams entered the 1924

Olympics, held in Paris again, and this time they did represent their country. In the opening match France defeated Romania by 61 points to 3, followed by a victory for the United States team when they beat Romania by 37 points to nil a week later. The United States then went on to win the Gold Medal by defeating France by 17 points to 3 at Stade Colombes in Paris in the final. All three matches are recognised as full Internationals. Rugby Union has not been represented at the Olympic Games since, although a Pre-Olympic tournament involving France, Germany, Romania and Italy was held prior to the 1936 Berlin Olympics. The United States are therefore the reigning rugby union Olympic champions.

## THE EVOLUTION OF THE TRY

In the early days gaining a try was the only way a team could score a goal and gain points. The number of goals resulting from successful kicks was used to determine the winner of the match.

In 1886, the value of the try was set at one point and a successful conversion would add a further two points to the total. Five years later, in 1891, the try was increased to two points and the conversion was simultaneously increased to three points. However, in 1893 there was yet another change with the try increased again to three points and the conversion reduced to two points, thus retaining the value of a converted try to five points.

The try remained at three points for nearly seventy years before it was increased to four points on 1 September 1971. Two months later, Jean-Claude Skrela became the first man to score a four-point try in an International match whilst playing for France against Australia in Toulouse on 20 November 1971.

When the try was increased again, to five points on 1 July 1992, David Sole of Scotland became the last man to score a four-point try in an International when playing against Australia in Brisbane on 26 June 1992. Eight days later on 4 July 1992, the Samoan, Va'aiga Tuigamala scored the first five-point try in an International match whilst playing for New Zealand against Australia in Sydney. Curiously, all three milestones have been achieved in matches involving Australia.

## THE DEVELOPMENT OF
## THE INTERNATIONAL RUGBY BOARD (IRB)

The IRB was founded in 1886 at a meeting in Dublin of the Irish, Scottish and Welsh rugby unions as a result of dissatisfaction with the English RFU's interpretation of the rules At that meeting of the Celtic nations it was agreed that the creation of an International Rugby Football Board (IRFB), as it was then known, would be the appropriate body to govern the rules of rugby union. The first formal meeting of the Board took place in Manchester on 5 December 1887, at which broad terms of reference were drawn up. The English RFU could not agree with the IRFB's role as lawmaker, so the dispute went to arbitration.

An agreement was finally reached in 1890, and England was allocated six seats on the Board, compared with two to each of the three Celtic nations. The IRFB's first set of rules was drawn up later that year. The RFU's allocation of seats on the IRFB Board in 1890 did, in fact, give the English an effective veto on law changes, so, in 1911, the RFU agreed to reduce its allocation to four seats.

In 1948, Australia, New Zealand and South Africa, known as the SANZAR nations, were each allocated one seat on the Board, and England's allocation was simultaneously reduced to two seats. Then, in 1958, the SANZAR countries were allocated two seats each, thus achieving parity with the four Home Nations. France was finally invited to the Board in 1978 and also given an allocation of two seats.

Despite rejecting the concept of a Rugby World Cup as far

back as 1957, the IRFB finally yielded to pressure from Australia and New Zealand, and a motion to initiate such a competition was put to a vote at the 1985 AGM. The motion was carried by 10 votes to 6.

In 1991, Argentina, Canada, Japan and Italy were given seats on the IRFB council and allocated one vote each. In 1998, the IRFB was renamed the International Rugby Board or IRB, and on 19 November 2014, the Board was further renamed 'World Rugby'.

## THE LAWS OF RUGBY – GENESIS

On 26 January 1871, a meeting of twenty-one English rugby-playing clubs was held at a restaurant in London's Pall Mall. The meeting was called to form a code of practice in order to standardise the rules of the game. Shortly afterwards, the Rugby Football Union, known as the RFU, was founded and the first laws of rugby football were drawn up and approved in June 1871. It is interesting to note that the very first International between Scotland and England was played before that date, on 27 March 1871. In 1877, a new rule stated that the ball must be released after a tackle. It was an immediate success and removed the congregation of a large number of players in the tackle area and furthermore encouraged the art of dribbling.

As stated earlier, the four Home Nations provisionally agreed a set of rules drawn up by the newly formed IRFB in 1890, but it took another 40 years before it was finally agreed, in 1930, that all matches between members would be played under the laws of the International Football Board.

## THE LAWS OF RUGBY – EVOLUTION

Prior to 1958, it was necessary for a player to play the ball with his foot before picking up the ball after a tackle. The removal of this rule greatly increased the flow of play. In the 1968-69 season a ban on kicking directly to touch outside the then 22-metre line came into experimental law. Known as 'The Australian Dispensation', on account of years of canvassing by the Australians, it was made permanent in 1990. Injury replacements were allowed for the first time in the Five Nations tournament at the beginning of the 1969 campaign. Jean-Pierre Salut became the first player to be replaced when he fell and twisted his ankle in the dressing room at the start of the France versus Scotland match on 11 January 1969. Three tactical substitutions were allowed in 1996, irrespective of whether the replaced player was injured or not. This measure went a long way towards eliminating faked injuries. Over the years, the number of substitutions has gradually increased to the present-day level of eight. There have also been many other rule changes, such as supporting a player at the line-out and the issuing of yellow and red cards to players for various rule offences.

## PROFESSIONALISM

In late 1894, Yorkshire clubs declared that the RFU view on professionalism was unreasonable, so in January 1895 eighteen of them proposed forming a society called the Northern Union. On 12 August, the RFU reissued its code on professionalism, which prompted the Yorkshire clubs to meet again on 27 August. Two days they later, they had a further meeting with their Lancashire counterparts, at the George Hotel in Huddersfield, and formed the Northern Rugby Union on the basis of 'payment for broken time only'. Twenty-two clubs were represented, and in 1922 the 'Union' was given the new title, the Rugby League.

Amateurism was again put to the test in 1896 when the Welsh Rugby Union decided to honour Arthur Gould, one of Wales' greatest players of that era, with a retirement gift. The Welsh RFU decided to buy his house and offer it to him as a present for services rendered. This kind gesture was immediately seen by the other three nations as a professional act. The Irish and Scottish RFUs were so incensed that their national teams refused to play Wales in the 1897 Home Nations tournament and Scotland further declined to play Wales in the 1898 competition.

In 1905, US President Theodore Roosevelt, appalled by the violence he had witnessed in a university match, threatened to ban that form of rugby as being too dangerous. This ultimately led to the development of the professional game we now know as American Football, in which the players wear padding protection.

In the late 1920s there was an uneasy situation in France whereby certain clubs were being subsidised. This put them at odds with their own Union, and also caused disquiet in the four Home Unions. The situation worsened in 1931 when twelve clubs broke away from the French Federation to form their own alliance. The Home Unions acted promptly and on 12 February, 1931, at a meeting in Twickenham, a resolution was passed that International matches would not be resumed with France until the French had resolved the professional stance of some of their clubs. France was ejected from the Five Nations Championship at the end of the tournament on 6 April, and the competition became the Home Nations Championship again between 1932 and 1939. France were then reinstated to the Championship in September 1939, which allowed them to compete in 1940. The Second World War intervened and they were finally readmitted in 1947.

At a special meeting of the RFU on 19 September 1985, professionalism in any form was outlawed and strict new by-laws were adopted to 'govern the structure of the amateur rugby union game'.

SANZAR, short for South Africa, New Zealand, Australia Rugby, was formed in 1995 with an objective of creating a provincial competition between teams from the three nations and an International tournament between the three Southern

Hemisphere teams. During the 1995 World Cup in South Africa, on the eve of the third place match between France and England, SANZAR leaders announced that they had signed a contract with Rupert Murdoch who had offered the organisation $550 million for the sole rights to screen the newly proposed annual Super 12 Rugby competition for the provincial teams and a Tri Nations tournament for the SANZAR International teams, on a home and away basis. The matches would be screened on his News Corporation network for a period of ten years. As a result of this deal, the IRB met in Paris on 26 August 1995, and declared rugby union as an open game, thus lifting restrictions on all form of payments to both players and clubs. The amateur days of rugby were well and truly over and the professional era had arrived.

## FAMOUS STADIUMS – THE FIRST INTERNATIONAL

The first match played at Lansdowne Road was between Ireland and England on 11 March 1878. It was Ireland's third home International, the first two having been played at the Leinster Cricket Ground in Rathmines in Dublin and at the Ormeau Ground in Belfast.

Wales' first International match at Cardiff Arms Park was against Ireland on 12 April 1884. It was also their third home game, the previous two having taken place at St Helen's Ground in Swansea and Rodney Parade in Newport.

On 15 January 1910, England first played Wales at Twickenham, thirty-eight years after their first home game at the Kennington Oval in London in 1872, while Scotland's first International at Murrayfield was on 21 March 1925, when they faced England. Their previous seventy home matches had been played at various venues in Edinburgh and Glasgow.

New Zealand played their first home game at Athletic Park in Wellington against the touring Lions on 13 August 1904, a match they won by 9 points to 3. Seventeen years later, on 27 August 1921, the All Blacks lost to South Africa in their first game at Eden Park, Auckland by 9 points to 5. The Australians played their very first match at the Cricket Ground, Sydney against the Lions on 24 June 1899, and continued to play at that venue until 1986. The Sydney Football Stadium was then built in 1988 and the Wallabies played their opening game, at that ground, again against the Lions, on 1 July 1989. Australia's second International match was against the same touring Lions at the Exhibition Ground, Brisbane on 22 July 1899. After nearly seventy years, Test matches in Brisbane were switched to the new stadium built in 1966 and named Ballymore Oval. Then on 22 June 1968, Australia played the first match at that stadium, against the All Blacks, which they lost by 19 points to 18.

South Africa's first International at Newlands Stadium in Cape Town took place on 5 September 1891. That match, only the team's third game, was against the 1891 touring Lions.

The Springboks' first match at Ellis Park, Johannesburg came much later, on 21 July 1928, when they were narrowly defeated by New Zealand by 7 points to 6.

France played their first International match at Parc des Princes in Paris on 1 January 1906, against New Zealand, who were on their first major tour of the Northern Hemisphere. Exactly two years later, on 1 January 1908, the French played their first game at Paris' Stade Colombes, against England. France's opening match at the Stade de France in Saint Denis, north of Paris, was played ninety years later on 7 February 1998, against England.

Italy's first International match at Stadio Flaminio in Rome, which took place on 22 April 1935, was against a France XV selection. This was Italy's first real test against strong opposition in eight Internationals and, as expected, they lost the game by 44 points to 6. With the increased interest in rugby, after Italy's admission to the Six Nations Championship in 2000, the venue was moved to the larger Stadio Olimpico in Rome on 11 February 2012. The Italians lost the first game, against England, at the new venue, by 19 points to 15.

Argentina's first recognised International match at the Ferro Carril Oeste Stadium in Buenos Aires was played on 16 July 1932, against a touring South African team known as the Junior Springboks, and the Pumas' first International at the Velez Sarsfield Stadium also in Buenos Aires, took place on 31 May 1986, when they defeated France by 15 points to 13.

## SOME AMAZING COMEBACKS

On 15 August 1998, in a Tri Nations match against the All Blacks in Durban, the Springboks came back from 3-23 down to beat New Zealand by 24 points to 23.

The Welsh tour of Argentina in June 1999 looked like being an utter disaster, when in the first match in Buenos Aires the Pumas raced into a 20-0 lead in the first half hour. However, Wales struck back strongly but were still 10-23 down at half-time. They staged a tremendous comeback in the second half, and eventually ran out winners by 36 points to 26.

Arguably the most remarkable comeback of them all occurred in the semi-final of the World Cup match between France and New Zealand at Twickenham on 31 October 1999. With the score standing at New Zealand 24, France 10, ten minutes into the second half the French suddenly sprang into life and, displaying their famous Gallic flare, scored thirty-three unanswered points in the space of twenty-seven minutes. Suddenly the scoreboard read: New Zealand 24, France 43. The match ended a few minutes later with France victors by 43 points to 31 following a late converted try by the All Blacks.

Four years later, at the 2003 World Cup tournament, New

Zealand were very nearly victims of an amazing Welsh comeback. Drawn in the same pool as Wales, the All Blacks entered the final match of the pool having beaten Italy by 70 points to 7, Canada by 68 points to 6, and Tonga by 91 points to 7. The Welsh had struggled somewhat against the same three opponents, so the All Blacks were expected to sweep them aside in a one sided match at the Telstra Stadium in Sydney on 2 November. Indeed things did look ominous for the Welsh when New Zealand raced to a 28 points to 10 lead after only 32 minutes. Then suddenly Wales discovered some magic and at half-time had clawed themselves back into the game, but were still four points behind at 24 points to 28. Six minutes into the second half, Wales were actually leading by 34 points to 28: they had scored twenty-four points in just fourteen minutes. There the Welsh luck ended. New Zealand soon regained their composure and eventually ran out winners by 53 points to 37.

## INTERESTING ANECDOTES

The final split between the soccer form of football and rugby football came in 1863 and later that year the Football Association (FA) was formed.

The first ever rugby union international match, which was between Scotland and England, took place in Edinburgh on 27 March 1871, with each team fielding twenty players. Scotland's line up comprised of fourteen forwards, three full-backs and three half- backs, and England lined up with thirteen forwards three full-backs, three half-backs and one three-quarter-back.

The selection of the Irish team for their very first International match against England at Kennington Oval on 15 February 1875, was rather more unorthodox. The selectors decided on the less contentious option of picking ten players from the Republic and ten players from Northern Ireland, rather than choosing the best possible combination of players. Most of them were unknown to each other and many played out of position and so, given these unusual circumstances, it is quite amazing that Ireland only lost by 7 points to nil.

Two years later on 5 February 1877, in the match between England and Ireland, the number of players each side was reduced to fifteen, with both teams fielding nine forwards, two full-backs, two half-backs and two three-quarter-backs.

The Calcutta Cup, a trophy awarded to the winner of the annual England v Scotland match, has an interesting history. In 1878 the Calcutta Rugby Football Club, which had been formed in 1873, disbanded owing to lack of support, so the members decided to melt down the funds, which were in silver rupees, and create a cup that was subsequently presented to the RFU by G. A. J. Rothney. The first match, which ended 3-3, took place on 10 March 1879.

Twickenham is located on a piece of land that was originally the site of a market garden. In 1907, committee member William Williams recommended that the RFU purchase the land so that the England rugby team could have a permanent home. A price of £5,572 was agreed, and to this day the so-called 'RFU Headquarters' is affectionately known as the 'Cabbage Patch'.

The first five nations match after the First World War was between France and Scotland at Parc des Princess in Paris on 1 January 1920, and it featured a most amusing incident involving Jock Wemyss, the Scottish prop forward, who played for his country before and after the War. In those days players were given jerseys on their International debut but were expected to retain them for use in subsequent International matches. So, when the Scottish baggage man started handing out jerseys to the players, he skipped Jock because he had been capped before the war in 1914. The baggage man told him he should have brought his jersey with him and even Wemyss' explanation, that he had swapped his jersey with an opponent six years earlier, was ignored. It was only when he lined up to enter the pitch bare-chested that he was finally handed a jersey. That match also produced an unusual coincidence, since both Wemyss and the French prop, Marcel Lubin-Lebrere, had each lost an eye in the Great War.

Internationals between the Southern Hemisphere nations resumed after the First World War in 1921 when South Africa toured New Zealand. After a long seven-year wait, the first Test on 13 August must have been a disappointment for the Dunedin spectators when 114 line-outs were awarded during the match. The count even beats the infamous 111 line-outs recorded during the Scotland v Wales game in Murrayfield on 2 February 1963, when the Welsh captain decided that gaining ground by kicking to touch as much as possible was the best tactic in such muddy conditions (the tactic paid off as Wales won the match by six points to nil).

On 18 August 1924, Western Samoa played a touring Fijian side in Apia. Both teams played this, their very first International, barefooted. The game kicked off at 7am to allow the Samoans to go to work after the match and also to give the Fijians sufficient time to catch the boat to Tonga, to continue their tour. The other unusual feature about the match was that there was a tree on the halfway line. Fiji won the game by 6 points to nil.

Vivian Jenkins became the first player to score a try from the full-back position in the International Championship. It occurred on 10 March 1934, in the match between Wales and Ireland in Swansea.

On 28 September 1935, Swansea became the first club team to beat all three SANZAR countries when they triumphed over New Zealand by 11 points to 3. This was also the first match that the All Blacks had lost to a club side. That win followed the club's 6 points to nil win against Australia on 26 December 1908, and the 26 December 1912, win against South Africa by 3 points to nil.

The Lions tour to New Zealand in 1950 was the last tour on which players travelled by ship. The route carried them through the Panama Canal on the outward journey, and via the Suez Canal on the return leg, more or less a journey around the world. On that tour, nineteen year old Lewis Jones was summoned to join the Lions as an injury replacement and became the first Lion to fly from the UK on a rugby tour.

The term Grand Slam, which means a side winning all four matches in the Five Nations series, was first coined in the press in 1957, when England achieved that distinction.

The legendary Colin Meads became only the second player in International history to be sent off by a referee. The man in charge, Ken Kelleher, gave Meads his marching orders on 2 December 1967, in the Murrayfield game between Scotland and New Zealand.

The Irish tour of New Zealand in 1976 included one Test against the All Blacks and a final game against Fiji on 9 June. The team arrived in Fiji only to find that owing to a scheduling error the Fijian team was on tour in Australia. The Fiji Rugby Union had to put together what was basically a reserve side, and the Irish team had to play a non-cap International as Ireland XV.

Upon his retirement in 1978, Welsh International Gareth Edwards had achieved the unique distinction of gaining fifty-three International caps in succession without missing a single match through injury or non-selection since his debut in 1967.

The International between the United States and South Africa, which took place on 25 September 1981, is often referred to as the 'Secret International'. It was scheduled at the height of anti-apartheid protests that followed the Springboks wherever they went. The venue was kept secret until the very last minute and the match went ahead at the Owl Creek Polo Field in Glenville, New York, in front of an estimated thirty spectators. This was the first International between the two countries and, after a brave performance from the US Eagles in the first half, when they trailed a full strength South African side by only two points, they eventually lost this historic match by 38 points to 7.

Dick (Red) Conway was so keen to tour South Africa with Wilson Whineray's All Blacks in 1960, that he took the extraordinary step of having an injured finger, which had been badly set, amputated. He was duly selected for the tour and played in three of the four Tests as a number eight forward.

An extremely unusual scoring sequence occurred in the Tri Nations match between New Zealand and Australia at the Carisbrook ground in Dunedin on 16 August 1997. The All Blacks were unstoppable in the first half and raced into a 36 points to nil lead at the end of that half. However, the tide changed in the second half and the Wallabies staged a remarkable recovery, scoring 24 points without reply. Unfortunately it was a matter of 'too little too late', and the home team eventually won by 36 points to 24.

The remarkable thing about that game was that all sixty points had been scored at the same end of the ground.

The match between Scotland and Wales at Murrayfield on 6 February 1999, will be remembered by both Scottish and Welsh fans for years to come. Fly half Duncan Hodge changed the direction of his kick-off and caught the Welsh defence napping. Confusion between the Welsh wing Matthew Robinson, in his debut International, and the full-back Shane Howarth, allowed Scottish centre John Leslie to snatch the ball from Howarth's grasp and race to the line for a try. Many re-runs of the move clocked the try at 9 seconds, making it the fastest in International history, surely unlikely to be beaten in the future. Scotland went on to win the match by 33 points to 20.

Another record, which is unlikely to be broken, is the one set by prolific Welsh kicker Neil Jenkins. During the 2003-04 season, playing for club side Celtic Warriors, he was successful with forty-four consecutive kicks.

Wales versus South Africa at the Millennium Stadium on 6 November 2004, featured six players in the Welsh team with the surname Jones. The front row, Duncan, Steve and Adam, wing forward Dafydd and, number eight Ryan, and, to complete the sextet, Stephen, who played at outside half. South Africa scraped home that day by 38 points to 36.

## SELECTED RUGBY MILESTONES

**1877:** On 5 February at Kennington Oval, the first XV-a-side International match took place between England and Ireland. The home team won by 8 points to nil.

**1883:** The first season when all four Home Nations played against each other.

**1910:** The first Five Nations match between Wales and France was played at St Helen's in Swansea on New Year's Day. Wales overwhelmed France by 49 points to 14.

**1920:** On 17 January, when Wales defeated England in Swansea by 19 points to 5, Gerry O'Shea became the first player to perform the so-called 'full house' by scoring a try, kicking the conversion, kicking a penalty goal, and dropping a goal. Thirty years would elapse before the feat was repeated by Lewis Jones, playing for the Lions, in 1950.

**1922:** Numbers appeared on the back of rugby shirts for the first time in the Five Nations Championship in the match between Wales and England in Cardiff on 21 January. Wales won by 28 points to 6.

**1925:** New Zealand faced England at Twickenham on 3 January, having won all twenty-seven matches between September and December 1924. The game was so ferocious that the referee Albert Freethy had to warn both teams three times in the first six minutes about dangerous play, stating that the next transgressor would be dismissed. After ten minutes, following a line out fracas, he blew his whistle and Cyril Brownlie of New Zealand became the first player to be sent off in an International. Even with just fourteen men, the All Blacks emerged triumphant, winning by 17 points to 11.

**1927:** The first BBC radio commentary on the match between England and Wales was transmitted live on 15 January. England won the Twickenham game by 11 points to 9.

**1938:** On 19 March, BBC television broadcasted the match between England and Scotland at Twickenham live to an audience in the London area. Scotland won the game by 21 points to 16 and with it the Triple Crown.

**1953-54:** This was the year when New Zealand became the first International rugby team to travel by air when they toured Britain, Ireland, France, Canada and the United States between October and March.

**1955:** The Lions travelled by air for the first time on their tour to South Africa, in a flight that took thirty-six hours.

**1987:** The year of the inaugural Rugby World Cup when host nation New Zealand won the first match of the tournament, played on 22 May, at Eden Park, Auckland by beating Italy 70 points to 6.

**1992:** On 23 March, the non-racial South African Rugby Union (SARU) and the South African Rugby Board (SARB) merged to form the South African Rugby Football Union (SARFU). The unification was signed at the Sun Hotel, Kimberley, which led to the readmission of South Africa to International rugby. On 15 August, the Springboks played New Zealand at Ellis Park, Johannesburg in their first game for eight years. They only narrowly lost by 27 points to 24.

**1993:** In January, with the Springboks now competing internationally, it was decided to award South Africa the hosting of the 1995 Rugby World Cup. Unfortunately, Dr Danie Craven, an iconic figure in South African rugby for decades, and the first co-president of the newly formed SARFU, died on 4 January, shortly before the award was made public.

**1994:** On 26 June, Philippe Sella became the first player to reach 100 caps when he led France on to the field against New Zealand at Lancaster Park Oval in Christchurch. The team celebrated the occasion in style, defeating the All Blacks by 22 points to 8. A week later on  3 July, they won again at Eden Park in Auckland by 23 points to 20, thus achieving a first ever series win in New Zealand.

**1996:** As a result of negotiations with Rupert Murdoch the previous year, the Tri Nations tournament, involving the SANZAR members, was launched. The inaugural match took place at the Athletic Park ground in Wellington on 6 July. New Zealand ran out easy winners when they beat old rivals Australia by 43 points to 6.

**2000:** The year when the Five Nations tournament was expanded to the Six Nations with the introduction of Italy to the competition. All three matches in the first round were played on Saturday 5 February. Italy played Scotland in Rome at 1pm, England faced Ireland in Twickenham at 2.30pm, and Wales took on France in Cardiff at 4pm.

With the dawn of the new millennium, video replay technology was introduced to rugby union to ascertain whether a try had been scored. The video referee or the Television Match Official (TMO), was called upon for the first time during New Zealand's match with Tonga in Albany on 16 June, when English referee Steve Lander requested the televised replay of a disputed try by the All Blacks forward and captain, Todd Blackadder. The melee that had developed on the Tongan line had made it virtually impossible for the referee to make a correct decision. After some discussion between Lander and TMO Steve Walsh, the score was eventually allowed and New Zealand went on to win the match by 102 points to nil.

**2001:** On 3 February, Welshman Neil Jenkins became the first rugby union player to score over 1,000 points. It was appropriate that this remarkable achievement occurred at the Millennium Stadium in Cardiff with Wales facing rivals, England. Included in the total was the 41 points Jenkins had scored for the Lions whilst on tour in South Africa in 1997. Yet another milestone was reached six weeks later when he reached 1,000 points for Wales in the International match against France at Stade de France in Paris on 17 March. It was fitting that his 28 point haul in that match, which Wales won by 43 points to 35, included the unique 'full house' of scores.

**2012:** Argentina was finally invited to participate in an expanded Tri Nations tournament, which was renamed 'The Rugby Championship'. The first two games, played on 18 August, featured a victory for New Zealand against Australia at the ANZ Stadium, Sydney and a South African win against newcomers Argentina at Newlands Stadium, Cape Town.

# APPENDIX I

## THE RUGBY TROPHIES
## AND COMPETITIONS

| TOURNAMENTS | COMPETITION | DATE | CODE | OPPONENT(S) |
|---|---|---|---|---|
| | WEBB ELLIS WORLD CUP | 1987 | WC | ALL NATIONS |
| **CHAMPIONSHIPS** | | | | |
| | TRI NATIONS | 1996 | TN | Aus, NZ and SA |
| | FIVE NATIONS TROPHY | 1993 | 5NT | E, F, Ir, S & W |
| | SIX NATIONS TROPHY | 2000 | 6NT | E, F, Ir, It, S & W |
| | TRIPLE CROWN TROPHY | 2006 | TCT | E, Ir, S, & W |
| | RUGBY CHAMPIONSHIP | 2012 | RC | Arg, Aus, NZ and SA |
| **AUSTRALIA** | BLEDISLOE CUP | 1931 | Bled | NEW ZEALAND |
| | TROPHEE DES BICENTENAIRES | 1989 | BIC | FRANCE |
| | COOK CUP | 1997 | CKC | ENGLAND |
| | HOPETOUN CUP | 1998 | HC | SCOTLAND |
| | LANSDOWNE CUP | 1999 | LC | IRELAND |
| | MANDELA CHALLENGE PLATE | 2000 | MCP | SOUTH AFRCA |
| | PUMA TROPHY | 2000 | PT | ARGENTINA |
| | TOM RICHARDS TROPHY | 2001 | TRT | B & I LIONS |
| | JAMES BEVAN TROPHY | 2007 | JBT | WALES |
| **NEW ZEALAND** | DAVE GALLAHER TROPHY | 2000 | DGT | FRANCE |
| | FREEDOM CUP | 2004 | FC | SOUTH AFRICA |
| | SIR EDMUND HILLARY SHIELD | 2008 | EHS | ENGLAND |
| **SOUTH AFRICA** | PRINCE WILLIAM CUP | 2007 | PWC | WALES |
| | LIONS / SOUTH AFRICA SERIES | 2009 | LSA | B & I LIONS |
| **ENGLAND** | CALCUTTA CUP | 1879 | CC | SCOTLAND |
| | MILLENNIUM TROPHY | 1988 | MT | IRELAND |
| | INVESTEC CHALLENGE CUP | 2013 | ICC | ARGENTINA |
| **IRELAND** | CENTENARY QUAICH TROPHY | 1989 | CQT | SCOTLAND |
| | ADMIRAL WILLIAM BROWN CUP | 2012 | ABC | ARGENTINA |
| **SCOTLAND** | DOUGLAS HORN TROPHY | 2008 | DHT | CANADA |
| **FRANCE** | GIUSEPPE GARIBALDI TROPHY | 2007 | GGT | ITALY |
| **BARBARIANS** | CORNWALL CUP | 2008 | CWC | AUSTRALIA |
| | MASTERCARD TROPHY | 2010 | MCT | SOUTH AFRICA |

# APPENDIX I

| COMPETITION | CODE |
|---|---|
| AFRICA CUP (2000 on) | AFC |
| AMERICAS RUGBY CHAMPIONSHIP (2009 on) | AMC |
| ANTIM CUP (2002) - ROMANIA v GEORGIA | AC |
| ASIA FIVE NATIONS CHAMPIONSHIP (2008 on) | A5N |
| ASIA GAMES (1998 & 2002) | AG |
| ASIA NATIONS SERIES (2007) | ANS |
| ASIAN (ARFU) CHAMPIONSHIP (1969-2004) | ASC |
| BALTIC CUP (1994,1995) | BC |
| CHURCHILL CUP (2003 - 2011) | CHC |
| CONFEDERATION OF AFRICAN RUGBY CHAMPIONSHIP | CAR |
| CONSUR CUP (2014 on) | CSC |
| CORNWALL CUP (2008) | CWC |
| EUROPEAN NATIONS CUP (2000 on) | ENC |
| FIRA CHAMPIONSHIP (1966-1997) | FIRA |
| INTERCONTINENTAL CUP (2005) | IC |
| IRB NATIONS CUP (2006 on) | INC |
| IRB PACIFIC NATIONS CUP (2006 on) | PNC |
| IRB TBILISI CUP (2013 on) | ITC |
| MASTERCARD TROPHY | MCT |
| MEMORIAL CUP (1997) | MC |
| PACIFIC RIM CHAMPIONSHIP (1996-2001) | PRC |
| PACIFIC TRI NATIONS SERIES (1998-2005) | PTN |
| PAN AMERICAN CHAMPIONSHIP (1995-2003) | PAC |
| SIX NATIONS 'B' CHAMPIONSHIP (2011 on ) | 6NB |
| SOUTH AMERICAN CHAMPIONSHIP (1951 on) | SAC |
| SOUTH PACIFIC CHAMPIONSHIP (1982-1997) | SPC |
| SOUTH PACIFIC GAMES (1963-1983) | SPG |
| SUNSHINE COAST CUP (1976) | SCC |
| VICTORY CUP (1959) | VC |

# APPENDIX II

## THE RUGBY TOURNAMENTS

NORTHERN HEMISPHERE

SOUTHERN HEMISPHERE

# THE RUGBY TOURNAMENTS

## THE RUGBY WORLD CUP
### (WEBB ELLIS TROPHY)

This is the premier competition in world rugby and has been staged every four years since 1987. The first tournament, co-hosted by Australia and New Zealand, was won by the All Blacks and featured sixteen teams who received special invitations from the International Rugby Board (IRB). However, subsequent tournaments required qualifying matches to determine the final list of contestants.

*World Cup venues / Winners:*

**1987** New Zealand and Australia – *New Zealand*
**1991** England – *Australia*
**1995** South Africa – *South Africa*
**1999** Wales – *Australia*
**2003** Australia – *England*
**2007** France – *South Africa*
**2011** New Zealand – *New Zealand*
**2015** England – *New Zealand*

## THE SIX NATIONS CHAMPIONSHIP

The Six Nations Championship started as a four-nations competition between England, Scotland, Ireland and Wales in 1883. It was expanded to a five-nations competition in 1910, when France was invited to participate. In 1931, when France was expelled from the competition for not abiding by the strict amateur rules of rugby union football, the Championship became a four-Home Nations competition once again. It remained so until 1939 and the outbreak of the Second World War. In 1947, France was reinstated and the revived Five Nations Championship continued uninterrupted until 1999.

In 1993 it was decided to present 'The Championship Trophy' to the winning nation and in 1994 a tie-break system was introduced for the first time to decide the champion if two or more teams ended with equal match points: the victor was then deemed to be the one with the greatest difference between total points scored and total points conceded over the whole tournament. In the event that the teams were also equal on points difference, the team who had scored the greater number of tries during the campaign was deemed to be the trophy winners. With the entry of Italy in 2000, rugby's oldest International tournament became known as the Six Nations Championship.

*Outright winners of the Five/Six Nations Championship between 1883 and 2015:*
England (26 times)
Wales (26 times)
France (17 times)
Scotland (14 times)
Ireland (13 times)
Italy (none).

## THE TRI NATIONS CHAMPIONSHIP

The Tri Nations Championship was contested each year from 1996 to 2011 by the three major Southern Hemisphere nations. During that time the tournament was dominated by New Zealand, who won the competition on ten occasions. Australia and South Africa both won three titles.

## THE RUGBY CHAMPIONSHIP

In 2012 the Tri Nations Championship was expanded to a four-nations tournament with the addition of Argentina, who had finished in third place in the 2007 World Cup. This new Southern Hemisphere competition was named The Rugby Championship. New Zealand were champions in the first three years (2012 to 2014) and Australia won the championship in 2015.

## THE FIRA CHAMPIONSHIP

The expulsion of France from the Five Nations Championship in 1931 led to the formation of FIRA, the Fédération Internationale de Rugby Amateur on 2 January 1934. The ten founding members were: Italy, Germany, Belgium, Spain, France, Holland, Portugal, Romania, Sweden and Czechoslovakia. In 1966 FIRA organised a second string European competition as an alternative to the Five Nations Championship.

France won the tournament on twenty occasions between 1966 and 1997, and they were the only team from the Five Nations tournament to compete in the FIRA league. In most instances France fielded an 'A' side. The Romanian team won the competition five times between 1968 and 1983, and Italy won the title once, in 1997.

## THE EUROPEAN NATIONS CUP (ENC)

The FIRA Championship was renamed the European Nations Cup (ENC) in 2000. The ENC consists of three divisions, with the first division renamed the 'Six Nations 'B' Championship' in 2011. Romania became the first ENC champions in 2000, followed by Georgia in 2001. From 2002 the tournament became biennial, with the winners declared every two years when each team had played the other five teams twice on a home and away basis.

Georgia, Romania, Spain, Russia, Portugal and Belgium competed in the 2013-14 Championship. In the nine tournaments played between 2000 and 2014, Georgia has won the title five times, Romania has had three title wins, and Portugal has won the title once in the 2003-04 season. Belgium was replaced by Germany in 2015 and Georgia are at present league leaders in the 2015-16 campaign.

## THE PAN AMERICAN CHAMPIONSHIP

Argentina won all five tournaments held irregularly in the Americas between 1995 and 2003. Except for 1995, when the United States did not enter, the four competing teams were Argentina, Uruguay, Canada and the United States.

## THE IRB NATIONS CUP
## WORLD RUGBY NATIONS CUP in 2015

The Nations Cup was first held in Lisbon in 2006 and has been staged annually at Bucharest ever since. The aim of this particular tournament was to provide competition between Tier 2 teams, Tier 3 teams and the 'A' sides representing Tier 1 teams.

In 2015 the four competing teams were: Romania, Spain, Namibia, and Argentina Jaguars. Namibia, who won in 2010, and Romania, who won in 2012, 2013 and 2015 are the only cup winners outside the Tier 1 'A' sides.

## THE SOUTH AMERICAN CHAMPIONSHIP /
## CONSUR CUP

The first South American Championship was held in Buenos Aires in 1951, involved four teams: Argentina, Chile, Uruguay and Brazil. The next three competitions were held in 1958, 1961 and 1964. In 1967, it became a biennial event and this continued until 1997; in 2000, it was agreed to run the competition annually. Over the years, the Championship has been expanded from one division to two divisions and, from 2012, to three divisions.

In 2014 a new competition called the Consur Cup was launched, with the top two teams from Division One of the South American

Championship competing with Argentina (who were seeded) for the title. Argentina, winners of the Championship thirty-four times between 1951 and 2013, did not enter the competition in 1981 and 2014. Uruguay won in both those years and Chile won for the first time in 2015. Argentina won the inaugural Consur Cup in 2014 and retained the trophy in 2015

## THE SOUTH PACIFIC CHAMPIONSHIP
The South Pacific Championship contested by Fiji, Western Samoa and Tonga, was held between 1982 and 1997. Western Samoa were title winners ten times, followed by Fiji, who won three times and Tonga, who won the title twice. There was no competition in 1989. The Championship was renamed the Pacific Tri Nations Series in 1998.

## THE PACIFIC RIM CHAMPIONSHIP
Between 1996 and 1998, the tournament comprised four teams: Canada, Hong Kong, Japan and the United States. Canada won on all three occasions. In 1999-2000 season, six teams were in competition when Fiji, Samoa and Tonga joined the Championship and Hong Kong dropped out. Samoa won the title that year, and in 2001, the final year of the tournament, the United States dropped out and Fiji won the title.

## THE PACIFIC TRI NATIONS SERIES
The series, a continuation of the South Pacific Championship, ran from 1998 to 2005. The same three nations, Fiji, Tonga and the renamed Samoa, were in competition.

The tournament was suspended in 2003 owing to the Rugby World Cup in Australia. In the seven years of competition Samoa won four titles to Fiji's three.

## THE IRB PACIFIC NATIONS CUP
## WORLD RUGBY PACIFIC NATIONS CUP in 2015

The IRB Pacific Nations Cup was originally known as the IRB Pacific Five Nations in 2006, the first year of the competition. The five nations competing for the title then were: Japan, Samoa, Tonga, Fiji and the Junior All Blacks, who won the inaugural tournament. They retained the trophy in 2007 when the tournament was renamed the IRB Pacific Nations Cup, and triumphed a third time in 2009. The New Zealand Maori team won in 2008. During the years 2010 to 2012, the Pacific Nations competition was reduced from five International teams to four: Samoa, Fiji, Tonga and Japan. Samoa were the Cup winners in 2010 and 2012, and Japan won in 2011. The five nations competing in 2013 were Tonga, Japan, Canada, the United States, and Fiji, the winners.

In 2014, the tournament was revamped and split into two separate competitions. The six competing teams were divided into two groups of three: Fiji, Tonga and winners Samoa formed one group, and the United States, Canada and winners Japan, the other. Fiji were outright winners of the trophy in 2015.

## THE AFRICA CUP

The Africa Cup is an annual tournament first held in 2000, run by the Confederation of African Rugby. Originally known as the CAR top9 / top10, the competition was renamed in 2006. Twenty-seven nations played in three divisions of the Africa Cup in 2015, and the most successful team since its inception has been Namibia, champions five times in 2002, 2004, the 2008-09 season, 2014 and 2015.

## THE ASIA FIVE NATIONS CHAMPIONSHIP

The Asian Rugby Championship was held between 1969 and 2004. In that period Japan won the championship fourteen times to South Korea's five wins. Japan also won the Asian Rugby Series in the 2006-07 season, which was then replaced by the Asian Five Nations Championship. This round-robin tournament was first held in 2008, and the competing sides over the years have been Japan, Kazakhstan, Hong Kong, Singapore, South Korea, the Arabian Gulf the United Arab Emirates, Sri Lanka and the Philippines. Japan has won all seven titles between 2008 and 2014, winning all twenty-eight matches in the process. The tournament reverted back to its original name The Asian Rugby Championship in 2015 and Japan were champions yet again.

## THE IRB TBILISI CUP
## WORLD RUGBY TBLISI CUP in 2015

The Tblisi Cup, with similar terms of reference as the IRB Nations Cup, was launched in 2013 when the hosts Georgia were joined by Uruguay, Emerging Ireland and the South African President's XV, who became inaugural champions after they won all three matches. Argentina Jaguars, were cup winners in 2014 and Emerging Ireland in 2015.

## THE CHURCHILL CUP

The Churchill Cup was held annually between 2003 and 2011. The competition was mainly between Canada, the United States and, in various years, representative teams from England, Ireland, France, Italy, Argentina, Scotland and the New Zealand Maori. In recent years, Georgia, Uruguay, Tonga and Russia were also invited to participate in the competition.

Past winners of the tournament are: New Zealand Maoris in 2004 and 2006; Ireland 'A' in 2009; and England 'A' on the other six occasions.

# APPENDIX III
## THE MAJOR STADIUMS

NORTHERN HEMISPHERE

SOUTHERN HEMISPHERE

# MAJOR STADIUMS IN ARGENTINA

| | | |
|---|---|---|
| 1 | BELGRANO STADIUM, BUENOS AIRES | A multi-purpose Stadium and home ground of Belgrano Athletic Club. |
| 2 | CLUB ATLÉTICO SAN ISIDRO GROUND, BUENOS AIRES | The club was founded on 24 October 1902, and rugby was first played at the ground in 1907. |
| 3 | CRICKET AND RUGBY CLUB GROUND, BUENOS AIRES | The club was founded on 8 December 1864. |
| 4 | ESTADIO DON LEON KOLBOVSKI, BUENOS AIRES | A multi-purpose stadium, mainly used for football matches, was opened on 5 May 1960, and renovated in 2009. |
| 5 | ESTADIO MONUMENTAL, RIVER PLATE, BUENOS AIRES | The stadium, also known as 'Estadio Antonio Vespucio Liberti', was opened on 25 May 1938, and renovated in 1978. |
| 6 | FERRO CARRIL OESTE STADIUM, BUENOS AIRES | The stadium was opened on 2 January 1905, and was given the often used name of 'Estadio Arquitecto Ricardo Etcheverry' in 1995. |
| 7 | GIMNASIA y ESGRIMA de BUENOS AIRES | The stadium, known in short as 'Estadio GEBA', and also as 'Jorge Newbery Gimnasia', was established on 11 November 1880. |
| 8 | VÉLEZ SARSFIELD STADIUM, BUENOS AIRES | Also known as 'Estadio José Amalfitani', the stadium was opened on 11 April 1943, renovated in 1951, and expanded in 1978. |
| 9 | ESTADIO OLIMPICO CHÂTEAU CARRERAS, CÓRDOBA | Opened on 16 May 1978 as a football stadium, it is also known as 'Estadio Mario Alberto Kempes' or just 'Estadio Córdoba'. |
| 10 | ESTADIO CIUDAD de LA PLATA, LA PLATA | The stadium, also known as 'Estadio Unico', was opened on 7 June 2003. |
| 11 | ESTADIO JOSÉ MARIA MINELLA, MAR DEL PLATA | This football stadium was opened on May 21, 1978, in time for the 1978 Football World Cup. |
| 12 | ESTADIO BAUTISTA GARGANTINI, MENDOZA | The stadium was opened on 5 April 1925, and is the home ground of Club Sportivo Independiente Rivadavia. |

# MAJOR STADIUMS IN ARGENTINA

| | | |
|---|---|---|
| **13** | ESTADIO MALVINAS ARGENTINAS, MENDOZA | The stadium was opened in 1978 to coincide with the 1978 Football World Cup, and is also known as 'Estadio Mundialista Malvinas'. |
| **14** | RUGBY CLUB CATARATAS, PUERTO IGUAZU, MISIONES | The home ground of Cataratas Rugby Club. |
| **15** | TACURU SOCIAL CLUB, POSADAS, MISIONES | The Tacuru Social Club ground is also known as 'Estadio Posadas' in Posadas, the capital city of the province of Misiones. |
| **16** | ESTADIO RAÚL CONTI, PUERTO MADRYN | This mainly rugby stadium was opened on 25 May 1967. It is situated in the Chubut region of Argentina. |
| **17** | ESTADIO GABINO SOSA, ROSARIO | The home ground of Club Atlético Central Córdoba in Rosario in the province of Santa Fe. |
| **18** | ESTADIO GIGANTE de ARROYITO, ROSARIO | The stadium was opened on 27 October 1929, renovated in 1957, 1963 and 1968 and also between 1974 and 1978. |
| **19** | ESTADIO PADRE ERNESTO MARTEARENA, SALTA | A multi-purpose stadium opened in 2001. |
| **20** | ESTADIO SAN MARTIN de SAN JUAN, SAN JUAN | The home ground of Club Atlético San Martin. |
| **21** | ESTADIO SAN JUAN del BICENTENARIO, SAN JUAN | A multi-purpose stadium opened on 16 March 2011. |
| **22** | ESTADIO BRIGADIER GENERAL E. LÓPEZ, SANTA FE | The ground was opened on 9 July 1946, as a football stadium, under its full name, 'Estadio Brigadier General Estanislao López'. |
| **23** | ESTADIO MONUMENTAL JOSÉ FIERRO, TUCUMÁN | This multi-purpose stadium, opened on 21 May 1922, is the home ground of the club Cancha (or Clube) del Atletico Tucumán. |

# MAJOR STADIUMS IN AUSTRALIA

1 BALLYMORE OVAL, BRISBANE — This mainly rugby stadium, opened in 1966, is owned by Queensland Rugby Union. The ground hosted five matches in Rugby World Cup 1987.

2 EXHIBITION GROUND, BRISBANE — The ground, formerly known as 'RNA Showgrounds', was opened in 1886 and was used for Internationals during the period 1899 to 1971.

3 LANG PARK, BRISBANE
renamed: SUNCORP STADIUM, BRISBANE — The stadium was opened in 1914 under the name 'John Brown Oval', before being re-named 'Lang Park' shortly afterwards. In 1994, under sponsorship, it was renamed 'Suncorp Stadium' and was refurbished in 2003 in time to host nine matches in Rugby World Cup 2003.

4 BRUCE STADIUM / CANBERRA STADIUM — The stadium was opened in 1997 and named 'Bruce Stadium' until 2002 when it was renamed 'Canberra Stadium'.

5 THE GABBA CRICKET GROUND, BRISBANE — Brisbane Cricket Ground, known as 'The Gabba', was established in 1895, and was used for Internationals between 1907 and 2002.

6 COLONIAL STADIUM, MELBOURNE
renamed: TELSTRA DOME / ETIHAD STADIUM — The ground was opened on 9 March 2000 and named 'Colonial Stadium' before being renamed Telstra Dome on 1 October 2002. On 1 March 2009, with a new sponsor on board, it was renamed 'Etihad Stadium, Melbourne. It is also known as 'Docklands Stadium'.

7 OLYMPIC PARK STADIUM, MELBOURNE — This multi-purpose stadium, built in 1956, was used for rugby Internationals until 1994. It was demolished in 2011.

8 SUBIACO OVAL, PERTH
renamed: PATERSONS STADIUM, PERTH — The stadium, established on 9 May 1908, was redeveloped in 1995, 1997 and 1999 and hosted five matches in Rugby World Cup 2003. Since October 2010, under a naming rights contract, Subiaco Oval now is known as 'Patersons Stadium', Perth.

9 CONCORD OVAL, SYDNEY — The 'Oval', opened in 1985 was used for Internationals up to 1998 and also during the 1987 Rugby World Cup. It is often known as the Waratah Stadium.

# MAJOR STADIUMS IN AUSTRALIA

**10  SYDNEY CRICKET GROUND**

Established as a sports ground in 1848, it was known as the SCG in 1894, and was used for rugby Internationals between 1899 and 1986.

**11  SYDNEY FOOTBALL STADIUM**
*renamed:* AUSSIE / ALLIANZ STADIUM.

This football stadium was opened in 1988 and was renamed 'Aussie Stadium, Sydney' in early 2002. It then reverted to its original name on 7 July 2007. Currently however, it is known by its sponsorship name 'Allianz Stadium'.

**12  ROYAL AGRICULTURAL SHOWGROUND, SYDNEY**

This ground, situated in Moore Park, was opened in 1882, and was used for rugby Internationals between 1921 and 1926.

**13  SYDNEY SPORTS GROUND**

The stadium opened in 1911 was used for rugby Internationals between 1914 and 1962. It was closed in 1986 and demolished in 1987.

**14  STADIUM AUSTRALIA, SYDNEY**
*renamed:* TELSTRA STADIUM, SYDNEY
*renamed:* ANZ STADIUM, SYDNEY

The stadium built to host the Sydney 2000 Summer Olympic Games, was opened on 6 March 1999. It was renamed 'Telstra Stadium' in July 2002 when the telecommunications company acquired the naming rights. The stadium's name was changed again on 1 January 2008 to 'ANZ Stadium' in a seven-year sponsorship deal with the ANZ Bank.

**15  YORK PARK LAUNCESTON, TASMANIA**

The sports ground was opened in 1921 and was renamed Aurora Stadium from 2004 to 2010 under a six-year naming agreement.

**16  DAIRY FARMERS STADIUM, TOWNSVILLE, QUEENSLAND**

The ground opened in 1994, and was known as Stockland Stadium between 1995 and 1998 and Malanda Stadium during 1998.

**17  WOLLONGONG SHOWGROUND, NEW SOUTH WALES**

The ground was opened in 1911 and took on the sponsored name of WIN Stadium Wollongong in 1997. It was upgraded in 2002.

## MAJOR STADIUMS IN ENGLAND

| | | |
|---|---|---|
| 1 | VILLA PARK, BIRMINGHAM | The stadium, opened in 1897, is the home ground of Aston Villa Football Club. It will host two pool games in Rugby World Cup 2015. |
| 2 | RECTORY FIELD, BLACKHEATH | The multi-purposed ground, opened in 1873, was regularly used for rugby Internationals between 1884 and 1909. |
| 3 | BRIGHTON COMMUNITY STADIUM, BRIGHTON | Known under the sponsorship name of 'American Express Community Stadium', it will host two pool matches in Rugby World Cup 2015. |
| 4 | ASHTON GATE, BRISTOL | This football stadium, opened in 1904, staged its first rugby International in 1908, and was used in Rugby World Cup 1991 and in Rugby World Cup 1999. |
| 5 | SANDY PARK, EXETER | This rugby stadium opened on 1 September 2006 is the home ground of Exeter Chiefs' rugby club, and will host three pool games in RWC 2015. |
| 6 | KINGSHOLM, GLOUCESTER | The stadium, opened in 1891, staged its first rugby International in 1900. It was used in Rugby World Cup 1991, and will host four pool games in RWC 2015. |
| 7 | McALPINE STADIUM, HUDDERSFIELD | Opened in 1994, the stadium, renamed 'Galpharm Stadium' in 2005, is currently known as 'John Smith's Stadium' and was used in Rugby World Cup 1999. |
| 8 | ELLAND ROAD, LEEDS | The ground was opened in 1897 and has been the home of Leeds Football Club since 1919. The stadium will stage two pool games in Rugby World Cup 2015. |
| 9 | WELFORD ROAD, LEICESTER | Opened in 1892, as the home of Leicester Tigers, the ground staged its first rugby International match in 1902, and was used in Rugby World Cup 1991 and in Rugby World Cup 1999. |
| 10 | LEICESTER CITY STADIUM, LEICESTER | The stadium, built in 2002, and home of Leicester City Football Club, has since then staged seven rugby matches. The ground will host three pool games in Rugby World Cup 2015. |
| 11 | KENNINGTON OVAL, LONDON | This cricket ground, also known as 'The Oval', was established in 1845. It staged seven rugby Internationals between 1872 and 1879. |

# MAJOR STADIUMS IN ENGLAND

12 OLYMPIC STADIUM, LONDON — The stadium, built primarily to host the 2012 Olympic Games, was opened in 2011. It will stage four pool games and the bronze match in Rugby World Cup 2015.

13 TWICKENHAM, LONDON — The land was purchased in 1907, the rugby stadium was opened in 1909, and the first International was played on 15 January 1910. It underwent many redevelopments between 1927 and 1995, the most recent being in 2006. It was used in Rugby World Cups 1991 and 1999. The stadium will stage five pool games, two quarter-finals, both semi-finals and the final in Rugby World Cup 2015.

14 WEMBLEY STADIUM, LONDON — This football stadium was opened in 1923, renovated in 1963, and demolished in 2003. The new 'Wembley Stadium', opened on 9 March 2007, was chosen to host two matches in Rugby World Cup 2015.

15 STADIUM MK, MILTON KEYNES — This football ground, known locally as "Denbigh Stadium", was built in 2007. It will stage three pool games in Rugby World Cup 2015.

16 MANCHESTER CITY STADIUM, MANCHESTER — Known as the 'Etihad Stadium' for sponsorship reasons, it was opened as a football stadium in August 2003. It will host the England v Uruguay pool game in Rugby World Cup 2015.

17 OLD TRAFFORD, MANCHESTER — This football stadium was opened on 19 February 1910 and staged its first rugby International in 1997.

18 WHALLEY RANGE, MANCHESTER — This football stadium staged seven Home Nations rugby Internationals between 1880 and 1892.

19 ST JAMES' PARK, NEWCASTLE — The stadium has been the home of Newcastle United Football Club from the time it opened in 1892. It will host three pool matches in Rugby World Cup 2015.

20 CROSS GREEN, OTLEY — This multi-purpose stadium, home ground of Otley RFC, hosted the Pool A rugby International between Italy and the United States in Rugby World Cup 1991.

21 ATHLETIC GROUND, RICHMOND — The stadium was used for ten rugby Internationals between 1891 and 1909.

# MAJOR STADIUMS IN FRANCE

| 1 | STADE ARMANDIE, AGEN | The ground, opened on October 9, 1921, hosted one pool game in Rugby World Cup 1991. The stadium was then renovated between 2008 and 2010. |
|---|---|---|
| 2 | STADE JEAN DAUGER, BAYONNE | Opened in 1937, and renovated between 2006 and 2009, this multi-purpose stadium was used in a pool match in Rugby World Cup 1991. |
| 3 | STADE de la MÉDITERRANÉE, BÉZIERS | Opened in 1990, the stadium hosted a pool game in Rugby World Cup 1991, and two pool games in Rugby World Cup 1999. It was renovated between 2003 and 2007. |
| 4 | PARC des SPORTS AGUILÉRA, BIARRITZ | This multi-purpose ground was opened in 1906, expanded in 1962, and renovated during the period 2003 to 2006. |
| 5 | STADE MUNICIPAL du PARC LESCURE, BORDEAUX *renamed:* STADE CHABAN-DELMAS. BORDEAUX | This municipal sporting ground, opened on 12 June 1938, was renovated in 1935, 1987 and 1998. The stadium hosted two pool games in RWC 1999, was renamed 'Stade Chaban-Delmas' in 2001 and staged four pool games in RWC 2007. |
| 6 | STADE PARC MUNICIPAL des SPORTS, BRIVE . *renamed:* STADE AMÉDÉE-DOMENECH, BRIVE | Opened in 1921, and used for one pool game in RWC 1991, the stadium was renamed 'Stade Amédée-Domenech' in 2004, and expanded in 2011. |
| 7 | PARC des SPORTS MARCEL MICHELIN, CLERMONT-FERRAND | The stadium was opened in 1911, and renovated between 2006 and 2008. It was further renovated in 2010-11, and is the home of ASM Clermont Auvergne. |
| 8 | STADE LESDIGUIÈRES, GRENOBLE | The stadium was opened in 1968 and renovated in 1991. The ground hosted one pool match in Rugby World Cup 1991. |
| 9 | STADE FÉLIX BOLLAERT, LENS | Opened in 1933 and renovated in 2004, 'Stade Bollaert-Delelis' hosted a play-off game game in Rugby World Cup 1999 and three pool matches in Rugby World Cup 2007. |
| 10 | STADE NORD LILLE MÉTROPOLE | Built in 1976 and situated in Villeneuve-d'Ascq, the stadium staged a quarter-final match in Rugby World Cup 1991. |
| 11 | STADE de GERLAND, LYON | Opened in 1926 and renovated in 1960, 1980 and in 1998, this mainly football stadium hosted three pool matches in Rugby World Cup 2007. |

# MAJOR STADIUMS IN FRANCE

**12** STADE VÉLODROME, MARSEILLE — Opened on 3 June 1937, and renovated in 1984 and 1998, the stadium staged four pool games and two quarter-final matches in Rugby World Cup 2007.

**13** STADE de la MOSSON, MONTPELLIER — This mainly football stadium, opened in 1972 and renovated in 1997, hosted pool games in Rugby World Cup 2007.

**14** STADE de la BEAUJOIRE, NANTES — The multi-purpose stadium, opened on 8 May 1984, staged three pool matches in Rugby World Cup 2007.

**15** STADE COLOMBES, PARIS — Opened in 1907 as 'Stade du Matin', it was renamed Stade de Colombes' in 1920, and hosted the 1924 Olympics. In 1928 the stadium was renamed 'Stade Olympique Yves-du-Manoir' but it is still known as simply 'Stade Colombes'.

**16** STADE DE FRANCE, PARIS — Opened on 28 January 1998 as the National Stadium of France, the ground is in the Saint Denis commune of Paris. It hosted a quarter-final match in Rugby World Cup 1999 and seven games, including both semi-finals and the final, in Rugby World Cup 2007.

**17** PARC DES PRINCES, PARIS — Opened as a multi-purpose stadium on 18 July 1897, and renovated in 1932, it became dedicated to football and rugby in 1967. Known as the National Stadium until 1998, the ground hosted a quarter-final in Rugby World Cup 1991 and five pool matches in Rugby World Cup 2007.

**18** STADE GEOFFROY-GUICHARD, SAINT ÉTIENNE — This mainly football ground, opened on 13 September 1931 and renovated in 1984 and 1998, hosted three pool games in Rugby World Cup 2007.

**19** STADE MAYOL, TOULON — This multi-purpose stadium, inaugurated on 28 March 1920 and renovated in 1947 and 1965, is the home ground of RC Toulonnais.

**20** STADE ERNEST WALLON, TOULOUSE — The stadium also known as 'Stade des Sept Deniers' was opened in 1982, renovated in 2000, and used in a pool game in Rugby World Cup 1991.

**21** STADE MUNICIPAL de TOULOUSE — This multi purpose stadium, opened in 1937 and renovated in 1998, hosted two pool games in Rugby World Cup 1999 and four pool games in Rugby World Cup 2007.

# MAJOR STADIUMS IN IRELAND

| 1 | BALLYNAFEIGH, BELFAST | The stadium was founded in 1877 and staged three rugby Internationals between 1891 and 1894. |
|---|---|---|
| 2 | BALMORAL SHOWGROUNDS, BELFAST | This venue was frequently used for rugby Internationals between 1898 and 1921. Eleven matches in all were played at the ground. |
| 3 | ORMEAU, BELFAST | The stadium staged seven rugby Internationals between 1877 and 1889, including the abandoned match against Scotland in 1885. |
| 4 | RAVENHILL, BELFAST *renamed*: KINGSPAN STADIUM, BELFAST | The stadium was opened in 1923 and was used continuously for rugby Internationals between 1924 and 1954. It was also used in both Rugby World Cup 1991 and Rugby World Cup 1999, and was renovated in 2009. It is now the home ground of Ulster Rugby. Ravenhill was upgraded during the period 2012 to 2014 and renamed in June 2014 as part of a ten year sponsorship deal with the Kingspan Group. |
| 5 | MARDYKE, CORK | The Cork County cricket ground, also used by University College Cork sports club, staged two rugby Internationals between 1911 and 1913. |
| 6 | MUSGRAVE PARK, CORK | The rugby stadium, opened in 1940, is one of two home grounds used by Munster Rugby, the other being in Limerick. |
| 7 | AVIVA STADIUM, DUBLIN | Mainly a rugby stadium, it was built on the site of 'Lansdowne Road' between 2007 and was opened on 14 May 2010. |
| 8 | CROKE PARK, DUBLIN | Headquarters of the Gaelic Athletic Association (GAA), the stadium was opened in 1913 and renovated in 2004. It was used for fourteen rugby Internationals between 2007 and 2010 during the Aviva Stadium construction project. |
| 9 | DONNYBROOK STADIUM, DUBLIN | The stadium was renovated in 2008, and became the home of Leinster Rugby until the club moved to the RDS Showgrounds. |

# MAJOR STADIUMS IN IRELAND

**10** LANSDOWNE ROAD, DUBLIN

The rugby stadium was opened in 1872, but the first rugby International did not take place until 11 March 1878. The last International was played on 20 November 2006. The, then, oldest rugby International stadium in the world was finally demolished in 2007. It was used in Rugby World Cup 1991 and Rugby World Cup 1999.

**11** LEINSTER CRICKET CLUB, RATHMINES, DUBLIN

The cricket club was founded in 1852 and the ground staged Ireland's first ever home rugby International on 13 December 1875.

**12** RDS SHOWGROUNDS, DUBLIN

Opened in 1868 to host equestrian events, the arena, expanded in 2007 and 2008, is now the new home ground of Leinster Rugby.

**13** UCD BOWL, DUBLIN

Part of the University College Dublin sports complex, the rugby ground section of the campus was renovated in 2007.

**14** GALWAY SPORTSGROUND, GALWAY

This multi-purpose venue in the west of Ireland was opened in 1927, and is the home ground of Connacht Rugby.

**15** THOMOND PARK, LIMERICK

The current stadium was opened in 1940, but the first rugby International was played on the old location on 19 March 1898. The stadium was used in Rugby World Cup 1999, and was modernised in 2008, to become the main home ground of Munster Rugby.

# MAJOR STADIUMS IN ITALY

1 STADIO SANTA COLOMBA, BENEVENTO
renamed: STADIO CIRO VIGORITO

The ground was opened on 9 September 1979 as a football stadium, and it was renamed 'Stadio Ciro Vigorito' on 2 November 2010.

2 STADIO RENATO DALL'ARA, BOLOGNA

Opened in 1927 as a multi-purpose stadium, it is used by Bologna FC. In 1995 the ground hosted the Italy match against the All Blacks.

3 CENTRO SPORTIVO SAN MICHELE, CALVISANO
*renamed*: STADIO PERONI

Opened in 1972, the stadium is the home of Calvisano RFC, and was renamed 'Stadio Peroni' on 19 May 2012.

4 STADIO SANTA MARIA GORETTI, CATANIA

A multi-purpose stadium, home of Amatori Catania, it is used mostly for rugby and American football.

5 STADIO ARTEMIO FRANCHI, FLORENCE

Opened in 1931 as a football stadium and renovated in 1990, it was previously known as 'Stadio Comunale Artemio Franchi'.

6 STADIO COMUNALE LUIGI FERRARIS, GENOA

Opened on 22 January 1911, the stadium is also known as 'Stadio Luigi Ferraris' or just 'Marassi'. The ground was renovated in 1989.

7 STADIO TOMMASO FATTORI, L'AQUILA

This multi-purpose stadium opened in 1933, is the home ground of L'Aquila Calcio and L'Aquila Rugby.

8 ARENA CIVICA, MILAN
*renamed*: ARENA GIANNI BRERA

Opened on 18 August 1807, and renovated in 1945, this multi-purpose stadium was renamed 'Arena Gianni Brera' in 2003.

9 STADIO SAN SIRO, MILAN
*renamed*: STADIO GIUSEPPE MEAZZA

Opened on 19 September 1926, renovated in 1956 and 1989, the stadium was renamed 'Stadio Giuseppe Meazza' on 3 March 1980.

10 STADIO PLEBISCITO, PADOVA

The stadium, mainly used for rugby, is the home ground of Petrarca Padova rugby football club.

11 STADIO EUGANEO, PADOVA

Opened in 1994, this football stadium, home ground of Calcio Padova, replaced the historical 'Stadio Silvio Appiani'.

# MAJOR STADIUMS IN ITALY

| | | |
|---|---|---|
| **12** | STADIO COMUNALE ENNIO TARDINI, PARMA | The football stadium opened on 16 September 1923. and renovated between 1990 and 1993, is the home of Parma FC. |
| **13** | STADIO XXV APRILE, PARMA | A dedicated rugby stadium opened in 2008, replaced 'Stadio Sergio Lanfranchi', and is the home ground of Zebre Rugby. |
| **14** | STADIO COMUNALE BELTRAMETTI, PIACENZA | Opened on 27 November 1966 as a rugby stadium, it is the home ground of Rugby Piacenza. |
| **15** | STADIO FLAMINIO, ROME | Opened in March 1959, the stadium was the venue for Italy's home games during the Six Nations competition between 2000 and 2011. The stadium was renovated in 2008, and was due expansion in 2012 which did not materialise. |
| **16** | STADIO OLIMPICO, ROME | Opened in 1937 as 'Stadio del Cipressi', the stadium was renovated and officially inaugurated on 17 May 1953, as 'Stadio dei Centomila'. In 1960, the stadium was given its current name when Italy staged the summer Olympics that year. It was further expanded in 1990. |
| **17** | STADIO COMUNALE MARIO BATTAGLINI, ROVIGO | Opened in 1970, as a multi-purpose facility, the stadium is the home ground of Rugby Rovigo. |
| **18** | STADIO COMUNALE DI MONIGO, TREVISO | Opened in 1973, mainly as a rugby stadium, it is the current home ground of Benetton Treviso rugby football club. |
| **19** | STADIO OLIMPICO di TORINO, TURIN | Opened on 14 May 1933, as 'Stadio Mussolini', and later as 'Stadio Comunale', it was renovated and reopened on 10 February 2006. |
| **20** | STADIO FRIULI, UDINE | This multi-purpose stadium was opened in 1976, replacing 'Stadio Moretti'. It was renovated in 1990, and also between 2012 and 2014. |
| **21** | STADIO LUIGI ZAFFANELLA, VIADANA | Opened in 1972, mainly as a rugby stadium, and owned by Rugby Viadana, it was the home ground of the now defunct Aironi rugby club. |

# MAJOR STADIUMS IN NEW ZEALAND

**1 NORTH HARBOUR STADIUM, ALBANY**

The stadium, opened on 8 March 1997, and situated in North Shore City near Auckland, hosted four pool games in Rugby World Cup 2011.

**2 EDEN PARK, AUCKLAND**

The ground was opened in 1900, and the first rugby International was played at that venue on August 27, 1921. The stadium staged many matches in RWC 1987 and in Rugby World Cup 2011, and is currently the only ground to have hosted two World Cup finals.

**3 LANCASTER PARK OVAL, CHRISTCHURCH**
*renamed:* JADE STADIUM, CHRISTCHURCH
*renamed:* A M I STADIUM, CHRISTCHURCH

The stadium was opened on 15 October 1881, and the first test at the venue took place on 29 September 1913. The ground was renovated many times between 1995 and 2009, and was renamed 'Jade Stadium' by its sponsor in 1998. It was renamed 'A M I Stadium' by another sponsor in 2007, but had to close in February 2011 because of an earthquake.

**4 CARISBROOK, DUNEDIN**

The ground, opened in 1883, staged three pool games in Rugby World Cup 1987, and closed in 2011. It was replaced by 'Forsyth Barr Stadium'.

**5 FORSYTH BARR STADIUM, DUNEDIN**

The stadium, opened on 5 August 2011, used the temporary non-commercial name 'Otago Stadium' during Rugby World Cup 2011.

**6 RUGBY PARK, HAMILTON**

Opened in 1925, the stadium hosted one pool game in Rugby World Cup 1987 and was replaced by 'Waikato Stadium' in 1999.

**7 WAIKATO STADIUM, HAMILTON**

Opened in 2002, to replace 'Rugby Park', the ground hosted three pool games in Rugby World Cup 2011.

**8 RUGBY PARK STADIUM, INVERCARGILL**

This rugby venue, which started as a cricket pitch in 1886, hosted one pool game in Rugby World Cup 1987 and three pool games in Rugby World Cup 2011.

**9 McLEAN PARK, NAPIER**

The ground, established in 1911 mainly as a cricket venue, hosted one pool game in Rugby World Cup 1987, and two pool games in Rugby World Cup 2011.

# MAJOR STADIUMS IN NEW ZEALAND

**10** TRAFALGAR PARK, NELSON

The ground was opened on 21 April 1888, renovated in 2008, and then upgraded in 2011 to host three pool games during Rugby World Cup 2011.

**11** YARROW STADIUM, NEW PLYMOUTH

The stadium, opened in September 2002, used the non-commercial name of 'Stadium Taranaki' whilst hosting three pool games in Rugby World Cup 2011.

**12** SHOWGROUNDS OVAL, PALMERSTON NORTH
*remamed:* ARENA 1, PALMERSTON NORTH
*renamed:* FMG STADIUM, PALMERSTON NORTH
*renamed:* ARENA MANAWATU PALMERSTON NORTH

The original ground, named 'Showgrounds Oval, Palmerston North' hosted one pool match in Rugby World Cup 1987. The stadium redeveloped in March 2005, was earlier known as 'Arena 1' and later as 'FMG Stadium', but is currently known as 'Arena Manawatu'. Under this name, the venue staged two pool games in Rugby World Cup 2011.

**13** ROTORUA INTERNATIONAL STADIUM, ROTORUA

Rotorua Stadium, built in 1911, hosted the third-place game in Rugby World Cup 1987 and three pool matches in Rugby World Cup 2011.

**14** ATHLETIC PARK, WELLINGTON

The stadium was opened on 6 April 1896, and demolished on 10 October 1999. The ground hosted four pool matches in Rugby World Cup 1987.

**15** WESTPAC STADIUM (TRUST), WELLINGTON
*renamed:* WESTPAC STADIUM, WELLINGTON

The stadium was opened on 3 January 2000, with the original name incorporating the word 'trust', which was dropped in 2004. The new name was changed to the non-commercial name 'Wellington Regional Stadium', during Rugby World Cup 2011.

**16** OKARA PARK, WHANGAREI

The ground was opened in 1965, renovated in 2008, and hosted two pool games in Rugby World Cup 2011.

# MAJOR STADIUMS IN SCOTLAND

1 PITTODRIE STADIUM, ABERDEEN — The football stadium was opened in 1899 and renovated in 1993. The ground has also been used for rugby Internationals since 2008.

2 INVERLEITH, EDINBURGH — The ground was opened in 1899 and was used continuously for rugby Internationals between 1899 and 1925.

3 MEADOWBANK STADIUM, EDINBURGH — This multi-purpose sporting facility was opened in 1970 and was renovated in 1994 and also in 1999.

4 MURRAYFIELD, EDINBURGH — The Stadium was opened in 1925, and the first rugby International was played there on 21 March 1925. It was used in Rugby World Cup 1991, and following renovation in 1995, it staged further matches in Rugby World Cup 1999 and Rugby World Cup 2007.

5 POWDERHALL, EDINBURGH — The stadium was built in the 1870s and staged two rugby Internationals during the 1897 and 1898 seasons.

6 RAEBURN PLACE, EDINBURGH — Staged the first rugby International between Scotland and England in 1871 and was used continuously for rugby Internationals until 1895.

7 NETHERDALE STADIUM, GALASHIELS — Home to Gala Rugby Club, in the Scottish borders, the stadium hosted one rugby International match, between Uruguay and Spain, during Rugby World Cup 1999.

8 FIRHILL STADIUM, GLASGOW — The stadium was opened in 1909 and was the home ground of Glasgow Warriors Rugby Club between 2007 and 2012.

9 HAMILTON CRESCENT, GLASGOW — Staged the first soccer match between Scotland and England in 1872, and was used for four rugby Internationals between 1873 and 1885.

10 HAMPDEN PARK, GLASGOW — This famous Scottish International football stadium was opened in 1903, renovated in 1999 and used during Rugby World Cup 1999.

11 HUGHENDEN STADIUM, GLASGOW — This rugby stadium was opened on 24 May 1924, and was the home ground of Glasgow Warriors RFC between 2005 and 2007.

# MAJOR STADIUMS IN SCOTLAND

**12** OLD HAMPDEN PARK, GLASGOW

This football stadium named Cathkin Park, when opened in 1884, staged just one rugby International on 14 March 1896. The ground was closed in 1967.

**13** SCOTSTOUN STADIUM, GLASGOW

The stadium, an athletics and rugby venue, was opened in 1915, and is the current home ground of Glasgow Warriors Rugby Football Club.

**14** RUGBY PARK, KILMARNOCK

This football stadium, opened on 1 August 1899, renovated between 1994 and 1995, staged Scotland's rugby International against Tonga on 22 November 2014.

**15** McDIARMID PARK, PERTH

This football stadium, opened in 1989, staged its first rugby International match between Scotland and Japan on 13 November 2004.

# MAJOR STADIUMS IN SOUTH AFRICA

**1** FREE STATE STADIUM, BLOEMFONTEIN
*renamed:* VODACOM PARK STADIUM

The original stadium was built in 1954 and was replaced in 1995 by the new 'Free State Stadium' in time to host three games in Rugby World Cup 1995. Renamed 'Vodacom Park' in 2002, the ground was expanded in 2007 and renovated in 2008.

**2** NEWLANDS STADIUM, CAPE TOWN
*renamed:* NORWICH PARK, NEWLANDS
*renamed:* FEDSURE PARK, NEWLANDS

The ground was opened on 31 May 1890, and was upgraded several times between 1990 and 1995 in preparation for Rugby World Cup 1995. In an agreement with sponsors, the stadium was renamed 'Norwich Park' in 1996, and again in 2000 to 'Fedsure Park'. Investec became the sponsor in 2002, followed by Vodacom in 2005. Both agreed to retain the original name 'Newlands Stadium'. The ground hosted four matches, including a quarter-final and a semi-final, in Rugby World Cup 1995.

**3** KINGS PARK STADIUM, DURBAN
*renamed:* ABSA STADIUM, DURBAN
*renamed:* THE ABSA STADIUM, DURBAN

Built in 1891, the stadium was opened by rugby icon Dr Danie Craven in 1958 as 'Kings Park Rugby Ground'. It was renovated throughout the 1990s, and its capacity was increased in 1995. In 2000, in a sponsorship deal, the stadium was renamed 'ABSA Stadium'. Then in 2005 it was renamed again to 'The ABSA Stadium', but is currently known simply as 'Kings Park Stadium'. The ground staged five games, including a quarter-final and a semi-final, in Rugby World Cup 1995.

**4** BASIL KENYON STADIUM, EAST LONDON
*renamed:* ABSA STADIUM, EAST LONDON
*renamed:* BUFFALO CITY STADIUM, EAST LONDON

The stadium, built in 1934, was originally named 'Border Rugby Union Ground' and later named 'Basil Kenyon Stadium'. It was then named 'ABSA Stadium, East London' until 13 October 2009, when it was renamed 'Buffalo City Stadium' or 'BCM Stadium, East London'. The ground hosted three pool matches in Rugby World Cup 1995.

**5** ELLIS PARK, JOHANNESBURG

The ground, established on 10 October 1927, was opened in 1928, then demolished, and rebuilt exclusively for rugby in 1982. The modernised stadium hosted five games in Rugby World Cup 1995, including a quarter-final and the final when South Africa beat New Zealand by 15 points to 12. Ellis Park was then rebranded 'CocaCola Park' on 4 July 2008, but the ground then reverted to its original name in 2012.

# MAJOR STADIUMS IN SOUTH AFRICA

**6** BOET ERASMUS STADIUM, PORT ELIZABETH
*renamed:* TELKOM PARK STADIUM, PORT ELIZABETH
*renamed:* EPRFU STADIUM, PORT ELIZABETH

The stadium, opened on 30 April 1960, was named 'Boet Erasmus' until 1999 when it was renamed 'Telkom Park' in a naming rights deal. It was further renamed 'EPRFU Stadium' in 2003, until it was officially closed in July 2010, to be replaced by the 'Nelson Mandela Bay Stadium'.

**7** NELSON MANDELA BAY STADIUM, PORT ELIZABETH

The stadium staged its first event on 6 June 2009, nearly nine months before its official opening on 28 February 2010.

**8** LOFTUS VERSFELD, PRETORIA
*renamed:* MINOLTA LOFTUS STADIUM, PRETORIA
*renamed:* SECURICOR LOFTUS STADIUM, PRETORIA

The stadium was opened in 1923 and named in honour of Robert Owen Loftus Versfeld in 1932 until its name change on 10 June 1998. It was then renamed 'Minolta Loftus' between 11 June 1998, and 4 February 2003, in a sponsorship deal with the Minolta Company. In a new sponsorship arrangement it was then renamed 'Securicor Loftus' from 5 February 2003, until 1 September 2005. Vodacom then took over the sponsorship, and agreed to use the original name. The ground hosted three pool matches, a quarter-final and the third place game in Rugby World Cup 1995.

**9** OLYMPIA PARK, RUSTENBURG

This multi-purpose stadium, opened in 1989 and used for both football and rugby, hosted three pool matches in Rugby World Cup 1995.

**10** ROYAL BAFOKENG SPORTS PALACE, RUSTENBURG

The sports palace, opened in 1999, is mainly used for football matches. It was renovated and expanded in 2009.

**11** P A M BRINK STADIUM, SPRINGS

The ground was inaugurated on 3 July 1949, and is used mostly for football matches. Two Internationals have been played at the stadium: in 1964 and 2002.

**12** DANIE CRAVEN STADIUM, STELLENBOSCH

Named after the famous Springbok scrum-half, the stadium built in 1979, staged the pool match between Australia and Romania in Rugby World Cup 1995.

# MAJOR STADIUMS IN WALES

**1 TALBOT ATHLETIC GROUND, ABERAVON**

A multi-purpose ground, known as 'The Central Athletic Ground' in the 1900s, has been the home of Aberavon rugby football club since 1913.

**2 BREWERY FIELD, BRIDGEND**

This sports stadium, opened in 1920, is the home ground of Bridgend Ravens rugby football club.

**3 ARMS PARK, CARDIFF renamed: NATIONAL STADIUM, CARDIFF**

The ground was opened in 1881 and renovated in 1912, 1934 and in 1956. The first International was played there on 12 April 1884, and the last International match against France took place on 23 March 1968. The stadium was then renamed 'National Stadium, Cardiff' in 1969, with the first match played on 8 March 1969. Although often referred to as the Arms Park in 1969, renovations at the stadium continued in stages during 1970, 1977 and 1980, and on completion the ground was officially opened, as 'The National Stadium', on 7 April 1994. The last match at the venue took place on 15 March 1997, just before it was demolished. The stadium had hosted four games, which included the third place match, in Rugby World Cup 1991.

**4 MILLENNIUM STADIUM, CARDIFF**

The new stadium, rebuilt on the National Stadium site, was opened in June 1999 in preparation for the 1999 Rugby World Cup, hosted by Wales. The first International took place on 26 June 1999, and the stadium staged matches during Rugby World Cup 1999 and Rugby World Cup 2007.

**5 CARDIFF CITY STADIUM, CARDIFF**

This relatively new multi-purpose stadium was opened on 22 July 2009, and is the home stadium of Cardiff Blues rugby club.

**6 PARC EIRIAS, COLWYN BAY**

The leisure centre, also known as known as 'Eirias Park', staged six International matches involving Tier 2 and 3 teams during November in 2012, 2013 and 2014.

**7 EUGENE CROSS PARK, EBBW VALE**

This rugby and cricket stadium was opened in 1919 and is the home ground of Ebbw Vale rugby football club.

**8 PARC Y SCARLETS, LLANELLI**

This new ground, which replaced Stradey Park, was opened 15 November 2008, and is the current home stadium of Llanelli Scarlets rugby club.

# MAJOR STADIUMS IN WALES

**9** STRADEY PARK, LLANELLI

The stadium was opened in 1879, and the first rugby International was played on 8 January 1887. The ground, home of Llanelli rugby football club until it was closed on 15 November 2008, was finally demolished in 2010. The stadium staged one pool game in both Rugby World Cup 1991 and Rugby World Cup 1999.

**10** THE GNOLL, NEATH

The cricket club was formed in 1848 and rugby was played from 1871. The current multi-purpose ground is the home of Neath Rugby Football Club.

**11** RODNEY PARADE, NEWPORT

Opened in 1877, this is the home of Newport-Gwent Dragons rugby club. The first rugby International took place at the ground on 12 January 1884.

**12** PONTYPOOL PARK, PONTYPOOL

First used for rugby in 1946, it is the home of Pontypool rugby club. The ground hosted the pool match between Australia and Western Samoa in Rugby World Cup 1991.

**13** SARDIS ROAD, PONTYPRIDD

Opened in September 1974, it is the home of Pontypridd rugby club. The ground hosted the pool match between Argentina and Western Samoa in Rugby World Cup 1991.

**14** LIBERTY STADIUM, SWANSEA

The multi-purpose stadium was opened on 10 July 2005, and is the home ground of the Ospreys rugby club.

**15** ST HELEN'S, SWANSEA

This rugby and cricket stadium, opened in 1873, staged Wales' first ever home rugby International on 16 December 1882. The ground continued to stage International matches until 1952, after which Welsh home matches were transferred to Cardiff.

**16** THE RACECOURSE, WREXHAM

Opened in 1864, this football stadium, known as 'The Racecourse Ground', hosted the pool match between Samoa and Japan in Rugby World Cup 1999. The ground also staged three Internationals between Wales and Romania between 1997 and 2003.

# INTERNATIONAL VENUES: LIST OF STADIUMS A TO C

AAMI Park - Melbourne

ABSA Stadium - Durban

ABSA Stadium - East London

Adams Park - High Wycombe

Adelaide Oval - Adelaide

AMI Stadium - Addington

AMI Stadium - Christchurch

ANZ Stadium - Sydney

Apia Park - Apia

Aranduroga Rugby Club - Corrientes

Arena Civica - Milan

Arena Giann Brera - Milan

Arena Manawatu - Palmerston North

Arms Park - Cardiff

Ashton Gate - Bristol

Athletic Club - San Pablo

Athletic Ground - Richmond

Athletic Park - Wellington

Aurora Stadium - Launceston

Ausgrid Stadium - Newcastle, NSW

Aussie Stadium - Sydney

Aviva Stadium - Dublin

Ballymore Oval - Brisbane

Ballynafeigh - Belfast

Balmoral Showgrounds - Belfast

Basil Kenyon Stadium - East London

BBVA Compass Stadium - Houston

Belgrano Stadium - Buenos Aires

BMO Stadium - Toronto

Boet Erasmus Stadium - Port Elizabeth

Boxer Stadium - San Francisco

Brewery Field - Bridgend

Brighton Community Stadium - Brighton

Brook's Field, Wilmington - North Carolina

Bruce Stadium - Canberra

Buck Shaw Stadium - Santa Clara, California

Buckhurst Park - Suva, Fiji

Buffalo City Stadium - East London

Camino Carrasco, Polo Club - Montevideo

Campo Ciudad Universitaria - Madrid

Campo de Pepe Rojo - Valladolid

Canberra Stadium - Canberra

Cardiff City Stadium - Cardiff

Cardigan Fields - Leeds

Carisbrook - Dunedin

Cataratas Rugby Club - Puerto Iguazu, Misiones

Central Coast Stadium - Gosford, NSW

Central Stadium - Krasnoyarsk

Centro Sportivo San Michele - Calvisano

Chalon-sur-Saone - Perpignan

Chanel College, Moamoa - Apia

Churchill Park - Lautoka, Fiji

Club Atlético Atlanta - Buenos Aires

Club Atlético San Isidro - Buenos Aires

Clube Atlético Ground - Sao Paulo

COC Stadium - Casablanca

CocaCola Park - Johannesburg

Colonial Stadium - Melbourne

Colorado Springs

Concord Oval - Sydney

County Ground - Gosforth

Cradock RC, Cradock - Eastern Cape

Cricket and Rugby Club - Buenos Aires

Cricket Ground - Melbourne

Cricket Ground - Sydney

Croke Park - Dublin

# INTERNATIONAL VENUES: LIST OF STADIUMS C TO F

Cross Green - Otley, Yorkshire

Crown Flatt - Dewsbury

Crusaders Ground - Port Elizabeth

Crystal Palace - London

Dairy Farmers Stadium - Townsville

Danie Craven Stadium - Stellenbosch

Donnybrook Stadium - Dublin

Eclectic Cricket Ground - Kimberley

Eden Park - Auckland

Edgeley Park - Stockport

Elland Road - Leeds

Ellis Park - Johannesburg

EPRFU Stadium - Port Elizabeth

Epsom Showgrounds - Auckland

Estad. Mundialista J M Minella - Mar del Plata

Estadi Olímpic de Montjuïc - Barcelona

Estadi Olímpic Lluís Companys - Barcelona

Estadio Bautista Gargantini - Mendoza

Estadio Brig General E. López - Santa Fe

Estadio Centenario - Resistencia

Estadio Charrúa - Montevideo

Estadio Ciudad de la Plata - La Plata

Estadio de Las Fuerzas - Asunción

Estadio de Vallehermoso - Madrid

Estadio del Colegio San José - Asunción

Estadio Don Leon Kolbovski - Buenos Aires

Estadio Gabino Sosa - Rosario

Estadio G.E.B.A - Buenos Aires

Estadio General Pablo Rojas - Ascunción

Estadio Gigante de Arroyito - Rosario

Estadio Gran Parque Central - Montevideo

Estadio José Maria Minella - Mar del Plata

Estadio La Carrodilla - Mendoza

Estadio Luis Franzini - Montevideo

Estadio Malvinas Argentinas - Mendoza

Estadio Moldanado - Buenos Aires

Estadio Monumental A V Liberti - Buenos Aires

Estadio Monumental José Fierro - Tucumán

Estadio Monumental - River Plate, Buenos Aires

Estadio Mundialista JM Minella - Mar del Plata

Estadio Olimpico Château Carreras - Córdoba

Estadio Padre Ernesto Martearena - Salta

Estadio Parque Artigas - Paysandú

Estadio Playa Ancha - Valparaiso

Estadio Raúl Conti - Puerto Madryn

Estadio San Carlos de Apoquindo - Santiago

Estadio S. Juan del Bicentenario - San Juan

Estadio San Martin de San Juan - San Juan

Estadio Sausalito - Viña del Mar

Estádio Sérgio Conceição - Coimbra

Estádio Universitário de Coimbra - Coimbra

Estádio Universitário de Lisboa - Lisbon

Etihad Stadium, Docklands - Melbourne

Eugene Cross Park - Ebbw Vale

Exhibition Ground - Brisbane

Express Advocate Stadium - Gosford, NSW

Fallowfield - Manchester

Fedsure Park, Newlands - Cape Town

Ferro Carril Oeste Stadium - Buenos Aires

Fili Stadion - Moscow

Firhill Stadium - Glasgow

Fletcher's Field, Markham - Toronto

FMG Stadium - Palmerston North

FNB Stadium, Soweto - Johannesburg

Football Stadium - Sydney

Forsyth Barr Stadium - Dunedin

Franklin Gardens - Northampton

Frascati Rugby Stadium - Rome

# INTERNATIONAL VENUES: LIST OF STADIUMS F TO O

Free State Stadium - Bloemfontein

Fritz-Grunebaum-Sportpark - Heidelburg

Galway Sports Ground - Galway

George Allen Memorial Field - Long Beach

Glover Field Anaheim - Los Angeles

Grand Stade - Lille Métropole

Great Strahov Stadium - Prague

Growthpoint Kings Park - Durban

Hamilton Crescent - Glasgow

Hampden Park - Glasgow

Hanazono Stadium - Osaka

Harder Stadium - Santa Barbara, California

Hartsfield Rugby Ground - Bulawayo

Headingley Stadium - Leeds

Heywood Road - Sale

Hughenden Stadium - Glasgow

Iffley Road - Oxford

Inverleith - Edinburgh

Jade Stadium - Christchurch

Johann van Riebeeck Stadium - Witbank

Kennington Oval - London

Kings Park - Durban

Kingsholm - Gloucester

Kingsland Rugby Park - Calgary

Kingsmead Ground - Durban

Kingspan Stadium, Belfast

Lancaster Park Oval - Christchurch

Lang Park - Brisbane

Lansdowne Road - Dublin

Leicester City Stadium - Leicester

Leinster CC, Rathmines - Dublin

Lia Manoliu Stadium - Bucharest

Liberty Stadium - Swansea

Life College Stadium - Atlanta, Georgia

Loftus Versfeld Stadium - Pretoria

Madejski Stadium - Reading

Mahamasina Stadium - Antananarivo

Makarska Stadium - Makaraska, Yugoslavia

Maksimir Stadium - Zagreb

Manchester City Stadium - Manchester

Mansfield Park - Hawick, Scotland

Mardyke - Cork

Mbombela Stadium - Nelspruit

McAlpine Stadium - Huddersfield

McDiarmid Park - Perth

McLean Park - Napier

Meadowbank Stadium - Edinburgh

Meanwood Road - Leeds

Millennium Stadium - Cardiff

Minolta Loftus Stadium - Pretoria

Mohawk Sports Park - Hamilton, Ontario

Murrayfield - Edinburgh

Musgrave Park - Cork

Nagai Stadium - Osaka

National Olympic Stadium - Tokyo

National Sports Stadium - Harare

National Stadium - Avarua, Rarotonga

National Stadium - Cardiff

National Stadium - Suva, Fiji

Nauka Stadion - Moscow

Netherdale Stadium - Galashiels, Scotland

Nelson Mandela Bay Stadium - Port Elizabeth

Newlands Stadium - Cape Town

North Harbour Stadium - Albany

Northland Events Centre - Whangarei, New Zealand

North West Stadium - Welkom

# INTERNATIONAL VENUES: LIST OF STADIUMS O TO S

Norwich Park, Newlands - Cape Town

Observatory Park - Denver, Colorado

Okara Park - Whangarei, New Zealand

Old Hampden Park - Glasgow

Old Trafford - Manchester

Olën Park - Potchefstroom, South Africa

Olympia Park - Rustenburg

Olympic Park Stadium - Melbourne

Olympic Stadium - London

Ormeau - Belfast

Otago Stadium - Dunedin

Owl Creek Polo Field, Glenville - New York

P A M Brink Stadium - Springs

Parc des Princess - Paris

Parc des Sports Aguiléra - Biarritz

Parc des Sports de Sauclières - Béziers

Parc des Sports et de L'Amitié - Narbonne

Parc des Sports Marcel Michelin - Clermont-Ferrand

Parc Eirias - Colwyn Bay

Parc Municipal des Sports - Bayonne

Parc y Scarlets - Llanelli

Parque Federico Omar Saroldi - Montevideo

Parque Mahuida CARR La Reina - Santiago

Parramatta Stadium - Sydney

Patersons Stadium - Perth

Pittodrie Stadium - Aberdeen

Police Ground - Harare

Police Ground - Salisbury

Polo Ground, Flores - Buenos Aires

Pontypool Park - Pontypool

Potter's Park - Auckland

Powderhall - Edinburgh

Prince Chichibu Memorial Ground - Tokyo

Prince of Wales Country Club - Santiago

R A S Ground - Sydney

Raeburn Place - Edinburgh

Ravenhill - Belfast

RDS Showgrounds - Dublin

Recreation Ground - Bath

Rectangular Stadium - Melbourne

Rectory Field - Blackheath

Rentschler Field - Hartford, Connecticut

Richardson Stadium - Kingston, Ontario

Richardson's Field - Blackheath

River Plate Stadium - Buenos Aires

Robertson Stadium - Houston

Rockne Stadium, Northfield - Chicago

Rodney Parade - Newport

Rotorua International Stadium - Rotorua

Route du Médoc, Le Bouscat - Bordeaux

Royal Agricultural Showground - Sydney

Royal Bafokeng Sports Palace - Rustenburg

Rugby League Park - Christchurch

Rugby Park Stadium - Invercargill

Rugby Park - Hamilton

Rugby Park - Kilmarnock

San Carlos de Apoquindo - Santiago

San Pablo Athletic Ground - São Paulo

Sandy Park - Exeter

Sardis Road - Pontypridd

Scotstoun Stadium - Glasgow

Securicor Loftus Stadium - Pretoria

Showgrounds Oval - Palmerston North

Singer Family Park - Manchester, New Hampshire

Sixways Stadium - Worcester

Skilled Park, Robina, Gold Coast - Queensland

# INTERNATIONAL VENUES: LIST OF STADIUMS S

Skra Stadium - Warsaw

Slava Stadion - Moscow

So Kon Po Stadium - Hong Kong

Soldier Field - Chicago

South West Stadium - Windhoek

Sparta Stadium - Moscow

Spartak Stadium - Kiev

Spartak Stadium - Moscow

Sports Ground - Sydney

Sports Ground, Avarua - Rarotonga

Sports Park Berg and Bos - Apeldoorn

Springbok Park - Bloemfontein

St Helen's - Swansea

St Ignatius, California Field - Berkeley

St James' Park - Newcastle

Stade Africain de Menzel - Bourghiba

Stade Aimé Giral - Perpignan

Stade Albert Domec - Carcassonne

Stade Amédée-Domenech - Brive

Stade Antoine-Béguère - Lourdes

Stade Armandie - Agen

Stade Auguste Bonal - Montbéliard

Stade Bourillot - Dijon

Stade Chaban-Delmas - Bordeaux

Stade Colombes - Paris

Stade d'Albert Domec - Carcassonne

Stade de France - Paris

Stade de Gerland - Lyon

Stade de L'Egassiairal - Narbonne

Stade de la Beaujoire - Nantes

Stade de la Chambrèrie - Valence

Stade de la Croix du Prince - Pau

Stade de la Méditerranée - Béziers

Stade de la Meinau - Strasbourg

Stade de la Mosson - Montpellier

Stade de Sapiac - Montauban Stade des Ponts, Jumeaux - Toulouse

Stade des Sports Aguiléra - Biarritz

Stade du Hameau - Pau

Stade du Moulias - Auch

Stade du Parc Lescure - Bordeaux

Stade du Ray - Nice

Stade E. Jean Baylet - Valence d'Agen

Stade Ernest Wallon - Toulouse

Stade Félix Bollaert - Lens

Stade Félix Mayol - Toulon

Stade Français - Santiago

Stade Geoffroy-Guichard - Saint Étienne

Stade Jacques Fouroux - Auch

Stade Jean Alric - Aurillac

Stade Jean Dauger - Bayonne

Stade Jules Deschaseaux - Le Havre

Stade le Bouscat - Bordeaux

Stade Leo Lagrange - Besançon

Stade Lesdiguières - Grenoble

Stade Louis II - Monte Carlo

Stade Marcel Michelin - Clermont Ferrand

Stade Marcel Saupin - Nantes

Stade Maurice Trélut - Tarbes

Stade Mayol - Toulon

Stade Méditerranée - Béziers

Stade Michel Bendichou - Colomiers

Stade Municipal de Toulouse - Toulouse

Stade Municipal du Parc Lescure - Bordeaux

Stade Municipal - Albi

Stade Municipal - Chalon-sur-Saone

# INTERNATIONAL VENUES: LIST OF STADIUMS  S

Stade Municipal - Chambéry

Stade Mustapha Ben Jannet - Monastir

Stade Nord Lille Métropole - Villeneuve-d'Ascq

Stade Océane - Le Havre

Stade Parc Municipal des Sports - Brive

Stade Patrice Brocas, Moulias - Auch

Stade Pershing,Vincennes - Paris

Stade Pierre-Antoine - Castres

Stade Roi Baudouin - Brussels

Stade Sébastien, Charléty - Paris

Stade Vélodrome - Marseille

Stade Yves-du-Manoir - Montpellier

Stadio Alberto Braglia - Modena

Stadio Angelo Massimino - Catania

Stadio Artemio Franchi - Florence

Stadio Arturo Collana - Naples

Stadio Brianteo - Monza, Milan

Stadio Cino e Lillo del Duca - Ascoli Piceno

Stadio Ciro Vigorito - Benevento

Stadio Comprensoriale - Fontanafredda

Stadio Comunale Beltrametti - Piacenza

Stadio Comunale Carlo Montano - Livorno

Stadio Comunale Censin Bosia - Asti

Stadio Comunale di Monigo - Treviso

Stadio Comunale, Ennio Tardini - Parma

Stadio Comunale Luigi Ferraris - Genova

Stadio Comunale Mario Battaglini - Rovigo

Stadio Comunale Rho - Rho

Stadio Comunale Sergio Lanfrachi - Parma

Stadio Danilo Martelli - Mantova

Stadio Dino Manuzzi, Cesana - Trieste

Stadio Euganeo - Padova

Stadio Flaminio - Rome

Stadio Friuli - Udine

Stadio Gigante de Arroyito - Rosario

Stadio Giglio - Reggio Emilia

Stadio Gino Pistoni-Ivrea - Turin

Stadio Giovanni Zini - Cremona

Stadio Giuseppe Meazza - Milan

Stadio Jesi Arriva - Jesi

Stadio Lamarmora - Biella-in-Piedmont

Stadio Leonardo Garilli - Piacenza

Stadio Luigi Zaffanella - Viadana

Stadio Lungobisenzio - Prato

Stadio Marc'Antonio Bentegodi - Verona

Stadio Mario Rigamonti - Brescia

Stadio Mompiano - Brescia

Stadio Nazionale del Roma - Rome

Stadio Olimpico di Torino - Turin

Stadio Olimpico - Rome

Stadio Omobono Tenni - Treviso

Stadio Oreste Granillo - Reggio di Calabria

Stadio Peroni - Calvisano

Stadio P. Perucca, St Vincent - Aosta

Stadio Pierluigi Penzo - Venice

Stadio Plebiscito - Padova

Stadio Renato Dall'Ara - Bologna

Stadio Rho - Rho

Stadio San Dona di Piave - Venice

Stadio San Paolo - Naples

Stadio San Siro - Milan

Stadio Santa Colomba - Benevento

Stadio Santa Maria Goretti - Catania

Stadio Silvio Appiani - Padova

Stadio St Vincent Perruca - Aosta

Stadio Testaccio - Rome

Stadio Tommaso Fattori - L'Aquila

Stadio XXV Aprile - Parma

# INTERNATIONAL VENUES: LIST OF STADIUMS S TO Y

Stadion Krč - Prague

Stadion Maksimir - Zagreb

Stadion Sparta, Krč - Prague

Stadionul 1 Mai - Constanta

Stadionul 23 August - Bucharest

Stadionul ANEF - Bucharest

Stadionul Cotroceni - Bucharest

Stadionul Dinamo - Bucharest

Stadionul Farul - Constanta

Stadionul Giulești-Valentin Stănescu - Bucharest

Stadionul Municipal Gloria - Buzău

Stadionul Municipal Brăilla

Stadionul Municipal - Brașov

Stadion Parcul Copilului - Bucharest

Stadionul Republican Chișinău - Moldova

Stadionul Republicii - Bucharest

Stadium Australia - Sydney

Stadium MK - Milton Keynes

Stadium Taranaki - New Plymouth

Stoop Memorial Ground - London

Stradey Park - Llanelli

Subiaco Oval - Perth

Suncorp Stadium - Brisbane

Swanguard Stadium - Burnaby Lake, BC

Tacuru Social Club Posadas - Misiones

Tahuna Park - Dunedin

Talbot Athletic Ground - Aberavon

Telkom Park Stadium - Port Elizabeth

Telstra Dome - Melbourne

Telstra Stadium - Sydney

Teufaiva Sport Stadium - Nuku'alofa

The ABSA Stadium - Durban

The Gabba Cricket Ground - Brisbane

The Gnoll - Neath, Wales

The Greenyards - Melrose, Scotland

The Kimberley Athletics Club - Kimberley

The Racecourse - Wrexham

The Sportsground - Galway

The Wanderers Ground - Johannesburg

Thomond Park - Limerick

Thunderbird Stadium - Vancouver

Toyota Park Stadium - Chicago

Trafalgar Park - Nelson

Tupapa Rugby Field - Avarua

Twickenham - London

Twin Elms Rugby Park - Nepean, Ontario

UCD Bowl - Dublin

Union Sportif Annecy Rugby - Annecy

University Ground - Sydney

Upper Park - Birkenhead Park

Varsity Stadium, Stanley Park - Toronto

Vélez Sarsfield Stadium - Buenos Aires

Vicarage Road - Watford

Viking Park - Canberra

Villa Park - Birmingham

Vodacom Park Stadium - Bloemfontein

Waikato Stadium - Hamilton

Wanderers Club Ground - Montevideo

Waverley Park - East London

Welford Road - Leicester

Wellington Regional Stadium - Wellington

Wembley Stadium - London

Westpac Stadium - Wellington

Westpac Trust Stadium - Wellington

Whalley Range - Manchester

WIN Stadium - Wollongong

Withdean Stadium - Brighton

Yarrow Stadium - New Plymouth

York Park, Launceston - Tasmania

York Stadium - Toronto